THE EMERGENCE OF
EUROPEAN CIVILIZATION

THE EMERGENCE
OF EUROPEAN
CIVILIZATION

From the Middle Ages to

the Opening of the Nineteenth Century

JOHN B. WOLF, University of Minnesota

Harper & Row, Publishers
New York, Evanston, and London

To my assistants, past and present,

who have helped me teach History 1, 2, 3

at the University of Minnesota

Contents

BOOK V. *The French Revolution and Empire*

Preface

This text is the result of several decades of thought and study on the problem of teaching American students the history of their own civilization. If we start with the assumption that the contemporary culture of these United States is, at its foundation, a subculture of occidental civilization, then the historian is confronted with the task of presenting the emergence of this remarkable society of Europe as an integrated whole rather than as a series of short national histories. This is a very difficult task. Traditionally European history has been written in terms of the national stories of the several European states, more or less under the direct influence of the historians of those separate states. But if we are to understand our society as a part of the larger whole of western civilization, we must resist the temptation to make it merely a story confluent with that of a half dozen or so national histories. Obviously at certain points it becomes necessary to dwell upon the history of this or that subculture, but if the American student is to become sophisticated about his past, the historian should never linger long in the alleys of national histories without trying to bring them into focus with the problems of European society as a larger and more significant whole. This approach should also be instructive to those who do see the history of Europe from the vantage point of Oxford, Paris, Heidelberg, or even Moscow, for it provides a natural antidote for the bane of historical writing, namely, provincialism. There is another advantage in this approach: it is thereby possible to make the sense of time more meaningful to American students when the presentation does not place the sixteenth to eighteenth centuries in a hodge-podge of national histories that dislocates time entirely. It is difficult enough to grasp the process of European development without adding the handicap resulting from an unintegrated presentation of the temporal processes.

A second problem that should be presented to American students is the fact that history is not a fixed and immutable academic discipline. Just as scientific knowledge, and hence the subject matter of courses in science, has changed considerably in the last decades, so also has the understanding of history available to the student. It is, unfortunately, impossible in a short history to explain the evolution of historical thinking on all the problems of European civilization; nonetheless, it seems incumbent upon the writer of history to indicate that historical interpretations have been subject to change, and, by inference, will probably change in the future as new information and insights become available. It does not seem necessary in an introductory text to burden the student with the arguments among historians of different generations or of different basic assumptions, but he should be made aware of the fact that such arguments do exist and may be worth further study. In this text there is a conscious effort to meet some of these problems head on, others are suggested as meriting investigation.

The organization of this history into five "books" is not based upon any assumption of "historical eras," for it should be obvious to any student that time is continuous and that the processes of human history present an inter-related web of events. However, if we are to comprehend this history, we have to make assumptions about its development. The five books are of unequal time periods, each shorter in duration as we move toward the present. Book I is an introduction, largely devoted to analyses, rather than to narrative history, of the seeds of Occidental culture up to the end of the fifteenth century. The four following books address themselves to the larger problems faced by western men in the next three centuries. In each there is a conscious effort to analyze the characteristic forms that were emerging in the process of western history. If it has been successful, this text should provide a sound underpinning for understanding our civilization's developments in religion, politics, economics, war, art, science, and learning. Book V deals with the great social and political upheaval that shook western civilization at the end of the eighteenth century and that has provided so much of the basis for subsequent thought and action of western man, but this great revolution is presented as an acceleration of the processes in western civilization rather than as a break in its onward progress.

Like all writers, I am deeply in debt to my own teachers, to my graduate students and assistants, to my colleagues and fellow students of history, and to my friends in other disciplines for ideas, suggestions, and friendly assistance. Anyone who has attempted to discuss the marvelous intricacies, the rich variety, the ever-baffling problems involved in the emergence of our civilization will fully comprehend why I am indebted to many people who have generously shared with me their knowledge and ideas over lunch, coffee, or cocktails, at family parties, at conventions, in seminars and classrooms, and indeed wherever I could find men willing to allow me to pick their brains. I only wish that I could acknowledge all of them, and at the same time excuse myself for failing to use as effectively as they might wish the ideas that they passed on to me. I do, however, wish specifically to thank those people who generously gave of their time to read all or part of this manuscript; they are not responsible for its faults, but have certainly added to whatever virtues it may possess. First of all, my erstwhile students who were in Minnesota when the manuscript was almost finished and who have all become college professors in their own right: Doctors Ivo Lambi, Lloyd Moote, J. Quintin Cook, Orest Ranum, and George Rothrock (the latter also helped with some of the pictures); next my colleagues past and present at the University of Minnesota, Professors John Bowditch, A. Clarke Chambers, Herbert Heaton, R. S. Hoyt, A. C. Krey, L. D. Steefel, and D. H. Willson; and then colleagues in other institutions, Professor Arthur S. Williamson of Hamline University and the late Professor Lucile D. Pinkham of Carleton College, both of whom read the manuscript with the critical eye of the classroom teacher as well as of the scholar, and to Professor W. B. Willcox of the University of Michigan and the late Professor Walter Dorn of Columbia University, both of whom were extremely helpful in suggestions and corrections; and finally to my wife Theta who is not only the bright spot of my life, but also my editor, critic, and friend—her support has been very important.

JOHN B. WOLF

BOOK I

Medieval Origins

In the twentieth century when the peoples of the whole earth are confronted with the dynamic movement of western civilization and forced to adapt their ways and customs to its on-going progress, it has become evident that this western society is a unique cultural development fraught with consequences for the future evolution of man himself. As we attempt to discover its origins, no simple solution presents itself to the historian as the obvious and necessary explanation for the wonderful development of this western civilization. One thing is obvious, namely, that its relationship with the cultural organizations of classical antiquity —Egypt, Greece, Rome—is one that was largely created by scholars who reactivated that part of the classical tradition which seemed suitable to western needs. The actual survivals of classical civilization in institutions or in the hearts of men were greatly altered by the iron years between the disorganization and decay of Roman society and the period when western European men were again able to organize their lives in a complex civilization. This does not mean that western men owed nothing to other civilizations that preceded them or that were developing contemporaneously; it is only to say that western civilization seems to have adopted only those ideas and institutions suitable to its own growth.

If this is true, then there is much justification in starting an account of the emergence of western Europe with the Christian Middle Ages when western Europeans developed the seeds of their political, religious, economic, social, and intellectual institutions, and perhaps even more significant, also developed the cultural diversities and pluralisms that have been so characteristic of the emerging forms of western society.

1

Thus, this first section will concern itself with the institutions and cultural trends in medieval Europe that seem to be at the roots of the civilization that was to come. Here we shall consider the rise to power of the Roman Catholic church, the emergence of feudal institutions and the rise of the several feudal states, the emergence of European agricultural patterns and the dynamic development of urban economy. We shall also study Europeans as they reached out in time and space to discover new worlds: the opening of the routes to Asia and America, the discovery of classical civilization's theology, law, science, medicine, and letters. Thus will unfold the picture of a moving, vital society in which tensions and differences, strife and competition, variety and uniformity are all deeply entwined in its evolution.

A century or more ago when western men looked back to their medieval past they were seeking colorful, poetic, romantic elements that would allow them to contrast the past with their own present to the disadvantage of the latter. The world of the immediate era was so distasteful to many sensitive souls (a Sir Walter Scott, a Chateaubriand, a Victor Hugo) that they sought escape from the reality of their world into an unreal medieval scene of their own making. This romantic tradition of the origins of western civilization still lingers on in fiction, but the historical studies of the last century have shattered that picture to a degree that even those most disillusioned with the world of atomic energy no longer seek refuge in an imaginary medieval past. What the historians have brought to light is a portrayal more useful to modern man than the Xanadus of earlier eras. In the medieval world discovered by modern scholarship we find delineations of political, economic, social, and intellectual patterns of development that throw great light upon the vital forces that have long been active in the shaping of western civilization. Far from being a field of antiquarian research, decorative but hardly useful, the study of medieval history is emerging as a powerful spotlight that gives significance to the whole story of western man as well as an interesting laboratory for the study of human behavior in a simpler cultural organization than modern society can provide.

It is with this in mind that we shall approach the study of the medieval beginnings of western society. Only through comprehending its origins can one understand the divergent evolutions of the subgroups in western culture, and, in turn, western civilization itself is inconceivable without the tensions created by these differences. Thus, any attempt to explain the forms taken by the developing process of western culture must start with the relatively simple structures that appear at the dawn of western civilization.

BIBLIOGRAPHY FOR BOOK I

General Books

There are a number of excellent textbooks covering the period that we call the Middle Ages; these listed below will provide a good introduction. The little book by Professor Joseph R. Strayer, *Western Europe in the Middle Ages,* is a brilliant short interpretation of the period, but it may be that a student should also read either Professor Hoyt or Professor Painter, or one of the other texts first in order to understand more fully Strayer's argument.

Two books in the series, *The Rise of Modern Europe,* deal with this period. *The Dawn of a New Era* (Cheyney) has been criticized because it does not take account of the disorders and economic distress of the fourteenth century, but the student should note that it is the introductory volume in a multi-volume series discussing the emergence of western civilization rather than an account of the economy of the latter Middle Ages. The other volume of this series, *The World of Humanism* (Gilmore), is an excellent survey and summary of Europe before the Reformation. The books listed below are not exhaustive of the subject.

Cheyney, E. P., *The Dawn of a New Era, 1250–1453,* New York, Harper, 1936.
Gilmore, M. P., *The World of Humanism, 1453–1517,* New York, Harper, 1952.
Hoyt, R. S., *Europe in the Middle Ages,* New York, Harcourt, Brace, 1957.
LaMonte, J. L., *The World of the Middle Ages,* New York, Appleton-Century-Crofts, 1949.
Painter, S., *A History of the Middle Ages,* New York, Knopf, 1953.
Previte-Orton, C. W., *The Shorter Cambridge Medieval History,* Cambridge, Cambridge University Press, 1952, 2 vols.
Strayer, Joseph R., *Western Europe in the Middle Ages,* New York, Appleton-Century-Crofts, 1955.
Strayer, Joseph R., and C. D. Munroe, *The Middle Ages,* New York, Appleton-Century, 1942.

Thompson, J. W., and E. A. Johnson, *An Introduction to Medieval Europe,* New York, Norton, 1937.

Specialized Studies

It is difficult to pick and choose between the many excellent studies of special problems. Some of the best have not been translated into English. The following list is only a suggestion of the possibilities. (The books in the first half of the list are available in paperback or low-price editions as well as standard editions which are cited.)

Gillespie, J. E., *A History of Geographical Discovery, 1400–1800,* New York, Holt, 1933.
Ferguson, W. K., *The Renaissance,* New York, Holt, 1940.
Haskins, C. H., *The Rise of the Universities,* Ithaca, Cornell University Press, 1940.
Huizinga, J., *The Waning of the Middle Ages,* New York, Doubleday, 1924.

Newhall, R. A., *The Crusades,* New York, Holt, 1927.

Packard, S., *Europe and the Church Under Innocent III,* New York, Holt, 1927.

Painter, S., *The Rise of the Feudal Monarchies,* Ithaca, Cornell University Press, 1951.

Power, E., *Medieval People,* New York, Doubleday, 1950.

Pirenne, H., *Medieval Cities: Their Origins and the Revival of Trade,* Princeton, Princeton University Press, 1925.

Stephenson, Carl, *Medieval Feudalism,* Ithaca, Cornell University Press, 1942.

Artz, F. B., *The Mind of the Middle Ages,* New York, Knopf, 1954.

Flick, A. C., *The Rise of the Medieval Church and Its Influence on the Civilization of Europe from the First to the Thirteenth Centuries,* New York, Putnam, 1909.

Flick, A. C., *The Decline of the Medieval Church,* New York, Knopf, 1930, 2 vols.

Ganshof, F. L., *Feudalism,* New York, Longmans, Green, 1952.

Heaton, H., *Economic History of Europe,* rev. ed., New York, Harper, 1948.

Painter, S., *French Chivalry, Chivalric Ideas and Practices,* Baltimore, Johns Hopkins University Press, 1940.

Perroy, E., *The Hundred Years' War,* New York, Oxford University Press, 1951.

Runciman, S., *A History of the Crusades,* Cambridge, Cambridge University Press, 1951–1954, 3 vols.

Thompson, J. W., *An Economic and Social History of the Latter Middle Ages,* New York, Century, 1931.

Vasiliev, A. A., *History of the Byzantine Empire,* Madison, University of Wisconsin Studies, 1952.

Although the concept "Renaissance" is often misused by historians, students should know something of its development.

Ferguson, W. K., *The Renaissance in Historical Thought: Five Centuries of Interpretation,* Boston, Houghton Mifflin, 1948.

The two classic books, J. Burckhardt, *Civilization of the Renaissance in Italy,* and J. A. Symonds, *Renaissance in Italy,* should be backed up by B. Berenson, *Italian Painters of the Renaissance.*

This print illustrates the type of warfare common at the opening of the fifteenth century. Note the weapons and the armor. (University of Minnesota Library)

Chapter 1

THE EMERGENCE OF THE POLITICAL INSTITUTIONS OF MODERN EUROPE

1. THE HEIRS OF ROMAN CIVILIZATION

The story of the rise and development of western civilization is one of the most dramatic sagas ever told. It is made up of elements of comedy, of large and somber scenes of tragedy, of periods of suspense, and, finally, of strophes of action more exciting than any adventure novel. It is from this history that western men—Europeans and Americans—can draw their strength and their understanding of their own lives, of their institutions, and of their beliefs. In this present era when western civilization is an all-pervasive force in the world, understanding of its origins has become particularly important.

In the first place it should be recalled that in ancient times the Roman Empire governed not only most of western Europe, but also the entire Mediterranean basin and much of the Middle East. In the first century of the Christian era the Empire must have seemed to its contemporaries an imperishable political fact destined to last forever. That Roman civilization was a mélange of Greek and Roman cultural achievements in many different areas of human activity: art and architecture, literature and philosophy, political and military institutions, religious and economic organization. Supported by the valor of the Roman soldiers and the political wisdom of the Roman statesmen, at the pinnacle of its power the Empire assured a measure of peace and tranquillity from Spain to the Indian Ocean. The spread of Christianity between the first and third centuries must have seemed to add another element of stability to that society by promising to provide a common religion for the entire great "community."

Like other things on this earth, however, the Roman Empire was destined to change. It was once fashionable for historians to speak of "the decline and fall of the Roman Empire." Indeed, one of the finest histories ever written carries that title. But that Empire did not actually "fall." What happened was a gradual unwinding of the cultural knots that held that society together. At times the process was slow, at others, accelerated; but from the high point of its power in the first century A.D. until the low point reached some six or seven centuries later, Roman society was in the process of internal decay. Many books have been written to explain this occurrence. Some have argued that the taxation system became too oppressive and so undermined the economy of the Empire. Others have pointed out that the Christians' interest in the next world diverted too much attention from the problems of this one; that the Church took into its service and into the monasteries the talented men who should have been the governors and soldiers. Still others have argued that the appearance of Christianity and other eastern religions indicated that the Romans had lost faith in their traditional institutions—that a moral crisis found them doubting the value of their own civilization. It has also been pointed out that the civil wars that made the crown the plaything of the armies created an impossible political situation at a time when changes in the economy of Italy were turning the common Roman citizens into mobs demanding bread and circuses. Nor have the barbarians been ignored as forces hostile to the Empire. They came first as allies and mercenary soldiers, but later they appeared as invaders who tried unsuccessfully to make the institutions as well as the territories of the Empire their own. There have been interesting and bizarre explanations: one book argues that the almost impenetrable Chinese Wall forced the barbarians westward; another points out that the malaria mosquito, by enervating the Italians, created a vacuum that was filled by more healthy and virile men from the north.

This is not the place to try to settle so momentous a question, but it is important to note here that the Roman Empire did not disappear everywhere at the same time. Indeed, it had three "heirs," each of them with a different history and a different heritage: (1) the Latin West, (2) the Byzantine-Greek Empire, and (3) the Syrio-Egyptian East. Each of these areas had had a different pre-Roman history, and so, when the Roman Empire began to waver, their basically different traditions began to assert themselves. Even the early Christian church felt the fissures that were opening up between these three segments of the Empire: differences in Christian art forms, in ritual, in Church government, and in doctrine had begun to separate the Roman Catholic church, the Greek Orthodox church, and the Syrio-Egyptian eastern church from the time when Christianity seemed to be triumphant

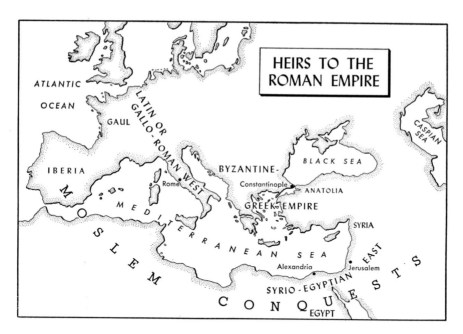

HEIRS TO THE ROMAN EMPIRE

ATLANTIC OCEAN

GAUL

LATIN OR GALLO-ROMAN WEST

IBERIA

Rome

MOSLEM

MEDITERRANEAN SEA

CASPIAN SEA

BYZANTINE-

Constantinople

BLACK SEA

ANATOLIA

GREEK EMPIRE

SYRIA

NEAR EAST

Alexandria

Jerusalem

SYRIO-EGYPTIAN

CONQUESTS

EGYPT

throughout the Empire. The barbarian invasions (after the third century) in the western Gallo-Roman lands, and, later, the Mohammedan invasions of the Syrio-Egyptian provinces (in the seventh century) completed the breaches in the three parts of the Empire as well as in the three sections of the Christian church.

By the eighth century the Byzantine-Greek community seemed to be the only direct descendant of Roman traditions. The Syrio-Egyptian lands had transferred their religious loyalties to the new conquering religion of Mohammed and had become the cultural center for the Islamic civilization that extended from India to Spain. These provinces were the foyer through which Graeco-Roman ideas entered the Arabic world. The third "heir," the Gallo-Roman West, lost contact with the great traditions of the Roman Empire more completely than either of the other two. When the barriers were down and the Germanic tribesmen found it easy to enter the Empire, new ethnic groups with non-Latin languages and non-Latin customs and culture imposed themselves upon the older settlements. In England and parts of the Rhineland the Roman culture disappeared entirely; in France and Italy it was drastically modified both by anarchy and disorder and by the cultural differences between the native populations and the invaders. In the north the Latin language disappeared; elsewhere it was vulgarized by the uneducated, illiterate populations. In some towns of Italy and parts of France vestiges of the old civilization remained, but by the eighth century there was less Roman civilization in the Latin west than in the other two "heirs" of that great society.

Both the barbarian "kings" in northern Europe and the popes at Rome attempted unsuccessfully to stem the tide of disorder in the Gallo-Roman West. The barbarian princes had no traditions that would allow them to understand Roman political institutions, and their contempt as warriors for men of the pen prevented their making a contact with Roman society through the written word. The church, too, had its troubles with the barbarian invaders; the Roman popes sent missionaries to convert them, but it was difficult to explain the Christian conception of God to these men, and it was often questionable whether the new converts would accept Christianity, or would turn the Christian God into a god of war in line with their own traditions. Furthermore, by the seventh century the church itself was suffering from the problems resulting from the decay of Roman society; there were not enough educated men available to operate the church and to carry forward its mission effectively. The curtains of ignorance that settled over the West also blanketed the Roman church and obstructed its mission. The popes came to pretend to the authority of the Caesars of the western Empire, but the actual power and prestige of the church were grievously weakened. The occasional monastery, the mission churches, and an insecurely established episcopal organization reflected only imperfectly the ideal of a united western European Christendom under papal authority.

Undoubtedly it was due to the Roman church, however, that the Gallo-Roman and Germanic peoples of the Latin west did not entirely lose the memory of a Europe governed by Roman law and assured peace by the Roman shield. This ideal of a unified society did not die in the West, but the reality of the political and cultural structure moved further and further from that ideal. The barbarian tribesmen with their varying languages and customs made many different adjustments to the populations among whom they settled. The linguistic and cultural diversity was further accentuated by the fact that there were no schools to provide men with a common language or a common body of information to hold the elite of the populations together. In France, Italy, and Spain many new dialects emerged from the corruption of the Latin tongue; in Germany, the Rhineland, and England, where Latin culture had never had deep roots, Germanic dialects became the speech of the people. These linguistic patterns merely reflected the deeper changes in custom that were taking place as new societies emerged from the debris of Roman civilization. Men continued to believe in the unity of the Gallo-Roman West, but when Charlemagne, a great soldier-statesman, momentarily brought most of what is now Italy, France, and Germany into a tenuous political unity (around A.D. 800) he quickly discovered that cultural diversity, not unity, was the basic political fact. Indeed, the church was the only Roman institution at his disposal that could be used to help unite and govern his state. Charlemagne was unable to reunite the West: the processes of history held a quite different historic destiny for Europe, a destiny in which the very diversity that emerged from the ruins of Roman society provided much of the stimulus for the creation of a new and wonderful civilization.

In the century and a half after Charlemagne's death (814), western men were put to their severest test, and the conditions of their political and social life probably touched the lowest point ever experienced after the disintegration of Roman authority. From the north came the Norsemen in their shallow draft ships that were capable of crossing the Atlantic ocean or of sailing up the rivers of France and Germany. These wild marauders came to pillage, and Europe had no adequate force to place against them. From the east came the Hungarians; mounted on fast ponies, they swept into Germany, stealing and burning wherever they went. From the south came the Moslem raiders seeking slaves and loot along the coasts of Europe, as far north as England and Ireland, and attacking even Rome itself. Western Europe did survive these iron years of the ninth and tenth centuries; indeed, some writers even see in them the real seedbed for the feudal political and military institutions that Europe was to create. To the men of the day, however, it must often have been questionable whether or not they would really survive.

2. FEUDAL INSTITUTIONS

At the base of all western European political institutions we find the political organization of feudal society; from feudal relationships the great modern states have evolved. In the method of all political institutions the feudal order developed out of the social, economic, and political problems of the society in which it came into being. For example, there was one Roman socioeconomic institution that never quite disappeared in Europe: the *latifundia* or large estates. These were basic social and economic units; an important landowner, his slaves or serfs, and the other people who grouped around his house to provide for the necessities of life formed a natural socioeconomic group with great resistance to the ravages of change. As the Germanic peoples settled down and became cultivators of the soil, they, too, tended to group themselves around the house of an important chief, and in the course of time the Roman and the barbarian landlords mingled their culture and their blood so that these manorial settlements took on forms that were the result of the mixture of the several cultures in the decaying Roman Empire. When Charlemagne attempted to recreate the western Roman Empire, he recognized that these manorial units could be used to provide local government by making their owners mutually interdependent, but his empire did not last long enough for the experiment to be tried. However, after his death, the attacks of the Norse, Hungarian, and Saracen invaders forced the owners of these manorial units to cooperate with each other and with the monastic foundations in their neighborhoods for defense. Out of these crises were born the institutions of feudal society.

Under such conditions the key person was the owner of the manor or *latifundia*—the landlord, the nobleman. He had enough capital to equip himself with the weapons of the soldier and to gather around his house a band of retainers. He had the leisure to train himself in the use of arms, and the money to build some sort of fortification to protect his villages. By the ninth and tenth centuries the peasants, even those of Teutonic origin whose forebears had been warriors, were no longer prepared to fight; the cost of arms and military equipment had become too great. Therefore, those who were not already slaves of a landlord were often willing to surrender some of their freedom and their right to personal ownership of land in return for the protection that a lord and his band of men-at-arms could provide. The economic and social relationships that developed between the lord and the people who worked the soil will be discussed in a later chapter; it is enough to note here that the lord provided a sort of justice, military protection, and whatever political organization the villagers had. The lord and his manor comprised the simplest cell in the political structure of feudal Europe. But the owner of a single manor could not alone provide for his defense against determined foes; he in turn had to league himself with other landlords in the neighborhood to protect his property. In this way the feudal fief came into existence.

The fief was composed of an indeterminate number of manors or estates. At its head was the richest and most important lord in the neighborhood, who might have the title of baron. The other landlords freely gave him their lands, but in turn received them back again as his vassals. In other cases the baron might give part of his own land to a landless soldier of valor in return for his services. The lord-vassal relationship that existed between these men was at the heart of the feudal contract. It was a personal relationship between two men rather than an impersonal one between men and the state. The vassal, upon assuming control over his lands, placed his hands in those of his lord and swore homage and fealty, thus establishing a relationship of reciprocal obligations between the two men. Since the most important problem was that of defense of the fief, the most important obligations were military in character. The vassal's obligations to defend the fief in case of attack were usually unlimited, but his lord could also require him to go on military adventures outside the fief for a limited number of days a year, in some cases thirty, in some as many as sixty. This latter fact made it difficult to assemble an army for an extended campaign without some further inducement to the men who filled the ranks. The vassal was also expected to do garrison duty for specific periods of time either at the baron's own castle or at one of the forts on the frontiers of the fief. He was obliged, too, to help with the political organization of the fief: he attended councils where his advice was solicited and, in general, helped to manage the fief. Furthermore, he was expected to attend his lord at ceremonial and festive occasions: when the lord's children were married, a son knighted, or a death occurred in the family. When the vassal's lands were transferred in one way or another to a son, a brother, a nephew, or to a widow who could find someone to do knight's service for her, there was a regular schedule of fees or fines that had to be paid. In fact, there was no rule that applied universally to all fiefs; each one had its own customs and developed its own law. When speaking of "feudal law" or "feudal customs" it is important to remember that there were many of them. The diversities within the society we call "feudal" were very great. It is perhaps this political pluralism that is responsible for the rich diversity that developed in western civilization in the following centuries.

Beyond the frontiers of the fief there emerged larger political organizations, namely the duchy and the kingdom. They might also be considered as fiefs for they came into being in much the same way: they were associations of a number of fiefs for political and military purposes. Thus the baron had his lord (a duke) to whom he swore homage and fealty, and the dukes in their turn had a lord (the king) to whom they swore homage and fealty. Some political theorists insisted that the Holy Roman emperors who emerged in tenth-century central Europe were in turn the overlords of the kings, but the kings of Europe very early developed the doctrine that "the king is emperor in his own kingdom," and, therefore, that the king held his lands from God. Therefore God was owner of all the land, and he, in turn, gave it to the kings to do his work on the earth, and they in turn gave it to their vassals to insure protection, justice, and tranquillity. Thus, in theory, God was at the top and the peasant tilling the soil was at the bottom of this chain of the feudal hierarchy; the church, as might be expected, was also closely involved in the system, with bishops and abbots becoming true feudal lords and serving in both political and religious roles. Thus feudal society came to include all of western European culture.

The theory of any political organization, however, may or may not correspond to the realities of everyday politics. Under the changing conditions of life between the hard years of the tenth century and the economic prosperity of the thirteenth, feudal institutions varied greatly. In the early years many of the kings were actually weaker and less important militarily and politically than their vassals. In the tenth century Hugh Capet was chosen by the French peers to be their king (after the Carolingian dynasty had died out) because he was one of the weakest of their number and therefore unlikely to try to impose his will upon them. They had to have a king from whom they could "hold" their lands; they wanted a king who would not interfere in their affairs. But the processes of history have a way of divesting some institutions of their power and giving other institutions unexpected weight, and so it was with those feudal institutions. As Europe began to recover from the harsh treatment of the ninth and tenth centuries, real power tended to migrate upward in the ranks of the feudal hierarchy. Europe was too large and decentralized for either the pope or the emperor to re-establish the old Roman imperium, but it also became too prosperous and complex economically and politically for power to remain in the hands of the petty knights or barons. The men "on the wave of the future" in the feudal society were the kings and princes who eventually were able to resist the encroachments of either pope or emperor and, at the same time, to impose their rule upon their own vassals. These men became the princes whose labors contributed to the creation of that unique institution, the European state. Historians, looking back at the disorders of feudal society with its petty baronial wars and numerous rebellions of vassals, have called the feudal era a period of "organized anarchy." The judgment is at once true and too harsh; feudal society was also the seedbed for the political institutions that molded western civilization.

3. THE ROMAN CATHOLIC CHURCH

The differences in concepts of church government, rituals, and even some items of dogma that had led to fissures in the Christian church during the latter years of the Roman Empire became more pronounced after the Roman power in the West had practically disappeared. The bishop of Rome, in the See of St. Peter, was the most important Roman official left in the Gallo-Roman West, and, as popes, the Roman bishops not only came to demand recognition of their See as the first in Christendom, but also to take over the government of the city of Rome. In the East the patriarchs and the Byzantine emperor refused to recognize the papal claims of the priority of the Roman See, and at the same time the differences in ritual and practices deepened the split between the Greek and Roman churches. After the Moslem conquest detached the Syrio-Egyptian community from the old empire, the split between the East and the West became definite: by the tenth and eleventh centuries the popes at Rome and the patriarchs at Constantinople mutually excommunicated and anathematized each other in language that reflected the crudeness of the era; by the eleventh century the breach was complete: the Christian community was divided between the Greek Orthodox church of the East and the Roman Catholic church of the West.

The years between the sixth and the eleventh centuries were hard ones for the Roman Catholic church as well as for the rest of the Gallo-Roman world. Missionaries sent out by Rome converted the barbarians, and the monks joined them as important agents of civilization in the neighborhoods of the monasteries, but it was a momentous task to make the Christian mission clear to the men of that rude age; by the ninth century the barbarians had become Christians of a sort, but the number of men who understood the subtleties of Christian theology—or, indeed, the basic moral teachings of the church—was small. As discussed above, Charlemagne discovered that the church was the only existing institution available to him to give unity to his empire, and so he greatly increased the number of bishops and strengthened their rule, as well as introduced schools where clergymen could be trained more adequately for their mission. After his death, however, the church suffered the same distress that overtook the rest of Europe. The churches and monasteries were natural targets for the marauding Norsemen and other disorderly bands. The tenth century, an age in which books and schools were practically unknown, witnessed catastrophic disorders in the church. Ignorant priests could not understand their mission, and the urgent demands of the day for defense entwined the clergy with the feudal institutions that provided the existing defense system. Eventually, the greatest evil was the fact that clerical appointments were made by secular authorities, and usually a clergyman was appointed for reasons that had nothing to do with the church. The candidate could handle a sword effectively; he had powerful friends or relatives; or he could pay money for his office. None of these reasons led to succcessful appointments, but what else could be expected from men who did not read and who had to fight for survival? The evil infected the church at every level. Even the papacy had become the plaything of the Roman nobles and the disorderly mobs at their disposal. As soon as Europe began to recover a little from the effects of the tenth-century disorders, it was evident to many that the church needed reform.

The reform movement really started in the tenth century with the rise of the Cluny monastic movement in France. The Cluny monks obeyed the strict monastic rule, opened schools, and impressed people in power with the necessity for reform. Within a century Europe was dotted with new foundations either directly subordinate to the Cluny monastery or inspired by the same high principles. In retrospect, it is astonishing to see how the reformers infused new spirit into the religious life of Europe in a short hundred-odd years. They sought, first of all, to lead the nobles and princes to understand the need to give spiritual content to men's lives, and depended upon them to help bring the mission to the people. All areas of religious life were affected by the movement: church government, ritual, theology, and the Christian mission, each in turn profited from the energy of the reformers.

One of the most important abuses attacked by the reform was that of secular interference with clerical appointments. The abuses of simony (purchase of office), nepotism (appointment of relatives), and pluralism (the holding of several offices by one person) were all directly connected with the secular appointment of clergymen. The Cluniac monks would not accept any grants of land that would force them to recognize a landlord who might be able to control appointments in their foundations. By word and deed the reformers attacked this problem at every level of church government; it would be quite untrue to suggest that they were able to cure all of the abuses, but they did win striking victories. Unquestionably the most important was the creation of the College of Cardinals as the body responsible for the election of the pope. By the inclusion of non-Roman clergymen in this body, the control of the Roman nobles over the papacy was broken, and the reformers were able to place men of their own choosing in the Chair of St. Peter. Thus the papacy itself was enlisted in the ranks of the reformers.

It would not have been enough to reform the government of the church. Students joined hands with administrators to purify its doctrines by recovering the writings of the early church fathers. For hundreds of years the theological speculations of the first centuries of the Christian era had been neglected or only partly understood. The task of recovering this intellectual heritage of the church and integrating it with the Christian mission was one of the great intellectual labors of the eleventh and twelfth centuries. Besides the students of theology, there were men who rediscovered and expanded the old liturgy of the church, and those who purified its mission. The impact of these labors upon the imagination of contemporaries is testified to by the great cathedrals erected in the later eleventh, the twelfth, and the thirteenth centuries, as well as by the popular tradition that would try to make us believe that the Middle Ages was primarily an era of piety and Christian works.

From the point of view of the political evolution of Europe, the most important result of the reform was the rise in the powers of the papacy. At the end of the eleventh century a Roman pope sent western soldiers to the Levant on a great crusade to liberate the Holy Lands, and within the next hundred years the prestige, wealth, and power of the Holy See had become the greatest single force in Europe. Papal courts, papal tax collectors, and papal agents were everywhere in Europe. The papal curia at Rome, while deprived of ordinary military forces, had tremendous moral powers at its disposal: by placing a kingdom under an interdict that would deprive the entire land of the services of clergymen—thereby endangering the soul of anyone who happened to die—or by releasing vassals from their oaths to either king or emperor, the pope at Rome could bring great pressure upon an opponent. Medieval theory assumed that society was governed by two officers, the one spiritual and the other temporal, but by the end of the twelfth century the papacy had reached the point at which the kings of Europe were its vassals: from England to Poland rulers accepted the overlordship of the papal throne. A great pope like Innocent III seemed on the point of establishing a new Imperium under papal control. As we shall see in a later chapter, this very power led to new troubles for the church: temporal interests too often obscured spiritual ones in the eyes of high clergymen, and the wealth and power of the church aroused envy and hostility in the hearts of both the princes of Europe and their subjects. Finally, in the fourteenth century conflicts between the papacy and the rulers of Europe resulted in victory for the latter.

4. URBANIZATION

Since the economic and social aspects of the rise of towns and cities will form an important part of a later discussion, at this point it is unnecessary to do more than call attention to the political and military significance of their development. From the eleventh century onward conditions of life improved steadily throughout western Europe, and with the return of a measure of security came considerable amelioration in the conditions of life. The population began to increase, and Europe started to expand toward its frontiers: swamps were drained, forests cleared, new settlements arose in the eastern borderlands, and, perhaps most important of all, towns began to spring up along the roads and watercourses to accommodate the new requirements of commerce, finance, and manufacturing that were becoming so important. By the beginning of the thirteenth century movement of goods in western Europe was probably as extensive as it had been at the most prosperous period of the Roman Empire. The growth of both commerce and the towns resulted in political and military problems unknown in the earlier period when country noblemen had been the only political forces in the land.

The townsmen had at their disposal military and financial power. The walls that they built became military installations, and the civic militia companies that were at first useful only for defense of the walls and street fighting finally became strong enough to challenge the feudal cavalry in the field. The financial power of the townsmen played an even larger role. The feudal nobleman received his income primarily in the form of goods and services, and his wealth—more or less in the form of land—was not flexible. He could get money in the form of gold and silver, but this was not easy. The townsman, on the contrary, possessed wealth which was more easily converted into money, and his commercial and financial affairs gave him a skill in the handling of money unknown on the country manor estate. This money was easily transformed into political power. The situation became more of a reality as the political ambitions of princes, stimulated by the rising military power of the West, led them to extend their activities toward the frontiers of Europe in the form of crusades in Spain, Sicily, and the Near East, and at the same time encouraged them to bring their vassals under tighter control. Money for these projects could be obtained from the townsmen in return for political privileges and concessions, and especially for protection of commerce on the sea and on the land. When changes in the art of war introduced a much greater number of foot soldiers to the battle-field, money became even more important because the foot soldier, unlike the feudal cavalryman, was a mercenary who fought for money under the banner of the captain who could pay for his services.

Care must be taken not to simplify unnecessarily what was essentially a very complex process. As the cities appeared on the European scene they developed special needs connected with their commerce and their desire for recognition within a society that was centered on the rural interests of the feudal nobility. They wanted the right to trade with a minimum of inter-ference in the form of tariffs or tolls, and, of course, they expected protection in return for the payments that were imposed upon them. They also required the establishment of courts capable of dispensing justice and applying busi-ness law. There were many ways in which these needs could be met. Some-times the townsmen found it wise to unite with the kings or great dukes against the marauding activities of the lesser nobility whose behavior was often similar to that of bandits. In other cases, they formed leagues with other cities and tried to impose their own terms upon the feudal society, if necessary by force of arms. The Lombard League in Italy, the Hansa League in the Baltic, the Leagues of Flemish and of Spanish towns were more or less successful in their efforts to force kings and emperors, as well as pirates and highwaymen, to respect their interests. Some of the towns, like Florence or Venice, invaded the countryside and brought the rural areas as well as other towns directly under their own government. It is probably a safe generalization to say that the townsmen used both their money and their military power to secure the political requirements resulting from their commerce and city life. In this way the urbanization movement became an important force among the processes that were establishing the characteristic forms of western European society. As we shall see, the townsmen (or bourgeoisie) came to play a significant role in the rise of the princes and the development of the new state.

5. THE RISE OF THE PRINCE: FEUDAL KINGDOMS

At the turn of the sixteenth century an Italian political philosopher, Ma-chiavelli, wrote a book entitled *The Prince*. One of the most famous of all political treatises, it has been variously called a "handbook for tyrants," a "do-it-yourself book" for rulers, and, more properly, "an analysis of the methods of exercising political power." Machiavelli was an historian as well as a philosopher. He was struck by the fact that in the preceding two cen-turies there had occurred a considerable concentration of power in the hands

of princes and kings at the expense of the other orders of the political hierarchy, and he assumed, rightly, that the process was going to continue. There
was too much anarchy in the political pluralism of the feudal era; it could
not be maintained in a society that was developing large commercial enterprises, a money economy with banks and exchanges, a new technology in
war and in industry, and finally, new conceptions of power. It was unquestionably necessary to suppress the anarchy inherent in the feudal contract by
a concentration of power and authority; there were many things involved
in this process of concentration, but, as Machiavelli well understood, the
princes who were creating the new states of Europe were at the center of
the movement.

These princes, however, had to contend with the fact that the political
power and the institutions with which they had to deal were rooted in
feudal contracts and feudal society. Thus, each of the kings and princes of
Europe was faced with widely divergent political problems. The feudal
kingdoms of Europe had quite different constitutions, and these basic institutions were the decisive influence upon the development of the European
states that succeeded them.

In Germany, for example, the Holy Roman Empire of the tenth and
eleventh centuries developed as a confederation of feudal principalities.
These principalities were offshoots of more ancient tribal states, and when
that Empire disintegrated with the death of Frederick II in 1250, the
principalities remained as the enduring political institutions of Germany.
The German dukes and princes had already long been semiautonomous,
especially in the control of problems within their own territories; the mere
fact that the emperors had been unable to give unity and meaning to an
Empire that pretended to include both Germany and Italy did not undermine the power of the German princes in their own little principalities.
Indeed, when the Holy Roman Empire of the German nation arose in the
fourteenth century as the successor of the medieval Empire, the confederate
structure of the state clearly reflected the earlier constitution. Emperor Charles
IV fixed the constitution of the Empire by the Golden Bull of 1356 which
provided for the election of the emperor by the seven electors (the king of
Bohemia, the princes of Saxony, Brandenburg, and the Palatinate, and the
archbishops of Cologne, Trier, and Mainz), and for a diet or *Reichstag*
(parliament) of three houses representing the electors, the princes, and the
towns. The further organization of the Empire into "circles" or local units
made up of several principalities under the leadership of the most powerful
prince in the neighborhood underlined the confederate structure of the Empire. This organization of power was destined to be one of the most significant facts in the political evolution of central Europe; even today Germany
is a federal state reflecting the historical organization of political power.

Italy also was involved in the collapse of the ideal of the medieval Holy

WESTERN EUROPE
ABOUT 1400

Roman Empire, even though the German emperors had never really succeeded in bringing the Italian peninsula under their control for any long
period of time. Political power in Italy tended to gravitate in the north into
the hands of the rulers of the city states of Venice, Florence, and Milan,
and in the south to the Papal States and the kingdom of Naples and Sicily.
The duchy of Savoy on the frontier between France and Italy and a number
of smaller states in the mountainous north had to adjust their interests to
the balance of power that developed in Italy among the five important Italian
states. Thus Italy did not even develop a confederation or alliance of principalities; the five Italian states governed their relations with each other, and
with foreigners, by a balance of power maintained by military as well as
diplomatic procedures. When this balance broke down, and foreign troops
from the north and from Spain entered Italy as allies of one or the other

of the Italian states, Italy lost all control over its own destiny. Foreign intervention may well be the cause of the decline of Italian cultural leadership after 1500.

The situation in France was quite different. As a result of shrewd political leadership, the French monarchy developed into a federal state rather than a confederation. By marriage and by war the kings of France gradually brought under their own hands the lands of their great vassals, the peers of France. But when the king installed himself on the ducal throne of his vassal, the province that he thereby took over did not lose its traditional characteristics. It was usual for the king to grant a charter guaranteeing the integrity of the ancient laws and customs of the province. Thus the gradual displacement of the quasi-sovereign vassals of the crown resulted in the creation of a federation of provinces, each with its own laws, customs, and even tax structures, but all of them under the government of the king. This federal character of the French monarchy became one of the striking facts in the history of France: from the days of the strong feudal kings to the French Revolution reformers struggled to give unity to the legal, fiscal, commercial, and political institutions of the entire kingdom, while the men who enjoyed the privileges guaranteed by charters and traditions labored hard to retain their special positions.

The English monarchy was more fortunate than any of the others. Duke William of Normandy who conquered England in 1066 organized his kingdom so that the more obvious difficulties inherent in a feudal monarchy were avoided. He did not allow his great vassals to acquire large tracts of land concentrated in one place in the kingdom; this policy was facilitated by the structure of landownership that he found in Saxon England, and the results were fortunate, for it was not easy for a great baron to retire to his estates and defy the king. William also prevented his barons from acquiring vassals who were not also subject to the king; thus it was difficult for the vassal to assemble a military force for rebellion since both the great and the small nobles owed loyalty to the throne. The result was that feudal England became a unitary state untroubled by the problems of confederation or federation, and the English kings were able to establish a government that could give unity to the laws and customs of the entire kingdom. England was to be troubled by civil wars and armed contests for the crown, but the English kings escaped many of the thorny problems that disturbed the continent.

The other kingdoms of Europe differed in turn from the ones described above. Spain, for example, developed several kingdoms with constitutions similar to those of France; then, at the end of the fifteenth century, these kingdoms in turn were united by marriages to result in a Spanish monarchy that was haunted by questions arising out of provincial differences in laws, customs, and ambitions. The Spanish grandees remained a problem for the king throughout the sixteenth century. In Poland, Lithuania, Hungary, and Bohemia where the king received his crown by election rather than by hereditary right, the great vassals of the kingdom remained largely independent: indeed, in both Poland and Hungary armed rebellion against the king was a "constitutional" right, and many of the great magnates of the land possessed power as great as that of their king.

6. THE RISE OF THE PRINCE: LAW AND POLITICAL THEORY

While the feudal origins of the kingdoms of Europe differed from one to another and thereby canalized the development of political institutions in divergent directions, there were also common forces working on the whole of European society that tended to give a sort of unity to the emerging political structure of Europe. It might be said that their feudal origins conferred a uniqueness on each of the political societies of Europe, but the fact that European society as a whole was developing new technology in war and industry, new needs in commercial and political organization, and new visions of the structure of law and political power tended to mould the evolution of these states in a common direction. The rediscovery of Roman law was one of the outstanding factors of this process, for it came to affect all the European states in one way or another.

Before the eleventh century it was rare for anyone except a clergyman to know how to read and write, and even the clergy were often so poorly educated that little could be said for their skills. Legal studies in that rude era were practically nonexistent. Trial by combat or some such test constituted the legal procedure that settled many cases, while a rough and ready system of justice based upon common sense and custom as recalled by living men served to fill the need for law. The Germanic traditional law and the feudal procedures were relatively simple and mostly unwritten; in any case, they did not require trained men or extensive institutions. The church had a body of law largely based upon the older Roman procedures, but before the eleventh century even this canon law was only partially understood by the men who governed the church.

After the crusades, however, a large number of legal problems arose. The crusaders usually left their property and their dependents in the care of the church, and since so many of them did not return from the east, it was not long before the bishops found themselves beset with complex legal questions that were difficult to unravel. By the end of the eleventh century it became common for many bishops to send one or more of their brighter young deacons down to the school at Bologna, where men were trying to relearn the legal teachings of the Romans. By the twelfth century, when business enterprise began to expand and the rise of the towns had started to complicate the structure of society, laymen as well as clergymen began to visit the famous university at Bologna or one of the newer schools in the north (e.g., the University of Paris) where Roman law was taught. The rediscovery of the legal procedures of classical society was a gradual process: by the thirteenth century, however, the great law schools were providing a continuous stream of young men with training in the science of Roman law.

At first glance this seems to have little to do with the rise of princely power. Nonetheless, it does have much to do with it. Roman law assumed a society in which the state was an abstraction above all men rather than a series of personal relationships between men. The feudal contract was between lord and vassal; the Roman contract was between state and subjects. Roman law also assumed a society in which the state commanded and the subjects obeyed, a society in which law rather than the whims of a ruler or the chances of combat determined justice. Furthermore, Roman law made the sharp distinction between free and unfree men as well as clear regulations about property and property rights. In all this the new legal learning cut sharply across the half-delineated lines of Germanic and traditional law, and also gave rulers a new vision of their role in society. It required no great imagination to identify the king's government with the state.

Perhaps equally important was the fact that the study of law tended to develop a new kind of individual. Whether they were laymen or clergymen, the men trained in the law tended to think more exactly and to conceive of society in new terms. These new men were soon to be the advisers of princes; their orientation was political and secular rather than religious, and their advice pushed princes toward the consolidation of power in the hands of the royal government.

With such men as their servants, kings were able to extend their power at the expense of both their vassals and the church. For example, it is interesting to observe the increased prestige of the royal courts. There were church courts, seignioral courts, town courts, and royal courts—all competing with one another for jurisdiction. The fact that the king's courts provided opportunity for appellate jurisdiction (that is, the right to appeal to a higher court if the decision seemed arbitrary or unfair) and at the same time tended to be manned by men who understood Roman law placed these royal courts in an advantageous position. By the end of the fifteenth century in many lands the king's courts had won a nearly complete victory over their rivals, with a consequent increase in royal prestige.

7. THE RISE OF THE PRINCE: THE ESTATES AND DIETS

The new conception of the role, as well as of the expanding needs, of the royal authority gave rise to several types of new institutions. The feudal monarchies before the thirteenth century had a relatively simple institutional structure. It was customary for the feudal king to consult with his peers on policies that affected the whole kingdom, but such consultation was only partly formalized, and the king was expected to raise revenue from his own lands to provide for his projects and to take care of the expenses of his government. His vassals owed the king military service; this might be paid in the form of money or in the traditional form of knight's service in the royal army. But they did not expect to pay him taxes. Toward the end of the thirteenth century, however, kings all over Europe suddenly found themselves in need of support other than military aid. The pretensions of the papacy to power forced kings to enlist the loyalty of their subjects against papal encroachments. Only if supported by their people, would kings be able to resist the papal demands. About the same time changes in the art of war and extended demands for bureaucratic servants forced kings to seek financial aid in the form of taxes to carry on their government. These needs arose from the expanding society that accompanied the economic and population booms of the twelfth and thirteenth centuries.

Since both money and moral support were needed, kings extended the practice of consultation to include the three orders of society: the clergy, the nobility, and the townsmen (third estate). English-speaking people usually think of the English Parliament as the first of these consultative institutions, but actually it may be that Spain rather than England was the "mother of parliaments" in the sense that the Cortés of the kingdoms of Castile and Aragon seem to have been the first medieval consultative assemblies to include townsmen as well as nobles and clergymen. The Spanish kingdoms had particular problems. They were the frontier between Christendom and Islam, and throughout the later Middle Ages they were almost constantly at war with the Moors. At the same time the Spanish towns developed *hermandades* (town leagues or brotherhoods) very early, and those gave the townsmen a new vision of their place in society. It is, therefore, not surprising that when kings needed money for their wars, the townsmen were consulted about the kings' projects. They were invited to send representatives to the Cortés because they would vote and collect taxes only if they also were consulted. Thus, as early as the end of the thirteenth century representative institutions became an important feature in the governments of the Spanish kingdoms. The Cortés of Aragon with its four houses or *brazos* (arms), writes Professor Cheyney, "occupied the most independent, influential, and well established position of all the parliamentary bodies in Europe. It imposed taxes, passed legislation, and controlled the king's government so that its powers appear coordinate with and in some respects superior to those of the king."

In Castile, Valencia, Catalonia, and Portugal we find a development parallel to that of Aragon. Throughout the fourteenth and well into the fifteenth centuries those representative institutions played a significant role in the development of the Spanish kingdoms and the conquest of Spain from the Moors. Toward the end of the fifteenth century the parliaments tended to become decadent, but they had already succeeded in bringing the towns and the territorial princes into a common political life.

The rise of the Estates-General in France resulted from a long history of provincial estates and feudal convocations, but not until the opening of the fourteenth century (1302) were the townsmen called as the "third estate" to deliberate on the king's business. This first meeting came as a result of the French king's desire to reject the pope's claim to superiority over temporal sovereigns. One might almost say that this 1302 convocation of the Estates-General marks a break with the medieval notion that the western empire could be recreated by spiritual or by temporal authority. Subsequently, the Estates-General was assembled to grant taxes (1314) and to exclude the English king from the throne (1317) by accepting or inventing the so-called "Salic Law" which assured the succession to the French throne solely through the male line.

By the middle of the fourteenth century, when the French and English kings were locked in war, the Estates-General began to assume a new importance. The king needed money on a scale theretofore unknown. In 1356 the Estates were considering his request for three million Parisian livres, and appeared ready to grant it on condition that the Estates would secure a measure of control over the government. Before the request was agreed to, however, the battle of Poitiers, in which the French feudal army was cut to pieces and the king captured, created a new situation. The Estates-General then offered to provide the money, but they also demanded the arrest and trial of eight of the king's officers and the appointment of a royal council drawn from the Estates-General to control the king's government.

This began a movement that was more of a revolution than a reform. One Stephen Marcel, the provost of the merchants of Paris, became the leader of the group that finally drew up the "Great Ordinance" which the Dauphin was forced to accept. This charter was a remarkable document, the nearest to a written constitution that was to appear in Europe until the seventeenth century, and, in a very real way, it was the first document in the long process that eventually was to place the government of France in the hands of the people. But this attempt was premature. In the fourteenth century Paris was not France, and the bourgeoisie were still few in number, weak, and disorganized. The revolutionaries lost their hold on the government; Marcel was murdered (1358), and with his death the short-lived attempt of the Estates-General to govern France came to an end. The kings, alerted to the danger inherent in the assembly of the Estates-General, continued to call on it from time to time for revenue, but the institution never became an instrument of royal power in the way that its counterpart did in England.

The situation in France was further complicated by the fact that in addition to the Estates-General which met periodically to consider the affairs of the kingdom as a whole, there were provincial Estates summoned to deliberate upon the problems of the separate provinces. This federal character of the French monarchy was often responsible for the failure of the Estates-General to act effectively, either for or against the royal interests. Many of its members were keenly aware of the privileges of their own provinces and quite unwilling to surrender their favored position for any legislation that might unify the whole kingdom. There was one important exception to this rule, and it greatly strengthened the position of the crown. The Estates-General of 1439 granted the king a war tax, the *taille,* under conditions that allowed him to continue to collect the tax as a permanent source of revenue. The Estates-General did not understand the implications of this act. The *taille* became as valuable to the French kings as the mines of Peru were to be to the kings of Spain; it freed them from dependence upon later sessions of the Estates-General for revenue. This deprived the Estates of a formidable source of strength—namely, the power of the purse.

The rise of the English Parliament parallels that of the Spanish and French representative institutions. In the mid-thirteenth century the king began to call townsmen and knights (landowners who might or might not have been nobles) to join the great nobles and clergy in deliberations on matters of state. The end of the thirteenth century (1295) saw the so-called "model parliament" in which all classes above serfdom had a measure of representation. The custom of meeting in two houses—the Lords Temporal and Spiritual and the House of Commons—became fixed in the early fourteenth century when the gentry and the burgesses started the practice of sitting together in the Abbey of Westminster whenever the Parliament met in London.

The power of the English Parliament grew apace in the course of the fourteenth century. The kings were almost constantly engaged in war with France, Scotland, and Wales, and they had to go to Parliament for money. There were forty-eight meetings between 1327 and 1377, and due to their actions, the rights and privileges of Parliament became ever more firmly fixed. At the same time, the institution became increasingly valuable to the king's government. During the troubled years of the latter fourteenth and most of the fifteenth centuries, when contests over the right to the succession disturbed the whole of the kingdom, Parliament made good not only its right to hold the purse strings, but also to interfere in the king's government by reorganizing the council and appointing a regency. At the end of the fifteenth century when Henry Tudor came to the throne (1485), and thus put an end to the civil wars, he recognized Parliament as an institution that could be used to strengthen his hold over the country. Thus cooperation between the king and the representatives of the estates of the land became a characteristic feature of English government under the Tudor rulers (1485–1603).

While Parliament in England expanded its power, in the Holy Roman Empire of the German nation a plethora of representative institutions prevented any of them from becoming really important. Each of the German principalities had a *Landtag* (meeting of the *Stände* or classes) of some kind or other, and each of these little assemblies was jealous of its power and of the privileges in the *Land* (province). At a higher level, in each of the twelve "circles" of the Empire there was a diet charged with the defense of the frontiers, and finally there was the Diet of the Empire composed of the three houses—electors, princes, and towns. This complexity of representative institutions reflected that of the confederative constitution of the Empire. The result was that instead of strengthening the imperial power, representative institutions tended to make it diffuse and ineffective.

In kingdoms like Poland and Hungary, even less tightly organized than the Holy Roman Empire of the German nation, the assembly of the diet only further emphasized the power of the magnates of the land vis-à-vis the king, for the great ones tended to control it and make it an institution subservient to their needs. Like all generalizations, this one will not hold universally for all times, but it is near enough to the truth to help to explain why those eastern kingdoms failed to effect the powerful centralized institutions that became characteristic of the western states. It may well be that the fact that the eastern part of Europe was behind in the growth of great urban centers—and consequently in the rise of both a bourgeois class and a money economy—contributed to the weakness of the royalist parties in those kingdoms and thus, by default, left power in the hands of the great landlords.

8. THE RISE OF THE PRINCE: THE ART OF WAR

The highways of fourteenth-century Europe were crowded with merchants and men going here and there—to fairs, market towns, parliaments, Estates, and conferences—but there were also other people on the highways and other forces at work in the political picture. In addition to the merchants with their pack trains or their wagons and the noble or bourgeois representatives to the parliament, a new kind of soldier was also on the march. The medieval soldier had been the mail-clad knight, mounted on a horse, and followed by his squires and attendants. These battle-ax and broadsword wielders had made Europe the scene of almost continuous private warfare, and had carried western military power as far as the Holy Land. Their descendants in the fourteenth and fifteenth centuries still wore armor, and rode forth to battle as errant knights and representatives of a decaying feudalism. The true successors to the medieval knights as the soldiers of

Europe, however, were the mercenaries who were beginning to assume their places on the battlefield. Interestingly enough, just when the real usefulness of medieval knighthood on the battlefield was under question, the nobility developed the "cult" of chivalry. Orders of knighthood were founded, tourneys were held, and every effort was made to retain the mythology of the feudal soldier. Like the American wild west show of the twentieth century, the tournament of the later fourteenth, fifteenth, and sixteenth centuries was a spectacle rather than preparation for the work of the world.

In fact, by the fourteenth century there were two distinct military forces that were merging into an army. The first was the emergence of the free companies of foot soldiers, usually bowmen or pikemen, who were to become the backbone of modern armies. The second consisted of engineers and artillerymen, who at first were not soldiers at all but laborers whose job it was to conduct siege operations to reduce a fortified place. It takes little imagination to realize that both of these new military forces constituted a desperate menace to the feudal lords who had heretofore ruled the countryside. The free companies could liberate the prince from his dependence upon the feudal levy; the engineer-artillerymen could break down the walls of the great feudal castles that dotted Europe and ruled the countryside. The time was not far away when the king would have the military power needed to compel his vassals to obey his orders.

The weapons of the foot soldiers were not yet the product of important technological advances. The most complex was the crossbow, which was a powerful weapon but a little cumbersome to operate; the simplest was a heavy pike, the "good day" as it was called in the Lowlands, that could be used to impale either horse or rider. The most effective weapon turned out to be the English longbow, which could rapidly and accurately launch an arrow capable of piercing most of the armor of the day. None of the new weapons was really effective against a large body of armored cavalry in the open field if the horsemen were intelligently led, but if the foot soldiers established themselves in a defensive position with either a body of water or some other barrier to slow up and channel the movement of the horsemen, the arrows and the "good days" could work havoc on feudal cavalry.

The rise of the engineers and artillerymen as vital components of military power had important results too. The knight clad in armor and mounted on a palfrey was the offensive force of feudal society. The same knight guarding the ramparts and towers of his castle was also the defensive force of feudal society. The discovery of gunpowder and its application to military problems originated the process that outmoded the feudal castle, just as the new infantry outmoded the feudal knight. Engineers learned to mine the ramparts of castles and to blow them up with powder; they learned how to build attacking earthworks that made the destruction of most castles only a matter of time and patience, while artillery fire provided an offensive weapon that decreased the time required to reduce a fortification.

The earliest artillery was of little use as a military weapon, although the noise and smoke might have frightened men and horses sufficiently to aggravate the lack of discipline already prevailing in the feudal armies. However, by the opening of the fifteenth century, men in Milan, Nuremburg, and a dozen other cities of Europe had learned to make cannons that were dangerous to the enemy. These early guns were things of beauty, covered with bas-reliefs and named—as we name battleships today. They were awkward to transport and inaccurate in their aim, but they could deliver solid shot or an assortment of rocks and metal chips that created havoc. Like the engineers, the men who operated these guns were not regarded as soldiers. They were workmen and technicians, unfit socially to associate with the knights. They were destined to remain in that category until the seventeenth century.

By and large these innovations in the art of warfare strengthened the hands of the larger territorial princes who could persuade their parliaments or *Landtäge* to provide money for foot soldiers, artillery, and engineers. Unquestionably, too, these new methods of warfare spelled the doom of the feudal knight as the key figure in political society by making him militarily out of date. Historical process, however, moves slowly: and changes in the art of warfare that began to be apparent at the opening of the fourteenth century were to be part of the development that in the next three centuries transferred power to the hands of royal governments.

In the fourteenth century the results of the changes in warfare were in fact often disastrous to all concerned. Free companies of soldiers seemed to spring up everywhere. The Hundred Years' War between the French and English kings, the interurban conflicts in Italy, warfare in Germany and on the eastern frontiers brought into being armies that the princes and cities of Europe were quite unprepared to support permanently. Europe's economy would long remain too primitive to allow the re-establishment of the Roman legions in any permanent form. Once assembled for a war, however, these soldiers were difficult to disband, and they became a scourge to the countryside, as France of the latter fourteenth century could well testify. Their leaders became a threat to urban independence in Italy and Germany, where condottieri chieftains found it easy to become rulers of towns. The Europe that found use for professional soldiers was not yet rich enough to support standing armies, nor was it politically strong enough to control them.

In the long run, however, the free companies and the engineer-artillerymen strengthened the power of the prince both by freeing him from dependence upon his vassals for military assistance and by providing him with a weapon that could curb the disorder of decadent feudal society.

9. THE RISE OF THE PRINCE: THE CHURCH

As we have noted, at the opening of the thirteenth century the papacy was the greatest political power in Europe. Emperors and kings had to bow before the papal throne, and the papal treasury grew rich from fees, tithes, and other revenues. Bishops, abbots, and religious foundations owned great tracts of land, and clergymen everywhere were so deeply involved in economic and political affairs that it often seems that their religious functions must have been overshadowed by these worldly activities. In a later chapter we shall consider the broader aspects of the situation created by these worldly matters. At this point, however, our primary concern is with the relationship between the papacy and the territorial princes who appeared in the lists as contenders for power in Europe. It was inevitable that the princes who were trying to bring their vassals under control, and who always felt the need for money, should regard the wealth and power of the church with covetous eyes. In both France and England the requirements of war led the kings to tax the church. This was the first assault upon the church's economic position; and naturally the papacy reacted quickly to what seemed to be a usurpation of its power. In 1296 Boniface VIII issued the Bull, *Clericus laicos,* which declared it unlawful for lay governments to tax church property. The English king responded by demanding a fifth of the income from the temporal property of the English church. The French king not only imposed a tax but also forbade the export of money from France to Rome. Furthermore, as we saw, he called the first Estates-General in which the townsmen took their places to assure general support for his program. The clergy's reputation with the townsmen was none too good; the stories they told about monks and bishops and their willingness to support their princes in conflicts with the papacy indicated a latent resentment against the clergy in bourgeois society.

At the same time that the conflict between the kings of western Europe and the papacy announced the princely threat to papal power, the papal curia weakened its position by abandoning the city of Rome and taking up residence in the Rhone valley. In 1305 Clement V, a native of the French province of Aquitaine, became pope. He was consecrated in Lyons and never found it convenient to go to Rome. For nearly seventy-five years his successors remained in southern France where they acquired sovereign control over the principality of Avignon. Several of them planned to visit Rome, but between 1305 and 1378 only one of them actually made the trip, and he returned to Avignon after a very short stay in Rome. The papal palace in Avignon had become a comfortable—even sumptuous—residence, while the palaces and churches at Rome had been allowed to fall into decay. The idea of returning to Rome, where a turbulent population and unruly nobles created all sorts of problems, seemed less and less attractive to the popes and their cardinals, most of whom now tended to be Frenchmen. This so-called "Babylonian captivity" not only resulted in a great scandal in the church, but also strengthened the determination of the princes to control the church within their own frontiers, for the papacy seemed to be losing its international character and becoming a French institution.

The Avignon popes took full advantage of their beautiful site on the Rhone river to construct a city and a papal palace that was at once a fortified point and a château for pleasure. Luxury and worldliness, perhaps corruption and sin, crept into the church, and to support it money was needed. The attempt of the papacy to expand its financial harvest came contemporaneously with the growing financial needs of the princes. As might well have been expected, new conflicts emerged. In these conflicts the princes had the advantage, for the papacy at Avignon, which could be accused of being a French puppet, did not have the majesty nor the independence of the early thirteenth-century popes at Rome.

To this point the papal authority had merely been tarnished, but the threat to its position became really serious when Gregory XI returned to Rome and died there in 1378. The Romans brought pressure on the cardinals and forced the election of an Italian to the papacy, but the austerity of the new pope ill-suited the tastes of the French cardinals, so they declared his election illegal and elected another pope. For almost half a century thereafter Europe had the scandal of two, and later even three, men claiming to be pope. This situation inevitably reacted in favour of royal authority. To secure support from the princes who ruled the land, the men contending for the right to be recognized as pope bid against each other with grants of privilege and rights that augmented the power of princes while undermining the authority of the papacy. The disasters of the schism between Avignon and Rome were increased in the early fifteenth century when, in an attempt to heal the schism, a third pope was elected to contend with the other two. This, of course, was a scandal in western Christendom, and finally the secular powers intervened under the leadership of the Holy Roman Emperor and called a church council at Constance to end the schism. The three pretending popes were all deposed, and Martin V was elected to the papal throne. The proud political position occupied by men like Pope Innocent III at the opening of the thirteenth century was completely destroyed. The fifteen-century popes had to become diplomats and soldiers just to keep their status in Italy. They could no longer aspire to universal power in Europe. Thus over a hundred years before Luther's rebellion, the princes of Europe had begun to discover the advantages that could be gained by bringing the church within their territory under their own authority; in the political life of Europe the sixteenth-century Reformation was merely the climax to the movement that really started two centuries earlier.

10. ROYAL POWER IN MID-FIFTEENTH-CENTURY EUROPE

By the middle of the fifteenth century the processes of history had already given firm contours to the emerging political structure of Europe. Instead of a rebirth of the western Roman Empire either as a secular or as an ecclesiastical universal authority, there had emerged a number of kingdoms and principalities governed by princes who were struggling to make good their authority. In Germany where the loose confederation of the Holy Roman Empire of the German nation still provided for an emperor, the princes enjoyed only a quasi-independent position, but in the rest of Europe the maxim that "the king is emperor in his own lands" made the rulers responsible only to God. This was possible because the German emperors who claimed to be the heirs of universal power actually had little authority outside of the lands that they governed as hereditary princes, and because the prestige of the papacy was so dilapidated after the disorders of the latter fourteenth century that papal interference with the affairs of princes was practically unthinkable. However, those monarchies and principalities that were assuming the right to organize European political civilization were not yet the proud political and military powers that were to create the European states' system several centuries later; rather, if their problems are looked at closely, they appear weak, torn by civil wars, and embroiled with each other in conflicts that seemed to be unsolvable, for none of them had power enough to impose a solution on his neighbor. The anarchy of the earlier baronial wars had been transferred to the larger arena of Europe.

While the process of strengthening the central authority of the ruler had made great progress, it was far from its ideal. Neither Roman law, nor new sources of tax revenue, nor new officials and soldiers were yet able to give the ruler the powers to impose his will upon the kingdom. The rulers had the right to appoint men to all sorts of lay and clerical offices, but since the appointees were supported by traditional sources of revenue outside of the royal treasury, the rulers found it difficult to control their behavior. The towns were still for the most part governed by officials elected and paid in traditional manners, and the countryside and villages were still governed by the nobility who owned the land or held royal commissions that might even be hereditary in the family. It was difficult to force either nobleman or townsman to obey the king's will unless it corresponded to their own. Princes everywhere talked about their royal absolutism, and in truth they could act arbitrarily if they could lay hands upon those men who disobeyed or defied their will, but that was the problem; sometimes full-fledged military campaigns were required to secure obedience. Thus, for all their pretensions, the expression "for this is my good pleasure" with which monarchs so often ended their royal decrees, was a literary flourish rather than evidence that the order of the king would be obeyed. If this fact is kept in mind, the terrible political struggles which took place over the growth of the power of central authority between the sixteenth and the twentieth centuries will be easier to understand.

The Fair of Lendit, from a miniature illustrating *Le Pontifical de Sens* (Bibliothèque Nationale). In this picture we see a fair in progress under the protection of the Bishop. The medieval artist indicates the relative importance of objects and people by differences in size. The fact that the sheep look somewhat like dogs bothered neither the artist nor his patrons.

Chapter 2

SOCIAL AND ECONOMIC PATTERNS OF MEDIEVAL EUROPE

1. RURAL ECONOMY

Medieval men lived under many different conditions. At first glance they seem to have been one people bound together by their Christian religion and similar political institutions (e.g., feudalism), but if we look a little closer, it soon becomes clear that there were great differences among them. Indeed, as we shall see throughout this history, diversity seems to be closely connected with the dynamic force that has been so characteristic of the history of western men. This diversity arises out of the variety of European geography as well as the numerous streams of historical culture that make up the European peoples. In Italy, parts of Spain, and southern France, for example, the social and economic institutions of Roman society were never completely extinguished. Indeed, some of the best preserved architectural remains of Roman antiquity are to be found today in the French cities on the lower Rhone river basin, and even a superficial study of the societies in these areas reveals their Roman roots. In northern Europe, on the other hand, Roman institutions were either never established, or were destroyed by the barbarian invaders so that few traces remain. In Slavic Europe there were practically no Roman influences, cultural or architectural. Then, too, the several Germanic peoples who settled down on the land with the older Latin and Celtic inhabitants did not have social and economic patterns common to all. Some of them were relatively civilized tribes; others were the crudest of barbarians. As a result, the rate of assimilation differed from place to place. The great variety of languages spoken from Portugal to the Polish frontiers is further evidence of the differences in the cultures of the peoples who live there.

Even aside from their historic differences, those that can be traced to geography alone would have accounted for great diversity. While many Europeans lived relatively close to salt water, there is enormous dissimilarity between the frigid waters of the Baltic and the North Sea and the warm waters of the Mediterranean. The different potential ways of life available to an inhabitant of the Swedish Baltic coast and another of Genoa are as striking as those offered a dweller in an Alpine valley and another on the estuary of the Rhine river in Holland, or a man living in the forests of Germany and another on the Atlantic coast of France or Spain. In other words, it is very difficult to write about the "culture of medieval Europe"— there were many "cultures" which may appear similar but were in fact very varied.

However, most of medieval Europe supported itself by agriculture. Even on the sea coasts, where fishing and commerce eventually took precedence, agriculture was the important economic activity of the people. There was one common characteristic of the agricultural pattern everywhere—namely, the surprisingly low yield from the fields. All over Europe the struggle to maintain soil fertility was a discouraging task. Even by the thirteenth century, when there had been considerable improvement in the methods of cultivation, it was rare for a village to secure a yield of more than ten bushels of grain from an acre of land that had required two bushels of seed to plant. This yield of five for one, or even less, was the most discouraging fact of medieval economy. It meant that the peasants had to cultivate all the available land for grain in order to supply enough calories to support themselves, and therefore they had little or no land left over for producing forage crops to carry farm animals through the winter. This was one of the links in the vicious circle of medieval agriculture; without adequate forage, there were few animals; few animals meant little manure; and without manure it was practically impossible to increase the yield from the fields.

A second virtually universal characteristic of medieval agriculture was the existence of common meadows or pastures. All the village animals were pastured on the common lands. These might be a meadow or a forest where pigs, fowl, and cattle were run together, watched by the children of the village. Such a system provided pasture, but it did not allow for selective mating of animals—even if the peasant had had any knowledge of breeding (which he did not). Pictures that we have of the hogs and cows of the fourteenth century suggest that the hogs were bred for speed, while the cows failed to meet specifications for either milk, meat, or traction. Nonetheless, the peasants could not have supported themselves without the common lands where their animals were pastured in the summer and the common woods where they cut fuel for the winter.

The systems of cultivation had one aspect in common. To maintain as much fertility as possible, medieval peasants had to let part of the lands lie fallow each year. The best practice seems to have been to rotate the crops on a two- or three-year pattern in the south and north respectively. However, not all Europeans were rich enough to allow one-third of their land to remain idle each year, and therefore we find many cases where the land was farmed four or even five years in succession. As a result, the yield decreased to such a point that they barely managed to retrieve the original amount of seed. In those poorer villages the lack of forage also reduced the number of animals, so the peasants not only had little grain, but they also had little manure, meat, and power to help cultivate the fields. Rural poverty has plagued Europe from the Middle Ages to the twentieth century, but it was particularly severe from the medieval era to the mid-eighteenth century.

Methods of cultivation differed from place to place, and the examples that are given here may have been typical, but only in a general sort of way. In northern Europe the soil tends to be heavy, and therefore effective plowing requires power. By the eleventh century the heavy wheel plow was in general use. It was pulled either by four or six oxen or by several horses. The tenth century had seen the invention of the horse collar and consequently the possibility of using horses in place of cattle for farm work. However, the advantage of the faster pace of horses was counterbalanced by the fact that they required grain for food, and therefore were more expensive to use than oxen which could be fed hay. In many localities, too, there was a feeling of prejudice against working horses in the fields for they were useful in warfare. In the south of Europe, where the soil is lighter, the plows were also lighter; they could be pulled by a yoke of oxen, or even by two cows, but since the plows were hardly more than pointed sticks, their usefulness was strictly limited. Both in the north and in the south there were no methods for cultivating the land by using animals for power after the crops had begun to grow. All cultivation and harvesting was done by hand labor with hoes and cutting tools that were of the crudest manufacture.

Grain was the principal crop everywhere. It was customary to plant a bread cereal such as wheat, rye, or buckwheat in one of the fields and a porridge cereal such as oats or barley in the second. Beans or peas might be used instead of oats and barley. The songs, "Oats, Peas, Beans, and Barley Grow," "Coming through the Rye," and others suggest the familiar pattern of medieval life. Of the bread grains, wheat was held in the highest prestige, rye next, and finally buckwheat; everyone looked down on the "buckwheat eaters" as inferior people. The choice, of course, was connected with the fertility of the soil and the length of the growing season. Buckwheat will grow on poor soil and ripen within the short summer of northern Europe. The porridge crops seem to have had traditional patterns behind them: some parts of Europe liked "Pease porridge hot, pease porridge cold," even "in the pot nine days old"; other sections lived on oatmeal, barley, or bean soup, and liked it that way. No matter what grain was used, the bread was made from whole grain in large heavy loaves. In some sections honey provided a sweetening agent to make the bread more desirable.

In the south of Europe, where classical patterns of agriculture never really died out, the vineyards and olive groves that had been characteristic of Roman culture still held an important position in medieval rural economy; in the north, the culture of the vine in Burgundy, the Rhine, and parts of France tended to expand as soon as a market could be found for the product.

Vine and fruit culture for local use was widely scattered. Every village provided its householders with garden plots where vegetables, fruits, and vines suitable to the soil and climate tended to flourish. Thus turnips and cabbages as well as other vegetables helped to keep the peasant alive. At best, however, the rural diet was poor; game and fish seldom graced the peasants' table, for those were the property of the lord and poaching was punished unless, like Robin Hood, the poacher could evade the long arm of the law. We often note the relatively short lives of most of the men living in medieval Europe; while germs, accidents, and violence probably tended to increase the death rate, undoubtedly the poor diet was an important contributing factor.

The system of "field cultivation" was responsible for the type of land distribution generally found in Europe. Since each of the fields would be left fallow periodically, every household had to have land in each field to assure its share of the bread and porridge crop of the year. This land distribution seems also to have been based on the theory that each household ought to have a share of the good, as well as of the poorer, land in each of the fields. Thus each peasant had strips or scraps of land scattered over the fields of the village. The methods of culture in a measure regulated the size of these strips. In Germany the strips were called a *morgen* (morning) of land, i.e., about the amount that could be plowed in a morning. In the north they tended to be long and narrow, for the method of plowing made it convenient to have a long furrow that would not require frequent turning of the plow and oxen. In the south, where lighter plows were used, the plots tended to be more nearly square; the shape may even have been fixed in Roman days.

The clothes of the peasants and the tools used in these village communities were almost entirely the product of local manufacture. The lord's household probably could support several individuals with particular skills (blacksmiths and shoemakers, for example), but most of the things that were used were made by peasants who otherwise tilled the soil. Since little or no money changed hands in these communities, this work might either be done on a barter basis or, more frequently, by each family for itself. This was partic-

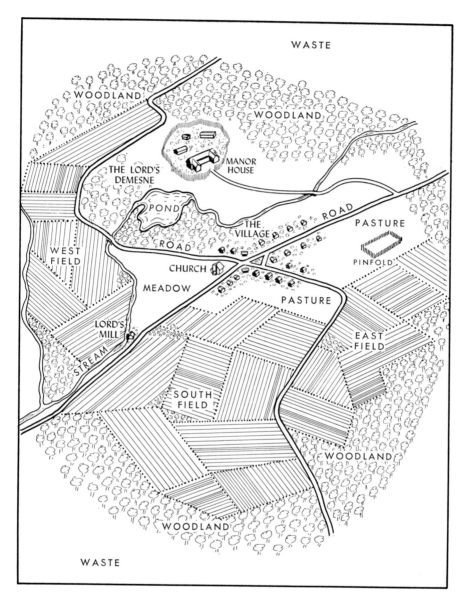

A Medieval Village.

ularly true for the cloth and the clothes that were made by the women, and for the tools and such furniture as existed which were made by the men. Thatching roofs, building houses, and other such work were usually accomplished by cooperative efforts on the part of the villagers. Throughout the Middle Ages most of the articles owned and used by the peasants of Europe originated within the village locale.

Scattered through the fields were the lands of the lord and those of the parish church. These reserved lands were almost universally characteristic of the medieval economy. Thus, the soil not only supported the men who tilled it; it also cared for the men who defended it, as well as those who interceded between God and man for the latter's salvation. As with the culture of the soil, the lord-peasant relationship in the south of Europe seems to have been linked with the society of Roman days; in the north it seems to have emerged out of the structure of German society and the cultivators' need for protection. Whatever its origins, by the twelfth century nearly every village had a lord who held legal right to land in the fields as well as to labor dues from the peasants to assure cultivation of his holdings. These lords also had the right to demand aid from the peasants—work on the roads, carting the crops to market, and even assistance in the lord's house. They also owned and controlled the "public utilities" of the village: the grist mill, the bake oven, the wine press, the brewery, and so on, which the peasants were obliged to use in return for the payment of a fee or a percentage of the produce.

The lord might be a king or great nobleman who controlled holdings throughout the kingdom; he might be a simple knight whose sole income and status were dependent upon a single village or manor; or the owner might be a bishop, a monastery, or some other clerical foundation. The village or manor would be ruled by a bailiff of some kind, and would be visited at intervals by the lord, who might find it easier to consume his share of the village income on the premises rather than transport it to a central location.

The relations between the peasants and their lords differed from one part of Europe to another. In the tenth and eleventh centuries most of the peasants tended to be serfs who were bound to the soil and whose lives were virtually at the mercy of their lord. In some places the church had to fight for the lords to recognize the serfs as human beings with the right to marry and have legitimate children. Even after his right to marry had been acknowledged, the serf could not do so without his lord's consent. Nor did the serf's dependence on his lord end there; his whole life from birth to death was completely bound up in a network of relationships to his lord. If he should by any chance accumulate more wealth than was necessary for his living, the lord could take that away without the serf's being able to obtain redress.

It should be noted that not all the peasants of Europe were in the status of serfdom. A very few were free men who held their land just as the lord held his—from the king or another great lord. Others were in varying degrees of servitude—some owing only dues or taxes in kind, others owing labor. These peasants could sell their holdings, but a new owner had to assume his predecessor's obligations. Such holding might be considered hereditary leaseholds in which both the peasant and the lord had property rights in the land. After the twelfth century the number of free or relatively free peasants tended to increase, but serfdom remained a characteristic social form, particularly in eastern and central Europe, until the nineteenth century.

To any one peasant in the eleventh or twelfth century it must have seemed that his life was bounded by a static universe; patterns of behavior changed slowly, patterns of institutionalized culture even more slowly. Yet to the student who examines the processes of life it becomes apparent that this concept was mistaken. Change, even if it occurs slowly, is in the nature of things, and from the eleventh century onward there were several important forces working in European society that were eventually to transform rural life.

The most obvious force of change was the rise of towns, and with them subsequent alterations in the demands for agricultural products. The early towns supplied themselves with food and most of their raw materials from the countryside around the town. As urban communities grew larger, however, they tended to expand along river courses or on sea routes, and thus began to make demands upon more distant agricultural communities. Demands for wine, wool, flax, leather, and food products stimulated the production of these commodities, and since the urban communities were developing money economies, those areas that were affected by the towns were drawn into the larger market economy of Europe. It must be remembered, however, that the urban communities, while they were to be found all over Europe, were mostly small enterprises; only a few of them became great towns like Paris, Florence, or Frankfurt which drew raw materials and supplies from afar.

The other persistent element of rural change probably accounts for even greater social mobility than the urbanization movement. It was the colonization of new lands on the frontiers as well as the reclamation of forest and marsh land to create new communities. From the eleventh to the fourteenth centuries the population of rural Europe grew continuously, and the increase could be provided for only by adding new fields or by migration. It was laborious work to clear forests and drain marsh lands with the primitive tools then at the disposal of society, laborious and expensive work that could be undertaken only by princes or great landlords who could afford to make the investment in the hope of realizing profits in the future. In the twelfth and thirteenth centuries, however, there was great activity throughout Europe and the amount of available arable land was enlarged. This work of clearing the forests and draining the swamp lands was one of the important engineering projects of the era; it rivaled the building of fortifications in importance and in the amount of capital involved.

In addition, the process of migration was a most important project of the nobility: emigrants could not pick themselves up and move to the frontiers unless there were soldiers to defend them against the savage Slavic and Magyar peoples who occupied those lands. The political society that sent soldiers to fight Islam in Spain, Sicily, and the Levant, that sent the Normans to England to establish continental institutions on the English island, also sent the German knights eastward and northward to establish settlements in the Wendish, Prussian, and Slavic lands. In some ways these settlements were very much like the outposts that the United States of the nineteenth century created in western North America to control the Indians. In both cases attractive conditions were offered the settlers, although, of course, the incentives varied in tune with the problems and opportunities of the different periods. In the medieval settlements a man was fortunate if he could have twenty-five to thirty acres of land to support himself and his family; on the frontier he was offered at least twice that much land, as well as other inducements, including a larger measure of personal freedom. From the eleventh to the fourteenth centuries the process of frontier settlement was constant. In some cases it was a prince who settled the peasants on the frontier; in others it was the work of the crusading order of the Teutonic Knights, who were fighting the Slavic and Wendish heathens of east Prussia. It is most interesting to note that the German capitals that later were to compete for hegemony in central Europe were founded in this fashion. Vienna was an outpost of Bavaria; Berlin and Koenigsberg were outposts of northern and middle Germany.

There were other ways in which the nobility acted as the agents of change. With the gradual rise of the money economy there were changes in the art of war: the feudal levy provided fighting men who would follow the king's banners on a temporary basis, but with money troops could be bought who would not go home as soon as their period of service was finished. Kings and princes were not alone in deriving advantage from the new patterns. Clergymen who owed knight's service preferred to pay a money fee rather than send a fully armed soldier to their lord's castle; many noblemen also preferred to pay cash rather than present themselves for military service. To obtain this cash, however, they had to be able to transform the goods and services that they received from the peasants into money values. Thus, many peasants were able to change their status—or at least the payments which they had formerly owed their lord in kind or services were replaced by ones in money values.

It must not be assumed, however, that the peasants found it easy to escape their obligations to the lord. A bad harvest, a catastrophic illness, or any other calamity that might easily befall a family usually resulted in the peasant's becoming deeper in debt to his lord. Moreover, the peasant's opportunity to obtain justice or redress for grievances was strictly limited. The village court was established by the lord, and in most parts of Europe these courts could dispense summary justice. The lord could hang or mutilate any peasant thought to be guilty of poaching, stealing, or murder, and only in a very few places was there any risk that the king would show displeasure at the lord's hasty action.

Under such circumstances, the only way the peasant could obtain redress against the clergy and noblemen who oppressed him was through blind, irrational outbursts of violence. Such uprisings were no more than acts of despair, for the peasant had little chance against the armed noblemen, and his probable reward was death. Yet peasant revolts were not uncommon. Nearly every chronicle recounts deeds of violence, and occasionally these outbursts swept through a whole province or a whole kingdom, but they inevitably failed. Their leaders were killed or won over to the enemy, and their crude weapons proved to be of little use against the feudal cavalry. Thus, even though several of these rebellions, aided by the element of surprise, won premature victories, none of them left any real mark on the institutional or cultural life of Europe. The peasants were too ignorant to organize a political program, too poor to secure adequate arms, and too scattered to respond to an appeal for united action.

2. THE RISE OF TOWNS

By the end of the eighth century the Saracens had largely converted the Mediterranean Sea into an Islamic lake, and the economic structure of Europe received a terrible shock. It used to be believed that practically all trade dried up at its roots, leaving western Europe with agriculture as the sole way of economic life. Such a severe picture has to be modified somewhat; yet by the eighth century most of the great commercial centers of the Roman era had, in fact, either disappeared or were in decay—mere pitiful reminders of the greatness of the past. Wild animals as large as the wolf roamed within the confines of the ancient city of Rome, while the miserable inhabitants of the city uncomfortably occupied ruins that were mute witnesses of a nobler age now past. Elsewhere a few ruined buildings, an ill-kept wall, or a broken aqueduct were often all that remained of once prosperous cities. Decay and evidences of economic stagnation were all that could be found in the western Empire. Five centuries later—say about 1150 to 1200— a vigorous town life again flourished in many parts of Europe, and great urban centers were rising along the highways of trade. This urbanization movement may well be medieval man's most important single contribution to the advancement of western civilization. In its wake came a host of political, social, economic, and intellectual trends that have given western society its characteristic forms.

As in so many aspects of medieval life, the church played a most important role in the revival of towns. Many an old Roman center survived because it was the site of a bishop's church, and many of the new towns came into existence because of a monastery, shrine, or cathedral. The needs of the clergy and the business that developed around a bishop's court tended to provide employment and encouragement for town dwellers. In many of the towns of the eighth to eleventh centuries it was the bishop who provided government and protection as well as the employment that kept the town alive.

In addition, the development of fortifications against Norse, Magyar, and Islamic raiders tended to encourage town growth. On important river crossings, at the forks of roads, and in natural harbors traders found it advantageous to cooperate with the soldiers who built the fortifications. Even in the rudest times of the seventh or ninth centuries peddlers from the east ventured into western Europe; these "Syrians," as they were often called, were at first loath to settle down and become merchants, but as military protection became available they began to take advantage of it. Soon artisans, servants, innkeepers, harlots, and entertainers of all types, as well as beggars and thieves, moved in. The townsmen must frequently have wondered why these people came to their towns, but the process was reasonably continuous, and in time each found his or her place. Dreary as these towns must seem to us—the narrow dirty streets, the wretched light at night, the lack of fuel in winter, and all the other inconveniences attendant upon so crude a society —they were places of excitement, interest, and safety to men who knew only the dull routine of the country. Thus, even in those early days, the "tinkle" of the city life and the freedom that it offered attracted country boys and girls. "City air makes man free" was the German proverb; and if a runaway serf managed to live in the town for a year and a day, he was free.

Soldiers were in many ways connected with the rise of towns. They not only guarded the city against dragons, Norsemen, and bandits; they also made demands upon the town's economy. War and preparation for war have always imposed activity on many who are not soldiers. Weapons have to be forged and supplies have to be assembled before any important military effort can be undertaken. The crusades provide an excellent case study. The port cities of Italy became centers for the assembly of food for men, fodder for horses, and ships for transport; they also became arsenals where broadswords, lances, battle clubs, and axes were made for the soldiers. Once the crusaders had established themselves in Syria and Palestine, those cities then became the receiving ports for loot as well as for goods that came as the result of trade. After all, opportunities for loot are relatively limited even for soldiers; trade has to follow or the supplies of desirable goods will come to an end. Once trade began to grow between the east and the west, those same Italian cities were in possession of the ships, the knowledge, and the privileged charters that allowed them to take advantage of it. To say that the Italian cities grew solely because they were supply dumps for soldiers would be an overstatement. Nonetheless, the war and the needs of the soldiers gave those cities a great boost and helped to make them the important commercial centers that they became.

It is very easy for a modern man to get an exaggerated notion of the extent of trade in earlier periods. We should, therefore, remember that only a very small segment of the population of Europe could afford to buy the goods that were to be found at the fair towns or in the peddlers' packs. Most of the rural inhabitants used none of these goods, and only a small proportion of the items in daily use by townsmen actually came from any distance. Keeping this in mind, we will not confuse the complex market of the twentieth century with its simple prototype of the twelfth and thirteenth centuries. Yet a medieval man in the year 1300 might have believed that commerce in his era had reached a high peak. He would not have had before him a vision of the world of the future, and if he had any realization of the progress that had been made in the two preceding centuries, he could well have concluded that his was an age of great commercial activity and importance. This is the historian's eternal problem; at any one point in time judgments must be made against the background of the flux of time.

Although the extent of trade was small, traders were important builders of the medieval towns. They carried on their business under varying conditions. The local and provincial fair towns provided the most characteristic type of market. All over Europe there were market towns that acted as distribution centers for goods in a province or country. Under the protection of a territorial prince or, in some cases, under the jurisdiction of the town government the market would be opened on certain days of the week or month; in others the town charter would provide for a "perpetual" market. This simply meant that the peasants could bring their produce to town, peddlers or traveling merchants could set up their booths, and the townsmen could trade with the visitors. The market towns usually maintained a very strict control over the activities of foreign merchants to prevent competition with local sellers, as well as to regulate prices so that buyers would hopefully receive full value. The lineal descendants of these markets can still be seen both in Europe and America; the farmers' market of many American cities and the traveling markets that are so characteristic of Latin Europe have their roots in these market towns. In a sense, these were the retail markets; the wholesale, or, as we might call them, "jobbers' markets," were held in the great fair towns.

There were many fair towns in Europe, but those of Champagne were the most famous. They were held at six towns in the lands of the Counts of Champagne on an annual circuit. The counts provided protection both in the market towns and on the highways between them; they also held courts that dispensed justice and maintained a sort of commercial law quite in advance of that found elsewhere at the time. Buyers and sellers from all over Europe came to these fairs, where goods from the Baltic, India, China, the

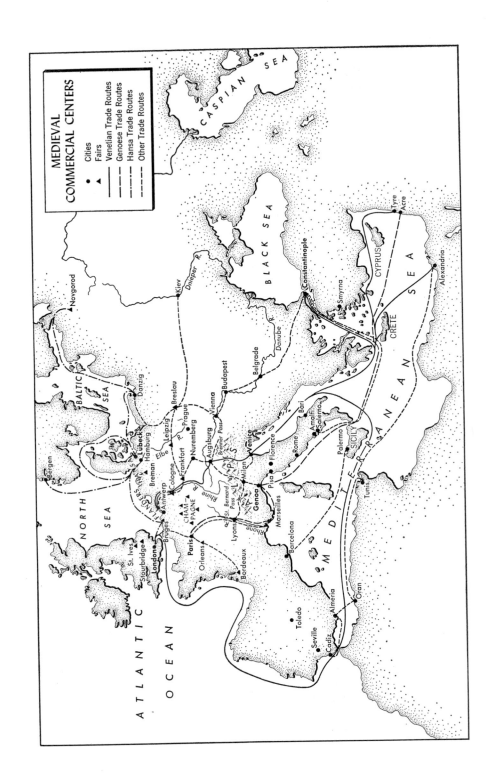

MEDIEVAL COMMERCIAL CENTERS

- Cities •
- Fairs ▲
- Venetian Trade Routes
- Genoese Trade Routes
- Hansa Trade Routes
- Other Trade Routes

CASPIAN SEA

BLACK SEA

Novgorod

Dnieper R.

Kiev

Danube

Belgrade

Budapest

Vienna

Breslau

Prague

Leipzig

Nuremberg

Augsburg

Brenner Pass

Danzig

BALTIC SEA

Lübeck

Hamburg

Breman

Elbe

Cologne

Frankfort

Main R.

A L P S

Venice

Florence

Rome

Bari

Amalfi

Salerno

Palermo

SICILY

Constantinople

Smyrna

CYPRUS

CRETE

Tyre

Acre

Alexandria

MEDITERRANEAN SEA

Bergen

NORTH SEA

St. Ives

Stoutbridge

London

Bruges

Antwerp

F L A N D E R S

CHAMPAGNE

Paris

Orleans

Bordeaux

Lyons

St. Bernard Pass

Rhine

Rhone

Milan

Genoa

Pisa

Marseilles

Barcelona

Toledo

Seville

Cadiz

Almeria

Oran

Tunis

ATLANTIC OCEAN

Iberian and Italian peninsulas, North Africa, and the Levant mingled with the products of central and western Europe. The fairs in Champagne dealt in all kinds of goods, but some of the other fairs came to specialize in one commodity. The book fair at Leipzig was a striking example of the latter type. Fairs were the most colorful commercial activity of the Middle Ages. To them came merchants from near and far, pickpockets and thieves, money-changers, women of easy virtue, confidence men and gamblers, monks, soldiers, and entertainers. They served as a mart for goods, ideas, and news for all Europe.

By 1200–1250 much of Europe was involved in the high commerce that was linking the world together, and the era of economic disorder and decay that had followed the disintegration of Roman economy had ended. Indeed, it is quite probable that by 1250 the actual volume of business was as great as it had been in Roman times. The seas around Europe carried sailing ships and oar-powered galleys from port to port, and the pack trains that plodded over wretched roads connected those interior cities that were far from navigable water. By 1250 traffic in spices, drugs, jewels, silks, cutlery, and other luxury goods had expanded to include many bulky items. On the Mediterranean, ships carried wine, olive oil, dried fruits, wheat, sulphur, alum, cotton, wool, furs, skins, as well as a long list of manufactured goods including rugs, cloth, hardware, and the like. In the Baltic, the North Sea, and the Bay of Biscay ships were loaded with wool, salt, fish, wine, tar, pitch, timber, lead, tin, copper, and even coal, as well as the luxury items and the manufactured goods of the south and east. This traffic extended to Russia and beyond to inner Asia by way of both the Black Sea and the overland routes from Novgorod, but the rivers and coastal waters of Europe, and the connections between the Levant and the markets of the Middle East accounted for most of the traffic.

This intercity and interprovince commerce comprised only a part of the economic activity of the towns. Most of the urban activity concerned the production of goods and services that were consumed in the town itself. Manufacture of hats, cloth, shoes, furniture, and iron ware, baking of bread, slaughtering of animals, and many other such activities were primarily oriented toward the needs of the townsmen. Probing beneath the surface of urban life, we discover that those early town dwellers carried the economic ideas of the villages in their bags when they came to the towns. They conceived of the town, just as they had the village, as a social institution to guarantee to each some degree of economic security. The village had been a self-sufficient economic unit; the towns tried to be the same. The village had operated on a subsistence economy system that assured to each his share according to the status to which God had called him; the towns tried to follow the same pattern. Thus we find that most of the towns operated agricultural enterprises outside the town walls, and tended to try to produce within their walls all the manufactured goods needed by the inhabitants. If the student concentrates his attention on the great cities that emerged, he will see that they developed more "modern" notions about economic life; but if he looks only at the vast majority of towns like Toulouse, Amberg, Lille, and hundreds of communities smaller than these, he will soon see that John Town Dweller, like his cousin in the village, used little that did not come from his own community.

Whether the town was a great city like London, Paris, or Florence, or merely a small provincial town, the guilds played an important part in the life of the community. The guilds can be divided roughly into two types: craft guilds and merchant guilds. The former were found everywhere; the latter were frequently the product of the great urban areas like Florence and Cologne. Both types tended to play an important part in the politics and economy of the town.

The primary function of the craft guilds was to control the production of goods. The techniques of manufacture were their secrets; the standardization of the quality and quantity of the items they made was their avowed objective; and, lastly, the maintenance of the workers in the status to which God had called them was their reason for existing. The guilds were usually organized with a dean as the head or president of the company. The dean and the master craftsmen of the guild regulated its affairs and governed the behavior of the whole body. The actual mechanics of government differed from craft to craft and from area to area, but in general the guild was organized more or less democratically. In most of the guilds a boy of eight to twelve years would begin his training as an apprentice to a master craftsman who, in return for his services, would teach him the secrets of the trade. After an apprenticeship lasting from five to ten years, the young man would be recognized as a journeyman craftsman, and might leave the town to find his fortune elsewhere. For a period he would take service in a master's shop until he had the money and the opportunity to set himself up as a master and assume responsibility for apprentices. Since the average life span of the workers of this era was probably somewhere between thirty and forty years, many who started as apprentices died without ever becoming masters of their own establishments. Death, the common interrupter of all careers, acted thus as a regulator that both denied and opened up opportunities. It was often easier for a man to marry the widow or the daughter of a fellow guildsman and thereby fall into his place than it was to start a shop of his own.

Merchant guilds were far more complex, and were undoubtedly indicative of a more advanced economy. They were primarily interested in commerce between cities rather than in production for local use, and many of them seem to have grown up in the process of developing this intercity trade. For example, the members of the Calimala guild in Florence dealt in woolen cloth: they bought rough woolen textiles in England and the Netherlands, imported them to Florence, where the lesser guilds (craft guilds) furnished the labor to dye, fill, shrink, and clip the cloth; it was then re-exported to the markets of Europe and the Near East—from Dublin to Baku. The guild organization furnished banking facilities for its members. It also had consuls who acted as agents for both the purchase of the rough cloth and the sale of the finished product. Some of the merchant organizations were formally organized, while others were simple associations of merchants for a single voyage. There was no one standard pattern for all merchant guilds. By the fourteenth century, however, the guilds were playing an important part in the economy and the politics of Europe as merchants and as bankers.

As was mentioned earlier, both the craft and the merchant guilds were active in city politics; the fact that their organization was such that it could easily be turned into a military force gave them the power necessary to take over the cities. Neither the bishop nor the nobleman could easily rule a town without the consent of the guildsmen. In the eleventh century the Italians showed the emperor how difficult it was to impose authority on the towns; in the twelfth, thirteenth, and fourteenth centuries in the Lowlands and Germany princes learned the same lesson. The guildsmen were already formed in "companies," and when armed with poleaxes or "good days," they could easily command the narrow streets of their cities, and even in the open fields they were able to make fighting difficult for the horsemen.

With military power came political authority. By the thirteenth century towns all over Europe had won the right to manage their own affairs, and town government tended to fall under guild control. It has been easy for those who are romantically inclined to transform these guild-controlled cities into a sort of poetic democratic idyll. Such a tendency should be resisted. The governments very early became oligarchies or aristocracies in which the patrician families of the towns controlled everything. The term "the people" did not mean everyone as they used it; "the people" were the wealthy who were in a position to rule. In certain cities interguild conflicts led to bitter disputes and often to armed conflict. Some of the Italian towns attempted to put an end to these bloody wars by introducing a city manager, or perhaps he should be called a city governor—the *podestà*. They got the idea from the sort of government that the emperor had tried to impose upon them. The *podestà* was usually appointed for only one year; if his accounts were satisfactory at the end of that period, he might be reappointed. Needless to say, it was not too uncommon for the *podestà* to try to set himself up as ruler of the town on his own account. Such was the penalty for conflict within the towns.

By the fourteenth century another factor was responsible for the guilds' loss of control over the towns. As the guildsmen became rich, they lost their taste for street fighting, and even for organizing the defense of the town.

This was not universally true, but it was of sufficient frequency to be of interest. Unwilling to do their own fighting, they had, therefore, to hire others to do it for them. The result was the rise of the condottieri or mercenary bands of soldiers. These condottieri soon became almost as dangerous to the liberty of the towns as they were to the enemies whom they were hired to combat. Like the *podestà,* the captains of the condottieri had a tendency to set themselves up as rulers of the community. In northern Europe it was not uncommon for a nobleman to maintain his position as town count, usually, however, with the cooperation of the guilds. In some cases there was a town council with a *Bürgermeister* as well as a town count (*Burggraf*) who performed a military function in the government of the community. In the troubled years of the fourteenth century those military officers were apt to gain prestige at the expense of the townsmen. The bourgeoisie were destined to see soldiers take precedence over them, at least until the nineteenth century.

The government of the medieval towns concerned themselves with many phases of the lives of the citizens. Just as the guilds held the idea that the work men did should support them in the status to which God had called them, so the town governments attempted to base the economy of the community on the theory that each man should be provided with his proper sustenance. They assumed the right to regulate the guilds within the walls; they also regulated the relations between foreign merchants and the inhabitants. To prevent anyone from getting a disproportionate share of the wealth, towns could enforce what they conceived to be a "just price" for any commodity. There were no ideas about free markets, supply and demand, or laissez-faire to interfere with economic regulation. Some of those town governments went further still. It was not uncommon for the city fathers at the town hall to legislate concerning the number of petticoats, earrings, and dresses that their wives and daughters might possess. These laws had to be passed repeatedly, and thus it would seem that the men were no more effective in controlling the expenditure of their women when they acted collectively than when they acted individually! Be that as it may, the medieval town was an institution that attemped more or less successfully to control the lives of its citizens on the general understanding that the community should assure to each his status as God had willed it.

As the townsmen became richer, their ideas about the part they should play in the world around them expanded. Their commercial and financial interests forced them to seek out ways to curb the disorders that made the trade routes unsafe, as well as to secure legislation that would support and facilitate their economic projects. In some cases, this meant the establishment of town leagues or "brotherhoods"; in others, cooperation with the territorial princes. Several of the leagues became very famous. The Hanseatic League, for example, included hundreds of towns on the coasts of the North and Baltic

Seas and in inland Germany; it maintained naval power that swept the pirates from the seas, and it negotiated as an equal with the powerful kings of western Europe. Town leagues in Italy and the Low Countries played nearly as striking political parts as did the German cities of the north. In other parts of Europe the townsmen made common cause with princes to assure peace and prosperity. Their leaders assumed places in representative institutions where they argued for the interests of the townsmen.

The impact of the townsmen did not end with the achievement of economic and political goals. Urban society and urban interests were of paramount influence on the development of secular culture, which was based upon the rediscovery of Latin and Greek authors. In short, the rise of the towns and the concomitant expansion of the interests and ambitions of the townsmen were dynamic forces in the evolution of European society. At every stage from the eleventh century to the present, the urban population has given a creative impetus to western civilization out of all proportion to its size. The compact life of the towns proved to be a source of great cultural energy.

3. MONEY AND BANKING

The story of the disorders in western Europe following the barbarian invasions and the recovery that was unmistakably well under way at the opening of the thirteenth century might almost be told in terms of coins. Coined money, or the lack of it, is a barometer by which to judge the status of civilized life. By the ninth century useful coins had almost ceased to exist in the West; by the fifteenth century, while they were still not abundant, coins had again become about as common as they had been in Roman days. Furthermore, in the ninth century banking, as we understand the term, was nonexistent; by the fifteenth century there were numerous banking facilities linking the West with the East, as well as serving the needs of the new political authorities.

The history of money is a long one. By the tenth century the two standard gold coins in western Europe were the Byzantine Greek bysant and the Moslem dinar. Like the British pound sterling in the nineteenth century and the American dollar in the twentieth, those two media of exchange were widely used by traders throughout the West. Their prestige in the commercial world demonstrated recognition of the cultural, as well as of the commercial superiority of the Byzantine and Moslem civilizations of the Levant. By the thirteenth century, two Italian coins, the Florentine florin and the Venetian ducat, had achieved a position of prestige that accompanied the rise in their manufacturers' commercial importance. At a time when the coinage of most of the princes of Europe from England to Hungary was often debased to meet the needs of the royal treasuries, these city states managed to retain a stable currency necessary to trade, and Europe paid them the compliment of using their coins as the standard. It was not until the seventeenth century that the kings of Europe began to strike or mint coins of parallel stability with those of the commercial cities.

However, even if their coins were not consistent in weight or metal content, princes and noblemen did not cease making them. There were literally hundreds of different coins in circulation, with an incredible number of values. At the fairs and crossroads of commerce, the men who could change this money were greatly in demand. A man required knowledge and native judgment to retain his shirt in those transactions, though there were many who made shirts of gaudy design for themselves from their profits. In the early medieval period most of this money-changing was left in the hands of Jews, for the simple reason that Christians were sure that such profits and business endangered a man's chances of salvation. It may seem to have been unfeeling, and even unchristian, of them to allow the Jews to damn their souls to eternal fire, but such was the reasoning. When the Jews became too rich, Christian princes or noblemen sometimes found ways to transfer the money to their own pockets without endangering their souls by trade or commerce in money. Outright robbery, if the victim were a Jew, did not seem as reprehensible as drawing profits from trade.

By the twelfth century, however, the profits were becoming too great to leave entirely in Jewish hands. The papal court was collecting taxes all over Europe, and remittances had to be made to Rome. Princes were finding it useful to borrow large sums of money and were willing to pay exorbitant interest rates. The Jewish moneylender was the first to exploit such avenues of wealth, but Christian merchants could not stand idly by and let them "corner the whole market." Thus, even though theologians argued learnedly that money could not beget money (for it was sterile) and expanded the concept of usury to include profits in business transactions, merchants pushed their way into the money business. Some of them may have had qualms, like the merchant of Cologne who advised his sons not to follow in his footsteps for the safety of their souls, but there were always others who were willing to risk the "usurious contracts, trickery, and hazards of traveling far from home" (i.e., hazards to the soul) that accompanied commerce in money.

By the thirteenth century, the moneylenders had developed complex banking establishments. The "banks" were first of all family affairs in which the money of the family alone was invested, but some "bankers" very early adopted the practice of accepting "deposits" from friends or fellow merchants. These family units were also "federated" in guilds or even intercity combines. The Florentine guild of bankers was a classic example; each member retained a high degree of independence, while the guild acted to unify and facilitate their efforts in foreign lands. These bankers offered a variety of services. They discounted bills, provided letters of credit, and issued notes that were not dissimilar to bank notes. Some of this paper actually circulated from port to port, and merchant to merchant, much as paper money does today. The fact that payments could be made from London to Tiflis through an Italian banker without the transmission of any coin speaks volumes for the complexity of the system.

The business of finance and the profits of usury may have been dangerous to men's souls. It was also dangerous for their bodies and their wealth. The usurious banker may have taken a rather large profit for the loan of his money, but the royal and clerical borrowers were not always above retaliation. After the Templars had loaned the king of France rather more money than he wanted to repay, he trumped up a charge of vice and black magic against the Order. Edward III of England, hard pressed for cash to continue the Hundred Years' War, simply repudiated the debts that he had contracted with two Italian banking houses. The Christian bankers of the fourteenth and fifteenth centuries did not usually suffer the same sort of treatment that had been given the Jews earlier, but there were cases where they did. Dick Whittington sent his cat to sea for trade, loaned money, and was thrice Lord Mayor of London, says the nursery story, but Jacques Coeur, who really did loan money to the king of France, landed in prison when the king could not pay.

4. PROSPERITY AND DEPRESSION

In the twentieth century, scholars have labored hard to explain the forces that underlie the cycles of prosperity and depression; the one clear point that has emerged from their researches is the complexity of the problem! Even now, we only imperfectly understand the mechanics of business cycles. When the situation is projected upon the stage of the history of the latter Middle Ages, it becomes even more difficult to grasp because the data that might give us insight are often nonexistent. Our evidence indicates clearly that Europe was suffering a severe depression in the ninth century, and that two centuries later economic conditions had improved to a point of considerable prosperity. By the thirteenth century the expansion of towns, the clearing of forests, the colonization of the frontiers, and the enormous expansion of commerce resembled an economic boom. Undoubtedly, in thirteenth-century Europe there was still an abundance of poverty and squalor, but the great investments in cathedral building, as well as the luxury goods produced by metal workers, cloth and tapestry workers, goldsmiths, and other artisans, are persistent witnesses to a prosperous society.

The fourteenth century apparently saw a reversal of this trend, at least in northern Europe. It was a period of severe storms and adverse weather changes, and those seem to indicate that the climate of Europe became colder and less favorable for agricultural activities. It was also a period of almost continuous warfare in northern Europe; and, as we have seen, the mercenary soldiers who fought those wars had little more respect for their "friends" than they had for their foes. Few of the nineteenth-century romantic novels written about those soldiers convey any idea of the disorder that they produced.

If famine and war were two of the "four horsemen," pestilence was the third. The fourteenth century is still remembered as the period of plagues, climaxed by the infamous visitation of the "black death" (bubonic plague) that struck with great ferocity. Wave after wave of this dread disease killed kings, noblemen, peasants, and paupers alike. Boccaccio's company, who told the tales of the *Decameron,* were seeking asylum from its ravages. The plague proved that war is a poor substitute for disease as a killer of men. In the main, war destroys men, and women are left to fulfil their childbearing function more or less unmolested. The bubonic plague took from forty to sixty percent of the populations without respect for age, sex, or status. Even though this calamity, like most population catastrophes, was apparently followed by a high reproduction rate (perhaps more children survived because there was more food), it was a half century before many sections of Europe recovered from the disaster.

The problems of the fourteenth century did not affect the whole of Europe to the same degree. While plagues did not fail to visit Italy, the political disorders characteristic of France during the Hundred Years' War were absent. The Italians organized their political life around the five important states of the peninsula (Venice, Milan, Florence, Naples, and the Papal States) and managed to prevent the disastrous conflicts that upset life in the north. Furthermore, since Italy was largely dependent upon the luxury traffic with the East, it proved reasonably easy not only to maintain this trade but also to increase it, despite the disorders in the north. After all, the prosperity of Italy rested on the ability of the wealthy to buy, not on a democratic market that included all the people. Thus, the fourteenth century that saw a definite decline in the artistic enterprise of the north (with the possible exception of the Netherlands), was the first great century of the so-called Italian Renaissance, and gave Italy the cultural traditions that were soon to make her the schoolmaster for the rest of Europe.

The fifteenth century, particularly the latter part, was a period of recovery and rapidly renewing prosperity for most of Europe. Wars continued, but the military forces were being brought increasingly under control, while the armies' need for supplies was becoming an important creative force in the economy. Perhaps of equal significance was the fact that new discoveries of silver mines in central Europe and new techniques for mining and smelting the silver greatly augmented the amount of precious metal available. This increase acted as an inflationary force on the whole economy: prices began to rise and goods to circulate. By the time the Spaniards introduced gold and silver from the New World, inflation had been in existence for half a century. Thus there was more money to oil the wheels of commerce, and the rising power of kings had reached the point where they could bring peace and order to the countryside more effectively and adopt economic policies designed to facilitate commerce and strengthen the economy of their kingdoms.

Italy, where the fourteenth-century disorders had not been so violent, seemed to benefit the most. Evidence of Italian prosperity in this period is to be found in every art gallery of the world, and in the form of brick, mortar, and marble in every important city of Italy today. This was a period in which there was a huge building boom and with it came decorative arts to embellish the new architecture. Northern Europe did not feel the impulse of this movement at once, but in the last quarter of the fifteenth century, from Geneva, Toulouse, Augsburg, Barcelona, Hamburg, and other cities, the pulse of the northern economy again began to quicken; the number of fine buildings dating from this period is still architectural evidence of the fact that men were investing in capital goods as well as in luxury housing. By the time that the Portuguese were ready to send their ships to India, Europe was once more on the verge of a new period of prosperity—perhaps greater than any that had occurred since Roman times. It was still prosperity solely for the elite classes of noblemen, soldiers, clergymen, and merchants, but that was the only kind the civilized world had known up to that time.

Sandro Botticelli, *Madonna of the Magnificat* (Florence, Uffizi Gallery). Botticelli crowned the work of a century of Florentine painters.

Chapter 3

CHANGING PATTERNS OF THOUGHT AND EXPRESSION

1. THE MEDIEVAL MIND

As in so many other aspects of western civilization, medieval Latin Christendom owed much to its intellectual and cultural contacts with Byzantium and Islam. In Spain, Sicily, and the Levant the westerners met civilizations more complex and more advanced than their own. The Saracens, Greeks, and Moors had kept in contact with ancient Greek and Roman culture, and had also retained commercial and cultural relations with India and China. It is not at all surprising that the rude men and poorly educated priests from the West were much impressed with the superior knowledge, as well as with the manners and economic system, of the people they encountered on their frontiers. Thus, the commerce that was encouraged by the Crusades both in Spain and in the East was not only one of goods and gold; manuscripts and ideas, too, were part of this traffic.

The process by which men recovered the ancient learning was slow and painful. By the tenth century the West had lost much of the knowledge of the ancient world that had once been the common heritage of the whole Mediterranean basin. What was retained was largely in the possession of the clergy who considered the first obligation of man to be the salvation of souls and who therefore often regarded pagan cultures as evil because of their emphasis on worldly things. Even the most enlightened churchmen were superstitious and credulous. They limited their mental horizons by taking it for granted that life on earth was important only as preparation for a life hereafter. The early medieval era was a rude age, and it produced rude men; only with the gradual improvement of living conditions and greater opportunity for men's activities on this earth could this society concentrate on more sophisticated ideas.

The fact that most educated men were clergymen was undoubtedly responsible for the interest that theology inspired as soon as it became possible for men to turn their attention seriously to the learning of the past. The church fathers of the early Christian era had been unable to erect a complete system of theology that would bring together Greek learning and Hebrew-Christian traditions. The task was begun both in the East and in the West by the early church fathers, but it was not yet complete when Roman civilization was overtaken by the barbarian invasions and Roman culture suffered a paralyzing shock. In the eleventh and twelfth centuries western scholars began to recapture that theological learning. It was a tremendous labor, for men had to redevelop concepts that had been lost for hundreds of years in order to understand St. Augustine and the other fathers. However, by the end of the twelfth century much of the theological writings of the fathers of the church was not only well known but also reasonably well understood in the advanced centers of learning in the West. In the thirteenth century western theologians were ready and able to crown the labors of the early fathers and to complete their theological work.

The discovery of Aristotle was an essential factor in this process. The West "found" Aristotle in Moorish Spain, where classical Greek philosophy was being studied. It would be a mistake to think that Christians and Moors spent all their time fighting each other; many of their contacts were confined to the exchange of goods and ideas. Indeed, it was not uncommon for Christian students to visit Moorish centers of learning, where they encountered Indian mathematics, Islamic science, and Greek philosophy. Aristotle was the greatest prize, for he was a writer who seemed to know everything; to men who had lost contact with large areas of the Graeco-Roman civilization he appeared a paragon of wisdom. The problem they faced was, of course, to adapt his worldly wisdom to the theological teachings of the church. Such a task was worthy of the efforts of the greatest intellects of the day.

Much has been written about those medieval scholars that will not stand careful scrutiny. For example, it is a great injustice to them to assert that they relied solely upon the authority of ancient books as the source of truth. While they did stand somewhat in awe of the wisdom of the philosophers and theologians of the ancient world, they were nonetheless rational men who assumed that they could explore and expand the areas of human understanding by drawing logical deductions from "self-evident truths" as well as from the "truths" that had been established by their predecessors. It is quite untrue that they slavishly followed the "authorities" that had come down to them; they were rationalists who established answers to their questions by logic as well as on the authority of ancient books. This was undoubtedly the reason Aristotle appealed to them; he was eminently a man of common sense. Furthermore, like medieval men, Aristotle assumed that the world had a logical pattern that was was always consistent, and ultimately discoverable by reason. Medieval men never considered the possibility that they could fail to explain the world in terms of man and his destiny, for both Aristotle and the Christian tradition assumed that man was the reason for the existence of the universe.

The characteristic institution for medieval learning was the university. Medieval universities must not be confused with modern institutions of higher learning. They had no endowments, no state appropriations, no administration in the modern sense of the term, and no buildings especially constructed for their use. Universities were groups of scholars and teachers banded together to pursue knowledge. They taught the arts, theology, law, medicine, and philosophy. By the thirteenth century the pattern for university education was already well established; students wandered from one center to another all over Europe to listen to famous teachers, who were on the whole allowed freedom to think and to teach the truth as they understood it. Nothing could be further from fact than the idea that medieval men lived in an intellectual straitjacket that prevented their having ideas of their own. The arguments and disputations of the schoolmen belie any such notion. They were limited by current assumptions about the world that were accepted without question, but within these assumptions they ranged freely in their quest of truth. Society was not dominated (as are totalitarian states today) by any "thought-control" that might smother free inquiry.

In retrospect, the greatest achievement of the medieval schoolmen or scholastics was the *Summa Theologiae* of St. Thomas Aquinas. His book might well be called the intellectual counterpart of the Gothic cathedral—a soaring structure, imposing in its outlines and satisfying to men who sought the security of religion buttressed by reason. St. Thomas roamed through all the categories of knowledge available in the thirteenth century, and so arranged them as to leave little room for doubt of the superior truth of Christian religious beliefs. He accepted Aristotle's philosophy, and as the Philosopher, Aristotle was made a pillar of the church. St. Thomas was not original in this. The church fathers in the third century had adopted the pagan neo-Platonic philosophy of their era as a tool for constructing Christian metaphysics, so that neo-Platonism had become an integral part of the Christian tradition. In much the same way St. Thomas incorporated Aristotelian philosophy in his great work so well that later centuries have called St. Thomas the greatest of the Catholic theologians.

The *pro* and *contra* method of presentation that St. Thomas used may be regarded as characteristic of much of medieval theological writing, and is dramatic evidence of the methodological debt that medieval scholars owed to their study of formal logic. St. Thomas first states the problem to be considered in the form of a proposition or assertion. He then musters all the objections that he can find either from logical deduction or from the writings of earlier teachers. Next he presents the supporting evidence in much the

MEDIEVAL CULTURAL CENTERS

- Universities and Schools
- Religious Centers
- Other Cultural Centers
- Famous Monasteries

same way. The final statement of proof is then buttressed by the opinion of Aristotle or of Holy Scripture, or, in some cases, the opinion of one of the church fathers. This *pro* and *contra* form of presentation was well established long before St. Thomas' time, and it continued to be the standard form for theological discussion for the generations that followed him.

However, St. Thomas' theology was not a binding dogma upon either his contemporaries or his followers, and the tradition of disputation inevitably brought changes and alterations in his teachings. Aristotle's writings came to Christendom by way of Spain, and from Spain there also came the beginnings of a philosophical conflict that raged through the fourteenth century. Theologians and philosophers became divided over the problem of nominalism versus realism. The nominalists were empiricists; that is, they believed knowledge came from experience or experiment alone. They did not recognize the validity of abstract theories or generalizations, and insisted that one could speak only of things—hard, concrete things that could be seen, felt, or experienced with the senses. The realists, on the other hand, insisted on the reality of abstractions. They had no trouble accepting the idea of one God in three persons, while the nominalists were forced to regard the Trinity as three different gods, and avoided heresy only by insisting that theology was a matter of religious belief and not of philosophy.

The argument that raged between nominalists and realists is illustrative of the intellectual climate of the Middle Ages. In the first place, since it was a discussion among educated men, it was conducted in Latin and therefore available only to the educated population. The masses, who might have drawn unorthodox conclusions through misunderstanding the philosophers' words, were entirely excluded from the discussion. Secondly, the whole debate fell within the broad framework of medieval man's postulates about the world. Neither realist nor nominalist ever questioned the basic assumptions of the existing political, social, or religious institutions. Finally, the debate was encouraged because the medieval church did not possess a large body of fixed dogma. One does not speak of the *teaching* of the medieval church, but rather of the *teachings* of the medieval church. Almost all the variety that can be found today in the hundred and more Christian churches could be found under the broad roof of medieval Christendom. Thus medieval society not only permitted, but also encouraged, intellectual freedom within the bounds of its assumptions. By and large, the only people who were persecuted for their opinions were those who doubted the basic teachings of the Nicene Creed or who questioned the efficacy of the services of the church. Such doubters were outside the pale, but the philosophers and theologians who attempted to give the world of men an explanation of the ways of God were not troubled.

As with so many human efforts in the past, the intellectual labors of the great scholastic teachers failed to continue to produce fruitful results when mere followers were writing the books. Their systems of logical deduction became more and more fanciful, and the problems they attempted to solve became less and less associated with the realities of the world. As a result, by the fifteenth century they often appeared ridiculous even to their own contemporaries who nevertheless accepted many of the same assumptions about the world. Too often, in discussing medieval learning, modern men consider only the fossilized patterns of decadent scholasticism rather than the really creative efforts of the men of the twelfth and thirteenth centuries.

There were other streams of thought that invaded the medieval West. Arabic interest in astronomy, mathematics, physics, and alchemy seems to have fascinated the western mind. The Arabs in Spain made important advances in several branches of these sciences, and by introducing the flexible Indian system of mathematical notation (Arabic numerals), they prepared the way for the great scientific discoveries of the future. Natural philosophy found its way into the studies of the universities early in the thirteenth century, and by the fourteenth Oxford, Paris, and Padua were already famous for their "scientific traditions." Those students of "natural philosophy" were interested in explaining such problems as the refraction of light and the laws of mechanics. They raised many intelligent questions about the world around them, but had few tools for obtaining exact answers. Greatest among them were Robert Grosseteste, Roger Bacon, Albertus Magnus, and above all, William of Occam, who actually introduced primitive versions of later experimental procedures. "By 1375," Professor Randall remarks, "the genius of Descartes, of Galileo, and of Copernicus had already been anticipated."

However, the society of the fourteenth century was not prepared for such developments on any large scale, and was therefore unable to exploit them. The men of that time were too much committed to the beliefs of their age to escape into a later one. As natural philosophers, they spoke of mathematical analyses, but often they were thinking of *number* as a magic property. Their *numbers* had mystical significance—for instance, because they were divisible by three, or because they were whole numbers, and so forth. The sixteenth-century historian who tried to establish "mathematical relationships" between events by the number of years between them or by the calendar number of the year when they occurred had the same ideas about the magic of numbers as inspired Roger Bacon to find mathematical significance in the length of Noah's Ark. Without instruments for exact measurement, numbers lost their real significance and easily took on magical properties. Thus we find in the fifteenth and sixteenth centuries that natural philosophy, along with scholastic theology, was to become the butt of ridicule from the humanists. Erasmus, for example, classed them together in his *Praise of Folly,* because he could see no difference between the natural philosopher's attempts to learn truth from nature and the philosophical hairsplitting of the schoolmen.

In two other areas the Arabs gave their learning (or pseudo-learning) to the West: astrology and alchemy. Accepting the idea that the universe had meaning only because man lived in it, medieval men were fascinated by the problem of discovering the secret meaning of the movements of the stars. Kings and noblemen employed astrologers just as modern governments employ economists to give them advice. The astrologers were not all complete charlatans; they helped to keep alive the knowledge of astronomy inherited from Greece (via Spain), and many of them proved to be shrewd advisers to their royal patrons. However, it is probable that they usually consulted their own wisdom rather than the stars. Alchemists were the men who sought an imaginary substance (called the "philosopher's stone") capable of changing baser metals into gold or silver, and of prolonging life. In their way, they, too, made discoveries about nature, but their magic formulas were unsuited for any serious understanding of chemistry. Princes kept alchemists just as modern governments employ physicists, chemists, and psychologists to control nature and men for their own purposes.

2. THE RISE OF HUMANISTIC STUDIES

It is, of course, untrue that the West ever completely lost contact with the classical world of antiquity. By the tenth century, however, the number of people in western Europe who had any idea about earlier civilizations, and indeed the number of classical writers remembered by anyone, was pitifully small. Curiously enough, the cathedral schools of twelfth-century France, particularly the one at Chartres, taught and appreciated many of the classical Latin authors; but by the thirteenth century this interest had declined as the prestige of scholastic philosophy rose. Thus, there is some truth in the idea widely held a generation ago that the "Renaissance" began in Italy in the fourteenth century when western Europe "rediscovered" the books of antiquity. However, we must not forget that there were westerners who were acquainted with some of the more important Latin writers long before Petrarch (1304–1374) and the other humanists, as we call the men who discovered and edited these books, appeared on the stage of history. Indeed, it is now evident that the humanists only extended and developed a trend that was already present in the Italy of their day. Nonetheless, in the century and a half between 1350 and 1500 Latin Christendom became more keenly aware of its Greek and Roman heritage. In that period, most of the works of classical antiquity known to us today were discovered, corrected, and edited. It was then that western men found in the cultures and society of Greece and Rome ideas that could be applied to their own lives.

By the mid-fourteenth century the levels of civilization found in the principal commercial cities of Italy approximated those of the Roman era. Opportunities for leisure, curiosity about the world, and desires for pleasure and comfort were present because the economy of the Mediterranean basin was producing considerable surpluses of wealth. Naturally those Italian city men wanted to hear about earthly, human affairs. The scholastic theologians and the church fathers (patristic writers) wrote about moral and theological problems; by contrast, the writers of classical antiquity dealt with the affairs and activities of men. Since the latter were human in contrast to divine, the men who discovered and edited Greek and Latin texts came to be called "humanists," the study of the classics became "humanistic studies," and interest in such writings became "humanism." These terms have continued into the twentieth century even though the study of Latin and Greek no longer has a monopoly on the interest in human affairs.

It was not a simple thing to recover and edit the texts of the great Latin and Greek authors. In the first place, knowledge of the Latin language as it had been used in antiquity was required. This was different from the Latin of everyday speech in the medieval universities. Medieval Latin was a living, vigorous language, and therefore its vocabulary as well as its syntax was in the process of change; the humanists had to uncover the changes that had developed in the Latin language between the second century before Christ and their own time. For example, the language of Cicero differed from that used by later Roman writers of, say, the fifth century, and both of them differed from the Latin taught in medieval schools. The task, therefore, was to recover the grammar, syntax, and vocabulary of the ancient tongue. How well they accomplished this is shown by Lorenzo Valla's demonstration that the famous *Donation of Constantine,* the document that justified the pope's temporal authority over Rome, was a forgery; it was written in a form of Latin unknown in Constantine's time.

The next problem was to find the manuscripts themselves. In the thousand years between the fourth and fourteenth centuries the hazards of fire, mildew, and rot made any book's chances of survival pretty small. It was a period when few men cherished books; only a few poorly trained scribes copied them—laboriously, by hand. It was no easy task to recover whole texts. Petrarch first dramatized the process by ransacking old monastery libraries and contacting Levantine libraries for manuscripts. One after another of the great Latin historians, essayists, and poets began to reappear, but the task was not finished when a manuscript was found. Scribes had made errors, and sometimes only a part of a text was found, with indications that perhaps the largest part of it was still to be discovered. It was therefore the task of the scholar to find several texts of each document, so that they could be compared, purified of errors, and properly edited. That was exciting, exacting work comparable to the scientific research of a later age, and within educated circles the discoveries were followed with avid interest.

The manuscripts that the humanists found were often copies made in the Carolingian period (ninth century) by scribes who had had only a limited understanding of the documents with which they were working. Ninth-century men did not fully grasp the differences between themselves and the Romans of the classical era for they had no conception of historical change. The result was that there were many errors in their manuscripts. The four-teenth- and fifteenth-century scholars, however, were better prepared to deal with the problems of the texts. They had an appreciation of the differences between classical Roman society and their own era, as well as an understanding of the history of the Latin language and a feeling for Roman civilization. Petrarch's self-conscious, egotistical letters to the Roman poets and essayists —letters written to enlarge his reputation rather than to edify his readers —clearly show that he comprehended the fact of cataclysmic changes and the more than a thousand years that separated him from the men to whom he wrote. Undoubtedly it was this understanding of change, as well as their superior knowledge of the Latin language, that made it possible for fifteenth-century scholars to re-establish the authentic texts of the literature of antiquity.

In the fifteenth century, many humanists added the Greek language to their armory, and began the collection of Greek manuscripts as well as Latin ones. It was once believed that the capture of Constantinople by the Ottoman Turks in 1453 was the stimulus for importing Greek culture to the West. Alluring as this picture of the West as the savior of civilization might be, it hardly conforms to the facts. The rule of the Ottoman Turks was as enlightened as that of their Greek predecessors, and furthermore, Christians in the West had already been collecting Greek manuscripts for at least half a century when Mohammed II made the cathedral of Santa Sophia into a mosque. It is true that Greek refugee scholars came to Italy in greater numbers after 1453, but this merely hastened a process that was begun decades before. Greek scholars, like Chrysoloras who arrived in Italy in 1396, had begun moving westward as soon as there was a public with enough wealth to "appreciate" (i.e., support) them in the Italian cities. Possibly fear of the Turks accelerated the exodus, but perhaps it was simply easier to make a living in Italy than in the Byzantine Empire.

After Greek, the Hebrew language became the next fortress for Western scholars to storm. The curious isolation of the Jewish culture within Christendom during the Middle Ages was in part the result of Christian ignorance of Hebrew. The beginning of Hebrew studies in the mid-fifteenth century centered in Italy and Spain, but by the end of the century there were Christian scholars in most parts of Europe who could read the language. The most celebrated was the humanist Pico della Mirandola, a petty Italian prince who became a famous scholar in Florence. He and others introduced Christians to the Jewish theological and philosophical studies. His most famous student, Johann Reuchlin, published a Hebrew grammar and became the center of a great controversy in the early sixteenth century when a converted Jew named Pfefferkorn tried to get the authorities in the Holy Roman Empire to destroy all Hebrew writings as dangerous to Christianity. He personified the sixteenth-century version of the book burners and witch hunters that have appeared from time to time down to our own day. Reuchlin entered the lists against him, and soon brought down upon himself the wrath of all the obscurantists of Germany. The conflict became a bitter one, for the opponents of humanistic learning hailed this attack on Hebrew studies as an assault upon the most vulnerable point in the humanists' armor. The learned world came to Reuchlin's defense; a book of their letters to him entitled *Letters of Famous Men* inspired the publication of another, *The Letters of Obscure Men,* which exposed the ignorance and superstitions of the opponents of humanism. Ridicule and sarcasm were effective weapons against the reactionary obscurantist opponents of the new learning.

The new learning was victorious everywhere because Latin Christendom was ready to accept and understand its message. Particularly in Italy, but also in other parts of Europe, the new urban culture was interesting men in temporal affairs. They were eager to find new meanings for life on this earth, as well as to discover pleasures and ideas that the ruder, cruder society of earlier centuries could not appreciate. The earlier medieval period, to be sure, had been concerned with worldly matters even when its assumptions were based on the rejection of this world. However, that worldliness was overlarded with crudity and coarseness unsuited to a more cultivated people. Thus, just as medieval men had formerly been interested in earthly matters, so fifteenth-century men retained their theological or other-worldly concerns even when they became intrigued with the Greek and Roman classics. Catalogues of the principal libraries of the fifteenth century reveal that the patristic and theological manuscripts still outnumbered the Graeco-Roman classics. Cicero, Tacitus, and Plato may have modified the humanists' thinking, but they did not turn the Latin West from Christianity. Obviously the humanists were simply adding to the intellectual fare of their clients, not supplanting all their former intellectual and emotional interests.

The new learning also prospered because its devotees easily found employment. Princes of the church, state, and countinghouses were eager to use the services of intelligent men who knew how to write elegant Latin and whose literary activities might bring fame to the patron. Consequently, humanist scholars might be found nudging clergymen off the benches in the chancelleries of Europe, while others became hangers-on in royal or ecclesiastical courts. Some appeared as teachers in the new schools that began to grow up at this time; still others appeared as editors for the new publishing houses which had developed as the result of the invention of printing in the mid-fifteenth century. Several of the most famous of these humanist scholars would be classed as publicists or public relations men today; their writings were often produced to justify their patron's actions or to attack his enemies. Thus, the practice of hiring writers to present the case for important men who were themselves unable to write so persuasively did not begin with the popular mass magazines of the twentieth century.

Perhaps the most important factor in the triumph of the new learning was the invention of printing. Once the presses were furnished with movable type and supplied with paper manufactured more cheaply by a newly discovered process, European men were prepared to extend their culture on a foundation of books and reading. The presses were the first harbingers of the age of universal literacy. In the fifteenth and sixteenth centuries their ability to print an unlimited number of copies of any book, free from copying errors and at a reasonable cost, led to the democratization of learning. Bibles, textbooks, treatises both secular and divine, and controversial discussions of all kinds poured from the presses in Germany, Switzerland, France, and Italy to provide for the men of Europe their first exhilarating experience with a broad forum for ideas.

The humanists also brought intellectual developments to other fields; among others was the extension of the vernacular languages. Latin was the language of the medieval universities, of the medieval church, and of the medieval state, but it was not the common vehicle of communication. Most of the people ordinarily used their local dialects. Without strict grammar, syntax, or vocabulary, the popular speech grew to meet the needs of the time, and as the culture became more complex and sophisticated, so did these vernacular languages. The story of the French language is illustrative. Early in the Middle Ages the French tongues spoken in the north and in the south emerged as different languages, both elegant in form and beautiful to the ear. The language spoken in the northern district, called the Ile de France, whose capital city, Paris, was the seat of the court and the university as well as a commercial center, outdistanced its rivals and eventually became "correct" French. There is a tale of a deaf and dumb man, cured of his affliction by touching the remains of St. Louis, who immediately began to speak in the "proper" French of Paris rather than in his native Burgundian dialect. This story may not have been literally true, but, like all myths, it symbolizes the historic development of the people—in this case, the triumph of the Ile de France over its competitors. By the opening of the fourteenth century other vernacular languages were appearing as suitable vehicles for literary expression; London English, Castilian Spanish, Florentine Italian— each in turn was purified and given elegance through literary usage.

Throughout the Middle Ages there had been occasional literary expression in the vernacular, though, as was pointed out, the most important language had been Latin. From the latter thirteenth century onward, however, more and more literary men used their native tongue to express their ideas.

The songs of the troubadours, the *Canterbury Tales* by Chaucer, the *Divine Comedy* by Dante, Petrarch's *Poems,* and Boccaccio's *Decameron,* to say nothing of the numerous chronicles and other works, pointed to a vigorous literary development in the vernacular languages. With this upsurge of writing in the language of the people, it may be said that modern European literature was well launched in its own characteristic pattern. The recovery of the classical authors and the fifteenth century's emphasis on purity of Latin style checked, but did not stop, this development. The humanists' insistence upon writing Latin as Cicero wrote it was a barren procedure when books and learning became available to larger numbers of people. Neither were men with a vital literary message long imprisoned in such dry formality; by the sixteenth century practically all literary works were written in the popular languages. After all, a writer first wants his books to be read and understood; if he is writing for the people, he must use their language.

Humanistic studies entered the realm of theology and religion as well. When the study of Greek introduced Plato's writings to the West, their impact was almost as impressive as the one produced by the introduction to Aristotle several centuries earlier. Plato's thought was already part of the Christian tradition, since many of the patristic church writers of the third century had been indirectly influenced by him through neo-Platonism. That, however, had merely been an experience at second hand with the lofty spiritualism of the master. Beside Plato's own words, those of the patristic writers whom he influenced seemed only poor carbon copies of a beautiful original. It was not difficult to "baptize" Plato, to make his ideas fit into Christianity, nor was it hard to find men anxious to listen to his ideas, for they have always had a fascination for men seeking to fathom the meaning of life. Even so, most of the Platonic studies were limited to Italy, and the most important Italian humanist to turn philosopher-theologian was Marsiglio Ficino who, under the patronage of the Medici family of Florence, undertook to translate Plato and to adapt his doctrines to those of the church. "In his general optimism, in his emphasis upon the freedom of the will and the possible glory of man, and in the development of a theory of love," writes Professor Gilmore, "Ficino has been regarded as the formulation of a Renaissance philosophy."

Platonism led to a contemplation of ideal universals; that is, Plato was writing about general ideas that could apply any time, anywhere, in the universe. He was further concerned with such problems as the sublime symmetry of the universe. In this framework, the medieval idea of God as an intimate force in constant contact with each man tended to become blurred. God became justice, love, and truth as abstract ideas, instead of a personal experience for the individual man. Thus Platonic thought in Italy at the end of the fifteenth century began a theological revolution that concentrated attention on God the Father, Creator and Sustainer of the universe; Jesus, the man of sorrows and of personal love, receded into the background of religious contemplation. The substitution of a religion based on God as a general force throughout the universe for one based on Christ the "man-God" led later generations to accuse the men of the Italian Renaissance of being pantheistic[1] and pagan.

---

[1] Pantheism is the doctrine that God is the transcendent reality of the universe, and that all material things, as well as man himself, are only manifestations of God. This belief identifies God with nature, but denies that God is a person.

In northern Europe the new learning tended to become closely associated with traditional Christianity. It is often said that humanism was baptized when it crossed the Alps. This is simply another way of saying that the northern humanists generally used their knowledge in the service of the church. This may have been because the works of the most important classical authors had already been discovered, edited, and published by the Italians, leaving only the Christian texts to be edited by northern humanists. The new learning did not attract much attention in the north until the end of the fifteenth century when Erasmus, Colet, More, and others attempted to show that the Christian tradition could easily be interpreted to teach the reasonable humanistic morality that was to be found in the more lofty classical authors. Life on earth might be a preparation for the next world, but there was no reason why a Christian could not also live reasonably and humanely during that period of "testing." Both the schools of the northern humanists and the books that they wrote for their contemporaries demonstrated a spirit quite different from the Platonic humanism of Italy: while the Italians concentrated on God the Father, the northerners gave much of their attention to the "man-God" who had died for the salvation of all men.

There were several ways in which this interest in the personality and teachings of Christ expressed itself, but most important was the attempt to purify and to popularize the New Testament. At the beginning of the sixteenth century new editions of the Bible appeared in both Spain and Germany. The Complutensian Polyglot Bible, edited under the direction of the great Spanish cardinal, Ximenes, printed the Old and New Testaments in the original Hebrew and Greek languages with the Vulgate translation (in Latin) in parallel columns. It was a great monument to the scholarship of the period. Although the editing was more in line with medieval traditions than with modern higher criticism, by providing a purified text of the original documents it permitted many comparisons that helped clear up problems of the Vulgate translation. The fact that its authors secured many manuscripts from Rome and elsewhere to establish the correct text gave the Complutensian Polyglot an authority not enjoyed by any earlier edition of the Bible.

The other new edition of the Bible was the publication by Erasmus of Rotterdam of the New Testament with the Latin and Greek texts in parallel columns. Although Erasmus (1466?-1536) had neither the number of manuscripts for comparison nor a command of the Greek language comparable to that of the editors of the Polyglot Bible, his edition was in many ways more important than theirs. While the Spanish scholars were trying to buttress the authority of the Vulgate edition, the notes of Erasmus raised many questions about the authenticity of its translation.

The humanists both in the north and in the south differed from the earlier scholastic philosophers less than is apparent superficially. Both fully accepted the Christian religion. Here and there an Italian humanist appeared who seems to regard paganism with nostalgic eyes, but the vast majority of them recognized the moral superiority of Christianity. Both humanist and scholastic believed that truth was to be found in the writings of the church fathers and the pagan or pre-Christian philosophers as well as in the Bible. Their attempts to bring Aristotle, Plato, and other philosophers into line with Christianity were made relatively easy, because Christianity itself had grown from the intellectual ferment of the Roman Empire in the first centuries after Christ, and from its very beginnings it had been deeply influenced by Greek and Roman thought. Doctrines like neo-Platonism, cynicism, stoicism, and epicureanism had competed for the allegiance of intellectuals in the later days of the Roman Empire; all had been incorporated in part into Christian teachings, so they did not seem strange to Christians a thousand or more years later. Neither the humanist nor the scholastic had any idea of an experimental, scientific approach to problems of the physical world. Both regarded man and his moral problems as the important subjects to be studied, and both believed that man's most important destiny was to achieve salvation in the world beyond the grave.

3. THE ARTISTIC EXPRESSION

The medieval era produced the great cathedrals that have since been the delight of tourists, as well as the source of inspiration for Christians. There were many streams of historical development involved in their construction. In the first place, European society between the eleventh and the fifteenth centuries became rich enough to afford the extensive investment of capital and labor needed to create these great churches. Secondly, the Christian doctrine proved vital enough to provide the inspiration needed to persuade men that this money should be spent on churches rather than on other projects. While the goal may have been spiritual, the building of the cathedrals was also an assertion of faith in material things; medieval men invested an enormous proportion of their total capital goods in religious edifices. Lastly, medieval men had to learn the architectural skills necessary to construct buildings of such magnitude. From the ruins of Roman buildings, men endowed with creative imagination were able to work out the architectural principles developed by classical civilization, but the great churches that they created were in no way mere copies of earlier buildings. The master mason architects of the eleventh and twelfth centuries were proponents of a "modern," indeed revolutionary, style. They were faced with the challenge of constructing buildings on a scale theretofore unknown in their society, and they solved it with new architectural principles that allowed them to cover vast spaces with vaulted ceilings. Their uses of the arch have given medieval architecture its two names: Romanesque and Gothic.

The difference between the Romanesque and the Gothic styles is, at first glance, the difference in the arches that vault or sustain the cathedral roof. The Romanesque has a semicircular arch, the Gothic a pointed one. Flying buttresses were introduced to sustain or to strengthen the walls and to help carry the thrust of the roof. Gothic cathedrals had as much window space as possible to let light into the structure. The doorways, the capitals (the tops of columns or pillars), the altars and altar screens, all provided places for statues and bas-relief carvings, while the windows were frames for the magnificent stained glass pictures that the men of the twelfth and thirteenth centuries learned to make. Even on a dull day, the cathedral at Chartres provides an unforgettable experience of the spell that those unknown artists could work with glowing glass.

In the south of Europe—in Spain, southern France, and particularly Italy —the problem of light was quite different from that in the north. While English, German, and northern French architects widened their windows to let in what light they could during the dull, foggy, northern winters, the Italians needed walls to shut out the brilliance of the southern sun. Thus, the architects of the south tended to produce churches more like the basilicas of classical Rome, which provided huge expanses of walls in place of the stained glass windows of the north. Medieval builders filled the walls with decoration: allegories, representations of Biblical stories, and the lives of the saints. A rich society like that of Venice or Ravenna used mosaics of colored glass or stone; elsewhere men used paint as a cheaper substitute. The designs might be a picture of the risen Son of God, triumphant over the grave, or of the Virgin, Mother of God, holding her Son for men to worship, or they might simply be geometric designs. In some of the churches in Spain, as well as in the cathedral of Le Puy—a holy city in central France from which pilgrims left for Spain—Moorish designs in stone or brick testify to the artistic influence of Islam on Christianity.

In the fourteenth and fifteenth centuries a new style of architecture developed in Italy. Like many other aspects of this so-called Italian Renaissance, it was inspired by the ruins of Roman monuments. The architects of the great cathedral of Florence, for example, made extensive studies of the ruins in Rome, particularly of the basilica of Constantine. Their work, however, was more than a copy of the Roman basilicas; the magnificent dome at Florence, created by Brunelleschi in the face of great odds, is one of the significant artistic achievements of western art, and the high vaulted cathedrals and free-standing bell towers of Siena, Pisa, and a dozen or more other Italian towns testify to the genius of Italian architects of that era.

Both in northern Europe and in Italy the walls of churches often invited decoration with some sort of pictures. Whether these were in stained glass, mosaic, or simply painted on plaster, the medieval decorations had a common factor: as with much of twentieth-century modern art, they were not

The Church of the Notre Dame la Grande at Poitiers.

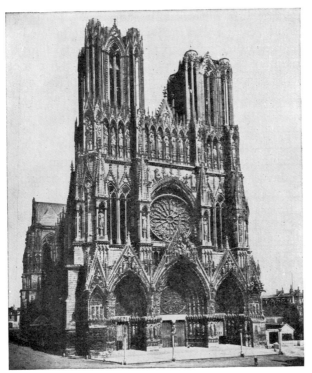

The Cathedral of Reims, an excellent example of Gothic Architecture. This great church was the scene of the consecration of the French Kings. It is still one of the most important monuments of France. Reims was severely damaged by war during the twentieth century but has been restored. (Ewing Galloway)

These three churches illustrate Romanesque, Gothic, and Renaissance styles of architecture. The Church of the Notre Dame la Grande at Poitiers was started in the eleventh century; the round arches and the severity of the lines on the side are typically Romanesque. The façade, which was not completed until the fifteenth century, illustrates the taste for decoration in the later medieval period. The Cathedral of Reims, with its pointed arches and soaring towers, is pure Gothic. Its sculptured figures include the famous "Smiling Angels of Reims" and some wonderfully diverse carvings of both strange and familiar animals. The Cathedral of Florence illustrates the Renaissance style; it is highly ornate with its colored marble façade. The dome was the most imposing in the Latin West before the construction of St. Peter's Cathedral at Rome.

The Cathedral of Florence. The dome was designed and built by Brunelleschi in spite of labor trouble, jealousy, and the meddlesome interference of the city fathers. Like most such structures, however, its present form is the work of many architects. Upon close examination one can see that the base of the dome is still unfinished. (Foto-Enit-Roma)

Mosaic from the Baptistry of St. John. This is one section (about one-eighth) of the mosaics in the ceiling of the baptistry at Florence. Christ is portrayed as judge, as the dead rise from their tombs for the last judgment. Above, Christ as God is surrounded by cherubin and seraphim.

made to look realistic. There was no attempt to imitate nature or to procure natural effects. Art historians self-consciously tell us that those styles were modifications of Byzantine art, and that they show the influence of the Greek East upon the Latin West. That may well be true, but we must remember that the purpose of the pictures was to produce religious emotions in the hearts of the viewers and to keep alive familiar religious stories. Whatever the source of the style, its flat, nonrealistic expression was best suited to concentrate the worshipper's attention on the story that was being told, rather than to distract him by details that were clearly earthly. The mosaics on the ceiling of the baptistry at Florence are magnificent examples of the emotional force that could thus be given to the traditional stories. Here in gleaming gold are told the principal stories of the Christian tradition. (However, one wonders how men could have seen these mosaics before the days of electricity!)

Another significant characteristic of the early paintings was the custom of following traditional patterns of representation. Each story came to have a definite symbolic organization for the figures represented. Each saint, for example, had a characteristic emblem that distinguished him from all the others, and in the great traditional scenes like the crucifixion and the resurrection there were fixed patterns that were rigidly followed. This might have led to an art with little content and less feeling, but some of the better pieces produced by twelfth- and thirteenth-century masters prove that these conventions could not shackle real genius.

Out of medieval Italy there arose one of the most remarkable schools of painters that the western world has ever seen. The term "Italian Renaissance art," which art historians use for this movement, is probably a misnomer; the movement was not a "rebirth" of any type of ancient art. Rather, it was a group of native schools of painting centered in Florence, Venice, Milan, and elsewhere that were to be merged in sixteenth-century Rome. However, the early Italian masters were "men of the Renaissance" in that they show all the individualism, versatility, and egotism that we generally associate with that period.

The man usually credited with beginning the movement is Giotto (1276–1337), the painter of the life of St. Francis of Assisi. St. Francis loved the out-of-doors and nature, and since he had only recently been sainted there was no established convention as to how he was to be represented. This gave Giotto an opportunity to paint more freely than his predecessors. Some unexplainable spark of genius made him want to paint real men and women rather than conventionalized types. The result was that he tried to make more accurate drawings of the human figure, and the props that surround it, and to give his figures perspective to make them seem real. Comparison of a painting by Giotto with one by an equally talented but more conventional contemporary such as Simone Martini (1283–1344) shows that the former tried to paint real people, while the latter hoped to produce a beautiful composition, charged with emotion by the force of his representation. Martini's "Annunciation" is every bit as striking a picture as any by Giotto, but it was Giotto who was to found a school of painters eager to recreate nature realistically and faithfully.

Giotto's immediate followers continued to paint flat, mosaic-like pictures

Giotto, "Lamentation over Christ" (Padua, Arena Chapel). Giotto was a precursor of the great Florentine school of the fifteenth century. This painting illustrates his departure from conventionalized representation of the human figure; the bodies are solid and appear to have weight, and the facial expressions portray real grief. The painting displays a deep dramatic sense in the story it tells.

rather than to imitate his efforts to get a feeling of space and depth through correct perspective, but early in the fourteenth century a young Florentine painter named Masaccio (c. 1401–1428) appeared on the scene as a worthy successor to continue Giotto's tradition. He died before he was thirty, but in the Carmine church in Florence he left frescoes that were to have a profound effect on every Florentine painter for a century after his time. In one step he seemed to have captured the reality and vitality that Giotto envisaged. His figures were real people with real emotions, ambitions, and fears. As he

Simone Martini, "The Annunciation" (Florence, Uffizi Gallery). This painting of the Annunciation illustrates the highly decorative and stylized form of the period. Gold leaf as well as paint is used to heighten the effect. The lilies between the Virgin and the angel are required by custom. (University Gallery, University of Minnesota)

painted Adam and Eve, they are not merely two middle-aged people uncomfortably bereft of their clothing, but two human beings who had lost paradise.

The generation of painters following Masaccio lacked his genius, but made up for it by hard work. They were really scientists grappling with the problems presented by the new style. Paolo Uccello (1396–1475), for example, worked at the problem of perspective. He painted battle scenes in which an array of "rocking horses" and puppet men were placed in serried ranks, and a mélange of spears and other equipment was scattered on the ground. Though his figures were stilted and wooden, he achieved correct perspective. Andrea del Castagno (1423–1457) followed Masaccio's efforts at visual realism, producing figures that often appeared as if they had been sculptured. One art critic has called this quality "tactile value"—that is, the appearance

Paolo Uccello, "Cavaliers in Combat" (Florence, Uffizi Gallery). This is one of the artist's several battle scenes in which he was concerned with perspective. It mattered little to him if his horses appeared wooden, as long as they illustrated successfully the problems that he was trying to solve. (University of Minnesota Gallery)

Masaccio, *Adam and Eve Expelled from Paradise* (Florence, Carmine Church, Branacci Chapel). This painting and Masaccio's "Betrayal of Christ" make the walls of the Branacci Chapel an important monument to the fifteenth-century Florentine school.

of reality that gives the impression that painted figures have weight and body. Another scientifically minded artist-sculptor was Antonio Pollaiuolo (1443–1496), whose primary interest seems to have been the problem of depicting motion (running, wrestling, and dancing) in a two-dimensional picture.

A drawing by Andrea Mantegna. This line drawing
by Mantegna, or one of his students, illustrates the scientific labor of fifteenth-century artists. Mantegna, like
Pollaiuolo, was interested in depicting motion on a flat
surface. (Minneapolis Institute of Art)

Several others of this first generation of fifteenth-century painters deserve
mention. Fra Angelico (1387-1455) portrayed a world of heavenly goodness,
kindness, and beauty, while Piero della Francesca (1406-1492) achieved astonishing vitality by carefully executed perspective and stark, brutal realism.
Not the least was the versatile Fra Filippo Lippi (1406-1469), a monk with
quite "unmonkish" ways, who left canvases and frescoes of great beauty.
With the possible exception of Fra Angelico, those painters of the mid-
fifteenth century were deeply affected by the worldly atmosphere of con-

Domenico Ghirlandaio, "The Last Supper" (Florence, The All Saints Convent). Ghirlandaio is often dismissed as merely Michelangelo's teacher, but he is a great painter in his own right. The painting is the traditional portrayal of the Last Supper; Leonardo's painting in Milan is similar. But compare Ghirlandaio's with Tintoretto's *Last Supper* on p. 90.

temporary Florence, which was the chief center of the movement at the time. The city was rich, its inhabitants luxury loving, and its society interested in earthly pleasures. Thus, even when they painted religious scenes, the artists ornamented them with the pomp and circumstance of the world; and, if anything, that tendency became more pronounced in the last generation of the century.

Florence had been the chief center or school of painters in the mid-fifteenth century, but in the next generation techniques and ideas from painters in Venice, Mantua, Milan, and elsewhere began to merge with the Florentine, and the resulting style might properly be called Italian. The rising tides of wealth throughout the peninsula brought artists together in Rome, as well as in the lesser capitals. In the Rome of that period the papacy lost much of its medieval piety; it became a state ruled by worldly, luxury-loving popes whose artistic tastes sometimes outran their spiritual interests. Lorenzo the Magnificent consolidated the Medici family's position of cultural and political leadership in Florence. Pope Leo X, Lorenzo's son and perhaps the most famous of the Renaissance popes, gathered together in Rome the great artists of the early sixteenth century and garnished that city with the fruits of

Pietro Perugino, "The Nativity." Perugino was Raphael's first teacher. He perfected the concept of space composition; note the recession of the horizon toward a center point. (Minneapolis Institute of Arts)

Italian renaissance genius. (It was during Leo X's pontificate that Luther first kindled the spark of the Reformation.)

The later fifteenth-century painters were faultless craftsmen, their sole limitation being that they sometimes lacked imagination in presenting their materials. Even this criticism is perhaps unjust, since their patrons often prescribed not only their subject matter but also the general scheme of the painting. Ghirlandaio (1449–1494), for example, has often been dismissed as important only as the teacher of Michelangelo, but anyone who studies his pictures can see that in his own right he was one of the great masters of

Luca Signorelli, "The Damned" (Orvieto, Cathedral). Signorelli was the most famous of Pollaiuolo's students. "The Damned" is an example of his frequent theme of masses of men in violent motion. (University Gallery)

Leonardo da Vinci, "The Virgin of the Rocks" (Paris, The Louvre). This painting is one of the few works that Leonardo actually finished, but even if it were the only one, it would secure his reputation as a master.

his craft. His ability to create large compositions with many figures against an ornate architectural background was unexcelled. Botticelli (1444–1510) painted lovely women and children; with his fine sense of color and balance he must be considered one of the great painters of all time. Perhaps the best place to compare works of this period is on the side walls of the

Sistine Chapel in Rome, where three masters are represented. Here we see that Botticelli's sense of the dramatic was overpowering, perhaps even beyond his great skill; and while Perugino (1446–1523) has superb technique, his work is shallow in content. It was Perugino who really learned to achieve a feeling of space, and in his canvases it seems possible to see far into the distance. The third artist, Signorelli (1441–1523), showed great skill at depicting masses of men in movement. In the works of these artists the ways in which ideas and techniques were passed from one generation to the next can be seen; of the three represented here, Botticelli was a student of Filippo Lippi, Perugino learned his art from della Francesca, and Signorelli's interest in motion went back to his early training under Pollaiuolo.

Perhaps the greatest master of this generation was Leonardo da Vinci (1452–1519). He studied under Andrea del Verrocchio, who was more renowned as a sculptor than as a painter and who, like Pollaiuolo, was interested in motion and realism. Da Vinci adopted all his teacher had to offer, and then developed a style uniquely his own. He left but little of his painting on canvas or walls (and that mostly unfinished), but what he did leave, along with his drawings from sketch pads and notebooks, has established his great reputation. His "Virgin of the Rocks" is one of the most beautiful canvases in the world; his "Mona Lisa," one of the most famous; and his "Last Supper," even in its present dilapidated condition, one of the most frequently visited. Even had da Vinci painted nothing, his drawings, his anatomical studies, and his superb sketches of men and animals would entitle him to a paramount place among artists of skill and inspiration.

Most of these latter fifteenth-century artists lived on into the next century, and before they were gone, there arose the last generation of artists who may properly be called "Renaissance" artists. Of these men, two tower above the rest: Michelangelo (1475–1564) of Florence, and Raphael (1483–1520), the Umbrian. Their styles of painting were, of course, the result of their own genius, but both always retained strong traces of their early schooling. Both were also affected by the mingling of the styles in Rome. Both could combine masterful technique with poetic imagination and deep feeling.

When Raphael arrived in Florence in 1504 the precise but unimaginative style he had learned in Perugino's workshop was not much in demand. The Florentines preferred forceful, vigorous painting such as the murals then being created by Leonardo da Vinci and Michelangelo for the Palazzo Vecchio. The young Umbrian painter learned to adapt some of the Florentine vigor to the modest dignity of his own work, and was soon a success. In 1509 Pope Julius II invited Raphael and Michelangelo to Rome, where the former was put in charge of decorating the four papal apartments (or *stanze*) of the Vatican palace. Here he created a series of pictures that were to be almost as famous as the frescoes which Michelangelo painted in the Sistine Chapel at the same time. Critics can show that Raphael got many of

Raphael, detail from "The School of Athens" (Rome, Vatican Palace). In this fresco on one of the walls in the papal chambers, Raphael emerges as the master of Renaissance humanism and intellectualism.

his ideas from Leonardo and Michelangelo, but the quiet dignity, skill in design, and deep emotional feeling were uniquely his own. Fame, fast living, and more contracts than he could execute marred many of his later works, since he left students or assistants to do much of the actual painting. However, some of his most striking portraits came from that period; they were the ones that were entirely his own work. He died before he was forty, loaded with fame, honors, and riches.

The universal artistic genius of the period was Michelangelo: poet, sculptor, painter, architect, and engineer—even Leonardo did not excel him in versatility. And Michelangelo had the added virtue of completing more of his projects than did the great da Vinci. More than any other artist of the age, Michelangelo reflected the philosophical and literary thought of his time. His Sistine Chapel ceiling and "Last Judgment" on the wall behind the altar are expressions of the Platonism of Renaissance philosophy and

Michelangelo, detail from "The Last Judgment" (Rome, Sistine Chapel).

theology. The emphasis is upon the universal ideals; the style is simplified and details are removed to bring out eternal forces. A figure reminiscent of God the Father, creator of the universe and final judge of the dead, occupies the center of the stage, while Jesus, as the man of sorrows, of mercy, and of love, is absent from the picture. Pope Julius II made Michelangelo take down the scaffolds when he had only half finished the painting to make sure it was going to be fine enough for the Chapel. Looking closely at the finished work, the spectator may see a face very like the old Pope's—among the damned!

Michelangelo also had much to do with the architecture of the cathedral

Gentile Bellini, "Procession in the Square of Saint Mark" (Venice, Accademia). Gentile Bellini was one of the important Venetian artists. He portrayed the pageantry and pomp of Venice, religious scenes, and historical events. The "Procession" illustrates the statuesque quality of his work.

of St. Peter in Rome, and he did the *Pietà* that graces one of its side altars. His other sculpture, for example the David or the figures on the Medici tombs, would rival the work of the Greek masters of Athens, and the few paintings he left on canvas show that he was a master of color as well as of form. His work, whether it was the central figure of God in the "Last Judgment" or the great church of St. Peter, was always monumental. His was the genius that could translate grandiose ideas into concrete realization.

Not until the sixteenth century did Venice produce a school of painters worthy of the traditions developing elsewhere in Italy. It is interesting that while Venice was the wealthiest and most powerful of the Italian city states, as well as being the one most secure from foreign invasion, she produced no first-rate humanist scholars, no philosophers, and no painters as versatile as Leonardo or Michelangelo. The wealth and luxury of the city, the self-complacency of its inhabitants, and the efficiency of the government in preventing civil strife, may have had a blighting influence on the creative genius of her people. Florence—with all her turmoil, civil warfare, and repeated foreign invasions—seems to have had the better climate for developing artists and philosophers.

The two Bellinis, Gentile (c. 1429–1507) and Giovanni (1429–1516), were the first native Venetians to appear as first-rate artists. Their father before them had been a painter influenced by the Florentines, and they in turn were influenced by the visit in 1475 of Antonello da Messina, a Sicilian painter who had learned much of the Renaissance style from his travels. Giovanni Bellini is usually credited with developing the characteristic tendencies of Venetian art, which are the elaborate, sensuous use of color and the rich decoration of pictures through detailed painting of fabrics, jewels, and fine furniture. The climate of Venice made frescoes (painting on wet plaster) impractical, so most Venetian painting was in oil. This medium easily lends itself to rich detail and brilliant color, and undoubtedly contributed to the character of the Venetian school.

The Bellinis' paintings almost always have a stage-like character. The designs are formal, the figures placed in tableaux. Calm dignity, almost absolute quiet, prevail throughout the pictures. Whether the characters are saints, madonnas, or Christ, they are all obviously modelled after patrician Venetians of the time. When Dürer (see below) visited Venice early in the sixteenth century, he wrote that Giovanni Bellini, then seventy-six years old, was the best painter in Venice. He did not seem to realize that out of Bellini's studio there was emerging a whole new school of painters who had begun to produce great canvases. Giorgione (1475–1510), Palma Vecchio (c. 1480–1528), Sebastian del Piombo (1485–1547), and the great Titian (1477–1576), all appeared in the second decade of the century as masters of the new Venetian school.

Tintoretto, "The Last Supper" (Venice, San Giorgio Maggiore). Tintoretto was severely criticized for this painting of the Last Supper, because he departed from the traditional representation and included more people than the Biblical text warranted. Note the use of light, shade, and motion that made him one of the forerunners of the seventeenth-century Baroque painters.

Titian, who lived to be ninety-nine years old and painted almost to the day of his death,[2] was the most versatile of the Venetians. He painted for the state, the church, and the great men of the day. Charles V sat for him several times; his painting of Pope Paul III is one of the most revealing of all portraits. Sometimes his draftsmanship was faulty, but his sure sense of color and design, as well as his ability to present his subject dramatically, made his pictures both masterpieces of art and documents of historical significance.

There are two other Venetian painters of the sixteenth century who cannot be ignored. Paolo Veronese (1528–1588) painted the pageantry of great festivals, huge canvases filled with people, sprinkled with interesting detail, and bejewelled with magnificent color. He had a penchant for painting crowds and this led to his appearance before the Inquisition, for his painting

[2] His last picture was a *Pietà*, or representation of the dead Jesus after the crucifixion. Titian painted himself as Joseph of Aramathaea kneeling before the dead Christ. Only a few brush strokes were unfinished when he died.

of the "Last Supper" depicted many more people present than tradition allowed. Veronese's defense was based on the artist's privilege to present his subject as he wished. Tintoretto (1518–1594) had in his studio the motto, "The drawing of Michelangelo and the coloring of Titian." His paintings with their characteristic purples and blues reflect that ambition. He, too, painted a "Last Supper," which provided an interesting comparison with those by Ghirlandaio or Leonardo, for he broke completely with the traditional presentations.

At that time the lands north of the Alps produced their own schools of painters. Since the Dutch school did not achieve its greatest importance until the seventeenth century, it will be discussed in detail later. However, there were two German artists of the Renaissance who deserve mention at this point. Albrecht Dürer (1471–1528) and Hans Holbein (1497–1543) were both influenced by visits to Italy, but they also drew their inspiration from native German traditions, including the use of different media such as woodcuts and etchings that developed in the north during the fifteenth century. Dürer's black and white designs are undoubtedly among the finest ever produced, and his ability to depict detail without losing sight of the drama of the story he was telling was unexcelled. Both he and Holbein were portrait painters of the first order. It is interesting to see that these German painters did not follow the Italian tendency to emphasize the universal aspects of the Christian tradition. Platonism did not take deep root in Renaissance Germany, and German artists were more likely to depict Christ on the Cross than God the Father and Creator of the universe, the nativity, or the Virgin and Child.

The era called the Renaissance has attracted considerable attention from historians. Men are always fascinated by the flowering of genius, and the later fifteenth and early sixteenth centuries seem to have been particularly productive of versatile, highly talented individuals. It is hard to believe that those men differed from preceding generations biologically or that they were born with greater intellectual capacities or artistic abilities. Therefore, we must assume that the questions presented by the appearance of so many talented men should be answered by studying the society that produced them. It must be remembered that both the literary humanist and the artist were products of the new urban and princely culture of the time. They flourished when there were enough princes, prelates, townsmen, and noblemen interested in supporting them. This pattern of support for the arts was to continue, with variations, until the nineteenth century. As we shall see in later chapters, the baroque and rococo styles of the seventeenth and eighteenth centuries were supported in much the same way. It might also be noted that they were to be worthy successors of the styles of the Renaissance.

Chapter 4

THE FRONTIERS OF EUROPE

1. EARLIEST EXPLORATION

The Saracen invasion that swept across the Mediterranean Sea in the seventh century dealt a deadly blow to Christian commerce, and also to western European knowledge of the peoples on the frontiers of Europe. We used to believe that East-West trade ceased, that the Mediterranean became a Moslem lake, and that European men were doomed to an agrarian and isolated existence. Recent studies, however, have demonstrated that the Byzantine naval units ranged from the shores of Anatolia to Sicily and the Adriatic Sea, and that trade between the Greek East and Italy, although small in volume, never quite came to an end. It is true that west European men, even the Italians, did not know as much about the world beyond their frontiers as the Arab geographers in Sicily and Spain, but there were a few Italian merchants and seamen who were well enough acquainted with the Levant to understand the commercial possibilities of that part of the world when western soldiers were ready to embark upon the first crusade. As soon as those Christian armies appeared in Syria at the end of the eleventh century, the Italians knew just what they wanted in return for naval support. After the crusades had introduced western soldiers to Anatolia, Syria, and Egypt, the interchange of goods and ideas went on rapidly.

This map of Europe is a fragment of "La Mappemonde Royale," executed at the request of Francis I of France. The modern student must turn it upside down to get the perspective to which he is accustomed. Close inspection will reveal that its anonymous cartographer was acquainted with the portolami of the Mediterranean and the Black Sea. Like the portolami, this map underestimates the land mass of Europe. Also, the further a place is from the Mediterranean, the more fanciful the cartography. The artist evidently believed that Christianity was outflanking Islam in Africa, for he placed a number of Christian figures at the top of his page.

Early Medieval Map of the World.

Genoa, Pisa, and Venice were the most important of the Italian commercial cities; in the twelfth century their ships passed both the straits of Gibraltar and the Bosphorus and Dardanelles to make an all-water contact between the Black Sea and England and the Rhine estuary. Even though their commercial and exploring activities were at times hampered by bloody wars with each other, those Italian cities continued to expand the horizon of the West. Their seamen ventured into the Western Ocean (the Atlantic). Almost three hundred years before Columbus, Genoese sea captains saw the Azores and Madeira Islands rising out of the sea. By the mid-thirteenth century they had reached the Canaries, and, if a map in the possession of the Library of the University of Minnesota may be trusted, by the early fifteenth century the Portuguese, in whose service many Italians sailed, believed in the existence of islands that Columbus actually "discovered" in the "New" World almost a century later.

As we have already seen in an earlier chapter, by the thirteenth century the Italian cities had become marts for international commerce—trading in fish, cloth, drugs, and a host of other articles that came from Asia as well as from the Atlantic Ocean basin. They possessed good maps of the Mediterranean and of the seas that joined it, maps that were not to be improved upon until the seventeenth century, and as we shall see, they even had considerable knowledge of the world to the east.

The Norsemen were the most adventurous of the north European travelers. As we have previously noted, they first appeared as pirates and robbers, but when European defenses proved equal to the task of repelling their predatory attacks, many settled down as merchants. There were two streams of Norse, or as it is sometimes called, Viking penetration. One group, under the name of Varangians, fanned southeastward through Russia as far as Constantinople. The sagas of the Varangian invasion tell of merchants and soldiers who came to control the great river systems of Russia and to govern the land as territorial princes. Some of them ended up in Constantinople as mercenary soldiers of the Byzantine emperor; others, as merchants, carried goods and ideas from middle Asia and the Black Sea basin to northern Europe. The other group of Norse adventurers steered their swift ships westward at about the same time that the Italians were beginning to re-establish contacts with the Levant. In the ninth, tenth, and eleventh centuries they reached Iceland, Greenland, and the mainland of North America; by the eleventh and twelfth centuries they had firmly established shipping lines across the top of the world, and on those they carried commerce and emigrants to Greenland and North America.

While knowledge of the Norse exploration and commercial enterprise was not the common property of all Europe, it was nonetheless known in most of the port towns of the north as well as in Rome. However, the sagas of these voyages were not translated into other languages, and so the records were necessarily confined to manuscripts without wide circulation. It was, therefore, difficult for most Europeans to learn of this story of the north. Even so, we now know that the Norse colonists in Iceland, Greenland, and Vineland (probably Labrador) had built up well-established settlements by the opening of the twelfth century. Nor was information about the settlements to the west completely lost when the severe climatic changes[1] of the thirteenth and fourteenth centuries drove the colonists out of Greenland and Vineland. In the latter fifteenth century Christopher Columbus visited Iceland in search of information before he asked for Spanish aid to make a westward voyage.

We do not know exactly what happened to those Norse settlements in North America. About the years 1150 to 1250, however, the climate of the northern hemisphere seems to have undergone severe changes; glacial ice drove the savage Eskimos southward to press upon the European settlements. The glaciers followed the Eskimos, and it was not until the twentieth cen-

[1] Meteorologists now call this climatic change the "little Ice Age"; they have several explanations for it.

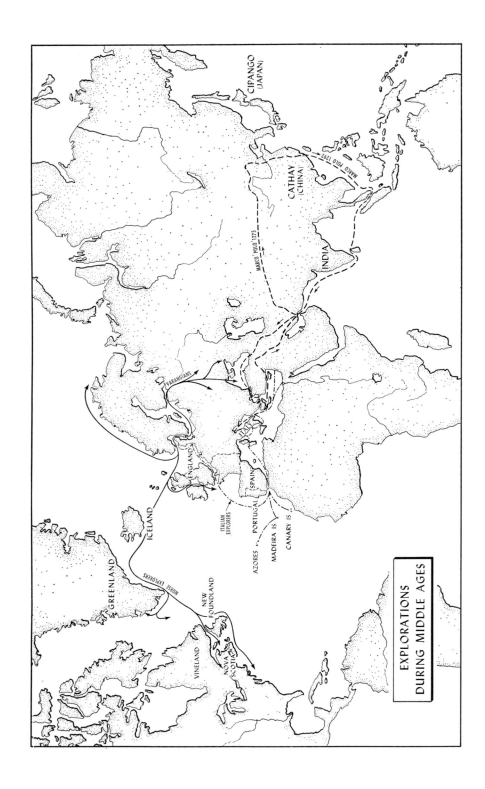

EXPLORATIONS
DURING MIDDLE AGES

CIPANGO
(JAPAN)

MARCO POLO 1292

CATHAY
(CHINA)

MARCO POLO 1275

INDIA

VARANGIANS

ICELAND

ENGLAND

ITALIAN
EXPLORERS

PORTUGAL SPAIN

AZORES

MADEIRA IS.

CANARY IS.

GREENLAND

NORSE EXPLORERS

NEW
FOUNDLAND

VINELAND

NOVA
SCOTIA

tury, when the rivers of ice were again in retreat, that they gave up some of the secrets of the early Norse settlements. We have found burials of Europeans dressed in English costumes of the thirteenth century that indicate clearly the advanced character of those Greenland settlements.

The early Italian and Norse seamen were only the harbingers of western Europe's pressure on its frontiers. They were followed by soldiers, adventurers, missionaries, and merchants who for reasons of power, curiosity, profit, or religious zeal probed into the lands beyond the confines of Europe and finally made the whole world Europe's province.

2. THE EMPIRE OF GENGHIS KHAN

The political and military situation of mid-thirteenth-century Asia opened another window for the West. The Tartars, who swept across high Asia and invaded eastern Europe in the first half of the thirteenth century, were part of the great Mongol movement under Genghis Khan and his successors. They conquered China as well as the wide provinces of central Asia, and spilled over into modern Russia. Before the movement exhausted its impetus, Tartar soldiers had seen the Adriatic Sea. Conditions within the empire, as well as the general problems of space, probably had more to do with checking the invasion than the battle of Wahlstatt (1244) which the central European Christians claimed as a victory. This Tartar conquest resulted in the founding of the most extensive empire ever created up to that time. From the frontiers of Poland to the Pacific Ocean, all Eurasia north of the high mountains was under one rule. Naturally this was no unitary state, but the khans had the advice of highly civilized and educated Chinese who gave their regimes both political strength and a sophisticated cultural veneer. The khans were tolerant men, uncommitted to any fanatical religious assumptions, and the Chinese tended to accentuate their urbane attitude. Thus they welcomed foreigners to their lands, and since a passport from the khan was good for travel from the frontiers of Europe to the Pacific, many travelers found their way across high Asia in the latter thirteenth and early fourteenth centuries.

Over this highway traveled Christian merchants, priests, adventurers, and political emissaries. One of the first, and by all odds the most famous of them, was Marco Polo, whose account of his voyages and activities in China was widely read throughout Europe. From Venice Marco Polo went with his father when he was still a boy to visit the Great Khan in 1271. For the elder Polo it was a return visit, so there were no problems for the family in the court of Kublai Khan, where young Marco gained favor, power, and riches. He became an official of the Khan's government, and traveled all over China visiting rich provinces and prosperous cities. His return to Europe was by sea to India and Persia, where he delivered a princess of the royal family as a bride for a distant relative of the Khan. Polo's story of the East,

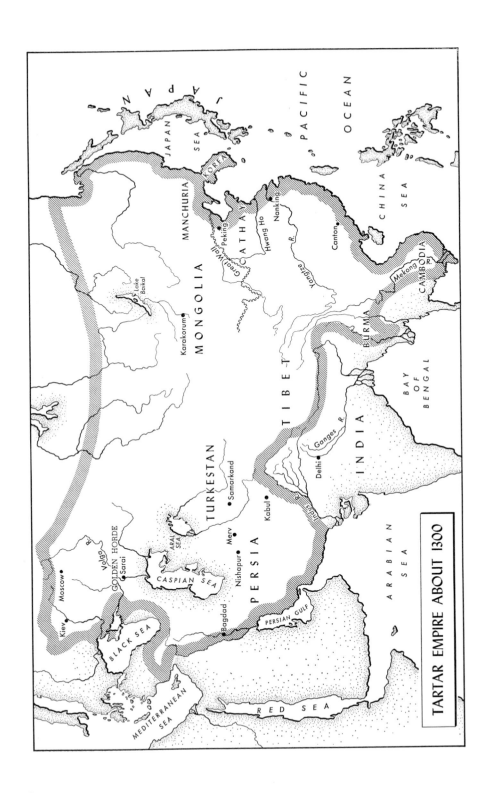

TARTAR EMPIRE ABOUT 1300

largely substantiated by other contemporary witnesses, was a merchant-administrator's account (probably somewhat exaggerated) of a fabulous land, immensely wealthy, with beautiful cities and enormous markets.

Within a few years after Polo's return, the highways over central Asia became well frequented with travelers—missionaries to convert the heathen and to correct the errors of Nestorian Christians, merchants, and adventurers pushed into Asia. As an indication of the extent of those contacts, there was a Roman Catholic bishop at Zayton (Canton) in China by 1308, and there were settlements of Christian merchants in many of the Chinese cities. It is impossible to say whether the zeal of the Dominican and Franciscan monks who preached the word of God was more pressing than the desire for gain or adventure that took other men to the lands of the Great Khan, but, be that as it may, in the mid-fourteenth century the Latin West knew much about the East. There were even emissaries from the Khan arriving at Avignon, Paris, and London to maintain political contact between China and the Latin West.

Moreover, knowledge of the East was not the monopoly of a chosen few. There were numerous travel accounts, and at the beginning of the fourteenth century most people who were acquainted with "affairs" would have had some idea of the Orient. The knight's story in the *Canterbury Tales* of Chaucer substantiates this notion, as does the fact that one of the great literary hoaxes of history was the false account of the eastern travels of one Sir John Mandeville, which in reality was written by a French physician who got all his ideas from other travel accounts. This would seem to indicate the popularity and extensiveness of Asiatic travel literature.

Because of the existence of the Tartar empire, China was more accessible to the West than was India. The trip to China could be made without traveling through Mohammedan lands. To visit India, Europeans had to penetrate the Arabian barrier, and the Arabs were not friendly toward non-Moslem visitors in Middle Eastern waters. Arab merchants had a monopoly on the trade of the Persian Gulf, the Red Sea, and the western water approaches to India. They were the middlemen between Europe and all of south Asia. That meant, in effect, Arabic control over the spice trade (pepper particularly) as well as the trade in Indian cloths, jewels, and drugs. The Arabs continued to maintain their position until the Portuguese reached India by way of the Cape of Good Hope at the end of the fifteenth century. The Mohammedans did not prevent Europeans from getting oriental goods; they merely stood on the route as middlemen. From the thirteenth century onward, Europeans sought ways and means to turn the flank of Islam.

In the latter fourteenth century the contact with China was broken; all of the economic and most of the religious institutions that had been created while the Tartars ruled China were destroyed. The last Mongol emperor was Toghon Timour (Ukhagatu) (1322–1368). After him a native movement, starting in the south of China, drove out the Mongols and all of the foreigners, and established the Ming dynasty (1368–1644). With a cultural egotism perhaps warranted by the actual status of the world of the day, the Chinese assumed their own superiority and decided to prevent cultural contamination from the outside. This isolationism was an attitude exactly opposite to the spirit of enterprise and curiosity that was to give the western Christians their first victories and to lead eventually to the political, cultural, and economic hegemony of western Europe.

3. THE OTTOMAN TURKS

The Ottoman or Osmanli Turks appeared on the frontiers of Europe about the same time that revolution in China excluded the foreigners. With the advent of the Ottomans, the Moslem assault upon the Byzantine Empire again became a paramount question for the Christian world. Of obscure central Asian origin, the Ottoman Turks accepted Mohammedanism and invaded Asia Minor. Their first two leaders, Osman and Orkhan, conquered all Anatolia; by the mid-fourteenth century they had crossed the straits and firmly established themselves in Europe. In the next hundred and fifty years they conquered Egypt, Mesopotamia, Syria, and the whole of the Balkans below the Danube river.

The Ottoman empire that they created retained its original character for centuries. Like the Mohammedan conquerors of India, the Turks resembled an army encamped on conquered land more than a state integrated into the lives of the people they ruled. Although they were Mohammedans, they made no great effort to force the people subject to them to adopt their religion, nor did they try to interfere with ancient laws and customs so long as those practices did not prevent the collection of taxes. The reason for such tolerance did not stem from the fact that the Turks recognized the rights of others, but probably from their inability to see what other courses of action might be open to them. After all, the Turks were few in number compared with the non-Turkish people who had fallen under their control. Ottoman rule was usually corrupt, with bribery as an integral part of the process of government. Such a charge, however, could be made of most of the governments of the world in that period.

The government of the Ottoman empire was and continued to be largely in the hands of people who were themselves not Turks. The mothers of the sultans were harem women, many of them slaves, from Greece, Russia, Persia, Georgia, and the trans-Caucasian lands, so that practically no Turkish blood was left in the House of Osman. Their political affairs were mainly managed by Christian or Persian renegades who renounced their own lands to serve the sultan, or by the Janissaries who had had Christians for parents. The Turkish people were above all soldiers, and some of them rose to high places, but at the top they had to compete with non-Turkish personnel who were usually cleverer and better prepared to operate the complexities of a government. It was not until the seventeenth century that men of Turkish blood and culture appeared as intellectuals rather than as men of the sword.

The most striking institution of that empire was the Janissary corps which may have been inspired by Plato's *Republic*. The Ottoman state imposed a tax of a certain number of boys between the ages of nine and eleven upon all Christian villages under its rule. As slaves of the sultan they were carefully trained and screened. They were his elite military corps and the recruiting ground from which he drew his viziers and generals. Those with brains—Plato's "men of gold"—became governors; those with brawn—Plato's "men of brass"—became soldiers. The Janissary corps was the very backbone of the Turkish military machine. Its members were the pampered darlings of the sultan; they occupied the place of honor in his marches; they were the guard of honor at his capital. The corps, however, was kept under strict discipline, and until the seventeenth century, the Janissaries were forbidden to marry and have legitimate children. If one of their number displeased the sultan, the slave's life was forfeit without any appeal.

In their first invasion, the Turkish armies came into Europe proper as allies of one faction in a civil war within the Byzantine Empire. As a result, Emir Orkhan married a princess of the Byzantine royal family. In 1354 his son crossed the straits as an invader, entitled by his blood to a share in the Byzantine emperor's inheritance, and subsequently established his rule on European soil. The extension of his conquest fell within the pattern of the feudal relationships of the Balkans. One by one the princes of Bulgaria, Serbia, Albania, and other Christian lands became vassals of the Turkish sultan, and each in turn assisted the Turks in the conquest of his Christian neighbors. The actual number of Turkish people who settled in Europe was small, and their settlements were widely scattered. The Turkish conquests were made by the Janissary corps, Christian vassals and allies, and a few Turkish soldiers, all fighting under the banner of the sultan. Thus at the battle of Kossovo (1389), when the Serbian army was crushed and all hopes of Serbian independence were destroyed, large contingents of Sultan Murad's army were furnished by his Christian allies.

Sultan Murad was killed in the battle of Kossovo, probably murdered by a faithless ally or a deserter. His successor, Sultan Bayazid, immediately took over, and killed all of his own brothers to prevent disputes over the succession. This practice was followed by later sultans, one of whom erected a beautiful tomb for the bones of his beloved brothers whom it had been necessary to murder in the name of the state.

European reaction to the rise of the Ottoman Turks provides insight into the misunderstanding the West had of the peoples on its frontier. Between the end of the crusading epoch and the opening of the fourteenth century,

Islam had gradually ceased to be a serious threat to most of Europe. Although there was still conflict between the Moors of Spain and North Africa and the Spanish kingdoms, in the East the Italians had come to terms with the Arabs so completely that Islam no longer seemed to be a danger to the West. When the Ottoman emirs appeared as a new military force under the banner of Islam, they were not at first recognized as a real danger, but once they had crossed the straits and established themselves on the flank of the city of Constantinople, it became apparent that Europe might again soon be under siege. There was, however, no single political or religious leader in the West to raise the call for military action. The papacy was crippled by the schism in the church, which had led to the election of a pope in Avignon as well as one in Rome; the Empire had ceased to have any real meaning, and Christian princes were more interested in fighting each other than in resisting the encroachments of Islam. Even after the Council of Constance healed the schism (1417), it was impossible to arouse Europe to the danger. The restored papacy had no means of uniting the Christian princes in a crusade against the Turks since its own prestige was low, and the most important of the princes were in conflict with each other. However, the popes did try to use the crisis as a lever to bring the patriarch and the Greek Orthodox community to recognize the supremacy of Rome.

The lack of vision in Europe was dramatically illustrated by the feeble attempt that was made to raise an army to go to the aid of the Byzantine emperor. The undisciplined band of crusader adventurers that marched south to assist in the defense of Constantinople seemed to have had only the haziest notion about the strength or fighting capacity of the Turks. Indeed, they acted as if their only reason for going to war was to take advantage of the opportunity for loot; long before they met Bayazid's Janissaries they had earned an unsavory reputation with both the Christian and Mohammedan populations in the Balkans. They stole from the Christians; they murdered and stole from the Mohammedans. In 1396 at Nicopolis the army of crusaders was utterly defeated by the Turks. Bayazid ordered that they all should be slaughtered in punishment for their treatment of the Mohammedans who had fallen into their hands. A small group of French knights who had the money necessary to buy their lives watched the butchery.

The Turks had hardly consolidated their hold on the lands below the Danube when they fell victim to another raider more ruthless than themselves. Out of Asia came a further assault from the hill people; this time it was led by a remarkable soldier named Timur the lame (Tamerlane in western tradition), who built an empire stretching from the Mediterranean to India. On July 20, 1402, Tamerlane's armies defeated the Ottoman forces, and captured Sultan Bayazid at Angora. Tradition has it that Bayazid was exhibited in Tamerlane's baggage train in an iron cage. The new conqueror, however, proved unable to establish an empire that could survive his own

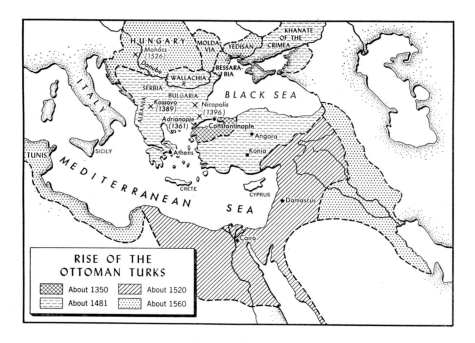

RISE OF THE
OTTOMAN TURKS

About 1350   About 1520
About 1481   About 1560

death, so the respite that Tamerlane gave the Christians in Constantinople and in Hungary was short-lived. Within fifty years the Turks had not only recovered completely, but also were ready to beat down the walls of Constantinople.

Again the Christians were unable to act effectively to check the Turks. In the West, England and France were playing out the last days of the Hundred Years' War and preparing for the civil conflicts that filled the midfifteenth century. In Germany the Hussite wars fully occupied the attention of the emperor; as we shall see, schism in the church led to heresy, and heresy to open rebellion. In Italy the five principal city-states had achieved a balance of power among themselves, but lacked the will or the means to join forces against an enemy abroad. Only in the Spanish kingdom was there still the disposition to crusade, but the Spaniards were more interested in fighting the Moors in their own backyard than in embarking on a campaign in the Levant. Christians called the Turks "the scourge of God," and damned them in sermon and pamphlet, but they left the great city of Constantinople to take care of itself.

The Turks were hammering at the walls of Constantinople by the midfifteenth century. In 1451 the talented Mohammed II came to the Ottoman throne; two years later Constantinople fell, and Santa Sophia, the greatest church in all Christendom, became a mosque. The conqueror was as civilized and sensitive a man as the Byzantine rulers had been; he assumed the role of Greek emperor along with his other titles as a Mohammedan ruler. The loss of Constantinople, however, was a terrible moral blow to Christendom.

Not only was it the largest and most important city ever lost to Islam, but with its fall collapsed the centuries-old Byzantine Empire, the last direct contact with the empire of classical Rome. When the "city protected by God" fell into the hands of the Turks, there were only two societies left on the Mediterranean: the Islamic East and the Latin West. Mohammed II was no Genghis Khan or Tamerlane; his was not to be a sprawling empire carved out by rapid conquest northward against Christian central Europe. For the next three-quarters of a century he and his successors consolidated their power over the Islamic Levant.

In the later fifteenth century, decked in the mantle of the Kalif (headship of Islam), the Turkish sultans emerged as rulers over the eastern end of the Mediterranean basin. Syria and Egypt, as well as Mesopotamia and the holy cities along the Red Sea, were combined in a great Mohammedan empire. The Arabs and Egyptians had no great love for the Turks, nor were they happy to recognize the sultan in the role of successor to the prophet. Still the power and authority that were brought together in the Ottoman House made it the most formidable force that had appeared on the frontiers of Europe up to that time, and for several generations it was to constitute a serious threat to European security.

4. THE WORLD ON THE EVE OF THE "DISCOVERIES"

A glance at the world about the time of the fall of Constantinople reveals that there were a number of relatively important societies existing in various parts of the world, but with only slight contacts between them. After looking at these societies, one distinguished historian remarked that in the mid-fifteenth century western Christendom seemed "least likely to succeed." The Western Empire was divided into dozens of principalities, none of which had any considerable wealth or power. The Eastern, or Byzantine, Empire had ceased to exist when its capital city fell to the conquering Turks. The West may have believed that God would never allow His people to be destroyed, but in 1453 it could well have seemed questionable whether there was any justification for this optimism. The simple fact was that the western Christians of the fifteenth century were seemingly intent upon self-destruction rather than upon any program of action that could strengthen their hold upon the lands they occupied. Roman Christendom still displayed the outer forms of unity, but the inner structure of the society was dividing Europe into petty, self-centered principalities, each anxious to affirm its independence and unwilling to act as a unit even against so dangerous an enemy as Islam.

One of the most interesting problems in world history emerges from this fact. How was it that between the sixteenth and the twentieth centuries west Europeans were able to establish domination over so much of the rest of the world in spite of those divisions and the almost continuous wars that they fought among themselves? Obviously no pat answer can be given to such a question. The total matrix of western society is involved. As we have seen, by the thirteenth century the decentralized structure of the West was already showing remarkable vitality in many areas of human activity. On the one hand, the diversity of strength of the economy, the reintegration of knowledge, the re-establishment of military force—all were evidence of the vigor of western men. On the other, the inability of any power to establish effective leadership seemed to argue that there was a fundamental weakness in the political organization of western society. It may well be that this "federal" order, for all its apparent disadvantages, was also the important source of strength. The frictions and differences developed by western men may have been the dynamic element in their society.

In the fifteenth century, however, the ascendant power was Islam. Led by the Ottoman Empire, Islam was knocking lustily at the back door of Europe from the Balkans and at sea from the Levant and the whole north coast of Africa. There was still a Moorish kingdom in Spain, and the Moriscos, scattered among the Christian population, created a potential "fifth collumn" to aid in the reconquest of that peninsula. In the Middle East a heretical sect (Shi'ites) of Islam prevailed in Persia, while all of north India was subject to a Moslem empire that, in a similar fashion to the Ottoman power, acted like an army of occupation rather than a state. There were isolated groups of Mohammedans scattered throughout the Far East. China, southeast Asia, and the Philippine and East Indian archipelagos had their Moslem colonies. Moslem missionaries were also moving up the Nile, converting the black tribes of the Sudan.

Islam traditionally made converts by the sword—as it did in Asia Minor, the Balkans, and India—but merchants and missionaries also acted as agents for the expansion of Mohammedanism. The merchants introduced their religion with their goods; they built compounds and mosques at the same time, and were followed by missionaries who pressed home the superiority of Mohammed's teachings. Unlike Christianity, Islam was not burdened by a difficult mystic doctrine like the Trinity; it was pure and simple monotheism adapted to the sensibility of relatively ignorant people. Its ethics and its picture of heaven also were well fitted to appeal to the societies of the East.

Thus, wherever Europeans looked abroad they saw Islam. A map of the western world of the middle sixteenth century emphasizes this fact by placing the south at the top of the page and putting the Arctic Ocean at the bottom. With this perspective, it becomes clear that Europe was surrounded by a huge semicircle of Islamic culture and proportionately threatened by it. Europe's great problem at the end of the fifteenth century was to turn the flank of this Mohammedan power. As the Turkish sultans extended their direct authority over the Berber states on the north African coast and pushed their conquest into the Danube basin and over the islands of the eastern

Mediterranean Sea, that problem assumed military importance. It was not simply the Mohammedan culture but the Mohammedan sword that was encircling Europe's living space. It should come as no surprise that Charles V, as king of Spain and emperor of Germany, should have had to spend most of his efforts in the first half of the sixteenth century fighting the soldiers and sailors of Islam.

Beyond the Islamic world were the societies of India and China, but Europe could not expect aid from either of them against the Moslems. India was in a state of complete decay, politically and militarily; her people did not know it, but they were only waiting for the Mogul conquest that was to come at the end of the fifteenth century. China, during the entire period of the Ming dynasty, was culturally isolated; foreigners were unwelcome in her ports, and the Chinese do not seem to have established firm contacts beyond their own frontiers. In the fourteenth and early fifteenth centuries they sent great fleets of junks on "sweeps" of the Indian Ocean to collect tribute and carry on trade, but in the latter fifteenth century that practice seems to have been discontinued. The weakness that was eventually to open the frontiers of China to the Manchu invasion became characteristic of Ming China about 1500. The government fell increasingly under the control of the empress-mother, the harem, and the eunuchs who served the women. It came to pass that ambitious young men would submit willingly to the knife, since only a eunuch could secure favor in the government of the harem. Such a society was in no position to give aid against so masculine a doctrine as the Mohammedan.

The island societies from Japan south to Malaya were not strong enough militarily to warrant consideration, and into many of them Islam had already infiltrated. The African tribes were both too backward in their political development and too deeply involved in their primitive religious rites to play a significant cultural or military role in the fifteenth century. Africa was apparently destined only to furnish the human chattels demanded for the harems of Islam and for labor in both Asia and, after their discovery, the Americas. Neither Islam nor Christianity made any important impression as religious movements upon black Africa.

Thus a superficial glance at the world when the "city guarded by God" fell into the hands of the Ottoman Turks would seem to indicate that Islam, guided by the Ottoman and Indian empires, might well develop as the world religion and the great political force. Yet at the very moment when that disaster seemed to stalk the gates of Christendom, there were strong forces at work that were destined to reverse such a trend and to give Christendom the initiative in the contest. As we shall see, only a few years after Constantinople fell and thereby reduced the "living space" of Christendom, Portuguese mariners pushed their explorations of the African coast and the south Atlantic to a point that gave the West a whole new empire upon which to build its power and prestige.

However, voyages of discovery alone could not have shifted the balance of power in the world. If this had been possible, Ming China would have appeared in the sixteenth century as the great power in the world. At the very moment that Portuguese mariners were painfully inching their way down the coast of Africa, Admiral Cheng Ho, with a fleet of fifty ocean-going junks and over 27,000 men, made an ocean sweep that brought the Chinese to India, Mecca, Madagascar, and east Africa. Cheng Ho had made a striking voyage of exploration, but its long-term importance was nil, whereas the Portuguese who so laboriously and modestly pushed around Africa to India were to upset age-old patterns of East-West commerce and to introduce the process of westernization of the whole Orient. Obviously the spirit that inspired the Portuguese was akin to the one that had sent crusaders to the Levant. Both were movements that had apparently been beyond the ken of the Ming admiral who swept the Indian Ocean.

5. THE PORTUGUESE VOYAGES

Much has been written to explain why the voyages that contacted the East and discovered the Western continents emanated from the Iberian peninsula. Iberia, like the Levant, was the scene of crusades against Islam. Indeed, at the very time that her mariners ventured forth, the last of the Moorish rulers were being driven from the European mainland. No doubt many noblemen and priests in both Portugal and Spain welcomed the voyages as an outlet for crusading ardor, as a chance to accomplish, as their fathers did, feats for the glory of God. The fact that in the Indian Ocean the Portuguese again encountered their old enemy, Islam, made the conquest of those waters both a Christian and a commercial victory. In the New World as well as in the Orient the prospect of harvesting souls for the true religion may not have been as strong a motive as lust for gold, but it would be wrong to ignore its existence.

Of course, no one can escape the fact that commercial considerations were also of paramount importance in the process that brought India and the Americas into the European orbit. The Italian seamen who first exploited the trade of Spain, Portugal, and the islands of the western sea did so for profit and, perhaps, adventure. The Venetian seaman, da Cadamosto, who entered Portuguese service in the mid-fifteenth century, testified to the continuing interest in strange sights, the service to God, and the possible increase in a man's investment six- or seven-fold on each voyage. The prospect of gain must have impressed Spanish and Portuguese as well as Italian merchants. Their conflicts with the Moors gave the Portuguese information

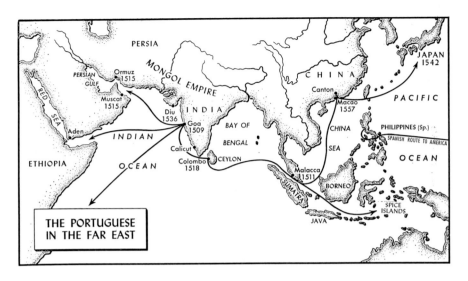

THE PORTUGUESE
IN THE FAR EAST

about the Africa of the Gold Coast, where Moslem caravans secured slaves, ivory, and gold. Thus their aim was twofold: to break Islam and to secure riches for themselves. The young and ambitious undoubtedly saw in exploration excitement and profit, as well as service to their God, that made ordinary voyages tame and uninteresting.

Yet before the story is told we must add to the desire for gain of some, and the urge to serve God or to see strange sights in others, the personality and interests of a remarkable man. Prince Henry of Portugal (1394–1460), surnamed "the Navigator," did not himself make the voyages that brought glory to his name. He might be said to have created an institute for navigation, for he gathered together in his court sailors, geographers, instrument makers, and merchants who improved their skills and knowledge. Inspired by his enthusiasm, his friends and associates plunged into the problems presented by the horizon beyond the last port of call. They were explorers interested in solving the problems of the earth's surface as well as men anxious to bring wealth to their country and themselves. In many ways this group of men combined in their several lives all of the interests and forces that sent western men to sea in ships. Portugal's pre-eminence in deep-sea navigation owed much of its force to Prince Henry the Navigator and the men who worked with him. Thus, the achievements of Portuguese mariners were in part based upon the systematic collection of evidence and scientific research. That story was to be repeated by the West many times in the following centuries.

It was no easy task to cut through the tangle of superstitions, wild tales, and natural fears that beclouded the horizon. Actually, the state of geographical knowledge in the fifteenth century was severely handicapped; the old routes across Asia had been closed for almost a hundred years, and the humanist scholars had imposed classical geographical concepts upon the learned of Europe. Freedom to travel eastward had ended with the coming of the Ming dynasty, and in an age of manuscript books much of the geographical knowledge that had been accumulated quickly disappeared. It is quite astonishing to learn that much of the geographical information that had been the common property of educated men in 1300 had been lost by 1430. In place of the books by travelers who had actually visited high Asia and the court of the Great Khan, the writings of Strabo, Ptolemy, and other first- and second-century geographers came into currency. The revival of the classical geographers was largely the result of humanist learning; the newly discovered ancient texts took the place of more accurate knowledge that was not so beautifully presented in classical Latin. Western men read Ptolemy, for example, without realizing, first, that much of his geography was erroneous, and, second, that in the thirteen centuries since he wrote some of his information had become woefully out of date. It was hard for men to understand that many of the basic postulates of the classical geographers had become untenable. The idea that the earth was a globe had long been accepted by learned men; so, too, was it understood that somehow all the seas were joined. However, their calculations gave them a wholly inadequate notion of the size of the earth, and of course they had no real idea of the structure of the continental land masses jutting out of the waters. Thus, even though men knew in general the shape of the earth, their ignorance about the details of its surface presented formidable problems for mariners.

The fifteenth-century Portuguese were sure that somewhere along the west African coast they would be able to turn north again and sail toward India, but throughout Prince Henry's lifetime they were faced with the appalling fact that a solid land mass barred the way. Africa was discouragingly large for men with fifteenth-century sailing ships. For several years after Prince Henry's death there was a tendency to exploit the lands already discovered rather than to continue the disheartening push southward, but in 1469 Fernão Gomes, a Lisbon merchant, received a monopoly on the Guinea trade on condition that each year he would carry forward exploration one hundred leagues beyond the last point of discovery of the previous year. It was a slow and painful process that achieved its goal at the end of the century. In 1483 Diego Cão reached the mouth of the Congo River; in 1486 he sailed to Cape Cross. In 1487 the Portuguese government sent out an expedition eastward by way of the Red Sea to establish the fact that it was possible to sail southward along the east African coast. However, before those emissaries had returned to Portugal, Bartolomeu Dias had embarked on the voyage in which he first rounded the Cape of Good Hope (1488) and demonstrated that from there on the route lay northward.

The first successful expedition reached India almost a decade later, a fact that gives us insight into the problems of navigation as well as the economic power of that age. Vasco da Gama left Lisbon in 1497. His ships picked up a pilot along the east African coast, and reached India in 1498. The next year he returned to Lisbon carrying a cargo worth sixty times the cost of the entire expedition. Looking at the century of labor crowned by this voyage, it becomes apparent that Portugal's contribution to geographical knowledge and to world commerce was the result of rational effort. Portuguese schools of navigation, geographical studies, technological discoveries, and hard work paid off only after some eighty years of labor. By way of contrast, Columbus' voyage (1492), though backed by great courage and fortitude, was the result of luck based on a monstrous error of judgment and faulty geographical understanding.

Within the first two decades of the sixteenth century the Portuguese had established themselves in the Orient. In the Indian Ocean they met their old enemy, Islam, now in the role of merchants who rightfully recognized the Portuguese as a threat to their own monopoly of East-West commerce. The military power of the Arabs, however, was not comparable to that of the Portuguese, whose tall ships were relatively more heavily armed. The sultan of Turkey and Doge of Venice, fearing for their own commerce, supplied the Arabs with money to fight the Portuguese, but victory went to the ships with the heavier guns and the best tactics. Through naval action, the Portuguese governors and seamen of the early sixteenth century cut the Arab routes via both the Red Sea and the Persian Gulf, and thereby added a further advantage to their monopoly of the all-water route.

At the end of the fifteenth century India was becoming subject to the rule of the Moguls at Delhi. Babar (1483–1530), a descendant of both Tamerlane and Genghis Khan, declared himself to be emperor of Hindustan in 1526. His conquest soon led to Mogul rule over most of the land, a rule, however, that did not greatly alter ancient institutions and laws. India's coastal cities were a mixture of all the races and creeds of the Orient—including Jews, Mohammedans, and even Nestorian Christians. There was no possibility that the Portuguese could rule such a land, and the Mogul conquest was only recent when Portuguese seamen appeared at Indian ports. They therefore sought only the privileges of merchants—the right to trade, to establish warehouses where goods could be stored, and to build compounds where they could live in their own way. The way was not always easy, for the Portuguese had to combat the intrigues of the Moslem traders whose business they were ruining, and to operate in a political climate where customs and practices were quite foreign to their own. Still, for almost a century they maintained their monopoly of the commerce of the all-water route, and made Lisbon the European gateway for oriental goods.

Portuguese activity was by no means confined to the Indian Ocean. In the course of the sixteenth century the Portuguese made contact with the spice islands, or East Indies, the Chinese mainland, and the island kingdom of Japan. Characteristically they did not attempt to establish more than trading posts from which merchants could operate to control commerce. When the Spanish fleet that rounded the Cape of Storms under Magellan (1520–1521) established rights for the Spanish king in the Philippines, the Portuguese tried to make them withdraw. Even though they could not close the oriental market to Spain, they were able to force the Spaniards to develop trans-Pacific trade routes. For a hundred years the trickle of goods that crossed the Pacific from the Philippines, the Isthmus of Panama, and the Atlantic was the only competition offered to the Portuguese possession of direct trade with the Orient. One further voyage at the turn of the sixteenth century should be mentioned: the landfall made by the Portuguese on the coast of Brazil. At the time the importance of the event was not recognized; and it was not until late in the sixteenth century that the dyewoods and other colonial products of Brazil made that territory important. Perhaps the Portuguese neglected Brazil for the same reason that they refrained from any serious attempt to conquer the Orient. The kingdom of Portugal was a mountainous land with a scanty population and insufficient wealth to exploit all the advantages of Portuguese exploration. Thus, they modestly contented themselves with the organization of a trading empire that gave Portugal a monopoly of eastern commerce; Lisbon became a rich city, and Portugal a great naval power.

The Portuguese maintained their monopoly by the strictest sort of regulations concerning the dissemination of information about the route to the East. They deliberately spread tall tales about the terrors of the southern sea, and ruthlessly attacked any non-Portuguese ships found in southern waters. However, they willingly left to others the carrying trade from Lisbon northward. Perhaps there was not enough manpower in Portugal to develop that trade as well as the Indian commerce, but, whatever the reasons, north Europeans—particularly the Dutch—became the middlemen who sold Portuguese imports to the rest of Europe. At the end of the sixteenth century the Dutch and English middlemen had acquired enough information and equipment to sail southward themselves and to establish direct contacts with the East, but that development only came after about a hundred years of Portuguese monopoly.

6. SPANISH EXPLORATION

At the same time that Portuguese explorers rounded the Cape of Good Hope and pushed on to India, the Spanish monarchy sent ships westward. Every schoolboy in the West today knows the story of Christopher Columbus. With the support of Ferdinand and Isabella of Spain he fitted out a fleet of three small vessels, and sailed westward to find India. It was a gigantic error in calculations. Had Columbus known how far India really was from Europe, he might never have had the courage to make the trip. But this does not detract from Columbus' feat of navigation, nor did the fact that

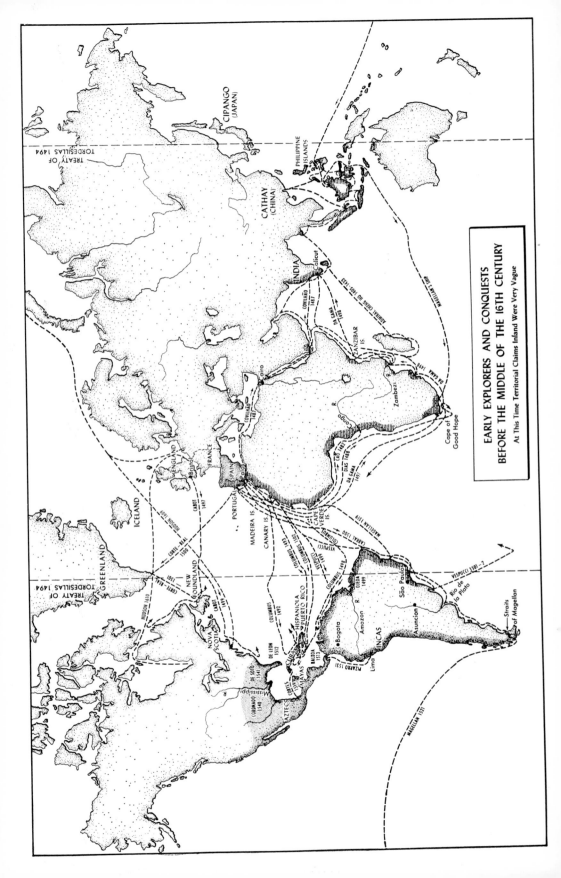

EARLY EXPLORERS AND CONQUESTS
BEFORE THE MIDDLE OF THE 16TH CENTURY

At This Time Territorial Claims Inland Were Very Vague

he ultimately found the land mass of the western hemisphere rather than Asia work to the detriment of his Spanish backers.

Fortunately for the Spaniards, Columbus blundered onto the island chain that protects the Gulf of Mexico and the Caribbean Sea, rather than making a landfall on the mainland itself. On the islands he found natives who had little military force, and harbors that were excellent bases for building up Spanish power. Those islands became, in effect, a "staging area"; men, materials, and horses could be accumulated there for the invasion of the mainland, where Aztec and Inca civilizations had already created powerful, if perhaps decadent, societies. Thus the Spanish conquest began at a weak point in the defenses of the New World, and built up the force necessary to carry the conquest to the mainland.

It was a motley crew of adventurers, soldiers, merchants, and missionaries who rallied under the flag of Spain for the conquest. They did not long ask by what right they appropriated the lands that they discovered nor by what authority they murdered and enslaved the people they found there. Those were to be questions that bothered the consciences of later men; the first waves of Europeans came to the New World avid for gold, power, and personal glory, untroubled by questions of conscience. The fact that the Spaniards did not encounter their old enemy, Islam, in the New World prevented their conquest from becoming a "crusade." The natives of the New World presented no serious obstacle since they lacked political and military organization comparable to that of the invader. The soldiers did not find them stubborn opponents, and the missionaries had little difficulty in bestowing on them a veneer of Christianity. The natives of the New World were quite unlike the men that the Portuguese encountered in India, and there were no Mohammedan missionaries to challenge the priests.

The American "Indians," as they were called, were at widely different stages of civilization. The ones that Columbus encountered first in the islands were really naked savages; on the other end of the scale, the Aztec and Inca societies of Mexico and Peru were highly complex and relatively sophisticated. But even those "high" civilizations were handicapped in face of the Spaniards. They did not understand metalworking, complex commercial relationships, or the military tactics that were needed against European troops. Furthermore, their political institutions seemed to indicate that the ruling classes had not integrated the masses into their government, for the Spaniards found it relatively easy to liquidate the rulers and place themselves in the vacated seats of power. Lastly, there were intertribal conflicts that made it easy for the Spaniards to find allies in attacking the more highly organized societies.

The Spanish government had neither the wealth nor the political machinery to supervise and direct so complex an operation as the discovery, conquest, and colonization of a continent many times the size of Spain. Thus, the conquest became a wonderful example of the effectiveness of individual initiative. The king granted hereditary privileges and governmental authority to private individuals; in return the latter assumed the expenses and risks involved in exploration and conquest. That system was not really different from the one used to organize military force by condottieri chieftains in sixteenth-century Europe, and so it is not surprising to find it extended to the New World. The territories and peoples brought under the Spanish crown by the conquistadors were consolidated under provincial governments and placed under the general administration of the Council of the Indies in Spain.

The actual conquest was facilitated because the Spaniards possessed military weapons superior to those of the natives. The cannon and arquebus were primitive firearms, perhaps not actually very useful in conflict, but to a people who knew nothing about gunpowder they were terrible weapons that suggested superhuman powers. Perhaps even more important in the early years of the conquest was the invaders' possession of horses. There were no such animals in the Americas before the Spaniards arrived, so their horses not only provided the usual advantages of cavalry mobility and shock force, but also added another quasi-superhuman attribute to the Spanish arsenal, for the superstitious natives did not understand that horse and rider were separate creatures. Nor did the superstitions that aided the invaders stop there. In Mexico, where Aztec military power might well have made the invaders pause, there was an ancient story about a white, red-bearded god who had once lived among the people and who would one day return. The superstitious Aztecs, seeing white men mounted on horses and commanding the destructive power of firearms, were sure that Cortes and his band were the fulfillment of that prophecy, and hesitated to take up arms against them. Did some Norse adventurer of an earlier century pave the way for Cortes' conquest of Mexico?

The Spaniards pushed forward both by land and by sea. On land, one group of explorer-conquerors invaded Mexico, another the Mississippi basin, another Florida, and still another group pressed over the Isthmus of Panama and then moved south toward Peru. At the same time the Spaniards made contact with the northern coast of South America by sea, moved down the east side of the continent, and, with Magellan in 1520, sailed around the Cape of Storms, across the broad Pacific to the Philippines, where Magellan was killed. His ships returned to Spain by way of the Cape of Good Hope (1522). Thus Spanish seamen not only proved that the world was round by sailing around it, but also established the foundation for the first empire upon which the sun never set.

The lands that fell under Spanish rule were fabulously rich. In Mexico gold and silver were discovered, and, once colonization was begun, fertile fields were found where great ranches could be established with herds of cattle. The climate on the islands encouraged a plantation economy, particularly the raising of sugar. On some of the islands the natives seem to have died rather than submit to slavery, but in their place the Spaniards soon introduced black slaves from Africa whose dispositions were more flexible than those of the Indians. Of all the lands they found, Peru was the richest; indeed, even to this day the French use the word "Peru" to mean fabulous wealth. The Inca civilization that they encountered there consisted of a highly developed social organization with skilled artisans and builders. The Incas had already discovered gold mines, and had even amassed considerable hoards of the precious metals; but since they lacked the military power to resist invasion, everything became forfeit to the Spanish conquerors.

To these lands of the Americas and to the islands of the Philippines the Spaniards brought their language, their religion, and their political and economic civilization. In the process of colonization Spanish culture underwent certain modifications as it adapted to the needs and superstitions of the conquered people. Nonetheless, there is no better example in history of the effectiveness with which a conqueror imposed his civilization upon another people. The Spanish empire lasted some three hundred years, a record in itself, but Spanish civilization transplanted to the New World is still a monument to the colonial efforts of Spain.

Spain could not long enjoy a monopoly over the New World. Before the sixteenth century began, the Portuguese laid claim to Brazil as their share of South America. Pope Alexander, acting as mediator, divided the New World between Spain and Portugal, and Brazil became a field for Portuguese exploration, colonization, and trade. Rio de Janeiro, one of the most beautiful natural harbors in the world, developed as a Portuguese town; its history was to be checkered by Dutch and English conquests. That sixteenth-century claim, however, was the determining factor in deciding, for example, that Portuguese rather than Spanish was to be the language of Brazil.

In the north, seamen subsidized by the British and French kings explored the American continent north of Virginia. Those men were lured on by the hope of finding a northwest passage to China and India. They were also on the lookout for gold. Spain's harvest in Mexico and Peru captured the imagination of all Europe, and actually blinded the early explorers to the real wealth that was available to brave and enterprising men. Not until the seventeenth century were English and French adventurers, colonists, and merchants ready to found colonies and tap the true wealth of North America. These sixteenth-century seamen founded fishing rights and established English and French claims to North America. The Cabots, Cartiers, and Hudsons with English or French flags at their ships' masts extended men's knowledge of the earth, while the Spaniards were lining their own and their kings' pockets with gold.

In the latter half of the sixteenth century English and Dutch seamen either in the role of privateers commissioned by their government, or as pirates operating on their own, invaded the Spanish colonial empire in search of booty. The lands that Spain claimed were so extended and the islands so numerous that it proved quite impossible to prevent these interlopers from establishing themselves in secluded harbors and bays from which they raided both the Spanish treasure fleet and the Spanish settlements. In the seventeenth century some of those lawless rovers elevated piracy to a profession, while others who still had a connection with their home government were responsible for founding the island and coastland settlements of England, the Netherlands, and France in the Caribbean basin.

Obviously the discoveries and the establishment of the Portuguese and Spanish empires were answers to the Ottoman conquests of the fifteenth century. Charles V helped to check the Turkish invasion both on the Danube and in the Mediterranean area with gold and silver from the New World. The Portuguese commercial empire in the Indian Ocean and eastern Asia also curbed Islam at about the time that Babar's conquest of India from central Asia crushed the Mohammedan power in that subcontinent. From the sixteenth century onward the Christian states seemed more "likely to succeed."

BOOK II

The Religious Rebellion

Book II deals primarily with the problems that accompanied the Reformation of the Latin Christian church. The Reformation put an end to the religious unity of the Latin West, and thereby accentuated the cultural and political differences that were already becoming important characteristics of the emerging civilization of Europe. Indeed, the religious disunity concomitant with the Reformation demonstrated the growing differences between the several Germanic, Latin, and Slavic societies that shared the land mass of western and central Europe.

The history of the Christian church underlines the idea that differences in religious forms are reflections of cultural variations. The primitive Christian church more or less divided itself along the cultural lines of the Roman Empire. The Roman Catholic (universal) church was obviously suited to the Gallo-Roman and Germanic culture of the West; the Greek Orthodox church reflected Byzantine culture; and in the Syrian-Egyptian segment of the Empire unorthodox rites and teachings were symbolic of the Orient's rejection of Greek and Roman culture. The latter easily fell victim to Islam; only small scattered enclaves still remained Christian. The schism between the Greek Orthodox and the Roman Catholic churches was deeply drawn. Even the awful threat of the Turk and the disappearance of the Byzantine Empire did not succeed in bringing the Greeks to accept the primacy of the Roman pope. Each regarded the other as inferior, and found it easy to believe that schism might only be a word to hide heresy.

The Orthodox community was further splintered since the Greeks encouraged the use of vernacular languages in church services. By the sixteenth century, the "national" Orthodox churches—such as the Russian, the Serbian, and the Armenian—had also developed interesting variations in ritual and teaching that reflected the cultural differences within the larger Orthodox community. Since the patriarch at Constantinople pretended to a moral rather than an administrative primacy over that church, those differences did not result in any attempt to enforce unity on the whole, and, furthermore, they were so small that it would have been difficult to define them for purposes of discipline. Had the patriarch at Constantinople had the power, however, some action might have been attempted.

The sixteenth-century Reformation of the Roman Catholic church produced more far-reaching differences than those that had developed within the Orthodox community. It would be interesting if we could find some simple racial or cultural factor to explain why some of the West accepted the Protestant (Lutheran) church, others the Reformed (Calvinist) church, while still others remained in the Roman Catholic fold. Unfortunately no such explanation exists. The most alluring formula—namely, that the lands where the Roman Empire left its greatest impression remained Catholic—falls down when we see how many Germans stayed with Rome and how many southern Frenchmen (the south was the most Latin part of France) joined the Reformed communion.

However, even if there is no simple formula, the fact still remains that the religious Reformation was an expression of the diversity of European societies. The most important problem of the history of the Reformation is to trace the development of the patterns characteristic of the emerging communities of Europe, and this will be the central theme of Book II. The sixteenth century is often referred to as the "confessional age," and there is justification for concentrating attention on the rise of confessional differences, but it was also an era when "confessional" flags covered political rebellion against traditional authorities, an era when "confessional" arguments were used to justify actions that were quite unconnected with the religious debates of the time. This aspect of the movement deserves as much attention as the theological controversy or the conflicts over church government.

The last chapter of Book II deals with the Thirty Years' War, 1618–1648. This conflict falls entirely within the seventeenth century, and to a considerable extent the problems connected with it lie outside the religious controversy. In other words, it could as well be considered in Book III as in this one. There is, however, one important reason for including it in the discussion of the Reformation. It was the last European conflict in which the religious question played any large part, and it ended with the peace treaties that may be said to mark the secularization of European politics (Treaty of Westphalia, 1648). After the Thirty Years' War European men might continue to regret that the western Christian community was not united, but they were no longer willing to risk war to achieve that unification. Secular goals rather than religious ones were henceforth the predominant guideposts for the emerging society of Europe.

BIBLIOGRAPHY FOR BOOK II

Historical scholarship on the Reformation era has produced a great many books, some slanted one way, some another, in the theological controversy. The following list is not complete, but it is a usable introduction.

Green, V. H. H., *Renaissance and Reformation,* London, Arnold, 1952.

Grimm, Harold, *Reformation Era,* New York, Macmillan, 1954.

Lucas, H. S., *The Renaissance and Reformation,* 2d ed., New York, Harper, 1960.

Smith, P., *The Age of the Reformation,* New York, Holt, 1920.

The following books were either first published in cheap editions or reissued in paperbacks.

Bainton, R. H., *Here I Stand: A Life of Martin Luther,* New York, Abingdon-Cokesbury, 1950.

Bainton, R. H., *The Reformation of the Sixteenth Century,* Boston, Beacon, 1952.

Mosse, G. L., *The Reformation,* New York, Holt, 1952.

Palm, Franklin, *Calvinism and the Religious Wars,* New York, Holt, 1932.

Salmon, Edward, *Imperial Spain: The Rise of the Empire and the Dawn of Modern Sea-Power,* New York, Holt, 1931.

Tawney, Richard, *Religion and the Rise of Capitalism,* New York, Harcourt, Brace, 1926.

The heroes of the Reformation era have many biographers. This list is at best partial.

Armstrong, E., *The Emperor Charles V,* 2d ed., London, Macmillan, 1910, 2 vols.

Bainton, R. H., *Here I Stand: A Life of Martin Luther,* Nashville, Tenn., Abingdon-Cokesbury, 1950.

Brandi, K., *The Emperor Charles V,* London, Cape, 1939.

Breen, Q., *John Calvin,* Grand Rapids, Mich., Erdmans, 1931.

Clayton, Joseph, *Luther and His Work,* Milwaukee, Bruce, 1937.

Grisar, H., *Martin Luther: His Life and Works,* St. Louis, Herder, 1930.

Harkness, G., *John Calvin: The Man and His Ethics,* New York, Holt, 1931.

Harvey, Robert, *Ignatius Loyola: A General in the Church Militant,* Milwaukee, Bruce, 1936.

Holborn, Hajo, *Ulrich von Hutten and the German Reformation*, London, Oxford University Press, 1937.

Jackson, S. M., *Ulrich Zwingli: The Reformer of German Switzerland*, New York, Putnam, 1900.

Neale, J. E., *Queen Elizabeth*, New York, Harcourt, Brace, 1934.

Pollard, A. F., *Henry VIII*, rev. ed., New York, Longmans, Green, 1951.

Schwiebert, E. G., *Luther and His Times*, St. Louis, Concordia, 1952.

Smith, P., *The Life and Letters of Martin Luther*, Boston, Houghton Mifflin, 1911.

Wedgwood, C. V., *William the Silent*, New Haven, Yale University Press, 1945.

There are several general histories of the sixteenth century and many specialized studies of that century's various problems.

Bindoff, S. T., *Tudor England*, Penguin Books, 1950.

Brown, George, *Italy and the Reformation to 1550*, Oxford, Blackwell, 1933.

Davis, Reginald, *The Golden Century of Spain, 1501–1621*, London, Macmillan, 1937.

Elton, G. R., *The Tudor Revolution in Government*, Cambridge, Cambridge University Press, 1953.

Janelle, P., *The Catholic Reformation*, Milwaukee, Bruce, 1949.

Johnson, A. H., *Europe in the Sixteenth Century, 1494–1598*, New York, Macmillan, 1925.

Kidd, Beresford, *The Counter-Reformation, 1550–1600*, London, Society for the Promotion of Christian Knowledge, 1937.

Merriman, R. B., *The Rise of the Spanish Empire in the Old World and the New*, New York, Macmillan, 1918–1934.

McElwee, William, *The Reign of Charles V, 1516–1558*, London, Macmillan, 1936.

Oman, C. W. C., *The Sixteenth Century*, New York, Dutton, 1936.

Parker, T. M., *The English Reformation to 1558*, New York, Oxford University Press, 1950.

Powicke, F. M., *The Reformation in England*, London, Oxford University Press, 1941.

Read, C., *The Tudors*, New York, Holt, 1936.

Taylor, Henry, *Thought and Expression in the Sixteenth Century*, New York, Macmillan, 1930, 2 vols.

Trend, John, *The Civilization of Spain*, New York, Oxford University Press, 1944.

The wars of the era also have a considerable bibliography; the following books are only an introduction:

Gardiner, S. R., *The Thirty Years' War*, New York, Scribner, 1874.

Geyl, P., *The Revolt of the Netherlands, 1555–1609*, London, Williams & Norgate, 1945.

Geyl, P., *The Netherlands Divided, 1609–1648,* London, Williams & Norgate, 1936.

Oman, C. W. C., *A History of the Art of War in the Sixteenth Century,* New York, Dutton, 1937.

Wedgwood, C. V., *The Thirty Years' War,* London, Cape, 1938.

John Hus, the Bohemian reformer who was influenced by Wyclif, was burned for heresy at the Council of Constance despite the safe conduct given him by the Emperor. Hus' teachings were similar to those of Luther. (The Bettmann Archive)

Chapter 5

THE LATIN CHRISTIAN CHURCH
IN THE LATER MIDDLE AGES

1. THE MEDIEVAL CHURCH

The medieval clergy was composed of a large body of men and women set apart from the rest of society by vows and ordinations that gave them status in the clerical hierarchy. The clergy occupied many different positions in the complex organization of the church: they were bishops, priests, deacons, nuns, friars, canons, curates, confessors, notaries, and students, to mention a few. Some of them actually administered the spiritual services of the church to laymen; others were cloistered in monasteries. Some were teachers, others administrators; some were impostors, others saints. At the top of the whole organization was the pope, the bishop of Rome. He appointed the members of the College of Cardinals, who in turn elected the next pope. Beneath the pope were the archbishops, bishops, abbots, abbesses, priests, and ultimately, at the bottom of the hierarchy, the humblest friar or the poorest hermit. The lines of command, authority, and obedience were complex and difficult to unravel.

The avowed mission of the church was two-fold: to worship God and to assist Christians to achieve salvation. Medieval man's world was a stage on which he worked out his destiny in the next world under the watchful eyes of angels and devils who supported or tempted him. The church played a critical role in this drama, for it stood by the Christian with aids—the seven sacraments—that supported him in his struggle with the forces of evil. At birth he received *baptism,* which washed away original sin and made him a child of God. When he came to the age of reason, he received *confirmation* from the bishop, which made him a soldier of God. About the same time he was also admitted to the confessional, where absolution and *penance,* administered by the priest, relieved him of sin. He was then in a state of grace so that he could receive the *eucharist* (holy communion), the sacred bread and wine that the priest's blessing at the mass had changed into the body and blood of Christ. If his vocation was to be that of priest, he received *holy orders*. If he married, he received the sacrament of *holy matrimony;* and before he died he was anointed with the sacred oils of *extreme unction* to assist his passage into heaven.

These seven sacraments were administered by the clergy. Without them salvation was considered to be virtually impossible. Many of the clergy, however, had no particular contact with the laity. As monks, nuns, hermits, and wandering friars, those men and women did good works and prayed for the salvation of men. The saints and holy men piled up more good works than they themselves needed, and those constituted a sort of "bank" that could be used for the remission of temporal punishment of others. Thus the holy men and women justified their existence. That treasury of good works in heaven was accessible to the popes for uses that they might wish to make of it. In the sixteenth century when men protested against the granting of indulgences for a fee, it became the center of a theological conflict.

The practices of the medieval Latin Christian church were complex and varied, reflecting the conditions of the conversion of western Europe. The early missionaries had "baptized" many pagan customs and incorporated others in the religious folkways of the people. These were largely administered or regulated by the clergy. The cult of the Virgin contributed to the erection of the magnificent cathedrals in France. There were many local saints, or otherwise specialized saints, who had special missions to perform, such as to assist in finding lost objects or to act as patrons for special groups like cobblers, hat makers, or butchers. Those were medieval developments perhaps especially suited to the mentality of the Latin West. Besides the cults of the saints, there were cults of holy places: pilgrimage cities like Canterbury or Le Puy, local shrines like Mont St. Michel, and of course, the capital city of the western Christian world, Rome. The theologians and other learned men made careful distinction between the purist teachings of the church and the popular practices that attracted the attention of the laity. However, such distinctions had little or no meaning for the ignorant people who loved the richness of the many traditions and customs associated with relics, saints, pilgrimages, and holy shrines. Since the church did not actually discourage the laity's use of those pious or near-miraculous agencies in the quest for salvation, it, in a measure, accepted them as part of the religious structure of western Christendom.

Inevitably an organization as large and complex as the church required considerable money to maintain itself. In the earlier Middle Ages the church, like the baron, the prince, or the king, was expected to support itself from its own lands, but by the thirteenth century, when feudal relationships were beginning to change, the church, like the political powers, found that new

values made the income from land inadequate. At the same time, the gradual development of a money economy allowed the collection of coined money
from various sources other than land, and thereby provided new potential
sources of revenue. Thus, the economic problems of the clergy multiplied:
they had to administer property and collect fees, dues, taxes, fines, and volun-
tary offerings. Of course, they had to account for that income and administer
its disbursement. If the correspondence of fourteenth- and fifteenth-century
churchmen is an indication of their activity, economic problems occupied
many of their waking hours. The church, as the largest institution of the
time, was also, very naturally, the biggest business.

As it became easier to get money, the tastes of the churchmen who had it
were perceptibly changed and their appetites increased. Some of them developed worldly ways and worldly outlooks often unbecoming to their office.
From the fourteenth century onward literary references to the clergy became
increasingly uncomplimentary to them as servants of the Christ who said,
"Sell all ye have and follow me." Chaucer and Boccaccio, to mention the
two most famous writers, leave no doubt about the worldliness of the clergymen they describe. The same phenomenon occurred in other areas of four-
teenth- and fifteenth-century life. Princes, too, found money easier to get as
trade and manufacturing expanded the money economy, and inevitably the
flow of money broadened both their conception of their political role in society and their tastes for a higher standard of living. However, the princes,
unlike the clergymen, were not committed to a religious ideal that made
virtues of poverty, humility, and weakness, while it frowned upon pride,
luxury, and the pleasures of the flesh. Thus, the secular authorities could
taste the new pleasures available to men without the same reproach that fell
upon their brothers who were ordained in the church. Of course, not all the
clergy were seduced by the world, but the stories that men told about those
that were acted to bring discredit upon the whole body of the clergy.

The flow of wealth into church coffers also proved a point of conflict with
princes. The clergy naturally wished to retain the sources of their wealth;
the papacy could see no reason why people should object to its collecting
money anywhere in Christendom. On the other hand, princes, like the king
of France for example, felt that the clergy should lend them financial assistance, and resented the flow of money from their lands to the coffers of the
pope in Rome. In earlier centuries, the conflicts between church and state
had been over the right to control and select bishops; by the fourteenth century questions of taxation had become even more important. Philip the Fair
and Boniface VIII wrangled over finances at the opening of the fourteenth
century, and their conflict was repeated, with variations, for the next two
centuries.

This, however, was not the sole problem that emerged from preoccupation
with money. The spiritual mission of the church suffered when some greedy

priests cynically used their religious offices or the religious presuppositions of the people to extort money. The indulgence problem is an excellent illustration of that tendency. Indulgences were first granted to men who kept their vows to go on a crusade to save the Holy Land from Islam; later they were granted to those who commuted their vows into fees to support a crusader, and, finally, just to provide cash for the church. In an era when the church's need for money had become so great that all sorts of favors and offices became objects for traffic, it was not difficult to find a way to make indulgences pay handsomely. Some churchmen nicely adjusted the doctrine of the church and their actions with clever arguments and sharp logical formulae that went far above the heads of ignorant and superstitious laymen who wished to save themselves or their loved ones from hell or purgatory. The clergy well knew that Christian doctrine would never allow them to "sell" the remission of sins. The fee paid could in no way assure any such result. They also knew that the humble people did not and perhaps could not read the "small print" on the indulgences that they bought. Revenge came when the people of Europe listened to "heretics" who came forward to purify the church and return it to its primitive ways.

2. THE BABYLONIAN CAPTIVITY

An unexpected development in the fourteenth century added to the difficulties faced by the church. When Clement V became pope in 1305, he had every intention of going to Rome eventually. So had his successors, but good Frenchmen that they were, they found it more convenient to stay in southern France where life was easy and good, and in 1348 they even secured the city of Avignon as a papal territory. Before long, Avignon became the most brilliant court in Europe, with a magnificent castle-fortification decked out with "modern" conveniences and sumptuously decorated by the foremost artists of Europe. Compared with the beautiful palace on the hill overlooking the Rhone river and the walled fortification of the city of Avignon, Rome looked sorry indeed. Rome was a turbulent city, shot through with conflicts among the noblemen and filled with a populace with violent traditions. Furthermore, during the years of the papal residence in France, the churches and palaces in Rome had fallen into a bad state of disrepair. French popes, elected by French cardinals, preferred to send French administrators to look out for their interests in Rome and the papal states rather than to go there themselves. When the Italians tried to rebel against the French "barbarians" who came to Rome to administer church affairs, the popes sent mercenary soldiers to suppress the revolts.

The Avignon period must have held considerable personal satisfaction for the popes but the church suffered from it. This period has been called the "Babylonian Captivity." We might dismiss Petrarch's scathing criticism of the manners and morals of the Avignon court and of the effects of the residence in France on the church as the complaints of another disgruntled Italian, if it were not that his was only the most literary of the chorus of voices that condemned this residence in France. The critics of the Avignonese papacy did not take into account the fact that in this period it was easier to get money, and that rulers everywhere were living more sumptuously: they merely noted that the head of the church and his court were losing the austere and holy way of life that had been associated with the Holy See. Pious men and women, as well as political leaders, literary men, and philosophers, all urged the pope to return to Rome.

Furthermore, the question was not solely one of the manners and morals of the papacy; a political issue was joined to the moral one. As long as the pope remained at Avignon, the rest of Europe felt, with some justification, that the head of the church was under the control of the French king. That feeling became more pronounced when the pope appointed French clergymen to important ecclesiastical positions in England, Italy, and Germany. The English were at war with France, so they particularly resented those foreigners who, they believed, were nothing less than spies. Thus, political tension, added to the fact that the papal court at Avignon had acquired a name for luxury unbecoming the vicar of Christ, created a situation that reached the proportions of a scandal.

3. THE SCHISM AND THE COUNCILS

The real scandal, however, was yet to come. In 1367 Pope Urban V journeyed to Rome, but did not stay there. His death shortly after his return to Avignon (1370) seemed, to superstitious Italians, to be God's punishment for leaving the city. Six years later, Gregory XI went to Rome. The chorus of protest, plus the fact that southern France was infested with bands of unemployed mercenary free companies, had made it advisable to return to the "Eternal City." Pope Gregory died in 1378, the date that nominally marks the end of the "Babylonian Captivity." When the Cardinal College met to elect a successor, the Roman mob demanded the election of an Italian. Urban VI, a Neapolitan, became Pope, and immediately indicated his intention to remain in Rome and reform the church of its evil practices.

The French cardinals, offended by the new pope, withdrew from Rome and, after declaring Urban's election illegal because it was made under threat of force, elected another French pope who took the name of Clement VII. After an ineffectual military venture that brought no credit to the soldiers of either claimant, the Frenchmen returned to Avignon. Western Christendom was now treated to the unedifying spectacle of two popes hurling anathemas and epithets at each other in the best fourteenth-century vulgar language. At the same time, both sought the support of secular princes. The wheel had come a full turn since the thirteenth century when secular princes had been forced to go to Rome to seek the support of the pope. Now there were two popes, and the secular princes could negotiate for the conditions of their recognition of one or the other. This disgraceful situation in the church was not corrected for a full generation.

Disorder grew apace. One part of Europe supported one pope; the rest of Europe, the other. The princes of France, Aragon, Castile, Navarre, Sardinia, Sicily, Scotland, and some parts of Germany supported the Avignonese pope, while those in England, the Netherlands, most of Germany, and Italy supported the Roman one. By dividing Europe between them, they created serious financial problems. Both courts were very expensive. Europe had objected to the money collected by one pope; now two competed for cash as well as for loyalty. Everything was for sale—indulgences, bishoprics, and special grants to princes, to cities, and to individuals. To the disorderly spectacle of two popes excommunicating each other and calling on Europe for a crusade against each other, were added the scandals that accompanied the introduction of marketplace techniques and morals into the spiritual and administrative life of the church. This was the period when princes subjected the church to their rule, while the heresies that had begun to plague the church early in the fourteenth century waxed vigorous in the face of the church's divided authority and reduced prestige.

Intelligent men realized that something had to be done. Even the rival popes understood that the schism could not go on indefinitely, but no one, after his election to the triple crown of St. Peter, was willing to give it up. The solution came with the revival of the old idea that a church council was the highest authority in the church. In the records of the early Christian church, the councils were obviously of the utmost importance both in matters regarding the purification of doctrine and the delineation of procedures. When the fourteenth-century crisis arose, learned men recalled that earlier practice. Furthermore, the fourteenth century was an age of parliaments, diets, estates, and convocations, for, as we have seen, with the rise of the towns and the money-economy, men had learned to settle their affairs by consultation. It was not, therefore, unnatural that men hit upon the idea of calling a council. Political theorists argued that a council would be able to depose both popes and elect a new one.

The French assumed the leadership. Guided by scholars from the University of Paris and backed by the king, a council of the French clergy withdrew their support from the Avignonese pope. This action threatened to establish the independence of the Gallican (French) church. A similar movement occurred in Bohemia and in Hungary. Unless the church were to become splintered into tiny fragments, a general council would have to be called to create order. In 1409 a majority of the cardinals from both the Roman and the Avignonese lines deserted their masters, and met with a General Council at Pisa, where they summoned the rival popes to appear before them. Failing to comply, both popes were deposed, and a third one, Alexander V, was elected. The Council broke up, but neither the Avignonese nor the Roman pope would resign, and there were then three popes in western Christendom. The Council had, in fact, aggravated rather than solved the scandal.

Therefore, Sigismund, the Holy Roman Emperor, intervened and called for a council outside Italy. He prepared the diplomatic groundwork so carefully that practically all western Europe was represented both by political as well as spiritual delegates. The Council met at Constance in 1414. It was said that a hundred thousand people swamped the little town and the surrounding countryside. Undoubtedly this was an exaggeration, but the conference was certainly well attended. When confronted with the will of the Council, John XXIII, the new pope of the "Pisan line," was forced to give up his claim to the papal crown. Gregory XII, the Roman pope, waived his claims in return for the position of cardinal-bishop. Only Benedict XIII, the Avignonese pope, refused to accept the majority will of Europe. A refugee in Spain and deserted by all but two of his cardinals, he obstinately declined to abdicate. He could not, however, stop the Council's action.

In the early fifteenth century communications, as well as the actions of deliberative assemblies, moved slowly. Negotiations between the Council, the claimants, and the princes who protected them took time. Not until the Council of Constance was in its third year were the members able to depose Benedict XIII and elect a new pope. The Council acted carefully, for then the leaders of Christendom really wanted to end the schism in the church. In April, 1417, Benedict was deposed as a heretic, schismatic, and disturber of the peace. Shortly thereafter the cardinals met and elected a Roman cardinal as pope; he took the name of Martin V and received the respects and congratulations of the crowds that passed before him at the High Altar for hours. The schism had ended.

4. HERESY AND HERETICS

The Council also attacked the problem of heresy; it was the Council of Constance that burned John Hus, the Bohemian teacher to whom Sigismund had given a safe conduct. Too often the Middle Ages are regarded as a period when everyone believed alike, a period when the doctrine of the church closed the door on arguments and differences. This, of course, is untrue; the doctrines of the church in many areas were very loosely defined, leaving considerable leeway for differences of opinion. Even where they were clearly defined, the sharp distinctions that later came to characterize western Christendom were not present. Heresy, therefore, was somewhat hard to define; indeed, the line between a heretic and a saint was often hazy. Furthermore, the church was slow to condemn men for heresy so long as the doctrinal disputes involved only the few people who could read, reason, and argue. Only when the masses seemed about to be affected by some idea that was obviously dangerous to the church, or when some teacher produced ideas that pretended to dispense with the services of the church, did the hue and cry against heretics become loud-tongued. This attitude is undoubted evidence of the wisdom of the medieval churchmen who wished above all to avoid hasty action as long as the church as an institution was not under attack.

The thirteenth and fourteenth centuries produced several doctrines that verged on heresy. The idea most dangerous to the church was that the services of the priests were quite unnecessary for a man's salvation. The fact that such an idea developed may well have been a reflection on the "unspiritual" lives of many of the clergy. Naturally, clergymen regarded any teaching that tended to dispense with their services as heretical. Some of the heretics were mystics who tried to identify themselves with the Godhead, to subordinate their every impulse to the will of God. They thus bypassed the clergy as intermediaries between God and man, and made the church's sacraments unnecessary. It was difficult to deal with the mystics; they were obviously deeply religious, perhaps even holy men, and many times it was not easy to draw a line that would separate a saint from a heretic. Others were hardheaded souls who had reached heretical conclusions from studying the Bible, where few of the practices characteristic of the medieval church were to be found. By rejecting tradition and the teachings of the fathers who had known Greek philosophy, some denied the efficacy of the sacraments as well as much of the symbolism and ceremony of the church. Still others combined those and other ideas to reach a notion of the "priesthood of all believers," a notion distinctly inimical to the organized institution of the church. Lastly, the fourteenth century saw the translation of the Bible into several vernacular languages. Historians have long noted that the Bible has been "the book of heretics." Unless it is rigidly controlled, the Bible opens many vistas and interpretations of religious experience, and if each person is allowed to give it any interpretation that seems proper, it is probably inevitable that a babble of doctrine will emerge. When people could read the Bible in their own language, the church fathers found it difficult to control their thinking.

Who were these heretics? Most were clergymen themselves. Abbot Joachim of Flora, a twelfth-century man, wrote mystical interpretations of the Bible that now seem unbelievably naive, yet were not too naive for his time. Anonymous writers added to his collection, and in the late thirteenth and early fourteenth centuries *The Everlasting Gospel,* a fantastic mixture of prophecy, religious ecstacy, and curious lore, was a popular book throughout much of Christendom although it was condemned as heretical several times. Mysticism of that sort had been as old as Christianity itself, and very difficult to control, for it was hard to draw sharp lines that would define the heresy.

During the schism, however, another sort of doctrine arose in England—a doctrine dangerous to the church and clear-cut enough to allow a sharp definition of the heresy. The doctrine began with the teachings of the famous Oxford professor John Wiclif; it extended itself into Bohemia through the teachings of Jerome of Prague and John Hus. The heretics—Lollards in England and Hussites in Bohemia—threatened the foundations of the church by questioning both its political and its spiritual mission.

The heresy started with John Wiclif, "the flower of Oxford scholarship," whose career as diplomat, university professor, and religious thinker was deeply influenced by the scandal of the schism in the church. As diplomat, he defended his king's interests at the papal court; as teacher, he attacked the exercise of temporal power by the church; and as religious thinker, he "discovered" that the primitive Christian church was much simpler than the church of his own day. His heresy came directly from his Biblical studies. He knew the Vulgate almost by heart; indeed, his writings were actually little more than biblical quotations held together by a running commentary. In the Bible he failed to find that Christ and the apostles knew many of the religious practices common in his own day. He therefore rejected the sacraments, pilgrimages, holy water, intercession of saints and the Virgin, the use of images, and many other current ceremonies and symbolisms on the grounds that "Jesus Christ and His apostles used them not." He also attacked the endowments of the church as harmful and dangerous to the spiritual needs of the church. If Wiclif's ideas had been allowed to influence the teaching of the church, the whole superstructure of medieval Christian practice would have been destroyed. He was the true forerunner of the sixteenth-century reformers who dismissed the sacramental system, the symbolism, the holy places, and the saints as practices foreign to true Christianity.

Wiclif's teachings spread rapidly in England. An English Bible, probably translated in part by Wiclif himself, appeared to strengthen his insistence that primitive Christian practices differed from those current in the fourteenth century. The conservative forces in the church in England were slow to move against this religious upsurge, perhaps because the papacy's prestige was at its lowest point during the third quarter of the fourteenth century. Avignon, it will be recalled, was regarded as a branch of the French government. Moreover, Wiclif himself seems to have had considerable prestige both at court and amongst neighboring townsmen and the scholars at Oxford University. In any case, he was called before church convocations only twice, and although the archbishop condemned his sermons as heresy, he was allowed to live out his life and die peacefully in 1384.

His followers, however, enjoyed no such good fortune as soon as there was a pope in Rome who could command the loyalty of the English crown and high clergy. Even though Lollardy seems to have had a considerable following at Oxford University, as well as among the gentry and the wealthy townsfolk and among the "little people" who were of small account in the councils of the world, it was quickly destroyed or driven underground. The statute of 1401 provided for the burning of the heretics so "that such punishment may strike fear into the minds of others." Thus, royal pressure was applied to exterminate the heresy. Lollardy smoldered underground in England for a century until the Reformation again released its force. Probably no small part of the enthusiasm that greeted the reform of the English church under Henry VIII can be traced to Lollard ideas still honored among the English people. It would be a mistake to believe that the king and Parliament could have so easily accomplished the sixteenth-century reformation in England if the people had not already been prepared for it in some way.

The accident of royal marriage and the medieval custom of scholars traveling from country to country introduced Lollardy to Bohemia about the turn of the century, and by 1415 it had become a vigorous movement among the Czech population. Its leader, John Hus, was summoned before the Council of Constance to explain himself and his ideas. Obviously Hus was a dangerous heretic. His teachings would make the church unnecessary, or at least would greatly scale down its power and activity. But he was more than that: he was also an obstinate and provocative debater; he would not budge an inch from his position, and he tried to make fools of those who disagreed with him. Controversial arguments during the fifteenth century were interlarded with abusive, sometimes vulgar, language, and Hus was a master of the jargon of the day. When he was summoned to Constance, there seems to have been every intention of honoring the "safe conduct" that the Emperor Sigismund had granted him. Even after his views obviously appeared at odds with the teachings of the church, his judges tried to find a compromise, a face-saving formula that would allow him to cover his heresy. Hus, however, adopted a stiff-necked, stubborn attitude. He not only refused any formula, he also abusively pressed home his contention that it was the church, rather than the Lollards and Hussites, which had departed into heretical ways. There seemed no alternative to burning him, and thus, in spite of the "safe conduct," Hus was burned as a heretic at Constance. The subsequent criticism of the Emperor Sigismund's failure to live up to his word may account for the fact that Charles V respected his grant of "safe conduct" to Luther a century later.

Burning Hus did not put an end to the heresy. Bohemia was not England, and Sigismund's authority there in no way resembled that of the king of England. An armed revolt broke out under aggressive leadership that was to make the very name "Hussite" a dreaded word in Bavaria, Saxony, Oberpfältz, and Austria. The Hussites developed military power that gave them an advantage over their neighbors, and their practices of pillage and destruction made the Hussite wars terrible scourges for much of central Europe. A hundred years later in Germany the word "Hussite" practically meant pestilence.

As the Hussite revolt continued, religious radicals of several varieties appeared. The people were given the Bible, and the Bible became an inspiration for several new heresies. A generation after the death of Hus, Rome came to a compromise solution with the more conservative groups in Bohemia, but the compromise did not stamp out the heretical ideas. Bohemia actually was the home of Protestantism of one sort or another for over a hundred years before Luther's break with Rome.

There were several things that England and Bohemia had in common in the early fifteenth century. Both were states with relatively strong parliaments and a long parliamentary history. The Bohemian Diet actually elected each new king. Both were lands in which the popular vernacular language was emerging victorious over a court or official tongue. English was victorious over French and Czech over German, when these vernacular languages emerged as a vigorous, colorful means of communication, and, in each case, the use of the vernacular language was, in a sense, an expression of the nationalism that was just beginning to be felt among the peoples of Europe. In both kingdoms the Roman church was in part associated with a hostile foreign power: the Avignonese papacy was as much an anathema to many Englishmen as the German rule was to many Czechs. For the Czechs an additional reason to dislike the Roman church was the fact that they had been Christianized by Greek monks, and still retained certain features of the Orthodox church in their ritual. Lastly, in both England and Bohemia there was an intelligent, vigorous, and literate middle class that readily listened to Hus and Wiclif when they taught that religious institutions should be simplified in the name of spiritual values and economy.

Were there reasons other than the problems created by the schism that made the fourteenth and fifteenth centuries favorable to heretics? This is a difficult question to answer. Many people have pointed out that in the twelfth and thirteenth centuries a large proportion of the wealth of society was put into cathedrals dedicated to the Virgin or to one or another of the saints. Was this a deliberate investment in salvation? Was it an attempt to influence the ways of God with men by stone, mortar, and stained glass? Perhaps fourteenth- and fifteenth-century men were questioning the efficacy of the materialism inherent in the building of those great churches. The wicked stories they told about their clergymen, many of them undoubtedly gross exaggerations, seem to indicate their anger at the clergy for forcing them to give so much to the church. It may well be that in the troubled times of the fourteenth century it appeared only too obvious that the materialism of the earlier era had not produced tangible results. Such speculation might lead to the conclusion that the heresies were in part caused by a crisis in morale that made men question former values. The austerity of sixteenth-century reformed churches suggests that this crisis actually did affect men's religious views.

5. THE RENAISSANCE PAPACY

The problems of the papacy did not come to an end with the healing of the schism. The conciliar movement had erected a new, or rather, had resurrected an old doctrine that made the pope subordinate to a general council. Pope Martin V and his successors throughout the fifteenth century were primarily concerned with combating this notion, and with re-establishing the monarchical constitution of the church. The age favored them, for, in contrast to the preceding one, it was an age of princes rather than of parliaments. Nonetheless, it was no easy thing to ward off the constant threat of a church council. Eugenius IV, who succeeded Martin V in 1431, did work with councils at Basel (1431–1449) and Ferrara-Florence (1438–1445) to deal with the Hussite wars and the question of aid for the Greeks against the Turks. However, he precluded the councils from considering any program of reform for the church as a whole. As we shall see, his successors, at considerable cost to the church, prevented the meeting of another general church council until the revolts of the sixteenth century led to the Council of Trent.

In practical terms, the political activity of the papacy seemed to be becoming more important than its spiritual mission: its ancient monarchical constitution could not be reaffirmed unless the pope could stave off attempts from all sides to give the general council of the church power to direct his activities. Thus, the popes needed men around them who were skilled in politics and diplomacy, and, as the century wore on, men skilled in war too. The latter became more and more necessary because there developed in Italy a balance-of-power system between Venice, Milan, Florence, Naples, and the Papal States. With worldly interests coming to the fore, it became necessary to appoint to the College of Cardinals men who had talents suitable to serve the needs of the papacy. Unfortunately, such attributes were not usually to be found in pious men, and so the College of Cardinals lost much of its religious character. The result was that it tended to elect to the papacy men who were representative of the worldly interests of the group, and some of those elected were quite unworthy of the spiritual offices they held. It is only necessary to read the works of the great Catholic historian, Ludwig Pastor, to see that pious Catholics of the contemporary era regard several of the pre-Reformation pontiffs as a source of shame and humiliation.

To maintain themselves politically in both Europe and Italy, the popes had to play the role of Italian princes and take part in Italian politics. They might have been able to defend themselves from the pressures of Italian political forces by calling in the northern kings to defend them, but that was just the thing that they had to avoid if they wished to re-establish the position of the papacy in Europe. If the popes called in the northern kings, they ran the risk of ending up as chaplains to those powerful princes or of being forced to recognize the supremacy of the Council and accept reform at its hands. The papacy's prestige depended upon each individual pope's ability to re-establish the monarchical structure of his office and to maintain his independence in Europe. Unfortunately, the cost of those operations was the momentary transformation of the papacy into an Italian principality.

The stories of the immorality and the crimes of several of the Renaissance popes and the worldly lives of most of them have furnished Protestant propagandists with fuel for four hundred years, and therefore need not be repeated. What is often overlooked in such diatribes is the fact that those men were quite characteristic of their age. They were reasonably typical manifestations of the culture of powerful men in Latin Christendom during the later fifteenth century, rather than unique and horrible examples of personal wickedness and wrongdoing. The Renaissance popes were surely no worse than the rulers in other states, and they may actually have lived more worthy lives than most of the great lords of their century. Although this may not say much in their favor, in justice it should be said.

One further fact may be mentioned to explain the Renaissance popes. The Rome that they inherited after the schism was in a terrible state of disrepair resulting from a century of neglect. At the same time, the expanding money-economy of the western world presented the opportunity to obtain the funds necessary to restore the churches and palaces of the city. However, to get that money many devious methods had to be employed. The Protestant propagandists who accuse the fifteenth-century popes of luxurious living, and indeed of a host of sins connected with materialism, rarely explain that the popes had inherited an immense job of repair and redecoration, and that the money to carry the work to a successful conclusion was available—for a price. The rebuilding and redecoration of Rome also suited their need for prestige and independence. It is small wonder then that, worldly men as they were, the popes were willing to sell offices, favors, indulgences, or anything at all to get the money for the reconstruction of their capital.

The reconstruction of Rome came at the precise time that the Renaissance schools of Italian art were reaching their greatest period (cf. Book I, Chapter 3). From all over Italy the best painters, architects, and sculptors were attracted to Rome. The results of their labors are today the artistic heritage of the whole western world, but the tourist in Rome should never forget that these beautiful walls, statues, and columns were frightfully expensive. It may even be true that they could never have been created if the Renaissance popes had not been willing to find money through channels that were, to say the least, questionable.

Thus, political needs forced those fifteenth-century popes to become diplomats and soldiers. Rebuilding the city tempted them with the beauty and the glamor made possible by the new art style. To supply money for their enterprises, they had to exploit all the abuses of the past and introduce new ones. Small wonder that they did not reform the church as well.

6. DEMANDS FOR REFORM

Even though the papacy was unable or unwilling to reform the church, other men continued to urge some action. The end of the schism did not remove the old abuses since the papal needs for money grew faster than the new sources of revenue, but when the popes did not remove those abuses, the reformers demanded that something should be done. The reformers, however, were largely isolated men and women who could not take effective action. They tried at the Councils of Basel and of Florence-Ferrara to introduce projects to reform the church "in its head and members," but were unable to do anything in the face of papal opposition. Thus, the reformers were left to their tears and their prayers or, at most, to local action within their own communities. They could scold the church for its abuses, they could beg the popes to make reforms, but as long as the papacy was not under their control, the reformers could do very little.

Reform, however, was obviously long overdue. Illustrative of the temper of the era was the career of Girolamo Savonarola, a monk in the Dominican convent of San Marco in Florence. He was a preacher, a thunderer against the worldly ways of both laymen and clerics. His eloquence brought him to the pulpit of the cathedral in Florence; his forcefulness made him into a quasi-dictator of the city. As a preacher he was partly responsible for a political upheaval in the city that, for a few years at least, placed Florence under a government dedicated to God and reform. His prophetic vision that an avenger would purify the church had seemed vindicated when Charles VIII appeared in Italy with his French soldiers. For four years Savonarola's hold on the city of Florence was almost complete.

Nevertheless, the "Kingdom of Christ" that Savonarola proclaimed in Florence proved to be popular with neither the wealthy nor the powers that ruled the church. Denouncing luxury and sin in general was all very well, but Savonarola tried to make worldly people into saints, and only a few of them were emotionally suited for the role. His religious program failed to take into account the needs of the vigorous economic society that had developed in Florence. His demands for the reform of the church as a whole were also unwelcome. Pope Alexander VI (whose personal life left a good deal to be desired) was not amused at the monk's exhortations. Pious people may have placed their follies on the bonfire as Savonarola exhorted them to do (the great painter, Botticelli, burned many of his canvases), but in the end Florence burned him as a heretic (1498). The dramatic trial and execution of that eloquent monk only slowed down the process of reform, however; the fire that stilled his voice could not entirely quiet the voices of men who wished to purify the church by correcting abuses.

While Savonarola tried to reform the church by eloquence and even by force, other men were working along more traditional lines. One group attempted to organize better instruction for parish priests, most of whom were woefully ignorant and quite unable to present the spiritual message of Christianity. Others organized meetings of pious Christians to pray and meditate; still others attempted to extend the traditional good works of the monastic orders, the care of the sick, the poor, and the downtrodden. The great Cluny reformation in the church had come about four or five centuries earlier by this sort of regeneration of religious activity. The church had long thought that the problem was to bring the Christian message to the elite of society or to create a Christian elite; once this had been done, the message would trickle down to the masses of men.

In line with this notion was the attempt of the Christian humanists to use their skill and knowledge to purify the church and its doctrines. Men like Pico and Ficino in Italy, who attempted to reconcile the spiritual teachings of Plato with the teachings of Christianity, were really trying to strengthen the theological doctrines of their church. Others like Erasmus, Colet, and Lefèvre, who edited the New Testament and urged the purification of religious practices through humanistic reason and the application of biblical studies, were also seeking reform. None of these men had any notion of breaking up the unity of Christian Europe; they merely wished to reform the abuses and purify the doctrines of their church. It might be pointed out that most of those Christian humanists did not support either Luther or Calvin in the sixteenth century, even though their demands for reform undoubtedly helped to prepare the ground for the rebellion against Rome.

Perhaps the great problem confronting all the reformers arose because the European world of the later fifteenth century was quite different from that of the Cluniac era several centuries before. The abuses of the church grew out of administrative and fiscal problems that cut across the political structure of Europe. The most important single movement revolved around the fact that the princes of Europe were then strengthening their power over their lands. In short, the sovereign states were clamoring for recognition of their interests, and one of the most persistent demands of the princes was for the right to share the wealth of the church within their country and to control appointments to high and lucrative clerical offices. Only in such a way could princes use the church most effectively as an instrument of power. This fact in turn affected the papacy, the organization of the church, and the moral climate of the era. The mild voices of reformers like Erasmus were soon drowned by the more strident tones of men like Luther who were willing to give the control of the government of the church into the hands of the princes in return for the right to reorganize its practices.

Albrecht Dürer, "The Four Horsemen of the Apocalypse." This magnificent print was one of many such illustrations depicting the evils threatening man. Devils, the death dance, and other devices were used to instill a fear of hell, perhaps to deter men from acts that might send them there. (Minneapolis Institute of Arts)

Chapter 6

THE LUTHERAN REFORMATION
OF THE SIXTEENTH CENTURY

1. RELIGIOUS PATTERNS AT THE OPENING OF THE SIXTEENTH CENTURY

The opening years of the sixteenth century have been described as a period of pagan Renaissance, an era in which worldly interests were more important than spiritual ones; this seems to be a sharp contrast with the Middle Ages. Those years are sometimes pictured as a time when secular rulers, merchant princes, condottieri captains, humanistic scholars, and "half-pagan" artists dominated the cultural life of western man. It is true that such people did loom large in the cultural elite of Europe, and that worldly interests claimed the attention of some men, but it does not follow that pagan ideals had captured the imagination of all the people of Europe. The intellectual life of any era is composed of many facets. In the Italy that saw renewed interest in Platonic philosophy, there also flourished among the educated and the illiterate a profound belief in the teachings of the church, as well as in superstitions with roots much deeper than those of Christianity, and it would be a serious error not to understand that throughout Europe the Christian idea, though perhaps inadequately understood, made up a prominent part of the intellectual furniture of all classes.

The invention of printing during the fifteenth century was just beginning to alter the texture of European intellectual life by making possible a civilization bound together by books and reading. If we examine what the printers were actually doing, it becomes clear that they reflected the predominantly Christian ideal of the epoch. It was not Graeco-Roman literature or philosophy that bulked largest in the new printers' shops established from Germany to Italy; it was rather the Christian Bible, books of prayer and devotion, and works on Christian theology. Men bought books written in the humanist

139

tradition, but they seem to have been even more interested in the problems involved in their life after death. As a distinguished American scholar has written, the best seller of the day was not "How to See Rome," but rather, "How to Avoid Hell."

Interest in the problem of salvation seems also to have captured the imagination of the print-makers who were just beginning to supply Europeans with reasonably cheap pictures for popular consumption. "The Four Horsemen," "The Last Judgment," "The Dance of Death," "Devils Waiting at the Deathbed," and similar themes dealing with the mystery of the unknown beyond the grave seem to have fascinated both the artists and their patrons. Clearly, the print-makers depicted scenes that their patrons believed would show the real problems of the world. No one studying them will miss the influence of the Christian tradition or mistake them for expressions of pagan ideas. However, concern with devils, death, and salvation did not mean that men were not also involved in worldly things. There were merchants involved in commerce, soldiers in war, young men with young women, and learned men in Greek philosophy. However, there can be no doubt as to the importance of the impact of religious interests upon the majority of men at the beginning of the sixteenth century.

Furthermore, the disorders current in the church of the later fifteenth century were not evidence of any fundamental European swing away from Christianity. As we have seen, those disorders were largely the direct result of the administrative anarchy (a term coined by a distinguished French Catholic historian) that had crept into the organization of the church. When the lines of authority no longer functioned, when ignorant, irreligious, and unworthy men were thrust into church offices, there was grave disorder in the church, but the very fact that reform movements or demands for reform sprang up in many places in fifteenth-century Europe seems to indicate that the mass of the people were still deeply imbued with the ideals and ideas in the Christian tradition. Viewed thus, Luther's rebellion was a natural process well within the framework of the development of European tradition.

2. MARTIN LUTHER, REFORMER

"So help me, Saint Anne, I will become a monk." Terrified by the rigors of a storm and shaken by a violent flash of lightning, Luther vowed to forsake his career in jurisprudence and enter a monastery. If the "Gothic" man ever existed, that is the way he must have behaved. We must remember that the world of the sixteenth century was peopled by spirits of all kinds, and natural phenomena were taken as the voice of heaven. The "divine warning" that forced Luther to "forsake the world" is in character in an epoch when men believed that God spoke directly to them in such a dramatic fashion.

The young man who entered the Augustinian monastery at Erfurt in 1505 was the son of a farmer turned miner who had done well for himself, but whose harsh and brutal discipline may well have given the young Luther a distorted vision of authority. As a child, he had been whipped for minor offenses until the blood came; as a young man he arrived at the horrible belief that he was doomed to hell for his petty sins. Thus, his childhood may well have predestined him to the career of a monk, a career that would almost certainly assure him of salvation from the horrors of hell.

Luther's early years in the monastery brought him no peace. Even by the most rigorous fasting, scourging, and prayer he was not sure that he would win the favor of God. No wonder that he later said, "Love God? I hated Him!" He was obsessed with the idea that he had found in St. Augustine and elsewhere that virtue without the grace of God may be even specious vice: God, he concluded, damns or saves men without regard to their actions. His confessor and superior, a man of great insight and true humanity, tried to comfort him, and finally assigned Luther to the task of teaching the scriptures at the young University of Wittenberg. From everything that we can learn of Luther at this period, he was an extremely earnest young man burdened with his own guilt and obsessed with the idea of an awful last judgment.

The Bible brought him some comfort. In Paul's Epistles he found the line, "The just shall live by His faith." Suddenly he believed that a man could be saved simply by abandoning himself to the will of God. Not good works, but faith in God's redemption was the key to salvation. The idea was surely not a new one, nor was it one that necessarily spelled heresy, but Luther was a single-minded man, and in the violence with which he seized this idea and the exclusiveness with which he interpreted it, may be seen the germ of the religious rebellion of the sixteenth century. The whole sacramental system, all the teachings about good works and indulgences, indeed everything about the church that made it necessary for man's salvation paled in significance and became unimportant in the face of the idea that man is saved by faith alone. What a weapon with which to shake the church that had constructed such an elaborate ritual to minister to men on their path to heaven!

Naturally the full implications of this idea did not come to Luther immediately. He visited Rome in 1511 on a commission for the Augustinian order. While there he tried to take advantage of the many opportunities to win spiritual favor for himself and others, but the earnest German monk seems to have been disillusioned by Rome. The Italians took their religion less seriously than he did; the apparently mechanical organization of salvation by good works raised new doubts in his mind. Luther crawled up the stairs that Jesus allegedly had trod to go before Pilate, but upon reaching the top he asked himself, "I wonder if it is so?" Even on such holy ground he was assailed by doubts. The Pauline Epistles probably strengthened his conviction, but it was the blatant sale of indulgences in Germany that hardened his belief that salvation cannot be earned by exterior, mechanical means.

The doctrine of indulgences was clearly defined in the mid-fourteenth century, and the practice of granting them had by then become ancient and respectable. The infinite merits of Christ's suffering as well as the efforts of saints, monks, and other holy people—so went the argument—filled up a bank of good works in heaven far beyond their own needs for the remission of temporal punishment for their sins: those holy people, then, were willing to allow their spiritual merits to be used for the satisfaction of the temporal punishment of others. The pope, as the representative of Christ on earth, held the key to the spiritual treasures given to him and his successors by Peter, and it was within his power to grant indulgences; that is, remission of temporal punishment to men who had received the sacrament of penance and who performed certain acts. The practice, as we have noted, started when men went on the crusades: to secure soldiers for the Cross, plenary indulgences were granted. At that time, both Christians and Mohammedans were confident of immediate entry into heaven if they fell defending their religion. According to Catholic doctrine, of course, indulgences could not remove the guilt of the individual for the sin he had committed; that could only be done by receiving the sacrament of penance. Indulgences could only remit temporal punishment. The theologians were well aware of the limited power of indulgences when they insisted that the recipient of one could expect it to be effective only if he were in the proper—that is, Christian—state of mind and grace, but the unscrupulous sellers of indulgences very often failed to call the buyers' attention to those theological subtleties—the fine print in the contract.

Luther was aroused by the unprincipled use of indulgences; those which immediately provoked his wrath had been granted to the young archbishop of Mainz, Albert von Hohenzollern, to allow him to raise money to pay the pope for his confirmation in the see of Mainz. The problem arose because Archbishop Albert had to have special permission to assume his post, since there were irregularities in his appointment. (Part of the money did also go toward the construction of St. Peter's cathedral in Rome.) The seller of the indulgences, a Dominican monk named John Tetzel, was completely without scruple in his claims about the efficacy of the papers that he offered. Anyone, it seemed, could save a deceased relative the pains of purgatory merely by putting cash in Tetzel's pocket; only the most ungrateful wretch would fail to take advantage of such an opportunity to help beloved ones who suffered there. If we give credence to contemporary accounts, Tetzel's sermons sounded like the cruder commercials on some television programs; he claimed a great deal for his product! Superstitious people saw no inconsistency in his teachings, and poured their money into the Dominican's coffers while they dreamed that their fathers, mothers, husbands, or wives flew directly to heaven armed with the papal pardon. There were many theologians of the period who would have objected to so simple an operation.

Certainly this proved too much for the man who believed that good works were of no avail; that man's salvation depended upon his faith in the goodness of God. On October 31, 1517, Luther nailed to the door of the castle church in Wittenberg a paper in which he argued against the validity of indulgences under ninety-five theses. While he did not yet absolutely deny that they had any value, he pared them down to a minute size, and among other things, asked why the pope did not empty purgatory if he had such powers. Luther emphasized the fact that German money was being sent to Rome to build a Roman church, when the Germans needed churches too. He assumed that the pope was not aware of this injustice.

Under "normal" conditions, Luther's invitation for a theological debate might not have attracted much attention, but in 1517 his remarks about the "economics" of the indulgence traffic struck a responsive chord in Germany, because many people resented the flow of money to Italy. The ninety-five theses were translated from Latin into German, and the translation was published. The attack on the "holy trade" found so ready a response that the ecclesiastical authorities had either to act promptly, or accept a considerable loss of revenue.

When the news of Luther's attack reached Rome, it was first assumed that the whole quarrel was between an Augustinian and a Dominican monk, and that when Brother Martin calmed down, all would be as before. Therefore, Pope Leo ordered the Augustinians to make Luther recant, but the Medici pope little understood the man with whom he had to deal. Luther not only refused to recant, but also, with a moral earnestness almost unknown to the Renaissance papacy, he took the offensive against the whole idea of indulgences as a key to salvation. In a sermon on indulgence and grace, he underlined his fundamental ideas more firmly. The fat was indeed in the fire. All Germany, in fact the whole of European society, had become involved in a controversy that was destined to give an important impetus to the process of western historical development.

3. THE GERMAN HUS

When Luther attacked the sale of indulgences, he assumed that he acted as a Christian theologian who had to defend the purity of the church's teachings. There is no evidence that he saw himself in any other light. Certainly he did not regard himself as a heretic, but when he was asked to recant, first by a papal command to the Augustinian order, then by a citation before the papal legate, Cajetanus, and finally by an order to appear in Rome for trial, he was forced to consider the full implications of his ideas. The Dominican Order championed their member, Tetzel; the Augustinians were soon to be hard put to defend Luther. However, his prince, Frederick the Wise of Saxony, saved him from a trip to Rome, where either a dungeon or the stake awaited him, and secured for him a trial before the Imperial Diet in Germany.

Luther's ideas unfolded rapidly as the German presses poured forth pamphlets of all kinds discussing the issues. Finally, in 1519, he entered into a full-fledged debate at Leipzig with the theologian Eck. The controversy led Luther to deny one authority after another, until there was nothing left but the Scriptures, which he insisted upon the right to interpret himself. Thus, he was inevitably led to the conclusion that the traditions and customs in the western church—at least from the time of Gregory the Great—were unfortunate deviations from the true primitive Christian church. During the Leipzig debate Eck skillfully pushed Luther to admit that he believed that both the pope and the church council could be in error. Eck then pointed out that the position Luther took was the heresy of Wiclif and Hus. At first Luther was shocked by such an idea, but Eck seems to have pushed him down the path toward heresy, for after the debate Luther began to study Hus, only to find himself in agreement with much of the Bohemian's teaching. When he read Valla's exposition of the forgery of the *Donation of Constantine*, he became further convinced that the church had fallen into grievous error, and that the pope (who was persecuting him, of course) was either Antichrist or his disciple. All the doubts that he had suppressed about Rome now welled up in the conviction that the city was a "devil's nest of wickedness" that needed complete reformation.

On the other side, the logical implications of his doctrine—that men are justified by faith alone—led Luther to attack prayers for the dead, commemorative masses, relics, pilgrimages, and most of the sacramental system. His insistence upon the Scriptures brought him to the doctrine of the priesthood of all believers and the individual's right to interpret God's words. His attack upon religious abuses and practices resulted in suggestions that cloisters should be closed and that priests should marry. Luther also rejected the idea of sacrifice in the mass, and urged that religious services be conducted in the vernacular. He questioned the idea that the bread and wine became the body and blood of Christ (i.e., the doctrine of transubstantiation), and taught that, while it remained bread and wine, the body and blood of Christ were also present (i.e., the doctrine of consubstantiation). Like Hus, he gave the chalice (the wine as well as the bread) to the people.

Luther's reforming ideas burst upon the German church in a torrent of pamphlet literature from dozens of pens. "The German Hus" became a national hero. Whether he expressed his ideas in vigorous earthy German or, as one critic has unkindly put it, bellowed in bad Latin, Luther struck a responsive chord among his people who disliked papal taxation and who were already prepared by the humanists to question the practices and ideas of the monks. That Luther went somewhat further did not seem to bother them; perhaps the readers of the pamphlets failed to notice that he was preparing to sweep aside the religious superstructure of the preceding thousand years or, if they did understand, perhaps they sympathized with his project.

In one particular Luther took care to fortify himself by erecting a new authority to replace the one that he was battering aside. In his *Address to the Christian Nobility of the German Nation* he proclaimed the doctrine that the civil power has the duty to reform the church. As Tawney has pointed out, Luther was probably sceptical of the existence of unicorns, but he believed in another rare monster, the "good prince." That doctrine tempted princes with the riches of the church as payment for their support. Ever since the fourteenth century, princes had been encroaching upon the power of the pope and the bishops; Luther invited them to bring both under their government.

The debate in Germany was allowed to run its course because the death of the Emperor Maximilian and the election of his grandson, Charles V, delayed any action until 1521, when Luther appeared before the Diet of Worms. The papal curia, by that time, had decided that Luther was a dangerous heretic. The monk's quarrel had blown up into a movement that threatened to lead all Germany astray. Therefore even before the Diet met, the papal court, urged on by Eck, had prepared a Bull, *Exsurge Domine,* condemning some forty-odd of Luther's propositions. This Bull was published in Germany in September, 1520, and Luther was given two months in which to recant. On December 10, 1520, Luther solemnly burned "this execrable Bull of Antichrist," and for good measure, a copy of the Canon Law. It was neither the first nor the last book to be burned in Germany. There was nothing left for the pope to do but to excommunicate the heretic. The Bull, *Decet Pontificem Romanum,* published at Worms in May, 1521, after Luther had left the Diet, cut Brother Martin Luther away from the church.

Therefore when Luther appeared before the Imperial Diet for trial, his case had already been judged in Rome, and the question was not whether he could be proved wrong, but, rather, whether he would recant. The young Emperor Charles V understood little or nothing about the theological dispute and probably less of the actual discussion that was carried on in Latin before him, but, like the pope, he had no sympathy with rebellion of any kind, so he too was against the "little brother" who stood before him. Nonetheless, Luther had friends at Worms; at no time in his career did he come closer to being a national hero than at this hour of his trial. Princes, knights, and the masses, even though they might not understand or fully agree with his position, saw him as the German hero defying Rome. He had a "safe conduct" to assure that he would not be treated as was John Hus at Constance, but his popularity was probably a better pledge of his safety.

"Unless I am convicted by Scripture or by right reason . . . I neither can nor will recant since it is neither safe nor right to act against conscience, so help me God, Amen." It was easy for the Catholic theologians to demonstrate that his teachings were heresy, but by denying any right except that of the Scripture, Luther could insist on his side that the church had fallen into error. He was undaunted by the question, "Can you alone be right?" He denied a thousand years of custom; in revenge the church secured the ban of the Empire against him. On May 26, 1521, the Edict of Worms forbade all to give aid to Luther or to read his writings. Luther the heretic had now come to the point of complete separation from the "universal church." When he left Worms, most men assumed that he would soon pay the extreme penalty for his heresy. In this they miscalculated both the sincerity of his friends and the political problems that would prevent the Emperor from acting against him. The "heretic" was spirited away to Wartburg Castle, and from there he began the construction of a new church free from the controls of Rome.

4. THE FORMATION OF THE LUTHERAN PARTY

When Luther nailed his ninety-five theses to the church door, he had no intention of forming a church of his own. When the pope excommunicated him and the emperor placed him under a ban, they had no idea that they were disturbing the religious unity of all of Europe. As with most great changes in the world's history, the decisions that created the Lutheran party were made with mixed motives and with no clear understanding of the possible consequences. Each step in the creation of the new church was a small one, but, piled one on top of another, they snowballed into a great decision that destroyed the religious unity of western Christendom. The "monks' quarrel" over indulgences led to an attack on papal financial policies and upon the authority of Rome over the Christian community. The discussion of indulgences involved the problem of salvation, and this developed into an attack on the sacramental system. It also led to a discussion of abuses on the part of the clergy, and, finally, to a demand for a complete reform of the church. But who could have known in 1517 or even 1521 that before Luther's death western Christendom would be hopelessly divided?

Had the authorities acted quickly to reform the abuses that Luther attacked, or had they done away with the men who objected to the religious practices, the crisis might have been averted or postponed. But Pope Leo X did not have the foresight to understand the need for reform, and the awakening spirit—that might be called nationalism—in Germany worked to Luther's advantage. Important men in Germany, unwilling to allow Rome to decide Luther's fate, forced the emperor to let him be heard before the Imperial Diet. Before a Diet could consider the question, however, the Emperor Maximilian had died (1519), and his death made Luther's trial unimportant compared with the election of a new emperor, for the election involved the ambitions of the kings of Spain, England, and France. Surely the plans, projects, and ambitions of those men were more important than the utterances of a mere professor of theology! Charles von Hapsburg (Charles V) was Maximilian's grandson and already king of Spain and duke of the Burgundian state in the Netherlands; he finally won the election after a considerable amount of money had changed hands. The bribery of the electoral college in 1519 was the largest financial undertaking of that kind in the history of the West up to that time; the wealth of the Fuggers decided the issue. Luther's case may seem more important from our position in time, but his contemporaries did not have our advantage of hindsight.

Many years later, when Charles had abdicated from the throne (1555), he once remarked that he wished he had burned Luther at the stake. This was the "wisdom" of an old man. As a young man Charles did not understand that Luther was really dangerous to his ideal of Catholic Christianity. In 1521, after the ban had been pronounced, Charles had not pressed the case against the heretic, nor did he take significant steps against the emerging Lutheran party until a quarter of a century later. The reason is not hard to find. When Charles left Spain to become Holy Roman Emperor, he repeated his coronation promise to "defend Christendom." In Spain, that promise meant only one thing: to make war against Islam. The Spaniards were as yet both ignorant of and uninterested in Luther. Islam in the guise of the Ottoman Turks threatened the Danube basin and the western Mediterranean, so it is not surprising that Charles regarded the Turkish threat as his greatest problem. A second problem that was to engage even more of his military power was the hostility of Francis I, king of France. In Italy, in Germany, in the Netherlands, and in the Pyrenees there were sources of conflict between Charles and Francis. In the four decades after the Edict of Worms, Charles and his successor were fully occupied with wars against the Turks and against the king of France.

While Charles' military power was tied down by the Turks and the French, Germany, too, was faced with other problems apparently more serious than the Lutheran. In 1522 and 1523 a rebellion of the knights, led by several men who had espoused Luther's ideas, violently upset the peace of the Rhineland. The rebellion, however, was not of a religious nature. The knights were gradually being squeezed out of existence by the new money-economy and the importation of Roman law. Their action was an expression of medieval feudalism in revolt against the new order, rather than a religious movement inspired by Luther. It was suppressed by both Catholic and Lutheran princes who were satisfied to cooperate against a common danger.

In 1524 and 1525 an even more serious rebellion swept through Germany in the form of a peasants' uprising. While there were some religious fanatics among the peasants, the revolt was also a protest against the economic and social order, rather than an expression of religious dissatisfaction. The same kind of peasant revolt had troubled Europe periodically for over a century and a half. Luther quickly came out against the rioters, and, as in the case of the knights' revolt, his followers joined the Catholics in slaughtering the peasants. Lutheranism may have been a monstrous thing in the eyes of many Catholics, but there were other evils even more dangerous. Therefore, in combination with the Turkish and French threats, the rebellions served to allow Luther's reformation to progress without being disturbed by the emperor and the Diet.

Rome, too, proved incapable of doing anything to stop Lutheranism. It was incredible to Pope Leo X that one "little brother" could lead all the others astray, but incredulity did not stop the movement. Upon Leo's death in 1521, the College of Cardinals elected a candidate picked by Charles V, Adrian of Utrecht. He was a pious, austere old man. Of Lutheranism he wrote, ". . . we frankly confess that God permits this persecution of the Church on account of the sins of men, especially those of the priests and prelates." Such an attitude was hardly likely to please the priests and prelates who held important political positions in the church. Adrian died within a year, and his hopes of reform were frustrated by the election of another Medici, Clement VII. The new pope was a politician rather than a reformer. He allied the papacy with France in the wars against Charles V, which resulted, among other things, in the sack of Rome by Charles' armies (1527). This deed, perpetrated by the army of a Catholic king, did not contribute to a reform of the manners and morals in the Catholic church, nor did it direct imperial energy against the heretics in Germany. Obviously neither in the emperor's court nor in the papal curia did men understand the meaning of the rebellion.

Without hindrance, the Lutheran reform developed swiftly. Within a decade, most of the northern German lands and their rulers had been converted. While religious conviction was not the sole cause for all the conversions, it would, on the other hand, certainly be wrong to assume that desire for the wealth to be had by looting the Catholic churches and monasteries was the primary motive of all the princes who deserted the Catholic fold. The reformers must have taken heart when such important people as the Electoral Prince of Brandenburg and his relative, the Grand Master of the Teutonic Order in Prussia, joined the new church, but there were also the millions of little people who worked for and made up an important part of the Lutheran movement.

It should be noted, however, that Luther's insistence upon the divine right of the princes to regulate and purify the church was undoubtedly an important factor in the conversion of many princes in Germany. Those men were seeking to establish their rule over their own territory, just as were the kings of France and Spain. The control of the church would give them the right to name the officers of the church and to use the churchmen as agents of their own power. In an era when there were no other means of mass communication, the spoken word in the church was a powerful political, as well as a social, force. It was that sort of power, as well as the money that could be obtained by disestablishing monasteries, religious foundations, and other wealthy religious institutions which made the transfer of allegiance to Lutheranism attractive. Furthermore, since Charles V as emperor did not join the movement, it was a natural rallying flag for all those elements dissatisfied with the encroachments of imperial power and with the "Spanish and Burgundian advisers" of the Emperor. Again, however, it should be remembered that some sixteenth-century princes were as much concerned for their souls as were some of their subjects.

The process of organizing the Lutheran church was not always simple. It was one thing to defy the papacy; it was quite another to build a new church. Luther himself was the real leader in this task. None of the men around him had his stubborn courage, his absolute faith in his destiny, or his ability to express himself in vigorous, popular language. Some might be willing to compromise, others might be undependable, and most simply lacked the genius or energy to lead. Luther suffered none of those failings; his energetic, single-minded resolution made him the natural leader of the new sect.

It will be remembered that when Luther left Worms his friends spirited him away to Wartburg Castle for protection. There he wrote pamphlets, letters, and began the translation of the Bible into German. This was an important period in his life, for he was safe from his enemies and had leisure to develop his literary interests. His version of the Bible may have given a Germanic cast to the Jewish characters and stories of the Old and New Testaments, but it also gave the German nation a literary document of importance both to the church and to the language. By translating the Bible into German and preaching that each believer might interpret it himself, Luther also left the door wide open for possible radical heresies. He did not seem to have foreseen that there would be many interpretations of God's word as soon as everyone could read it himself. He, of course, was unwilling to allow the diverse opinions that did emerge. In the development of new religious rituals, Luther also had an important influence on the movement that bears his name. His hymns were to affect the development of German music as well as of German religious life.

His early followers were not as conservative as Luther, nor did they share his good judgment. While he was hidden at Wartburg, some of them tried to implement what they believed to be his conception of the church. They began to confiscate money given to pay for masses for the dead, to destroy images, relics, and other pious objects, and they simplified the divine services. Soon monks and nuns left the convents and priests took wives. People began to realize that the movement really was revolutionary when services were conducted in the vernacular language and the communion was distributed in both bread and wine. The reforms were all based on Luther's teachings, but the radicals applied them too quickly. Raids on the churches recklessly destroyed art objects, while the radically different church services repelled many of the more conservative people. The more respectable elements in Germany were not ready to break away so far from established practices, and Luther himself believed that his church was only for good Christians, perhaps only for good Catholics.

The news of such violent action brought Luther back to Wittenberg, where he acted as a brake on the radicals. He was aware that his whole program might be endangered if it became identified with the more radical elements of the reform movement. He re-established many of the former rites, including even the use of Latin in the church, until such time as the changes could be made without shocking the people whose support he needed. Perhaps only the fact that Luther identified his reformed church with the power of the princes saved the movement from destruction in the early years. Thus, when the peasants, despairing of social and economic justice, rebelled against their landlords, Luther wrote a blistering attack, *Against the Thievish, Murderous Horde of Peasants,* in which he assured salvation to soldiers who might die in battle against them. He urged every man to avoid the peasants as he would the devil, and to join forces to slay them as he would a mad dog. This was language to reassure the conservative princes and noblemen.

Not only were the rebellious peasants who tried to find religious cloaks for rebellion the objects of Luther's attack, but also the Anabaptist sectarians, who wished to return to what they conceived to be the Christianity of the first century. The Anabaptists were uneducated, simple-minded people, who took seriously the Biblical messages that their limited understanding allowed them to discover. In their simplicity, they believed that they could separate the community of Christians from the larger community of the world. Thus all Christians would become monks. The Lutherans and Catholics of the sixteenth century showed as little sympathy for the Anabaptist millennial beliefs, socialistic teachings, and religious enthusiasms as the pagan first century had shown toward the primitive Christians. Luther approved the execution of those religious radicals as completely as did the church at Rome, and, later, the Calvinist church at Geneva.

The repudiation of rebellious peasants and overzealous Anabaptists tended to circumscribe the Lutheran cult. Princes, noblemen, and burghers found Lutheranism congenial, and they were in a position to force their poorer neighbors to conform. So, even though the ignorant peasantry may have felt that Luther's attack on them excluded them from his church, Lutheranism was assured of a measure of success. Indeed, in the first few years it secured the loyalty of over half of Germany, and began penetrating into Scandinavia. Nonetheless, by refusing to have anything to do with the radicals and by associating his church with the princes and noblemen, Luther did limit its expansion. Even before his death, the Lutheran clergy were becoming conservatives who depended on government backing rather than on their spiritual mission to strengthen their hold on the people.

The attitude of the humanist scholars also condemned Lutheranism to a limited victory. While Luther regarded the Anabaptists as wild radicals, most of the Christian humanists rejected him as an overzealous fanatic. In the early days of the controversy with Rome, Erasmus and his friends more or less took Luther's side; the same ignorant, superstitious people who attacked them were also attacking him. They assumed that most of the agitation in the papal curia resulted from Luther's assault on the flow of gold from Germany to Italy. However, as Luther's program unrolled in the heat of controversy, it became obvious to them that he was not a Christian humanist like themselves but rather a religious reformer overwhelmed with a single idea. He was not just bent on weeding out superstitious practices, nor did he emphasize that Christ's teachings were essentially humanistic. Rather, Luther was a prophet violently denouncing everyone who did not agree with him, and overbearing in his insistence that his was the only true creed. Instead of applying the humanists' learning to the purification of the church, Luther was intent on returning the church to what he thought were the practices of primitive Christianity. Erasmus exemplified the humanists' objection to the reformed religion in a pamphlet entitled *A Diatribe on Free Will,* in which he attacked Luther's doctrine of salvation by faith alone. He also attacked the doctrine of predestination, which taught that some men are selected for salvation and others are doomed to hell without regard for their virtues or good works on earth. Like other humanists, Erasmus came to regard Luther's dogmatic position with almost the same horror that he felt in the face of the superstitions of the monks. Therefore, one by one the Christian humanists decided that they were more at home in the old church. Luther replied by vilifying those aristocratic scholars who he felt had been corrupted by their learning. Nevertheless, the loss of Erasmus' backing was a severe blow to his party and prestige.

The movement that Luther began in Germany showed an early tendency to split up into sectarian groups that were to prove the bane of the Reformation. In Switzerland, a clergyman named Zwingli, trained in humanist studies, followed Luther's lead and successfully led Zurich and other parts of German Switzerland into the rebellion against the papacy. He and Luther agreed on many things. They both disapproved of images, indulgences, pilgrimages, fasting, and the like; but eventually they disagreed on a very important point.

It will be remembered that at the communion service of the mass the

Roman Catholic church insisted that the bread and wine actually became the body and blood of Christ (transubstantiation). Luther taught that it remained bread and wine, but that the body and blood of Christ were also present (consubstantiation). Zwingli insisted that bread and wine were bread and wine, and that the whole ceremony was simply a symbolic service. A debate between the two men failed to reconcile their differences, since neither would budge from his stand. As a result, the reforming churches became divided. Zwinglian ideas eventually merged with those of Calvin and others, and, as the "Reformed" church, spread through Switzerland, down the Rhine to the Netherlands, and into France and the British Isles, as well as to Hungary, Transylvania, and Poland. Luther would have nothing to do with the ideas of the "Reformed" church, and did not hesitate to take common cause with the Catholics against reformers more radical than himself.

The Lutheran church that took shape in the 1530's was something less than its promise had been when Luther had defied the papacy's right to collect money in Germany. Controversy sharpened points of dogma, and not only brought out the many problems of church reform, but also split off Anabaptists and Zwinglians to the one side and men who preferred the old church to the other. In the process, Lutheranism became the state church in many of the principalities of northern Europe. Its adherence to princely power gave it its characteristic political form which well satisfied the needs of many princes in Germany and Scandinavia who were struggling to establish power over their lands. At the same time, Luther's religious and moral teachings suited the nobility and the patrician city dwellers in a large section of Germany, and they had no serious difficulty in forcing their less educated fellow countrymen to follow their faith. Strangely enough, as soon as those northern peoples had seized the right to determine their own religious destiny, Lutheranism lost its revolutionary character and became a conservative force in central Europe.

5. RECOGNITION OF THE LUTHERAN PARTY

Unquestionably Charles V had originally had every intention of enforcing the ban against Luther, but, as we noted, wars with the French and the Turks took up most of his time and energy. Because of the wars the emperor also needed the help of the Lutheran princes. The first war against France (1521–26) came just as the Turks were conquering Hungary (the battle of Mohács, 1526). The second French war, in which Charles' soldiers sacked Rome (1527), ended the year that the Turkish army of Suleiman the Magnificent reached Vienna (1529). Both the French and the Turks were defeated, but these were busy years for Charles V, with his personal dominions, extending from the Danube to Spain, under assault from two very dangerous foes. The support of the north German princes could not be obtained if Charles insisted that they return to the Catholic church, so it is not surprising that he failed to enforce the ban against the Lutheran leader.

The story of the compromises that Charles had to make is also the story of the rise of the Lutheran Party in Germany. At the Diet of Speier (1526) there seems actually to have been a majority of the princes favorable to the Lutheran cause. Charles needed their aid, and so, even though he did not legalize the Lutheran practices, he recognized the right of each prince to organize Christian worship in his own lands until such a time as a German church council could be called to rule on the question. This church council became a sort of shield for Charles; hiding behind it, he could grant religious freedom of a restricted sort and still not commit the empire to any fixed solution. Three years later (1529) a second Diet at Speier saw a reversal of the majorities. This time the Catholics wished to impose religious uniformity on all of the princes. The result was the famous "Protestation" that gave to the Lutherans their name of "Protestants." The principal Lutheran princes publicly avowed their faith, and protested any effort by the Catholic majority to suppress it.

The next year the Lutherans drew up a statement of their religious position and presented it to the Diet of Augsburg (1530). The "Augsburg Confession" actually minimized the difference between Catholics and Lutherans, and rather stressed the differences between the Lutherans and Anabaptists and Zwinglians. Hard pressed by the Turkish menace, Charles would have accepted the Augsburg Confession as a basis for peace, but the papal legate and Catholic theologians would not agree to any compromises. Although Charles was troubled by the failure to find any solution to the religious problem, he was able to salve his conscience by reminding himself that religious questions should be solved by a church council rather than by imperial force. The idea of settling matters by a council did not appeal to the papacy nor to the Lutherans, but in this at least Charles had a program which he could advocate, allowing him to temporize.

Failure to reach a satisfactory compromise at Augsburg caused the Lutherans to form a formal party called the Schmalkaldic League (1531)—a military alliance to guarantee their liberties and rights. They were genuinely concerned about their ability to retain their religious liberty and, therefore, founded the League. The Catholics were equally determined to reunify the Christian church and responded to the Schmalkaldic League by electing Charles' brother Ferdinand king of the Romans, that is, heir to the imperial throne. After the battle of Mohács Ferdinand had also been elected King of Bohemia and of Hungary. Thus, he had become the center of a coalition of central European states against the Turks. The Catholics hoped also to make him their champion against Lutheranism. The threat of Islam, however, was still more important than doctrinal problems of the church, for

everyone realized that conquest by the forces of Islam would mean slavery. So Catholics and Lutherans momentarily stood together against the Turks, whom both believed to be the scourge sent by God to punish the sins of Germany.

Suleiman's armies were checked and driven back into Hungary, but the victory did not provide Charles with a breathing space. In 1533 Pope Clement VII, fearing the Hapsburgs would be able to dominate all of Europe, made another treaty with Francis I of France. Clement was a member of the Florentine Medici family, and a Medici princess, Catherine, went to France to marry Francis' son, Henry. In return, the French agreed to prevent the calling of a general church council as Charles had proposed. (It will be remembered that the papacy insisted that the pope, not a church council, should decide all church matters.) Within a very short time the third war between Charles V and Francis I was in progress. Not content with his alliance with the pope, Francis also made one with Suleiman, and the French port of Toulon then became a base for the Turkish fleet. It was not until 1544, when the Treaty of Crespy momentarily ended the war with France, that Charles could turn his attention to Germany. By this time almost a quarter of a century had passed since Luther stood trial before him at Worms.

Once he was free from the French and Turkish menaces, Charles moved his army into Germany. If, however, we concentrate our attention upon the religious problem in Germany, we will not understand the full meaning of the so-called Schmalkaldic War that followed (1546). Charles still hoped that the religious question would be solved by a church council, and his Catholic theologians continued to negotiate with their Lutheran counterparts in an effort to find a compromise. The formation of the Lutheran party and the military Schmalkaldic League was another matter from the simple question of religious organization; in the constitution of the Empire there was no place for a "party" military alliance. The League was a military-political organization that undermined the traditional character of the Empire. The fact that Charles was able to associate the Protestant Elector of Brandenburg and the Protestant Prince of Albertine Saxony as well as the Catholic Duke of Bavaria with his forces seems positive evidence of the predominantly political interests involved in the conflict. The German armies, aided by the forces from Spain that Charles brought over the Alps, soon had Germany at their mercy (1547), but the military victory brought neither religious nor political peace to the Empire. It was a triumph for Charles as emperor, and as such eventually frightened both the Catholic and the Protestant princes whose "liberties" were endangered by any increase in imperial power. It was not a victory for the Catholic forces, for Charles still held that the religious question should be settled by a church council.

Charles' attitude toward the religious question can be understood only in terms of his belief that a church council would eventually settle the long-standing problem of reforming the church in its "head and members." In Wittenberg he visited Luther's tomb as a conqueror, but he refused to desecrate the grave. "He has met his judge. I wage war on the living, not on the dead" was the emperor's verdict. Instead of using his military position to enforce a Catholic solution, he arranged the so-called *Interim of Augsburg* (1548). This was a compromise that allowed the *status quo* and postponed all final solutions of the religious question until a church council had pronounced its verdict. Thus, it settled nothing; pleased no one; and failed to hold out any promise of future religious peace.

In 1548, at the time of the *Interim of Augsburg*, Charles' power in Germany was at its height. The presence of Spanish soldiers and Spanish and

Dutch advisers underlined the fact that the emperor might be able to dictate a new political order in Germany. At this critical juncture, however, the princes in Germany—Catholic and Protestant—became fearful for their traditional rights, and listened to the counsels of the new French king, Henry II (the son of Francis I), who was anxious to reopen the Hapsburg-Valois conflict that had troubled the peace of Europe since the early 1520's. French intervention dramatically changed Charles' position. When his own allies joined the French, there was nothing for him to do but withdraw with the Spanish troops into Italy. In 1552, at the Peace of Passau, Charles was forced not only to recognize the traditional rights of the German princes but also to grant to them the new privilege they had recently won, namely, that of determining the religion of their subjects. The formula, *cujus regio, ejus religio* ("to him who rules, his the religion"), was an affirmation of the Lutheran principle of the divine right, as well as the duty, of princes to guard the church.

Charles refused to be responsible personally for such a solution, since it violated every principle in which he believed. He therefore renounced his thrones and, weary from thirty years of warfare, withdrew to a monastery. His son Philip became ruler of Spain, the Netherlands, and Hapsburg Italy; his brother Ferdinand I became emperor and ruler of the Danubian lands of the Hapsburgs. In 1555 at the Diet of Augsburg, Ferdinand formally recognized the Lutheran solution as the religious settlement for the empire. Each prince was allowed to decide whether his subjects should be Catholic or Protestant. "Protestant" meant Lutheran; the "Reformed" (Calvinist) church was given no status. The Diet also proclaimed that no more Roman Catholic church property was to be confiscated and that none of the church states (territories governed by bishops or other high clergymen) were to be changed from Catholic to Protestant control. The Diet formally recognized the breach in the western Christian community; henceforth, there was no institution that could claim the allegiance of all men in the West. The 1555 solution remained the basic law for Germany until 1648, and it assured an uneasy peace in that country until 1621.

Titian, "Pope Paul III" (Naples, National Museum) (*left*). Pope Paul III (1466–1549) was the first reforming pope of the sixteenth century. The reforms he introduced into the government of the Church were largely responsible for beginning the Counter-Reformation. (The Bettmann Archive)

Hans Holbein the Younger, "Erasmus" (Museum of Chartres) (*right*). Erasmus' humane advice failed to stay the violence of the Reformation. (The Bettmann Archive)

Chapter 7

THE EXTENSION OF THE REFORMATION

1. THE REFORMED CHURCH

The religious reformation of the sixteenth century must be seen as a series of movements rather than as a single stream. Luther's attack upon the abuses in the church was only one voice, a strong one to be sure, but only one of a chorus demanding reforms of the administrative disorders in the church and urging some reconsideration of Christian theology. There might well have been a rebellion against Rome without Luther, for in the first quarter of the sixteenth century there were reform movements as demanding as his. These movements may be grouped under four main lines of development. The first was the Lutheran movement in Germany which depended heavily upon the support of the German princes for its existence. The second was the Zurich-Geneva reform led by Zwingli, Calvin, and others; it drew political and intellectual support from the urban populations of Switzerland, the Rhine and Rhone valleys, southern France, and elsewhere. The third was the Anabaptist movement—the most radical of all. It drew its membership from the humble people of Europe, and was almost stamped out through lack of political support. Finally, there was the so-called "Counter-Reformation" within the Roman church, bolstered by both the papacy and the Catholic princes. The English Reformation, while politically important, was in fact not a separate stream. As we shall see, it borrowed heavily from the other movements for both theological and governmental reforms. These four movements shared a common determination to eradicate the abuses that had invaded the church, though they differed in the means that they adopted to achieve this goal.

Of those four, the movement that began in Switzerland spread over the widest geographical area, and was the only one of the reformed religions that successfully defied the power of the princes who refused to join with the reformers. From Zurich, Basel, Berne, Geneva, and other Swiss towns, this movement spread down the Rhine and Rhone river valleys into the Netherlands and France. It eventually reached the British Isles, Poland, Hungary, Transylvania, and northern Germany. In the first bloom of the Reformation, the Swiss movement was confused with the Lutheran, but, as we have seen, there were significant differences between the Swiss reformers and those at Wittenberg that very early led to a disassociation between the two. Indeed, these differences were so great that cooperation between them, even against the Roman church, was nearly impossible. Luther would have nothing to do with Zwingli's teaching that the communion was a "commemorative service," and the Lutheran party excluded the "Zwinglians" from the religious peace in Germany (1555). In Lutheran eyes, the Swiss reformers and their followers were a kind of "Christian Mohammedan" sect, an intolerable heresy. Differences in conceptions of church government and organization were added to those on doctrine to make the two religions almost completely mutually incompatible. Thus, while Luther's church was called "Protestant," the Swiss church took the name "Reformed." Eventually the latter found a theologian, John Calvin, from whom it got the additional title "Calvinist."

From the very beginning the Swiss Reformed church was largely confined to the walled towns and cities. The forest cantons (the rural areas) of Switzerland would have nothing to do with it, but urban dwellers found it congenial. Perhaps the security of the town walls gave men courage to break with the traditional religion; perhaps the Reformed doctrine with its austere moral code and simple ritual appealed particularly to the bourgeoisie and artisan classes. It may also be that the church that defied the territorial prince provided the townsmen with a flag of rebellion against the centralizing political tendencies of the day. It is significant that the towns in the Rhineland, the Lowlands, France, and Switzerland, where the Reformed religion was successful, were also those that took up arms against their territorial princes, sometimes in the name of religion, sometimes for political or economic reasons. The Reformed religion had no prejudice against the sword provided it were drawn in a "just" cause.

Much ink has been spilled to prove that the Reformed religion was well suited to the emerging capitalist civilization. Such a thesis overlooks the fact that a capitalist society developed in Catholic Italy before it did in the Calvinist countries, though there is something to be said for the fact that merchants and artisans found satisfaction in the Reformed religion. Undoubtedly its ethical doctrines, as well as its conception of "vocation" (all professions from laborer to preacher became "callings" or "vocations" from God), appealed to city people. Not all the converts, however, were urban dwellers. In France, Transylvania, Hungary, the Netherlands, and elsewhere a relatively large segment of the nobility also joined the Reformed church. No one can say that those men, like their city brethren, were not sincerely convinced that they were serving their God well. Yet it is also important to note that in each case the Reformed religion provided its adherents with an excuse for political rebellion against a Catholic prince. Although those revolts might have been in defense of their religion, it is fair to say that factors other than religion probably played an equally important part. In a very real way that political aspect of the Reformed church marked it off from Lutheranism. While Luther assumed the divine right of the territorial prince, the Swiss reformers taught that divine right rested with noblemen, magistrates, and other institutionalized orders (even professors!), as well as with princes. They added that it was justifiable for the former to rebel against their prince to force him to do God's will. Thus, the Reformed religion in the towns and in the country was both a way of salvation and a flag of rebellion against princes who refused to do God's will or to protect God's church.

It was no easy thing to turn a whole community away from its traditional religious practices. On his estate a nobleman could do as he pleased, but in the towns there existed several layers of authority, any one of which could resist change. The town council, the bishop and the cathedral chapter, the guilds, the local noblemen, and the territorial prince were all interested in the religious forms of the community, and each of them possessed varying degrees of political and military power. Thus, when the reformers managed to convert the political and the religious authorities of a town, they could take over the church buildings and thereby impose their will upon everyone. When they failed to secure the church, they opened their own conventicles in the house of a member, in a warehouse, or in any available room. Such action very often created a scandal in the town and led to bloodshed. In many communities the struggle for control seesawed back and forth for decades before one party emerged victorious. If the Reformed church finally achieved victory, it closely associated itself with the municipal authorities to assure its power. It may, then, be argued that the Reformed church was as dependent upon the government as was the Lutheran. Town governments, however, were organized in a more democratic manner and were more responsive to the opinion of churchmen than princely governments. Furthermore, the missionaries of the Reformed church did not wait for the town authorities to sanction their services. They were apt to convert the people and then try to impose their will on the town council.

Since the Reformed churches resulted from the labors of the congregation rather than from those of a prince or bishop, they soon assumed their own characteristic form of church government that was to be a pillar of strength for the Reformed religion. Control over the church was vested in the congregation, acting through presbyters, elders, or deacons who chose the ministers and, with them, governed the church. Those congregations found it useful to form federations, usually on a territorial basis, to forward and protect their common interests, and those soon assumed the character of political ruling bodies so that they resembled the beginnings of a state within a state. After Calvin had become the guiding theological light of the movement, his political ideas influenced the whole Reformed religion in the direction of theocratic government, and so, whenever the movement came into conflict with a territorial government, it was easy to justify rebellion on the grounds that princes must do God's will and must be forced to respect and protect God's church.

The theological doctrines of the Reformed church were not fixed until many years after it had achieved success as a movement. Zwingli, as we have already noted, was more a product of the teaching of Erasmus than that of Luther. Indeed, in the first years of the Reform movement Erasmus and the French humanist, Lefèvre, both had an important influence on the theological teachings of the Reformed clergy. Erasmus and Lefèvre attempted to place the New Testament and the ideals of Christ at the core of Christian teaching; by ignoring the theology of the schoolmen and condemning many of the practices of the monks as superstitions or paganisms, the Christian humanists taught that through Christianity a man could experience a reasonable and ennobling life on this earth without prejudice to life after death.

Zwingli, as a humanist priest in Switzerland, had begun to teach Erasmus' ideas before Luther became famous for his ninety-five theses. He urged simplification of church ritual and Christian doctrine to make them more understandable to the common man. Like the Lutherans, he noted that the practices of the early Christian church had been much simpler than those of the church of his day, and concluded that reform was necessary. Armed with Erasmus' edition of the New Testament, Zwingli insisted upon the essentially human character of the teachings and personality of Christ, as well as the simplicity of the original Christian church. He convinced the town authorities of Zurich that the Bible did not mention celibacy of the clergy, abstinence from meat on Fridays, fasting during Lent, and many other practices that had become common in western Christendom. In the first years of the Swiss reformation, the study of the New Testament had the most important influence upon the movement. After the middle of the century, when Calvin's prestige became ascendant, the Old Testament with its emphasis upon law and custom and a sterner ideal of God came to have a greater influence, but in the early years the Reformed churches emphasized the practices of primitive Christians and the teachings of Christ rather than any rigorous theological pattern.

Even more than the Lutheran church had done, the Reformed church simplified the Christian service. Wherever the movement was successful, there ensued a wave of iconoclasm that destroyed art objects accumulated over the centuries. The whole idea of the "sacrifice" of the mass was rejected along with the belief in the real presence of God in the bread and wine. Thus vestments, the altar, indeed the whole exterior paraphernalia of medieval religion disappeared. In its place the sermon, congregational singing, and a simple communion service emerged as the new ritual. In the process of reforming the old church, those pious, psalm-singing men destroyed some priceless art treasures. They rejected as superstition much of the religion of the Middle Ages, and presented men with an austere interpretation of Christian practices. They were the first Puritans in that, unlike the Anabaptists, they insisted that everyone—members and non-members alike—should lead a life of austerity and give up the pleasures of this world. In a sense, they strove to make everyone accept the ideals of the medieval monks.

With the rise of John Calvin (1509–1564) to intellectual leadership, the austerity of the Reformed church was reinforced by a dogmatic theology that was at once the hope and the despair of its adherents. Calvin's *Institutes of the Christian Religion* was first published in 1536, when he was only twenty-six years old. In four successive editions brought out in the next three decades, the *Institutes* were enlarged and enriched and became a *Summa Theologiae* for the Reformed religion. Calvin's writing was not as colorful nor as earthy as Luther's, but his logic was effective and his style clear. He alone of the reformers produced a theological treatise that can be compared with the works of the great medieval theologians. It matters little if his critics say that there was not a single original idea in his work; the emphasis is original, and the vigor with which he presented his argument places Calvin among the greatest of the Christian theologians.

Calvin was trained in France as a lawyer and a humanist scholar. Like the other Reformed teachers, he first turned to the New Testament, but before long the Old Testament with its Jewish law and its picture of God, the Creator and Judge, fascinated him. Almost singlehanded, he turned the emphasis of the Reformed church to a theology based upon the Old Testament more than on the New. Calvin's postulates were simple. Man was a lost creature. The sin of Adam encompassed all of his descendants, and made them into evil, sinful beings who of their own will could do no good. Like Luther, he saw the weakness of man in the face of God's omnipotence; like St. Augustine, he argued that man was not only weak but wilfully sinful. God, on the other hand, was all-powerful and all-knowing. He was everything that man failed to be, and in His infinite goodness He had elected some men for salvation. To them He freely gave His divine grace. With the aid of this grace the elect could do good and could achieve heaven. The rest, and Calvinists assumed them to be the vast majority of men, were eternally damned because of their sinful natures. This doctrine of predestination had been present in the ideas of St. Augustine and Luther, but neither of them insisted on it with the rigor that is found in Calvin's work.

The state of morality in the sixteenth century undoubtedly convinced Calvin's followers of the essential correctness of his thesis. Public morality was at a low point. Rulers used judicial murder and sometimes simple assassination to remove their enemies. Traditional sexual morality was surely never more openly affronted than it was by princes, statesmen, and prelates at the opening of the sixteenth century; and public faith in moral commitments simply did not exist. From all we can learn, private morality followed the examples given by the great. A woman in Calvin's own family was punished as an adulteress; and her sin seems to have been common in her times. Reformers in every age usually insist that theirs is the time when men have fallen lowest in the sight of God, when public and private morality is at its lowest point. However, if the evidence available to us is at all reliable, sixteenth-century men may well have justified the condemnations that the reformers hurled at them. Perhaps it is no wonder that many men were ready to believe that the majority of their fellows was so wicked as to deserve eternal damnation.

By the middle of the sixteenth century, Calvin's Geneva had become a sort of "Rome" for his followers elsewhere in Europe, but to achieve that distinction the city had had to undergo a radical reorganization that changed the luxury-loving commercial center of the fifteenth century into a city of "saints." Geneva was the most important city in the French-speaking part of Switzerland; and although French or "Roman" Switzerland did not experience the bloody religious conflict that disturbed the German cantons in the 1520's and 1530's, the reform was not accomplished without considerable violence. Troops from Berne introduced the Reformed religion to Geneva, stabling their horses in the cathedral. French and Swiss preachers continued the work of converting the population. William Farel, also a Frenchman, brought Calvin into the ranks of those who were preaching against the Romish doctrines by assuring him that God would certainly send him to hell if he did not dedicate himself to the will of the Lord. Both Farel and Calvin were determined to make a new Israel of God out of the city. In doing so, they roused both the Catholics and the wealthy patricians against them.

In 1539 the patricians secured the upper hand and expelled "that Frenchman," but two years later Calvin was recalled. The next decade saw the transformation of Geneva. The Catholics were expelled; heretics who believed in Unitarianism or who denied the immortality of the soul were beheaded or burned; and those who refused to accept the doctrine of predestination were banished. Some of Calvin's political opponents were executed; some were banished; and the rest seem to have gone into exile voluntarily or accepted his leadership. At the same time, refugees from Catholic or Lutheran persecution flocked to Geneva for haven. It has been estimated that about six thousand refugees were taken in by the city, which originally had had a population of about thirteen thousand. Since those who were not members of the church were driven out, the city of Geneva and the Church became one and the same thing. The Calvinists were not always able to reproduce this pattern elsewhere, but in Scotland, seventeenth-century New England, and many of the French Huguenot towns they approximated the Geneva ideal. In the Netherlands civil war almost created a similar situation, and in Scotland the victory of the kirk came near to forcing the whole community into the Reformed church.

As the first city of the Calvinist church, Geneva exemplified most of Calvin's ideas. The puritanical "blue laws" that attempted to regulate dress, food, drink, and other behavior may have been merely a continuation of the medieval sumptuary legislation, but now they had behind them the sanction of religion. The public power was freely used to prevent the behavior of evil men from scandalizing the elect of God. Even though those evil men could do nothing to save themselves from bad impulses and eternal damnation, the law insisted that they must lead exemplary lives or be subject to its rigors.

Geneva thus became the inspiration for other communities of the elect to create a democracy of the chosen of God, a holy commonwealth where men could live serene in the knowledge that their lives glorified God. Calvin often pointed out that it was useless to worry about salvation, useless and unworthy since God had already decided the question. Therefore the Christian man should live his life, in tranquillity and without anxiety, exemplifying God's will on earth.

In spite of the fact that Calvin well understood that no one could penetrate the intentions of God, both he and his followers could live lives exemplifying their doctrine of tranquillity and serenity because they believed that they knew the signs of their own election. Those to whom God had granted His grace would lead lives like the saints, indicating their holiness. Thus they gloried in their pale cheeks, their plain dress, their austere behavior; those were the outward signs of the fact that they enjoyed God's grace to lead good Christian lives. Like the early Christians, the elect testified publicly to their faith in God's salvation and publicly confessed their sins. They also advertised their acceptance of God's grace and His church by participation in the communion service. Once assured of God's grace, they could rest secure in the knowledge that it was an irresistible force that would bring them to salvation.

Calvin's doctrines were teachings for heroes, and before the sixteenth century was over heroes had risen who were eager for religious, and perhaps many other, reasons to build holy commonwealths in many parts of Europe. This is the other side of the story of the Reformed church—the side dealing with religious wars and rebellions. In the Netherlands, it led to the creation of a new state; in France, to three-quarters of a century of civil war or uneasy truce; in Germany, to a conflict that altered the structure of the empire; and in England, to civil war and sectarianism. These stories will unfold in succeeding chapters, when we shall see that Calvinism, unlike Lutheranism, remained a radical and aggressive force even in the seventeenth century.

2. THE ANABAPTISTS

While the Lutherans earned the name "Protestants," and the Calvinists the term "Reformed," the Anabaptists probably should be called the "Restored" church since they, more than the others, rigorously searched the Bible to recover the pattern of the early Christian church. They were most impressed with the fact that the early Christians were persecuted, despised, and rejected by the state and the world, and they argued that this was only natural, since Christians could not really accept the world. Hence the compromises that were made *after* the Roman emperors became Christians were departures from the true church. The world, they believed, could not be Christianized; and if Christians compromised with the world, they abandoned their faith.

Thus, the Anabaptists tried to withdraw into Christian communities apart from the world, much as the monasteries of the medieval church had been. In those Christian communities the ethical urge to exemplify by their lives the teachings of Christ could be achieved. If the testimonies of many contemporaries are to be trusted, the Anabaptists really did try to live in humility, patience, meekness, temperance, honesty, and straightforwardness. One Catholic observer found in them "no lying, deception, swearing, strife, harsh language; no intemperate eating and drinking, no outward personal display. . . ." Their outward manifestation of Christian good works at one time made the Catholic church willing to accept some of the Anabaptist communities back into the fold as a sort of monastic order, provided that they in turn would accept the mass.

Anabaptists were generally simple people who had not developed complex theological teachings. They earned their name "rebaptisers" because they discovered that Christ had been baptized as an adult, and therefore they rejected infant baptism. They accepted the idea of the priesthood of all believers, and thus allowed each of their members to ransack the Bible for inspiration. This resulted, in effect, in many points of emphasis, but in general they took the Sermon on the Mount and the Ten Commandments literally, including the commandment forbidding men to kill. They also tended, like the primitive Christians, to expect the end of the world in their own lifetime. Their ritual consisted of hymn singing, prayers, sermons, and public confessions of guilt as well as of faith. Since their communities were separate from the world, all members were saints, and the church, weeded of sinful and worldly elements, was an Israel of the true believers.

Sixteenth-century "men of the world" found the Anabaptists unacceptable.

If men refused to fight the enemies of society, who was going to stop the Turks in their drive up the Danube? Who would enforce religious conformity on the Lutherans or the Catholics? Furthermore, if every man could be his own priest, what would happen to the institutionalized church? And lastly, how could "people believe such things"? Both the Catholics and the Lutheran and Zwinglian reformers were aghast at the progress such "absurd" doctrines made with the people. The common men of the sixteenth century were heavily burdened with hunger, insecurity, poor housing, disease, and all kinds of troubles: they did not ask for sophisticated theological argument; they only wanted some assurance that in another world things would be different. When Anabaptist "missionaries" came among them with teachings that would assure heaven, the poor and the downtrodden flocked to the new doctrine. At Speier in 1529, when the Lutheran princes made their famous protest, Catholics and Lutherans alike voted for the death penalty for the Anabaptists. If those teachers continued to make conversions, the walls of Christendom would be destroyed and the Turks, who were attacking Vienna at that very moment, would triumph!

The "Code of Justinian" had provided for execution by drowning of the Donatist heretics (an obscure heresy of the early Christian era), and designated those who rebaptized as Donatists; and that code was turned against the Anabaptists. Professor Bainton has pointed out that few of the leaders survived the persecutions; in the Anabaptist hymnbooks beside the names of the authors may be found the notations, "drowned 1525," "burned 1526," "beheaded 1527," "hanged 1528," and so on. Sometimes a whole congregation would be drowned; at other times simply the leaders. It is hard for a modern man to understand the savagery that developed against those simple-minded folk.

For the most part, the Anabaptists allowed themselves to be led to the slaughter like sheep, but at Münster in 1534 the pacifism of one group of Anabaptists broke down when they carried arms to the market place. They revolted, and took over the town. Perhaps the saner heads of the movement had already been executed and only the unstable element remained in control, but whatever the reason, the reign of the "saints" at Münster left behind it an unsavory history. They tried polygamy, as mentioned in the Old Testament; they ran nude like the prophet Isaiah. Both the immoralities and the eccentricities of Old Testament characters shocked Lutherans and Catholics. Münster was taken by the sword, and the "New Jerusalem" was exterminated. Even though this episode was not typical of the entire Anabaptist movement, it so discredited all its members that they were literally rooted out of Germany, Switzerland, and the Rhineland—so completely, in fact, that later generations did not even remember that Germany, rather than England, was the seat of the first "sectarian" movement.

The Anabaptists who survived migrated to the frontiers of Poland, Moravia, and other eastern provinces, where noblemen in need of honest, industrious workers for their lands did not ask too many questions about religious conformity. Their communal groups operated Christian communistic societies, not to improve the standard of living of the members, but rather so that each could live in Christian poverty. St. Francis rather than Karl Marx would have understood their ethical urge.

3. THE ANGLICAN COMPROMISE

The dynastic ambitions of England's King Henry VIII were the immediate cause of the breach between the Anglican (English) church and Rome, but the eventual development of that church as one of the reformed churches of the sixteenth century grew out of problems and conditions deeply rooted in English soil.

England had been the home of Wiclif and Lollardy, and both Luther and Calvin found sympathetic followers on the island. When Henry VIII asked Englishmen to reform their church, he found them willing to go well beyond his own original idea. Henry apparently had no real intention of breaking with Rome if he could avoid it, and once the break appeared, he was anxious that it should not be widened by theological and liturgical differences from Catholicism. However, when the reform movement was released, many Englishmen were prepared to extend and develop its significance for English life. The speed with which Englishmen adopted many of the ideas from Germany and Switzerland is striking evidence of the movement of books and "tourists" in this period. Long before their king was ready to "lead" them, many Englishmen had become converted to the ideas of the continental reformers. Thus, though Henry VIII unquestionably led his nation in revolt against Rome, it was an activist segment of his people who reformed the church, and their reasons for action were often more important than the personal desires of the king.

Henry VIII was not a man to conceive and execute policy. Indeed, if one compares him with either his illustrious father, Henry VII, or his famous daughter, Elizabeth, it becomes clear that he was a vain, fatuous, selfish, extravagant, pompous, and, at times, even stupid king. As the distinguished English historian, Maurice Ashley, has written: "As a crowning example of 'how not to do it' his career is almost unrivaled." Yet this sensuous, promiscuous king did play an important role in the reform of the English church, and the development of England's constitution.

Henry's problem was a relatively simple one. The Tudor dynasty had finally established itself on the English throne, killing most of the other claimants to the crown. Both Henry VIII and his father had used judicial murder as an instrument of dynastic policy to prevent the recurrence of the civil wars that had troubled the mid-fifteenth century (the so-called Wars of the Roses). However, if Henry did not have a male heir to succeed him, problems over the succession might again lead to conflict. Henry had married Catherine of Aragon, a redoubtable woman several years his senior and the wife of his deceased elder brother. The marriage had produced only one daughter, although several other children had either been stillborn or died almost immediately after birth. When there was no hope that Catherine would produce a son, Henry was faced with a great problem of state: he had to consider ways of securing a queen who could bear him an heir. His lawyers assured him that his marriage was illegal, since it was contrary to church law to marry the wife of a brother. Therefore, it seemed reasonable to ask the pope for an annulment. The king's desire for an annulment became an imperious demand when he fell in love with Anne Boleyn, the sister of one of his mistresses.

Under normal circumstances an annulment might well have been possible, but Catherine was also the aunt of the Emperor Charles V. Furthermore, she insisted that her first marriage had not been consummated, and that therefore her marriage to Henry was not irregular. The request for an annulment arrived in Rome after Charles' troops had sacked the Eternal City (1527), forcing the papal court and Pope Clement VII to respect his will, and so Catherine's claims gained strong support. A political deal might perhaps have been arranged between Charles V and Henry VIII to secure the divorce if it had not been for the personal ambition of Henry's chief minister, Cardinal Wolsey, who was consumed with a desire to be pope, and therefore did not wish to make a deal with the emperor. As a result of Wolsey's inept diplomacy, Henry found himself summoned before a papal court (which his own first minister had allowed to be domiciled in England), instead of securing the simple annulment that he had been led to expect. It was an impossible situation: the king's case was to be tried in his own country by a court under foreign jurisdiction.

At that point, Henry dismissed Wolsey, and summoned Parliament (1529) to (1) assure for the crown the support of the people, (2) overawe the clergy in England so that they would recognize his power, and (3) frighten the pope into yielding on the question of the divorce. The so-called Reformation Parliament (1529–1536) succeeded completely in the first two projects, but failed in the third.

In its first years the Reformation Parliament thoroughly enjoyed venting the anticlericalism of the nation in a series of reform laws limiting clerical fees for funerals and wills, and forbidding the grosser forms of pluralism and non-residence. (Many high churchmen held several church offices for which they collected the salaries but did not do the work!) At the same time, because of their recognition of Wolsey's legatine authority, the two Convocations of the English clergy were forced, under dire threats of confiscation of their goods, to accept the reforms of Parliament and buy a royal pardon with a huge amount of money. The assault continued with further legislation controlling the church in England and isolating it from Rome. One important measure even arranged for the consecration of archbishops in England, even though the necessary documents might not be forthcoming from Rome. Those measures had no effect upon the papal curia, for Clement VII was still under the thumb of the Emperor Charles, who did not have a high opinion of England's king. Thus the "cold war" continued.

Late in 1532 the situation changed radically. Anne Boleyn, after holding Henry at bay for several years, finally agreed to the conditions under which she would live with him. She became Marchioness of Pembroke with £1,000 a year in land, and shortly thereafter she became pregnant. To answer Henry's and England's prayers for an heir, however, the child had to be born in wedlock. Swift action was then needed, for the processes of Nature would not wait for diplomatic delays! Henry then recalled Thomas Cranmer to England to become Archbishop of Canterbury, and Cranmer married the king and Anne Boleyn in January 1533. In May 1533 he declared Henry's first marriage null and void, and on June 1 Anne Boleyn was crowned Queen of England. Three months later Elizabeth Tudor was born, and the whole world knew that all the king's efforts had been wasted. No one could then foretell that this baby girl would later become the "great and good Queen Bess."

After the marriage, there remained no reason to temporize with Rome. Henry therefore pressed Parliament to pass an Act in Restraint of Appeals (February 1533) by which all foreign jurisdiction of any kind was denied. England was declared "an empire," and her king subject to God alone. In Rome, the anticlerical legislation, the rejection of papal authority over both the English episcopate and the throne, and the "illegal" marriage appeared as all of a pattern. Such irregularities could not be explained away or tolerated. The new pope, Paul III, replied by excommunicating Henry, annulling his divorce from Catherine, and declaring that all his children by Anne Boleyn were illegitimate. For good measure, he absolved Englishmen from their oath of allegiance to their king. Henry replied by the Acts of Succession and Supremacy (1534): the former vested the inheritance to the crown in the children of Anne Boleyn; the latter declared that the king's majesty "justly and rightfully is and ought to be supreme head of the Church of England." The limits of the royal powers were not clearly defined; neither Henry nor his successors presumed to say mass, yet their political and economic rights over the church were considerable. English Caesaropapism (union of offices of Caesar and pope) was of the same order as that established in Germany by the Lutherans, with the sole exception that Henry's association of Parliament with the reform made that body a responsible agent in the direction of the English church.

The marriage marked Henry's breach with the church of Rome, but he did not intend to carry out a comparable breach with the teachings of the Roman Catholic church. Years before, the Pope had conferred upon Henry the title of "Defender of the Faith" for a flimsy refutation of Luther's doctrine that had appeared under the king's name. Henry proudly accepted the title, and probably rewarded the ghost writer. Even though he no longer accepted the Pope's jurisdiction, Henry fully intended to defend the traditional religion against heretics. Thus we see a curious situation. Lutherans as well as Catholics were persecuted and executed in England, at the same time that the king was despoiling the church of its property and bringing its entire organization under his own control. Changes in church doctrine had to wait until after Henry's death.

It would be quite useless to dwell on Henry's subsequent history. In the political field, it proved as unfruitful for England as had the period before the break with Rome. His marital career had only begun with the wedding in 1533! He was to have more wives than the Koran allows the Grand Turk. Anne, accused of being unfaithful, *had* to be sent to the block; she was followed by four more princesses, both foreign and domestic, and one of them also followed Anne to the block. The royal bluebeard was as hard on his wives as he was on his ministers, who also lived under threat of judicial murder. Catholics canonized Sir Thomas More, who was executed for refusing to agree to Henry's breach with Rome. Other ministers whom he beheaded received no such treatment, since they, like the king, were outside the fold of the Roman church.

Henry's break with Rome was solemnized and institutionalized by the confiscation and sale of monastic properties in England. There had been no such gigantic transfer of land in England since the Norman conquest, nor would it occur again in the centuries that were to follow. The crown's "take" from the transfer was not equal to the market value of the land; nonetheless, it profited handsomely. Such a shift of property inevitably had its effect upon the political and social organization of society, for men who bought church lands understood that their title depended upon the reformation of the church. The two principal gainers were the new peers that Henry created and the gentry. Those classes bought or otherwise acquired most of the monastic lands, and thereby became financially involved in Henry's politico-religious revolution.

At Henry's death in 1547 his weak, sickly son, Edward VI, mounted the throne. Soon after the boy king's accession, the Duke of Somerset became Lord Protector. Immediately the reform of doctrine and ritual in the Anglican church became possible; but the reformers in the higher clergy were divided between followers of Luther and those of Calvin. Foreign theologians appeared in England to help the natives decide; they added their voices to those of the natives without successfully producing a unanimous opinion. However, both the Protector and the prelates recognized that Parliament (that is, king, Lords, and Commons assembled) had the final say in the doctrine, as well as in the organization, of the church. In 1549 an Act of Uniformity imposed the first English Prayer Book as the basic pattern for religious worship. The Prayer Book moved in the direction of Calvinism, but still retained much of the ceremony of Rome.

The religious settlement was completely tied up with the political problems of the reign. Somerset was unable to maintain his position. In 1552 he was arrested and sent to the block, and the Duke of Northumberland assumed power. A revised Prayer Book and a second Act of Uniformity (1552) made Anglican services more aggressively Calvinistic. References to the mass and the idea of transubstantiation disappeared. At the same time a commission of bishops attempted to edit a definite statement of the articles of faith. On June 21, 1553, the young king's signature was fixed to a list of forty-two articles upon which the theologians (including the Scottish Calvinist, John Knox) had agreed. The Anglican revolution against Rome had led to a reformed church, but the conflict was not yet settled.

In July 1553, Edward VI died, and the Catholic Mary Tudor, the daughter of Henry VIII and Catherine of Aragon, became queen of England. It was now the Duke of Northumberland's turn to be executed. The personnel in the prisons changed. Bishops who were too Catholic for the last regime emerged; the Calvinists either went to jail or into exile. However, even though England was apparently loyal to the Tudor family, Mary's reign was destined to be both short and unpopular. Her immediate aim was to secure the country's return to the Catholic fold, and she underlined her intention by marrying Philip II, king of Spain and the leading figure of the Catholic Counter-Reformation, a marriage which resulted in frustration for Philip, herself, and her people.

Mary's short reign (1553–1558) proved to be no more than an interlude in the process of reforming the Anglican Church. Her Parliaments readily agreed to repeal the Acts of Uniformity and to re-establish the mass, but they would not agree to the return of the church lands, and, although the English people may have been ready to return to the Roman fold, no Parliament would actually agree to that. At first Mary moved slowly against the reformers. Foreign Calvinists and their English "fellow travelers" were urged to migrate peacefully, and the Catholic bishops re-established the traditional services in the churches. Unhappily, however, Mary's desire to bring her people back to Rome culminated in lighting fires to burn heretics, and with those fires she and her church earned the hatred of succeeding generations of Englishmen.

Further, Mary's marriage proved no more successful. Philip never loved the middle-aged woman who demanded from him an heir. Mary accumulated a mountain of unpopularity only to learn that she was hopelessly sterile, both physically and politically. She died in 1558, a gray-haired, broken woman who had faithfully followed her religious convictions although they could end only in disaster.

Her successor was the Lady Elizabeth, the daughter of Henry and Anne Boleyn. If she were a Roman Catholic, her birth was illegitimate, for the pope had not accepted the marriage of Henry and Anne. If she adhered to the reformed Anglican church, her birth was legitimate and she was England's queen. There seemed to be little choice between these positions; only the latter was possible for an ambitious woman. Elizabeth proved herself to be as astute a politician as Mary had been obtuse. She had no fixed principles, no guiding star except the maintenance of her throne and her kingdom by any means. Under Elizabeth a new Act of Uniformity with a new Prayer Book and the Thirty-Nine Articles of Faith (1563) gave the Anglican church its characteristic form. The Prayer Book strengthened, and in a measure satisfied, a large segment of the "Catholic" population, and at the same time provided for a ritual rich in emotional content that came to have a strong hold on the hearts of men. The Thirty-Nine Articles emphasized the "Calvinistic" theological patterns and thereby tended to satisfy the more radical parties in the church. Both could be interpreted to suit individual consciences, and they thereby established a broad roof over the English church. The government of the church remained subject to the throne and retained the episcopal hierarchies that assured authoritarian control over the whole of the church. Both Catholic and Calvinist extremists found that the government of the church was a barrier to their plans. Although the Elizabethan compromise did not assure lasting peace to the English church, for the reign of Elizabeth, at least, England enjoyed a high degree of religious tranquillity, and the compromise finally did emerge as the basis for the Anglican church.

4. THE REFORM OF THE ROMAN CATHOLIC CHURCH

Luther's assault upon the church, followed as it was by blasts from other reformers, might lead one to think that western Christendom had no piety, no true religious feeling, and no concern for religious teaching before the rebellion developed in Germany. Such an assumption would, of course, be utterly false. The disorders that undermined the church were real, but so were the sincere men and women who, long before Luther, had urged reform. In a very true sense, however, it is also correct that without the rebellion in the north, it would have proved hard to accomplish any reforms. The various groups of men who wanted reform had no common program upon which they could agree. Theologians, mystics, Christian humanists, and pious men, scandalized by the disorders in the church, knew that something had to be done, but they could not see any constructive course of action that would bring results. For almost a century the demand had been to reform the church in its "head and members," but the Renaissance papacy had been too clever and too strong to be reformed.

The problem of reform had been tied up with the project for calling a church council. A century earlier the Council of Constance had healed a scandal in the church, but it had done so by proclaiming the supremacy of the church council over the pope. This doctrine was opposed by every pope after the Council of Constance. Indeed, in 1512 an assembly at the Lateran under the control of the papal court had condemned the conciliar doctrine and proclaimed the *plenitudo potestatis* (fullness of power) of the Holy See. If a council could not be called to reform the church and if the pope himself would not institute reform, there was no easy way to accomplish it. Such was the problem facing men who were deeply disturbed by the Renaissance papacy, by the ignorance and the venality of many of the clergy, and by the pressing need for new spiritual values.

Luther's first demand for reform was not taken seriously. Pope Leo was not the man to don a hair shirt at the request of a monk in Saxony, nor did the College of Cardinals contain men who could understand the force of Luther's protests. As we have already noted, on Leo's death the Emperor Charles managed to have his own tutor, Adrian of Utrecht, elected pope, but Adrian died before he could do much more than anger the whole papal entourage by his carping criticism. Of the next pope, Clement VII, a distinguished Catholic historian says: "Unfortunately Clement VII did not seek salvation outside and above the ordinary game of international politics." Clement VII, the second Medici pope, feared the overwhelming power of the Hapsburg emperor, Charles, and willy-nilly led the church into the political arena. In 1527 his policy reaped its disastrous dividends when the Spanish-German army of Charles V besieged and looted Rome. This was a shock for Christendom, and it dramatically underlined the necessity of reform. "Never had Christianity fallen so low," writes the Catholic scholar, Janelle. "Never, it seemed, would the Church flourish again."

There were, however, recuperative powers in the body of Roman Christendom that were able to withstand the assaults from Germany as well as the poisons in Rome. The church was an old institution; it had a solid foundation in the hearts of men, and it filled many needs, both personal and social. In Spain and France the connections between the altar and the throne were strong. No Lutheran rebellion would be able to give either the French or the Spanish kings more advantage from the church than they already possessed, and in the third decade of the sixteenth century those two princes ruled most of Europe. Furthermore, most of the Christian humanists finally came to agree with Erasmus that the old church offered more to men than any of the reformed ones could, so there was available an intellectual elite to support the political powers, and the strength of the old church did not end there. Throughout the West there were pious men and women who were deeply attached to the church of their fathers. Some were laymen, some were clerics, but all were ready and anxious to serve as soon as there appeared leaders capable of healing the disorders that were corrupting the church. All that was required in the Catholic church was leadership to bring together the efforts of the reformers.

The necessary leadership had to come from the papacy, or at least it had to have the cooperation of the papacy. When Clement VII died in 1534, the Sacred College elected a man, Paul III, who provided that leadership. Actually the past life of the new pope showed that he was a man very like the others of his day, but he was also a sound administrator and a man convinced that reform must come. He did not want to see reforms imposed upon the papal curia either by secular princes or by a church council. Thus we see him laboring to arrive at some measure of reform through the efforts of the papacy itself. In this program, however, Paul III was handicapped by the fact that Charles V not only believed that a church council alone could heal the religious conflict in Germany, but also wanted to effect a compromise between the theological views of the papal doctors and those of the north. Thus, the ghost of the conciliar movement haunted every step that was made to reform the church. Charles wanted the council to be held in Germany with German and Spanish bishops in control. Paul III was willing to hold a council only if it could be kept under his own control. This conflict delayed the course of the Roman Catholic Reformation, and prevented the compromise with the reformers that first Charles V and then Henry II of France wished to impose on the church to make reconciliation in their own realms easier.

The Roman church reformed itself by its traditional methods: first of all, by the appointment of pious, God-fearing men to the College of Cardinals and the episcopal (bishops') sees; secondly, by introducing reforms in the manners and morals of the clergy; thirdly, by reforming existing religious orders and creating new ones; and, lastly, by the establishment of schools and the extension of missionary activity. Such a program of action was in line with the traditions of the church; it rested upon the assumption that reform could be accomplished by purifying the patterns of the lives of the leaders of the church. They in turn would then provide proper and edifying examples for the rest of mankind. Under Paul III the papacy assumed the initiative in carrying out the reformation of the administrative structure of the church, as well as of the manners of the clergy. There was no intention of reforming church doctrine, but the attacks from the Protestant and Reformed theologians forced the Roman church to sharpen and define church dogma so that the Roman faith became more rigid in its teachings than ever before.

The first wave of the reform might well be called "Erasmian." In Spain, Italy, and France Erasmus enjoyed both a reputation and a following that had been accorded to few literary men in western society. Influenced by his teachings, the first reformers of the church were men anxious to eradicate superstitious practices, to emphasize the evangelical roots of Christianity, and to reconcile the lofty thought of the pagan philosophers with the Christian creed. In Italy, too, men influenced by Erasmus formed the Oratory of Divine Love, an association of highly intellectual and deeply religious clergymen who were determined to raise the standards of the clergy by education and example. It is significant that when Paul III created his first cardinals (1534) the men he named were nearly all followers of the Christian humanists. Erasmus himself was offered a cardinal's hat, but declined because he was old and so ill that he was near death.

Erasmus, however, had much in common with Luther. The emphasis upon the New Testament rather than on tradition, placed him on the fringe of the teachings of Wiclif, Hus, and the sixteenth-century rebels. His unwillingness to accept Luther's propositions about faith and predestination, and perhaps his feeling of security within the old church, kept Erasmus from joining the rebels, but this did not silence his enemies among the theologians who relied upon the scholastic traditions of the Middle Ages for their religious beliefs. The monks could not forgive his attacks on them in his *In Praise of Folly*, nor could the traditionalists accept his evangelical emphases. By the mid-1530's the Inquisition in Spain had begun to trouble the "Erasmians"; by the 1540's Erasmus' gentle conception of Christianity was regarded with disdain throughout the Catholic world. Sterner stuff than Erasmus had to offer provided the backbone of the Reformation within the Roman Catholic church.

The most effective weapon of the Catholic Reformation was forged by a Spaniard, St. Ignatius de Loyola, who founded the Society of Jesus (1540), more commonly called the Jesuits. A Spanish nobleman and a soldier, Loyola saw his military career ruined by a broken leg, and then, like Luther, Calvin, and others of his generation, had a religious experience that convinced him of his mission.

The line between heretic and saint is often very narrow. Ignatius de Loyola got in trouble with the Inquisition in Spain before he decided to equip himself properly for his career. He studied philosophy and theology at the University of Paris; he visited the Holy Land; he came to understand himself and others by rigorous introspection and hard labor. Here was a man who prepared himself to be a soldier of God by the most effective education in religious, intellectual, and mystical matters that his generation offered. The

Society of Jesus was not founded by a barefooted saint coming out of the wilderness crying the name of God, but rather by a man whose brain and emotions were strictly disciplined to create a sophisticated, if saintly, conception of the role of the new order. Along with Calvin and Luther, he deserves a high place in the list of sixteenth-century reformers.

The Jesuit Order reflected the vision and the ideals of its founder. It became an elite corps, rigorously selected to insure the finest personnel possible. Each member undertook education that was both long and intensive to assure that only men equipped to work effectively in the world would be included in its ranks. Loyola not only defined the course of instruction; he also prepared a manual of *Spiritual Exercises* that each member must perform to assure the hardening of his mystic understanding of the faith, just as the theology and philosophy guaranteed an intellectual grasp of the church's teachings. Lastly, the Order was organized along military lines with absolute and unquestioning obedience imposed upon each member. It was placed directly at the disposal of the pope to be used as he saw fit.

The Jesuit soon took the counteroffensive against the reformed religions by teaching, preaching, and missionary work. Their principal concern was to educate young princes and others who might occupy positions of power. To accomplish this, they founded schools from one end of Catholic Europe to the other. At each level of instruction they studied to bring together the best possible methods of education in the classical languages and humanities with the purest teaching of their church. Their philosophy was pragmatic, anti-intellectual, and mystical; they adopted St. Thomas as their theologian, but they were careful to teach in their colleges both theology and Christian humanism. Jesuit priests also became missionaries to extend the boundaries of the Latin Catholic church. While Luther and Calvin detached part of Europe from Catholicism, Jesuits in the New World, China, India, and Japan labored to bring new populations within the fold.

They were, too, preachers and confessors, especially the confessors of rulers. In its role as director of morals, the Order eventually got into serious trouble. They tried to hold wide open the gates of heaven, so that everyone could hope to get there. This spiritual democracy is perhaps laudable in its charity, but in opening heaven's gates to everybody many Jesuits also argued away the existence of sin; and the practice of justifying men's sins by flimsy arguments became as much a source of weakness as it was of strength. While they might thereby successfully "fish for souls for God," the Jesuits also offended the righteous by their easy-going moral teachings. In the late seventeenth century the papacy rebuked the Order for its moral doctrines.

While the Jesuits seem almost to have been the very embodiment of the Catholic Reformation, it was not the only religious order to enter the lists for the old church. Reform movements in the Franciscan and Dominican orders also produced soldiers for the church. Indeed, the Capuchins, at least in France, rivaled the Jesuits as leaders of Catholic reform. The Theatines emerged as teachers of priests. The Oratory of Divine Love provided teachers, preachers, and confessors. In the later sixteenth and early seventeenth centuries other new monastic orders for both men and women undertook to perform good works, to teach, and to provide centers for spiritual retreat and rejuvenation. The church had always reformed its abuses and won support from its people by the devoted work of men and women in monasteries and convents; thus the sixteenth-century reform merely repeated the pattern that had been characteristic of the church's past history.

The Inquisition was another institution that had a share in the reform of the Roman church. The idea and the institution of an inquisitorial court to deal with heresy were several centuries old, but only in Spain do we find such a court functioning when the Lutheran heresy appeared. The Spanish Inquisition had been founded at the end of the fifteenth century to meet the problem raised by Mohammedans and Jews who joined the Christian faith to avoid persecution but who never actually accepted it in their hearts. Those Moslems and their sympathizers were a serious problem in Spain, for at any time they might become a treasonous element aiding a new Moorish invasion of the peninsula. We know now that Islam did not have the power to accomplish this task, but sixteenth-century Spaniards did not, of course, have the advantage of our hindsight. The Spanish Inquisition was, therefore, an instrument of the crown as much as it was a court of the church, and the Spanish kings were quite unwilling to give up their control over its personnel and actions. The papal or Roman Inquisition that appeared in the 1540's was a different and separate institution from its Spanish counterpart. It was primarily charged with the task of uprooting the new heresies and disciplining the church rather than protecting society against Islam.

The Spanish Inquisition actually had very little to do with the northern heresies; only a few followers of the reformed teachings were found among the Spanish people. In Italy, however, the Roman Inquisition found many people who had been tainted by the new doctrines. The inquisitorial courts operated on the theory that the fallen brother must be weeded out and imprisoned or burned to prevent him from leading others astray. In an age that did not understand the word "toleration" such a court may not have seemed quite as brutal as it does today. It is useless to dwell upon the smoking piles upon which Christians burned Christians in Rome, Spain, Germany, Switzerland, France, and England because of differences in the interpretation of the word of God. All of them *knew* that they had the truth. The courts also concerned themselves with other things. It might be noted that fewer witches were burned by the Inquisition than by courts in Protestant Europe, for the Inquisition understood the nature of evidence.

On the other hand, the Inquisition's interference with the scientific and speculative thought of Italy undoubtedly contributed to the decline of intellectual life there in the seventeenth century. The intellectual freedom that had been reasonably characteristic of much of the Middle Ages suffered severely from the presence of a court which was empowered with the right to impose conformity.

The Inquisition was never formally established outside of Italy. The Parlement in France resisted any encroachment upon its right to supervise heretics and literature; and in Germany Catholic emperors did not give up hope of converting the Protestant princes by a compromise.

Closely akin to the "Holy Office" of the Inquisition was the Congregation of the Index of prohibited books. The invention of printing presented a problem in regard to heretical or immoral books even before Luther's revolt. In the early years of the sixteenth century several measures had been taken to censor such publications before they could be printed; and after the flood of literature poured from the pens and presses of the reformers the whole question again came to a head. Like the Inquisition, the Congregation of the Index was founded on the assumption that the church must prevent the faithful from becoming tainted by heresy by any means whatsoever. If books carried the germs of heresy, let them be burned and let none of the flock read them. However, it was not always clear upon what basis a book would be placed on the list. The lists of heretical and immoral books drawn up by the Congregation of the Index have very often represented the moral scruples of the censors more than the theology of the church. Thus, so many of the world's most famous Catholic and Protestant writers have been placed on the Index that inclusion may almost be evidence of literary success. It is hard to estimate the effectiveness of the Index as an instrument to control heresy. The threat of excommunication for reading one of the books must undoubtedly have prevented some people from dabbling with ideas that might have undermined their faith. It might also be true that the meddlesome interference of the Congregation of the Index had an unfortunate blighting effect upon some Catholic thought.

The crowning action of the Catholic reform was the labor of the Council of Trent. From the first days of the revolt the idea of a church council had been in the air. Charles V saw such a council as the only certain solution for the German question, and after him Henry II took up the Council as a means of restoring religious peace to France. In addition to the princes who wished to use the Council to work out a political compromise, many of the bishops, particularly in Spain and France, wanted to establish a theory of episcopal divine right which, in effect, would reduce the pope to the position of first among peers. On the other hand, the reforming popes wished to prevent the assembly of a council until their own labors had accomplished the reforms necessary to heal the disorders in the church. Even after the convocation of the Council of Trent, the papacy used every means at its disposal to control its action. The ghost of the Council of Constance at which three popes had been dethroned and another placed on the throne continued to haunt the papacy into the sixteenth century.

The Council first met at Trent in 1545, but its work at that time was inconclusive, and it quickly adjourned. It reconvened in 1551, only to fold up again in the face of a Lutheran military threat. It met again from 1562–1564, and in that session triumphantly proclaimed the canons and decrees that clarified church doctrine and reformed church practices. That final statement was as far a cry from the compromise that the Emperor Charles had hoped to effect as it was from the program of those men who wished to strip the papacy of its power. Even though it cannot be said that the papacy actually "ran" the Council and "dictated" its final decrees, it was directly or strongly influenced by the papal party and other prelates, the most important of them Jesuits, who pleaded the papal cause.

Taken as a whole, the Council's work falls into several broad areas. First, it reaffirmed the doctrines of the church regarding good works, the sacraments, veneration of saints, prayers for the dead, and so forth, that were under fire from the reformers in the north. It not only reaffirmed them, but also clearly defined and strengthened the church's dogmatic teaching to give it distinct form. Second, the Council took up numerous abuses within the church, from the disorderly garb of some clergymen to the sale of indulgences, from the problem of clerical concubinage to the question of the bishops' power to regulate the clergy. Many of the decrees only reaffirmed the work of the reforming popes; others broke new ground in an effort to arrest the evils in the church. The Council was also responsible for many other decrees and orders that were aimed at the purification of the church: the creation of a seminary for the training of priests in each bishop's diocese was perhaps the most important of those measures. Taken together, the reforms and decrees of the Council of Trent provided a legal structure for the reformed Latin church, and sharpened its rivalry with the other reformed churches of western Christendom.

In the latter sixteenth century a new type of man occupied the chair of St. Peter and filled the College of Cardinals. Pious Christian prelates armed with the moral force of reformers had forged the institutions and the laws necessary to give new strength to the church. In their insistence upon their own interpretation of the Christian tradition and their conception of the road to salvation, those reformers of the church of Rome were as rigid and unyielding as their rivals in England, Germany, or Switzerland. For a half century after the initial breach in the Christian community men could hope that the unity of Europe might be restored, but by the opening of the fourth quarter of the sixteenth century that hope had nearly vanished. The Roman Catholic church, like the Lutheran, the Reformed, or the Anglican churches had begun to assume the form that was to be characteristic of its development in the modern world. United western Christendom had become a thing of the past, inviting to students of history, but no longer vital as a force in the organization of Europe.

A Contemporary Drawing of the Battle of Lepanto (1571). This Christian victory over the Turkish navy made a tremendous impression on Protestant and Catholic alike, for it was a striking defeat of the arch foe of Christendom. Don Juan, the Christian commander, became the idol of thousands of young noblemen throughout Europe. (Paris, Bibliothèque Nationale, Cabinet des Estampes)

Chapter 8

THE HEGEMONY OF SPAIN
AND THE WARS OF RELIGION

1. THE PROBLEMS OF THE EMPEROR CHARLES V

As we have already seen, in the opening years of the sixteenth century Charles von Hapsburg inherited the Burgundian throne, the Spanish thrones, and was elected Holy Roman Emperor. Not since Charlemagne's time did any prince come so close to dominating the Latin West, though, of course, he ruled over a series of more or less unrelated provinces and kingdoms rather than over a single united state. Each of his territories jealously watched to see that he only employed its resources for purposes which were important to its own welfare. In other words, even though Charles V ruled a vast collection of territories, his power was never as universal as it appeared.

The government of Spain was unquestionably the most important segment of Charles' power. His predecessors, Ferdinand and Isabella, had done much to bring the several thrones of Spain under a common rule. Even though each of the Spanish kingdoms still had the traditional Córtes and the traditional royal officials, they were all more or less governed by a superior council for Spain which gave some unity to the administration of the kingdom. Charles, however, knew well that he governed a federation of medieval kingdoms; indeed, several separatist rebellions that he had to suppress underlined the fact that the old kingdoms of Aragon, Navarre, and Castille retained their identity within the government of Spain.

In Charles' time, the Spanish kingdom was a vigorous and prosperous community: its handicraft industry was one of the foremost in Europe, while its wool, wine, and olive oil supported the countryside. The blight that unhappy fiscal policies and war were to place on the Spanish economy did not begin to undermine its society until the third quarter of the sixteenth century. In addition to the prosperity of Spain itself, the flow of gold from the New World added sinews to the strength of the crown. Moreover, in the first half of the sixteenth century Spain still had an adequate supply of men, imbued with the crusading spirit of their ancestors, who could be enlisted in the armies of the king. Those Spanish soldiers, whose prowess was displayed on battlefields for the next century and a half, were among the foremost fighting men in Europe and the very backbone of the hegemony of Spain in the sixteenth century.

As king of Spain and emperor in Germany, Charles V inherited the task of defending Christendom against the assaults of Islam. By the sixteenth century, the Greek East had been completely absorbed by the Ottoman Turks, and in both the Mediterranean and the Danube valley the Latin West was under siege. This was, in fact, the first time that the crusaders in Spain and the crusaders in the East fought the same political, as well as religious, enemy: the Ottoman Empire and its vassal states. The North African corsairs, now a part of the Turkish navy, were threatening the commerce and the coastal cities of Spain. It is little wonder that the Córtes demanded that its king fight in Algeria and Tunis to ward off the Spanish foe. In central Europe, Charles' reign as emperor coincided with the high tide of the Turkish invasion up the Danube. In 1526 at Mohács the Hungarian nobility was crushed by the Turks; and in 1529 Suleiman's forces besieged Vienna. Frightened Bohemian, Hungarian, and south German peoples turned to the Hapsburg emperor and his Spanish-educated brother, Ferdinand, to save them from the Turks. From this originated the Hapsburg Danubian state composed of Germans, Hungarians, and Slavs that was to play a role in Europe from the sixteenth to the twentieth centuries.

In addition to his conflicts with the Ottoman Empire, Charles V also became involved in wars with France, largely because he had inherited the Burgundian crown. The "Burgundian inheritance" represented a curious political entity. It included the provinces of the Netherlands, a complex of territorial rights and privileges in the Middle Rhine (Alsace, Lorraine, Luxembourg) and Franche-Comté on the western frontier of Switzerland. There was neither ethnic nor cultural unity in those provinces. The people spoke Flemish and Netherlandish German, and Walloon and Franche-Comtian French. Their political organization and institutions varied from province to province, depending upon local estates and town charters; and the whole complex of territories was held together solely by the fact that they were all under a single prince.

It was the "Burgundian inheritance" then which brought Charles into direct conflict with France. His great-grandfather, Charles the Rash, had ruled the French duchy of Burgundy as well as the other provinces of the "Burgundian crown." The death of Charles the Rash without a male heir gave the French king the "right" to reattach that duchy to the French crown, but Charles V, as the heir of Charles the Rash, would not recognize that "right." Naturally, when Charles became king of Spain and Holy Roman Emperor, the dispute over Burgundy became serious from the French king's point of view. However, Burgundy was only one of several points of conflict between Francis I, the king of France, and Charles V; in Italy and on the frontiers of Spain and France their interests clashed as well, so there was almost continuous conflict between 1521 and 1559. Those so-called Hapsburg-Valois wars were a keystone of European politics during the entire sixteenth century; they occupied much more of the emperor's time than the religious conflicts in Germany.

Wars with the French, wars with Islam on the Danube, in North Africa, and on the Mediterranean, and finally, political and religious wars in Germany occupied Charles throughout his lifetime, and he died without having successfully solved any of his problems. After the disaster that stalked his armies in Germany and forced upon him the Peace of Passau (1552), Charles, as we have seen, turned over his German interests and with them the crown of the Holy Roman Empire to his younger brother, Ferdinand I. Since Ferdinand already held the crowns of Hungary and Bohemia, it was he who thus became the founder of the Hapsburg Danubian state, and to him and his heirs was left the task of holding off the Turks on the Danube and providing some kind of government for the Empire.

Charles then gave to his son Philip II the crowns of Spain and the "Burgundian inheritance," and the Hapsburg territories in Italy (Milan and Naples). Thus Philip acquired the tasks of defending the Mediterranean and meeting the French. Charles probably did not understand that he also left on his son's shoulders the whole weight of the Counter-Reformation in the West.

2. THE EMPIRE OF PHILIP II

The lands that Charles V turned over to his son Philip made up the first world empire upon which the "sun never set." In Europe, Spain, the Netherlands, and part of Italy came under his hand; beyond the sea, Spanish America in the west and the Philippines in the orient provided the basis for a great colonial empire. His childless marriage to Mary Tudor failed to attach England to his world empire, so on Mary's death Philip proffered his hand to Elizabeth. In doing that, he was following a traditional Spanish policy of friendship toward the island kingdom. When Elizabeth evaded and later actually mocked his offer, Philip married the princess of Portugal and succeeded in bringing that kingdom and its immensely wealthy trading empire under his government.

Philip's empire was not like a unified modern state, but Charles' rule of nearly half a century had gone far to giving it a common government that

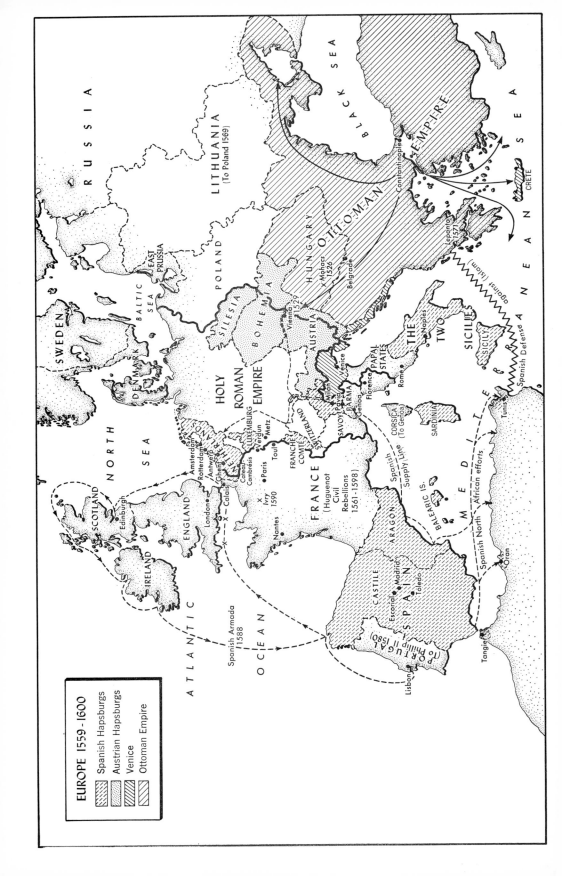

EUROPE 1559 - 1600

Spanish Hapsburgs
Austrian Hapsburgs
Venice
Ottoman Empire

RUSSIA

SWEDEN

DENMARK

NORTH SEA

SCOTLAND
Edinburgh

IRELAND

ENGLAND
London

ATLANTIC OCEAN

Spanish Armada 1588

BALTIC SEA

EAST PRUSSIA

POLAND

LITHUANIA
(To Poland 1569)

BLACK SEA

OTTOMAN EMPIRE

Constantinople

CRETE

SILESIA

BOHEMIA

HUNGARY
Mohacz 1526
Belgrade

AUSTRIA
Vienna 1529

Lepanto 1571

HOLY ROMAN EMPIRE

SAXONY

Amsterdam
Rotterdam
Antwerp
Ghent
Calais

Cateau Cambrésis

LUXEMBURG
Verdun
Metz
Toul

FRANCHE COMTÉ

SWITZERLAND

Milan

SAVOY
PARMA
Genoa

Venice
Florence

PAPAL STATES
Rome

THE
TWO

Naples

SICILIES

SICILY

against Islam

MEDITERRANEAN SEA

Spanish Defense

Paris

Ivry 1590

Nantes

FRANCE
(Huguenot Civil Rebellions 1561-1598)

ARAGON

CASTILE

Madrid
Escorial
Toledo

SPAIN

PORTUGAL
(To Philip II 1580)

Lisbon

CORSICA
(To Genoa)

SARDINIA

BALEARIC IS.

Spanish Supply Line

Spanish North African efforts

Tunis

Oran

Tangier

MEDITERRANEAN

had not existed earlier. It was ruled from the top by a series of royal councils that operated directly under Philip's supervision. Of those councils, the most famous were the Council for the Netherlands, the Council for Italy, the Council of the Indies, and the several councils for the Spanish kingdom. Over all of them was the Council of State, which acted as an integrating force for the whole. The several lands and provinces were governed by vice-roys who operated within the framework of the traditional government of the lands they ruled. That meant that the local nobility and the town councils also exercised power over the land. The central government, however, possessed military forces that could reach more or less effectively to all parts of the empire, and so it was able to direct the policies of the viceroys and military officers. Therefore, although Madrid was far from the center of the empire and local officials had considerable authority, Philip was, in fact, the real ruler over his extended empire.

It was, however, the reality of Philip's rule that turned out to be the Achilles' heel of his own regime and of the empire that he tried to unify. Effective operation of the system of councils and vice-regencies was dependent upon the personality of the ruler. Even a strong king like Philip II proved incapable of understanding all the political ramifications of his realm; the weaker kings who followed him were completely unable to operate the political machine. A king either became overburdened with details, which in Philip's reign paralyzed his government because everything had to wait upon his royal will, or he might—like Philip's successors—leave the government to favorites and see the whole system deteriorate.

Philip's government of his empire was motivated by two central policies. The first was to strengthen the authority of the ruler as against that of the local governments. That process of centralization was the characteristic form taken by practically all governments in the West during the sixteenth and seventeenth centuries, but Philip tried to impose Spanish conceptions of autocracy on Italy and the Netherlands, as well as upon the Iberian peninsula. In Italy and Spain, where there was a common Latin culture, such a policy had a chance to succeed; in the Netherlands it led to rebellion. The second, intimately related to the first, was Philip's attempt to suppress the reformed churches that had withdrawn from the Roman Catholic communion. Philip II was undoubtedly the most important European prince ever to place his power behind one faith, but it was Spanish, rather than Roman, Catholicism that he wished to see triumph. So we find Philip II often at odds with the papacy, while at the same time defending Catholicism against Protestantism. He saw the church and the Inquisition as adjuncts to his own crown, which he held by the grace of God. He wished to use the church and its teachings to bind his subjects more closely under his regime. Thus to Philip II, as to many princes of his age, religion served the same role that nationalism, communism, fascism, or one or the other of the modern political ideologies serves the states of the twentieth century. His subjects rightly understood that rebellion against Philip's political control could best be expressed by rebellion against his religious beliefs.

In Spain, Philip's policies were relatively successful. The sons of the noblemen who had revolted against Charles V in defense of the "rights" of the Spanish kingdoms were willing to take service either in Philip's armies or as adventurers in Philip's overseas empire. Inflation of the currency and the decline of Spanish agriculture had undermined their position at home, so that they had either to seek favor from the king or perhaps perish like their caricature, Don Quixote. The townsmen who had shown such an independent spirit in the earlier centuries of Spanish history were unable to secure military power to resist the centralizing force of the royal government. Charles had crushed much of their independence, and the disruption of the Spanish economy completed the process that reduced them to the royal will.

Only the Moriscos found revolt and either death or deportation preferable to Philip's government. As converted Moors, the Moriscos had been under suspicion by their Spanish Christian neighbors ever since the conquest. Their very presence seemed not only an invitation to the Moslem princes of North Africa to try to reconquer Spain, but also an assurance of aid to the Moslem corsairs that harried Spanish commerce and coastal towns. The Spaniards regarded the Moslem customs that the Moriscos retained even after their "conversion" to Christianity as sure evidence that they were only waiting for the return of Islam to Iberia. Such a population very naturally presented problems that Philip's government could not solve without drastic measures, and the result was that the Moriscos were goaded into rebellion and finally deported en masse from the kingdom. It was one of the first attempts made by a government to force the migration of an undesirable and alien population. Historians and moralists have condemned the policy, but their condemnations are based upon ideas of "right" and "wrong" unknown and unaccepted either by Philip II or by modern totalitarian societies.

In Italy, as in Spain, the policy of centralizing authority in the hands of the prince's government was relatively successful. Spanish viceroys, troops, and officials found native Italians who would cooperate. The preceding century and a half had seen the decay of quasi-democratic institutions in Italy and the rise of princely power. The Spanish regime seems to have been a continuation of that process. Italy, divided and discordant, had called in foreigners (French and Spanish armies) at the end of the fifteenth century. Philip's regime in both northern and southern Italy was the fruit of Charles' victory over France; and the Italians could do nothing but submit to his rule once France had been removed from the scene. Italy had lost all control over its own political destiny, and thus she ceased to have a "history" in the grand sense of the term.

In the Netherlands, quite a different picture emerged. Philip's first speech in those provinces after his father had invested him with the Netherlands-Burgundian crown was in *Spanish*. The Netherlandish German and the Walloon French languages of the land were unknown to him. Neither did Philip seem to know—or at least he did not appear to appreciate the fact—that those provinces were inhabited by a people who had traditionally had recourse to arms against prince and king in defense of their local rights. Their walled towns and their networks of canals aided in the defense of their ancient privileges and assumed rights. Moreover, it was not just the unruly townsmen who might reject authority; the nobility—Netherlandish, Walloon, and Burgundian (Franche-Comté)—too had traditions of independence and pride in their local institutions. Thus, Philip's first speech, in an alien tongue, boded ill for the future of his regime. Charles V, who had been born among the people of the Netherlands and spoke their language, had been able to strengthen his authority by emphasizing certain aspects of the traditional government of the lands, but, as we shall see, Philip, with his Spanish background and advisers, succeeded only in whipping the provinces into revolt.

The Netherlands revolt was doubly embarrassing because of the problems that developed between England and Spain. In England, Queen Elizabeth and many of her subjects came to see Philip as the arch enemy of their religion, as well as a potential threat to their security. With Elizabeth's connivance, English seamen made piratical attacks upon the Spanish treasure fleets and the Spanish-American colonies, although England and Spain were technically at peace. Furthermore, Elizabeth gave aid to the rebels in the Netherlands and the Huguenots in France. England thus came to represent a menace to Philip's plans, and Englishmen who set out to "singe the beard of the Spanish king" constituted a threat to his treasury. To achieve his ambitions in Europe, Philip tried to force England to submit to his regime, but failed utterly.

By a curious twist of fortune, Philip's problems in the Netherlands also became subordinated to a civil war that ravaged France in the latter sixteenth century. Philip's role as principal defender of the Catholic faith placed obligations upon his government and led to political involvement. In France, it almost resulted in a scheme that might have integrated Franco-Spanish power, and placed it at the disposal of the church and the Hapsburg family. As we shall see, his involvement in French affairs relaxed Philip's pressure upon his rebellious Dutch subjects and gave them an opportunity to extend their revolt.

3. *THE PROBLEM IN THE WEST: FRENCH PHASE*

Henry II of France was killed (1559) in a tournament accident shortly after he had signed the Treaty of Cateau-Cambrésis with Philip II. His Calvinist subjects, sorely pressed by Henry's persecution, exulted that the lance blow was a sign from God that He was watching over the Huguenot party. In actual fact, the Huguenots had merely exchanged one system of oppression for another more severe, for Henry's eldest son, Francis II, turned the government over to his wife's uncles, Francis, Duke of Guise, and the Cardinal of Lorraine, both ardent Catholics and workers for the Counter-Reformation.

The Reformed religion had made considerable progress in France between 1535 and 1560 in spite of the hostility of the royal government. Neither Francis I nor his son Henry II was willing to accept it since the Concordat of Bologna (negotiated by Francis I with Pope Leo X in 1516) had ensured for them control over the church as complete as they could expect. By the terms of the Concordat, the king of France had the right to appoint all high church officials and to collect revenues from church properties during the periods between the death of a bishop or abbot and the appointment of his successor. Since, in addition to those political and financial advantages, there were many other tangible gains to be had from the support of the clergy and the traditional association with Rome, Francis I and his son certainly had good political reasons for remaining in the Catholic tradition. (It is highly questionable in any event whether either would have felt any religious scruples about deserting Rome if they believed it to be politically necessary.) The towns of the south, some of the great nobles, and a large segment of the lesser nobility joined the Huguenot "cause" for their own reasons—some religious, some political.

It is interesting that the towns of the south rather than those of the north became the headquarters of the Reformed religion. The south of France was the last part of the kingdom to be brought under the government of the king. Provincialism and localism were especially strong there, and particularly so in those towns where an educated bourgeois class was conscious of its interests. In part, those townsmen joined the Reformed religion in protest against the authority that the king was exercising in their affairs. In part, too, they joined because the austere moral code prescribed by Calvin well suited their outlook on the world, while the doctrine of predestination provided them with the assurance that they, as well as the noblemen, were an elite group. It is very difficult to penetrate the spiritual and moral forces at work in a society, yet it would be folly to assume that they do not exist simply because they are hard to define. In any case, the Reformed preachers who taught the theology of John Calvin and organized religious services in which sermons and psalmody were of the greatest importance converted a large part of the townsmen in the south and the southwest of France.

The religious conquest was not just confined to ritual. The Huguenots, as they came to be called, organized themselves in loose confederations so that the scattered Huguenot communities resembled a state within the kingdom. They held regular meetings, organized military forces, and elected "protectors" to look after their interests. By 1570 they probably numbered about twenty percent of the total population of the kingdom of France, but their location in walled towns and the relatively high cultural level of their members gave the Huguenot party an importance out of proportion to their actual numbers. Even though they were unable either to free themselves from the rule of the French king or to capture his government, from 1560 to 1630 they played a significant and often decisive role in the history of the kingdom.

The Huguenot party, of course, was not confined to the sons of weavers and other craftsmen; many of the proudest names of France contributed blood and brains to its cause. The princes of Bourbon-Condé, descendants of the Constable de Bourbon who had betrayed Francis I, were Huguenots intermittently. As heirs to the throne of Navarre, and, after the House of Valois, to the throne of France, the Bourbon-Condé princes counted as princes of the "blood of France," and therefore were the natural rallying point for elements dissatisfied with the government of the kingdom. Thus, the king of France was faced with one of his most serious problems: his near relatives were always potentially his most dangerous political rivals. Other important nobles supported the Huguenots: the names of Coligny, Rohan, and others may have little meaning today, but in the sixteenth century everyone knew that those names were among the proudest and most powerful in the kingdom of France. Those men had many "political axes to grind"; they resented the ever-growing authority of the crown as long as they were unable to control royal policy. For many of them the Huguenot church provided a flag and a political philosophy to justify their rebellion against royal power. The lesser nobility also acted from mixed motives. Many of them had been soldiers who had become unemployed after the Treaty of Cateau-Cambrésis only to find that they not only had lost their income as soldiers, but also that inflation had ruined them as landlords. When Henry II was killed, the plight of such men tended to become desperate. Francis II, the new king, was a stripling enamoured of his beautiful wife, Mary Stuart, later Queen of Scotland; he had had nothing to do with the wars, and therefore had little interest in the plight of the soldiers. The government was in the hands of the Duke of Guise and the Cardinal of Lorraine. The latter did not endear himself to the ex-soldiers when he declared that he would hang the next one who asked for a pension! That proved a most unsuccessful way to treat veterans and heroes, for during the next two decades a very high percentage of the veterans of the late wars fought against the king on the side of the Huguenots.

The civil wars were about to break out under Francis II, but his reign was cut short by his death in 1560—just in time to prevent his uncles from executing the Prince of Condé as a rebel. (Many of the Huguenots believed that the premature death of the king was God's intervention on behalf of Condé— though that may be considered doubtful!) Francis was succeeded by a minor,

Charles IX, and thus the queen mother Catherine de Medici, became the regent and also the center for all the plots in the kingdom. She had no particular love for either the Catholic party of the Duke of Guise or for the Huguenot faction of Condé; both constituted menaces to the royal authority and the government of her son. Catherine understood that the crux of the problem was political rather than religious, and that the wars, once unleashed, would threaten the existence of the monarchy rather than offer any real solution of the religious question. So we find her returning time and again to the proposal of the Chancellor, l'Hôpital—namely, that the religious question be solved by granting toleration to the Huguenots. That, at least, would prevent the use of religion as an excuse for rebellion. However, until it was shown that the Huguenots could not be suppressed, there were men who insisted on trying. Neither Catherine nor her sons were strong characters; she tried to rule by guile, by flattery, by persuasion, and even by assassination. One of her favorite tricks was to assemble a bevy of beautiful young women at court—her "flying squadron"—to give the men something to think about besides politics. However, she proved unable to prevent civil war.

It would be tiresome to recount the story of the French civil wars in detail. Unlike the contemporary rebellion in the Netherlands or the Thirty Years' War in the next century, the French rebellion was not a continuous conflict. Some nine distinct wars, divided by short periods of uneasy peace, filled the years between 1562 and 1598. Any one of them might be the plot for a tragic opera, several of them for a semicomic one. Taken together, they constituted a major catastrophe for the French kingdom. The actual battles in the field were often relatively unimportant, since the armies of the period were still small and shock action between them infrequent. The innumerable vicious outbursts of violence in all parts of the kingdom—where neighbor was set against neighbor, where marauding troops pillaged from friend and foe indiscriminately, where bands of armed men roamed the land under no control other than their own will—those were the actions that made life, property, and trade insecure. There were some proud names that fell on the battlefield; others, both Huguenot and Catholic, fell by the blows of assassins.

The religious wars can be divided into roughly two periods: the first from 1562 to the death of Charles IX in 1574; the second from 1574 to the Treaty of Vervins and the Edict of Nantes in 1598. During the entire period both sides drew sporadic and clandestine aid from foreign powers. In the last period, however, Philip II openly aided the Catholics with money and soldiers to the point that the civil war in France actually became a Franco-Spanish war. The Huguenots also received slight assistance from England and the central European Protestant states, but never on the scale that Philip II was willing to invest for the Catholic cause.

The climax to the first period came with the massacre of St. Bartholomew (1572). The Huguenot chiefs were all assembled at court to witness the marriage of one of their number, Henry of Bourbon, to the king's sister, Margaret of Valois. The marriage had been arranged as a means of bringing peace to France, and at the same time uniting Huguenots and Catholics in a plan to aid the Dutch rebels against the Spanish king. The story behind the massacre is a complex one, but the brutal fact was that the king's forces fell upon the Huguenot chieftains and murdered them. It was neither the first nor the last of such violent outrages, nor were the Catholics the only ones to commit them, but the massacre was surely the most dramatic outrage and the one which was remembered longest. The immediate result was the elimination of most of the great nobles in the Huguenot party, and consequently the bourgeois politicians and Huguenot preachers acquired a larger voice in the direction of the "cause." Those men were more seriously committed to the religious interest of the party, and hence were less willing to compromise.

The most important factor in the second period of the wars was the realization that Henry III (1574–1589) would not be able to sire an heir to the throne. None of the sons of Catherine de Medici and Henry II was able to father an heir. In accordance with the ancient Salic Law of the kingdom, which laid down that the throne could only be inherited through the male line, Henry of Bourbon, king of Navarre and the military champion of the Huguenots, became the next in line for the French throne. Henry had escaped the massacre of St. Bartholomew since he had become brother-in-law to the king and pretended to be converted to Catholicism, but he fled from the court as soon as he could and rejoined the remnants of his party. Thus, the heir to the throne was not only an avowed heretic but also the leader of a party in rebellion against the throne. This had a curious effect upon the political teachings of both the Catholics and the Huguenots. In the first stages of the war, the Huguenots had insisted upon their right to rebel against a king who persecuted God's church. Their most important book, *Vindiciae contra Tyrannos,* still remains a ringing defense of liberty against tyrants. In this period many of the Huguenots in France seem to have had the idea that they could create a state within the kingdom of France or even, like the Dutch provinces, achieve independence. But when Henry of Bourbon appeared as the next in line and then as the contender for the throne, those psalm-singing Calvinists saw the Salic Law as God's work and Henry's right to rule as a divine right. It was a dramatic reversal of the argument that had allowed subjects to rebel. Rebellion against a Huguenot king would, of course, be treason.

The Catholics made an equally drastic about-face. Before Henry of Bourbon had appeared as heir apparent, they had supported the idea of divine right. The possibility of a heretic on the throne by divine right forced them to seek another argument. Their theorists "discovered" that the nation, i.e., the Estates-General, had the right to depose a king and to elect another, and they accepted the current Jesuit teaching that a tyrant who persecuted God's church could be killed by the first man who met him. It was to be a long time before the kings of France forgot those arguments proposed by their "loyal" subjects.

The Catholics proceeded to form their own political party, the Catholic League. Led by the Duke of Guise, most of the great Catholic noblemen and the bourgeoisie of the northern cities (particularly Paris), the League soon became an instrument of revolution. Henry, Duke of Guise, could trace his ancestors back to Charlemagne through the House of Lorraine. He was a dashing and popular prince, the darling of the Paris mob as well as the hero of the Catholic Church. When King Henry III learned that the Paris crowds would obey the Duke Henry of Guise and not the king, the threat that an Estates-General might dethrone the Valois family and raise the House of Guise to the throne seemed very real, and the king resolved to do away with his dangerous Catholic subject.

This phase of the conflict is sometimes called the War of the Three Henrys. Henry III (Valois) resolved on a coup d'état. At Blois he lured the Duke of Guise into his apartments, and then caused him to be murdered. (Today the visitor to the castle of Blois is given a vivid description of the murder and shown "the very spot" where it occurred.) Poor Henry had thought he would thereby really be king; but instead, he had to flee from the wrath of the Catholic Leaguers and join Henry of Bourbon. A few months later he was himself murdered by a Catholic fanatic, leaving Henry, prince of Bourbon and king of Navarre, the "rightful" heir to the throne.

The Catholic League refused to recognize the Huguenot Henry of Bourbon as king. Paris barred its gates to him, and France braced herself for another stage of the religious civil wars. At that point Philip II not only offered the support of his arms but also proposed that his daughter, an issue of his marriage with a Valois princess, might be given the throne of France. The Catholic League had no suitable candidate available after the death of Henry of Guise, and yet Frenchmen hesitated to let the Spanish king determine French policy. Most Frenchmen remembered the era of the Hapsburg-Valois wars, and were unwilling to reverse the decision that had been reached by those conflicts. Thus, when the Spanish ambassador presumed to play an increasingly greater part in the deliberations of the League and the Catholic Estates-General, fear of the Spaniard grew apace.

In the meantime, another party had emerged from the conflict and demanded the attention of Frenchmen. The ferocity of the wars and the obvious fact that neither side could exterminate the other made the proposal for toleration first put forward by l'Hôpital and Catherine de Medici more and more attractive. The party that emerged called itself the *politiques* (political men); Jean Bodin was its intellectual leader. His principal argument was simple and cogent: religious unity in society might be a good, but it could not be the supreme good. When it was possible to secure religious unity only by destroying society itself, it was wise to accept toleration as a policy. Those men were also "good Frenchmen," and as such hostile to foreigners. Therefore, they placed the Salic Law at the very core of the French constitution, and resisted any attempt to introduce a Spanish solution to the French throne. Interestingly enough, however, even Bodin refused to give his allegiance to Henry of Bourbon until he had become a Catholic; it was one thing to tolerate the practice of the Reformed religion in the kingdom and quite another to accept a heretic king.

The *politiques* were to play an important role in the struggle for the throne, because their support of the Salic Law led them to support Henry of Bourbon. This saved his cause from being identified only with the Huguenots. The Catholic League tried to equate the Bourbon monarchy with heresy. The *politiques,* who stood with Henry of Bourbon when the Spanish armies invaded France to dethrone him, made it evident that some Catholics as well as the Huguenots would not accept foreign dictation. They thus were the men who found the "solution" that allowed the rest of France to join Henry and expel the foreign "invader."

There was only one possible solution that could bring internal peace: Henry IV must renounce the Reformed religion and return to Roman Catholicism. He himself had few religious scruples, but the fact that he had been "in and out" of the Catholic fold several times already made him reluctant to parade his religious opportunism further. There was, however, no other alternative; if he wanted to be king, he had to become a Catholic. In 1593 Henry IV was again received into the Roman church at St. Denis, just beyond the walls of Paris; and thus broke the stubborn resistance of the Catholic League. All that remained for him to do was to bribe its chieftains with grants of money, privileges, and offices. Henry's oft quoted remark, "Paris is worth a mass," is misleading. Paris and the affection of the Catholic party could be *bought* only after the king had heard mass, but bought it was at costs that weakened—almost bankrupted—the monarchy. Once their own political and financial positions were assured, the Catholic Leaguers were ready to help Henry drive out the Spaniards.

Henry's apostasy was a blow to the Huguenots, and almost immediately they began to look around for a "champion" to take the place vacated by Henry of Navarre. With the Spaniards still occupying part of France, their readiness to desert him appeared shocking to the king. He had to make a settlement that would allay Huguenot fears. The famous document issued in 1598 as the Edict of Nantes was therefore a negotiated settlement between the Huguenot party and their late leader. It embodied Catherine's ideas about toleration and gave guarantees that the Huguenots would be treated the same as the Catholics in France. Actually, the guarantees were stronger than those possessed by the rest of the nation, for by the Edict of Nantes the

Huguenots secured possession of walled towns, soldiers, tax revenues, and the right to hold assemblies to discuss common interests. They thus became almost a republic within the kingdom. Henry could not do anything else. The Edict was the bribe that secured Huguenot support for the throne of the Bourbon family.

Philip II, too, had to recognize Henry IV as King of France. By 1598 Spain had been bled white. Philip had failed to bring England to heel; he had been unable to suppress the Dutch rebellion; and his French policy was bankrupt. There was not enough money in his treasury nor gifted soldiers in his army to warrant continuing the war. Thus the Treaty of Vervins in 1598 brought peace to the northern provinces of France, and ended the second phase of the sixteenth-century Franco-Spanish conflict. Henry of Bourbon was left on the throne of France to establish his dynasty and heal the wounds of forty years of warfare.

4. PROBLEMS IN THE WEST: THE NETHERLANDS AND ENGLAND

Philip II would probably have experienced difficulties ruling the Netherlands-Burgundian state even if there had not been a religious rebellion in Europe. He was and remained a foreigner in language and in ideas, and he ruled the land from Spain through viceroys to whom he granted power and then withdrew it alternately. Furthermore, his ideal of government, indeed that of any sixteenth-century prince, inevitably resulted in conflict with the traditional liberties of the nobles and townsmen. When that conflict was inspired from abroad, it more easily became violent. In addition to the political problems, there was a religious one. In 1560 about ten percent of the population was Protestant or Reformed. All three branches of the Reformation, Lutheran, Anabaptist, and Calvinist, were represented. The movement had not made greater progress because it failed to convert either the ruler or any large segment of the great nobles. However, there were many people who had been influenced by Erasmus and who, in a crisis, would side with the reformers. The masses, both rural and urban, were like the masses elsewhere, bound by tradition and yet converted with relative ease to the Reformed religion if military and political power fell to the reformers.

As we noted, Philip's government was exercised by viceroys. The first, his half-sister, Margaret of Parma, was a well-intentioned woman, but her power was limited because Philip placed his favorite, Bishop Granville, beside her as adviser and guide. At the same time, he tried to direct the policy of the government from Madrid. Almost at once the regime ran into difficulties. In the first place, the Netherlands—both the Catholic and non-Catholic regions—disliked executions by burning for religious beliefs. The fires burned not only martyrs but also the people's affection for the House of Hapsburg. Philip also attempted to give his Burgundian lands a rational ecclesiastical constitution, and this brought further protests. At the time, several Netherlands bishops were under archbishops residing in neighboring states, and Philip decided to divide the whole land into three arch-episcopal provinces appropriately subdivided into bishoprics. At the head of the whole ecclesiastical organization he proposed to place Bishop Granville as primate of the Netherlands-Burgundian state. The new organization would increase the power of the central authority considerably and allow for closer supervision of heresy. It became an immediate target for both noblemen and townsmen who saw it as a threat to "liberty."

By 1566 opposition to the regime had reached the point where several important noblemen had resigned from the Council, and a petition was prepared to be presented to the viceroy vigorously protesting the religious policy. That petition should have proved a warning; it was signed by some five hundred notables, among whom were Catholics as well as Protestants. One of Margaret's courtiers advised her to pay no attention to the "beggars" who were petitioning her. He thus gave the party of revolt its famous name, "the Beggars."

Deeds inevitably followed the words. By midsummer of 1566 the Calvinists apparently believed themselves strong enough to act. In a wild orgy of destruction, they shocked their Catholic neighbors by their violence. Armed with axes and malls, they stormed into churches throughout the Netherlands, and wrecked statues and paintings as well as relics, books, and manuscripts. That burst of iconoclasm destroyed art treasures accumulated through five centuries. That action was characteristic of the Calvinists: in Switzerland, the Rhineland, southern France, and Scotland those stern men saw only idols in the works of art that decorated churches. By their violence, they excited the anger and indignation of men who still loved the traditional religious forms. They also earned for themselves the dislike of future generations of art lovers, for it is difficult to see what "religious" needs were satisfied by such wanton destruction.

Philip II was determined to punish the outbreak. He assumed that Margaret's policy had been too soft, so he sent the Duke of Alva at the head of a Spanish army to institute a harsher regime. Alva began to make wholesale arrests: those who were responsible for the outburst of iconoclasm and those who objected to the government's policy alike were taken into custody. Along with little people whom the world does not remember, he arrested great nobles like the Counts of Egmont and Hoorn who, after the Prince of Orange, were the richest and most influential men in the land. He would have arrested Orange, but that wily prince withdrew to live with relatives in Germany and to plan an armed intervention against the unpopular regime.

When that intervention came, the lives of Egmont and Hoorn, as well as a host of other notables, were forfeit; they were the martyrs for the independence of the land.

The Dutch war for independence may be said to have started in the late 1560's when Alva's army became a necessary instrument of his government; it did not end until 1609, or perhaps even 1648. In 1609 the twelve years' truce forced the Spanish king to recognize the *de facto* status of the rebellious United Provinces; in 1648 under the terms of the Treaty of Westphalia the Spaniards also recognized the *de jure* existence of the new state. The last thirty years of the sixteenth century, however, were the critical years; it was then that the civil war in France and conflict with England drew off enough Spanish military pressures to allow the Netherlanders to establish their republic in the northern provinces.

It was no accident that the rebellion was successful in the north but a failure in the south. No rebel army could stand up to the Spanish infantry unless it had advantages of terrain that incapacitated the Spaniards. Thus, in the provinces of Zeeland and Holland, where the sea, islands, canals, and rivers conspired to hold off the Spanish *tercios* (infantry), the rebels were able to organize their forces. At first they were little more than pirates, the "Water Beggars" whose marauding voyages harassed Spanish commerce, and who maintained a hold upon the island curtain of the Netherlands. In time, however, Calvinists from all over the Netherlands came to the northern provinces for safety from the Spanish fury. Alva's "council of blood" sent a stream of *emigrés* to the north. At the same time, the anti-Roman Catholic excesses of the "Water Beggars" made Catholics leave the northern towns for the south.

The rebellion developed into a religious war, but it would be a mistake to see in it only religious issues. Catholic historians have taunted the Dutch with the fact that it was a sales tax rather than religious edicts that drove the Netherlanders into revolt: in other words, that their pocketbooks rather than their God were the critical issue. The Prince of Orange, himself more an "Erasmian" than a Calvinist, tried to keep the religious issue in the background to unite the Netherlands-Walloon peoples against a foreign regime. He and many of the other leaders saw the issue in political and nationalist terms as much as in religious ones. Others were driven to revolt when Alva's arrests, executions, and confiscations resulted in the destruction of trade and disruption of economic life. There is no doubt that economic, political, and national interests were involved in the rebellion, but religion provided both its flag and its ideology.

The war was often a sordid affair of sieges and relentless massacres. The world knows most about the bloody record of the "Spanish fury," but both sides had records of pillage, rape, and murder. Philip II came to understand dimly that Alva's brutal methods were not going to succeed, but he was

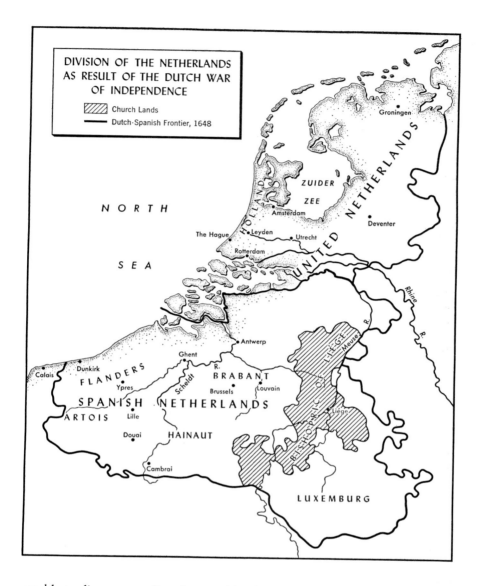

DIVISION OF THE NETHERLANDS
AS RESULT OF THE DUTCH WAR
OF INDEPENDENCE

///// Church Lands
——— Dutch-Spanish Frontier, 1648

NORTH

SEA

Groningen

ZUIDER
ZEE

Amsterdam

Deventer

The Hague

Leyden

Utrecht

Rotterdam

HOLLAND

UNITED NETHERLANDS

Rhine

R.

Meuse

R.

Antwerp

Ghent

R.
Scheldt

BRABANT

Brussels

Louvain

BISHOPRIC OF LIÉGE

Liége

Calais

Dunkirk

FLANDERS

Ypres

SPANISH NETHERLANDS

ARTOIS

Lille

Douai

HAINAUT

Cambrai

LUXEMBURG

unable to discover a policy that would. Alva's successor, Don Luis de Reque-
sens, was as Spanish and as bigoted as Alva, but lacked the latter's ability.
Instead of placating the rebels, those two men were probably responsible
for the ready acceptance in the northern provinces of the idea that a Spanish
soldier or a tyrannical prince might be murdered without a sin having been
committed. Violence begat violence and failed utterly to quell the rebellion.

As with any conflict as lengthy as the Netherlands rebellion was, its history
was comprised of battles, negotiations, conferences, and, finally, the creation
of new institutions. Out of the war there emerged two states, where formerly
there had been one: the United Provinces in the north and the Spanish

Netherlands in the south. This division was to continue to divide the old Burgundian lands even down to the twentieth century, when the Benelux union again established a sort of unity between the states of the United Netherlands, Belgium, and Luxembourg. The political theory that justified these states in the sixteenth century was itself the product of the conflict that produced them, and the political institutions that emerged to govern the states were hammered into place by the force of the war. Surely the rebellion did not achieve exactly what its originators expected, but it stands as a constant reminder that war does change the *status quo,* and sometimes greatly.

The effects of the rebellion were not just confined to the Netherlands. It was inevitable that the Huguenot conflicts in France would become intertwined with this rebellion. Actually, there were two points of juncture. The Huguenots naturally sympathized with the Calvinists in the Netherlands, but within the Catholic population of France there were many who had not forgotten the Hapsburg-Valois wars, and regarded the rebellion as a chance to strike a good blow against the Spaniards. The marriage of Henry of Bourbon and Margaret of Valois on the eve of the St. Bartholomew's Day massacre had been inspired by the idea that both Huguenots and Catholics in France should join ranks to help the rebels in the Netherlands. That idea again became important when Henry III was struck down by an assassin and Parma's Spanish army appeared in France to impose a Catholic-Spanish solution to the problem of the French succession.

Equally if not actually more important was the role of Elizabeth's England. Many refugees from the harsh Spanish regime had fled to England in the 1550's and 1560's, where they found friends and assistance. When the revolt began, the English queen gave aid to the rebels, although not too generously. Some few English troops and an incompetent English commander were engaged in the early years of the struggle. Enough English money and military aid went to the Netherlands to convince Philip II that the revolt could not be broken as long as England contributed to it. Indeed, English harassment of Spain did not end there: with Elizabeth's connivance, English seamen like Drake, Hawkins, and Raleigh attacked Spanish commerce and the Spanish colonies in America. From the Spanish viewpoint, those men were pirates since England and Spain were at peace. However, the Spanish ambassador could get no satisfaction in London. It was profitable business to rob the Spanish treasure fleet, and at the same time Protestant England was doing her bit for the "cause."

Finally Philip II felt obliged to take action. War with England had not been a part of his program; indeed, throughout the sixteenth century alliance with England was one of the central points of Spanish policy, but Elizabeth had left him no choice.

The story of the great Spanish Armada has been told so often that it requires no lengthy recital. Philip's great naval armament was imposing in its bulk, but as a fighting machine it lacked the speed and maneuverability characteristic of the English navy. It was folly to send the Armada against England without first planning a way to bring it safely into an English port, for the Armada was in fact a great fleet of troop transports rather than a fighting navy. But up to that time, the western world had not seen a fleet on the scale of the Armada. Who knew then that it would not succeed? In July, 1588, the Armada appeared in the English channel. For nine days a battle raged in which the heavy guns mounted on the sides of their light vessels gave the English a great victory. The Englishmen had been trained to fight as buccaneers; the Spaniards were prepared to give battle if they could land their army on English soil. A great storm completed the havoc begun by the English, and Philip's dream of subjugating England melted into the sea. It had never been more than a dream; the disaster that overtook the Armada only hastened the defeat that Spain was facing in northern Europe.

In the next decade Philip's armies were as much engaged in the war in France as they were in the Netherlands, and in both fields their efforts were frustrated. To a considerable extent, this failure can be traced to the disaster that overtook the Spanish Armada, for from that time onward it was impossible for the Spaniards to supply their army in the Netherlands by sea. Thus gold, supplies, and men used in northern France and the Netherlands had to travel the tortuously slow and dangerous route across the Alps and down the Rhine. In the end, the Spaniards were happy to cut their losses and make peace with the Dutch rebels.

Neither a linguistic nor a religious frontier emerged as the dividing line between the rebellious provinces and the Spanish Netherlands. True, there were more men subscribing to the Reformed church in the north, and a larger percentage of Catholics in the south. Still the line that divided the provinces did not really reflect a religious boundary. The language frontier between the Netherlandish Flemish dialects and the Walloon French did not coincide either with the new frontier. The only determining factor in regard to the frontier was the ability of the military forces of the two opposing sides to defend it. The survey had been made with soldiers: to the north of the line the rebels were successful; to the south the traditional Hapsburg-Burgundian state still ruled. Like many frontiers in the world, it represented the military realities of the age; in time, customs and institutions were to give it a relative hardness and stability that assured its permanence.

Rebels often find it easier to agree upon common action against an enemy than to agree on common institutions and programs. The rebellious northern provinces were no exception. Each province had its own traditional estate or parliament and its own traditional local government. Since one of the provinces, Holland, was much larger, more populous, and more wealthy than any of the others, there were strong prejudices in favor of retaining the local institutions rather than creating a new system in which the smaller provinces might be swallowed up entirely. Thus, from the very beginning each of the rebellious provinces maintained its ancient identity. The institution of an Estates-General, where representatives from the several provinces would meet, had long been established in the Burgundian state, so it was an easy step for the rebellious provinces to bring together an Estates-General representing them to direct the rebellion. As the war continued, political theory and political institutions developed apace. The officers, institutions, and political traditions of the United Provinces, as they came to be called, were hammered into place by the war on land and on sea.

Two traditions developed. On the one side, the House of Orange came to be almost the uncrowned royal family. The office of stadtholder (governor) was hereditary in the Orange family in several of the provinces, and whenever the family could supply the soldier he became stadtholder for the Estates-General as well. The Orange faction came to be made up of the nobility in the country and the poorer classes in the towns. It recognized the republican form of the United Provinces, but in fact worked toward a monarchy. Whenever the United Netherlands were in trouble with their neighbors, the Prince of Orange tended to assume leadership and power as head of the military institutions of the state.

The other party was truly republican. It was made up largely from the wealthy and comfortably well-to-do city people. The Oldenbarnevelts, the De Witts, and other bourgeois republican politicians were the leaders of this group. When the republic was at peace or the head of the House of Orange was a minor, those men were the leaders; during a war the House of Orange tended to assume control. Conflicts between the two groups often resulted in sanguinary civil wars which upset the peace and quiet of the cities and the countryside.

The most important fact about the United Provinces concerned their economy. The seamen and merchants of the Netherlands had prepared for their prosperity in the early sixteenth century by entering the carrying trade between Spain and Portugal (India and the Americas) and northern Europe. Clever traders, sharp dealers ("It's hard to beat the Dutch," says the proverb), and able men of affairs, they managed to create a trade situation centered upon their homeland that gave them a near monopoly of the seaborne trade of Europe. Every harbor of Europe sent its goods to the Netherlands, and there picked up goods from the rest of Europe and the colonies. The war at first interrupted this development, for Dutch merchants were unwelcome in Iberian ports while they were in rebellion against the king of Spain, but by the end of the sixteenth century the Dutch sailors did not suffer much from their exclusion from Iberian ports for they were ready to sail around Africa and make their contacts directly with the east, a fact that strengthened the commercial position of their homeland. The men of the United Provinces became rich from commerce and the booty of warfare at sea, and thereby laid the foundations for the future greatness of their country.

At the opening of the seventeenth century, the two most important commercial institutions of the United Provinces began to take form. One was the Dutch East India Company, which was virtually a sovereign state connected with the United Provinces by interlocking directorates. The East India Company had a monopoly on Asiatic trade; it could acquire territory, make treaties, and declare war. It operated ships, maintained soldiers, and paid enormous dividends. The other was the Bank of Amsterdam, which rapidly became the most important financial institution of Europe. Like the East India Company, it was connected with the state by interlocking directorates. The Bank acted as a discount and transfer agent for the merchants of Europe. Anyone in the north who wished to participate in international trade kept funds on deposit in the Bank. Everywhere in Europe the commercial paper of this Bank circulated as if it were gold.

In 1621 the Dutch West India Company came into being to complement the two other institutions. Its field of enterprise stretched from Brazil to New York, but the Netherlands eventually proved to be too small to maintain its activity in North America along with its extensive holdings in the orient. In the course of the seventeenth century nearly all of its holdings in the western hemisphere were liquidated.

Philip II had died in 1598. He probably never understood why he failed to win back the Netherlands. His successors were anxious to cut their losses and end the drain on Spain, for it had become increasingly evident that it was impossible to subdue the rebels who had created a state strong enough to be counted as a great power. Peace came in 1609, in part through the intervention of Henry IV of France, in the form of the Twelve Years' Truce that recognized the *de facto* independence of the United Provinces.

With the truce, the form of the southern or Spanish Netherlands also began to take shape. Philip III established his daughter Isabella and her husband Albert von Hapsburg (Austrian branch) as independent sovereigns, but a Spanish-Walloon-Italian army under General Spinola remained to guarantee its security and to act as a threat to the northern provinces on the expiration of the truce. Actually, this inaugurated a new period in the history of the southern Netherlands. Control from Spain was gradually loosened, so that the destinies of the land, inasmuch as they were controlled by anyone, were in the hands of the local nobility and burghers. Albert and Isabella failed to produce an heir, and sovereignty eventually did revert to Spain, but never again were the southern provinces governed completely from Spain. In the course of the next two centuries, they were ruled by Spain (until 1714), by Austria (1714–1815), by Holland (1815–1830), and have existed as the independent kingdom of Belgium since 1831. Their northern cousins, however, held control over part of the economy of the southern provinces which had long had manufacturing interests (cloth, leather, metal, and so forth) that transcended purely commercial ones. After 1609 their market contacts with the world were hemmed in by the control exercised by the United Provinces over the mouth of the Scheldt river, the natural artery for the export of their goods. Although this did not completely blight the economy of the land, it did accentuate the differences that were developing between the two Netherlands. As time went on, the Spanish Netherlands became more and more completely Catholic. The interiors of their churches were regarnished with paintings and sculpture to take the place of the medieval art destroyed by the iconoclasts. The new decorations were Spanish baroque rather than Gothic, and the rich sensuous colors and lines perhaps fitted in badly in the Gothic cathedrals and churches, but they yet remain as mute evidence of the iconoclastic outrages and also of the connections between Spain and the southern provinces.

5. PHILIP AND ISLAM

During the sixteenth century Spain's interests in the Mediterranean sea were considerable. From Spain to Sicily to Naples, from Genoa (independent, but still under Spanish influence) to the Balearic Islands and back to the mainland, the commerce and communications of the whole western Mediterranean area depended upon Spanish power. The problem that both Charles V and Philip II had to contend with there stemmed from the pirate states in North Africa, where Islam and buccaneering joined hands. Since the pirates were nominally dependent upon the Sultan of Turkey, their presence posed the further threat of an Ottoman thrust into the western Mediterranean. By the middle of the century Spanish conquests had established Christian garrisons in some of the North African harbors, including Mélilla, Mers-el-Kebir, Oran, and Bougie, but it was quite impossible to control the whole northern coast of Africa. As we have noted, the problem in Spain itself was complicated by the fact that the Moriscos were potential allies of every marauding North African emir, and constituted a constant threat that Islam might again invade Europe. The Spaniards regarded them with the same suspicion that twentieth-century Americans reserve for communists.

Philip's general policy was to attempt to seal off the Islamic forces in the western Mediterranean from Turkish aid by establishing a defense position from Italy through Sicily and across to Tunis. That line was intended to confine the Ottoman navy to the eastern Mediterranean. As we have seen, it also required a full-dress military operation in Spain to expel the Moriscos, but in Philip's eyes that was an essential condition to ensure the safety of his kingdom.

The Moriscos shouted their complaints against the cruelty and bigotry of

Spain from one end of the Moslem world to the other; and Turkish ulemas demanded redress in the form of a holy war against Spain. The Ottoman situation, however, was complex. Sultan Suleiman was more interested in expelling the Venetians from Cyprus and extending Turkish authority in Hungary than in an adventure in distant Spain. When Suleiman died during the campaign in Hungary, his son Selim proved incapable even of continuing the great sultan's policy, let alone extending it westward. In the Mediterranean basin the Ottomans contented themselves with the conquest of Cyprus (1570–1571), which a tragic explosion of the Venetian arsenal in 1569 temporarily left almost defenseless.

The attack on Cyprus aroused the fears of Italy, and, with Italy, those of Philip II whose Italian lands formed the most important part of the peninsula. A "Holy League," comprising Venice, Spain, the papacy, and several small Italian towns put an armada to sea under Don Juan, an illegitimate son of Charles V. The Christians encountered the main Turkish navy at the mouth of the Gulf of Corinth. In the ensuing fight (the battle of Lepanto, 1571) the Turks lost over a hundred ships, about four hundred cannon, thirty thousand men killed, and over a hundred thousand captured. Christian galley slaves on the Turkish ships aided their co-religionists. The Turkish admiral was captured, and his head was mounted on a pike to serve as an emblem of victory. The Christians lost sixteen ships, eight thousand dead, and fifteen thousand wounded. Although the battle had blunted the power of Islam, the Christians did not follow up their victory. Within a few years the Venetians made a separate peace, recognizing the loss of Cyprus in return for Turkish money and trading privileges. The Spaniards were content to establish a vassal state in Tunis, and thus hold the narrow waist of the Mediterranean.

His success against Islam was Philip's most important achievement. He put an end to the Moorish threat to Spanish security, and he more or less succeeded in maintaining Spanish authority in the western Mediterranean. However, the cost of his victories and defeats struck too deeply into the economic and political life of his state, and the roots of Spanish weakness and decay in the seventeenth century are to be found in the wars of Philip II. Into France, the Netherlands, the English Channel, and the Mediterranean Philip had poured the military and economic strength of Spain in a vain attempt to stem the enemies of his family, to consolidate the power of his empire, and to reimpose Catholicism over the whole of Europe. In conclusion, his reign was a colossal failure and contributed to the decadence of Spain: she had been quite unable to sustain the efforts that Philip demanded; the ever-mounting taxes, the drain on manpower, and the inflation resulting from the influx of precious metals from the New World and the monetary policy (debasement of the coinage) of the Spanish government—all weighed heavily upon the nation. By the end of the sixteenth century, the depopulation of the countryside and the impoverishment of the people that was to characterize seventeenth-century Spain had already begun; by 1700 her population had decreased about fifty percent. Spain was never strong enough to sustain the burdens imposed upon her by the Hapsburgs. A sparsely populated, mountainous country without many natural resources, she could not supply either the money or the manpower needed to invest an empire beyond the seas and at the same time provide forces for governing Europe. The treasure ships from America helped to some extent, but inflation prevented Spain from keeping, or indeed even using effectively, the treasure. In the sixteenth century, however, she was the great power of the western world; but in the centuries that followed, exhausted by bad government and completely overburdened, Spain dropped out of the grand stream of European history to become a political, social, intellectual, and economic backwash, no longer of importance in the story of western civilization.

Siege Operations Before Nördlingen. In the battle between the Imperial and Spanish armies and the Swedish forces, the Swedes were defeated. Note that the besieging camp has set up a gallows, but as yet has no victim hanging from it. (The Bettmann Archive)

Chapter 9

THE THIRTY YEARS' WAR,
1618-1648

1. THE HOLY ROMAN EMPIRE OF THE
GERMAN NATION

Unlike the western kingdoms, the Holy Roman Empire failed to develop any strong central government before the Reformation era. As we have seen, medieval Germany was a confederation of feudal states. The emperor's government was unable to control the internal affairs of either the great or the small territorial princes, and by the fourteenth century, when the Holy Roman Empire of the German nation emerged as the political institution for Germany, the confederated structure was firmly established. The Emperor Maximilian (1459–1519) tried to strengthen the central authority of the Empire, but, as we have noted, his successor, Charles V, had to recognize the rights of the princes in order to secure their aid against the French and the Turks.

Luther's religious reform further emphasized the decentralized nature of power in Germany by securing for each prince the right to determine the religion of his subjects. The process of decentralization was exactly opposite to the political trend in western Europe, and it was therefore to be expected that a strong emperor would either try to strengthen the imperial power or to create territorial power of his own. The larger territorial princes, on the other hand, resisted the extension of imperial power, and at the same time attempted to extend their own territorial authority.

Legally, the constitution of the Empire had remained much the same since the fourteenth century. It provided for an emperor to be chosen by seven electors: the archbishops of Cologne, Mainz, and Trier, the princes of the Palatinate, Saxony, and Brandenburg, and the king of Bohemia. The government of the Empire was divided between the emperor and the Diet. The latter consisted of three houses: the Electoral College, the House of the Princes, and the House of the Towns. In addition, there was a supreme court that, in theory at least, had jurisdiction over all cases involving succession to the various thrones and titles. It was also supposed to act as a court of final appeal. However, by the beginning of the seventeenth century the court no longer functioned effectively because its judges were at loggerheads over the religious issue. The Diet was not in a position to act decisively because it was torn by conflicts over precedence, religion, and "the splintering of votes" (inheritance policies had created a situation where as many as five or seven princes shared in one vote in the Diet). The emperor's prestige was still important, and the breakdown of the imperial court of justice led to questions concerning succession being judged in his courts, thus increasing his authority to some extent, although his powers remained limited. The emperor did not have the right to tax all of Germany, nor could he be sure every prince would obey his summons for military aid. So, although the office carried privileges and prestige, the emperor's real power had to originate in the lands where he ruled as a territorial prince. As a territorial prince, the emperor owned lands which he could exploit, enjoyed the right to levy fees, fines, and tolls on commerce within his principalities, and might persuade his local Estates to vote taxes for his use. Those revenues, of course, came to him as a prince, not because he was the emperor.

The organization of the Empire was further complicated by its division into twelve territorial subdivisions called Circles, each with its own diet and a president who was usually the most important prince in the Circle. The Circles settled local problems and acted together as the first line of defence if the Empire was attacked. Actually, they could become involved in a war on the Empire's frontiers without needing to inform the emperor officially. The existence of the Circles obscured the fact that the imperial military system was defective. Not only was there no uniform system within the Circles, there was no effective over-all military authority for the Circles as a whole. The Holy Roman Empire of the German people had become, as Puffendorff was to call it, a political monstrosity, a confederation of two thousand conflicting, overlapping jurisdictions without any strong central power. In that hodge-podge of German principalities, a few princes were beginning to develop military forces of their own. In time, those princely armies were to become the only substantial force in Germany.

The German Hapsburg provinces and the crowns of Bohemia and Hungary were cemented together by the threat of Turkish aggression. After the battle of Mohács (1526) the Danubian peoples realized that the Ottoman armies could be stopped only by united Christian action. In effect that meant, of course, the united action of the people on the frontiers of the Ottoman empire. It was, therefore, not love for the Hapsburgs, but fear of the Turks that brought the divergent Christian peoples together under a single dynasty.

After the death of Suleiman (1566), weaker sultans proved unable to continue the onward march of the Turkish conquests, and the pressure on the Danubian states was eased; almost immediately the Bohemian and Hungarian magnates became restive under their German Hapsburg rulers. However, the threat of Turkish invasion was not completely removed until after 1683 when the last Turkish army to besiege a major Christian city in central Europe (Vienna) was defeated; so until the end of the seventeenth century the Hapsburgs were necessary for the defense of central Europe against Islam, and that was their major role in the eyes of many of their subjects.

However, it was not solely as defenders of Christianity against the Turks that the German Hapsburgs gained their prestige and power. They profited from their connection with the rich and powerful Spanish branch of the family, and they also controlled the political patronage of the capital cities of Vienna, Prague, and Pressburg. But the Hapsburg emperors who followed Charles V to the throne in the sixteenth century showed a surprising lack of political ability. They allowed their inheritance to be divided among several heirs, and failed to organize effectively the power that was available. The last two of the line before the Thirty Years' War (Rudolph II and Matthias) were weak, ineffectual men whose rule nearly brought to an end Hapsburg government on the Danube.

2. CATHOLICS AND PROTESTANTS

The religious settlement of 1555 (which gave to princes the right to determine the religion of their subjects) could not be considered a permanent solution. It ignored the Calvinists, and it assumed that German society would not change. By 1600 all the parties in the Holy Roman Empire realized that some revisions were necessary. The Lutherans had by now become the conservative party. They had lost their revolutionary vigor, and their pastors and princes seemed anxious only to preserve the status quo of 1555, which, of course, no longer really existed. On the other hand, the rejuvenated Roman Catholic church and the Calvinists became the aggressive forces in German society. Neither was strong enough to win an absolute victory over the competing religions, but their efforts to gain power created tensions throughout central Europe.

The Jesuits were the spearhead of the Catholic thrust—the Counter-Reformation: their teachers, preachers, and confessors made every effort to reconvert Protestant princes and noblemen to the old religion, as well as to keep all the faithful within the fold. However, the Catholic successes were not just limited to moral and spiritual victories: the Catholic League—a political body which supported a military force under General Tilly—had been formed. Maximilian, Duke of Bavaria, was the political leader of the League and the real director of Tilly's army. He firmly believed in the Catholic mission in Germany, and he was an astute politician fully capable of looking out for his own as well as Catholic interests. Backing him, but not necessarily in complete accord with all of his political aims, was the Catholic House of Hapsburg. It was divided into several principalities, but was still strong and assured of its place as the leading Catholic power in central Europe because of its contact with the Spanish Hapsburgs. But such a simple statement fails to bring out the great moral power behind the Catholic party. The Counter-Reformation was building an imposing religious force in which universities and colleges, monasteries and religious orders, artists and architects, kings, politicians, and soldiers were all banded together to reunite Christendom. Thus, as the seventeenth century opened, the Catholic party had become a formidable religious and political force on both the German and European scenes.

The Protestant (Lutheran) and Reformed (Calvinist) churches lacked unity of purpose. The Lutherans regarded the Calvinists as hardly better neighbors than the Mohammedans, while the Calvinists were as anxious to convert Lutherans as Catholics. However, both recognized the Catholic church as a common enemy, and princes of the two churches formed the Protestant Union, which became the obvious opponent of the Catholic League; but the Union did not succeed in creating an army comparable to the one Tilly and Maximilian commanded in Bavaria, nor could it marshal the moral enthusiasm for its cause that was to be found among the Catholics, for the division between Calvinist and Lutheran was too great to allow any real unity. Each Protestant prince had his own forces which presumably could be pooled to defend their common interests, but their division made the Protestants relatively weaker than the Catholics in spite of the apparent vigor of the Calvinist group.

The German situation almost led to a war in 1610 when a crisis arose over the succession of Jülich-Cleve, a small but important principality on the lower Rhine. The emperor immediately occupied the territory with a military force to assure his jurisdiction over the succession; the Protestants answered by sending out a call to arms that was answered by Henry IV, king of France, as well as by most of the Lutheran and Calvinist princes. The fact that the French Catholic king was ready to join the Protestants in Germany shows that the crisis was as much political as religious. The House of Hapsburg stood to gain by a Catholic victory in Germany, and this revived French fears of encirclement and the princes' fears of the revival of imperial power in the Empire. In 1610 war was averted; an assassin's blade put an end to the life of Henry IV, and since the emperor really did not intend to take the provinces for himself, a compromise solution satisfactory to both Catholics and Protestants was agreed to for Jülich-Cleve. However, the crisis was a warning of the explosive events to come, for the religious and political situation in Germany had now become a powder keg waiting only for something to ignite it.

The internal problems of the Empire were not alone responsible for the danger. As we have seen, in 1609 the Spanish government had signed the Twelve Years' Truce with the rebellious Netherlands provinces recognizing that the United Provinces were independent in fact, but not in law. The truce was unsatisfactory to both Spain and the Catholic part of the Netherlands, and it had seemed probable that war would be resumed after the truce had expired. The Spanish House of Hapsburg still had interests in the Netherlands, even though the southern Catholic provinces (today's Belgium) were no longer ruled from Madrid. Isabella of Spain and her husband, the Austrian Archduke Albert von Hapsburg, were independent rulers of the Catholic Netherlands, but, by agreement between their government and that of Philip III in Madrid, General Spinola's Spanish army, the best in Europe, was stationed there, ready to resume the war as soon as the truce expired.

Spinola's army exerted a disturbing influence far beyond the Netherlands. Spain could not supply it by sea, because Dutch and English ships controlled the English Channel, so a long and involved supply line from Spain to Genoa, to Milan, and thence by way of the Valtelline Pass in the Alps to the headwaters of the Rhine, and on down to the Lowlands had to be established. Across the line were the territories of the most important Calvinist prince in Germany, the Elector Palatine, who was a potentially dangerous roadblock to the Spanish line of communications. Thus, when he became the leader of the Protestant Union, Spain's interests in the Netherlands became deeply involved with the political situation in the Empire.

In 1617 the Palatinate was ruled by Count Frederick, a naïve young man with no particular talent or ability. However, he was the nephew of the Prince of Orange, the political and military leader of the United Netherlands, and the French Duke of Bouillon, the leader of the Huguenot party in France. He was also the son-in-law of James I, who had succeeded Elizabeth on the English throne, and finally, he was the titular head of the Protestant Union. His charming, vivacious wife was as ambitious as his principal adviser, Anhalt, was scheming. Dazzled by the possibility of bringing all the Calvinists and Lutherans in Europe together (under Calvinist leadership) in a grand alliance against the Catholics, Anhalt failed to measure both the instability of his allies and the strength of his enemies. Frederick did not fully understand the implications of his minister's plans, and therefore allowed himself to become the center of the great Calvinist plot that failed to destroy the German House of Hapsburg, because the plotters were never able to achieve the necessary unity.

The other leading actor in the impending political drama was Ferdinand von Hapsburg, Prince of Styria and eventual heir to all the Hapsburg lands in central Europe. As we have seen, the Hapsburg lands had been divided among several heirs in the late sixteenth century, but several deaths in the family and the failure of princesses to produce sons made it apparent after 1611 that Ferdinand would probably reunite these lands. Therefore his personality and ideas became of importance in European affairs. He was a zealous Catholic, absolutely convinced that God had placed on his shoulders the task of winning Germany back to the Catholic Church. He appeared to be an easygoing man who delegated much authority to his ministers, and many of his contemporaries were, therefore, led to underestimate him. However, while Ferdinand's ministers might change, his policies did not. He was determined to establish both his own authority and religious unity in all the lands under his control. He created a bureaucracy with which he undermined the authority of his nobles, and he consolidated power in his own hands. His assault on the "traditional privileges" of the nobility and his insistence that Protestants either be converted or leave his lands made Ferdinand a dangerous foe of any man who feared either the royal power or the Catholic Counter-Reformation.

As we shall see, it was Ferdinand whom Count Frederick lightheartedly challenged when he accepted the crown of Bohemia from the hands of rebels. Each was convinced that God was on the side of his religion; neither of them was to know peace from that moment until his death.

3. THE BOHEMIAN CROWN, 1618–1621

At the opening of the seventeenth century, the crown of Bohemia brought little real power to its wearer for the constitution of the kingdom limited the royal privileges. However, since the king of Bohemia was also one of the electors of the Holy Roman Empire, the possession of the crown was of great importance to the Catholic Hapsburgs and to the Protestants. Three electors were Catholic archbishops (those of Cologne, Trier, and Mainz) who would naturally vote for a Catholic. The three Protestant princes (of Brandenburg, Saxony, and the Palatinate) would probably vote for a Protestant if there were a possibility of electing one; thus, the king of Bohemia could cast the deciding vote.

The Bohemian Diet elected its king. Throughout the sixteenth century, the Turkish menace had assured the election of one of the Hapsburgs, but since that menace had been momentarily eased, the Bohemian crown had become a potential prize for any vigorous Protestant prince who might win the election. Not only would the crown itself lend prestige to the prince's family, but the Protestants, if they held the crown, might elect its wearer to be the next emperor. Naturally, the Catholics were also aware of the importance of the election in Bohemia, and the Austrian House of Hapsburg was quite determined not to give up the rights that it had established in that kingdom.

The religious picture in Bohemia was complex. The kingdom had originally been converted by monks of the Greek Orthodox church, and even though it had long since transferred its allegiance to the Roman Catholic church, it was customary in many parishes to conduct religious services in the Czech language. The Hussite wars of the fifteenth century had added another change to the usual Catholic services: in some of the churches (called *Utraquist*) the laity received communion in both bread and wine, and the Utraquist Catholic church, thus, existed alongside those practicing more orthodox Roman Catholic rites. The Reformation had brought Lutheran, Calvinist, and Brethren (Anabaptist) churches to Bohemia. Altogether then, in the early seventeenth century a religious map of the kingdom would have been a composite of many patches and colors. The various groups tended to be distributed in fairly well-defined territories, but no one group had a majority in the whole kingdom. By the opening of the seventeenth century, the Hapsburg kings had granted religious toleration to all, for, like Henry IV in France, they recognized that they could not wipe out heresy without ruining their kingdom. In 1611 King Matthias (who was also the Holy Roman Emperor) reaffirmed the grant, but there were many who feared that toleration might be revoked. The spirit of the Counter-Reformation era was not one to give men any real confidence in toleration; the very idea was foreign to all groups, Catholic or Protestant.

Somehow those fearful for their religious liberties failed to assert themselves when Matthias persuaded the Diet to elect his nephew Ferdinand von Hapsburg as his heir to the throne. Bribery and promises controlled the votes, as they had in so many elections. It soon became apparent that Ferdinand did not favor religious toleration, for even before Matthias died the government began to do everything it could, without violating the edict of toleration, to limit the religious freedom of the Protestants. On Matthias' death, the Calvinist noblemen felt convinced that they must reverse Ferdinand's election. The result was a revolution in Prague (1618). The crowd stormed the royal palace, and the Calvinist leaders threw two representatives of Hapsburg authority out of the upper story window of the palace at Prague. That was the most famous and fateful "defenestration" of history. Fortunately for the victims, they landed in a pile of manure in the royal courtyard, and so were not physically harmed. The revolution marked the opening of a war that was to last thirty years in Germany, involving the German states and most of Europe, followed by another ten years of war between France and Spain in the Lowlands, Italy, and the Pyrenees.

As fortune would have it, Matthias' death left the thrones of both Bohemia and the Empire in question. His nephew, Ferdinand, claimed the former, even though the crown was in the hands of the Calvinist rebels, and proceeded to Frankfurt to ensure his election to the Imperial throne. He encountered no serious problem in the Imperial election; even Count Frederick's ambassador, representing the Palatinate, voted for him after it became evident that there was no other candidate. However, at almost the exact moment that Ferdinand's election was proclaimed in Frankfurt, news arrived from Prague that Ferdinand had been deposed as king of Bohemia and that Frederick had been elected in his place. The Bohemian Diet, led by the most extreme Calvinists, had refused even to consider some compromise solution such as the election of the Duke of Saxony, who hoped to make peace between the Hapsburgs and Bohemia. Counseled by Frederick's adviser, Anhalt, the Calvinists believed that England, the Netherlands, the Palatinate, the Protestant Union, and Transylvania would all join with Bohemia to put an end finally to Hapsburg power in central Europe.

The selection of Frederick as king of Bohemia did not prove to be a success. James I of England proved surprisingly unmindful of his son-in-law's needs, and the military help anticipated from other sources did not materialize. Furthermore, the French government intervened decisively in favor of the Hapsburgs. This action was as unexpected as it was disastrous to Frederick's cause. France's young king, Louis XIII, was deeply engaged in military action against his own Calvinist subjects, and so it was easy for him to see that Ferdinand, like himself, was confronted by a "Calvinist plot." The French ambassador in Germany not only neutralized the Protestant princes who might have aided Frederick, but also helped prepare the way for Lutheran Saxony to join Ferdinand and Maximilian of Bavaria in an assault on Bohemia.

Count Frederick and his attractive wife went to Prague to receive the crown, but their stay in Bohemia was destined to be very brief. In 1620 the Bavarian and Imperial armies reached the outskirts of Prague, and at the White Mountain Frederick's army, commanded by Count Mansfeld, was utterly defeated. The royal couple fled so hastily that they left the queen's French novels in the palace to shock the puritanical Catholic Bavarians.

The battle of the White Mountain sounded the death knell for the ancient liberties of Bohemia. Ferdinand changed the constitution so as to guarantee his family's hereditary succession to the throne. It was not the policy of the Hapsburgs to destroy the form of ancient institutions; Ferdinand and his successors merely changed the personnel in conquered kingdoms to assure themselves of solid support in the government. So in Bohemia he shuffled the landholdings by a process of confiscation so as to assure a nobility dependent upon his family. The new nobility of Bohemia were men from all over Europe who owed allegiance to the Hapsburg family, and the old families either came to heel or lost their lands and fortunes. Thus Bohemia, which had hitherto been more or less of a liability for the Hapsburgs, became a source of military and political power.

The war did not end with the Catholic occupation of Prague; there were too many problems left unsolved. In the first place, Frederick's army under Count Mansfeld retreated into the Upper Palatinate, and then fell back toward the Rhine. Secondly, and even more important, was the fact that Ferdinand had promised Maximilian of Bavaria that Frederick's electoral vote would be transferred from Protestant Palatinate to Catholic Bavaria in return for Bavarian military assistance against Bohemia. This was, of course, illegal and completely contrary to Ferdinand's assurances that the Bohemian war was simply a local affair. Maximilian, greedy to secure new honors for his family, had tied himself and his army to Ferdinand's policy so that he became an accomplice of the emperor's attack on "German liberties," that is, the "rights" of the princes.

The direction of the new political situation became apparent when the Bavarian army followed Mansfeld across Germany and invaded the Palatinate from the south. At the same time, fearing the actions of English soldiers who had recently arrived in the area, Spinola brought his Spanish troops down from the Netherlands, and invaded the Palatinate from the north. Thus, at one stroke, two problems were joined. First, the question of the Empire and the emperor's right to transfer an electoral vote from one prince to another became a German problem; and, second, the strategical question of Spanish control in the Lowlands became a German, and ultimately a European, problem.

4. THE WAR FOR GERMANY, 1621–1635

In the years following the battle of the White Mountain, the factors that had led to the conflict were twisted and altered almost beyond recognition, and new problems, born during the course of the war, tended to become the central axis for policy. The religious issue that seemed on the surface so important in 1619–1621 never did become the clear-cut, single motive that determined men's acts. As the war progressed, the vague idea of "German liberties" which, in effect, urged the rights of the princes against the emperor became of much more significance. "German liberties" were obviously grounded in the ancient confederative structure of the Holy Roman Empire, and they had been considerably strengthened when the Reformation endowed each prince with the right to determine the religion of his subjects. In seventeenth-century dress those "German liberties" appeared as constitutional rights. However, the constitution of the Holy Roman Empire was not clearly defined, and when the Emperor Ferdinand found himself endowed with military power, he could insist that he too had "rights" as emperor, rights that might undermine the claims of the princes. There was a problem that could easily transcend religious issues, for if the emperor should establish his right to rule Germany, both the German princes and those who ruled the kingdoms on Germany's frontiers would be vitally affected. It was that threat that turned the war in Germany into a European war, for princes to the west and north of Germany could not ignore the danger that Hapsburg hegemony might make the Holy Roman Empire the first military power of Europe.

However much this might seem a purely political problem to twentieth-century men, in the seventeenth century it could not be separated from religious issues. Statesmen of that era were not able to separate God's church from His state, and so their political ambitions were intertwined with their religious convictions. That association of religion and politics gave great intensity to the actions of statesmen and soldiers, for they never doubted that God had appointed them to their task, nor that He would assure for them final victory. Lest we conceive of such ideas as hypocrisy or cant, it is well to remember that some of those men—the Emperor Ferdinand among them —actually flogged themselves to atone for their sins. It would be a mistake to think that such a man did not really believe the words he uttered about God's intentions on earth.

On the other hand, it is unquestionably true that popes, emperors, and princes all at one time or another acted from strong political motives, and that politics often made strange bedfellows. Lutheran Brandenburg and Saxony were reluctant to help the "Protestant cause" at one time because of their distrust of the intentions of Frederick of the Palatinate, at another because of their fear of the ambitions and policies of the Swedish king. Likewise Catholic France, even though governed by a devout king and a cardinal of the church, did not hesitate to ally itself with Protestant Sweden against the Catholic Hapsburgs. The complex of forces that led to the invasion of the Palatinate by Imperial and Spanish armies underlines the fact that military and political problems were of the utmost importance in extending the war in Germany. The emperor's political ambitions, Maximilian's desire to become an elector, Spinola's need to control his supply lines—those were the most important factors that changed the war from a conflict in Bohemia to a struggle for power, first in Germany, and then in Europe.

The invasion of the Palatinate and the renewal of Spain's war against the United Provinces set off a chain of military reactions from France to Denmark. Several German princes arose to defend the Palatinate, and Christian of Denmark in the triple role of president of the Lower Saxon Circle of the Empire, king of Denmark, and Protestant champion, also entered the lists to stop Imperial and Spanish aggression. At the same time, Cardinal Richelieu, who had recently become chief minister to the French king, seized the Alpine pass of the Valtelline to cut the Spanish supply line to Germany.

THE THIRTY YEARS' WAR
1619-1648

—— Holy Roman Empire
---- Spanish Supply Line

Thus by 1624 the Bohemian rebellion had grown into a central European war for the control of the Rhine valley.

At the opening of that phase of the war, the Emperor Ferdinand gained sizeable additions to his power. Confiscation of immense amounts of land from the Bohemian rebels had brought wealth to his treasury, while the reorganized Bohemian constitution provided a more secure basis for power. In addition, a new personality named Wallenstein, who had been an important purchaser of confiscated lands, emerged as a first-rate general who knew how to enlist and supply an imperial army. As long as Ferdinand had to depend on the Bavarian army, his policy was tied to that of Maximilian. When Wallenstein recruited an imperial army that actually overshadowed Tilly's Bavarians, Ferdinand could afford to act on his own.

The new military power soon made its influence felt. The Protestant armies were divided; Wallenstein followed one of them into Silesia, where it broke up and disappeared, while Tilly soundly defeated the Danish king at Lutter am Barenberge, in 1626. War was a slower business in the seventeenth century than it is today, and although Christian of Denmark had been defeated and much of his territory occupied, he did not officially withdraw from the war until 1629 under the Treaty of Lübeck. Richelieu had long since been forced to withdraw the French forces from the Valtelline. He had hardly occupied the pass when a Huguenot revolt and a threat of military retaliation from Austria forced him to make a truce with the Spaniards that freed their supply lines.

Victory in Germany opened up new vistas of power for Ferdinand and the Catholic party, but it also presented a problem. If Ferdinand seized the opportunity to grab more authority for himself as emperor, he must invade the rights and privileges of Catholic princes as well as Protestant. Wallenstein urged him to do so, depending on the new imperial army to ride roughshod over many of the so-called "German liberties." Such action would have been in keeping with the way Richelieu and Louis XIII were using force to suppress the nobles and Huguenots who were opposing the centralization of power in France. On the other hand, if Ferdinand used his new power only to reestablish the rights of the Catholic church in Germany, he would merely be trying to put the clock back to the period before the Reformation—a program that offered little chance of success. Actually he landed between the two policies, and compromised by issuing the Edict of Restitution in 1629. The Edict ordered that all lands taken from the Catholic church since the Peace of Passau in 1552 must be restored to it. In concrete terms, this meant that two archbishoprics, twelve bishoprics, several hundred monasteries, and other foundations would be returned to the church. It also involved the fate of great towns like Augsburg, Magdeburg, Minden, and Bremen, as well as the territories of several important Protestant princes. The Edict was in effect a punitive religious measure. Furthermore, since it was issued without the consent of the Imperial Diet, it was a declaration of the emperor's new power.

Almost immediately a storm of protest arose, for the Calvinists had lost all legal standing, and the Lutherans were deprived of the gains of three-quarters of a century. The Edict of Restitution was the high tide of the Catholic Counter-Reformation in Germany, but it could not be enforced unless there was adequate military power to back it up. As it turned out, Ferdinand was not the man to manipulate the complex problems of Germany in 1629. Those problems existed on several levels. In the first place, the Edict of Restitution aroused great opposition, especially when it became apparent to the Catholics as well as to the Protestants that it might be simply a foretaste of the exercise of new imperial authority. Thus a formidable political party began to grow up to oppose the Edict. There was, further, a second factor of equal importance to many people in Germany. Wallenstein not only controlled the most powerful military force in Germany, he also assumed the right to advise the emperor, and he had pushed himself into the ranks of the German princes by becoming Duke of Friedland. Which of his offenses angered his contemporaries the most? His meteoric rise from a mere Bohemian nobleman to sovereign prince over a Baltic principality had aroused jealousy and irritation. His advice to the emperor seems to have been audacious and dangerous to the rights of the princes. Men said that he hired astrologers to advise him; they seem to have understood politics as well as the stars. Finally, he was feared as the commander of the greatest military force in the empire. But that was not all. As Duke of Friedland, Wallenstein was in the act of creating an imperial navy on the Baltic. His intentions, however, were not clear, since he refused to cooperate with the Spaniards, and so they joined the German princes in testifying against him. Ferdinand, too, seems to have been fearful of his commander; the emperor was not a revolutionary by nature, and perhaps only a revolutionary could have made use of so dangerous a tool as Wallenstein and his army.

Ferdinand's own position was not completely secure; he was concerned about his family. He wanted to be sure that his son would follow him on the imperial throne. If the House of Hapsburg should fail to get the crown, what use was there in building up imperial power? But to get the electors to name his son King of the Romans (i.e., heir to the imperial throne), Ferdinand had to find the right kind of bribes. The Catholic and Protestant electors together demanded the dismissal of Wallenstein. Maximilian wanted Wallenstein's army to be placed under the command of his own General Tilly. Ferdinand reluctantly agreed to a modification of the Edict of Restitution, and less reluctantly perhaps he relieved Wallenstein of his command. Even so, the electors avoided electing a King of the Romans. They had further concessions yet to wring from the emperor.

The German princes were not the only ones who viewed the rise of Wallenstein, the Edict of Restitution, and the new imperial authority as dangerous. Cardinal Richelieu, first minister of the king of France, sympathized with any program that would roll back the Protestant advance, but he was even more anxious to check the power of the Hapsburgs. He could not intervene actively because he was engaged in a life and death struggle with the Huguenots and the nobles at home. However, he could help in other ways; he negotiated a peace between the kings of Sweden and Poland, so that Sweden would be free to fight in Germany, and he paid the Swedish king, Gustavus Adolphus, a subsidy to help fight the war.

Gustavus Adolphus had by this time also realized that Swedish intervention in Germany would serve his best interests. He saw himself as the protector of the Protestants, as the builder of an empire along the Baltic Sea, and finally as the creator of a new empire for all of northern Europe. All this could be accomplished with French money and Swedish arms. Thus,

Ferdinand found himself confronted by powerful new enemies just when he had dismissed his leading general, Wallenstein.

Gustavus Adolphus landed in Germany in July 1630. His intervention was not really welcomed by anyone there. His brother-in-law, the Elector of Brandenburg, as well as the Elector of Saxony, wished to remain neutral; most of the other princes also hoped that some sort of peace treaty could be formulated. Gustavus Adolphus' past history was anything but reassuring; he was then thirty-five years old, and already had about twenty years of war behind him. He knew how to fight, he had no limits to his ambition, and he had no real desire for peace. He would have had great difficulty to get any foothold in Germany had not the imperial army under Tilly committed a terrible act of brutality by sacking and almost completely destroying the city of Magdeburg in an attempt to enforce the Edict of Restitution. As a result, the scale was tipped in favor of the Swedish invaders, as Saxony and Brandenburg were prompted to join them against Tilly. The first Swedish army was, therefore, made up of some two thousand veterans of Gustavus Adolphus' Polish wars and about thirty thousand Saxons, Brandenburgers, and other miscellaneous troops. As it passed through Germany, it grew by making enlistments from the population and by enrolling deserters from the imperial and Bavarian armies.

The Swedish forces met and defeated Tilly's army at Breitenfeld near Leipzig (September 17, 1631). With this reversal of the military situation, middle Germany lay open to the invaders. Gustavus Adolphus then marched westward to the Rhine, imposing huge money fines upon the church principalities as he went. It was only then that Richelieu realized that he was not just a condottiere general in French pay, for the Swedish hero paid no attention to the fact that France was also allied with Bavaria and the Catholic states. He was willing to accept French money, but used it to make war on France's allies as well as on her enemies. Adolphus was also dreaming of founding a great Protestant Swedish empire that would include all of northern Europe, and that might easily become an even greater menace to France than the Hapsburg Empire.

From the Rhine, Gustavus Adolphus turned southward, and invaded Bavaria, driving off both Maximilian and Tilly, who was killed. The meteoric career of the Swedish king forced Ferdinand to recall Wallenstein, although all his advisers warned him against this move. No one but Wallenstein had the prestige or the ability to raise a new army to resist the Swedes. Gustavus Adolphus then turned north again to meet Wallenstein at the battle of Lützen (November 16, 1632). The result was a victory for the Swedes insofar as their army remained in possession of the field of battle, but Gustavus Adolphus' death deprived them of the leadership necessary to follow up the victory. Wallenstein lost his best general, Pappenheim, but he withdrew in good order, and was soon in a good position to defend himself and the emperor against the enemy. On their side, the Swedes, unable to carry out the dead king's plans for a Swedish empire, were still determined to retain their position on the Baltic. Neither side was strong enough to impose a peace on the other, but both were strong enough to defend themselves.

The events of the next three years were a jumble of intrigue and politics in which Spaniards, Swedes, and Frenchmen, as well as the several factions in Germany, struggled for supremacy. The most dramatic intrigue resulted in the assassination of Wallenstein, who had become convinced that the emperor stood in the way of peace and had therefore opened negotiations with the enemy. He was murdered in February 1634 with the consent of Ferdinand; perhaps so dangerous a servant could expect no other treatment. A more important event of the same year was the battle of Nördlingen, in which the Imperial and Spanish forces defeated the Swedes. That victory seemed to offer a chance of peace that would remove the Swedes from Germany. Early in 1635 a treaty was drawn up at Prague between the Catholic and Protestant German princes to settle the religious and political problems and to pave the way for common action against the Swedes. Were this treaty of Prague actually to become imperial law, the war would be ended, leaving the emperor with a considerable amount of power in his hands. Such reasoning led to Richelieu's decision that France should enter the conflict as an ally of Sweden and a friend of any enemy of the House of Hapsburg. It was to be thirteen more years before peace would be written.

The situation in 1635 illustrates the character of the Thirty Years' War well. There had been five decisive battles—those of the White Mountain, Lutter am Barenberge, Breitenfeld, Lützen, and Nördlingen. The imperial forces had won four of them, and yet had been unable to impose a peace. Fundamentally, their failure stemmed from the fact that the war was not merely a German civil war. It was closely related to the conflict between Spain and the United Provinces in the Netherlands, and victory in Germany did not spell defeat for the Dutch. It was also related to the struggle for European power that had first manifested itself in the wars between the French Valois kings and the Hapsburgs. In the seventeenth century, the French Bourbons, Henry IV, Louis XIII, and Louis XIV, continued that conflict. Thus, even if Ferdinand had been able to suppress "German liberties," he would still have had the French, the Dutch, and other powers like the Danes and the Swedes with whom to contend. Of all of those, the French were the most dangerous, and after 1635 the Thirty Years' War entered the French stage.

5. THE WAR FOR EUROPE, 1635–1648

German historians tell the story of those last years of the war as a tale of horror that has not been surpassed even by the awful destruction that Germany suffered in the Second World War in the twentieth century. Possibly self-pity has exaggerated the tragedy that overtook the nation, but even so there is evidence of destruction and devastation on a colossal scale. The soldiers who fought the war marched with the "four horsemen" at the head of the column. Wherever they passed, villages were pillaged and burned, people were murdered, and disease and famine were left as mementos. The armies could keep their ranks filled only by enlisting the peasants from captured lands; they destroyed the peasants' chance of making a living except in the ranks. However, the armies could not visit all Germany each year. There were few districts that were not visited at least once, and there were several that suffered a number of invasions, but between the visitations the crops grew as usual and men labored to mitigate the suffering. However, it is true that Germany did not recover from the war for half a century or more.

The armies were all about the same, regardless of what flag they fought under or who led them. Although there were men from many nations in the ranks, the vast majority were Germans, uprooted by the war. Their discipline was poor, their training sketchy, and their equipment nondescript. The uniformed army that responded to "spit and polish" discipline was still in the future. The pikemen were the hard core of the infantry. Along with the pikemen, and usually placed where they could be defended from cavalry charges, were troops armed with muskets and arquebuses. Their firepower was too weak to be really effective, but they were already becoming an important part of the army. The cavalry, armed with sabers, lances, and pistols, were an element for shock action and pursuit, but pikes had considerably reduced the cavalrymen's function on the battlefield. The thrust of the pike was the decisive factor, and the pike was thus "queen" of the field. Artillerymen were still considered to be laborers and engineers rather than soldiers; their weapons were principally useful in sieges rather than in field battles.

The soldiers were accompanied by hordes of camp followers. Some authorities estimate that there were three to five women and children for every soldier. The camp followers cared for the soldiers' needs on the march, and nursed them if they became ill or wounded. They served the functions that commissary and hospital corps were later to assume. They also increased the disorder created by the armies. If the discipline among the troops was lax, there was none at all among the rabble that followed in their wake. They brought disease wherever they went, and removed everything that was not defended with considerable force. A disorderly army marching through a province would leave it stripped of everything that could be carried away.

By bringing France into the war in 1635 as an ally of Sweden Richelieu destroyed the possibility of a peace being negotiated which would leave the Empire intact. There were to be thirteen years more of desultory, indecisive war before treaty could be arranged. France did not by any means escape unscathed in the disaster that engulfed Germany. Richelieu had declared war before he had any army worthy of the name, and before he could as-semble one, a Spanish-Imperialist force had invaded France. The invaders failed to reach Paris (more because of their own lack of power than because of French valor), but they ravaged the border provinces. Finally Richelieu secured the services of an army (that of Bernhard of Saxe-Weimar) and eventually built up a force capable of meeting the Spaniards and the Imperial veterans in the field. He died in 1642, a year before the French forces under a young prince of the House of Condé won France's first great victory over Spain at Rocroi.

It would be fruitless to follow the last years of the war in any detail. One by one the original actors followed Gustavus Adolphus and Wallenstein to the grave, leaving behind younger men who did not remember a world at peace to direct the course of events. Those younger men were more interested in their own problems than in the issues that had been important at the be-ginning of the war. It was hard to justify the destruction of a province in terms that included God's will, and after about 1640 most of the actors in the drama relied less and less upon religious or ideological arguments of jus-tify policies that were obviously opportunistic in nature. For instance, after having fought Spain for three generations, the Dutch became convinced that they must defend Spanish holdings in the Netherlands to prevent them from falling into French hands. After the battle of Rocroi, France had become too strong to suit the politicians in Amsterdam. France, they decided, was a good friend but an unfortunate neighbor. They preferred a decadent Spanish authority on their southern frontier.

In Germany, the new Emperor Ferdinand III was much less a man of the Counter-Reformation than his father had been. He realized that the Edict of Restitution could not be enforced, that the imperial power could not really be given new authority, but he was determined to hold together the Hapsburg Danubian territories. It would be one thing to admit the right of the German princes to control their own affairs or even to cede to France imperial territory in the Rhineland; it would be quite another to lose Bo-hemia. In other words, the emperor recognized that his interests as emperor could be sacrificed to strengthen his position as a territorial prince.

The Spaniards wanted peace too, but their situation was somewhat more complicated. After Richelieu's death, French policy had fallen into the hands of the queen mother (a Spanish princess) and Cardinal Mazarin, one of the cleverest statesmen of the era. They were resolved to raise the throne of the boy king, Louis XIV, to the primary position in Europe. That would entail, of course, the submission of Spain and the annexation of Spanish territory. To achieve those ends, Mazarin was willing to separate the war in Germany from the war in the Netherlands and Spain, where French and Spanish forces were engaged in desperate conflicts. Thus, at the peace conference in Germany the Franco-Spanish war was kept out of the negotiations.

The Swedes were willing to make peace if their Baltic empire were recognized. After the death of Gustavus Adolphus, Sweden's policy had turned entirely on her demand for control over the south coast of the Baltic Sea. Fortunately for Sweden, Mazarin regarded the Baltic empire as a necessary check upon the German Hapsburgs, and therefore the Swedish demands were backed by the power of France.

The Congress of Westphalia that wrote the treaties of peace took five years (1643-1648) to complete its task. The political problems it faced were difficult, but the most important reason for the delay was the fact that war continued after the Congress first met. Without an armistice to end the fighting, the basic fact that war is a continuation of politics became the most important factor at the peace table. Both sides eagerly followed the fighting, and stiffened or relaxed their terms in response to news from the front. In the meantime, Germany suffered cruelly from the continual devastation.

The Treaties of Westphalia were finally completed in 1648. In a way they became a sort of basic constitution for the new Europe in that they provided a reasonably clear-cut definition of the "modern" sovereign state, as well as a territorial settlement for all of central Europe. In those treaties, the medieval organization of politics with its multiplicity of feudal relationships and its religious orientation had completely disappeared: they were civil treaties that announced the secularization of politics and the end of inter-Christian wars fought under religious flags. The new states that emerged were both sovereign and independent, owing no responsibilities to any power on earth. Those states, rather than any ideal of pope, emperor, or Christendom, were henceforth to be recognized frankly as the central forces of political life. Even in Germany most of the Holy Roman Emperor's power was effectively ended by the recognition of the political rights of the princes. The treaties reaffirmed the power of the prince to impose his religion on his own subjects, *cujus regio ejus religio;* they also endowed each prince in Germany with the right to make alliances and treaties and to form leagues with any other prince in Europe. There was the essence of sovereignty: the emperor had recognized each prince's right to control the internal and external affairs of his principality.

The territorial settlements within the Empire, by and large, benefited the more important princes—Brandenburg, Prussia, Saxony, Bavaria, and Hanover. They were among the states that had enlarged their holdings at the expense of their smaller neighbors and ecclesiastical lands. Frederick William of Brandenburg was particularly fortunate in the territories that came to his House, for he managed to get a foothold on the lower Rhine, to increase his holdings near Brandenburg, and to retain his lands in east Prussia. Thus Brandenburg began its career as a Protestant counterweight to Hapsburg Austria. The Count Palatine of the Rhine (Palatinate) recovered Frederick's electoral vote, and an eighth Electoral Hat was created for the Duke of Bavaria. There were many other changes in the German map, but most of them were of no great significance for the future of either Germany or Europe.

The situation on the frontiers of Germany was as important as the settlement within the Empire. Sweden's Baltic empire retained its foothold in Pomerania, and with it Sweden acquired a vote in the Diet of the Holy Roman Empire. Sweden's relative military power was due to decline, but, as a French ally, she fitted into the new balance of power as the ruler of the north.

In the west, the United Netherlands and the Swiss Confederation were both formally recognized as independent states, no longer even nominally within the Holy Roman Empire. The Swiss were still important, primarily as a source for mercenary soldiers. The Dutch provinces were one of the great military, naval, and commercial powers of Europe. The most important power in the west, France, did not finally establish the full extent of her gains from the wars until 1659 when the Treaty of the Pyrenees ended the war between France and Spain; but at Westphalia her foothold in the Rhineland at Metz, Toul, Verdun, and Alsace was formally recognized, while her role as ally and protector of both Catholic and Protestant German princes emphasized the fact that France had become the most important power in Europe.

In the south, the Hapsburg holdings in Austria and the neighboring German provinces in Hungary and Bohemia emerged from the Thirty Years' War as the embryo of the Danubian monarchy of later generations. Ferdinand II had been unsuccessful in his attempt to give real power to the imperial throne, but he was a veritable founding father of the state that his descendants were to develop. In a very real sense the Hapsburgs gave up much of the questionable dignity of the imperial crown in return for a chance to make an empire out of Hungary, Bohemia, and Austria.

In conclusion then, the Treaties of Westphalia formally ended an old era and opened a new one. It should be noted, however, that much of the political structure that they recognized as a legal fact had already been functioning for several generations. By formally recognizing political institutions such as the independence of the United Provinces and the Swiss Confederation, the treaties recorded the facts that the historical evolution of the preceding generations had completed. By recording the new powers of Sweden, France, and Hapsburg Austria, they recognized the outcome of the wars.

Obviously the Thirty Years' War did not achieve many of the objectives that the men of 1618 had had in mind, but it settled a considerable number of issues in Europe, and in a very real way the treaties ending the war became the basis for central Europe of the future.

With the end of the Thirty Years' War there came also the end of the Reformation era. For almost a hundred years European men had organized civil and international conflicts under religious flags as justification for their behavior; after 1648 it became increasingly difficult to justify war in the name of God. This is not to say that the complete secularization of society had been accomplished; men still believed that God inspired their actions and blessed their projects, but they no longer so readily justified wars and rebellions by appealing directly to His sanction. After the middle of the seventeenth century European men discovered other bases on which to organize their projects for society.

BOOK III

The Seventeenth Century: Tension and Conflict

In the seventeenth century, European men experienced a series of crises that drastically altered many aspects of their civilization. As we look back on the period, there seem to have been two movements that were particularly significant. The first was the rise of the bureaucratic state as a political institution capable of mobilizing political and military power on a scale theretofore unknown. The new state organization emerged amid more or less violent disturbances of the traditional political life in both the internal and international politics of Europe. The second movement was the development of a new approach to the problems of the natural world: a scientific revolution that forced men to discard many of their traditional explanations. Whether the political evolution that concentrated power in the hands of centralized authority and the scientific revolution that overthrew Aristotle and enthroned mathematics were related to each other, or rather, whether both depended on deeper forces at work in the seventeenth century, are questions that we shall not try to answer.

Marxist historians have an advantage over us at this point. They "know" that art, politics, religion, and science—indeed all aspects of man's life—are determined by the economic forces at work in society. If we could be content with this faith, it would be easy to relate the whole process to the economic structure of the seventeenth century. Such an explanation would be disarmingly alluring. How better can one explain the rise of the military-bureaucratic states than by the fact that Europe's economy became mature enough to support these political and economic institutions? At first glance, it seems harder to explain the scientific revolution, and yet Marxist historians have "succeeded" in doing this too. By the opening of the seventeenth century, so their argument goes, man's technological development—mining, weaving, navigation, metal working, and so forth—had reached a point where it created questions regarding the nature of the world, and it was to answer those that men turned to science. Galileo's interest in motion is thus reduced to his desire to solve the problems of firing cannons, making clocks, and controlling water. We should be careful not to deride that idea, for even though the Marxist explanations are too simple, there can be no doubt that there is a relationship between economic life and politics, between technology and science, and yet it is imperative to question whether or not there are other forces that may also be significant.

As we shall see in this Book, it is clear that there are many factors involved in political evolution. Theorists of the seventeenth century were deeply concerned with the problems of constitutional forms. The onward march of society would not permit political institutions to be frozen, and yet there were conservative forces in every section of Europe that stood ready to protect traditional rights and liberties. Frequently, this conflict resulted in civil war. In some of its aspects the Thirty Years' War in Germany was a manifestation of this strife, and as we shall see the Puritan rebellion in England, the Fronde in France, and the conflicts between princes and their rebellious noblemen in Germany, Sweden, Hungary, Poland, and elsewhere were expressions of the political crisis of the era. In studying these conflicts and the resultant constitutional developments, the most interesting problem for the student of history is the *form* of the process. The past history of the German, French, and English crowns and the legal structures within those lands had already set characteristic patterns for constitutional development in each kingdom. In this Book we are concerned with developing both the forms of the constitutional evolution of the major European states and the differences among them. Therefore the reader should keep in mind the earlier discussion of feudalism and the feudal monarchies, as well as the problems of the Renaissance princes.

The political tensions of the era were not confined to problems within states. The broadening horizons of the seventeenth century involved all Europe and, toward the end of the century, parts of the world beyond Europe in a larger political process. In the earlier eras, the dynastic interests of princes were the paramount factors in their relations with each other, but in the course of the seventeenth century the idea of "interests of state" growing out of economic, strategical, and political considerations gave new direction to international politics. Perhaps most important of all, the rise of France under Louis XIV to the position of a great military power that might create a new universal state by absorbing the Spanish and the German empires created problems for all the rest of Europe. In coping with the threat of France, Europe learned to organize coalitions that became the basis for a balance of power and a sort of constitution for the continent as a whole.

At the same time that the emergence of new constitutional forms mirrored the political crisis of the seventeenth century, tensions in religion, philosophy, and learning reflected the fact that a crisis in the conscience of men was also a problem of the period. The scientific revolution is undoubtedly the most dramatic component of this crisis, and yet to the discoveries about the nature of the physical world we must add the information contributed by travelers who had visited the greater world and by historians who probed into past societies. When men became convinced that the earth was not the center of the universe, when they learned that physical phenomena on the earth could best be described in terms of mathematics rather than of human motives or feelings, and when men realized that there were other human beings, non-Christian in religion, who had a morality as lofty as that of European men, many of the traditional views about man and the world had to be drastically revised. This is a story as significant for the development of western civilization as the story of the emerging political and economic institutions of Europe.

There is a school of historians that insists that the crises of the seventeenth century can best be approached by studying the art forms of the period. Just as the medieval era may be called "Gothic" and the fifteenth and sixteenth centuries "Renaissance," so the seventeenth century may be summed up by the word "Baroque." There can be no doubt that the baroque style is one of the great art forms created by western man and that it evolved in the atmosphere of the crises of that century, and it is probably true also that the baroque style mirrors part of the social and political forms of the period. It may not be equally true that one can isolate all the factors that are uniquely baroque and weld them into a synthesis that will explain the era, yet discussions of the seventeenth century that omit the baroque artistic movement cannot explain its problems and its triumphs. It might even be said that in the "flowers" created by artists and architects we find the truest expression of the ideals and ambitions of seventeenth-century European man.

BIBLIOGRAPHY FOR BOOK III

The three volumes of *The Rise of Modern Europe* for the seventeenth century (Friedrich, Nussbaum, and Wolf) present a general picture of the period and also an interesting problem in the interpretation of history. They each start with widely different assumptions about the historical process; taken together then, they provide the student with an interesting object lesson in historiography. The general textbook histories of the seventeenth century are all written by Europeans. In the United States popular courses on seventeenth-century history are rare to nonexistent.

Friedrich, Carl, *The Age of the Baroque, 1610–1660*, New York, Harper, 1952.

Nussbaum, Frederick, *The Triumph of Science and Reason, 1660–1685*, New York, Harper, 1953.

Wolf, John B., *The Emergence of the Great Powers, 1685–1715*, New York, Harper, 1951.

Clark, George, *The Seventeenth Century*, Oxford, England, Clarendon, 1929.

Ogg, David, *Europe in the Seventeenth Century*, 4th ed., London, Black, 1943.

Wakeman, O. H., *The Ascendency of France, 1598–1715*, New York, Macmillan, 1897.

Notestein, W., *The English People on the Eve of Colonization*, New York, Harper, 1954.

Packard, Laurence, *The Age of Louis XIV*, New York, Holt, 1929.

Perkins, J. B., *France under Mazarin*, 4th ed., New York, Putnam, 1894.

Perkins, J. B., *Richelieu and the Growth of French Power*, New York, Putnam, 1900.

Schevill, F., *The Great Elector*, Chicago, University of Chicago Press, 1947.

Sumner, B. H., *Peter the Great and the Emergence of Russia*, New York, Macmillan, 1951.

Trevelyan, G. M., *England under the Stuarts*, 15th ed., New York, Putnam, 1930.

Trevelyan, G. M., *The English Revolution, 1688–1689*, London, Butterworth, 1938.

Wedgwood, Cicely, *Richelieu and the French Monarchy*, New York, Macmillan, 1950.

Willson, D. Harris, *King James VI and I*, London, Cape, 1956.

ECONOMIC, MILITARY, AND DIPLOMATIC HISTORY

Heaton, H., *Economic History of Europe*, rev. ed., New York, Harper, 1948.

Clough, S. B., and C. W. Cole, *Economic History of Europe*, 3rd ed., Boston, Heath, 1952.

Cole, C. W., *Colbert and a Century of French Mercantilism*, New York, Columbia University Press, 1939, 2 vols.

Earle, E. M., ed., *Makers of Modern Strategy*, Princeton, Princeton University Press, 1943.

Heckscher, E. F., *Mercantilism*, London, Allen and Unwin, 1935, 2 vols.

Mahan, A. T., *The Influence of Sea Power on History, 1660–1783*, Boston, Little, Brown, 1890.

Petrie, C., *Earlier Diplomatic History, 1492–1713*, New York, Macmillan, 1949.

Vagts, A., *A History of Militarism*, New York, Norton, 1937.

CULTURAL HISTORY

(Paperback editions are cited whenever possible.)

Bronowski, J., and B. Maglish, *The Western Intellectual Tradition*, New York, Harper, 1960.

Brinton, C., *Ideas and Men*, New York, Prentice-Hall, 1950.

Bukofzer, M. F., *Music in the Baroque Era*, New York, Norton, 1947.

Butterfield, H., *The Origins of Modern Science, 1300–1800*, New York, Macmillan, 1951.

Clark, George, *Science and Social Welfare in the Age of Newton*, Oxford, England, Clarendon, 1937.

Guerard, Albert, *The Life and Death of an Ideal: France in the Classical Age*, New York, Scribner, 1928.

Hall, A. R., *The Scientific Revolution, 1500–1800*, Boston, Beacon, 1956.

Hazard, P., *The European Mind, 1680–1715*, London, Hollis & Carter, 1953.

Lang, P. H., *Music in Western Cvilization*, New York, Norton, 1941.

Randall, J. H., *The Making of the Modern Mind*, rev. ed., Boston, Houghton Mifflin, 1940.

Smith, P., *A History of Modern Culture*, vol. 1, New York, Holt, 1930.

Smith, T. V., and Marjorie Grene, *From Descartes to Kant: Readings in the Philosophy of the Renaissance and Enlightenment*, Chicago, University of Chicago Press, 1940.

Whitehead, A. N., *Science and the Modern World*, New York, New American Library.

Willey, B., *The Seventeenth Century Background*, New York, Anchor, 1953.

Wolf, A., *A History of Science, Technology, and Philosophy in the Sixteenth and Seventeenth Centuries*, rev. ed., London, Allen & Unwin, 1950.

Louis le Nain, "Family of Peasants" (Paris, Louvre). Louis le Nain liked to paint peasants, but evidence would indicate that these people were among the two or three percent of the population that might be considered wealthy.

Chapter 10

EUROPEAN ECONOMIC SOCIETY IN THE SIXTEENTH AND SEVENTEENTH CENTURIES

1. CONDITIONS OF LIFE

We often think of the great discoveries that opened the routes of trade to Asia and the Americas as the really decisive events in the economic history of Europe after 1500, yet most of the men who lived in Europe during the sixteenth and seventeenth centuries had only the vaguest notion of the world beyond their own provinces, let alone of the world that the explorers were discovering beyond the seas. A few intellectuals, a few merchants and seamen, and a few officials were aware of that greater world, but even those people, as we read their papers today, had an incomplete conception of its meaning. The great mass of men who tilled the fields or followed some craft lived out their lives without even any clear idea of the existence of people and countries outside Europe. It was not until the latter eighteenth century that the world commercial organization began to assert itself as a dominant factor in the life of European men.

An overwhelming majority of the people of Europe in the sixteenth and seventeenth centuries still lived in villages and small towns. Historians used to give descriptions of those villages and towns, but the research of the last half century has indicated that the one characteristic that seems to apply to all of them is diversity. There was no single pattern: each village had its own history, its characteristic architecture and building materials, and its traditional social patterns. Within a province or a district, there frequently was considerable similarity, but a whole kingdom, like France for example, defies easy generalization. The same is true of the towns. Most of them had walls for protection, but each of them had its own past, peculiar to it alone.

The one generalization that seems to hold for each town is that the walls created congestion within it which must have resulted in somewhat less than sanitary conditions, even by primitive standards.

In addition to the thousands of villages and hundreds of towns, there were a few large cities. In Paris, London, Florence, Rome, Amsterdam, Venice, and perhaps a dozen others where the pulse of economic life was brisk, the inhabitants, or at least the important inhabitants, were in contact with each other and with the centers of commerce on the edges of Europe's world (the Far East, the Americas, and the Levant). Each of those cities had developed its own characteristic pattern of life, its own particular style. The diversity that we see in our own day was even greater three hundred years ago when local architects depended upon the models about them rather than international styles for their inspiration, and when traditional patterns of society were less affected by cosmopolitan intercourse than they are today. The large cities, like the towns, were surrounded by walls that restricted the area of their growth. Not until the eighteenth century could they rely on the king's army to protect them from marauders. Thus, at least until 1715 the constricting effects of the walls continued to be a primary conditioning factor in urban growth.

One fact stands out in considering villages, towns, and cities—namely, the poverty of the great mass of men. It does not matter what province or what country is studied; poverty seems to be the general rule for all, and in times of stress—that is, of war, drought, or pestilence—poverty became acute. The French have a word for it—*misère*—which means total privation, poverty that becomes want. Naturally *misère* was unusual, but poverty was not. Few men in the villages ever used or even handled anything that originated more than a few miles from their homes. Two French painters, La Tour and Le Nain, have left us magnificent pictures of peasant life. In their pictures the iron or copper kettles that served as universal cooking utensils and the glasses from which peasants were sipping wine may well have come from a distance, but all the other articles—cloth, tools, furniture—betray local peasant manufacture. We know that iron kettles were handed down from generation to generation as valued possessions; we do not have much literary confirmation of the notion that many peasants had glasses from which to drink their wine. Indeed, most of the descriptions of the peasants do not seem to be about the idealized people depicted on Le Nain's canvases. A recent sociological study of the district around Beauvais has discovered that one or two percent of the peasants might own fifty to a hundred acres of land and the horses necessary to exploit it. These men were "well off," but the vast majority of the peasants were living on the edge of *misère*. Reports presented to the regent of France at the Estates-General of 1614 or the literary pictures painted by La Bruyère are almost brutal in their description of peasant needs. La Bruyère speaks of "wild animals" living in "hovels" constantly haunted by want. Similar pictures can be found for German, Scandinavian, and English country people; not all were in want, but nearly all were poor, and all were dependent upon the village for practically everything they had, for everything they used. This was the same culture pattern that we described for the medieval era: the economy depended upon self-sufficient and self-sustaining villages. Such an economy can provide for minimum human wants so long as things go well, but in times of stress (crop failure or war), want and starvation were the peasants' lot.

The study of the Beauvais area exemplifies sharply the problem of the poor people. Their incomes were enough to provide the family with bread as long as the harvest was normal, but whenever there were crop failures, they found their obligations to the church, the state, the lord, the money lenders, and others who lived off the peasants too heavy to bear. Frequently the terrible result was simply starvation. During at least four periods of the seventeenth century large numbers of the poor had to die for lack of enough to eat. Those were harsh years when the population was kept firmly in control by the grisly hand of death.

Towns were hardly less self-sufficient than villages. When we talk about the urban commerce of this period we think of the great cities like London or Amsterdam, but recent studies have shown that even reasonably large provincial cities like Toulouse or Zurich were only to a small degree involved in the great commerce of the metropolitan areas. Provincial towns tended to produce nearly everything that their inhabitants used and most of the things that they considered to be their cherished possessions. The Dutch painters have provided us with pictures of the interiors of urban dwellings, some of them owned by wealthy bourgeoisie, others by humble craftsmen. A striking feature of the paintings is the relative lack of household goods. The furniture is of local origin, the cloth and utensils of domestic manufacture. We see the women spinning, weaving, and sewing the garments worn by the family; the toys of the children are simple and crude, obvious made by "do it yourself" craftsmen at home.

The difference between poverty and comfort in the urban dwellings seems to have been more widespread than that found in the country. Some of the merchants and master craftsmen were well to do; most of the townsmen seem to have lived in comfortable poverty; some of them were in desperate want. But in any case the lot of the townsmen could change drastically. A plague or a famine in the district could have disastrous effects in spite of the fact that the town usually tried to maintain a year's supply of bread stuffs in reserve; a war or a siege could be even more catastrophic. Richelieu's siege of La Rochelle, for example, cut its population by two-thirds in one year; some of the German towns in the Thirty Years' War suffered similar casualties; and towns in the Lowlands (present-day Belgium) were under threat of siege during most of the seventeenth century.

In contrast to the towns, the large urban centers exhibited greater extremes of wealth and poverty. Like great cities in any age, they were the haunts of adventurers, beggars, thieves, merchants, prelates, princes, and every other sort of man. Life in the great cities was almost as insecure as it was in the rural villages, for while famine could not ordinarily exhaust all the stores of grain piled up to stave off want, it did raise the price of bread to a point where many could hardly afford to eat. Furthermore, fire and plague were the near-constant companions of the great cities: in some years plague and pestilence seemed to abate; in others it broke out with great destructive force. The annals of mid-seventeenth-century London give striking illustrations of the destructive power of fire and plague; superstitious men of that period believed that God had visited these evils upon them because of the Puritan revolution. With rather more realism, Huxley pointed out that control of refuse and better fire-fighting equipment were the factors that reduced the destructive force of these twin agents of evil.

When catastrophe overtook the harvests, the poorer people in the towns were in much the same position as the poorer people in the country. In Beauvais, for example, during a good year the poorer workers (and they made up well over three-fourths of the community) had an income amounting to about three times as much as they had to pay for bread. In a year of bad harvests, if the price of bread doubled, those people had to live in straitened circumstances; if it tripled, they faced misery and death. The price of bread in Beauvais doubled in 1609, 1618, 1623, 1627, 1631, 1632, 1643, 1647, 1674, 1679, 1699, and 1714; it tripled in 1649, 1651, 1661–1662; it quadrupled in 1693–1694 and 1710. It is not surprising to find that the years when bread prices soared were the same years in which there was a heavy mortality rate. Of the "four horsemen," Famine seems to have been the greatest scourge on the community; "he" was, of course, closely followed by Pestilence, War, and Death.

Population statistics for this period are very difficult to assess. There were no census reports, and such figures as do exist are often suspect. Even so, there is pretty good evidence to support the thesis that the population of Europe in 1700 was about the same as it had been in 1500. In any three decades the population of a district might vary between ten and, in extreme cases, fifty percent, but over a century or so the total change was slight. Taking the period 1400–1789, the population of France, for example, varied between fifteen and twenty millions; both of these limits seem to have been controlled by the checks and balances inherent in the society of the period. This sort of population problem is very different from the one confronting the world of the twentieth century. In our time we seem to be faced with ever increasing numbers. Between 1500 and about 1750 the population of Europe was apparently nearly stable; since 1750 it has been growing apace.

At the opening of the nineteenth century Malthus discovered, amongst other things, that there were two factors controlling population: the number of births and the number of deaths. By his time, the population of Europe was beginning to increase, and Malthus became greatly concerned about the supplies of food needed to feed the ever growing number of mouths. Had he lived a hundred years earlier he probably would not have noticed the problem at all, for the conditions of life that had prevailed for several centuries before 1730 had assured a balance of births and deaths. Recent studies seem to show that young women usually married early in their twenties, and that each marriage produced about five children; some of them had only one child for they died in their first childbirth; others had ten or more. The harvest of death matched the flow of births: some twenty-nine percent of the children died in their first year; another fifteen percent died between the ages of one and four; four percent between the ages of four and nine; and another four percent between nine and nineteen. Thus, about forty-eight percent of all children born lived to the age at which they normally began to reproduce. If the figure of an average of five children per marriageable female is considered with the fact that a sizeable number of girls entered the convent or remained unmarried, it becomes clear that the population was nearly in balance.

There are numerous studies of the population problems of pre-eighteenth-century Europe. One of the best ones produced the chart below. This breaks down the number of deaths per thousand of the population by age groups and also by "normal" and "crisis" years. The latter were years of severe plague or famine. From this study it can be seen that at least 88.9 percent of the population was under fifty-five years old, and that, in spite of the high rate of infant mortality, over fifty percent of the population was under twenty-five years old. The other interesting discovery of this study is the fact that in "normal" years the absolute number of deaths in each age group tended to be the same after the age of four. In years of crisis people over forty-five years tended to have a slightly larger number of funerals than their juniors. The percentages of the age group that died each year became larger every year after the fifteenth.

This was the pattern of deaths. The newly born died from a host of problems associated with childbirth and the care of infants; those who were lucky enough to reach five years of age could take their chances with the annual "fevers" at the end of summer, the respiratory illnesses of winter, and the epidemics that struck at unannounced times. People became physically old earlier than they do now in the twentieth century. The diet was poor, there was no dental care, and the labor needed to keep alive was heavy. Among the peasants, a woman of forty was old, worn out by pregnancies and hard labor; a man of forty-five was old, bowed down by illness and hard work. There were some who reached eighty, but such were the rare exceptions. Among the townspeople, some families fared better, perhaps because of im-

Population Per 1000	Annual Deaths for Normal Year			Deaths in Years of Severe Crisis	
Ages	Number of People	Percentage of Age Group	Absolute Number	Percentage of Age Group	Absolute Number
0–1	36	23.0	8 or 9	69.6	25
1–4	94	7.2	6 or 7	21.6	20
5–14	204	1.0	2	3	6
15–24	184	1.2	2 or 3	3.6	7
25–34	147	1.5	2 or 3	4.5	7
35–44	124	1.9	2 or 3	5.7	7
45–54	100	2.6	2 or 3	7.8	8
55–64	66	4.3	2 or 3	12.9	8
65–74	34	7.8	2 or 3	23.4	8
75–84	10	16.1	2	48.3	6
85 and over	1	28.8	2	86.4	6

From Bourgeois-Pichat, *Population*, n° 4, 1951.

proved diet and lesser need for labor; but, on the other hand, the townsfolk were more exposed to epidemics than the peasants. We need only follow the fortunes of a family—even a royal family like that of Louis XIV—to see the harvest of death; there was hardly a year between 1660 and 1715 that Louis did not receive news of a death in his family. The most persistent news was of the deaths of young children, but adults also died in what we would consider to be the bloom of life.

There were many factors responsible for this grisly harvest. Bad teeth, skin diseases, hernias, and goiters were apparently very common; all four drastically cut down vitality. Teeth especially caused trouble; even today Europeans are particularly prone to tooth decay. Three hundred years ago the only cure was to pull out the offending tooth; a tooth or two can be lost without too much penalty, but the loss of five or six may go far toward making a cripple. Plague and endemic diseases were even more effective causes of death. The microbe and the virus traveled with the merchants and the soldiers; smallpox (the dreaded killer), scarlet fever, diphtheria, tuberculosis, influenza, syphilis, and gonorrhea, as well as the plague, moved from place to place with merchandise and troops. It was rare for an epidemic to reach the proportions of the fourteenth-century Black Death (bubonic plague), but it was not entirely uncommon for one to kill ten to fifteen percent of the population of a district or town in a single year. In reading the records of the era, one is constantly struck by the fact that these diseases were no respecters of position or place; men of royal blood died of smallpox just like poor people. Perhaps the townsmen were more often exposed to disease, especially typhoid fever and amoebic dysentery (water pollution), than were the peasants, but townsmen, too, had immunities to diseases that the peasants failed to acquire.

The greatest check on the population was infant mortality and the death of young mothers. A father who reached the age of forty-five had a good chance of having had from five to fifteen children—not all by one wife, of course. Many of those children died at birth; most of them never reached the age of ten. Even a king could count on losing more children than survived in spite of the fact that his children had better care and better diet than that of the multitude. The death of young women of childbearing age also tended to keep down the population. Among the poor, girls began to bear children between the ages of eighteen and twenty-five; by thirty-five, if they survived, many of them had often lost their beauty and become old women. Among the wealthy classes, the women fared somewhat better, for servants were cheap and superior diet and care prolonged their lives somewhat. Both rich and poor women, however, were threatened with death in childbirth; the midwives may have had children themselves, but their "old wives' tales" were poor substitutes for twentieth-century obstetrical care. In a recent study of peasant families, it was interesting to see that in the early years of marriage, males tended to become widowers, but after the couple reached thirty the female was more apt to become a widow. If they could get past their first or second pregnancy, women had a reasonable chance of survival.

2. THE FRAMEWORK OF AGRICULTURE

As we have seen in the discussion of medieval agriculture, the methods of farming, the structure of land tenure, and the conditions of life varied from place to place. This variety was still manifest at the end of the seventeenth century and continued to be true into the twentieth. By the end of the seventeenth century, however, much of Europe showed little change in agricultural technique from that practised in the fourteenth. This apparent timelessness of rural life is deceptive, and yet, were a peasant of the fourteenth century miraculously transferred into the latter seventeenth, he would have had little difficulty understanding most of the conditions of life in his village. On the other hand, an early eighteenth-century peasant dropped into a twentieth-century environment would find it very hard to comprehend.

Even so, changes were taking place. The forces which control man's economic life are difficult to assess. In general, it may be said that throughout Europe control over land and the right to the surplus fruits of the soil tended to remain concentrated in very few hands. Yet there were changes in the personnel of land ownership. The Reformation in Protestant Europe transferred large tracts of land from clerical to secular hands. In many cases the new owners were more alert to effective methods of exploitation than the clergy had been. The same observation can be made of the merchants all over Europe who retired from business and purchased land—the only suitable investment for funds. They were accustomed to making profits, and they rearranged the contracts with the peasants to assure continued income. Rising prices in the sixteenth century also forced changes in land ownership. Many petty noblemen could no longer make a living from their ancestral holdings since their income was based on fixed money rents that could not be changed. The result was that the rising prices forced them to sell their property to city people, royal officials, or more prosperous noblemen. However, those changes in land ownership did not always result in new patterns of land exploitation, nor did they really revolutionize the entire structure of land-holding inherited from the past.

There were, however, several interesting results. Throughout England, France, the Rhineland, and western Germany the peasants freed themselves increasingly from the traditional servile land contracts. Serfdom did not disappear in western Europe, but its incidence was reduced to a relatively small percentage of the rural population. The contract that became most common was a sort of hereditary leasehold by which the peasant obtained the right to work, sell, and will certain lands in return for a fixed annual payment (a *cens*). Those peasants (*censitaires* as they were called in France, since they owed a *cens*) behaved as if they were proprietors. The obligations of some of them whose contracts were fixed in money dues were nearly erased by the inflation of the sixteenth century. A careful study of any neighborhood, however, tends to show that only a tiny fraction of the peasants "owned" enough land to support themselves without either becoming day laborers or renting land from the church or their landlord. Another group of peasants— the *metayers* or sharecroppers—was less well off as a result of the changing patterns of land contracts. While the sharecropping type of contract was most common in vine, olive, and fruit culture, where considerable capital was necessary to establish orchards and vineyards, it was also not uncommon elsewhere. The landlord furnished seed, farm implements, and land, while the peasant might provide draft animals as well as his own labor. In these contracts the lord usually got the lion's share of the production. However, in England, and to a lesser degree in the Lowlands and France important changes in land tenure began to appear: the land was often rented to farmers for an annual cash rent and the renters often gained control of relatively large tracts which they farmed with hired labor. By the latter seventeenth century the English renter who knew his business had no trouble finding all the land he could farm, and he was able to make the landlord shoulder full responsibility for the taxes that came with the great wars of the period.

It is not difficult to discover the reasons for the development of more efficient agricultural exploitation in England and certain parts of France and the Lowlands. By the seventeenth century the amount of grain raised in the immediate neighborhoods of the larger cities of western Europe was no longer adequate for their needs. Grain merchants, particularly in England, France, and the Netherlands, began to reach out to Danzig, Stettin, and other east European centers, where grain could easily be assembled from the interior by river traffic. Naturally they also tried to get as much grain as possible nearer the city market by stimulating peasant production in the neighborhood of the cities. Both the fact of the ever growing grain market and the attractive prices offered for grain stimulated production, but it would be unwise to stress too much the changes that resulted. Even western Europe had to wait until the road and canal building era of the latter eighteenth and early nineteenth centuries created cheap transportation, and new methods of crop rotation developed to improve land usage before a great agricultural transformation could occur.

In England the fact that it became more profitable to raise sheep than wheat in many sections of the country produced another significant change in the rural pattern. The practice of enclosure introduced sheep grazing in place of field crops and drove the peasants from the land. The lord had first secured the right to exclude the peasants from the common pastures, and then, since the peasants could not make a living without using them, the lords either bought or appropriated the peasants' rights to the land they had traditionally tilled. Professor Charles A. Beard has pointed out that by driving the peasants from their farms, the surplus population needed to colonize the North American mainland was acquired by England. The social problem exemplified by the debtors' prisons and the almshouses that plagued England well into the nineteenth century was also created then. Goldsmith's poem, *The Deserted Village,* explores the emotional content of the process, while the village moralist explained that it was against the law to steal a goose from the common, but perfectly legal to steal the common from under a goose.

The general trend in western Europe was toward a reduction of the number of servile contracts, even though the peasants did not thereby gain full control over the land they tilled. In eastern Europe exactly the opposite was the case. In the area beyond the Oder river, and particularly in Poland and Russia, a combination of government pressure and landlord aggression forced an increasing number of the peasants into the status of serfs. By the second half of the seventeenth century in Russia the only way a peasant could remain free was to flee to the northern forest lands or to Siberia where the economy was not profitable enough for the landlords to follow him. At the opening of the eighteenth century, Peter the Great completed the subjection of the peasantry by giving the landlords complete control over the peasants in return for their collecting taxes and recruiting soldiers from the peasant villages for the czar's government.

The methods of cultivation and the crops harvested changed very little between the fourteenth and eighteenth centuries. Some historians have argued that agriculture did not change because it satisfied the needs of the period, but such a thesis begs a whole series of questions about the conditions of human life. From our point in time, it becomes apparent that agriculture in the seventeenth century suffered from a series of interrelated vicious cycles that were almost impossible to break. It was not until the nineteenth century that European men found ways to attack those problems.

In the first place, the same basic problem that had plagued medieval men still persisted. There was no known way to retain the fertility of the soil except by allowing it to remain fallow periodically. Crop rotation was unknown, and since the grain (wheat, rye, and buckwheat) and the porridge (oats, peas, and beans) crops provided the largest amount of calories per acre, the peasants had to use their fields for those crops. Even so, the yield was pitifully small: a good yield might produce five to seven bushels of grain for each bushel sowed, but three to five bushels were more common. Under such conditions, peasants could not use much of their land for fodder crops, and therefore they could not have many animals and so did not have much manure. Until crop rotation and artificial fertilizers were introduced, there was no way to break the circle.

Another great problem confronting peasants was their lack of power and tools. Their cows were nondescript animals, resulting from haphazard breeding on the village common. Yet they were still forced to provide both traction and milk, and finally meat. It is not surprising that they did none of these things very well. There are parts of Europe today where this "cow economy" can still be seen, but today's cows are somewhat better animals than those of earlier periods. Even those peasants fortunate enough to own oxen or horses were not too well off because of the primitive plows with which they tilled the soil. We have pictures of those plows; they were heavy, awkward tools made of wood. An ox tired quickly pulling such a plow. By the later seventeenth century we find pictures of other implements, including seeders; they, too, were awkward, heavy, and inefficient as were the carts and wagons and roads. In other words, the peasants were caught in a cycle of poor power, poor tools, and poor roads. There was no remedy for this until metals became cheap enough for farmers to afford iron machinery and wagon wheels, and until animal breeding produced animals capable of sustained hard work, and in 1715 those factors were still in the future.

3. THE URBAN CLASSES

While the population of rural Europe was undoubtedly greater than that of urban Europe, there is considerable justification for spending more time in the study of the latter. It was urban Europe that provided much of the driving power that shaped the characteristic patterns for the emerging civilization in the West. The towns and townsmen furnished the fluid wealth that made princes strong; they also furnished the personnel that managed the princes' governments. They provided the marts of commerce that sent ships out to sea; and were the cradles for education and research that transformed the ideas of men. Peasants and noblemen may have furnished the men and the officers for the kings' armies, but the townspeople had the money and the intelligence needed to organize and control those forces.

The process of differentiation of the urban classes was centuries old, and the class structure of the towns reflected that history. At the summit of urban society were the magistrates and judges who managed the kings' affairs and ruled the towns. With a few wealthy merchants, bankers, and professional men, they constituted the elite class, almost indistinguishable from the nobility in the pattern of their lives. They owned town homes and country houses well staffed with servants; they educated their children to follow them in the positions of authority that they had acquired. Perhaps the most interesting thing about urban society in that period was the successful effort of the upper bourgeoisie to establish a sort of hereditary caste for themselves. In some countries like France officeholding became venal; that is, offices were sold and became the personal property of the purchaser. This made the effort to fix their status easier. In other countries—England, for example—wealthy townsmen relied upon the purchase of landed property to stabilize their family position. It is interesting to watch the bankers and tax farmers use their wealth as a lever to give permanence to the family status. A line was drawn by the nobility between men with "blue blood" and the "parvenus"; nonetheless, that line began to break down as the financial needs of the nobles and the size of the doweries of the daughters of the bourgeoisie increased together.

Not all townsmen were wealthy merchants, tax farmers, bankers, and lawyers. By the seventeenth century the petty business establishment, still so characteristic of provincial European towns, was to be found everywhere. Those were the shops that made shoes, hats, barrels, beer, knives, candles, guns, and bread. Those were the people who sold wine, colonial goods, fine cloth, and notions, and all the things that were needed to carry on life with the accustomed comforts of the age. Those little shopkeepers and craftsmen along with their servants, apprentices, and journeyman assistants made up the bulk of the population of the towns. Even in our day much of the activity in a European provincial town seems to consist of "taking in each other's washing," but this local interdependence was much more marked three centuries ago.

If we can rely upon the accounts of travelers, the innkeepers, their servants, and the entertainers of one kind or another who haunted the public houses played a significant role in town life. It was not until toward the end of the seventeenth century that the coffee house took the place of the inn as a gathering place for travelers and local inhabitants in search of entertainment and companionship. Some of those inns were large establishments with extensive stables for horses as well as reasonably good quarters for men, but most of them seem to have been miserable places that preyed upon the traveler. Erasmus in the sixteenth century and Locke in the seventeenth agree with scores of other literate travelers that the inns of Europe left something to be desired. Nonetheless, the inn, the *auberge,* the *Wirtschaftshaus,* all played an important part in supplying warmth, color, and excitement. Except in a few great cities, it was not until the eighteenth century that the theaters and opera houses began to supply formal entertainment for the towns.

For all except the larger towns, agriculture continued to provide employment for a sizeable percentage of the population. The fields for a mile or more outside of the town walls were usually cultivated by people living within the gates, and provided a significant part of the food needed to support the population. Sheep, goats, and cows were herded daily from the towns to pastures along the roads or in the fields so that the typical town smelled and sounded like the rural village at least from sundown to sun up. The townsmen who exploited the land usually did not own it; they were the renters or the hired men of their richer neighbors.

These farmers, along with the porters of loads, the pullers of hand carts, hewers of wood, beggars, thieves, prostitutes, and other marginal people were on the bottom of the urban society. They had little or no contact with the high culture of the towns; they always lived on the edge of misery without hopes for bettering their lot in the world. In the twentieth century, one must go to the Orient or the Middle East to see men performing the menial tasks our contemporary society reserves for animals or machines, and to see the swarms of beggars that were characteristic of European society several centuries ago. It is important to recall that western civilization was not always the efficient, humane society that is in a prosperous twentieth-century American town.

4. INDUSTRY AND COMMERCE

Unquestionably the most important functions of urban society were to be found in industry and commerce, and this fact became even truer as changes in the military structure of society, manifested by the rise of princely armies, reduced the military and political importance of most of the towns. If we look at the over-all economic picture of Europe, commerce appeared more important than industry, but in the everyday lives of men most of the items of commerce had to be transformed by some sort of manufacturing process before they could be used.

Manufacturing, however, was largely confined to small-scale operations;

most of it was either done at home for the producer's own use (usufacture) or carried on in small shops by craftsmen who manufactured their products at the consumer's orders. It is astonishing to a modern man to see how many of the things used or worn, even by the relatively wealthy bourgeois families, were made at home. This "do it yourself" economy provided such things as thread and cloth as well as clothing; it also included mattresses, tables, and thatching for roofs. The work was done by the family and its domestics, sometimes assisted by wandering craftsmen who worked for board, lodging, and a small fee.

Many of the articles that could not be made at home were made in the town or village by craftsmen working under age-old methods. The shoemaker, the hatter, the silversmith, and many other craftsmen operated shops where a master, assisted by an apprentice and perhaps also a journeyman craftsman, produced goods on order. The butcher, the baker, the candlestick maker fell into that category, except that they produced for a relatively stable market rather than on the demand of the customer. Production was organized by guilds or corporations that regulated the quality and price of products as well as the training and conditions of labor of the workers. Sometimes the regulations only covered the guilds of a city; sometimes of a province; sometimes of a kingdom. This pattern of production has, with some modifications, lasted into the twentieth century in certain places in western Europe: for example, the author visited a shop in southern France where craftsmen were making wooden shoes very much as they had been made for the last five hundred years. The economy of artisans and small enterprises is very much a part of the contemporary Middle East and the Orient, but the majority of the craftsmen in western Europe has been forced out of business by mass production factories. In the seventeenth century, however, they were still reasonably efficient economic units.

Nevertheless, the developing characteristic pattern of western economy was not to be usufacture or the craftsman's shop. In the port cities, the larger towns, and the fairs there was an ever-growing demand for greater quantities of goods that could be produced by small craftsmen. Cloth and hardware, particularly, but also china, glass, bullets, cutlery, guns, soap, and a host of other things were in demand for intercity and overseas trade. It was to be a long time before these items bulked as largely in commerce as naval supplies, metals (iron, copper, tin, zinc, and lead), wines and liquors, grains, wool, sugar, and other colonial products, but from the sixteenth century onward manufactured items played an increasingly important role in international commerce.

To supply these items Europeans developed two methods of production: first, the shop system which was a modification of the small craftsman's enterprise and the manorial mill, wine press, and forge; second, the "putting out" or "domestic" system which was a development based upon the usufacture of the peasant household. In some enterprises, for example, the manufacture of cloth in the Beauvais area, the entrepreneurs actually combined both of these methods of production to prepare cloth for the market. In these systems we see the roots of the contemporary mass production factory. The basic idea involved the breaking down of the process of production into a series of steps. By this division of labor, it was discovered that relatively unskilled workers could be taught to produce goods of a quality approximately equal to the work of the craftsmen.

The shop system required relatively large amounts of capital for the merchant-manufacturer was obliged to supply tools and work room as well as raw materials for his employees. It could be successful only in those industries for which there was a relatively stable demand and in those places where there was an abundant supply of labor. It also required comparative immunity from the ancient guild controls. Thus we see enterprises like the new book industry adapting itself to the shop system. (Indeed, in German the word *Verlager* means both printer and entrepreneur.) The manufacture of soap, starch, gold wine, weapons, armor, mirrors, china, velvet, tapestry, rugs, and many other such items came to be organized by the shop system. In many cases a patron (king or nobleman) would assure the entrepreneur a reasonably steady market by placing a standing order for the commodity. Even today in Europe we still see firms advertising their connection with a king or some member of a royal family.

The metal industries were particularly susceptible to shop organization, but their reliance upon wood for fuel limited their size and development. The forge that made pig iron had to "follow" its wood supply. Thus, in spite of important technological advances in the sixteenth and early seventeenth centuries, the iron industry remained a "forest industry." The wood had to be turned into charcoal before it could be used in the forge, so the forges had to be relatively peripatetic installations, easily transported when the wood was exhausted. By the latter seventeenth and early eighteenth centuries the ever-increasing demand for iron made dependence upon the forests a problem of the first magnitude. In many places the iron industry was causing progressive deforestation, threatening to exhaust the most important national resource, namely, wood. The forests supplied most of the fuel and building material upon which the civilization of the epoch rested.

Certain other industries, particularly that of textiles, developed the "domestic" form of organization. In the rural communities there was a large potential labor supply, and the traditional usufacture had given these people a relatively high degree of skill. Yarn and cloth (woolen or linen) produced for home use could also be sold to merchants, and in the centuries following 1500 there arose a class of merchant-manufacturers (entrepreneurs) who specialized in assembling and selling the products of rural labor. At first, the entrepreneur probably only bought the surpluses that had been processed in the village, but it was not long before the peasant either bought larger quantities of raw materials or had them provided for him by the entrepreneur. This so-called "putting out" or "domestic" system was extremely varied in its forms, but essentially it involved the organization of rural labor by the merchant-manufacturer for the production of marketable goods. For example, in the Irish linen industry the market was organized by entrepreneurs who acted as bleachers for the cloth in their district. They bought the entire output of the peasants' linen, and finished it for the market. In theory the peasant was free to sell to the highest bidder; in practice he was frequently in debt to a certain entrepreneur, and therefore committed to sell to him alone. In the woolen industry the pattern was often extremely complex. One group of peasants spun the yarn, another dyed it, a third wove it, and then the merchant-manufacturer "finished" the cloth, perhaps by filling and shaping it in his own shops. This was a system that utilized division of labor, but required the worker to supply his place of labor and often his own tools, although there were examples of the merchant-manufacturer supplying the tools as well as the raw materials.

While this "putting out" system was particularly advantageous to the textile industry of the day, it was also employed in other manufacturing processes in which relatively unskilled labor could be utilized. It had the disadvantage that it was difficult to discipline labor, and it was not always possible to maintain standards. Nevertheless, the advantages of a system that allowed the employment of women and children in their own homes, and peasant farmers when they were not needed in the fields, were enough to offset the lack of disciplined organization.

The "putting out" system has been depicted as an ideal manufacturing method that allowed peasant workers to supplement their incomes and produce valuable goods without imposing unhealthy urban conditions upon the workers. This school of thought emphasizes the rosy-cheeked peasant, living in the country and gaining an honest living by agriculture and craft labor. Another picture of the same system shows the peasant as a man who early fell into debt to the merchant-manufacturer and lost his freedom to sell his labor on the open market. The scheming merchant-manufacturer thereby exploited the peasant, made of him a sweat shop laborer and economic slave. Like so many apparently contradictory historical pictures, both of these are true but incomplete statements of the facts. In fact, the relations between rural workers and merchant-manufacturers varied so much from one section of Europe to another that any generalization would have to include both extremes.

Another industry that became increasingly important after 1500 was mining. From the silver and zinc mines of southern Germany to the coal mines on the English coast, Europeans dug in the earth for copper, iron, silver, lead, and other metals. Mining methods were refined in the sixteenth century by the introduction of new pumps and the use of explosives as well as by a better understanding of timbering the shafts. The mines were, of course, capital industries, requiring large investments and careful organization of labor. In some areas they were undertaken by territorial noblemen, in others by bankers and financiers (the Fuggers, for example), and in others by bourgeois entrepreneurs. However, by the seventeenth century, mining throughout Europe had become a relatively important enterprise employing considerable quantities of both capital and labor. The importance of the industry is clearly demonstrated by the varieties of mineral products offered for sale at the markets of Amsterdam about 1700.

If we were to characterize the period by a single term, we would call it a commercial rather than an industrial society. The production of goods for use at home and for sale in the community undoubtedly loomed large in the everyday lives of most of the people, for the mass of men and women of Europe were little involved in any economy except that which directly affected their daily consumption of goods. Yet when we see the large enterprises of Europe—those that engaged fluid capital on a considerable scale—we find that commerce rather than industry was most important. This all-European economy, in contrast to the local economy of a country village or a small town, concerned the transportation of so-called colonial goods (sugar, tea, coffee, chocolate, rice, indigo, tobacco, hides, etc.), of oriental goods (spices, silks, drugs, jewels, etc.), of naval supplies (pitch, tar, hemp, timber, etc.), of grains (wheat, rye, oats, etc.), of spirits and wines, wool, fish, metals, cloth, hardware, drugs, furs, etc. A glance at the commodities mentioned shows that only a few of them were produced in western Europe; the majority would be classified as raw materials or foreign importations. A study of the goods available at the great markets of Amsterdam in the latter seventeenth century would emphasize the generalization even more completely.

This does not mean that the sale of such goods occupied most of the labor of Europe, but rather that the manufacturing processes were still small-scale enterprises. They did not loom as large in the world market as the commercial enterprises that distributed raw materials and overseas goods. Students familiar with the industrial economy of the twentieth century must adjust their thinking to fit the commercial economies of earlier eras. In any age or society in which the craftsman is the typical laborer, commerce rather than industry will probably loom larger in the economic pattern of the society as a whole, even though it may play only a minor part in the daily lives of individuals who make up that society.

The characteristic form for large-scale commerce in that period was the monopolistic trading company operating with a state charter. The India companies of England, the Netherlands, and France and companies chartered for the Levant, Africa, Muscovy, and the colonies of the New World assumed considerable importance on the economic scene after 1600, and continued to hold a central position up to the nineteenth century. The organization and privileges of the chartered companies varied from country to country. Some of them, like the India companies, were almost sovereign states endowed with the right to raise armies and make peace or war. Others, like the Massachusetts Bay Company or the French Senegal Company, were charged with both the colonization and exploitation of specific areas. Still others, like the English Levant Company or the Muscovy Company, merely had a monopoly on the trade of one section of the globe. In each case the chartered company was given a monopoly on the trade between the country of its origin and the section of the world covered by the charter.

As might be expected, there was often a close connection between the personnel directing the companies and the government granting the charter. Usually there was also a legal relationship, making the company dependent upon the government for many aspects of its activity. In the case of the various French companies founded in the seventeenth century, the government actually acted almost as a godparent to the company. It encouraged members of the royal family, officials of the government, and great nobles, as well as city merchants, to buy stock. Members of Parliament, great lords, as well as London city merchants, were interested in the English enterprises; and the governing personnel of the Dutch India Company was nearly identical with that of the government of the United Provinces. Indeed, the great Dutch companies might almost be said to have been in a position to dominate the policy of the United Netherlands.

The legal forms of ownership for those enterprises had very ancient origins. Medieval merchants had early established the practice of joint ventures. The pooling of funds or merchandise for a voyage lessened individual risks and at the same time assured the larger amounts of capital necessary for more ambitious adventures. From those joint ventures, it was only a short step to the establishment of a joint-stock company in which the partners established a permanent association for a mercantile enterprise based upon shares. Permanent joint-stock companies were a departure from the earlier mercantile practices that had kept all enterprises as individual or family concerns associated with other such concerns only through a guild association or for a single voyage. The chartered companies were usually joint-stock companies with shares that could be bought and sold on the exchange.

Methods of control over the companies varied from company to company and from country to country. In most cases, executive control was vested in a board of directors or governors who employed managers and established the general rules for business action. Not all companies were successfully or even honestly managed. The most famous of the fiascos that developed out of speculation came in the early eighteenth century when in both England and France speculative companies started booms in the stock market which were quite unjustified by the actual facts of their situation. The resulting deflations wiped out speculators and investors, and greatly discredited the stock company system of enterprise.

While the large mercantile enterprises were usually organized as chartered companies, the greatest part of the commerce of Europe was still in the hands of smaller merchant houses. They were usually family concerns, organized around the head of a house and his sons or near relatives. There was no easy way to assemble large amounts of capital from the sale of stock or shares for anything less than a great chartered company operating a state monopoly. Thus, for smaller enterprises a family concern or a partnership became the rule.

The partnership in which ownership might be divided among several individuals was the nearest approximation to the corporation of later generations. In some cases the partner might be silent—that is, he might supply money but not participate in managing the concern; but the usual pattern was for all the partners to be active in the direction of affairs. Not until the nineteenth century did it become common for an investor to entrust his money to an enterprise over which he had little or no control.

The most interesting point about the whole process was the extension of the influence of those merchant houses in the society of Europe. In the latter Middle Ages those merchants began to loom up as important factors in the political and social life of Europe, but their influence was overshadowed by that of the landed nobility. In the sixteenth and seventeenth centuries, in spite of the disorders caused by the religious and political wars, the merchant class grew rapidly. Perhaps the wars may even have encouraged commercial activity. Thus, by the opening of the eighteenth century in western Europe the merchants and their allies, the lawyers and bankers, were well on the way toward the goal of overshadowing their rivals, the rural landlords, for political power. As we have seen, the merchants first challenged the nobles and kings as early as the fourteenth century; by the opening of the eighteenth they were almost ready to elbow them aside and assume control of society themselves. However, this is the story of the eighteenth and nineteenth centuries.

5. *PRICES, MONEY, BANKS, AND BOURSES*

Even though the average peasant and many of the townspeople were largely unaware of the significance of the discoveries, all Europe was affected by a price movement that was in part attributable to the New World. From the middle of the sixteenth to the middle of the seventeenth century, the price of wheat and most other commodities increased about four and a half times. After about 1650 prices tended to level off or actually decline, except when bad weather drove up the price of grain. That sensational rise in prices followed by a leveling off was perhaps the most significant single economic fact of the period. Contemporaries only vaguely understood what was happening. The rapid price rise brought in its train all sorts of problems. Noblemen who depended upon a fixed income found their incomes dwindling to nothing. Taxes often continued to yield the same amount of money, but the purchasing power declined. There was, of course, a reverse side of the coin. Rising prices or inflation brought benefits to some and disaster to others. Debtors especially benefit when the value of money declines. The contemporary explanations for the rise in prices included everything from malevolent extraterrestrial influence to the influx of gold and silver from the Americas.

We understand now, of course, that the exploitation of silver mines in Europe, and even more, the flow of precious metals from the New World probably accounted for this inflation. The Spaniards imported more and more silver every decade of the sixteenth century (in 1591–1600 the amount imported reached 2,707,626 kilos); in the seventeenth century imports declined (in 1631–1640: 1,396,759 kilos; in 1651–1660: 433,256 kilos). The metal did not stay in Spain; indeed, it hardly benefited Spain at all. By trade with France, Italy, the Netherlands, England, and the German cities, it was spread over all Europe. For a century the flow was too heavy for the commerce of Europe to absorb, and when there is too much more money in circulation than there are goods to buy, prices have to rise. As the flow of metals tapered off, the growing commerce began to absorb the metal that did not enter the economy without pushing up prices. After all, silver was a commodity just like wheat, and when the amount of silver available increased more rapidly than the production of wheat, more silver was paid for the wheat. When a balance was reached between the new wheat and the new silver on the market, the price of both stabilized.

It is an historical problem of considerable importance to discover whether the abatement in the flow of precious metals after 1640 and the subsequent stabilization and even decline in prices actually had a deleterious effect upon the economy of the West. In some sections of Europe—the Netherlands, for example—the expansion of business activity seems to have slowed down after 1650; in others—like Germany—there was an absolute increase in the rate of expansion after 1660 greater than in the preceding half century. The problem in each case is complicated by other factors: war, taxes, drought, and pestilence were variables that make it difficult to estimate accurately the effects of rising or declining prices. England and Germany experienced prosperity after 1660 greater than they had had between 1620 and 1660; France was reasonably prosperous until about 1690, and then experienced hard times. But the important factor in each case seems to have been war or peace rather than price levels.

The coinage of Europe during the three centuries following the discoveries was in a state of chaos. The Florentine and Venetian gold coins and, later, the Dutch taler tended to become the standards of value and to circulate—in international exchange, at least—freely all over western Europe. After 1696, when the government in London recoined all its metal currency, English coins also became standard for commerce. However, in every country local coins, often of very dubious value, circulated freely, and usually drove the good coins out of the market.

There were several sources for bad coins. In the first place, deliberate devaluation of coinage was a standard practice; many governments temporarily solved financial problems by debasing the metal in their coins. In the long run, such financial brigandage was usually proved disadvantageous to the economy of the country, but often it momentarily eased princely burdens. Tudor England, Hapsburg Spain, Bourbon France, Petrine Russia, and many of the states of Germany and Italy at one time or another resorted to the practice of reducing the amount of precious metals in the coins. Another source of bad coins came from "clipping." Coins were "struck" rather than "minted," and it was then difficult to give them a good edge. It was therefore possible to "clip" off little bits of precious metal without destroying the appearance of the coin. Clipping became a serious menace to commerce in England in the seventeenth century when some of the coins had actually lost a third or more of their intrinsic value, and the problem was solved then by the recoinage of silver coins in 1695–1696; but in many continental countries it was not until the nineteenth century that good coins appeared in circulation.

The relationship between gold and silver coins also presented a serious problem, for the flow of the two metals from the mines was not always in the same ratio. Money-changers, and particularly the *changes* or *bourses* of the principal commercial cities, acted as agents to adjust the ratio of exchange between the two metals. In the sixteenth century gambling on the gold-silver ratio could be as exciting as horse racing. It is interesting to note that the nineteenth-century American formula, 16 to 1, is not far from the average ratio for those three centuries.

Since medieval times banking procedures had been developing to meet the needs of princes and of commerce. The earliest function of bankers was to loan money to the rulers of church or state, to be repaid by taxes or other anticipated revenues. The practice of charging interest on loans was frowned upon by the theologians, but popes, emperors, and kings all had recourse to the wealthy bankers. Normally private individuals did not borrow from the bankers; most private loans were made by usurers and pawnbrokers who operated locally and exploited their victims more viciously than the bankers.

In addition to loans to the church and state, however, the bankers provided another important service—namely, the discount of commercial paper and the issuing of bank notes for the payment of accounts. As we have already noted, even in the Middle Ages bank notes became famous instruments of trade; some of them bearing almost a hundred endorsements have survived to prove that they circulated as currency. By the eighteenth century they had become universally used throughout the western commercial world. Thus banking houses served both government and commerce. A closer inspection of their activities will also show that they acted as tax collectors, as managers of mining enterprises, as factors in international trade, and in many other such operations.

The first banks had been private family affairs, like the Medici and Fugger houses. Some of them developed their banking operations as a side line to commerce; others emerged from the goldsmith business, for the goldsmiths knew about precious metals, and it became customary for people to deposit their gold with them for safekeeping; in turn the goldsmiths used the deposits to make loans to princes. By the seventeenth century most of the bankers also accepted accounts on deposit.

The emergence of the city or state banks, such as the ones in Geneva, Amsterdam, Stockholm, and, later, the Bank of England in London, somewhat altered the character of the banking business. These chartered banks were usually partnerships or joint-stock companies in which several families or groups pooled their resources. They often acted for the specific purpose of loaning money to the state or handling commercial paper. Some of them, like the Bank of Amsterdam, became so important in world commerce that almost anyone who pretended to do business on an international scale had to have money on deposit in their books. Others, such as the Bank of England, almost became an extension of the royal treasury, for their notes actually circulated in the commercial and governmental world in place of currency. The English wars against Louis XIV were financed to a large extent by loans floated by this Bank.

The sixteenth century also saw the development of the *bourse* or exchange as an institution serving the business community. Its early function was to act as a money exchange, as a commodity market, and as a primitive sort of insurance agency. When a merchant sent a ship overseas, he would secure odds that the vessel would be lost at sea; he would bet that it would be lost, while the insurer would bet that the ship would return. It then became customary to extend the areas that could be "insured" by such an arrangement. There were many other items that could be bought and sold on the exchange. Naturally commodities such as wool, wheat, and the like were often sold on the *bourse,* and by the eighteenth century specialized commodity exchanges had begun to appear in the principal port cities.

After the emergence of the great chartered companies the sale of their stock became an important part of the business of the exchanges. Even so, we have early seventeenth-century accounts of times when there was so little real business available in the bourse that its members placed bets on such things as the probable sex of a child about to be born or the vagaries of the weather. The exchange always had an element of the gambling hall in its structure.

By the opening of the eighteenth century, the commercial economy of Europe had matured to the point where its institutions were fully rooted in society and its directors were prepared to assert their right to political power. Throughout the history of western civilization we encounter the bourgeois merchant, banker, and lawyer who played important parts in the political history of the continent. By the seventeenth century they were ready to elbow the noblemen from the benches of the king's councils; by the opening of the eighteenth century they were almost ready to assume power in their own name.

The rise of the bourgeoisie from its tenth-century obscurity to a position of dominance has fascinated historians and philosophers ever since. Karl Marx found in the conflict between bourgeoisie and noblemen the "inevitable dynamic process of history"; the French historian, Guizot, saw in it the fulfil-ment of the destiny of western men. It is not necessary to seek grandiose explanations to discover the importance and the drama in the rise of the economic institutions that frame the lives of western men. In the course of the sixteenth and seventeenth centuries the new economy provided the money required to finance the growth of centralized governments and the standing military establishments necessary for their support. Since the "pen" became as important as the "sword" in regulating the affairs of princes, men educated in the urban civilization also moved to assume control over those govern-ments. Thus, the immediate impact of the burgeoning bourgeois civilization was a matter of political as well as of economic importance. The economy and the politics of Europe have always been closely intertwined. In the fol-lowing chapters we shall see that fundamental developments in the constitu-tional organization of Europe in the seventeenth century were interrelated, *inter alia,* with the economic structure of the era.

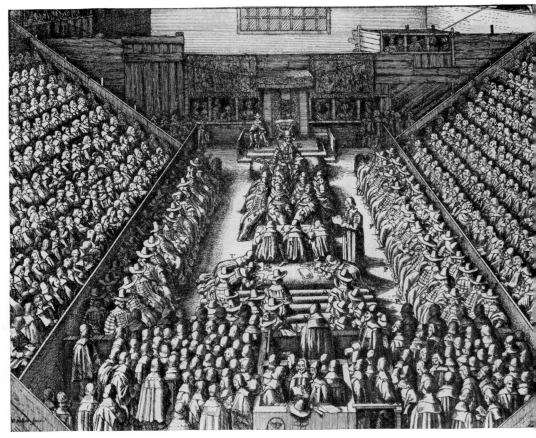

"The English Parliament in Session," a Seventeenth-Century Print. (Paris, Bibliothèque Nationale, Cabinet des Éstampes)

Chapter 11

SEVENTEENTH-CENTURY ENGLAND

1. ENGLAND AT THE DEATH OF ELIZABETH

The Tudors[1] (1485–1603) left an indelible mark on English society. After years of civil war they established a strong central authority capable of curbing the lawlessness of the great feudal barons. They reformed the church, redivided the land, and laid the basis for economic prosperity. With the exception of Mary, they were popular; both their internal and foreign policies captured the support of their politically articulate subjects. As a result, there was little criticism of their rule by royal prerogative or of their courts, where judges were really "lions under the throne." The courts could commit a "judicial murder" if royal policy required it. They could act outside of the traditional system of justice to deprive a subject of life, liberty, or property. The Tudors used their judges to compel the great lords to obey the crown. Towards the end of Elizabeth's reign, however, there was grumbling about her autocracy and her arbitrary actions, but her age, her sex, and the aura of glory surrounding her name kept those objections from coming to the surface.

Since the problem faced by Elizabeth's successors stemmed from the relations between king and Parliament (king, peers, and commons), it is important to understand how the Tudors used that institution. While they often made Parliament an integral part of their government, there was no question about the role of Parliament. The power and the leadership belonged to the king; Parliament was a sounding board to advertise his intentions and also a legislative institution to give added authority to his laws. The distinguished historian, Professor Conyers Read, has pointed out that the Tudors were able parliamentarians. They knew how to "manage" parliamentary majorities;

[1] Henry VII, 1485–1509; Henry VIII, 1509–1547; Edward VI, 1547–1553; Mary, 1553–1558; Elizabeth, 1558–1603.

they were not above "rigging" an election or bribing deputies. In this way the Tudor monarchs took advantage of the fact that in the preceding centuries Parliament had become a popular national institution. By associating Parliament with their enterprises, they assured for themselves a large measure of support in the kingdom; by manipulating it, they assured their own personal power.

The fact that the Tudors used their power to curb a disorderly nobility, to reform the church in a popular direction, to expand commerce, and to fight popular wars made their control easier. Furthermore, Henry VIII and Elizabeth did not need to rely heavily upon Parliament for money, since there were confiscated lands that could be sold by the crown and Spanish treasure fleets which would yield loot. This placed them in a strong position vis-à-vis the members of that body; but it was those same Tudor rulers who prepared the way for the problems that the next dynasty (the Stuart) was to meet. By making Parliament a partner in their government the Tudors gave it significance, while social and economic movements begun in the sixteenth century prepared the way for new roles for Parliament to play. Henceforth, when the great lords of the church and the countryside and the representatives of the towns and the gentry assembled to deliberate on policy, they were prepared to insist that the king make them a partner in his enterprises.

The most important social development at the end of the sixteenth century was the rise of the squires to importance in the countryside. The rural gentry, a class with leisure and education but relatively limited means, began to grow from several sources. In some cases wealthy peasant yeomen moved up the social ladder, while cadet sons of great families moved down the ladder to the gentry. Perhaps most important was the fact that city merchants and professional people came to regard the purchase of land as a suitable investment and life in the country as crowning a successful career. Thus, there came into being a vigorous class that expanded under the protection of the strong Tudor government. It would be folly to assert that the gentry class was a natural source for statesmen, yet among their numbers there were men with education and political vision. The majority may have been mere followers, often ready to limit their political ideas to the boundaries of their county, but the few leaders who did emerge were men capable of pressing for their own and their country's interests.

The other class that grew in strength was that of the city bourgeoisie. The extension of trade and manufacturing created a class of wealthy city people who had money and were experienced in handling business affairs. They were able to educate their sons through formal schooling and travel, so that they gradually emerged as a reasonably enlightened group, conscious of the impact of royal policy upon their economic interests and of the possibility of using the royal power to satisfy their political and social, as well as their economic, ambitions. They were linked to the squires, for many of them retired to the country; they were also an integral part of the new commercial groups that were to make England the mart of the world.

The House of Commons in Parliament was elected from the country gentry and the city bourgeoisie—men accustomed to commanding affairs—and, as their numbers grew, they demanded a larger voice in the government of the kingdom. Even in the latter years of Elizabeth's reign they were becoming restive, and when a new dynasty appeared they became more and more assertive. In the first quarter of the seventeenth century they insisted that their demand for a larger voice in government represented simply a return to the ancient practices of England. In point of fact, they were actually revolutionaries trying to take over powers that traditionally belonged to the crown. This is, of course, a familiar phenomenon in politics, for most men like to pose as defenders of ancient rights rather than as usurpers of new privileges. Thus when Members of Parliament tried to use their position to expand their powers over the king's government, they based their claims to these powers on presumed ancient traditional usages. In this way they could demand revolutionary changes and pretend to do no more than protect their rights.

Furthermore, the impact of gold and silver from the New World prepared the way for conflict between king and Parliament. At the opening of the seventeenth century, all western Europe was feeling the effect of the inflation that was so dramatically upsetting price levels. The English government was in trouble. The taxes that came to the crown from various sources had become "fossilized" so that they returned only a minimum of revenue, and the income from the crown lands also tended to remain at a fixed money rate. Thus the traditional revenues at the disposal of the crown were becoming less and less adequate. They simply did not yield the revenue needed to run the government. Elizabeth had felt this pinch. Despite the money she had received from selling crown lands and robbing the Spanish treasure fleets, she had needed more. At her death she owed £400,000. Her successor had no choice other than to ask Parliament for more money.

In another area, Elizabeth left her successor a problem. Her settlement of the religious question had created a church that included Calvinists and Anglican Catholics. The Thirty-Nine Articles, the Book of Common Prayer, and the Episcopal constitution of the church had left unsettled many questions of theology and ritual. The English church was broad enough to include almost everyone, but still not all the people were satisfied. Like Henry's first reform of the church, Elizabeth's settlement had been enacted by Parliament. No one in England really questioned Parliament's right to legislate in matters regarding the church, and thus the Lords and the Commons were as concerned with religion as with finance.

By the beginning of the seventeenth century, there were several strong currents in England which urged further reform in the church. Congregational and Presbyterian movements urged the abolition, or at least the modification, of the Episcopal organization; they felt that the bishops were tainted with "Romanism," and they disliked their control over the churches. Calvinist theologians urged doctrinal and ritual changes. Those "Puritans" wished to purify manners and morals as well as the constitution of the church: they were stern, tight-lipped men who were convinced that they knew God's will and were determined to enforce it. Naturally they aroused the opposition of the Anglo-Catholics and traditionalists. The lines were not clearly drawn, but the reformers tended to convert, in varying degrees, many of the gentry, most of the city bourgeoisie, and a segment of the artisan class; the most radical were usually people of lesser means, but many of the leaders were substantial citizens. Their feeling of righteousness born of their Calvinist theology gave them greater will to act than their opponents possessed.

Elizabeth's death released many of the conflicts that were already developing at the end of her reign. However, James I did not meet the revolutionary forces in English society all at once, but under him and Charles I the next half century marked the development of revolution in English government.

2. THE FIRST TWO STUART KINGS, 1603–1649

The new king, James I, was above all anxious to ascend the English throne; as king of Scotland he had enjoyed neither the revenue nor the power that he believed to be his due. He had been discreetly quiet when Elizabeth beheaded his mother, Mary Stuart. (After all, James had not known his mother; she had left him before he could walk.) He had also carefully cultivated friends in England to support his candidacy. He had the best claim to the throne, and a union of the English and Scottish crowns promised peace for the whole island; but Elizabeth consistently refused to name her successor, and James well knew that England's throne in the past had had a checkered history. He watched the events in England with greedy eyes, and regarded Elizabeth's long life as an attempt on her part to cheat him of the throne. He could not be sure that somehow another claimant might be preferred before him. When it had finally been settled that he was to be king, James shook the dust of poverty-ridden Scotland off his feet as quickly as possible, and headed south to what he believed was an opulent country that had become his own. He was quite unprepared for all the problems that were soon to confront him.

The new king was a man of parts. One of the few monarchs who were also scholars, James I could debate with theologians and discuss with grammarians; he wrote learnedly about political philosophy and theology, and he knew Latin well. But all his learning was not always supported by wisdom. His personal life left him open to charges of alcoholism and favoritism. His pedantic insistence upon divine right and the royal prerogative aroused almost as many enemies against him as the acts themselves. Henry IV of

France (who once remarked that *he* had enough trouble getting his orders obeyed without worrying about divine right), called James I the "wisest fool in Christendom."

Unlike his Tudor predecessors, James I understood the subtleties of theological debate, but his learning made him arrogant. Thus he not only knew what the theologians were talking about, but also *knew* what was correct, and he was, of course, then led to take sides; his experience with the Calvinists in Scotland had made him violently prejudiced against their party. Financially, unlike Elizabeth, James I did not have large holdings of confiscated monastery lands to sell nor could he depend upon war with Spain to provide him with gold. Yet inflation made every aspect of his court and government more expensive. He needed money—more money than Elizabeth had ever requested. Thus, the twin problems of internal policy with which he was faced were religion and finance, and in each James soon ran head on into the squires in Parliament who were willing to argue with the king.

In foreign affairs, James also ran afoul of Parliament as well as of much of the articulate public opinion in the country. It had been popular and profitable to "singe the beard of the Spanish king," but James came to the throne when it was time to make peace, and he soon made a personal favorite of the Spanish ambassador. The Hapsburgs were the most important royal family in Europe; perhaps James was a "social climber" in his efforts to be friendly with Philip III. In any case, James' policy of friendship was unpopular with the men who recalled the sagas of the Elizabethan "seadogs"; nor did they like to hear the king forbid them to interfere with foreign affairs, which he claimed was his royal prerogative. As they became aware of public policy, the men who were clamoring for the right to a voice in the king's affairs rejected his insistence that those were matters that alone concerned him and his ministers.

Toward the end of his reign, James aroused further criticism when he failed to act vigorously to save his daughter (the wife of Frederick of the Palatinate) from the combined power of the German and Spanish Hapsburgs. Instead of coming to her aid by attacking Spain at sea in the grand old English manner, James tried to arrange a Spanish marriage for his son Charles and thus regain the Palatinate by diplomacy. When he failed on both counts, England's prestige as a European power diminished greatly at home and abroad. James was blamed because he insisted upon his sole right to conduct foreign policy. When Prince Charles came back from Spain without a Spanish bride and crying out for vengeance against Spain, he, rather than James, got the credit for the change.

James' favorites were unfortunate choices and a cause of antagonism between him and his people and Parliament. The first, Robert Carr, came down from Scotland with him and was made in turn Viscount Rochester and the Earl of Somerset. He became rich, and then was involved in a murder scandal. The king's next favorite, George Villiers, who became Duke of Buckingham, was at least an Englishman, but his vanity, his arrogant stupidity, and his immense greed made him a target for critics of the king. Unfortunately for England, Buckingham survived James and, as the favorite of Charles I, continued his career of folly.

Even though he fought with all his Parliaments, James I was able to avoid an open break with them. He was not an astute politician, but when Parliament refused to grant him enough money, he found that his right to regulate trade allowed him to impose new rates. In religious affairs, the folly of certain Catholic conspirators who sought to blow up both king and Parliament (the Gunpowder Plot, 1605) led to increased penalties against Catholics, and for a time introduced an element of good humor into the relations between James and Parliament. On the other side, his persecutions of the religious radicals led to their migration, first to Holland and then to New England (the Pilgrim Fathers). James bickered with Parliament on questions of money, religion and foreign policy, but he never came to the point of warfare. Perhaps the fact that he did not call a Parliament between 1614 and 1621 accounts for the fact that there was never a clear break.

James I died in March 1625, and his son, Charles I (1625–1649), ascended the throne amid the cheers of his subjects. The war with Spain that followed Charles' unsuccessful attempt to marry a Spanish princess was popular in England, and in view of his hostility to Spain, his subjects were willing to overlook the fact that his French bride, the daughter of Henry IV, was a Catholic. After all, the king had to marry someone, and there were few eligible Protestant princesses.

It was a mistake, however, to assume that a new day had dawned. Charles exhibited even less political sense than his father had demonstrated. The English historian Dr. Maurice Ashley says of him: "A good father and a faithful husband . . . he might have made an excellent Italian duke . . . but his lack of insight and humor, his customary silence, and his intellectual shortcomings were poor protection against the coming storms." He needed money as much as his father had; he was disposed to be friendly toward the Catholic religion of his queen; and he was determined to retain the royal prerogatives of his crown. Any one of these things would have assured a conflict with Parliament, even if Charles had shown wisdom in his conduct of foreign affairs.

With Buckingham as his favorite, wisdom was out of the question. The first fiasco resulted from an ill-considered attack on the Spanish mainland; it is hard to guess just what Buckingham had thought he would do if he were successful, but in any event he failed. Then he led England into a foolish conflict with France. Sympathy for the Protestant rebels of La Rochelle and some absurd notions about his own relationship to the French queen were involved. (Buckingham believed that Anne was enamored of him.)

Needless to say, with Richelieu and Louis XIII as his antagonists, his folly led to catastrophe. Fortunately for Charles, Buckingham was murdered (1628), and the fall of La Rochelle ended the war (1629).

Charles' experiences with Parliament were not as fortunate as those of his father. Buckingham came under criticism at the very beginning of the reign, but Charles refused to discuss his choice of ministers. His wars with Spain and France cost money, and his court was even more costly than his father's had been. When Parliament proved tight-fisted, Charles searched the records to find precedents for levying taxes without Parliament's consent. Those taxes, fines, and assessments, many of them medieval in origin, were branded "illegal" by Parliament, and they succeeded in producing more enemies than money. By the late 1620's the men who were to lead the revolution of the 1640's were beginning to make their influence felt. Pym, Eliot, Cromwell, and others stood up to criticize the king. In March 1629, they tried to curb the royal prerogative by questioning the king's right to adjourn Parliament without its consent. The cup had run over: Charles decided to rule the kingdom without the benefit of advice or assistance from Parliament.

Let us pause to see what was involved in the king's decision. The Tudor kings had used Parliament as an instrument for translating the national will into legislation, but their Parliaments were largely under the control of the king. They never had the intention of giving Parliament the right to dictate policy or to supervise the royal government, or even to criticize the actions of the royal courts. James I and Charles I, however, encountered the doctrine that Parliament had the right to criticize the king's government, to initiate legislation, and to control the king's ministers through threats of impeachment. Along with those pretensions came denial of the king's power of arbitrary arrest and imprisonment, and of the collection of taxes not specifically granted by Parliament. No matter how reasonable parliamentary controls may seem in the twentieth century, they were revolutionary ideas in the seventeenth.

In the past, kings had shared power with the great interests of the realm. Especially when the monarchy was weak the great lords had controlled the king, if necessary, by civil war; but strong kings like the Tudors had created special courts (the Star Chamber, for example) that could and did exercise summary powers to curb the "lawlessness" of the great lords. Under Henry VII such courts were popular with the people, most of whom had nothing to fear from the royal prerogative, but to exercise such power a king had to be a strong man or at least employ able ministers. The Stuart kings were not strong men, nor did they occupy the political and economic position of the Tudors. In 1630 land ownership was no longer concentrated in the hands of the great lords, and therefore it was not the great lords who were in the forefront of the attack on the king's power. A member of the Commons boasted, "We could buy the Upper House (his Majesty only excepted) thrice over." The squires and burghers in the Commons represented the wealth of England; they also possessed the education and the will to translate that wealth into political power. With wealth in their hands, they demanded the prerogatives of power that have so often accompanied wealth, and attempted to find legal arguments to prove their right to that power.

On the other hand, both James I and Charles I were "modern" (seventeenth-century) princes. They fully accepted the current doctrine of the divine right of kings, and, like their continental contemporaries, they were anxious to strengthen their authority both within their kingdoms and against other princes on their frontiers. The first Stuart kings were not always wisely advised nor was their government strongly administered, but their political intention was in line with the political ideas of their age. It is not at all surprising that they should reject the demands of their subjects as illegal usurpations of royal prerogative. Princes elsewhere were ruling their unruly subjects; English kings saw no reason why they should not do likewise.

Between 1629 and 1640 Charles I governed without Parliament. His enemies called the period "eleven years of tyranny." Actually, those were not harsh years for most of England. The poor rates were levied more effectively than before or after, and the rights of the landless were vigorously defended. The Court of the Star Chamber moved to prevent illegal enclosures of arable land. The king's government did collect taxes that had not been voted by Parliament, but apart from the squires and city merchants who claimed they thus were "illegally" taxed, there was no widespread complaint against the king's government. On the other hand, many of Charles' policies were constructive and far-sighted. For example, it was then that the royal government began to build the English navy. Elizabeth's navies had been more or less informal affairs; a sixteenth-century merchant ship used to become a warship in time of war. The seventeenth century, however, saw the beginning of naval specialization. James had made a half-hearted start; his son, Charles, gave a real impetus to the development of the navy. A navy was a necessity for the protection of England's growing commerce. Of course it cost money, and Charles had to get the money wherever he could, and his devices led to a famous case at law. John Hampden, a squire from Buckinghamshire, contested the legality of the ship-money tax which had not been granted by Parliament. The Court of Exchequer decided the case in favor of the king, though not unanimously. Hampden became the squires' hero, and the income from the ship-money tax declined precipitously as others joined Hampden in refusing to pay it. It did not matter what the money was to be used for; those potential revolutionaries wanted to win the right to pass upon the policy themselves, and thereby curb the royal power.

Not all the actions of Charles' government were as wise or far-sighted as the naval program. His religious policy, for example, fell under the influence of Archbishop Laud, who was determined to stamp out Puritanism, Sabbatarianism, and Presbyterianism. Episcopal visitations and the removal of radical ministers from their "livings" led to complaints. The Calvinists felt that Laud's hostility toward their party contrasted badly with the tolerance shown toward the Catholics. Charles I had fallen in love with his French wife, and favored her co-religionists. The total number of persons involved in Laud's "persecutions" was not great, but the squirearchy and the bourgeoisie furnished a large share of them. The same people who objected to the political and economic policies of the king felt themselves attacked by the religious policies of his minister; the squires and the moneyed men cried, "tyranny and oppression." It was the same story elsewhere. The French kings discovered that political grievances and Huguenot leanings were often intertwined. The German Hapsburgs encountered religious flags leading political rebellions in Bohemia and Hungary. The seventeenth century still regarded religious unity as a social cement; it is not surprising then that religious dissent provided a flag for civil war.

Charles I got into serious trouble when his desire for uniformity within his lands led him to attempt to impose a new prayer book on the Scottish Kirk. James I had introduced a sort of episcopacy in Scotland, but the Scottish Calvinists were not prepared to accept all the Anglican forms without a struggle. Riots broke out in the churches when the new prayer book was introduced, and the Scots subscribed to a national covenant binding them to reject all changes in the religious constitution not approved by their own church. They also insisted that their general assembly must be recognized as supreme even over the bishops. Charles had either to give in completely or face a war in which the whole population of Scotland would be involved. His religious adviser, Laud, was unwilling to compromise. His new and most able favorite, the Earl of Strafford, had been successful in suppressing an Irish rebellion, and advised the king to fight. However, to pay for the war Charles had to summon Parliament in England and end the "eleven years of tyranny."

3. CIVIL WAR

The Irish Parliament "granted" Charles £180,000; the English clergy "gave" him £120,000. He needed £840,000 more from the English Parliament if the Bishops' War in Scotland were to be won. When Parliament met in 1640, its members showed little intention of considering the king's request. In their opinion the Scottish war was not the first item of business.

A surprisingly large number of the members of the House of Commons were Puritans or Presbyterians in religion, and an even greater number was offended by the king's "illegal" collection of taxes. Thus, their aim was to list their grievances against Charles I and his use of the royal prerogative, and this took precedence over the war. They also opened up a direct assault upon the king's ministers, Laud and Strafford, who had "misled" the king and so must go. They paid no attention to Charles' insistence that the first order of business was to grant him money. Parliament was in session less than three weeks, when Charles, despairing of help from that source, ordered its dissolution. This so-called "Short Parliament" broke up with everyone angry and dissatisfied. Pym and some of his comrades began to tour rural England, urging the squires to stand firm against the king.

The first brushes with the Scots proved the impossibility of carrying on a war without a Parliamentary grant. Princes in 1640 did not have any considerable military power at their disposal; if they needed an army they had to hire one. There was no way out; Parliament had to be summoned again. This fifth Parliament of Charles I's reign has been called the "Long Parliament" for it met on and off over a period of twenty years (1640–1660).

When Parliament met again, the royal prerogative and the king's ministers were definitely under attack. Unable to convict Strafford by any regular legal process, the House of Commons condemned him by a bill of attainder, and Charles I, weakly yielding to Parliament's lust for blood, signed the order that sent his strongest minister to the block. Archbishop Laud was likewise imprisoned in the Tower, and in 1645, at the age of seventy-three, he too was beheaded by a bill of attainder. Parliament then began to pass acts to reform the realm; the revolutionary element was definitely in control. To prevent the king from neglecting to call Parliament in the future, the Triennial Act made it necessary to summon Parliament every three years. The prerogative courts, that had been the backbone of Tudor justice, were abolished. All taxes levied without the consent of Parliament were declared illegal. As a crowning act of defiance, a treaty was signed with the Scottish Covenanters on their terms. His advisers put aside, his war repudiated, and his power emasculated, Charles I was in a most unenviable position. His chance of resisting the revolution lay in the possible excesses which the revolutionaries might commit, and thereby create a "king's party."

The revolution proceeded apace. An army was required to put down a rebellion in Ireland, but Pym was determined to make its officers subject to Parliament. At the same time, the Commons began the impeachment of a number of bishops, and discussed abolishing the episcopacy and the Book of Common Prayer. In November 1641, the Grand Remonstrance listed all Charles' misdeeds since his accession. Clearly James I had been right when he had muttered "no bishop, no king." Parliament determined to do away with the royal prerogative entirely and make the king's government dependent upon it. The crowds in London were crying "no popery, no bishops, no popish lords." There were those who talked of impeaching the Catholic queen as well as the bishops. It was at this point that some of the conservative Members of Parliament drew back; the king was soon to have a party to defend his interests.

In 1642 civil war broke out between the supporters of the king and those of Parliament. In general, the great lords, particularly the Catholic ones, and the conservative gentry supported the king; they came to be called the Cavaliers. The puritanical squires, city merchants, and professional people supported Parliament; their failure to wear wigs led to their name, the Roundheads. But no simple statement can explain the divisions that the war caused in England. Before it was over, hundreds of families had been split, brother against brother, uncle against nephew, by the impact of the conflict. The Roundheads had the sympathy of the Scots excepting the northern clans. The Cavaliers tended to get more support from abroad, where the royalist cause appeared the only just one. The navy that Charles had so carefully built up rewarded him by promptly joining the Parliamentary party. Both sides brought in foreign mercenaries to help fight the war, but native Englishmen formed the bulk of the armies.

In the civil war the cavalry proved itself the most important arm for shock action, and at first the Cavaliers had the advantage, but the Puritans learned to ride, and under the command of the only really great captain to emerge in the war, Oliver Cromwell, they finally created cavalry regiments that proved to be unbeatable. The fortunes of war went back and forth, until Cromwell's so-called New Model Army emerged as the real force behind each new step of the revolution—from the beheading of one king to the restoration of the next.

The greatest battle of the war, Naseby (1645), broke the backbone of the Royalist cause. The following June two of Charles' ablest commanders surrendered with their armies, and Charles himself sought refuge with the Scots, who shortly thereafter turned him over to the English commissioners in return for £400,000. Thus ended the first part of the civil war; the king's only hope was that the victors would not be able to agree among themselves, and that they proved unable to do.

The army that Cromwell had created was made up largely of Puritans and Independents; that is to say, men who believed that each religious congregation was responsible to God alone, and denied the right of any assembly to establish religious conformity. There were many elements in the army hostile to the aristocratic Presbyterians. The majority in Parliament, in order to obtain aid from the Scots, had subscribed to a League and Covenant to bring the churches of England and Scotland to religious conformity. Thus between the Puritan Model Army and the Presbyterian majority in Parliament there emerged a gulf that widened with each new issue. Parliament tried to establish its authority over the army, or disband it. By July 1647, Parliament and the army were ready to fly at each other's throats. Charles, a prisoner, was the third party; his chances seemed to be rising.

In November 1647, Charles escaped to the Isle of Wight, and thereafter he signed an agreement with the Scots. The army would have nothing of it, and the civil war began again with Cromwell as the key figure. Cromwell was convinced that no deal could be made with the king, and so when the leaders of Parliament continued to negotiate with both the king and the Scots, Cromwell intervened with military force. Colonel Pride, a former drayman, purged Parliament of its Presbyterian majority, leaving only a sectarian "rump." The Puritan soldiers who drove out the Presbyterians were completing the process that had previously excluded the Royalists and Anglicans, and finally left only a handful of Puritan "saints" in control of the government of England.

About the same time the Army again captured the king, and Cromwell forced the "Rump Parliament" to set up a high court of justice to try him for treason. The army and its general were determined to create a republic. "We will cut off the king's head with the crown on it," Cromwell assured his fellow judges. In January 1649, Charles I was tried for high treason, convicted, and sentenced to the block. Cromwell's influence obtained the necessary signatures from the reluctant commissioners; it was clearly the will of the army that the King must die. At his trial and execution Charles' behavior was more worthy of a king than his life had been. His death gave to English royalists a great myth and to the Anglican church a new saint, just as it gave a great tradition to all those who opposed royal prerogatives.

4. THE COMMONWEALTH AND PROTECTORATE, 1649–1660

Between 1649 and 1660 England was governed without a king by the small group of soldiers and politicians that controlled the army. In 1649 the monarchy and the House of Lords were abolished. A Council of State composed of forty-one members assumed the administrative functions, while the "Rump Parliament" was the law-making body. Much fancy language about England being a Commonwealth or "free state" could not cover up the fact that the army officers and their civilian friends had seized the government.

The right of the new regime to govern was challenged both by men more radical as well as by men more conservative than themselves. A so-called "Levelers" movement was operating in the rank and file of the army and in a fanatically religious segment of the population. Those men were vague democrats; perhaps they might even have been a sort of Christian communist group. Had their ideas prevailed, differences in wealth and status would have disappeared, and all men and women would have become "monks" of a sort in a Christian society. This was only one of several such radical sectarian movements. To property- and class-respecting squires like Cromwell, they were a great menace, and had to be broken as "anarchists." Much more dangerous were the forces behind the pretender, Prince Charles, who was to become Charles II. The execution of his father had shocked the western world. Throughout Europe, as well as in much of the British Isles, the execution seemed a sacrilege against divine law and an act of tyrannical violence. In Ireland and Scotland Charles Stuart found men who would support him. In Scotland that support was brought by subscribing to the political doctrines of the Presbyterian Kirk. Scottish aid was important to the pretender since it produced an army. Thus, in its first years, the Commonwealth had to fight for its existence, but in both Ireland and northern England Cromwell and his veterans won the day. The Royalists were unable to create a military force capable of meeting the Puritan army. Cromwell's work as a military organizer had been well done, and his victories in Scotland and Ireland firmly established the authority of the "Lord General" Cromwell and the "grandees" of the army.

The rise of the army in turn created new problems, for with every increase in the prestige and power of the soldiers, there was a corresponding decrease in that of the politicians. The army and the "Rump Parliament" had only a tenuous alliance, and the civilian politicians came to resent the rule of the major generals and the expense of maintaining the rank and file. The soldiers in turn became disgusted with the lawyers and debaters in Parliament. Finally Parliament, in an effort to rid itself of the military dictatorship, decided that a "fitting moment to change the Lord General" had arrived. Cromwell acted promptly. He invaded the hall of the "Rump Parliament" with troops, and announced its dissolution (April 20, 1653). "Thus," says Dr. Ashley, "the Long Parliament which had first raised the sword against the king, perished by the sword. . . ." The course of the revolution was complete; only the military power that it had created remained to govern the nation.

However, Cromwell did not now have a constitutional basis for his power. The army gave him the force necessary to rule England, and he believed that God intended him to exercise that power, but it was hard to find a demonstrable authority to which all England could subscribe. The army produced (December 1653) an "Instrument of Government" which made Cromwell "Lord Protector" of the Commonwealth. There was to be a Council of State with both civilian and military members to act as a check on the Protector and a parliament elected from England, Ireland, and Scotland for lawmaking and taxation. The franchise requiring voters to possess property valued at £200 assured that the radical Levellers would not come to power.

Had the ghost of Charles I been able to visit England then, it would have enjoyed Cromwell's plight. War with Spain, civil rebellion and plots for rebellion, and conflict with the Presbyterians and others who objected to the "Instrument of Government" provided ample grounds for friction between the Lord Protector and Parliament. Money and religion—those were the problems of the Stuart kings, and they remained problems for Cromwell. He dissolved his Parliament as soon as he could, and the government again rested its control upon the army. The government had become a military dictatorship no matter how it was described. The regime of the "major generals" was surely more tyrannical than the "eleven years of tyranny" of Charles I. The problem of power had come a full circle without finding a compromise that would work satisfactorily.

In addition to following many of the same patterns, Cromwell adopted many of the policies initiated by his Stuart predecessors. The Stuarts had begun to build up the English navy to protect commerce and had established the first colonial settlements of Englishmen in America (Puritan New England). Cromwell continued those policies vigorously. There were "cavalier" migrants to the middle and southern colonies in North America who disliked the rule of the "saints" as much as the "saints" had disliked that of the early Stuarts. Cromwell also passed the Navigation Acts by which he attempted to break the Dutch trade monopoly in favor of English merchants. The Acts led to war with the Netherlands, which we shall discuss in a later chapter. He also allied with France in the war against Spain, and secured Dunkirk as a base of operations for the English fleet. Those measures, undertaken for the advantage of the city merchants who largely favored his regime anyway, did not reduce the hostility that was growing in England against the arbitrary military dictatorship.

In other ways, too, the rule of the "saints" offended large segments of the English population. Puritanism has rightfully been associated with the "blue laws" that try to regulate public manners and morals by law. For example, traditional English practices, such as the Sunday games (outdoor exercises and sports) were forbidden because they "violated the Sabbath." The theater disappeared, the sporting fights between dogs, bulls, and bears, and, indeed, almost any entertainment that gave pleasure to man was made illegal. Such straight-laced meddlesome interference with innocent pleasures, with art, indeed with all aspects of life, earned for the "saints" the profound hatred of many of their fellow citizens. The mere fact that the Puritans also produced a John Milton and a Bunyan to decorate English letters seemed small compensation for their interference with so many aspects of English life. The rule of Cromwell, his major generals, and the religious fanatics associated with the Puritans, lasted only as long as there was a strong man at the helm to choke back the discontent that it generated.

Cromwell died in 1658. For a few months his son, Richard, became Lord Protector, but he was not a man of the stuff to retain power over a revolutionary regime. A military conspiracy overthrew the Protectorate (1659), and recalled the members of the "Rump Parliament" that Oliver Cromwell had dissolved in 1653. However, the members proved unwilling to do the bidding of the major generals, and so were again dissolved by force a few months later. At that point General Monk, one of the strongest and most levelheaded officers of the army, intervened to prevent the situation from becoming one of anarchy. Backed by military power, he joined with civilian politicians to secure the election of a "Free Parliament" which everyone understood would recall Charles Stuart to be king.

Charles was anxious to return. He was quite ready to meet any reasonable terms. By his Declaration of Breda in April 1660, Charles announced his intention to grant liberty to "tender consciences" and to leave to Parliament any punishment for persons not included in a general pardon. On May 29, 1660, he returned to London as Charles II, king by Grace of God. The invitation of the Parliamentary committee had been evidence that Parliament had accepted him as the rightful king. England received the son of the recently beheaded king with outward signs of joy. Charles II, with obvious irony, expressed astonishment over his popularity; even he realized that it was freedom from the rule of Puritan "saints" rather than the arrival of an unknown king that pleased Englishmen. Clearly no other solution could bring peace to the realm, and those who were skeptical held their peace or bided their time to see how the new king would behave.

5. THE RESTORATION, 1660–1688

When the dust had settled a little and men could take stock of what had happened, it became clear that the restoration of Charles II to the throne of his ancestors was only part of the picture of England after the civil war. The king's right to raise money and govern without Parliament had been abolished and with it the prerogative courts that had played so important a role in the preceding century. The Privy Council had lost its jurisdiction over criminal cases, and the king could no longer arrest members of Parliament without cause. Parliament was restored on its ancient basis in such a way that it became practically impossible either to alter the franchise or to redistribute the seats. Lastly, the Church of England with its hierarchy of bishops, deans, and canons was restored, purged of the Puritan and Presbyterian element. A new code was soon to make dissent a crime again and place Jesuit priests and Calvinist preachers in the same jail.

The new king was a handsome, charming man. His French mother, his years of exile, and his natural disposition gave him an attitude toward life considerably less straight-laced than that of the Calvinists who had ruled England before him. The court of the restored Stuarts soon became famous for its laxity, its immorality, and its brilliance. The theater in London that catered to those tastes after two decades of Puritanism became equally famous for its racy, amoral tone. Whatever else he may have done, Charles II reversed the rigorous moral regime that the Puritan saints had tried to impose upon England. He was also a skillful politician obsessed with the desire to live out his life as king rather than return to exile. Thus we see him making compromises where necessary, playing politics at all times. He did not permit his religious beliefs (he died a Roman Catholic) to interfere with the religious measures necessary to maintain his government. Without the royal prerogative and the special courts to fall back upon, he had to use skill and personality to achieve his ends. French-educated and a grandson of Henry IV of France, Charles II proved to have a greater portion of those attributes than either his Stuart father or grandfather had possessed.

The Restoration also saw the rise of the relatively stable political parties that were to become characteristic of English parliamentary life. In earlier Parliaments the House had been divided between the Court and the Country parties. The former were the favorites, placemen (officeholders), and pensioners of the king's government. The latter was composed of the suspicious souls who had little confidence in the king and probably had received but little of his bounty. Charles II's first Parliament was largely made up of men fervently loyal to the Restoration and the monarchy. It was so satisfactory a Parliament that Charles kept it in being most of his reign. He saw no reason for elections as long as Parliament supported his purposes. However, questions of religion, foreign policy, and domestic administration came to divide politically minded people into two camps, and between 1670 and 1685 there emerged two reasonably distinct political parties. They took their names from terms of derision: "Whig" meant a Scottish cattle thief; "Tory," an Irish robber. The parties elevated these names to a position of honor.

The Tory party came to be composed largely of the conservative squires and gentry, many of whom were former Cavaliers and who had been alarmed by the excesses of the civil war. Largely ignorant of the greater world of affairs, they were isolationist in foreign policy, Anglican in religion, and almost blindly loyal to the idea of divine right. The clergy and the conservative theologians at Oxford furnished them with a comfortable religion that did not tax their intelligence or their conscience severely, and at the same time provided a dogmatic basis for action. These men stood by Charles II even to the extent of supporting his Roman Catholic brother's claim to the throne. At the same time they insisted upon legislation to try to force all England into a kind of religious conformity. They passed the Test Act (1673) that prevented James, Duke of York, from ruling the Admiralty because he was a Catholic, but refused to back legislation to keep him off the throne if he remained a Roman Catholic.

The backbone of the Whig party was the city merchants and financiers and the Puritan and Presbyterian squires. While the Tories were usually the sons of Cavaliers, the Whigs were often the sons of Roundheads. Thus the late Presbyterian and Puritan elements tended to become Whiggish in politics and dissenters in religion. They were joined by many great landed magnates (old feudal lords and newer political and military officials who had consolidated their position as landlords and peers of the realm). The alliance between Whig lords and city men was to be a commonplace in English politics for almost two centuries. The Whigs tended to be more aggressive in foreign policy, more liberal toward religious dissenters (except Roman Catholics and Unitarians), and more insistent upon the rights of Parliament rather than those of the king. They were willing to ignore the doctrine of divine right of kings if the king did not satisfy their own political aims. They tried to exclude James II from the throne on the grounds of his Catholicism.

However, compared to political parties of later centuries, both the Tory and Whig parties were largely formless. There was no way of securing party discipline, and many of the chiefs were not immune to blandishments of favor, money, or other political bribes. Thus, as we watch them evolve toward more stable political forms the early Whig and Tory parties resemble rather a disorderly crowd struggling more or less toward a common goal than a disciplined army storming a fixed objective. It was to be over half a century after the Restoration of 1660 before the institutions of England would evolve to a point where political parties could pretend to responsible direction of the affairs of the kingdom.

The Restoration of 1660 created a relationship between king and Parliament that boded ill for the future because the basic question of the location of authority had not been resolved. The Tudor constitution had made Parliament subservient to the crown. Under the first two Stuarts this relationship had been challenged, and the second Stuart king had lost both head and crown. The Restoration created an uneasy partnership between king and Parliament, with both parties of about equal power. As long as they agreed with each other, government of a kind was possible; if they disagreed, government would have to revolve around a dead center or face a coup d'état, for there was no machinery to break a deadlock. Even without such a crisis, the solution was an unhappy one, for neither king nor Parliament was in a position to adopt a strong policy or to embark upon any important project, since neither had any way of assuring continued support from the other. The result was weakness in domestic and in foreign policy. A strong king like Louis XIV regarded England and Poland as comparable regimes. In both lands the Diet or Parliament curbed the king, and consequently both monarchs willingly accepted French money to escape from poverty; in return they were forced to assist Louis in his foreign projects. Internal policy also suffered, for inevitably the king and Parliament when they differed on a program reached a point where nothing could be accomplished, or even worse, where demagoguery took the place of statesmanship. Charles II marked a path between the emerging Whig and Tory policies with great skill. It was a path that kept him on the throne, but it did not necessarily allow a reasoned consideration of the state interests of England.

In 1685 Charles II died, and his brother, James II, mounted the throne. Only a few years before, Parliament had passed the Test Act that required all officeholders to receive the sacraments in the Church of England. It was reasoned that a Catholic might swear a false oath, but would hesitate to endanger his soul by sacrilegiously receiving communion from a heretic. James, a Catholic, had been forced to retire from the Admiralty. The Whigs, however, had failed in their effort to pass an act excluding James from the throne. The parsons and squires piously reminded their opponents that kings ruled by divine right, and God in His wisdom knew what He did. James' first Parliament was strongly Tory and more generous with money than any Parliament had heretofore been. When an illegitimate son of the late king led a rebellion to oust James from the throne, Parliament granted funds for an army to put down the revolt. The Tories were not happy to see their king practicing the Roman Catholic religion, but they knew that his heirs, Princess Mary, wife of William of Orange, and Princess Anne, wife of a Danish prince, were both Protestants, and so the church was really not in danger.

James II was more purposeful than his brother had been, perhaps more intelligent, but surely not as wise. He _knew_ that God had called him to the English throne to reconcile England with the Roman church, and in spite of the advice of the pope, the Catholic emperor at Vienna, and the most Christian king of France, James insisted on pushing this reconciliation as rapidly as possible. He apparently did not plan to force all his subjects to become Catholics, but he planned to make the Catholic church dominant in the kingdom. Above all, he tried to achieve his ends quickly.

The courts gave James II the loophole he needed. They found that the king could excuse his subjects from the obligations of the Test Act. James then proceeded to grant dispensations on a large scale, so that the army and government came more and more to be staffed by Catholics and Protestant dissenters. James exempted both groups from the provisions of the Test Act. One of the ironical facts of history was the willingness of the Protestant dissenters to take advantage of this royal bounty that was primarily intended for their bitterest enemies, the Catholics. Many good men of Anglican faith were actually confronted with the demand to become Roman Catholics or to give up their positions to make room for Roman Catholics. Oxford University, the very center of the doctrine of the divine right of kings, was also tested to the extreme when James turned one of the colleges over to Roman Catholic priests to create a seminary. A crisis arose when the king ordered his bishops to read a general Act of Indulgence sanctioning officeholding by Catholics and Dissenters as well as good Anglicans. It appeared that James II intended to staff the royal offices with Catholics, elect a Catholic Parliament, and then make Catholicism the religion of the realm. Thus, all his illegal acts would be legalized.

Seven bishops refused to read the Act, and James II brought them up before the court for seditious libel. Their jailers asked their blessings, and the rank and file in the army as well as many of the officers cheered loudly when the court acquitted them (June 1688). It was a scandal to bring such holy men before a court. Curiously enough, most of them lost their ecclesiastical positions a short time later because they would not swear allegiance to William and Mary as the rightful successors to James II. They believed in divine right, even if a "rightful king" arraigned them unjustly.

The case of the bishops showed the temper and intention of the king. When his wife gave birth to a son, James Edward, the king's intentions posed a fearful threat to the Anglican church and English liberties. The queen was thirty when her son was born. As the distinguished English historian, Sir George Clark, put it, "the people of the seventeenth century would believe anything." The Catholics said that the birth was "a miracle"; the Protestants insisted that the child had been introduced into the queen's bed in a warming pan. Both were wrong, but miracle or impostor, the baby, James Edward, would be a Catholic, and, if he lived, would assure the Catholic succession to the throne.

At that point the Whig leaders and some of the Tories agreed that action was necessary. Other Tories, whose tender consciences would not allow them to act against a king endowed with divine right, agreed not to interfere in any action that might be taken. The plotters invited William of Orange, James' son-in-law and Stadholder of the Netherlands, to bring an army to England to intervene in the political crisis. William was the foremost Protestant statesman in Europe and one of the leaders of a great military coalition that was being built up against Louis XIV. He also knew England well, and had long been in contact with English politicians. His acceptance of the invitation was conditioned by war in Hungary, Louis' invasion of the Rhineland, and his desire to force James II to join the coalition against France. Whether or not William foresaw that he would dethrone his father-in-law is an academic question; his problem was to force James to listen to reason, and England to join the alliance against France. Once his army had landed on English soil, he had enough power to decide the political issue, and James' "trusted lieutenants" joined the victor without delay.

The revolution of 1688 has been called the "Glorious Revolution" by English statesmen and historians. It cost practically no blood, and it gave a new constitution to both England and Europe. James fled to France; and a new Parliament, freely elected, declared the throne vacant and then called on William and Mary to become king and queen. Both had the blood of England's royal family in their veins, but no argument could alter the fact that

James Edward was the legitimate heir to the English throne. Thus the principle that Parliament could depose and elect the king became an established fact. The old contest for power between king and Parliament was being settled in favor of the latter. Parliament became the senior partner in the government of the realm. Henceforth the king would have to obey the law or face the fate of Charles I and James II.

The revolutionary settlement included a series of laws that gave Parliament control over wide areas of the king's government. The annual Mutiny Act placed the army under the king, but made its continuance as a disciplined force dependent upon Parliament. The practice of granting a civil list for the king's household expenses and annual appropriations for the conduct of his government made, in effect, government policy dependent upon parliamentary approval. Another act required regular periods for election to Parliament to prevent the king from keeping a Parliament friendly to his government in permanent session. In regulating the succession to the throne, Parliament reaffirmed its right to name the king, and added a provision that created an independent judiciary. Henceforth judges ceased to be "lions under the throne," and Englishmen's lives ceased to be at the "mercy of two false witnesses."

These laws gave new direction to the evolution of the English constitution. Overnight the center of political interest shifted from the king's court to Parliament, for it was the latter that passed the laws and granted the money. The king's government, however, was not thereby eclipsed, for henceforth it was assured of considerably more money than any English government had ever enjoyed before, simply by the expedient of securing parliamentary consent for its policy. Thus, the treasury officials undertook to educate the squires in Parliament in the intricacies of government, and the king called to his ministry men who could in one way or another find solid support in the House of Lords and the House of Commons. Such practices encouraged the growth of the party system as well as of corruption and graft; it also assured to England an executive authority endowed with more real power than was enjoyed by any of the so-called despotic rulers of that age.

William of Orange was not entirely in sympathy with all the measures strengthening parliamentary powers, but by securing the entry of England into the war against France he accomplished his primary mission. His interests were always more European than English, and he was happy to cooperate with any English politicians who would help him fight the king of France.

With Parliament as his ally in the war, William could tap financial resources greater than those available to any other ruler in Europe, and in the great war that raged in the West between 1688 and 1697, this financial power definitely checked the ambition of Louis XIV to rule the continent.

This war and the one that followed it (the War of the Spanish Succession) established the balance of power as the central mechanism of the constitution of Europe. The decisive political and military role of England that became possible only after the revolution of 1688 had far-reaching effects on the development of European society as a whole, and continued to have them into the twentieth century.

This aerial view of Versailles is one that Louis XIV never saw, but it illustrates better than any other the imposing structure of the palace and the way in which the whole area is subordinated to it. If the view took in more of the gardens, we would see that they, too, are centered upon this great building. (French Government Tourist Office)

Chapter 12

THE RISE OF
BOURBON FRANCE

1. THE NEW DYNASTY

Tourists who visit the Basilica of St. Denis just outside Paris are shown the tombs of the kings of France; the final thing that they see is the crypt where the Bourbons are buried, apart from their predecessors. Their symbolical aloofness did not preserve the Bourbon graves from desecration at the hands of the revolutionaries in 1789, but it does, somehow, express the dynasty's separate place in the history of the nation. When the first Bourbon (Henry IV) claimed the throne (1589), France was tormented by civil war; under the third of the line, Louis XIV (1643–1715), France achieved a political, military, and cultural leadership that dazzled Europe. Of the last three Bourbon kings, one (Louis XVI, 1774–1792) was beheaded, one (Louis XVIII, 1814–1824), after a lifetime of exile, died on the throne, and the last (Charles X, 1824–1830) was chased out of France by his irate subjects. The history of the Bourbon dynasty, however, is the history of France rather than the story of the royal family.

As we have seen, the Bourbon family came to the throne of France at the end of an era of civil warfare. Indeed, Henry IV not only had to fight for his throne, but also had to change his religion and to bribe his subjects before he could mount it. The great Catholic lords were willing to allow themselves to be bought after Henry had received the sacraments in their church; they wanted hereditary governorships over provinces and towns, the right to collect tolls on roads and rivers, and huge grants of money. However, the act that made him acceptable to the Catholics brought frowns of suspicion to the brows of his erstwhile friends, the Huguenots. They, too, had to be bribed, or they would seek another "champion" to take the place that Henry had vacated. Their price was the Edict of Nantes, which not only granted them religious liberty but also control over walled towns, revenues, and soldiers to assure their positions in the kingdom. By the Edict the Huguenot community practically became a republic within the kingdom of France. The *Parlement* that was asked to register the grants of vast powers to Catholic noblemen as well as to the Huguenots tried to prevent Henry's "give away" policies by refusing to register the edicts, but the king forced them to do so rather than risk further civil wars.

Thus the new dynasty began its career by stripping the royal authority of much of the power that its predecessors had acquired in the preceding century or so. Henry had no choice. He needed the support of both the Catholics and the Huguenots to drive the armies of Spain out of the land. He also needed their recognition of his right to occupy the throne, for no matter how good his claim might have been, he could not have become king without the consent of his subjects.

The last dozen years of Henry's reign marked the recovery of the kingdom and with it a rise in the popularity of the new dynasty. It was once believed that the economic policies instituted by Henry's finance minister, Sully, were largely responsible for the return of prosperity, but scholars now agree that the recovery was primarily due to the return of peace and tranquillity in the countryside. Like any good politician, Sully claimed the credit for everything that happened while he was the king's trusted man, and Bourbon propagandists of later eras re-echoed his words. However, it is improbable that there was "a chicken in every pot," and such pots as did contain chickens might well have held them even if Sully had not been the finance minister, for the first years of the seventeenth century were prosperous ones for Europe wherever there was peace.

Nonetheless, the fact of general European prosperity should not detract from the real work of Henry's government. When he came to the throne the treasury was in a deplorable condition. Interest on the royal debt was two decades in arrears; taxes were either uncollected or were collected but in the main not remitted to the treasury; the crown lands brought in little income, and the expenses of the war and reconstruction were crushing. Henry's marriage to Marie de Medici was designed, though only in a small measure, to bring relief to the treasury; she was a banker's daughter and brought a good dowry. Of more importance was the work done by Sully as Superintendent of the Finances, for which he had a right to claim honors. He was the prototype of all later effective French royal finance ministers. He was not a bold innovator, but such a role was not possible in France for the tax structure was a patchwork of special privileges and rights that could not be changed without a social revolution. Sully was an administrator; he studied the whole tax structure, and then insisted upon complete returns. It was a shock to tax collectors to be forced to pay into the treasury not only the current tax but also taxes that they had collected in the past. He also studied the obligations of the treasury, that is, the debts, to see how many of them were legitimate. He cancelled one after another on the grounds that they had been falsely created; on others, he reduced the interest rate. Bourbon France never succeeded in developing a sound fiscal system, but Sully's reforms saved the dynasty from bankruptcy in the first years that it was on the throne.

Henry fully supported his minister's economies. Since most of his life had been spent in the company of soldiers, his idea of a court was simple to the extreme. The stable rather than the salon was the principal scene of his exploits. His Italian wife and his many mistresses found it difficult to extract money from him. Poor Marie loved diamonds; Henry would give her a bill on the treasury to buy them with, but would neglect to tell her that the bill could not be cashed because no money had been provided in the account. Such jokes caused considerable friction in a household that was not altogether unified anyway. After Henry died, Marie was able to govern the kingdom for a few years on the results of his parsimony: the king had a "war chest" filled with money that he had saved.

In another area, too, Henry was an enlightened monarch. Concerned about the drain of French gold to Italy for luxuries of one kind or another, he tried to introduce industries into France to end foreign purchases. The silk industry, stocking manufacture, rug making, tapestry weaving, and other such enterprises were started in France with varying degrees of success. Henry and Sully also began work on canal construction that Louis XIV and Colbert were to continue and extend half a century later.

However, when Henry was murdered in 1610 by a religious fanatic, it became evident that he had not been able to undo the damage that the civil wars had worked on the French constitution. Although he tried to clip back the privileges of the "great ones" and to undermine some of the rights of the Huguenots, he had not re-established the prestige of the crown. The greatest problem for the French nation lay in the fact that those who opposed the royal authority had no intention of governing the kingdom in place of the king; they were merely selfish men seeking to decentralize all authority so that their own interests could be served. None of them had the slightest intention of creating a national government to take the place of the royal authority that they wished to weaken or even to destroy.

Since the new king, Louis XIII, was only nine years old at the time of Henry's death, Marie de Medici became regent; and her regency acted as a signal for every unruly force in the kingdom to move against the crown. The Huguenots feared the clerical advisers around the queen-regent, and wished to regain the privileges that Henry had usurped. The great nobles who had lost ground through Sully's fiscal policies as well as those who recalled that in earlier times a regency had been considered the occasion for extending their privileges banded together to blackmail the government. The Prince of Condé, cousin to the late king, became the leader of the "great ones." Thus, just as Henry had bribed the nobles to accept him as king, Marie now had to bribe them to recognize her rule. All went reasonably well as long as the proceeds of Henry's war chest held out, but when it had been emptied some new basis for government had to be found.

The complex nature of the problem in France became apparent in 1614–1615, when Marie was forced to call the Estates-General into session. The great nobles under Condé were opposed to her government. They objected to her ministers, to her internal policies, and to her pro-Spanish policy. (The Bourbon and Spanish Hapsburg families had exchanged princesses—Louis XIII married Anne of Austria.) When the Estates-General met other unsolved problems emerged. The Third Estate was largely made up of members of the *parlements* of the kingdom (law courts) and other officials. They demanded action in the church that might have made the Gallican church of France as independent of Rome as the Anglican church was in England. It also became evident that the two upper houses (the clergy and nobility) had no sympathy with the interests of those men of the "robe" in the lower house who were about to become hereditary magistrates and judges. The result was that the three houses fell into conflicts among themselves that simply could not be resolved. The Estates-General was as powerless to act as Marie's government seemed to be. The spokesman for the Estate of the Clergy, the young Bishop of Luçon (later known as Cardinal Richelieu), expressed the hopes of the majority of the Estates-General, when he urged the queen-regent to create a government of "authority"—in other words, to govern. Unlike the English Parliament, the Estates-General in France willingly gave up its right to direct the affairs of the country.

This was the first as well as the last time that the Bourbons called the Estates-General until the eve of the Revolution of 1789. Henry IV had never summoned the Estates-General, perhaps because the last to meet during the Valois regime had tried to place another dynasty on the throne. After the fiasco of 1614–1615, Henry's successors found it easier to govern without the advice and assistance of the elected representatives. Thus, when Louis XVI summoned it in 1789, there was no one alive who had any personal knowledge of the institution.

When the Estates-General failed to support Condé and his friends and urged the queen-mother to govern, Marie called to her counsel an Italian, Concini, the husband of her favorite confidante. He tried to give France a "strong" government. The young Bishop Richelieu became one of his secretaries of state, and the great nobles were excluded from the council. But Concini was a foreigner and much disliked by the French: like all the favorites of seventeenth-century rulers, he graspingly loaded himself with riches and honors. (Sully, too, had become one of the richest men of the realm.) French historians have had few good words to say for Concini, even though in many ways his policy was almost identical to that of Henry IV before and

Richelieu after him. When the great nobles left the court and raised the flag of revolt, Concini refused to bargain with them, and prepared to use military force to make them obey. While this may have been sound policy, the fact was that Concini, the foreigner, was making war on native-born Frenchmen, and his enemies called attention to the fact that he was becoming rich thereby.

Concini made many mistakes, and one of them proved to be fatal. While he was trying to force the nobles to respect the royal authority, he seems to have overlooked the fact that Louis XIII and not Marie was really king of France. Louis was a morose, ill-favored, sickly adolescent whose education had been neglected and whose ill-health seemed to promise an early death. Marie obviously favored her second son, the Duke of Orléans. The boy king hung around the stables, played with the dogs, and nursed his grievances; it was not surprising, therefore, that someone should sympathize with him and show him a way to revenge himself. Concini ignored him, and in retaliation Louis ordered the arrest of the minister with the understanding that he should be put to death. Louis' action led to a coup d'état. Concini was shot, his wife stripped of her wealth and honors, and Marie de Medici and her friends—including Richelieu—went into exile. The boy king's act had nothing to do with the revolt of the nobles that Concini was trying to suppress, nor did it end the rebellions. The coup d'état brought a new favorite into power, Luynes, a simple gentleman who soon became a duke and one of the richest men of the kingdom, but who failed to provide France with a strong government.

2. LOUIS XIII AND THE RISE OF AUTHORITATIVE GOVERNMENT

Marie de Medici in exile acted as a magnet for the crowd of great nobles who hoped to extract favors and wealth from the king. Paradoxically, she now took Condé's place as the vortex for rebellion against royal authority, in the person of her own son. However, the young king's problems did not end with a new revolt of the "great ones," for the other discordant political force in the kingdom, the Huguenots, also defied the king. Louis XIII seems to have welcomed the revolts at first, for he envisaged himself as a soldier king like his father, but with Luynes as his minister he could not really play that role since the favorite lacked both political and military skill. Thus his first years of personal government proved frustrating for the young king. With Richelieu as her adviser and diplomatic agent, Marie de Medici extracted one favor after another for herself and her friends. Even when the king's armies were victorious in the field against the nobles, Richelieu won the victory at the conference table. The fight with the Huguenots was equally disastrous. Luynes was unable to win a military victory against the great walled towns of the south, and the party of the Reformed religion secured a peace on its own terms. Luynes' death (1621) saved him from dismissal, but it was not until 1624 that Louis found a minister who could carry out his policy.

Richelieu was the man who gave meaning to the royal authority in France. Marie forced her son to take him into the royal council, and then discovered that her favorite had transferred his loyalty to the king and no longer obeyed her wishes. The partnership between the two men is one of the most important facts of French history. Until recent years most historians have described Louis XIII as a sort of puppet of the great minister, a dull king who knew only enough to hold fast to the tower of strength that gave his government force; but this picture has been radically altered in the last few decades, as new material has revealed that Louis was a strong and enlightened king and a real partner to the brilliant minister who directed the government. Richelieu's own correspondence leaves no doubt about his opinion of the king; he knew him to be a strong-minded man who was determined to be "master of the shop." The minister always presented his advice by giving all alternative policies, in such a way, to be sure, that his own opinion would prevail, but he never tried to force the king to follow a path contrary to the royal will. It now is evident that Louis and Richelieu supplemented each other, and apparently they both understood how completely they were dependent on each other for the success of their joint enterprise—the development of the royal authority.

Richelieu tells us that when he entered the council he assured the king that his policy would be to ruin the Huguenot party, to humble the great lords, and to raise French prestige in Europe. This meant, in effect, that he had thrown down the glove to the two great powers in France that opposed the royal authority. He did not have to wait long to test his skill in handling rebellious and intriguing noblemen. The "great ones" who had rallied to Condé and then to Marie de Medici now turned to Louis' younger brother, the Duke of Orléans, to lead their opposition. With this frivolous prince as front, they hoped to "unhorse" Richelieu. The fact that Marie also soon deserted, or was deserted by, her erstwhile favorite when he did not follow her pro-Spanish policy, added the queen-mother to the party of opposition. In the past, opponents of the king who had such patrons had been assured of personal immunity from reprisals if their plans failed, but neither Louis XIII nor Richelieu was willing to make compromises with rebels and plotters. The first plot planned by the "great ones" was not even allowed to come to a head. It was discovered and broken up before it could develop into a civil conflict. The Duke of Orléans was forced to marry at his brother's command, and the principal plotters, including a prince of the House of Talleyrand, lost their heads. Richelieu and Louis arranged for the executions to coincide with the marriage of the Duke of Orléans to show future plotters that they should not presume on the ability of the king's brother to secure a pardon in case their plots failed. Not since Henry IV had cut off the head of Biron (1602) for treason, had a cabal earned such punishment. Later plots, as we shall see, were treated with equal severity.

The most important addition to the royal authority came from the destruction of the political and military privileges of the Huguenot party which had been a continuous threat to the king. Great lords and rich fortified towns were ready to defend the party, and behind them was the cohesive power of religious fanaticism. As a young man, Louis had experienced their ability to resist with military power. Richelieu's first attempt to intervene in the Thirty Years' War (1624) had been frustrated by their rebellion. The Huguenots were practically a sovereign republic within the kingdom: with their synods and their armies they presented a formidable threat to any policies of which they did not approve. Richelieu did not attack the Huguenot stronghold directly, but by one means and another he goaded the most important of their cities, La Rochelle, into a revolt. This great city was one of the major trading centers on the Atlantic seacoast. Its sailors and merchants competed on equal terms with the Dutch and the English. Its government, secure behind high walls and assured of contact with the sea, had long regarded itself as an independent power with the right to regulate its own commerce and to control its own religious and political, as well as economic, affairs. When La Rochelle came into conflict with the king, its citizens did not hesitate to ally the city with England. For England, the alliance was perhaps the most irresponsible of a long list of foolish actions committed by Buckingham, the chief minister of Charles I. It was folly, too, for the people of La Rochelle: they got little aid from the English, and they provided Richelieu with an argument that isolated them from the rest of the Huguenots in France since no Frenchmen really like to see foreigners invited to participate in a domestic quarrel.

The conquest of La Rochelle was one of Richelieu's greatest triumphs. He was both soldier and statesman in the operation, preparing the plans for the siege and fending off the attacks of enemies from without and within his own ranks. The king's support was constant, for he had come to understand Richelieu's policy and supported it against all intrigues in the court. The English were driven off, and the city was starved into submission. In many ways the siege marked a new step in the history of the royal authority. It was the first occasion on which the king's armies had been able to stay in the field all winter: it was also the first time in many decades that the royal forces had imposed an unconditional surrender on rebels. This surrender (1629) marked the new policy toward the Huguenots. The king and the cardinal did not make war on the Reformed religion: they left the city with complete freedom of worship, but they made war on the military and political pretensions of the Huguenot party. La Rochelle's fortifications were destroyed, and a royal garrison was established in royal fortifications that could dominate the city.

Within the next two years the Huguenot cities of the south were also provoked to the folly of revolt, and each was forced to receive a royal garrison. The Peace of Alais (1631) finally confirmed Louis XIII's victory over the party. Huguenot religious practices were untouched, but the party of the Reformed religion had to give up the political and military power that the Edict of Nantes had placed in its hands. By the use of military force and moral restraint, Louis and Richelieu had thus removed a dangerous check upon the royal power. The Huguenots came to appreciate the tolerance of the king, and, rather than becoming a dissident element in the kingdom, they remained both loyal and royalist for over a generation. When the Fronde erupted in the middle of the seventeenth century, the members of the "pretended Reformed religion" did not joint the rebellion.

However, the end of the Huguenot threat did not assure peace. The great nobles, the anti-Richelieu party in the court, the queen-mother, and her second son, the Duke of Orléans, continued to threaten the stability of the government and the peace of the countryside. Their opposition to Richelieu stemmed both from their dislike of his stern, authoritarian government and his hostility to Spain and Hapsburg interests in Germany. Marie and her second son opposed the policies that allied Catholic France with Protestant interests in Europe. There were two severe crises, both of which sent men to the block, before Marie de Medici and the Duke of Orléans were finally exiled from the kingdom. The first occurred in 1630 (the so-called Day of Dupes), when Marie tried to force Louis to give up his minister by pulling all the maternal emotional stops. Unfortunately for her friends, several of whom lost their heads, she failed to move the king. The second crisis culminated in an "invasion" of the kingdom by the Duke of Orléans and his friends (1632). The rebels were defeated, and Orléans retreated across the frontier. However, the Duke of Montmorency, who was a godson of Henry IV, brother-in-law of the Prince of Condé, and one of the most popular young noblemen of France, was captured, tried, and beheaded. In spite of all sorts of pleading by the Duke's family, Louis refused to grant clemency. Montmorency's execution dramatically illustrated the fact that not even the greatest noblemen of the realm could successfully defy the king.

In the last decade of Richelieu's life there were to be several further plots against his government, but they invariably ended the same way. Even the Marquis of Cinq-Mars, who was one of Louis' own favorites, lost his head when he tried to interfere with the government of the realm. The king never faltered in his support of the great cardinal to whom he owed so much.

This tendency toward severity was not the only blow that the new government struck against the nobility's political freedom. Richelieu called an Assembly of Notables, nominated by himself and the king, to become a "sounding board," and presented them with a plan to destroy all the fortifications within the kingdom except those belonging to the king and those guarding the frontier. The subsequent destruction of great "places of security" deprived the nobility of much of their ability to resist royal authority.

Furthermore, the nobility's contempt for royal authority came under stricter surveillance in another area. Every nobleman virtually regarded himself as a sovereign power; his sword assured him justice. In practice, the nobles' attitude resulted in wholesale spilling of blood from irresponsible private quarrels. As many as four thousand young noblemen died in one year as a result of duels. There were stories of fights with ten to twenty men on each side that began because some stupid fellow felt that his "honor" had been attacked. Swordplay may look exciting in the movies, but in actual life it creates disorder in the streets and results in unnecessary deaths. There were laws against dueling, but they were not enforced. Louis and Richelieu decided that the blood which had been spilled could be used to better purpose in fighting the king's enemies, and therefore made a special effort to end the custom. Again the measures taken were severe. Several important noblemen were beheaded to show the nation that the king desired the practice of dueling to end; and in the decades following 1630 the incidence of dueling declined rapidly. It would be erroneous, however, to credit the king's government with this change completely. While Louis and Richelieu probably did discourage dueling, there were changes in the social and political patterns of life that also acted powerfully to discourage the practice. On the other hand, neither the government nor social pressure could completely suppress dueling, and while it was not common, the practice continued into the twentieth century.

The plots and the severity with which they were repressed were outward signs of the revolution that Richelieu and Louis XIII were effecting in French society. They were dramatic evidence of the tension that was developing as a result of the rising power of the royal authority. The king's government was taking over powers that had heretofore been the prerogative of the feudal authorities, the town governments, the royal governors of the provinces (great lords), and the sovereign courts (*parlements*) of the kingdom. Wherever possible the king suppressed provincial estates (that had the right to grant or refuse taxes to the king), and replaced them with treasury officials who could impose taxes at the king's pleasure. The traditional military offices of constable, admiral, lieutenant-general of the infantry, and the like were suppressed or their real functions were taken over by a secretary of state who was eventually to emerge as Minister of War. Provincial officials found that their functions were being assumed and their work checked by traveling agents of the king. Toward the end of Louis XIII's reign some of those "circuit riders" were already becoming royal *intendants*, established as representatives of the king. Royal governors found that bishops acting under royal instruction were also cutting down their power to act independently. Often Richelieu and Louis merely arranged for powerful political forces to "knock each other's heads" when it was impossible to bring them under royal surveillance, but the object was the same: the subordination of all independent forces in the realm.

The sovereign courts (*parlements*) were treated rigorously. Under weak kings they had increased their right to remonstrate against a royal edict to a point approximating the right of judicial review. They assumed that it was their right to refuse to register the king's orders if, in their opinion, those were contrary to the constitution of the kingdom. Thus, especially in financial matters, the *parlements* aspired to the right to dictate royal policy. Louis rather brutally told them to concern themselves with justice and "not to interfere with *my* state." It is highly questionable that his famous son, Louis XIV, ever used such arbitrary language; it was rather Louis XIII who might have said, "*L'état, c'est moi*" ("I am the state").

In the realm of economics Richelieu also showed himself to be a statesman with vision. He encouraged the establishment of French colonies as well as the creation of trading companies to compete for commerce. Years later, Colbert often offended Louis XIV by prefacing so many of his proposals with the words, "Sire, that great statesman, Cardinal Richelieu, proposed" this or that measure. It was true that wars and rebellion prevented Richelieu and Louis XIII from achieving much of their economic program, but it is also true that they were important in shaping the so-called mercantilist doctrines that later played such a significant role in French policy.

3. FOREIGN AFFAIRS: LOUIS XIII AND RICHELIEU

As we have seen, Richelieu was responsible for France's intervention in the Thirty Years' War in Germany. Nineteenth-century French historians, who wished to emphasize their own version of a desirable foreign policy for the nation, used to tell us that Richelieu's policy was to extend the boundaries of France to their "natural frontiers, the Rhine, the Alps, and the Pyrenees." This undoubtedly represented the ideals of the later nineteenth-century historians, but there is little evidence that Richelieu shared their notions of policy. Early seventeenth-century map makers had not yet produced the beautiful maps that "clearly" showed the "natural" frontiers, and treaties of that era never actually mentioned the exact lines of frontiers. Richelieu, like his age, thought in terms of "provinces and their dependencies" rather than in terms of lineal frontiers, and he regarded public policy in terms of the prestige and advantages of the Bourbon dynasty rather than in terms of the "French" nation. The "France" of his day was still a federation of provinces with diverse constitutions and civilizations speaking different languages (French, German, Flemish, Provençal, Spanish, Breton, and Italian) rather than a national state. Without realizing it, he and Louis XIII were laying the basis for a national state, but it would be a serious error to conceive of their foreign policy in nineteenth- or twentieth-century terms.

When Richelieu joined the king's council there were two "parties" or points of view about French foreign policy: the "patriots" and the "devouts." The patriots regarded the threat of Spanish hegemony in Europe as a direct danger to France. The Spanish Hapsburgs with their provinces in the Netherlands, the Rhineland, Franche-Comté, and Italy, practically surrounded France, just as they had in the sixteenth century. Furthermore, the victories of the Austrian Hapsburgs in the early years of the Thirty Years' War and the obvious close connection between Spanish and Austrian policy, seemed to point to a Europe completely controlled by the Hapsburgs. The "patriots" did not forget that Philip II had tried to place his daughter on the French throne, and believed that they had every reason to fear that Hapsburg designs on France had not come to an end. The logical policy to follow, therefore, was that of Francis I, Henry II, and Henry IV: namely, an alliance with the English, the Dutch, and the Lutheran powers of Germany and the Baltic. The fact that this made Catholic France the leader of Protestant Europe did not bother their consciences, for the "patriots" separated politics and religion.

The "devouts" were the men of the Counter-Reformation, and since Spain was the spearpoint of that movement, they felt it was France's duty to support Spain: they had wide support in the kingdom. Those men who "remembered" that Philip II had helped them to prevent Henry IV from becoming king as long as he was a heretic, urged alliance with Spain. Both the queen-mother, Marie de Medici, who was proud of her Hapsburg blood, and the queen, Anne of Austria, who was the daughter of a king of Spain, pressed for a pro-Spanish policy. To these voices were added those of priests and bishops, theologians and monks, several of whom have since been canonized as saints, who saw the Hapsburgs as the leaders of their Catholic cause. The king's own confessor believed that any other policy was contrary to God's will. It would be a serious mistake to underestimate the political and moral power of the "devouts"; even though Richelieu did not agree with them, he frequently found it necessary to take them into account. Whenever he opposed them, he courted plots and rebellions. For example, the two queens nearly succeeded in overthrowing him once when Louis was very ill; their principal complaint was based upon the cardinal's foreign policy. As a priest and pious Catholic, Richelieu himself was troubled by the interrelations between politics and religion. When a French princess was sent to England to become the bride of Charles I, he tried to provide guarantees for her soul as well as relief for English Catholics; but he did not forget that princesses were pawns in the game of politics, and, therefore, if France did not supply a queen for England some other state surely would do so.

Richelieu's apparent reluctance to adopt the "patriot" program for war on Spain undoubtedly developed from his experience during the first years of his ministry. At the time that the Danish king entered the war in Germany (1624), Richelieu tried to intervene by action in Italy and Switzerland, only to find that he had to withdraw because of a Huguenot rebellion and a plot of the great nobles. Therefore, not until his internal policy of suppressing those two groups had achieved a measure of success did he actively enter the German war. By 1635 both the Huguenots and the great nobles had succumbed to the royal whip, and thus it was safe for France to join the Swedes and Dutch against the Hapsburgs.

The course of Richelieu's intervention in the war seems to indicate that his policy was inspired by a desire to undo Hapsburg power rather than by any notions about "natural frontiers"; no other explanation will justify his Italian and Swiss policy. Obviously, when Richelieu and Louis XIII acquired control over the Italian fortresses of Casale and Pinerolo and influence over Mantua, they were trying to set up a French "roadblock" in the Po valley that would interfere with the Hapsburg supply lines between Spain and central Europe. In Switzerland the attempt to control the Valtelline was also clearly aimed at Spanish supplies. In the Netherlands, where the French armies eventually won a great victory (Rocroi, 1643), there were no "natural frontiers": French policy aimed at the acquisition of the great fortress towns that could hold off invaders from the east. In Germany, Richelieu supported any force that would undermine the authority of the emperor and keep central Europe from acquiring a strong government.

Neither Richelieu nor Louis XIII lived to see their policy crowned with success. Suspicion of the great nobles and inadequate finances had combined to limit the military power that they could mobilize for the war. Furthermore, French soldiers had to learn the art of war, as it had emerged in the German theater, before they could successfully lead their armies. After 1643 the young Prince of Condé and the Count of Turenne emerged as great captains whose victories led to the triumph of French policy in the Treaties of Westphalia (1648) and the Pyrenees (1659).

4. THE REGENCY, THE FRONDE, AND THE VICTORY

When Richelieu and Louis XIII died (1642–1643), the real import of their internal policy became apparent. They had successfully concentrated the government of France in the hands of the king by suppressing ancient offices and developing bureaucratic machinery to govern the state. The secretaries of state, who had formerly been mere writers of letters at the order of the king and council, emerged as heads of departments of government and members of special councils to make policy. Furthermore a newly created royal official, the *intendant,* had become established in the provinces to make the king's authority felt at the "grass roots" of society. They supervised justice, taxation, public works, the recruitment and care of soldiers, and any other task that might be assigned to them by the government in Paris. As the king's men, they undermined the power of the people who had traditionally governed the countryside, and thereby earned for themselves the hostility of the nobles and the town authorities. However, the work of the king and cardinal was not finished. Indeed, in the decade after their deaths it was put to the severest of tests, and only the political genius of their successor, Cardinal Mazarin, saved it from being reversed.

French historians rarely give Mazarin credit for his achievements, even though they value the glory and internal unity that he gave their nation. Like Concini, he was a foreigner; like all royal favorites, he became very rich. Mazarin also profited from clever financial enterprises; he was a speculator as well as a statesman. For his nationality and his wealth he is criticized and hated, perhaps also because his victories were won over Frenchmen as well as over foreigners. Nonetheless, Mazarin, supported by the Spanish queen-mother, first saved France from disruption within when the great nobles and the parlementarians tried to undo the Richelieuan revolution, and then they brought the kingdom to a pinnacle of power in Europe by victories over the House of Hapsburg.

Mazarin's power rested on the affections of the queen-mother and the boy, King Louis XIV, just as Richelieu's had on the affections of Louis XIII. Anne's position in France had long been difficult. A queen without children is a useless appendage to a throne, and Anne's first child that survived did not come until she was almost forty years old. After the birth of Louis, the *Dieu-donné* ("God given"), she had one consuming goal—namely, the glory and power of her son. She discovered soon after Louis XIII died that Mazarin was the one man whom she could trust to carry out her desires for her son, and this led the relationship between the Spanish-born queen and the Italian minister to become love between a woman and a man. Anne's letters leave no doubt about her passionate affection, and Mazarin's letters are surely not those of a minister to his queen but rather of a husband who expects to be obeyed. The probability is that they were secretly married, if for no other reason than Anne's religious beliefs which would never have condoned irregularity. Since Mazarin was not a priest, there was no fundamental objection to such a marriage. Both of them concentrated the care and affection of parents upon the young king.

The regency government was less harsh than the preceding regime. Where Louis XIII might have demanded the head of a plotter, Anne and Mazarin merely jailed him. Anne was less cruel than her late husband had been, and the Italian was more of a diplomat than Richelieu. Mazarin preferred to rule by finesse, even though he was capable of using force when necessary.

His most important achievements were in the field of foreign policy. The

Treaties of Westphalia were extremely satisfactory to France, and they were in no small part Mazarin's handiwork. By securing France's position in Alsace and destroying the old constitution of the Holy Roman Empire, he paved the way for French control over the Rhineland and French influence throughout Germany. The war with Spain did not end with Westphalia; another decade of fighting was necessary to induce the Spanish government to make the Peace of the Pyrenees (1659) that France demanded, and that peace, too, was Mazarin's handiwork.

At home, Mazarin was unable to ward off the rebellions called the Fronde ("slingshot"). Those conflicts arose over the pretensions of *Parlement* to control taxation. The first Fronde (1648–1649) was largely confined to Paris, where barricades and riots imperiled the young king's person and threatened to establish parlementary control over his government. The hereditary judges in the *Parlement* followed the events in England that led to the execution of Charles I closely, and somehow confused themselves and their own role in French society with that of the elected "Puritan saints" who took over both the Parliament and the government of England. Like the English Parliament they tried to control taxation. The *Parlement* of Paris, however, was unable to enlist strong popular support in France as a whole, and so this movement was eventually suppressed by royal forces laying siege to the capital. No sooner was the first Fronde brought to an end than a second, more dangerous one, erupted. This time it was led by the Prince of Condé, and allied with the Spanish king. It looked like a palace family quarrel, but it was, in fact, a rebellion of the great nobles against the centralizing tendencies of the regime and the "patriot" foreign policy. Like the parlementarians, the nobility were really fighting against the policies of Louis XIII and Richelieu, now represented by Anne and Mazarin.

The actual sequence of events during the Frondes makes a complex and difficult story that cannot be abbreviated without damage. Throughout, however, we see Mazarin and the queen acting as the protagonists of royal authority. Even when the Italian resigned and withdrew to Germany, he continued to direct the queen's policy by courier. Louis, who was entering adolescence during this period, learned from his mother that Mazarin was the man who could hold the kingdom together in the face of all destructive forces. Therefore as soon as he reached his "majority" (fourteen years of age) he recalled the cardinal to reassume the position of first minister. Mazarin was the important personality responsible for the defeat of the Fronde. The other factor in its suppression was the obvious selfishness of both the parlementarians and the princes. Neither group ever seemed to grasp the grand design of the state that had been the dream of Richelieu and Louis XIII; they saw only their own party interests. Thus Mazarin's enemies were never able to work together, for the parlementary leaders, who considered themselves to be counterparts of the English revolutionaries, were as repulsive to the great nobles as to the queen. On the other hand, Condé's treasonable alliance with the Spaniards was scandalous to all concerned. After experiencing the disorder and violence of civil wars inspired solely by the selfish ambitions of the contestants, the French were willing to accept a government of authority that could guarantee peace and tranquility within the kingdom.

The final victory over the Fronde came at the same time as the peace with Spain. By the Treaty of the Pyrenees (1659) Mazarin agreed to readmit Condé to the French court, but for all purposes the King's authority had been recognized by most of France by 1653.

The Peace of the Pyrenees was Mazarin's final diplomatic triumph. Here we see Richelieu's promise to elevate French prestige completely fulfilled. Spain surrendered the provinces of Artois and Roussillon to France, and her king sent his daughter, Maria Theresa, to become the bride of the young Louis XIV. In the marriage contract the Spanish Infanta renounced her claim to the Spanish throne, but the other clauses in the contract nullified her renunciation. Most important was the tacit recognition that the treaty marked the end of Hapsburg leadership and the beginning of the era in which France became the first power in the western world.

5. THE PERIOD OF BRILLIANCE

Mazarin died on March 7, 1661. Louis XIV ordered full mourning, usually reserved for members of the royal family, and then announced that he would henceforth be his own first minister. In his *Mémoires* Louis tells us that he had hoped for a little more time to prepare himself for his role. Mazarin had brought him up to rule, but he had not expected to assume that task when he was only twenty-three years old. Later in his life Louis regretted his lack of education, and his enemies accused him of ignorance or worse. Actually what they meant was that Louis never really mastered the Latin language. He spoke passable Spanish and Italian; he spoke and wrote elegant French, but beyond a schoolboy's translation of Caesar's *Gallic Wars* he knew no Latin. In point of fact, however, he was better educated than most kings. Mazarin had initiated him into the ways of statecraft by teaching him the business of government during the decade following the Fronde. By inviting the young king to council meetings and giving him documents to study, he had prepared Louis for the oral instruction that he gave him in the art of government. Mazarin, one of the best informed and cleverest statesmen of the century, was no mean teacher, and the testimony of foreign ambassadors who knew Louis in the early years of his reign gives ample evidence that the lessons had been effective. Later errors of judgment that were to cost so dearly can hardly be blamed on a lack of early instruction.

Mazarin not only educated the king, but he also left him a group of ministers capable of serving a brilliant regime. Through the two decades that

Anne and Mazarin corresponded with each other in code, they always referred to Le Tellier as "the faithful one." Le Tellier and his even more famous son, Louvois, were the architects of the new professional army that was created in the latter half of the seventeenth century. They had the assistance of engineers such as Vauban and soldiers such as Turenne, but the actual process of subordinating soldiers to a war ministry was their personal triumph. Colbert, another "gift" from Mazarin to his king, had been the Italian cardinal's trusted agent who managed his personal affairs. He was the financier who brought some order into the treasury, directed the economic policy of the kingdom, created a French navy, and expanded the colonial empire. His brother, son, and nephews all served the king in the foreign ministry, in the treasury, and in the councils for colonies, commerce, and marine. Hugh de Lionne was the diplomat that Mazarin had trained from the days of the Congress of Westphalia to help direct the policy of government, and as long as he lived he was Louis' right-hand man in foreign affairs.

Just below those men there were a number of soldiers and bureaucrats who were becoming a new kind of servant for the king. In his *Mémoires* Louis XIV takes personal credit for appointing men whose lack of noble blood and titles made them dependent upon him, but actually the rise of these new officials goes back to Richelieu who had tried to avoid using the great nobles as royal officials. Under Louis XIII and then under Mazarin this group matured to a point where it could operate the complex governmental machine that had come into being. Since they owed their entire fortune and their position to the king, they were less dangerous than the noblemen who had formerly been royal officials. Furthermore, since their position depended upon their ability to serve, they were, on the whole, much more effective than their predecessors had been.

The fact that he had able associates should not detract from Louis' reputation as king. He took his obligations seriously. It was no idle boast when he asserted that he spent many hours every day working at his job. He sought the advice and wisdom of his ministers, but he knew what they were doing and participated in directing their tasks. None of his ministers ever felt that the king could be ignored. Mazarin had told him that he had the capacity to be a great king if he would only apply himself to the position, and Louis religiously carried out this advice.

It is extravagant to claim that Louis organized his kingdom on "rational" principles, but it is undoubtedly true that he tried to systematize and bring order into his government. His first problem was to curb the lawlessness that had always infected many parts of the kingdom but that had increased during the long period of warfare. This was not a question of subordinating great noblemen to the king's government; they had seen their power disappear in the Fronde. It was lesser fry who were disturbing the countryside and showing disrespect for the king's peace. The "grand days of Auvergne" were the most famous of Louis' forays against these bandits, kidnappers, and others; but all over the kingdom his soldiers hanged or beheaded malefactors to convince the people that the king intended to keep the public peace. Of course banditry, kidnapping, and assault did not disappear from France; they simply became less prevalent and more liable to punishment.

Louis also undertook a reorganization of the law. He wished to become a French Justinian, to leave behind him a codification of the laws as a monument to his reputation. That proved too great a task, but the work that was accomplished became the basis upon which later French legal codes were built. Louis' most important codifications affected the operations of the treasury, the war office, the navy, and other government bureaus. Much of his legislation lasted throughout the eighteenth century; some of it was incorporated in the revolutionary codes and still exists today. Thus, even though there was no "code Louis XIV," his edicts sketched out the constitution of the modern bureaucratic state.

Colbert also set out to systematize the tax structure, but, like his predecessor Sully, he was unable to effect a thoroughgoing reform. He tried to bring some order to the tariffs and tolls within the kingdom and to distribute the tax burden more evenly. His great problem arose from the fact that the French upper classes (the clergy and noblemen) were largely exempt from direct taxation. This led to the seeming paradox that Colbert raised excise taxes to force the privileged classes to pay their share into the king's treasury. In England, on the other hand, excise taxes came to be imposed to force the "little people" to pay their share into the treasury. At the end of his life Colbert felt frustrated because the ancient system of privilege had defeated his best efforts. Nonetheless, his regime had, in fact, collected more taxes and let less money slip through its fingers, so that Louis XIV had at his disposal wealth undreamed of by his predecessors.

The program of legislation aimed at increasing the national wealth was also the work of Colbert, and is often called Colbertism. Actually, as Colbert so often told Louis, "the great Cardinal Richelieu" had proposed much of the legislation that Colbert carried out. No matter what the inspiration, the founding of chartered companies to trade abroad, the importation of foreign workers to introduce their crafts in France, and the legislation regulating and controlling the production of goods, conditions of apprenticeship, and the like, were all measures that Colbert and Louis used to strengthen French economy. It is customary to criticize their labors because they insisted upon close regulation by the government. Such criticism, however, is based upon several assumptions that simplify the historical process. There may have been —indeed, undoubtedly were—many factors at work on the French economy, and regulation may not have been the most important.

Perhaps the most successful effort of the regime was the creation of the new army. Louis' experience with the Fronde and the long history of rebellion pointed to the need for an overwhelming military force at the disposal of the king. For a century Europe had been moving toward the development of standing armies, and they came into being in France after 1661. The soldiers ceased to be composed of temporary bands of hirelings, loyal, if at all, only to their captain. Clothed in the king's coat, paid, fed, and equipped by the king's commissioners, and commanded by officers who took orders from the king's war minister, the new soldiers were truly a reincarnation of the Roman legions. As such, they gave an original form to the political society of Europe. This was the great achievement of Le Tellier and Louvois.

A comparable development occurred in the formation of the French navy by Colbert. Even though France was primarily a land power, by 1683 Louis' minister of commerce and finance had built the foremost navy of the day. Colbert appreciated the importance of sea power in the development of commerce; his navy was a shield for French merchants and colonies and a spear pointed at commercial rivals, for example, the Dutch, as we shall see later. Like the army, the new navy was under the command of the king's ministers, controlled by the king's agents, and completely responsive to the royal authority.

Seventeenth-century governments from England to Hungary regarded dissent from the state religion as evidence of treasonous intent. The men of that era still believed that the church was the principal source of social cement, the arbiter for ideas of good and evil, and therefore refusal to accept the state church was tantamount to rejection of the king's authority. The mere fact that Henry IV, Richelieu, and Louis XIII were willing to allow the French Huguenots to practice their "Reformed" religion did not indicate that France was really an exception to the general tendency in Europe. It was simply too difficult, perhaps impossible, to suppress the Huguenots, so they were tolerated. Louis XIII and Richelieu had so many other things to do that they were willing to submit to the "scandal" of Reformed religious services so long as the Huguenots were no longer able to interfere with their wider policies through military revolts. After Louis XIV assumed control of the government, it was natural that the question of religious uniformity should again be raised.

By 1660 the Huguenot community had become almost completely royalist. The era of their rebellions seemed forgotten, and with it the slogans and arguments against the king's government: but there were many people in the French court who had not forgotten that era and who regarded the Reformed religion as a danger to the realm as well as an outrage to Catholic sensibilities. The Act of Uniformity in England and the Calvinist rebellions in Hungary encouraged the ardent Catholics in France to believe in their own justice and wisdom when they urged action against the Huguenots.

Thus though the Huguenots had become royalists, their newly found love for the king did not impress the Catholic zealots.

At first Louis XIV merely continued the policy inaugurated by his grand-father, Henry IV, of bribing important Huguenots with money, favors, and royal offices to get them to change their religion. However, this method proved to be too slow, so more vigorous ones were used to encourage conversion. By the 1670's it was not unusual for Huguenot families to have soldiers quartered in their homes until they were prepared to renounce their religion. These sterner measures made the Huguenots reconsider their loyalty to the crown, and led to a stream of emigrants to England, Holland, and Germany where Calvinists could practice their religion peacefully.

Louis was led to believe that his policy of conversion had been much more successful than it in fact had. It is not uncommon for people in power to be supplied with faulty or even false information. If they base their policy upon such intelligence, the results are seldom successful. So it was in the case of the "Reformed" religion in France. Thinking that it would affect but very few people, Louis issued the famous Edict of Fontainebleau (1685) which revoked the Edict of Nantes and forbade the practice of the "so-called Reformed religion" (the words of the Edict) in France.

The result was further migration and the establishment of articulate spokesmen who agitated against Louis XIV from pulpits and presses all over Europe. The Electoral Prince of Brandenburg-Prussia answered Louis' Edict with the Edict of Potsdam in which he invited the refugees to his lands. The migration was comparable to the one caused by the French Revolution of 1789 or the Nazi Revolution of 1933, both of which sent enemies of the regime abroad to preach against the iniquities of their erstwhile fatherland. Neither the nobles who emigrated in 1789 nor the Jews driven from Nazi Germany felt more hatred toward their oppressors than the Huguenots who left France.

While Louis struck at the Huguenots as out-and-out heretics, he was also hostile toward the Jansenists, whose probable religious heresy and unquestionably antistatist theories had earlier aroused the ire of Richelieu. The Jansenists, however, were more difficult to attack, since they managed to find a way round charges of heresy until the first decade of the eighteenth century. Louis' hostility toward those pious people can best be explained in terms of his dislike of their independence of thought and the fact that his closest advisers hated the party. When the Jansenists were finally declared to be heretics, the king's wrath extended even to the entombed remains of their "saints," but for all his violence he was unable to crush the Jansenist movement within the church.

While he was defending orthodoxy at home, Louis also engaged in a running fight with the papacy in Rome. One pope in particular, Innocent XI, came into violent conflict with the king. There were several factors involved in the controversy, but the most important was the fact that Louis and his religious advisers were trying to extend the king's authority over the Gallican (French) church to a point where the pope would only be able to deal with the church through the king. There was also the question of church revenue which both the king and the pope wished to control. Finally, Innocent XI was a crusader against Islam, and when Louis XIV aided the Turks against the Hapsburgs the old pope was scandalized (as we shall discuss in a later chapter). There was, however, no real danger that the Gallican church would actually break with Rome. After the death of Innocent XI and the reversal suffered by the French in Europe, a series of compromises patched up the conflict with the papacy, leaving the king essentially in control of church government, while the lines of communication between the French clergy and Rome remained free.

Many writers emphasize Louis' mistresses, his bastards, and the expensive court that he maintained for his pleasure, and all are important. The king elevated himself above the great nobles and princes of the land by building palaces more sumptuous than they could afford and by creating a court etiquette that made them his servants. Even his mistresses served to separate him from the mass of men. He well understood that his position was unsafe unless he placed himself above the great nobles, who had made the throne unstable from the era of the religious wars to the Fronde. He used his assumption of magnificence as well as his soldiers to keep them in submission. As the "Sun King" he was the unquestioned ruler of the kingdom.

The elaborate court etiquette and the sumptuous palace at Versailles epitomize the achievements of the first twenty-five years of Louis' government. When the king moved into a palace which was not protected by moats and walls, he showed confidence in his ability to keep the peace. It was perhaps his greatest triumph that he could build his palace at Versailles rather than at Vincennes, where Mazarin had begun a beautiful structure within the great walls of the fortress. The palace at Versailles was in a very real sense a challenge to Europe to match the grandeur of the French king and a notice to the unruly forces in the kingdom that the king's government no longer feared their power.

In the days of Louis' grandmother, Marie de Medici, if a great nobleman "left the court," it was tantamount to the latter raising a flag of rebellion. All that had now been changed. At Versailles the great noblemen were reduced to the role of servants of the king through an etiquette that made every action of the monarch important. Indeed, the lives of great noblemen lost all significance other than that of serving the king, and to be "sent from the court" became a sign of disgrace rather than a symbol of rebellion. Thus Versailles with its magnificent salons, its gardens and reflecting pools, its crowds of courtiers about the king, and its lack of walls and moats, announced the fact that the labors of Richelieu and Mazarin had been successfully completed. The "great ones" of the land had been subordinated to the king. Actually, they had not only been subordinated but also deprived of any important role in the new political order that was coming into existence. It was for this achievement that Louis was known to his subjects as the "Sun King." He chose the emblem of the sun to emphasize the fact that the other forces in his kingdom, as well as in Europe, had become the satellites of his grandeur.

To Europe, Versailles was an announcement that France had taken the place of Spain as the leading power in the western world. One hundred years before, Philip II had built the Escorial, the great palace on the Sierra Guadarrama near Madrid to show the world the glories of Spain. Philip's great-grandson, Louis XIV, built Versailles eleven miles from Paris to underline the fact that France now held the hegemony of Europe. For the next century and a half the princes of the world lived under the shadow of his magnificence. Versailles, as an artistic monument, became the symbol of the new period of the baroque age in which secular structures were more important than religious ones. Its influence was destined to be felt as far away as Washington and St. Petersburg (Leningrad).

Later in the reign when Louis' armies had suffered defeat and his lands were ravished by tax collectors and soldiers, the glories of the early part of his reign seemed to have been forgotten. However, every prince in eighteenth-century Europe, even the great Frederick of Prussia, lived under his influence. Louis may not have been the first "enlightened despot," but he was surely the model for all those who followed him. Even Napoleon, who posed as a son of the Revolution, looked wistfully to Louis for inspiration in the art of government. The France that appeared as the great power of Europe in 1685 was the first bureaucratic state in Europe, and as such became the model for those states that emerged in the following decades.

French-Dutch Naval Battle. In the seventeenth century naval battles were still fought as "ship against ship" actions. It was not until the end of the century that the "line" took the place of the individual ship as the center of the naval battle.

Chapter 13

INTERESTS OF STATE AND
OF DYNASTY

1. THE MAINSPRINGS OF POLITICS

The important political movements of the sixteenth century seemed to revolve around questions of religious and dynastic interests. As we have seen, religious slogans then were frequently little more than flags to cover other motives, but even so they could arouse men to political and military action. In the seventeenth century, however, men gradually came to realize that religion no longer provided a useable flag for conflicts between Christian states. The pope and the emperor could still preach "holy war" against Islam, but after the Thirty Years' War it was no longer fashionable to dress up European political conflicts in religious terms. At the same time, dynastic politics continued to play their traditional role, and the interests of states expanded to take a central place in the stage of European affairs.

Dynastic interests could not be ignored, for the seventeenth century stands at the mid-point between the era when European rulers justified their right to rule by "divine right" and the period during which men would insist that the "right" to rule rested with the governed who delegated power to rule to princes. As long as the right to rule and the organization of empire were dependent upon the accidents of birth, death, and the inheritance of thrones, men could say that God's will determined the fate of states. Thus princes like James I of England and Louis XIV of France could insist that they ruled by divine right as an expression of God's will; and yet revolutions and rebellions in the Netherlands, England, France, Hungary, and elsewhere strongly suggested that the right to rule was conditioned upon the explicit, or at least the tacit, consent of the governed. Inevitably these basic postulates about the source of power became involved in the organization of high politics. No European prince could forget that Charles V had come close to inheriting all the important crowns of Europe. Louis XIV, a great-great-grandson of Charles V, might achieve even greater grandeur. His dynasty was heir to the throne of France, a claimant to the throne of the Spanish Empire, and it had a chance to be elected to the throne of the Holy Roman Empire. If all three crowns were actually brought together, an empire more extensive than Charlemagne's would be created. Thus dynastic politics offered the chance to recreate the Roman Empire of the West. Such a throne could be "legitimately" created only by the rise of a dynasty that ruled all Europe.

However, dynastic combinations depended upon marriages, births, and deaths, which were fortuitous, hazardous, and uncertain developments, and in the meantime many other problems arose to becloud dynastic ambitions. The seventeenth century also witnessed expansion in trade and political interests. Its wars called attention to problems of defense, while new military institutions created a series of problems in regard to finance and the organization of military supplies. The steady rise in expenditure for soldiers and sailors forced the consideration of sources of revenue and of the organization of state economy. It also brought new men into the councils of princes.

Perhaps the revolution in personnel and the subsequent change in the status of princes was the most important outward sign of the change in political emphasis. One historian has called the process "the victory of the pen over the sword." What happened was simple enough. In 1600 most of the men who sat on the councils of princes were high-ranking noblemen, princes of the blood, great landlords; their points of view, their attitudes toward politics were grounded in the feudal past. A hundred years later, those men had in the main been replaced by a new kind of adviser who was often of bourgeois origin and usually trained in law or finance. The "new" men owed their whole fortune to the success of their career in the state and to the favor of the prince. They thought in terms of the collection and administration of taxes, the organization and exploitation of colonies and commerce, the regulation of armies and navies, and the erection of fortresses. They understood that the glory and grandeur of the prince was dependent on his power to raise armies, build palaces, and to subsidize allies, which in turn involved the political and economic interests of the state to a great extent. By the end of the seventeenth century the rise of bureaucratic machines manned by the new advisers and servants had already begun to change the character of princes. Even a Louis XIV was becoming the "first servant of the state," and therefore the interests of the bureaucratic state tended to transcend the interests of dynasty.

Closely related to this shift to state interests was the realization that Europe as a whole presented a problem for statesmen. Before the seventeenth century there had been alliances that could be interpreted as attempts to maintain a balance of power, but it was the seventeenth century which saw the rise of coalitions of powers and more or less permanent combinations of powers organized to defend the "liberties of Europe." In this and the next chapter we shall trace this development that men came to see as a "government" for Europe. With the rise of physical science to a position of high prestige, men thought they saw society as a "machine." Those political "physicists" eventually came to believe that the "balance" of power in Europe as a whole was a basic law of its constitution just as "gravity" was the basic law in Newton's universe. This idea of the "equilibrium" of power resulted, in European affairs, in the establishment of many centers of power representing various magnitudes of political and military force. By the mid-seventeenth century France was emerging as the most important power, but in addition to Paris there were a half dozen or more other cities that counted in the government of Europe. Paris, London, Amsterdam, Madrid, Vienna-Prague, Rome, and Berlin, as well as some other lesser capitals, were component parts in the pluralistic picture of power. Since no European prince ever actually succeeded in "inheriting" all these capitals, and no conqueror managed to unite them by force, the maintenance of the balance of power in Europe became of primary importance to the politics and government of European states.

2. TRADE AND "MERCANTILISM"

Even while Charles V and his son Philip II were trying to unify Europe on the battlefield and in the council chamber, there were economic factors operating in society that eventually proved to be more influential than either the Hapsburg victories or defeats. The Spanish and Portuguese colonial empires brought the goods of the Orient and the Americas to the Iberian peninsula. The high-walled ships that rounded the Cape of Good Hope or sailed across the Atlantic carried spices, sugar, hides, jewels, gold, silver, silk, and many other items to the ports of Spain and Portugal. Other nations were forbidden to enter that trade, and their ships were treated as pirates if they were found sailing on the routes to the Americas and the East. However, they were welcomed at Iberian ports of entry where they could buy or exchange colonial goods for wine, cloth, amber, pitch, hemp, hardware, and the like.

Philip's wars interrupted the Iberian monopoly. When Dutch and English seamen were barred from the Spanish markets, it was only natural that they should seek alternative methods of continuing their business. The English, who had the more predatory traditions, turned to robbing Spanish treasure ships (Elizabeth's seadogs), and raiding South American ports. The Dutch, whose commercial position as middlemen was already strong, got around the barriers by establishing direct contact with both the Orient and the New

World. At the opening of the seventeenth century, it was the Dutch rather than the English or the French who profited most when the Iberian nations lost their monopoly.

The Dutch market became a fabulous place, where the goods of all Europe as well as wares from the colonies were offered for sale. Only on the Dutch market could buyers be assured of standard quality, and, therefore, the Dutch market tended to set the prices for all Europe. Their splendid commercial position was the result of many things. First, the estuary of the Rhine river (the Lowlands) was centrally located for trade deep into the continent by the Rhine and Elbe rivers, as well as for trade from the Mediterranean to the Baltic. Second, the Dutch had early developed a shipbuilding industry, and they built vessels that could be operated more economically than any others in Europe. With those ships their merchants had captured a large part of the carrying trade. The growth of the Dutch fishing industry was soon followed by other economic activities, until the Netherlands became a place where the goods of the world were brought, refinished, and transported to other markets. This led to the development of banking, insurance, and bourse (exchange) activities that made the Netherlands the financial, as well as the commercial, capital of the western world.

When rivals sought to explain Dutch prosperity, they saw first of all the great chartered companies that acted as the agents for colonial government. The East India Company established factories in India, then moved its operations to the spice islands around Java, so that it became the most important power in the Far East. Spice production was rigidly controlled to "rig" the European market; coffee and sugar were both developed as colonial products, but the Company rather than the natives made the profit. Dutch traders ranged from Canton to Japan, backed by the Company's power and prestige. Fabulous profits poured into the coffers of the stockholders, while the Company's activities in Europe and the East provided an outlet for the energies of young Dutchmen who sought wealth and adventure in the exotic lands beyond the seas.

The West India Company was never so powerful or so profitable. It was founded primarily as a war measure, chartered to attack the enemies of the Netherlands in the expectation that it would be able to make war a profitable enterprise. It established the Dutch flag from New Amsterdam (New York) to Brazil, and during the Thirty Years' War it proved a useful weapon against Spain and Portugal, even though it was not as successful a commercial venture as the East India Company. Except in precious metals, the American trade was not as valuable as the oriental trade during the seventeenth century.

The unilateral organization of trade centering on the Netherlands was as important as the two great chartered companies. The fact that the Dutch established standards for everything from Swedish iron and Danzig wheat to Cornish tin and Madeira wine gave European commerce a curious twist. It became the tendency for all goods of international trade to pass through the Netherlands. In other words, merchants of each country bought French, English, Spanish, Swedish, and German goods from the Dutch rather than directly from each other. Of course there was some other trade, but it was easier to pay for goods and sell wares by going to the Dutch: and much of the trade was carried in Dutch ships. Thus, Dutch merchants not only profited by being middlemen for Europe, but they were also the porters of Europe's goods. Only by understanding the unique position of the Dutch market is it possible to grasp the meaning of the so-called "mercantilist legislation" of the second half of the century.

Dutch theories of commerce were based upon the economy of the Netherlands. Very little raw material for trade or manufacture originated in the Dutch provinces. Wood for their ships came down the Rhine or from the Baltic; wool for cloth from Spain or England; iron from Sweden and Spain; and wine from France, Portugal, and the Rhineland. Therefore the Dutch tried to prevent restraints on the movement of those goods. Such tariffs, tolls, and port dues as were charged were restricted to the amounts necessary to provide naval protection and to service the ships and goods in the harbor. Thus, we see that the idea of a protective tariff was not of Dutch origin, for the commercial supremacy of the Netherlands depended upon its merchants' abilities to undersell all competitors, and therefore to keep their prices low.

Dutch commercial ideas, however, were not suitable for export to the other major countries of western Europe. France, England, and Spain produced raw materials of many kinds. Wool, iron, tin, wine, copper, and lead were the raw stuffs demanded by the more advanced economies of Italy, the Levant, and the great port towns of the Atlantic. The buyers of those goods often re-exported them in finished form to the countries of origin at a considerable increase in cost. Furthermore, the Levant, Asia, and Italy, as sellers of all kinds of luxury goods, seemed to be draining the less highly developed economic society of the western states of their precious metals. The first introduction of sugar and tobacco from the Americas was regarded in the same way. Here were luxuries that had to be paid for with gold or silver, and therefore, in the eyes of many writers who feared the loss of precious metals, this was an evil trade. Later those luxury commodities became the backbone of the excise taxes of the treasuries of Europe, and hence were regarded with favor.

European statesmen generalized the lessons of the Spanish, Portuguese, and Dutch empires something like this: gold and silver made a nation strong; precious metals represented wealth that did not decay or deteriorate; thus one object of a nation's policy should be to obtain large amounts of those metals. Concentration on gold, silver, and jewels as imperishable wealth made economic theorists consider commercial enterprise that would bring such items to their lands as of primary importance. Spain had wealth because she controlled the mines of the New World; the United Provinces had wealth because they engaged in trade that brought profits of gold and silver into the country. This line of reasoning made foreign trade of paramount importance to all countries that had no mines of their own. Thus it was wise to adopt measures that would stimulate exports and reduce imports, since such action would stock the kingdom with precious metals. The argument was simple in the extreme: goods purchased abroad had to be paid for in money that left the kingdom, while goods sold abroad were paid for in money that entered the kingdom; purchases drained gold; sales attracted it. Therefore anyone could understand the advantage of selling more than was purchased, since the difference would necessarily be paid in silver or gold which would enrich the kingdom. To continue this reasoning—colonies that produced precious metals were of great value; colonies that produced goods not found in the mother country might also be valuable, for some of those goods (sugar, tobacco, indigo, for example) could be sold for gold, and those retained would not have to be paid for by exporting precious metals.

Thus a complete theory of political economy emerged as an answer to the need for metallic reserves. The theorists argued for the erection of tariffs, the encouragement of exporters, the development of industries and plantations that would free the kingdom from the necessity for importing goods, and the foundation of colonies to supplement the mother country. Naturally such policies, when adopted, became mainsprings for political action that was in the states' rather than the dynasty's interests. In the course of the development of those politico-economic theories, another proposition emerged that turned them into veritable sources of international conflict. Sixteenth- and seventeenth-century men knew very little about the nature of commerce. They assumed that the total amount of trade was fixed, limited, and static. Thus, increase in the trade of one country was necessarily at the expense of others. This was an era without statistics, without the understanding that was to come from the study of political economy, and without realization of historical processes. It is not, therefore, surprising to find some of the conclusions that were reached about commerce strange, if not virtually incomprehensible to modern men, but they were conclusions that easily stimulated policies that led to war.

Another source for the politico-economic theory of the era was the traditional practices of the preceding centuries. It must be remembered that seventeenth-century men were still close to the economy of medieval Europe. Medieval towns had established legal control over their economies to assure monopolies for their own manufacturers and to prevent inroads by foreign merchants. The medieval practice of controlling quality and price by town or guild legislation was a corollary to the policy of maintaining the monopoly for local producers. Medieval kings had tried to control the commerce of their realms to increase their own revenue and also to give protection to their subjects. The sixteenth- and seventeenth-century state builders had good precedents to follow; they had only to devise means of applying medieval practice effectively to the entire state.

Thus we find during the first three-quarters of the seventeenth century the development of a body of political theory and practice designed to make the holdings of princes into economic units. In some cases, like England, the process had already gone far toward creating a politico-economic unit. In others, like Brandenburg-Prussia or the Hapsburg holdings along the Danube, the seventeenth century saw the rise of economic legislation aimed at consolidating ancient, disconnected provinces into new political units. Man's habit of inventing names for programs of action has led to several different terms to designate this diverse political and economic legislation. Adam Smith, in the latter eighteenth century, termed it "mercantilism." In the late nineteenth century was added the name "Colbertism," after the distinguished statesman whose career was associated with the economy of France. In Germany, where the problem was complicated by confusing the prince's personal wealth with that of the state, it has been called *"kammeralism,"* because the *kammer* or financial office of the prince became the agency for politico-economic legislation. These terms were nearly always invented as "words of reproach" by men who were hostile to the movement; they would have been largely incomprehensible to seventeenth-century men who did not know that they were developing an "ism." In any event, whatever it was called or wherever it was developed, the statesmen and political economists of the seventeenth century had one central idea upon which all else was based. They believed that the object of all policy was to make the prince (government) strong, and that meant militarily powerful. This was the epoch that saw the development of the standing army and navy backed up by arsenals, warehouses, and all the paraphernalia that made them ready for action. Most of the tax revenue in all states was used for this purpose. Thus, the object of legislation and administration was to increase the wealth of the country so that the king's loyal subjects could pay more taxes, and thereby could support a more powerful military force. If, as a result, the subjects became more wealthy, more comfortable, and more satisfied, so much the better, for they would be more willing to pay for the state's projects.

"Mercantilist" legislation took many forms. As we have seen in the case of France, the government encouraged new industries so that goods need not be imported from abroad. In each of the "advanced" states that was the practice. Foreigners with "industrial skills" were encouraged to enter those countries, and young men were urged to go abroad to acquire skills to bring back home. The government granted tax exemptions, bounties, tariff protection, rebates, and all sorts of subsidies to encourage new industrial enterprises. Adam Smith and other critics of this legislation asserted that it was merely a means of preventing the purchase of goods abroad and the consequent payment for them with gold. This, of course, was not the whole picture. By domesticating new industries, the "mercantilists" provided opportunities for employers and workers who could pay taxes and keep the kingdom prosperous; and this was as important as the gold that need no longer be exported to pay for foreign goods. To see "mercantilism" simply in terms of gold and silver is to miss the wider meaning it came to have.

The "mercantilists" also tried to achieve economic unity in their lands by making it easier for their subjects to trade with each other rather than with foreigners, thus enlarging the volume of internal trade, though problems in that regard were great. In the first place, the roads of Europe were at best in a deplorable state. Since Roman times there had been no systematic road construction, and the half-hearted patching of trails and paths that had been done left much to be desired. The really great work of rebuilding Europe's roads was not to get under way until the latter eighteenth and early nineteenth centuries, but the first steps were taken in the seventeenth. The same was true for the system of inland waterways. Today a large proportion of Europe's goods is still moved by water because of the splendid system of canals and dredged rivers that links the whole continent; and the system that we see now was begun in the seventeenth century; it was not completed—if one could say that it ever will be completed—until recent times. France took the lead in both road and canal construction, perhaps because she was the wealthiest country, perhaps because her government was more alert, or perhaps because she had great need for internal communications to tie the kingdom together.

We must be cautious, however, in dealing with the actual accomplishments of the seventeenth-century road and canal builders. Costs of construction were extremely high, and the time required for the completion of a project was considerable in an era when engineers had no machines to do their work. It was not until the nineteenth century that Europe became sufficiently rich and technologically skilled to build an extensive and effective network of roads and canals. Seventeenth-century statesmen had the vision, but not the means to accomplish their objective.

In another area, too, the "mercantilists" had more vision than power. There were toll stations and tariff gates along all the roads and watercourses to impede internal commerce. Many such dues were of ancient origin, all of them had vested interests behind them, and often they seemed absolutely necessary to the prince's treasury. State builders like Colbert or the *kammeralists* in Austria realized that those obstructions to commerce were unfortunate, but they were usually unable to do anything about them.

The different systems of weights, measures, and coinages further obstructed trade. For example, John Locke, on two voyages to southern France in the late seventeenth century, noted several dozens of different weights and measures. Had he gone to Germany, he would have found even more. Those differences were not ironed out until after the French Revolution, not because men did not know that uniform systems would be beneficial, but because savants had not yet devised a "rational" system of weights and measures, and no king was strong enough to establish his own traditional standards in his own kingdom, let alone over all Europe.

It was not difficult for those seventeenth-century political economists to see the relationships between wealth, sea power, and the merchant marine. The Dutch near-monopoly of coastal shipping was so obviously a source of wealth that every statesman worthy of the name wished to see his own people "cut into" that business. Furthermore, as the seventeenth century moved toward its third quarter the development of proper warships and naval organizations underlined the need for merchant ships, since the navy largely depended upon the merchant marine to train seamen. But the real "nursery" for sailors was the fishing fleet, for the small ships that fished the nearby coasts—as well as the larger ones that ventured to the cod fisheries off North America —provided excellent training for sailors. Thus, a large fishing fleet that would assure an abundance of seamen who could be enlisted or impressed into the navy and the merchant fleet became an object of solicitude for statesmen. The so-called "mercantilist legislators"—Cromwell in England, Colbert in France, and others—gave particular attention to the fishing industry. They wanted their people to eat herring, cod, and other fish caught by their own seamen. This was the first step taken to break the Dutch mercantile power.

The other side of the legislation dealt with the carrying trade. By regulating the right of sea captains to bring goods into the country, the legislators were really trying to break up the near-monopoly of the Dutch market, as well as to encourage their own shipping industry. The Dutch market was a depot for the goods of all Europe, and Dutch ships played the most important part in carrying those goods both to and from the Netherlands. Hence legislation that would restrict the right of Dutch ships to carrying goods that originated in the Netherlands would tend to break into the advantages held by the Dutch. The English Navigation Acts, proclaimed by Cromwell and Charles II, restricted the importation of goods into England to English ships or the ships of the country in which the goods were made or grown. By those measures, goods from Asia, Africa, or the Americas had to be carried in English or English colonial ships, and goods from Europe in English ships or in those of the exporting country. The Dutch were thereby not allowed to carry goods to England that had been previously imported to the Netherlands from another country. It was "hard to beat the Dutch"; but there was no reason for not trying. In the mid-seventeenth century there seemed to be no other way to interrupt the Dutch monopoly.

Another attack on commercial rivals was made by the imposition of tariffs and port duties. Foreign ships could be harassed and those of nationals favored by preferential port dues, dock space regulations, and the like. Even more direct was the imposition of protective tariffs or embargoes to cut into the trade of rivals. Colbert's tariffs of 1664–1667 were aimed directly at the Dutch. The English tried numerous ways of excluding both French and Dutch goods from their ports, and other states followed suit. However, it must be remembered that such measures were never completely effective, for at that time there was no adequate machinery to prevent smuggling.

The creation and encouragement of colonial trade was a further method of building up the power of the king and at the same time ruining rivals. The great India companies (Dutch, English, and French), the Levant and Muscovy Companies, and the companies and concessions for trade in the New World, are examples. In many cases those companies were extensions of the sovereign power of the state, with rights to raise armies, develop navies, annex territory, and make treaties. In the East, the Dutch, English, and French India companies carried on the rivalries and wars of their respective states throughout most of the seventeenth and eighteenth centuries.

The rivalries between colonial establishments were extended and deepened by legislation that attempted to restrict the benefits of colonial trade to the mother country alone. Like the Spaniards in the sixteenth century, the "mercantilist" statesmen of the seventeenth forbade their colonies to trade with foreigners. This theory seemed sound enough to seventeenth-century men, for, since colonies were intended to complement the mother country, it was their role to exchange sugar, furs, and such goods for the manufactured goods of the mother country: but it was hard to put into practice, for regulations were difficult to enforce in face of a smuggling trade bordering on piracy. However, men did not cease trying to guarantee their monopoly positions.

3. ANGLO-DUTCH CONFLICTS

Commercial rivalry inevitably led to military conflict. The first of the purely economic wars broke out in the early 1650's between England and the Netherlands. The English Navigation Act of 1651 tried to ruin Dutch trade and replace it by English shipping. As a result, war broke out between the two powers (1652).

In the mid-seventeenth century the Republic of the Netherlands was able to go to war with England on equal terms. Indeed, the Dutch actually possessed more fluid wealth than the English could muster, but they were not able to use their advantage fully, in part because their naval forces were not administered by a single admiralty. Each of several Dutch provinces managed part of the fleet through provincial admiralties. The English, on the other hand, administered their fleet through the agency of the lord admiral, and therefore could control their naval actions more easily. In another way, Dutch wealth proved disadvantageous. The Dutch had a larger merchant marine and therefore their shipping was a better target for the predatory English warships and privateers. The conflict between the two powers went on for two years with neither able to gain control of the Channel and the North Sea. In 1653, however, the British navy won a victory that left the Dutch merchant marine temporarily unprotected. Since the merchant marine was the very lifeblood of the Netherlands, the Dutch had to come to terms; but the peace that they made with Cromwell (Treaty of Westminster, 1654) was little more than a truce. The Dutch admitted the supremacy of the English flag in the Channel, accepted the navigation acts unchanged, and agreed to pay damages. They even signed a secret clause that was as agreeable to the Dutch Republicans as to the English revolutionaries—to prevent the House of Orange (relatives of the English Stuarts) from gaining command of the Netherlands. However, the Dutch could not really accept the restrictions placed on their commerce, nor were the English satisfied to see the Dutch remain so rich. Thus, in the Orient and the Americas, as well as along the African and Mediterranean waters, Dutch and English seamen continued to regard each other with hostile eyes.

When the Restoration of 1660 replaced the Stuart kings on the English throne, the time had arrived for England to take the initiative again. Charles II needed something to attract support and loyalty from his bourgeois subjects, most of whom had been his late enemies; a war with the Dutch for the express purpose of ruining a commercial rival was sure to be popular. There were plenty of pretexts for war. Charles II sent his brother, the Duke of York, to take over the Dutch Colony at New Amsterdam (New York thereafter) on the grounds that the Dutch were interlopers on land belonging to the English crown. In 1665 the conflict between the two powers again broke out into open warfare.

The Dutch prevented the English from getting any effective allies on the continent. In Germany, the Bishop of Munster tried to intervene, but Louis XIV, honoring his alliance with the United Netherlands, checked the move. Thus, the second Anglo-Dutch war, like the first, was fought at sea. The English had the worst of the fighting, but both sides suffered from the destruction of commerce. Finally the belligerents met at Breda to make peace. Charles, short of money, foolishly decommissioned much of his navy in anticipation of peace, only to see a Dutch squadron raid the Thames estuary and burn a large number of his ships. The Treaty of Breda (1667) was as inconclusive as the earlier one. It did, however, leave New York in English hands. Perhaps the Dutch would have been more demanding had it not been for the dangerous situation that had developed after the death of the king of Spain in 1665.

4. DYNASTIC PROBLEMS COMPOUND COMMERCIAL RIVALRY

The death of Philip IV of Spain dramatically called attention to the fact that the basic organization of Europe still rested on dynastic considerations: the right to ascend the throne was acquired by inheritance. When Louis XIV came forward with claims for an important segment of the Spanish inheritance as the rightful possession of his family, no one in Europe missed the fact that trade, fortifications and the problem of the balance of power were all deeply involved in the dynastic "rights" asserted then by the king of France.

The problem was complicated. Throughout most of the sixteenth and the first half of the seventeenth centuries Hapsburg Spain was the most important power in Europe. However, the forty years of warfare that was terminated by the Treaty of the Pyrenees (1659) also put an end to Spanish dominance, and left the Bourbon king of France the heir to the Hapsburg Empire both physically and politically. Louis XIV was the great-grandson of Philip II and a great-great-grandson of Charles V. His mother, his father, and his wife all had Hapsburg blood in their veins. Thus the dynastic policies of the sixteenth and seventeenth centuries had again produced a king who might claim most of Europe as his heritage, as we noted earlier. Unfortunately for him, the claims were not as clear-cut as those that had made Charles V almost a universal emperor a century and a half earlier, for Louis' German cousin, Leopold von Hapsburg, had a nearly identical family background. Louis, however, was king of France; Leopold was only ruler over a disorderly complex of kingdoms and provinces in the Danube River basin.

Mazarin had tried to arrange for the Bourbon prince to be elected Holy Roman Emperor in 1658, and he had thus first emphasized the rivalry that was to exist between Louis and Leopold throughout their lives. The attempt proved unsuccessful, but the idea that a French prince might occupy the German imperial throne was one that continued to motivate policy in France. The Treaty of the Pyrenees and the marriage of Louis XIV to Maria Theresa, the eldest daughter of Philip IV of Spain, provided another reason for rivalry between Leopold and Louis. Maria Theresa had formally renounced her rights to the Spanish throne in favor of her sister, who married Leopold. However, the fact that Maria Theresa's dowry had not been paid could be used to deprive her renunciation of legal force. Moreover, it was questionable whether a marriage contract could actually deprive an heir of the throne; inheritance was the result of the will of God and not of men. Thus, although Leopold I was elected emperor in Germany and perhaps had a prior legal claim to the throne in Spain, it was still possible that both the Spanish and the Holy Roman Empire might be joined to the throne of France.

The sensational rise in French military and commercial power in the sev-

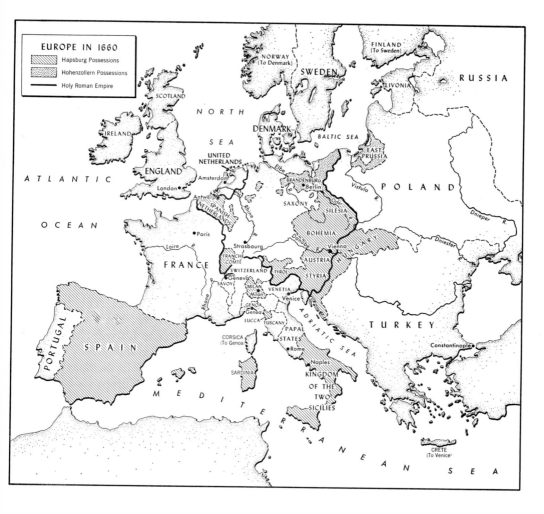

EUROPE IN 1660
- Hapsburg Possessions
- Hohenzollern Possessions
- Holy Roman Empire

enteenth century made the possibility of a French-controlled Europe both feasible and dangerous from the point of view of the independent states of Europe. Henry IV, Richelieu, Mazarin, and the men who surrounded the young Louis XIV had created the foremost military power in Europe; Colbert and Louis XIV were also determined to make France the foremost naval, commercial, and colonial power in the western world. If the crowns of Spain and the Empire could be added to that of France, the empire of Charlemagne would be reconstituted with power undreamed of by that semibarbarian.

When Philip IV of Spain died (1665) he left a sickly, dimwitted boy, Charles II, as his sole male heir. No one expected the young king to live long enough to produce an heir. Thus, a rich prize might soon be available for either the German Hapsburgs or the French Bourbons. Spain, the Catholic Netherlands, Milan, Naples, Sicily, Spanish America, and the Philippines: an empire on which the sun did not set was apparently about to have a new master. All Europe was interested in the outcome, for while succession to the Spanish throne may have been a dynastic question, it also had great military and commercial implications.

The German Hapsburgs had foreseen that such a problem would arise, and had attempted to prepare for it. In 1664 Leopold's armies, supported by a few thousand French soldiers, defeated an Ottoman invasion of Hungary. Instead of following up his advantage as the pope urged, Leopold made a twenty-year truce with the Turks: presumably this would guarantee his southern and eastern frontiers so that he could turn his attention to the Spanish inheritance.

In France the problems of the succession were also well understood, and Louis XIV wanted to be in as strong a position as possible to press his claims. Upon the death of Philip IV, he decided not to wait for his sickly cousin Charles to follow his father to the grave before trying to grab a part of the inheritance. In the private law of the Spanish Netherlands there was a ruling that allowed daughters to secure a portion of their father's estate. This rule of *devolution* had nothing to do with international law, but Louis used it to demand that the Spanish Netherlands be turned over to his wife, Maria Theresa, as her rightful due. A French army marched into the territory in 1667 to enforce Louis' claim. The presence of a French army in the Spanish Netherlands forced the Dutch to reconsider their position in Europe vis-à-vis England as well as Spain.

For almost a century (1560–1660) France and the United Netherlands had been friends and allies against the Spanish Hapsburgs. However, after France's victory at Rocroy (1643) many Dutch politicians had begun to wonder whether it would not be better to have a declining Spanish power rather than a vigorous French one in control of the neighboring Spanish Netherlands. France was a fine friend, but she was not a very satisfactory neighbor. This idea governed Dutch policy at the Congress of Westphalia, and became even more pronounced when Charles II of England sold Dunkirk to France (1662). It was, therefore, hardly surprising that the Dutch reacted quickly when Louis XIV claimed the whole of the Spanish Netherlands for his wife. For Bourbon France, dynastic interests may have been involved, but for the Netherlands, states' interests were concerned. The Dutch responded then by forming the Triple Alliance (1668, England, Sweden, and the Netherlands) which offered its good offices to settle the Franco-Spanish conflict. The threat of intervention on the side of Spain was only thinly veiled; for France it obviously meant either submission or a serious war. Louis XIV was not prepared to fight against Spain, England, Sweden, and the Netherlands, so he accepted the "good offices" of the Triple Alliance and made peace with his cousin, the king of Spain (Treaty of Aix-la-Chapelle, 1668). The peace gave France certain minor readjustments on the frontier, but the bulk of the

Spanish Netherlands remained in the hands of Spain; it did not put an end to Louis' ambitions, but it had momentarily checked his program of action.

In the French court, the Dutch intervention on behalf of Spain seemed to be an act of gross ingratitude. Henry IV, Louis XIII, and Louis XIV had aided the Dutch; now they had been repaid perfidiously. The Dutch thus acquired an enemy more dangerous than either Cromwell or Charles II.

5. FRANCE VERSUS THE DUTCH

The Dutch had commercial as well as military reasons for wishing to prevent Louis from taking the Spanish Netherlands. A French army so near to their frontiers could exercise undue pressure upon them, and perhaps even more important, French control over the industrial cities of the Spanish Netherlands would greatly enhance France's commercial position. The cities in the Spanish Netherlands were highly developed manufacturing centers producing cloth, hardwares, and leather goods; if they became part of the French kingdom, their importance in Europe would grow apace. Futhermore, it would be unlikely that the French would submit to the regulations that the Dutch imposed upon those cities through their control of the transportation routes out of the Spanish Netherlands via the mouth of the Scheldt river. Even without the control of those provinces, French commercial interests were beginning to conflict with those of the Dutch Netherlands, and were the French to rule the industrial towns of Ghent and Brussels, the Franco-Dutch conflict would be greatly accelerated. Thus military strategy and political, as well as commercial, rivalry had driven a wedge between the erstwhile allies. Here was a clear-cut case in which interests of state and dynasty were intertwined.

There were further causes of rivalry between France and the Netherlands. Once the long war with Spain had ended (1659), French commercial interests had received a strong impetus from the king's government. Richelieu had had plans for enlarging French commerce, but war had delayed their execution; after 1660 Louis XIV and Colbert began to implement those earlier projects. The India trade, the Levant trade, the African trade, the American trade, each in turn became projects that ran into Dutch competition. Louis had naïvely believed at first that the Dutch would help their old ally to find a place in the oriental market where Dutch merchants had had so much experience, but he was soon to learn the facts of the business world from the most rugged of seventeenth-century businessmen. The Dutch were no more willing to share the markets with the French than with anyone else. They could not treat French merchants the way they treated the Russians, who tried to carry their own goods from Archangel to Amsterdam only to find that no one would buy the furs until the Russians had returned them to Archangel. Nonetheless, the French received rough treatment.

On their side, the French, too, were willing to play rough. Just as Crom-well and Charles II in England had tried to curb their business rivals, by the tariffs, embargoes, rebates, and eventually by cannons, so Louis' govern-ment was also willing to take drastic methods. The growth of the French navy and commercial interests pointed to a Franco-Dutch conflict even be-fore the Netherlanders dared to organize Europe against Louis' demands for possession of the Spanish Netherlands. Not for nothing have the political and economic theories of the seventeenth century been called "Colbertism." Like all men of his century, Colbert recognized war as the normal method of settling disputes. It used to be customary for historians to paint Colbert, the man interested in trade and the king's treasury, as the man of peace who was opposed to Louvois, the war minister, who urged war. Such a view over-looked the fact that Colbert built up the French navy to a force equal to that of the combined English and Dutch fleets. He had no scruples about using the sword in a "just cause." It is an open question as to what his advice would have been in the years that followed his death (1683) when Louvois became the king's chief adviser.

The experience of the two Anglo-Dutch wars was enough to warn the French that any conflict with the Netherlands would mean serious business. Thus Louis XIV, unlike his English cousin, did not embark upon a Dutch war without considerable preparation. He recognized that his foes were for-midable opponents, and they turned out to be even more dangerous than he had expected. Louis' methods were simple and direct. At home, he organized a magnificent army and strengthened his fleet; abroad, he bought allies with subsidies. The king of England, the regency government in Sweden, the Rhine bishops, the electors of Bavaria, Brandenburg, and Saxony, were all put on his pay roll. None of those rulers could get as much money from his own people as he needed, so a subsidy from the king of France was welcome. There were, of course, other reasons for accepting French money and alli-ances. Both England and Sweden were as jealous of the Dutch commercial monopolies as were the French, and their rulers believed that war with the Dutch would strengthen their government's position with the merchant classes that would welcome a chance to injure a rival. The situation in Ger-many was somewhat more complicated. There the princes were anxious to get French money; they also were involved in intrigue against the Hapsburg emperor. Louis attached the condition to his subsidies that the recipients would vote for a Bourbon emperor in the next election. While the princes were thus "tied" to French policy, the Emperor Leopold was also persuaded to stand aside and permit the French to throttle the Dutch by promises that the Hapsburgs and Bourbons would divide the Spanish inheritance on the death of Charles II. All these preparatory actions left the Dutch alone to face the military pressure of the "Sun King."

However, events did not turn out as Louis had expected. The war that started (1672) as a military promenade for the French army and the Anglo-French navies developed into a conflict that lasted six years. The failure of the French to achieve a speedy victory cannot be explained without a complicated analysis of the military tactics and theory of the day. However, that failure gave the Dutch the chance to organize European resistance which saved them from destruction at the hands of the "Sun King." The Dutch were quite unequal to the task of matching the Anglo-French forces that moved against them. Even though Admiral de Ruyter defeated the allied navies, the Dutch had no land army capable of matching blows with the two French armies that invaded the Netherlands. All that was left to them was the chance that, by cutting the dykes, they could flood the lowlands and stop the invader. Fortunately, the French were slow to exploit their initial advantage, and thus the Dutch had time to cut the dykes. A great part of the Netherlands was abandoned to the enemy; some of it was covered with water, ruining the peasants, but the province of Holland virtually became an island inaccessible to the armies of Condé and Turenne. It was a tiny territory to resist the combined power of France and England.

The Dutch were ready to negotiate, but the terms offered them were ruinous. Their enemies wished to destroy the economic and political foundations of Dutch wealth. There was a revolution in Holland against the government that had led the Provinces into this predicament. The republican de Witt brothers and their friends were made the scapegoats, sacrificed because someone had to be blamed for the crisis. In their place arose the government of the stadtholder, William III of Orange. For generations the conflict between the aristocratic Orange party and the bourgeois republican party had see-sawed back and forth. When the Provinces were in extreme danger, the Orange party tended to come to the fore. Such was the case in 1672 when fanatics murdered the de Witts, and William III became the leader of Dutch resistance to France. The new government would not come to terms unless the commercial prosperity of the United Netherlands remained intact.

The Dutch decision to fight rather than to accept annihilation gave the rest of Europe time to think over Louis' policy, and within a relatively short period a coalition to aid the Dutch came into being. In Germany the emperor and the powerful electoral prince of Brandenburg-Prussia became rallying points for Catholic and Protestant German opposition to France. They were joined by the Spaniards, who saw that Louis' goal of possession of the Spanish Netherlands had not been abandoned. While the coalition was emerging on the continent, the English Parliament, suspicious of the relationship between Charles II and Louis XIV, forced England's government to withdraw from the war (1674). Even though the French were unable to secure a decisive victory, the power and ambition of Louis XIV had frightened the rest of Europe to the point where only Sweden was left as his ally.

Well might Europe be fearful. As the war progressed, the world saw that the French might not be able to impose their will on Europe, but neither could Europe defeat France. The French state was the only great military power of the day; French armies easily held off the attacks of Spain, Germany, and the Netherlands, and at the same time campaigned successfully in the border provinces of the Spanish Netherlands and the Franche-Comté. In the Baltic, France's ally, Sweden, enjoyed no such advantage. The forces of Brandenburg-Prussia overran Pomerania, while Dutch, Danish, and Prussian forces swept the Baltic and actually ravaged the coast of Sweden. Louis' efforts to bring Poland and Turkey into the war to aid Sweden were unsuccessful. Thus, the war that had begun as an effort to smother the commercial, political, and military power of the United Netherlands became a general European war as soon as the neighbors of France realized what was at stake.

The Spanish king, the emperor, and the North German princes had not joined the war merely to preserve the commerce of the merchants of Amsterdam, nor had England's Parliament forced Charles II to withdraw for that reason. They had acted to check the ambitions and the power of France, or, like Brandenburg-Prussia, to extend their own territory. They were, therefore, beginning to strive for a balance of power in Europe. The rise of the coalition against France was one of the first manifestations of the balance of power that was to become the basic constitution of Europe for the next two and a half centuries. From the end of the seventeenth century until 1919, when a global balance of power replaced it, the European balance of power was the governing mechanism in western society. However, the so-called Dutch war also revealed the fact that the balance of power principle was not yet sufficiently developed for Europe to fight a coalition war to a decisive conclusion. In part, the problem developed out of the military strategy of the day. Later seventeenth-century military conflicts were wars of position; that is to say, of sieges and countersieges rather than of battles in the open field. In this "fortress" warfare, attrition played a decisive role; the powers that could hold out without going bankrupt or facing internal revolt had the best chance of winning, or at least of securing a favorable treaty. By 1676–1677 all the parties concerned were weary of war, but as long as neither side could force a military decision and as long as the coalition presented a united front against France, there could be no peace. The French problem was to break up the coalition; if that could be done, French power would remain intact.

The French let it be known that they would reduce their demands to the acquisition of the Spanish province of Franche-Comté. Since Spain would then have to pay the bill, the Dutch were willing to negotiate. When one member of the coalition broke away, the others rushed to salvage what they could, and a general peace became possible. This was to be the pattern of coalition warfare for the next half century; it was not easy to hold a coalition together for each of the allies rightly suspected the others of seeking selfish interests rather than those of the coalition as a whole.

The peace conference met at Nijmwegen in 1678–1679, but the actual negotiations were not conducted at the conference table. Louis XIV negotiated separately with each of his enemies, and the conference of Nijmwegen merely confirmed the decisions already reached. There, too, was the pattern for future peace conferences in which coalitions of powers would struggle to maintain some sort of equitable government for Europe as a whole. It was not a very "rational" process, but it was the best that could be devised to meet the problems of western society at that time. The Treaty of Nijmwegen revealed two important facts about the European society that was coming into being. The first was that peace treaties would be concerned with commercial relationships as well as with territories. The second was that provinces could be won or lost by military engagements far from the provinces themselves. The Brandenburg armies had overrun Pomerania, and their prince was determined to hold that province, but Louis XIV forced him to return Pomerania to Sweden, even though the Swedes had been driven from the land. Lastly, Louis forced Spain to cede Franche-Comté and its "dependencies," thus adding an important province of the old "Burgundian crown" to France and giving her a claim to all the territories that had been "dependencies" of that province. This reaffirmed the fact that in the Europe of the future provinces and peoples were to be "pawns in the game" of politics, and therefore "bartered" about at peace conferences. No one—except, of course, the losers—seriously questioned this practice until Woodrow Wilson raised his voice against it in 1918. The Treaty also provides nice evidence of the status of European development in 1679. The idea of interest of state, rooted in economic, strategic, and political realities, was firmly established as a motive for political action and had become so much an integral part of the programs of governments that dynastic considerations might be overruled. On the other hand, the fact that French policy broke up the coalition that opposed France only emphasized the fact that Europe had not yet learned how to conduct a coalition war successfully. However, that first great coalition did provide experience in governing Europe through the balance of power. Thus, the Treaty of Nijmwegen was an important harbinger of the future political organization of the western world.

A Popular Contemporary Print Depicting a Sortie by the Defenders of Vienna. The sortie took place when a Turkish mine caused havoc at another point in the walls. The heroic defense of Vienna (1683) against Kara Mustapha's Turkish army aroused the admiration of the entire western world. Pictures such as this one were responsible for the stream of volunteers that filled the emperor's armies. (University of Minnesota Library)

Chapter 14

WAR AND REVOLUTION: THE EMERGENCE OF THE DANUBIAN MONARCHY AND ENGLAND AS GREAT POWERS

1. THE PROBLEM OF 1680–1714

The seventeenth century was an era filled with civil and international wars, a veritable age of conflict. As we have already noted, the so-called Thirty Years' War (1618–1648) that was brought to an end in Germany with the Treaty of Westphalia, in fact continued as a Franco-Spanish war in western Europe until the Treaty of the Pyrenees (1659). At first, the war had flaunted flags of religion; it ended in the secularization of politics and the recognition of France as the leading power in the West. The commercial wars that England and France fought against the Dutch and the political conflicts generated by the ambitions of Louis XIV followed as emphasis of the fact that the interests of states and dynasties had ousted religion as the motive force in high politics. After 1680, when a new series of wars again bathed European soil with blood, states' and dynastic interests were joined by a new political force, namely, the struggle to maintain the balance of power in Europe. The idea of a balance of power had been fully developed in fifteenth-century Italy, but it was not until the end of the seventeenth century that it became the basis for the government of the continent of Europe as a whole. Only if we see the great wars that raged from 1683 to 1721 in this light do they become intelligible.

The wars of the second half of the seventeenth century have caused historians endless trouble. Since most historians have been Europeans writing the history of their own land or writing European history from the viewpoint of their own country, they have tended to see the wars in terms of one or another particular national or geographical problem or theater of conflict. This approach, however, has resulted in certain distortions and really blinds the reader to the larger European significance of the period. Those wars were not simply struggles over commerce in the Atlantic basin, or the Spanish inheritance, or even the ambitions of Louis XIV. Since they also involved the first retreat of Islam from the heart of Europe and the first introduction of Russia (however unimportant at the time) into European politics, they can only be understood if we see them as general European problems rather than as questions involving France, England, Germany, or the Netherlands.

If we may look ahead to the end of the conflicts to get a clue to the significant forces operating in Europe of this period, we discover a striking fact. By 1715 there were three great military powers in Europe—England, France, and the Danubian monarchy—and a balance of military power had become the mechanism for the government of the continent. This is in sharp contrast to the situation of 1680 or thereabout, when France was the only great military power and the will of the French government seemed to be the supreme arbiter for most of the West.

Thus the problem of this chapter is to see how, out of an era of warfare, England and the Danubian monarchy managed to develop the power necessary to check the rise of France and also to establish a government for Europe.

2. THE HAPSBURG STATE ON THE DANUBE

An eighteenth-century wit remarked: "If Austria did not exist, it would be necessary to create her." While this remark reveals that century's naïve conception of political society as something that men might "create," it also points up the fact that the Danubian monarchy (Austria) had assumed its historic role in central Europe. It is difficult to say whether it was "created" by historical accident or historical necessity. Many factors were involved, but the most obviously important one was the dreaded pressure of Islam up the Danube. To meet this threat to independence and Christian civilization, the people of the upper Danube basin rallied around the Hapsburg princes who ruled Vienna.

The Hapsburg family first emerged as an important German dynastic house in the later Middle Ages, but, as we have already seen, the really significant rise of the family did not come until the later fifteenth century when a combination of marriages and elections made it the most powerful house in Europe. The Spanish and Burgundian holdings of the family that were brought together in the person of Charles V were not the ones that created the Danubian monarchy. It was Charles' brother Ferdinand I who was the "founding father" of that central European Hapsburg state. He was the first Hapsburg to bring together the crowns of Bohemia, Hungary, and German Austria. After the siege of Vienna (1529), when the Turkish armies were forced back into Hungary, those three peoples, bound together by a common fear of Islam, accepted a common ruler, but they were far from admitting any common loyalty or common sense of cooperative unity.

Furthermore, it did not prove an easy task to give those states even a semblance of political unity. Ferdinand I and his immediate successors failed to establish a firm basis for military power in any of the kingdoms, perhaps because the danger from Islam had relaxed in the second half of the sixteenth century. As soon as the Turks ceased to "knock at their gates," many Hungarian and Bohemian noblemen regretted their decision to accept the Hapsburgs as their protectors. They resisted any further surrender of powers, and rebellions and plots of rebellion became commonplace. Many of them joined a reformed religion, usually Calvinist, perhaps as symbolic of their opposition to their "foreign" king. The immediate successors of Ferdinand I were unable to check these disintegrating forces, but in the first half of the seventeenth century, as we have already seen, the rebellion in Bohemia and the Hapsburg-Catholic victory at White Mountain (1620) gave Ferdinand II the opportunity to reorganize the Bohemian constitution. The Bohemian throne became hereditary in the Hapsburg family, its authority was strengthened, and by reshuffling land ownership, loyal pro-Hapsburg noblemen came to dominate the diets of Bohemia, Moravia, and Silesia. Ferdinand II also strengthened his authority in the German Hapsburg provinces (Austria, Tyrol, Styria, and Carinthia) by the introduction of bureaucratic government and the reduction of the powers of the *Landtäge* (diets). He failed to gain a comparable control over Hungary, neither did he give organic unity to his lands as a whole. Nonetheless, the Thirty Years' War had given great impetus to the development of the Danubian monarchy, and the fact that a significant result of the war was the further weakening of the Holy Roman Empire acted as an additional incentive for the strengthening of the Hapsburg Danubian state. The crown of the Empire ceased to endow its wearer with much real power; therefore Leopold I (1658–1708) and his successors had to turn to their lands on the Danube which they governed as territorial rulers, to buttress their power and authority in Europe.

Of those lands the kingdom of Hungary presented the most problems. Two-thirds of that kingdom was ruled directly by, or as a fief of the Ottoman empire. The Turkish pasha at Ofen (Budapest) did not interfere with the religion or customs of his Hungarian subjects as long as they paid their taxes, but his presence was a constant reminder that Hungary was still a springboard for a further Ottoman thrust into central Europe. The Turkish vassal state of Transylvania, more or less ruled by native princes, was equally dangerous to both the Hapsburgs and the Turks. Transylvanian Calvinists saw themselves as the core around which a new Hungarian state would arise. They were, if anything, more hostile to the Catholic Hapsburgs than to the Turks, for they saw the Hapsburgs as rivals for the loyalty of the Hungarian people.

The third of Hungary under Leopold's rule was also a constant source of trouble. It retained the ancient Hungarian crown of St. Stephen, and with it the quasi-anarchic constitution of the kingdom. As a province bordering Islam, it was organized for war; in point of fact, however, Hungarian noblemen, Calvinist in religion, were in rebellion against their Christian king as often as they were under arms against the Turks. The German Hapsburgs were necessary to Hungary, but they were disliked by many of the great families of the kingdom because they were "foreigners" and because, as kings, the Hapsburgs wished to enhance their control over the land. The Hungarian magnates found it easy to rebel against their king: the rebels bore almost the same relation to their Hapsburg ruler that Dutch or Huguenot rebels had borne to the sixteenth-century Spanish and French rulers.

Hungary was thus a source of weakness to the Hapsburgs in Vienna, but since it was also the first line of defense against the Turks for their German and Bohemian lands, they could not do without Hungary, and therefore had to defend her.

In the second half of the seventeenth century Ottoman power showed signs of rejuvenation. The government at Constantinople was reorganized, and Turkish armies were again on the march. Leopold defeated them in 1664 and signed a twenty-year truce that presumably would give him time to secure his share of the Spanish inheritance. The Turks had only been checked, not stopped; their leaders in Constantinople were convinced that their empire could survive only if it expanded. They turned their warlike efforts toward Persia and the Venetian possessions in the eastern Mediterranean, and even before the truce of 1664 had expired they were again ready to try their luck in central Europe, which meant, of course, a challenge to the Hapsburgs.

However, there was another side to the coin. In Germany many men were beginning to say that, in spite of its apparent vigor, the Ottoman Empire was ready to fall apart. In Leopold's government there were those who believed that Turkish Hungary could be reconquered: they argued that if Hungary were "liberated" and integrated with Bohemia and the Hapsburg Austrian provinces, a state would emerge equal to France in economic and military power. The popular pamphlet of 1683 entitled "Austria Has Trumps If She Will Only Play Them" argued that the conquest of Hungary would pave the way for the rise of a great military power on the Danube. This was the vision that spurred Leopold on when the situation became desperate in 1683–1684.

3. FRENCH ANNEXATIONS IN TIME OF PEACE

While the Ottoman Empire presented both a challenge and an opportunity for the rulers of Vienna, a threat of a very different sort demanded attention on the other side of their lands. In the years immediately following the Treaty of Nijmwegen (1679), French expansion and French demands for recognition of her king's rights kept much of Europe in turmoil. When Genoa displeased the "Sun King," a French squadron appeared before the city and systematically destroyed a large part of the harbor by bombardment. The Muslim pirates at Chios received the same treatment when one of their number raided a French merchantman. Where French guns were not employed, French gold served almost as well. In Sweden, Germany, the Netherlands, Italy, Hungary, and Transylvania, princes and politicians became pensioners of the French monarch and jumped when he called the tune. Both Charles II of England and John III Sobieski of Poland were in his pay. The elector of Brandenburg, Frederick William, announced that opposition to France was fruitless; the princes must, therefore, get what crumbs they could from Louis' table.

In the upper Rhineland this period saw the establishment of a new French court, the Chambers of Reunion, that presumed to decide upon the sovereignty of the border provinces. At Westphalia and Nijmwegen no frontier had been clearly demarcated (no seventeenth-century treaty drew a frontier line). The treaties gave France certain provinces "and their dependencies." The word "dependencies" was ambiguous: did the term include the dependencies of the dependencies? Seventeenth-century Europe was still a welter of overlapping dependencies that dated back to the feudal tenures of earlier periods. At the suggestion of legalistically minded advisers, Louis XIV used his newly created Courts of Reunion to determine the exact extent of the territory that had been ceded to France. The Courts, assuming the roles of judge and advocate, began to award lands in Alsace and the Saarland to France. In 1681 the Free City of Strasbourg was adjudged as belonging to France, and was occupied. In the same year Louis' soldiers also entered Casale in Italy without bothering to obtain a court decision.

The whole of Europe, but particularly all Germany, was aroused by Louis' actions. The Emperor Leopold announced that he would not accept the annexations. His military power was inadequate to force Louis to give them up, but his ministers began to negotiate with other German princes, with the king of Sweden whose territory in the Saar basin had just been annexed, with the king of Spain whose land of Luxemburg was obviously threatened, and with William of Orange, stadtholder of the Netherlands. The negotiations proceeded slowly, however, for Europe was afraid of Louis' guns and discouraged because of France's success in the recent war, but by 1682 the crisis provoked by French expansion had reached a serious point. An alliance of the central European princes, organized by the Emperor Leopold and a close friend of William of Orange, was beginning to emerge. At about the same time, due to the deaths of the princes of electoral Saxony and Bavaria, young men who were resolved to break their fathers' connection with France ascended the thrones in Munich and Dresden. The German princes seemed ready to go to war with France to save the Rhineland from Louis' aggressions. At that point, however, the Turkish threat to central Europe—at least as dangerous as that of the French king—appeared from the east. The Ottoman Turks were again on the march and prepared to invade Germany.

4. *THE CRISIS OF 1683 AND THE RECONQUEST OF HUNGARY*

In 1683 Kara Mustafa led a Turkish army of two hundred thousand men up the Danube to besiege Vienna. In its ranks were the Hungarian Calvinist malcontents, soldiers from Transylvania, and the finest Muslim troops that the sultan could muster. The Turks had the assurance of the most Christian king of France, Louis XIV, that French soldiers would not assist Leopold's armies, and they knew that French diplomacy had worked to isolate the German Hapsburgs. The Ottoman leaders did not know how vigorously Vienna would defend itself or that Duke Charles of Lorraine and John Sobieski of Poland would raise armies capable of lifting the siege.

The French part in the Turkish invasion was no mystery. Leopold was the chief opponent to Louis' expansionist policies in the Rhineland and Italy. He was arousing German opposition to the Courts of Reunion; he was the principal actor in the league that was being organized against France; and he had demanded that the French leave Strasbourg. Furthermore, Leopold was Louis' rival for the Spanish inheritance. If Kara Mustafa could break the power of the German Hapsburgs, Louis XIV would remain as the sword and shield of Christendom against Islam; Europe would have to appeal to him to save itself from the Turks, and his Hapsburg rival for the throne of Spain would be eliminated. But Vienna did not fall. Leopold's commander, Duke Charles of Lorraine, and King John Sobieski of Poland overran Kara Mustafa's army, captured his camp, and sent the Turks fleeing down the Danube. The Christian army clamorously demanded to pursue the enemy and liberate Hungary, but before that could be done, Louis XIV insisted with arms that France's "rights" in the Rhineland be recognized.

The Turkish war was Louis' signal to invade the Spanish Netherlands and Luxembourg to demand recognition of the annexations made by his Courts of Reunion. The Spanish king declared war, but his declaration was futile unless Leopold, the Dutch, and the German princes could come to his aid. The Estates-General in the Netherlands, yielding to French threats and bribes, excused itself. The more important north German princes, in French

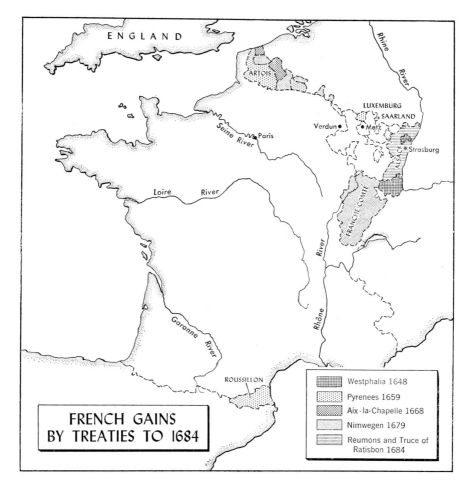

ENGLAND

ARTOIS

Rhine River

LUXEMBURG
SAARLAND

Verdun • • Metz

Seine River • Paris

Strasburg

ALSACE

Loire River

FRANCHE-COMTÉ

Rhône River

Garonne River

Rhône River

ROUSSILLON

**FRENCH GAINS
BY TREATIES TO 1684**

▦	Westphalia 1648
▨	Pyrenees 1659
▦	Aix-la-Chapelle 1668
░	Nimwegen 1679
▤	Reumons and Truce of Ratisbon 1684

pay, also refused to act, and Leopold's advisers preferred to fight the Ottoman Empire rather than risk a war with France in which victory appeared improbable. No army was available to save Luxemburg from the French the way the German and Polish force had saved Vienna, nor was there any likelihood that an army could be raised unless the emperor made peace with the Turks. Leopold's advisers decided that it was now possible to reconquer Hungary, but to do so peace would have to be made with France. Therefore, a truce was concluded for twenty years (Regensburg, 1684) whereby the Hapsburg princes of Spain and Austria agreed to tentative recognition of France's annexations in the Rhineland. Louis felt sure that the truce would in fact mean final recognition of his conquests. Leopold convinced himself that the recognition was only a temporary expedient; once the war with Turkey had been brought to an end, he expected to insist on an accounting with France.

With France pacified by these concessions, the Christian armies pressed forward their war against Islam. Much of the credit for their success should be given to Pope Innocent XI (1676–1689) who played the role of a crusading pope as well as any of his medieval predecessors had done. He organized the so-called Holy League that fought the war—an alliance of Austria, Venice, Poland, and Russia. He levied "taxes" on all Catholic Europe to provide the sinews of war for the Christian captains. His appeals to the crusading spirit rallied noblemen and commoners from all Catholic Europe to the Emperor Leopold's standard. It was Innocent XI who sparked Leopold's victories in the Danube and Venetian victories in Greece and then ordered that they should be celebrated in Catholic churches all over Europe.

However, even though Innocent XI envisaged the war as a crusade, the belligerents realistically saw it as an opportunity for conquest. Austrian and Bohemian bureaucrats followed the victorious imperial armies down the Danube. Jesuit priests joined them to consolidate with religion the Hapsburg victory over Calvinist Hungarians. In Greece, Venetian businessmen and Catholic monks landed just behind the armies that conquered the Morea and captured Athens. In both cases the men who followed the armies were intent upon establishing a new power relationship in the territory that had been liberated from Islam. Neither the Russians nor the Poles made any serious contribution to the war; the former were badly beaten by the Turks, the latter too divided internally to act.

By 1688 the Christian armies had overrun all Hungary, occupied Transylvania, and were besieging Belgrade. The Turks, badly shaken by defeat, had gone through several internal "reorganizations" involving considerable bloodshed, and were ready to sue for peace. All at once the full meaning of the conquest became apparent to Europe. This was not just a crusader's victory. The Emperor Leopold was changing the Hungarian constitution to make the crown hereditary in his family and to deprive the great noblemen of their legal right to rebellion. He was also reorganizing the administration of the kingdom and redistributing the land so that his loyal soldiers, bureaucrats, and courtiers would become important political forces in the kingdom. He had his son Joseph crowned king of Hungary (1688) without the usual crippling coronation diploma. It was clear that a revolution had taken place in Hungary and that a new force had been introduced into the European balance of power.

Furthermore, the new king of Hungary was elected King of the Romans (1688); that is, successor to Leopold I as Holy Roman Emperor. This act formally ended Louis XIV's hopes of securing that crown for the Bourbon family. The Hapsburg victories had been won in Hungary; the act in Germany merely underlined their significance.

Before the year 1688 was out, Louis XIV had again invaded the Rhineland, loudly proclaiming his grievances against the German empire. His candidate for the post of archbishop of Cologne had not received the office.

His sister-in-law's claims to the Palatinate had not been honored, and the German princes were leagued against him in warlike array. Simply reading what Louis had to say, it would seem that France was an injured party in a dispute. But Louis' words were only half of the story. He saw the Austrian victory in Hungary as a threat to his Rhineland conquests and was determined to save what he could by an aggressive act in Germany. His ambassador at Constantinople assured the Turks prior to the invasion that the French action would allow the Ottoman empire to remain in the war and regain its lost lands. What it actually did was to make the war an all-European struggle for the balance of power.

5. THE ENGLISH REVOLUTION OF 1688

The revolution in Hungary that brought Louis XIV into the war created a situation that had repercussions in England. The English king, James II, had provoked his Protestant subjects to a point where they were ready to revolt. But James II had an army at his disposal, an army in part officered by Catholics whose loyalty was unquestionable, but to a greater extent by opportunists. No rebellion was possible without foreign aid. Foreign aid was available in the Netherlands, where Prince William of Orange was stadtholder in command of a motley army of Germans, French Huguenots, and Dutchmen. The Estates-General of the Netherlands, however, deemed that that army and its commander were necessary for the defense of the state up to the day that the main body of the French army invaded Germany (1688). The French invasion lessened military pressure on the Netherlands, and the Estates-General then gave William permission to sail to England. His argument was that he could thereby persuade England to join the coalition against France.

As we have already seen, the revolution of 1688 in England revolved around a domestic question involving James II's right to bring England into the fold of the Catholic Church. The trial of the bishops and the birth of a son had prepared the people for rebellion, but it was William's army that made the revolution successful, and it was his policy that turned the revolution into an instrument for mobilizing the power of England against France. James II, fugitive from his throne, persuaded Louis XIV to help him regain it. This was exactly what William had hoped for since he was vitally interested in the anti-French coalition and wished to bring England into the war against Louis XIV. When French soldiers and sailors came to James' assistance in Ireland and on the sea, the English politicians agreed to become allies of the Dutch, the emperor, and the German princes to save their revolution and curb the power of France.

As we have seen, the English revolution of 1688 shifted the balance of political power in England to the advantage of Parliament. This was soon to have fateful consequences on the European scene, for when Louis XIV came to James' aid, the politicians in Parliament readily understood that their revolution was at stake in the conflict. Parliament had powers of taxation that no English king had ever enjoyed, and it could borrow money on a scale that no king had yet been able to establish. Although it was not apparent in 1688, Parliament's power to tax and borrow became the decisive factor before the war was over, for, with money granted by Parliament, England was able to raise armies, build ships, and pay subsidies to allies. These were the measures that forced Louis XIV to recognize the limitations to his power. For the first time in the century England had become a great military power. The revolution of 1688 and the war against France laid the foundation for her role as the arbiter of the balance of power in Europe, a role that she was not to relinquish until the end of the first war of the twentieth century.

Thus the revolution of 1688 in England, like the one that occurred the preceding year in Hungary, laid the basis for a new military-political state in Europe. England's change in status first became apparent with the rise of her navy to a preponderant position in the West. In 1688 the French navy was equal to those of England and the Netherlands combined; by 1698 the English navy was the largest afloat, and by 1708 it was clearly the preponderant sea power in the world. English armies on the continent and beyond the seas followed a similar pattern of growth, although, for obvious reasons, they never became as important relatively as the navy. The so-called "Glorious Revolution" was also to become the basis for interesting constitutional experiments in England that we shall discuss later, but for Europe as a whole its importance lies in the fact that it released the military power of England and placed it firmly as a weight in the new balance of power that was becoming the constitution for Europe.

6. THE FIRST WORLD WAR, 1688–1697

English historians have called the war of 1688–1697 the "War of the English Succession"; American historians used to call it "King William's War." French and German historians, noting that the war in the west merged with the one on the Rhine, called it the "War of the League of Augsburg" or the "War of the Palatinate"; certain Dutch and English historians call it the "Anglo-Dutch Trade War against France." In Austrian history, it merged with the War of the Holy League. In fact, this was the first European war to embrace the whole continent from Russia to Spain and spill over into the Americas and Asia, so that it is perhaps properly called the "First World War."

By 1690 most of the belligerents had taken their places. In the West, England, the Netherlands, Spain, Savoy, the emperor, and most of Germany faced France; in the East, the Empire, Venice, Russia, and Poland fought with the Ottoman Empire. Sweden, after honoring her alliance with the sea powers at the opening of the war, retreated into neutrality before the conflict was well under way. The pope tried to make the war in the East into a Catholic crusade against Islam; the Huguenots who had been expelled from France tried to turn it into a Protestant crusade against bigoted Catholicism. Obviously, the religious issue did not determine the combatants nor were the issues that brought one section of Europe into the struggle the same as those that affected another. Russia, Savoy, and England, for example, had little in common, yet they were all fighting against either France or her friend, the Ottoman Empire.

The conduct of the war was very similar to that of the so-called Dutch War of the preceding decade. Soldiers were no longer hired condottieri bands but rather members of the king's army, wearing *his* coat and carrying *his* musket. They were directed now by bureaucratic officials from the king's war ministry and cared for by the king's commissioners. Those cautious, time-serving, bureaucratic commissioners regarded the conservation of the army as their principal objective. They had nothing but suspicion for soldiers who wanted to risk the whole army on a single battle. They recognized that the other side of the assertion "the war could be won in an afternoon" was that it could be lost just as quickly. The time had arrived when soldiers were becoming too valuable to be used up in battle; an army "in being" gave military power to a prince and he could not afford to lose it.

Thus, on land the war became an affair of maneuvers and sieges; at sea, it was a matter of blockades and raids on commercial shipping. Only when a general like Marshal Luxembourg broke loose from the bureaucrats was it possible to press for a field battle. Some historians have insisted that after Turenne and Condé died, France had no great generals. That statement is not true, but it is true to say that after Condé and Turenne were dead, there were few generals who could stand up to bureaucrats like Louvois or the king to demand freedom of action. The enemies of France were in the same predicament. Leopold's armies, conditioned by the siege warfare in Hungary and under the direction of the imperial war office, were prepared for a war of position. William of Orange, himself a mediocre if stubborn soldier, was continually urged by the civilian commissioners from the Dutch government to follow a role of caution. The outcome of the military conflict was decided then by attrition rather than direct military action; each side sought to wear down the other, to destroy its will to fight. Control over the sea turned out to be of great importance. In the first years of the conflict, the French had control or at least preponderance at sea, but early in the 1690's the Anglo-Dutch fleets surpassed them. Even though French privateers harassed Anglo-Dutch commerce, commerce was ruined. In addition, a series of bad harvests made the loss of her merchant navy a major catastrophe for she could not import food, particularly grain from the Baltic.

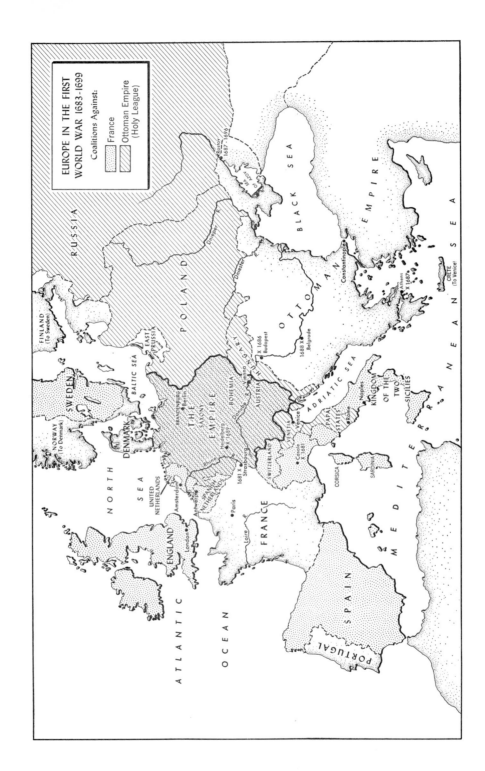

EUROPE IN THE FIRST
WORLD WAR 1683-1699

Coalitions Against:

France

Ottoman Empire
(Holy League)

RUSSIA

FINLAND
(To Sweden)

POLAND

BLACK SEA

OTTOMAN EMPIRE

Azov
1687-1696

Dnieper R.

Dniester R.

Constantinople

Athens
X 1687

CRETE
(To Venice)

SWEDEN

NORWAY
(To Denmark)

DENMARK

BALTIC SEA

EAST
PRUSSIA

BRANDENBURG
• Berlin

SAXONY

BOHEMIA

HUNGARY

AUSTRIA

Danube R.
• Vienna

X 1686
Budapest

1688 X
• Belgrade

ADRIATIC SEA

KINGDOM OF THE TWO SICILIES

NORTH
SEA

THE
EMPIRE

• Heidelberg

Rhine R.

1689 X

SWITZERLAND

VENETIA

• Venice

PAPAL
STATES

• Rome

Naples •

Casale
X 1681

UNITED
NETHERLANDS

Amsterdam •
Antwerp •

SPANISH
NETHERLANDS

1681 X
Strasbourg

ENGLAND

London •

• Paris

FRANCE

Loire R.

CORSICA

SARDINIA

MEDITERRANEAN SEA

ATLANTIC
OCEAN

SPAIN

PORTUGAL

In any war of attrition, the real test lies in the belligerents' ability to find the money or credit to pay for the contest. It has been said that wars were fought with "money and money and money," for only money could buy soldiers, supplies, and ships. Therefore, the real wealth of the belligerents and their ability to tax and to borrow became crucial. Here was the Achilles' heel of Bourbon France; Louis XIV could neither tax nor borrow as readily as the United Provinces and England. His soldiers might win fortresses, his fortresses might withstand sieges, for he had more effective military organization and better officers than his enemies, but after a decade of war his kingdom's credit was sorely strained, and his people's ability to pay more taxes was nearly exhausted. However, this deficiency was not the final one of Louis' problems. The coalition against France included Spain as well as Hapsburg Austria, England, the Netherlands, Savoy, and the German princes, and Spain's sickly King Charles II was expected to die any moment from the time he first mounted the throne in 1665. By 1695 it was certain that his death was not far away. Were he to die while the war raged, the coalition would undoubtedly recognize Leopold's second son as Charles III, king of Spain, thereby putting an end to the dream of a Bourbon succession to the Spanish throne. This, almost as much as the disorder in his finances and the war weariness of his people, caused Louis XIV to work to make peace.

Peace in the West came as a result of two treaties, both of which were disadvantageous to France; but considering the fact that all Europe had combined in a coalition against Louis XIV, they almost seem to be a French victory. The first was the Treaty of Turin (1696) between France and Savoy. By this treaty Louis XIV surrendered all the territories that France had gained in northern Italy since the time of Richelieu, and thereby recognized that France would not attempt to dominate the Po valley. When Savoy had made peace, the other powers of the coalition hurried to do the same. The second was the Treaty of Ryswick (1697) between France and the rest of her enemies. Actually, the negotiations were effected at Paris by direct contact between Louis XIV and the agents of William III of England and the Netherlands. This treaty left France with all she had gained by the treaties of Westphalia (1648) and Nijmwegen (1679) and even with some of the lands acquired by the Courts of Reunion (1680–1682), but it also marked limits to French expansion and forced Louis XIV to recognize the "rights and interests" of England and the Netherlands. To insure that those interests were respected, the treaty provided that the Dutch were to be allowed to garrison the fortresses in the Spanish Netherlands; only thus could they be secure against French aggression. The big issue of the hour, namely, the Spanish succession was left unsettled: there seemed to be no common ground for agreement in 1697.

Two years later Leopold made peace with the Ottoman Empire at Karlowitz (1699). The treaties of Karlowitz, along with those of Turin and Ryswick, ended the first great world war. They gave Leopold Hungary and Transylvania; Poland and Russia also secured frontier rectifications, and Venice was given the Morea in Greece. They revealed the true extent of the French defeat in the great war. The Austrian House of Hapsburg, Louis' rival for both the Spanish succession and control over Germany, emerged from the peace conference with the territory and the political organization to create another great military power on the continent. It was this Danubian monarchy that was to be a counterweight in the balance of European power for the next two centuries.

7. THE SPANISH SUCCESSION

In the interval between the Treaty of Ryswick (1697) and the outbreak of the next war (1703), western Europe enjoyed a period of unprecedented prosperity. It is small wonder that politicians and princes hesitated to plunge their peoples into a new war that must necessarily bring misery and destruction.

The most difficult problem before Europe was still the succession to the Spanish throne. Charles II was seemingly unable either to produce an heir or to die so that an heir could be decided upon, so all the courts of Europe seethed with discussion of the question. The Spanish throne involved important stakes. In Italy, Milan and Naples-Sicily were of interest to the Mediterranean powers as well as to the Danubian monarchy. The Spanish Netherlands were regarded as vital interests of France, the United Netherlands, and England; and all the trading nations were concerned about the disposition of Spanish America and the Philippines. Spain itself was of less immediate significance than the Spanish dependencies, and yet Spanish trade as well as the Spanish harbors in the Mediterranean and the Straits had important implications for Europe as a whole.

Both William III and Louis XIV wanted to avoid a war. As spokesman for England and the United Provinces, William III proposed to partition the Spanish inheritance between the several heirs. The First Treaty of Partition (1698) gave the bulk of the empire to a young Bavarian prince, a grandson of Leopold I, but the ink on the treaty was hardly dry when the young man died (1699). Life in the seventeenth century was of very uncertain duration; Louis XIV and Leopold I both lived to a ripe old age, but they outlived most of their children and grandchildren. A Second Treaty of Partition was immediately drawn up (1700), dividing the Spanish empire between Leopold's second son and Louis' grandson. The only trouble with this treaty was the fact that neither Leopold nor the Spanish king, Charles II, was willing to accept it or recognize its validity, and it was by no means certain that either England or the Netherlands would fight to support it.

In Spain the prospect of partition was appalling to proud grandees and ambitious politicians who regarded the empire as an important source of personal profit. Great pressure was brought to bear upon the dying king to make a will that would prevent partition. They had no particular love for France or for Louis' grandson, Philip of Anjou, but the Spanish politicos rightly reasoned that only France could hope to master the military power necessary to prevent partition. The Danubian monarchy was too far away from Spain and the Netherlands, and it had no navy. Therefore, a French prince must be invited to become king. The will also provided that in case Philip should refuse to accept the *entire* Spanish inheritance, it should then be offered to Archduke Charles of Austria. The will had hardly been made when Charles II died, leaving Europe to untangle his affairs.

Louis XIV found himself in a dilemma. The will gave the entire Spanish inheritance to his grandson, Philip. The treaty with England and the Netherlands provided for a division of that inheritance between Philip and Archduke Charles. However, Leopold insisted that Archduke Charles must inherit the *entire* Spanish empire, and had refused to sign the partition treaty. Would England and the United Netherlands fight the Danubian monarchy to force Leopold to accept partition? Probably not. Would they fight to prevent Philip from accepting the throne as provided by the will? French agents surmised that they probably would not, for the sea powers were tired of war and would recognize a Bourbon king in Spain if they were properly assured that the Spanish and French crowns would not be joined together. Thus Louis XIV had to decide to fight the Danubian monarchy either to make Philip king of all the Spanish empire or to secure for him the share granted by the partition treaty. In either case he had to fight! In November 1700, Louis XIV introduced his grandson as Philip V, king of Spain.

Leopold I prepared for war. He could not accept the exclusion of his son from the throne. England and the United Netherlands, however, were disposed to accept Philip as king of Spain. Had Louis XIV not pushed his luck too far, the peace parties in the Netherlands and in England would probably have allowed the will of Charles II to be executed much as it was written. They actually recognized Philip as Spain's lawful king in 1701.

However, it was too much to expect wisdom from the aging French king. He had seen his hopes for the installation of a Bourbon prince as emperor of Germany vanish into thin air when his cousin Leopold reconquered Hungary and secured the election of his son to both the Hungarian and the German crowns. The crown of Poland, which Louis had hoped to secure for the cadet line of Bourbons, had gone, under Hapsburg pressure, to the elector of Saxony. Louis wanted to be sure that by obtaining the Spanish crown he would fulfil some of his ambitions in the west. It was only through his grandson's becoming king of Spain that France could now expand to achieve some of Louis' ambitions. At his insistence, French merchants received preferential positions in all Spanish markets at the expense of their English and Dutch

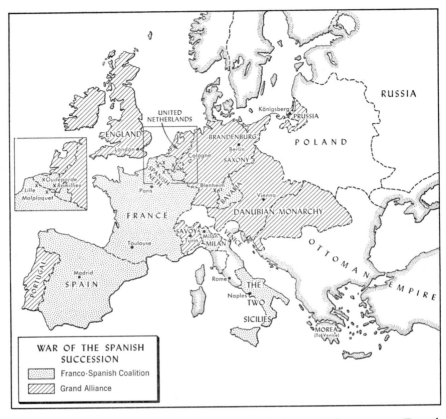

counterparts, and then, with the connivance of the Spanish governor, French troops invaded the Spanish Netherlands, and expelled the Dutch soldiers from the so-called "barrier fortifications." The response in England and the United Netherlands was the emergence of a war party. William began to negotiate with the Emperor Leopold for the recreation of the Grand Alliance. At the moment that an agreement was about to be reached by the Anglo-Imperial negotiators, James II died in France, and Louis XIV recognized his son, James Edward, as the rightful king of England.

A new Grand Alliance against France came into being in 1701. As in the previous war, England, the United Netherlands, and the Danubian monarchy made up the heart of the coalition. Prince Frederick of Brandenburg-Prussia joined in return for recognition of his new title, "King in Prussia." Most of the German princes followed the Emperor Leopold, with the striking exception of Maximilian of Bavaria and his brother, the electoral archbishop of Cologne, both of whom joined France. (After all, Philip, the new king of Spain, was their nephew.) On Louis' side, the most significant fact was that Spain and the Spanish dependencies were his allies in the war. Actually, he was in full possession of all the disputed territory; his sole problem was to retain it. France seemed to be in a most fortunate position; the Franco-

Spanish-Bavarian armies dominated Italy, the Lowlands, and all western Europe, and extended into Germany dangerously near the Austrian frontier. At sea, even though their enemies had the preponderant power, the Franco-Spanish navy was not to be ignored.

Hardly had the war begun when the Grand Alliance was threatened with destruction by the death of William III (1702). Fortunately for the allies, however, the king-stadtholder had entrusted the negotiation of the alliance to John Churchill, Duke of Marlborough, and John Churchill and his wife, Sarah, were the favorites of Anne, William's successor on the English throne. Anne was a stupid woman, but Marlborough turned out to be a political, and, even more, a military genius. He quickly rose to command over the Anglo-Dutch forces, and soon made contact with the other great soldier of the coalition, Prince Eugene of Savoy, who commanded the armies of the Danubian monarchy and became president of his master's war council. Those two men were not only the most important statesmen of the coalition, but also the soldiers who taught the world a lesson in military strategy.

With the notable exception of Prince Eugene's invasion of Italy, this War of the Spanish Succession began in the same way as the last war had ended, namely, as a war of sieges. Prince Eugene, however, had already given an indication of things to come when he had assumed command of the Emperor's forces in Hungary in 1697. Instead of waiting for maneuvers and sieges to wear down the sultan's army, he had attacked the Turks in the field at Zenta (1698), destroyed over half their army, and captured most of the sultan's war chest and supplies. The same resolution and daring characterized his conduct of the war in Italy (1701-1702). In a rapid campaign that surprised all Europe, he cleared much of the northeastern part of Italy of the French. This was a style of warfare that cautious bureaucrats regarded with horror; they much preferred the "safer" tactics of siege and maneuver.

In the west, the timid Dutch commissioners were perfectly willing to play Louis' game and fight another war of attrition, but Marlborough also had other ideas. In 1704 he moved his English army up the Rhine in a bold maneuver that tied down every French army in the west, then turned eastward into Germany, where he joined Eugene. They fought two battles, Donauwörth and Blenheim (1704) with decisive results; the French were driven out of Bavaria, out of Germany, and beyond the Rhine. It would have taken years of siege warfare to accomplish such results. However, their tactics had cost blood—so much blood that the bureaucrats in England, the Netherlands, and Austria combined against the daring commanders and chained both of them by regulations. In 1706, however, the soldiers again threw off the restraints. At Ramillies Marlborough fought a battle in the open field, one of the greatest cavalry actions of all time; and in Italy Eugene, with about half the number of men that opposed him, broke up the French siege of Turin and destroyed the morale of another French army. As a consequence of those two victories, Savoy and the Spanish Netherlands fell into the hands of the coalition.

In 1707 peace was discussed unsuccessfully, and again the dangerous captains were "chained," permitting the French to reoccupy much of the Netherlands. However, in 1708 at Oudenarde Marlborough and Eugene again teamed up against the French and destroyed another of Louis' armies. All of the Spanish Netherlands was occupied, and the French were pushed back to their frontiers. Marlborough wanted to march on Paris to dictate peace, but the bureaucrats insisted on reducing the frontier fortifications first. In 1709 the last of the great field battles was fought. The French forces were then also commanded by an able soldier who believed in field battles and who understood the lessons that Eugene and Marlborough had been teaching. In the extremity of defeat Louis XIV had proclaimed the "fatherland in danger," and entrusted command of a new army to Marshal Villars, a hardbitten soldier whose talents were better exercised in the field than at Versailles. At Malplaquet (1709) the French had to withdraw, leaving the field in the hands of the coalition, but the Anglo-Dutch-German losses were so great that winning many such victories would actually mean to lose the war.

From the time of the battle of Oudenarde (1708) and the capitulation of Lille (1709) onward, Louis XIV had been ready to make peace. The military disasters had coincided with the worst French crop failures in the memory of man; drought and plant disease joined warfare and excessive taxation to make France look like a country occupied by a foreign army bent on its destruction. Many Frenchmen, including the king, became convinced that God had turned his back on France, that He was punishing her. Thus, even the moderate French success at Malplaquet did not hearten the nation.

But while France was losing the war in the Netherlands and Italy, Philip V, Louis' grandson, was winning the war in Spain. It was a strange conflict. French, Spanish, English, Portuguese, Dutch, and German troops maneuvered and marched back and forth. As a war, it was brutal and disastrous; as a tale of confusion, it could be used as the plot for a tragic opera. The allied armies were Protestant and puritanical. They failed to win the Spaniards to their side, while Philip, and especially his wife (whose brother was one of the captains of the coalition's armies in Italy) endeared themselves to the Spanish people. By 1710, then, the war situation was approximately that the coalition had defeated France in the Netherlands and in Germany, but the French-born king had defeated the coalition in Spain. To defeat the French there as well as in the Lowlands would require greater military effort than the English were willing to undertake, and since England was the paymaster for the Grand Alliance, it was in England that the decision had to be made.

Continental historians have often described the making of peace (1711–

1713) as an example of English perfidy. What actually happened was that the Tory peace party, isolationist in spirit and hostile to both the Dutch and the Empire, succeeded in driving Marlborough and his Whig friends out of office. Rural England was tired of heavy taxation, continual bloodshed, and restricted wartime commerce; and the plotters introduced the religious issue at the critical moment much as modern politicians use the Communist one. Once in power, the Tories proceeded to make peace with France behind the backs of their allies! It was hardly a "peace at any price" movement, for they richly filled England's chests with spoils, but it was a peace at the "expense" of England's allies.

The big question of the war had been that of the succession to the throne of Spain. The Tories accepted the fact that Philip V had not only won the affections of the Spanish people but had also successfully checked the military intervention of the coalition. The death from smallpox of the Emperor Joseph I of Austria (1711) added one further reason for letting Philip remain in Spain, for Archduke Charles, the Hapsburg pretender to the Spanish throne, now became emperor and ruler over the Danubian states. Were he also made king of Spain, the Empire of Charles V would again have been restored. Naturally the English Tories would not fight for such a cause, especially when Philip V and Louis XIV were both willing to guarantee that the crowns of France and Spain would remain separated. That was the basic compromise; Philip gave up his rights to the throne of France for recognition of his right to rule Spain and her overseas empire in the Americas and the Philippines. The English merchants were well suited by this for they believed that they could easily deal with the Spanish government in America. The treaty with Spain provided for special trading privileges—the famous *Asiento* that placed the slave trade with Spain's colonies in the hands of an English merchant company. This concession did not work out as well as the English had hoped, but that was to be a problem for the future. The Spanish dependencies in Italy and the Lowlands were given to the Austrian Hapsburgs. The Dutch retained the right to garrison the so-called "barrier-fortification" in the new "Austrian" Netherlands, a right that had much greater economic advantages than military for the United Provinces in that they were able to recoup some of their losses from war at the expense of their Catholic cousins. The English gains were largely colonial. In America they secured Acadia (Nova Scotia), Newfoundland, and St. Kitt's Island as well as recognition of their rights in Hudson Bay. Spain ceded Gibraltar and Minorca to England, thereby enabling the English navy to dominate both the western Mediterranean and the Atlantic approaches to Europe. The commercial clauses of the treaties were too complex for simple description, but, as the Tory politicians explained, they secured an economic "feast" for England's merchants which would make them forget the Whig politicians.

The Tories were to be disappointed, for the merchants kept the advantages and the Whigs came back to power in 1714 when Anne died and George I, of the House of Hanover, became king of England.

The provisions above, as well as the many minor ones such as the recognition of the title "King in Prussia" for the Hohenzollerns, the rectifications of frontiers in Germany, Italy, and the Lowlands, and the like, were embodied in a series of treaties signed in 1713–1714. Since the Anglo-French and Franco-Dutch treaties were signed at Utrecht, the whole settlement is usually referred to as the Peace of Utrecht, even though the Franco-Imperial and the Anglo-Spanish treaties were negotiated elsewhere. The treaties closed one epoch and opened another. They put an end to the hegemony of France and the possibility, for the time being at least, that one nation could dominate Europe; they opened the epoch in which a continental balance of power provided the constitution for Europe, an epoch that was to last until the second great war of the twentieth century.

8. AUSTRIA AND ENGLAND: EPILOGUE

The War of the Spanish Succession presented the Hungarian malcontents with a further opportunity to rebel against their Hapsburg king. The aftermath of the "liberation" of Hungary had seen the rise of bureaucratic government, a considerable shift of land from the hands of old Hungarian families to those of Leopold's soldiers and statesmen, and an aggressive campaign for the reconversion of Hungary by German Jesuits. None of those events was welcomed by the Hungarian magnates, and when revolt became possible they took up arms. This time the fate of Hungary was decided in the West. The battles of Blenheim, Ramillies, and Oudenarde decided the Hungarian rebellion, and the new emperor, Joseph I, less harsh than his father, made it easy for most of the rebels to accept the political realities of their world. Hungary's relatively independent role in the Danubian monarchy was not to be recognized until the period of the War of the Austrian Succession (1740–1748).

The wars (1683–1714) not only brought Hungary into a more intimate relationship with the rest of the Hapsburg Danubian state but also proved to be the force that cemented those lands more closely together. As early as 1702–1703 there was talk of a *Generallandtag* (Estates-General) for all the German, Bohemian, and Hungarian lands under the Austrian House of Hapsburg. That never came to anything, but several times after 1702 royal pronouncements proclaimed the inseparability of those provinces. By the time Joseph I died in 1711, the way was prepared for the Pragmatic Sanction. This famous document was, in essence, a proclamation of the fact that the Hapsburg Danubian principalities had become in law and in administration an organic state. The statesmen and politicians in Vienna at the opening of the eighteenth century could hardly be expected to understand how the doctrine of nationalism would react on their work two centuries later.

In England, too, the revolution of 1688 continued to influence the course of events. Both in England and Scotland William and Mary, and then Anne, were accepted as rulers. But the Scottish revolution of 1688 had, for the first time, freed the Scottish parliament of royal control, and it was not ready to accept the English Act of Succession (1701) that nominated the members of the House of Hanover as the heirs to Anne's inheritance. If Scotland chose another king, there would again be two independent kingdoms on the island. To avoid splitting the dual monarchy of England and Scotland that had come into being with the accession of James I, the English Parliament brought pressure on Scotland to agree to an Act of Union. After much negotiation, name calling, and breast beating, the Act of Union was accepted by both kingdoms in 1707, and henceforth Scotland and England were united under the name of Great Britain.

The crisis that drove Marlborough and his friends from office threatened to have drastic internal results on England's history. When Queen Anne died (1714), the isolationist Tories became tarred with the brush of Jacobitism; that is to say, they were suspected of wishing to place James' son, rather than George of Hanover, a Protestant heir, on the throne. Fears of civil war were dispelled when the Whigs and certain of the Tory supporters moved in at the critical moment and assured the throne for George I. However, the fact that some Tories had shown Jacobite leanings kept them from office for the next half century; the first Hanoverian kings put their faith in Whig politicians.

The wars gave England considerably more than a new dynasty. By the time George I mounted the throne, the necessities of war had forced England to build a preponderant naval establishment, and victory had assured a flourishing and widespread colonial empire. A new constitution guaranteed a government capable of mobilizing the wealth and power of the nation in the interests—real or supposed—of the state. The sixteenth century had seen the hegemony of Spain; the seventeenth, that of France; and at the opening of the eighteenth century Europe was prepared for an era in which England was in a position to influence the direction of affairs on the continent by manipulating the balance of power.

Jean Marc Nattier, "Peter the Great." This portrait is somewhat romanticized. Peter was a tough barbarian, a man of lusty appetites and crude behavior. (The Bettmann Archive)

Chapter 15

EASTERN EUROPE: RUSSIA AND
THE WAR OF THE NORTH

1. PRE-PETRINE RUSSIA

In this history, Russia has heretofore played only a small role, for it was not until the seventeenth century that she became a part of western European society. Some Europeans were vaguely aware that Russia existed before 1600, and some Russians knew that there were people to the west who lived and worshiped differently from themselves, but the contacts between Russia and the West were few and their importance small. She was isolated from western Europe by geography, history, and culture; and it was difficult to bridge the gap that existed between them.

The geography of Russia was a fundamental factor in her isolation. We are accustomed to think of Europe as separate from Asia, but in the so-called frontier land between Europe and Asia the line is not so clearly marked. The Ural Mountains and the steppes of the Caspian Sea basin are both low hills and, in reality, they present no greater barrier than do the plains that stretch out on either side. The striking difference between Europe and Asia may well be that the important Siberian rivers flow north into the Arctic Sea, while those of Russia flow south into the Black and Caspian Seas. Neither in European Russia nor Asiatic Siberia do the rivers act to unify the plains: they are transportation highways that direct the attention of men toward the frontier. The location and the direction of the flow of the river systems play a vital role in the shaping of the character of Russia. The great Volga river that rises on the plains of Moscow empties into the Caspian Sea, and has acted from early times as a link between the Russians and the Turkoman and Cossack peoples to the southeast. The Don also rises on that Moscow plain, but it empties into the Sea of Azov and the Black Sea to link the Russians with the Cossacks of the north coasts of those seas. One branch of the Dnieper rises near

Moscow too, the other in the Pripet marshes that separate Poland and Russia; it flows by the ancient Slavic city of Kiev and through the Ukraine into the Black Sea. While these three rivers have their headwaters within a very few miles of each other, their mouths are almost a thousand miles apart. Thus, they have tended to divert the interests and attention of the Russian people to widely separated frontiers. Furthermore, the Volga flows to a landlocked sea, and the other two flow into the Black Sea, which has only one narrow outlet to the waters of the world, and that controlled by non-Russian peoples. This means that none of these rivers provides an open route to the highways of the world; and this fact has been an important factor in Russian history from the days of Peter I to the present. The Russians have long resented the fact that others controlled the waterways that they had to use to reach the seas of the world.

Almost all European Russia and Siberia lies north of the forty-fifth parallel (St. Paul, Minnesota; Halifax, Nova Scotia; and Portland, Oregon), and most of it is above the fiftieth parallel (Labrador, Edmonton, and Prince Rupert, Canada). It is a land of short summers and long winters, and since there is no barrier for air currents, the summers, controlled by the winds from the south, are hot, while the winters, formed in the Siberian "ice box," are cold. Confronted with great temperature extremes, a short growing season, and considerable variations in the annual rainfall, the people of this Russian plain have had problems of adjustment more difficult than those encountered by the men who lived to the west under the milder influence of the ocean climate. Europe may truly be said to be in the "temperate zone," but there is little "temperate" about a climate that varies from 110° above to 50° below zero.

In the seventeenth century the great plain of Russia was relatively sparsely populated. Siberia, to the east, was almost uninhabited except for a few nomadic peoples. The Russians lived in the lands between Kiev and Moscow. Their frontiers were not clearly marked, but to the southeast on the Caspian Sea was the decaying Tartar government of the Golden Horde. To the south the Turks occupied the coast of the Black and Azov Seas. To the west were the Poles and the Swedes.

Since the dukes of Moscow had freed themselves from Tartar control, they had a tendency to regard the Tartars as their enemies, but in the course of the seventeenth century they came to see that the Turks were politically and military more dangerous than the Tartars. Of the western peoples, the Poles were the most dangerous, for the Polish politicians assumed that their kingdom should extend from the Baltic to the Black Sea including Kiev and the Ukraine. They also interfered in Russian affairs to try to get control of the Russian crown. When it proved impossible for them to control the government at Moscow, the Poles, with the Swedes, closed the frontier, shutting Russia off from the West.

In the north the Russians encountered the Baltic peoples (Finns, Letts, Esthonians, and Germans), who were more or less armed in the German style. In the seventeenth century all of those peoples came under the Swedish Baltic empire. After driving the Russians from the Baltic, the Swedes helped create the seventeenth-century "iron curtain" that kept the Russian "barbarians" from obtaining western military tactics and material. Both Swedes and Poles hated and despised the Russian peoples that they encountered. Thus, the extreme north was left as the only direct outlet between the Russians and Europe. It was a long overland trip to the Dvina river and thence down to the White Sea, but worst of all, a traveler arriving at Archangel was still at the outer edge of the world. The White Sea was icebound about half the year, and from the White Sea to Europe was a long, arduous trip. It actually was as easy to go from Moscow to Peking when the Tartar posting stations were open, as it was to travel from Moscow to Rome; but neither trip was one to undertake for pleasure.

The inhabitants of Russia were a part of the Slavic peoples who settled in eastern Europe. Their pagan culture seems to have had at least one important difference from that of the Germanic and Latin peoples of the West. These primitive Slavs did not worship anthropomorphic gods like Wotan, Thor, Jupiter, Venus, and Mars, who were supposed to have human form. Their pagan deities were more general: the bowl of the sky, the wind, an all-encompassing mother deity without form or substance. It has been suggested that Russian mysticism is ultimately rooted in pre-Christian conceptions of God and the universe.

When the Russians were Christianized the missionaries came from the Orthodox church of the Byzantine Empire. This Greek Christianity permitted the church services to be read in Russian. Thus from early translations, which seventeenth-century scholars discovered to be faulty, the Russians acquired the holy books and rituals of Christianity in their own language. The effect was to give their church a national character that gradually encouraged a cultural isolationism. In their eyes, Moscow became the third center of the Christian church after Rome and Constantinople; and after the Turks had conquered Constantinople, they believed that Moscow was the only truly Christian capital under Christian rule. In the opinion of the Russians the Latins were schismatics, perhaps even dangerous heretics. Thus, Russia's form of Christianity tended to create a gulf between Russian culture and that of the Latin West. In the seventeenth century, after meeting a westerner a pious Russian washed himself carefully to cleanse himself of contamination. Russians feared to travel among heretics in the West, for fear that death might overtake them far from their own priests, and so might easily claim their souls for hell. Their religion became an "ideology" separating the Russian community from their "less fortunate" neighbors who were probably to be damned for all eternity.

The Russian Orthodox church of the seventeenth century was shot through with superstitions; its ritual was bedecked with misunderstood practices that often overshadowed any spirituality that it might possess. The ignorance of the clergy made trifles into questions of great moment, and in the mid-seventeenth century was the cause of a schism within the church. In the early seventeenth century, when certain Greek monks came to Russia and learned the Russian language, they discovered curious mistranslations in the holy books. The introduction of purified translations, however, split the church and created a sectarian movement. Those who refused to accept any change in the traditional holy books became the "old believers," and by the end of the century the movement had developed several sects with extravagant beliefs and practices. Since the government was at first unable to repress the schism and later uninterested in doing so, it continued into the succeeding centuries.

Considering its cultural and geographical isolation, it is not surprising that the political history of Russia also differed somewhat from that of western Europe. The Russians never knew the classical Roman Empire even as a frontier outpost. Their contact with Mediterranean culture came entirely from the Byzantine Empire at Constantinople, and even this influence was slight, since the Russian plains are far from the Black Sea.

The Norse and Hungarian invasions of Europe in the ninth and tenth centuries had their counterpart in Russian history. The Norsemen in particular played an important role in Russia. They were called Varangians, and they not only made themselves masters of the overland commerce from the Baltic to the Black and Caspian Seas but also of the land itself. As traders and conquerors they came to rule Russia, establishing themselves as land owners and governors of the Slavic peoples whom they had conquered. Under the Varangians the ties with Constantinople became closer. It was in that period that the Christian missionaries from the Greek Orthodox church completed the conversion of the people. Under the Varangian chieftains, Russia began to evolve a sort of feudalism not dissimilar in spirit to that of western Europe, and Russian towns like Kiev, Moscow, Novgorod, and others became centers of commerce that had many contacts with the western world. That western orientation, however, was abruptly broken at the turn of the thirteenth century when the Tartar conquest swept over Russia and made it politically part of Asia. For the next two and a half centuries Russia faced eastward, while her contacts with the West, though unbroken, languished.

As we have already noted, the empire of Genghis Khan broke up within a century of his death, but Russia was not thereby freed from the Tartars. The end of the "Great Empire" was probably a political and economic misfortune for Russia, since it cut the western part of the Khan's conquests off from the rich civilization of China and left Russia under the Tartar government in south Central Asia known as the Golden Horde. The Tartar government was neither close nor strict; Russian noblemen governed the country in the name of the rulers, and paid tribute for the privilege. It did, however, teach the Russians the lessons of Tartar culture and politics. The eighteenth century recognized this background with the quip: "Scratch a Russian, and you will find a Tartar." That may not have been literally true, but Russian political forms, for all their western veneer, have consistently reflected oriental influences.

By the fifteenth and sixteenth centuries, however, Russian political development again paralleled, in a fashion, that of the West. Ivan III (1462–1505), who freed the Grand Duchy of Moscow from its Tartar overlords, had the same impulses to unify his lands and to consolidate his power as did Louis XI in France and Henry VII in England. He was surnamed "the money-bags," because he accumulated wealth to buy soldiers to fight the Tartars as well as to force his own vassals to obey his will. He was clearly the prototype of the Russian "reformers" who have followed him even into the twentieth century.

Ivan IV (1533–1584) even more exactly exemplifies the same state-building tendencies of his western contemporaries. In many ways this prince, surnamed "the Dread" or "the Terrible," deserves to be called the father of the modern Russian state. He rigorously suppressed the power of the *boyars* (the great landed aristocrats), and created an aristocracy to serve the state. His ruthless methods were slightly more brutal than those employed by his contemporaries, Elizabeth of England, Philip II of Spain, and Henry IV of France, but they were in the same spirit of state building. Perhaps even more than Ivan III, Ivan the Dread foreshadowed Peter I (the Great), Catherine II (the Great), Alexander II (the Liberator), Lenin, and Stalin.

Ivan the Dread's work was interrupted at the beginning of the seventeenth century by the failure of the dynasty to provide an heir to the throne. There followed a period of civil and foreign wars. In that so-called "time of troubles," the nobility attempted to regain some of the status it had lost. Russia was also open to intervention by foreigners, particularly the Poles, who were invited by the opposing factions to intervene in Russian affairs. It would be a mistake to overemphasize the parallel with the West, yet the "time of troubles" was unmistakably the same sort of movement against princely authority that we have noted in most of western Europe at about the same period (the Fronde in France, civil war in England, the Thirty Years' War in Germany). In other words, while there are striking differences between the political structures of eastern and western Europe, there are also striking similarities. Characteristically for Russian society it was the church that healed the civil wars and enabled a new dynasty, the Romanovs (1613–1917), to rule the land.

Almost from the very beginning, the Romanovs showed a tendency to establish closer relationships with the West. Since the Russians had not had the advantages of the movements we call the Renaissance and the scientific revolution or of the technological progress that western Europe had made between the twelfth and seventeenth centuries, Russian technology, both civilian and military, was far behind that of the advanced countries on the Atlantic and North Sea coasts. Few Russians could read and write; fewer still had any notion of mathematics beyond addition and subtraction. There were clever craftsmen, but they did not understand metalworking, shipbuilding, gunmaking, and dozens of other trades as they were practiced in the West. The first Romanovs vaguely realized Russia's backwardness, and began to encourage the migration of Europeans to Russia. It used to be customary to give Peter I entire credit for the early westernization of Russia. He undoubtedly accelerated that movement at a revolutionary pace, but it is not correct to state that he initiated it. By the time Peter I came to rule Russia (1689), the so-called "German quarter" in Moscow was a flourishing section of the city. Foreigners were still not allowed to live where they wished; they were isolated in this "foreigners' ghetto" so that they would not contaminate the Orthodox Christian Russians; but they had already made their quarter the most comfortable and handsome part of the city, mute evidence of their superior technical civilization. Foreigners and their skills were becoming indispensable to the czars' government.

The pre-Petrine Romanovs also began the military reform that was to be the core of Peter's program. Russia's ancient military institutions were quite unsuited to meet the power of its neighbors to the west and south. The so-called *Streltsy* corps was a sort of pretorian guard, or perhaps janissary corps, formed on a hereditary basis and governed by military thinking that was completely obsolete. This corps continued on into the first years of the eighteenth century, but by 1685 under the Regent Sophia two "modern" infantry regiments based on "German" military practice had already come into existence. Those regiments and the two so-called "pleasure regiments" that the boy Peter I recruited for his amusement became the basis of the Russian army that fought the War of the North. Before Peter's time the standing army was not as large as the one possessed by Louis XIV, but it is interesting to note that Russia developed a professional army wearing the king's uniform about the same time that such a force was becoming common elsewhere in Europe.

The pre-Petrine Romanovs also attempted to make political contact with the West. Such contact was difficult as long as both Sweden and Poland screened off their "barbarian" neighbors from western influences, particularly to prevent their obtaining western military techniques. Nonetheless, the resurgence of the Ottoman Empire in the latter seventeenth century broke down that barrier for the West then needed help against the Turks. Czar Alexis (1629–1676) was the first Russian to discover that the Turks rather than the Tartars were his dangerous enemy. He received no response in Europe to his proposal for an alliance, but Kara Mustafa's Turkish army that besieged Vienna impressed upon Europe the need to recruit any help that could be found, and none other than Pope Innocent XI arranged a treaty between Poland and Russia, and Russia's entry into the Holy League (1684). The Regent Sophia understood the importance of this association with the West, but Russian military prowess was not equal to the tasks that the alliance imposed; and the Russians were beaten off with terrible losses by a second-rate Turkish army.

Peter the Great came to power as the result of a coup d'état (1689) that was in part a manifestation of antiforeign feeling among a segment of the *boyars* who resented the fact that Sophia had joined in an alliance with the westerners. They backed Peter as the rightful, duly anointed czar, without realizing that Peter, too, would continue the process of western orientation. His half-sister Sophia had ruled the land as regent. Her government was overthrown, when Peter's *boyar* friends and relatives rallied the army, the church, and the state officials to his side, and Sophia was placed in a convent in semiprotective custody. The revolution is a fabulous story that might make a good tragi-comic novel, yet it decided the fate of millions of men then unborn, for Peter's government was soon to undertake a great revolution in Russia's way of life.

2. PETER'S EARLY YEARS, 1689–1700

Peter I had been anointed as co-czar with his dull-witted half-brother Ivan, in 1682 when still a child; it was almost a decade before a palace revolution gave him real control over the government of Russia. In the interval, even though his sister Sophia did little to provide him with an education, he prepared himself for the role that was to make him famous. He played with boats on a fresh-water lake and learned that the Dutchmen living in the German quarter knew more about sailing than did native Russians. He organized his playmates into "military companies" that eventually became two regiments of soldiers, and he discovered that foreigners knew more about war than his own people did. Peter's education would have pleased an "advanced modern educator"; he learned by doing rather than by "being told," and all his life he continued to "learn by doing." He was in turn a petty officer (sergeant) in his army, an apprentice shipwright, and even an art student. At every point he discovered that westerners knew more than his own people, a revelation at once humiliating and challenging to him.

It must not be assumed, however, that Peter set his mind on reforming his land because he had "studied" western techniques. Peter was an impulsive, almost scatterbrained fellow who loved to eat and drink too much, and who got "great ideas" from the last person who talked to him. He was really a barbarian with only a thin veneer of civilization of any kind. On the other hand, he also was a new kind of ruler for the Russians. Former czars had assumed a religious role and a religious character that kept them aloof and above their people. Peter took his government into the streets and on the highways. His was a rough-and-tumble approach to politics, completely divorced from the ceremonialism of his predecessors.

In the first few years of Peter's personal government, he contented himself with playing with his soldiers. However, holding parades, mock campaigns, and maneuvers soon palled; he wanted to try his hand at war. In 1695 Russia was still technically a member of the Holy League and still at war with the Ottoman Empire; Peter's advisers believed that there would be real commercial and political advantage in controlling a port on the Black Sea. Thus Azov, at the mouth of the Don river, was fixed upon as the target for his war. His sister had practically withdrawn from the Turkish war after disastrous defeats a decade earlier; Peter's advisers felt that the time was again propitious to act. The first Azov campaign (1695) ended in failure. Russia's armies were not prepared to meet even so poorly equipped an enemy as the Turkish force in that city. The defeat was humiliating and sobering, but, characteristically, Peter asked what could be done to prevent its happening again. His foreign advisers pointed out that he needed to employ western military techniques to besiege a fortified river town: artillery and naval power were required, and Peter's forces were not equipped with either in any real sense.

This need for a western army led to the rapid Europeanization of Russia. Peter sent for Swedish, German, and Dutch teachers and for Swedish guns. He also ordered fifty of the sons of his *boyars* to go to Europe to study. Equally important was the activity in Russia. A river fleet was built under Dutch supervision; more soldiers were recruited and trained, and European officers were placed in command. Peter was a sergeant in the army that marched on Azov in 1696. The Turks were unprepared for the attack; they had not even filled in the Russian trenches of the campaign of the preceding year, and they were forced to surrender. The victory, even as the previous defeat, simply emphasized the necessity for creating a military force along western lines if the conquest were to be retained. His advisers persuaded Peter that this could only be accomplished by creating the economic and political machinery to support such a military establishment. They also convinced the young czar that he should visit the West and see for himself how things should be managed.

Peter's visits to Holland, England, and Germany have become almost a saga. He worked in a shipyard, he visited shops and factories, he talked to princes and statesmen, but even more important, he saw a different kind of society than any he had ever known. Following his visit, hundreds of young Russians were sent annually to learn Europe's languages and techniques. Scores of Europeans of all walks of life were tempted to come to Russia by offers of wealth and opportunity. On his return, too, Peter had tried to force his subjects to look and act like Europeans, even though many of their holy traditions might be violated by such behavior. The demands that he made upon his subjects to clip their beards, to smoke tobacco, to wear western clothes, and to include both men and women in the same social gatherings sometimes seem ludicrous to western ears, but their significance for Russian history should not be underestimated. In Peter's day clean-shaven faces, pipes, and western clothing were the outward signs of the foreigner. Neither Peter nor the rulers that followed him were ever able to do more than get their soldiers, courtiers, and officials to adopt western habits. By introducing western manners, and by educating his officials with western tours and foreign teachers, Peter divided the mass of the people from his officials, noblemen, and soldiers who became westerners. It seemed almost as if Russia was being governed by people who were no longer Russian.

Peter's first European tour led to new adventures in the field of foreign policy. On the way home he stopped at Vienna to enlist support for continuing the Turkish war, but the Emperor Leopold was ready to make peace with the Ottoman Empire so that he would be free to insist upon his rights in the Spanish inheritance. Disappointed, Peter proceeded to Warsaw where he met August the Strong, king of Poland and duke of Saxony. Those two were kindred souls: they ate together, drank together, made fireworks, and plotted war against Sweden. When he could not persuade Austria to aid in a Turkish war, Peter was willing to join Poland in a war to strip Sweden's young king of his Baltic provinces. It was not the world's first example of political immorality, but it was one of the most striking. The two plotters, soon to be joined by the Danish king, little understood the character of the young prince whose lands they coveted. They saw only an opportunity to acquire territory at the expense of a young, awkward youth who was as yet unknown.

3. CHARLES XII AND THE WAR OF THE NORTH

The Swedish empire in 1700 controlled most of the shores of the Baltic Sea. It was, however, neither rich nor well integrated. The German provinces were part of the Holy Roman Empire, while the so-called Baltic provinces from Lithuania to Finland were still organized as semi-independent states under the Swedish king. Only Sweden itself had reached the point of being a modern bureaucratic state, and Sweden was a country inhabited by poor people who wrested a living from the soil or from the Baltic Sea. It was an unpromising core for a great empire, but history had cast Sweden for that role.

Gustavus Adolphus (1611–1632), the man who led Sweden into the Thirty Years' War, was the great figure in the creation of Sweden's Baltic empire. As we have seen, he was a man of war who fought all his life against Russians, Poles, and the Imperial party in Germany. He won for Sweden control over the Baltic. Charles XI (1660-1697) was the king who developed a modern government in Sweden. His story is a familiar one in the seventeenth century. When he came to power he found that the great barons had enriched themselves at the expense of both crown and people and had usurped control over the state. Fortunately for him, they had also become disastrously engaged in Louis XIV's war against the Dutch (1672-1679) and had brought ruin to Sweden. King Charles XI instituted court action against the offenders and secured from the *Riksdag* (parliament) a law allowing him to occupy all crown lands illegally alienated in the past. Thus he economically ruined the great nobles, but at the same time he created a bureaucracy staffed by men utterly dependent upon himself. He also built a new army that assured him a corps of soldiers and officers loyal to the crown. When Charles XI died in 1697, he left for his young son Charles XII a reasonably tightly knit state with a full treasury, substantial military power, and strong political alliances with England and the Netherlands.

The young Charles XII (1697-1718) was afraid of the princesses and their matchmaking mothers who visited his court, but he liked to hunt bears armed only with a spear. He was brave to foolhardiness; he was loyal to his father's memory and to the Swedish tradition, but he was naïvely personal in his conception of politics. He never acquired the wisdom of a real statesman, but he was one of the great military captains of his era and he did develop into an astute politician. Such was the prince whose Baltic provinces Peter of Russia, August of Saxony-Poland, and Frederick of Denmark planned to take. When Charles XII learned of their plot, he was determined that each of them should be punished in turn for this treachery. It seems almost incredible, but for the next decade the fundamental aim of Charles' military and political policy was the personal chastisement of these three monarchs.

At first, Charles was overwhelmingly successful. The Dutch and English fleets, honoring their alliance with Sweden, secured control of the waters between Sweden and Denmark and allowed Charles to land an army in Denmark. Within a matter of weeks Frederick had to sue for peace and accept Swedish terms. Then Charles embarked a tiny army for the Baltic campaign. The Russians with forces six to eight times greater than his own were at Narva behind fortified lines. Charles launched his little army at the Russian camp; six thousand Swedes against forty thousand Russians: but the Swedes knew "modern warfare" which the Russians did not, and the latter were annihilated. It was a victory that taught Charles XII to scorn his Russian adversary too quickly—a scorn that cost him dearly.

After Narva Charles turned to Poland to bring August to justice. The Swedes won victories whenever they could force a battle, but they could not seem to force either August or Poland to surrender. The Polish nobles insisted that August's war was not theirs and that Charles was in their lands illegally. When Charles forced the assembly of the Polish Diet, dethroned

EUROPE AND THE
WAR OF THE NORTH
1701-1721

August, and "elected" another king, a large section of the Polish nobility
held aloof. In Poland men could rebel against the king, but the Poles did
not like to have a foreigner tell them who should be their king. This was
only a small matter. For six years (1701–1707) Charles and August fought
in Poland; their armies prowled the countryside with disastrous results to
the Polish people. Neither the Huns nor the Tartars worked as much havoc
as these Christian armies. Charles finally secured peace by invading Saxony
and imposing a treaty upon his adversary. The Treaty of Altrandstädt (1707)
required August to give up the Polish throne and to recognize Sweden's
puppet, Stanislas Lesczynski, as king. Charles, copying his hero ancestor,
Gustavus Adolphus, also forced Saxony and the Emperor Charles to right
certain "wrongs" done to Lutherans in the Holy Roman Empire. However,
he had no intention of taking part in the War of the Spanish Succession, for
of the trio that had tried to rob him, Peter of Russia was still unpunished.

Charles invaded Russia in the winter of 1708–1709. Cold, the immense distances, and a ferocious peasantry who burned their villages, opposed him as effectively as did the Russian army. Like Napoleon, Hindenburg, and Hitler in later centuries, Charles discovered that Russia was difficult to invade. Only the stubborn courage of the Swedish king and fear of the raiding Cossack horsemen who cut off stragglers kept his little army together. Early in the spring of 1709 the Swedes laid siege to Poltava; in the battle that followed the Swedish army was surrounded and overwhelmed by the Russians. Charles escaped with a handful of followers, and reached safety in the Ottoman Empire, but his army was either killed or captured and forced to labor on the projects of the Russian czar. The battle of Poltava was one of the decisive conflicts in shaping the history of Europe; it marked the entry of a new power onto the stage of European politics.

Like the rest of Europe, Charles XII had failed to notice that developments had taken place in Russia after the disaster at Narva. While Charles was involved in Poland, a new Russian army had come into being. Peter's soldiers may not have possessed the morale of the Swedes, but they were better equipped and there were many more of them. With this army Peter occupied part of the Baltic and began building both St. Petersburg and a Russian navy. After Poltava there was a new balance of power in eastern Europe and the Baltic, with Russia replacing Sweden as the dominant power. The war continued for more than a decade but it only resulted in the further impoverishment and weakening of Sweden.

4. THE PETRINE REVOLUTION

Peter's revolution was not a planned assault on ancient Russian society. Unlike the twentieth-century reformers in Russia, Peter had no real ideology, no substantial notion of objectives and goals. The two Azov campaigns showed him how important it was to learn European military techniques. His association with foreigners from the German quarter and his subsequent visit to western Europe made him see the gulf that existed, culturally, between Russia and Europe. He realized that Russia's military backwardness was but a symptom of Russia's social and economic backwardness. However, it was neither the Turkish war nor Peter's European trip that created the urgency for reform: that was the result of his war with Sweden and the swift military retribution that Charles imposed upon him at Narva. Peter ran away from Narva with the conviction that he had to reorganize his lands or face destruction. Just as he had asked what to do to retrieve the disaster at Azov in 1695, he again determined to take the steps necessary to repair the damage. In the following two decades reform followed reform in rapid confusion; for a while confusion was more evident than reform, but eventually at least part of Russia began to assume a new aspect.

Upon his return from Europe in 1700 Peter had an opportunity to smash

certain forces that might conceivably have threatened his program. While
he was away, the old-style army, the *Streltsy,* had revolted. Their rebellion
was suppressed, and on his return Peter took awful vengeance upon its members. An army of torturers examined them, and literally thousands were
hanged or beheaded. Peter himself swung the axe for exercise. The bodies,
stacked in frozen piles, were left about Moscow all winter as grim reminders
of the czar's authority. While seventeenth-century Europe was accustomed
to "judicial murder," the ruthlessness of Peter's vengeance made men's blood
run cold. A short time later the patriarch died, and Peter prevented the appointment of a new head for the church. One of his own men became "temporary guardian of the pontifical throne" and administered the church under
Peter's orders. Thus the old army and the church were brought to heel with
a show of authority that discouraged any questioning of Peter's right to rule.
After removing those two potential threats to a reform program, Peter could
drive ahead with the reformation of his empire.

Following the defeat of Narva Peter's problems were even more direct
and urgent. He needed soldiers, money, war materials, more soldiers, more
money, more war materials. He needed to train men and officers to make an
army; he needed to train men to administer the collection of taxes, the organization of supplies, and the regulation of soldiers; he needed diplomats,
judges, secretaries, and clerks. To get all these, Peter almost had to turn
Russia upside down; he had to import foreigners to improvise institutions.
For a decade he ruled Russia from horseback, traveling from one part to
another issuing cryptic orders, some of which countermanded those given
shortly before, some of which radically upset old traditions. It would be a
mistake to think that this reform effort developed clear-cut, rational institutions, or that at any one moment the government of Russia achieved any real
sense of balance or order. Nonetheless, out of twenty years of warfare (1700–
1720), there emerged a new governmental structure that, superficially at
least, was western in its appearance and rational in form.

The new army might be considered the most important creation of the
revolution, since for Peter's governors, commissars, and tax collectors the
army's requirements were their first concern. The "holy Russian army" was
formed by expanding the original four European regiments from four thousand to one hundred thousand soldiers. A system of forced recruitment made
each district of Russia responsible not only for a quota of troops, but also
for continual replacement. Thus the Russian soldier became immortal. If he
were killed, lost, or if he deserted, another stepped into his place. No single
ukase made this form; it emerged from a welter of conflicting orders that
provided the men for Peter's armies. As difficult as recruiting men was, the
provision for training them and finding officers to command them was even
more so. The Russians had a national proverb: "Flight is not very noble, but
it is very safe." Such an idea was not conducive to bravery. The Russian

illiterate, often drunken, noblemen were at first glance poor material for officers' training. It was a heartbreaking task to make an army of such people; still, between Narva and Poltava great progress was made. Foreigners, of course, continued to play a great role, but Russians did begin to take over their tasks.

The navy had the same story. Without seagoing traditions and without a shipbuilding industry, it was hard to create a navy. Yet by 1710 a Russian Baltic fleet was in being, and by 1720 it dominated the Baltic Sea. Dutchmen and Germans helped, to be sure, but Peter's determination to have a fleet was the most important factor. Shipbuilding yards and naval bases were built on the Gulf of Finland so that the new navy could be fitted, repaired, and reinforced. Before the war with Sweden ended, the Russian navy had landed marines on Sweden's coasts and burned Swedish towns and villages. It had become *the* fleet in the Baltic.

The treasury during these years presented the most complete picture of confusion. Money is necessary for warfare, and Peter ordered his officials to gather it in from all sources. Old taxes were extended and new taxes imposed; nothing escaped the collector. There were excise taxes on weddings, christenings, coffins, and graves; on soap, candles, liquors, and wines; on wheels, beards, springs, ponds, and taverns. One writer calls Peter's policies "fiscal brigandage," for he taxed everything. However, out of these taxes emerged new fiscal institutions and better methods of control. The old treasury had been wholly inadequate. Peter actually tried several alternative schemes *contemporaneously,* but eventually developed a system that allowed some decentralization of collection and disbursement, and still provided for a unified budget. However, even on Peter's death treasury operations were still somewhat chaotic.

While reorganizing the finances and methods for closer control over his lands, Peter gradually evolved a system of provincial governments. Russia proved to be too large a land to be governed from a single capital. As long as there was little for it to control, Moscow had been a satisfactory seat for government, but Peter's wars and taxes made much closer supervision necessary, and some means had to be devised to make Peter's authority real in the distant provinces. Thus, by the end of his reign there were eight provincial capitals or "governments" dependent upon the czar's authority, but at the same time flexible enough to take local differences into consideration. A congress of the governors met annually in St. Petersburg to give unity to their program. These "governments" had not been created as the result of a rational plan; they emerged from the confusion as a practical method of governing the provinces. Each "government" had its own history; each had come into being to meet a crisis or a problem, and the annual congress of governors developed almost as an afterthought. This story is typical of Peter's reform epoch.

The reorganization of the central authority was accomplished with the same disorderly procedure that marked all of Peter's efforts. One bureau (*prikazy*) after another was created, often with overlapping authority, to meet specific problems. After Poltava, when the pressure relaxed somewhat, Peter imported scores of Slavic-speaking foreigners from Bohemia who had had some experience with the organization of German bureaucratic governments. With these men as an administrative core, the whole central authority was reorganized (1712–1718) into "colleges" for foreign affairs, for military affairs, and so forth; and the Administrative Senate, a sort of *duma*, appeared as the central organ to interpret the czar's will and to bring order into the chaos of his government. By the time of Peter's death, little remained of the old regime that Ivan the Dread and his successors had used; the new machinery often did not work as it was supposed to, but it did give Russia a government that looked something like those of the West, and managed to give a sort of unifying direction to the political life of the land.

An agency of investigation and inspection emerged to supervise the whole machinery of government. The *Oberfiscal* was the secret police, and characteristically enough, one of the first chiefs of the Russian secret police, after sending important noblemen and officials to Siberia or the gallows, was himself convicted of malfeasance in office. The Soviet Union's GPU in the twentieth century was destined to repeat that performance.

Perhaps the most important symbol of the Petrine revolution was the building of the new capital, St. Petersburg. Peter wanted a "window" on Europe from which commercial, intellectual, and political communication would be easier. He also wanted a capital city not associated with the ancient past or with the religious life of his empire. St. Petersburg was a secular city in contrast to Moscow or Kiev, which were holy cities of the church. From his first city built of wood on a swampy bit of land on the Neva river to the beautiful city of stone that became his capital, St. Petersburg was an expression of the czar's will to break with the past.

In many ways Peter's reign was a turbulent epoch for Russia. His exuberant enthusiasm combined with the grim necessities of war to give great force to his reform activities. Many of his subjects with their religious outlook on all aspects of life were shocked and repelled by his actions. His insistence upon razors and pipes violated religious taboos; his calendar reform "stole eight days from God"; his riotous personal behavior (Peter liked strong drink, boisterous parties, and fast women) convinced many that he was an impostor, perhaps Antichrist, who masqueraded as czar. When Peter changed his title to emperor, they were sure that an impostor hid behind the new title. These beliefs rekindled a wave of religious extravagance in Russia similar to those that had occurred several times earlier in the seventeenth century. Convinced that the judgment day was at hand, many men sold their goods, slept in coffins in the open fields, and awaited the second coming of

Christ. Their calculations were wrong as to "the Day," but the movement had great influence.

Peter's regime, however, was secure from the religious authorities that had often been able to bring pressure upon former czars. In the first place, the schism in the Russian church that had developed a half century before was not healed. Indeed, on the contrary the "old believers" (those who refused to accept new translations of the holy books) had become the source of several sectarian movements. The patriarch had been unable to check these developments, and the government had been unwilling to do so. During the last quarter century of Peter's reign, there was no patriarch, and the government was so interested in securing troops and money that it had little time for doctrinal problems. Furthermore, Peter probably would not have appreciated the differences between the sects; it made little difference to him *how* his soldiers made the sign of the Cross so long as they kept in line and obeyed their officers.

The Petrine religious settlement abolished the patriarchate as an institution of church government and established in its place a board of governors called the Holy Synod. Since the czar appointed the Holy Synod, the church came more securely under his government than it had been when a patriarch ruled the church. Peter's need for money also led him to pillage the monasteries as well as the church's landholdings to secure revenue. Interestingly enough, the eighteenth-century French *philosophes,* led by Voltaire, hailed Peter as "an enlightened despot," largely because he brought the church under secular control and robbed it of its wealth. It may be questionable whether this was more "enlightened" than the rest of Peter's reformation. The same *philosophes* glossed over the fact that Peter ruthlessly killed the *Streltsy* and even that he had his own son executed. Such stories might have robbed their hero of his halo.

When considered as a whole, the Petrine revolution presents an imposing array of reforms in Russian society. Hardly any segment of life remained untouched. Western military and political forms, western technology and commercial institutions, even western ideas about society, invaded that semi-oriental country. We must take care, however, in evaluating the effects of these novelties. There is no doubt that they changed Russia, but it is also certain that they did not Europeanize Russia except in a formal sort of way. Russia revenged herself on Peter's efforts by giving her own twist to the new institutions. Perhaps they were at times grotesquely twisted because Peter had insisted upon such speedy adoption, but in any case the Russification of the European institutions that Peter had imposed upon Russia was a result as important as the innovations themselves. No one can know whether Peter's reform, by hastening the westernization of his kingdom, was responsible for the direction that Europeanization subsequently took in Russia.

5. *RUSSIA: A EUROPEAN POWER*

After the disaster at Narva (1700), most men in Europe assumed that Russia was little more than a military vacuum, waiting, perhaps, for a conqueror to give it order. The fact that Peter later reorganized the army and again invaded the Baltic provinces was not convincing, since Charles XII and the flower of Sweden's army were in Poland and therefore were not able to prevent the Russian intrusion. The battle of Poltava, however, served notice that Russia was no longer a negligible force. The Swedish "lion" had not only failed to drive Peter from the Baltic, but had also suffered a humiliating defeat. Europe had to take the "barbarian czar" seriously after Charles XII had fled to Turkey for refuge and the Swedish soldiers had virtually become slave laborers for their captor.

However, the story of the War of the North did not end when Charles lost his army at Poltava. The Swedish king had a fabulous reputation as a soldier, and as a guest of the sultan he proceeded to exploit it to recover from the disaster that had overcome him. He succeeded in involving the Ottoman Empire in war with Russia. The Turks had little taste for war at that time; their whole internal structure had been badly shaken by the recent war with the Holy League (Austria, Venice, and Russia). Nonetheless, under the prodding of Charles XII the war did get under way, and in 1711 a huge Turkish force surrounded Peter and his Russian army at the Pruth river. The Turks let Peter go free after he had signed the Treaty of Pruth (1711) that returned Azov to them and forced Russia to recognize the Ottoman Empire's possession of the whole north coast of the Black Sea.

The signing of the treaty was a shock to Charles. The Turks had had Peter in a trap, and had allowed him to escape. Charles vowed that he would get his revenge. He failed to realize that he was too late to save much of Sweden's former prestige. Both in Sweden and in Europe time had run out. A decade and a half of warfare had bled Sweden white. The treasury was empty, the number of possible recruits had been reduced, and the kingdom wanted only peace. In western Europe the War of the Spanish Succession was over, and the German powers were ready to concentrate on the Baltic question. Augustus the Strong of Poland-Saxony prepared to re-enter the war. The king of Denmark, the king of Prussia, and several other German princes were also willing to play jackal, since the Swedish lion was so severely wounded. Against such a force, Charles XII could muster only his own genius and the warlike traditions of Sweden, which were not enough. He managed to return to Sweden and to reorganize his army, but he was never again able to regain the initiative in the war. On December 11, 1718, the Swedish king was killed at Friederikshald, and with his death was removed the principal driving force that had kept Sweden at war. His sister, Ulrika

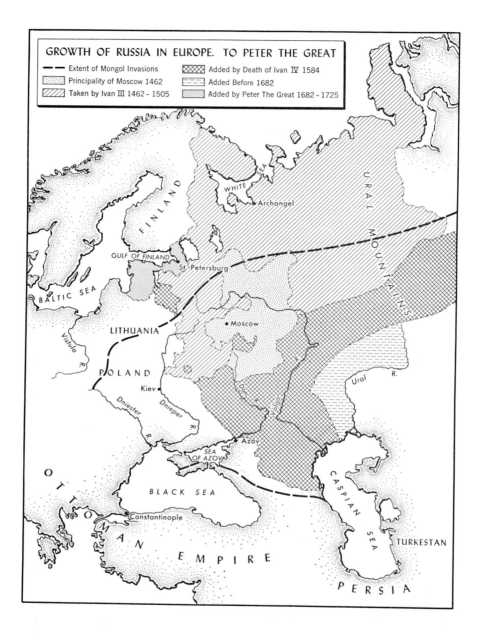

Eleonora, succeeded him, and she sued for peace. The War of the North was brought to a close by a series of treaties drawn up between 1719 and 1721 (treaties at Stockholm, Frederiksburg, and Nystadt). Sweden lost most of her territory on the southern Baltic coast; she lost the provinces of Livonia, Estonia, Karelia, and the fortress of Viborg. Sweden gave up her claims on the Sound, as well as her pretensions in Poland. Of her great Baltic empire, only Finland remained as a reminder of Sweden's greatness in the seventeenth century. The real victor was Russia. The Treaty of Nystadt firmly established Peter's control over the Gulf of Finland and a large section of the Baltic coast. This in turn placed Russia in a position to impose her will upon Poland and to exercise political influence upon north Germany. It was to be another generation before a Russian army would be able to penetrate as far as Berlin and almost a century before Russian arms would reach Paris. Nonetheless, after 1721 Russia was well on the way to becoming a great European power, and Peter had amply proved his right to be known as "the Great."

Philippe de Champaigne, "Louis XIII" (Paris, Louvre). This is an excellent example of Baroque portraiture. Notice that the armor worn by the king is beginning to decrease in size and weight. Louis, wearing the order of the holy spirit, is being crowned by fortune.

Chapter 16

THE BAROQUE ERA

1. THE BAROQUE STYLE

A twentieth-century tourist visiting Europe is shown a few Gothic cathedrals, some Renaissance paintings, and something of the modern developments in architecture, but the things that he mainly sees are the monuments and artistic achievement of the baroque era. From the magnificent cathedral of St. Peter in Rome to the equally impressive château of Versailles, the tourist is made vividly aware of the society of sixteenth- and seventeenth-century Europe that had been dominated by popes, princes, prelates, and noblemen. The North American tourist is particularly interested in these monuments because they were produced by a society that had no counterpart in the English-speaking colonies. When the artistic forms we call baroque were first developed, the North American countryside was a wilderness; when they reached their peak, colonial America was still a rude society with few cultural amenities. The tourist from Latin America knows a counterpart of this baroque era in some of the churches and palaces built by his forebears, but the colonial baroque was often an exaggerated form of the style that emerged in seventeenth-century Europe.

The word "baroque" is hard to define, and the period of the baroque is equally difficult to delineate. We have become used to calling the art forms of the Middle Ages "Gothic," those of the fifteenth and early sixteenth centuries "Renaissance." Similarly, the art forms of the latter sixteenth and seventeenth centuries (1550–1715) are generally called "baroque." Many of the forms that we see as most typically baroque were already in evidence in the earlier "Renaissance" period, and many remained vigorous well into the later so-called "rococo period." In other words, the idea of a baroque period is simply a useful device for discussing the emerging forms of the cultural life of man; we must never lose sight of the fact that this idea is an artificial creation of the historian. The processes of human life are continuous and uninterrupted; it is only after the historian has established norms character-

istic of certain stages in that process that we develop the idea of a period or
an era. If we keep this conception in mind in discussing the baroque era,
it will facilitate the unfolding of the story without creating the false impression of a static tableau called an historical period.

If we exclude the traditional culture of the peasants and poorer townsfolk,
there are good reasons for discussing together the art, architecture, music,
and perhaps the literature of the century and a half from 1550 to 1715.
The culture that we call baroque was essentially an aristocratic development;
the princes of church and state, the wealthy nobles and bourgeoisie, these
were the men who paid for the high culture of Europe, and their interests
are reflected in its monuments. The poor had little or nothing to do with it
except to pay the taxes that provided the money. This split in the cultural
pattern of Europe did not begin to develop until the later Middle Ages; by
the sixteenth century it was well established, and in the seventeenth it had
reached a point where there were two cultures in Europe, one for the rich,
another for the poor. It is worth a passing remark to note that a similar split
was developing between the learned and the ignorant; their notions, too,
about the world and its meaning, man and his destiny, were growing so wide
apart that neither could understand the other.

If we take it for a primary fact that baroque culture was developed for
the elite of the society, we can further assume that the interests of that elite
were expressed by the art forms. In a very real sense this is true. At the
opening of our period, the great question that moved men was the religious
debate; at the end of it the bureaucratic state had emerged as the characteristic political form, and the role of kings had transcended that of priests.
Thus we find that the artistic energy of men was first used to extol the glory
of God and to affirm the belief of men in certain theological propositions;
at the end of the period it had been altered to express the grandeur of kings
and the power of the new state. In 1600 men painted pictures of God and
the saints, built great churches, and wrote music to be sung in them; by 1700
their successors painted pictures of men and landscapes, built châteaux, and
wrote operas or concert music. Of course there were châteaux built in 1600
and churches in 1700, but the emphasis had shifted along with the interests
of the men who had the power to command talent.

This changing orientation corresponds with other developments of the
period that indicated a progressive secularization of society. In the sixteenth
century theological assumptions were still the important ideas of men. The
great questions of the Reformation era concerned salvation, God's grace, and
the role of the church in society; the religious wars and the civil wars that
used religion as an excuse for rebellion are evidence that men were willing
to die for their theological convictions. In the latter seventeenth century, after
the destruction caused by the civil wars in France and the Thirty Years' War
in central Europe, it became increasingly difficult to justify such violence in

the name of God. On the other hand, the general increase of wealth, the concentration of political power, and the new intellectual interests that resulted from the new learning all tended to turn men's attention to worldly things. The earth ceased to be a vale of tears to those who could afford comfort, and worldly interests ceased to be vanities to men who could appreciate them. The secularization of men's thoughts and ambitions was inevitably reflected in the artistic forms of the society. There were still men who were willing to go to prison or even die for their religion and there were still churches to be built, but these facts only show that secularization was not universal in 1700. It is still not universal in the twentieth century.

Whether religious or secular in orientation, the ways of living and the notions of personal prestige shared by the upper classes greatly influenced the directions of artistic style. That was an era when rulers liked to dramatize their actions with pageants and shows; princes of both church and state seized every opportunity to put on a grand display to impress the masses. Perhaps it was their best means of holding the imagination and the obedience of the people. A religious feast day, the inauguration of a high church official, a military victory, the birth of an heir, and any number of other such occasions provided excuses for tableaux, fireworks, bonfires, religious ceremonies—all requiring costumes, stage settings, and suitable props. This love of display extended itself to the construction and decoration of churches and palaces, to the composition of music, to the development of clothing styles and patterns of behavior. The huge bonfire on the Ile de la Cité, when Louis XIV was born (it almost "took" a monastery on the other side of the river), was an expression of the same sense of the dramatic. A similar inspiration stimulated Philip de Champaigne (1602–1674) to paint Richelieu in all his splendor and Richelieu dead and ready for the grave, the nuns of Port Royal praying for the recovery of Champaigne's daughter, and Louis XIII with the Knights of the Holy Spirit dressed up as for a costume ball. The dramatists like Corneille who portrayed the splendor of the *Cid* and the colorful notion of honor and duty to father, the architects who designed the Louvre or St. Paul's in London, were also reflecting this love of dramatic display. When Louis XIV ordered his architects to show him no plans for anything that was not big and dramatic, he was merely following the pattern laid down by laymen and churchmen for over a century.

Tradition has it that the Jesuits of the sixteenth century urged the architects and painters to treat their subjects as dramatically as possible, to give them a monumental character, even to paint pictures of the crucifixion that would make men cry. Undoubtedly the Jesuit fathers who had won such brilliant victories at the Council of Trent, on the borderlands of Protestantism, and in the field of foreign missions, did give such advice, but they were only reinforcing the characteristic pattern of the age. The baroque style by definition is monumental in its conception and stirring in its execution. Perhaps

it is even true that Catholic Europe developed this style to reaffirm its traditional belief in stone and paint as vividly as possible, so that the people would
feel the emotional impact of those beliefs. It is also true that men of that
period were flamboyant in their personal behavior, dramatic in their sense of
personal self-consciousness, and anxious to express their importance. Such
characteristics shine through the literature of the period and are reflected
in its art.

Another important characteristic of the baroque style is the expression of
motion. In painting, sculpture, music, and even in architecture the quiet
patterns of the earlier period are given a dynamic feeling of movement. The
era was one in which men were finding movement all about them: astronomers discovered the movement of heavenly bodies, anatomists the circulation of the blood, physicists the laws of inertia, and historians the notion that
change was movement, perhaps progress. It may be that the bodies of men,
women, and children flowing across one of Rubens' canvases, the marching,
repetitive lines in a baroque cathedral, palace, or garden, the moving vitality
in a Bernini statue, are the same sort of characteristic expressions of this age.
It would be unwise to press this point too far, yet it is interesting to speculate
on the fact that the music of a Handel or a Lully oratorio repeats the motifs
with something of the same marching, monumental cadence that is found
in the great baroque architectural forms as they repeat themselves in a
church, a garden, or a château.

Another universal characteristic of the baroque style is its tendency to create a unity. The Gothic cathedral soars to heaven, storming the heights without much concern for unity of effect; the baroque church or château is not
only self-contained but its architects also tried to impose its pattern on the
whole area around it. In a very real sense the baroque architects created
Greek temples on an imposing scale undreamed of by the Greeks, while their
interest in developing the area around the buildings and the roads approaching them, so that the whole was dominated by the single structure, led them
to unify space as well as architecture. The city of Paris today is an excellent
example of the beauty inherent in this unifying conception. Modern Paris,
of course, was not built in the baroque era, but it is conceived in that style.
The same tendency toward a unified conception can be found in the baroque
painters' work. A Renaissance canvas can often be cut up into three or more
separate pictures; their unity is only in the physical juxtaposition. Not so can
a baroque picture be divided. It matters not whether the school was Italian,
Spanish, Flemish, or French, the baroque painters created their designs so
that the entire canvas was focused on the center of interest and would be
more or less meaningless except in terms of that central point.

It is also possible to find in the baroque style a surging sense of power
over the world of man and of nature. The men who fought the battles of the
Counter-Reformation, who watched the conflicts over the control of political

authority, who followed the scientists and philosophers in their efforts to fathom the mechanics of the universe, somehow captured the idea that man's destiny is tied up with his will to power. Perhaps the notion that man was on the verge of imposing his will upon the world is best expressed by the monumental architecture, the turbulent drama, and the exciting canvases of the baroque artists. Obviously this concept must not be pressed too hard or it will fall apart for lack of adequate proof, and yet it should not be over-looked as a partial explanation for the dramatic force of the baroque style.

Like every art style, the baroque has had its interpreters who found many different spiritual, ethical, and aesthetic meanings in its development. Some of these interpretations make sense in terms of particular artistic creations, others in terms of particular philosophical assumptions. They are all inter-esting, stimulating, and even at times amusing to the initiated, but they have no place in a relatively abbreviated account of the baroque.

2. *ARCHITECTURE*

The prototypes of baroque architecture were the two great churches built in Rome in the latter sixteenth century: the papal church, St. Peter's Cathe-dral, and the mother church of the Jesuit order, the Gesù. The former was started under Pope Julius II to provide a site for his own grave; it achieved its final form only after several architects had labored over the plans, and, though many popes are buried there, Julius' memorial is in another church. The Gesù was built by one man and his student as an imposing monument to the glory of God and the Society of Jesus. In the following century the Gesù inspired churches all over Europe, as far west as Mexico, and as far east as Macao in southeast Asia. The dome of St. Peter's inspired churches and capitol buildings in London (St. Paul's), in Paris (Les Invalides), and in many other cities including Washington, D.C., Denver, and St. Paul, as well as Berlin and Brussels. Wherever an imposing monumental structure is needed, these two churches offer models that must be considered.

Like all other art forms, the new style developed from several roots. The city of Rome abounded in architectural remains: there were the ruins of the great public baths, one of which Michelangelo turned into a huge church and a monastery, still with enough space left to house a fine museum. There were also the ruins of pagan temples and of early churches, like the so-called Basilica of Constantine, that provided models of the architecture of the Ro-man Empire under the Caesars. The dimensions of the Hagia Sophia in Constantinople were well known, and the dome of the imposing cathedral of Florence, built in the fifteenth century by Brunelleschi, provided another example for consideration. In addition to these object lessons, there were Ro-man as well as contemporary architectural theorists who discussed the prob-lems. Of these Andrea Palladio (1518–1580) was so important that later

The entire complex of St. Peter's Cathedral in Rome can be seen clearly only from the air. At ground level the colonnade dwarfs the façade, and, in turn, the façade cuts off the dome.

generations have used the word "Palladian" as a descriptive term for classic adaptations of the baroque style. Palladio was deeply influenced by the writings of the Roman theorist Vitruvius and the fifteenth-century Italian writer Alberti. He produced several works on architecture, but his *Four Books on Architecture (Quattro Libri dell' Architectura*, 1570) were translated into all western languages and became the very foundation of academic architecture for the following three hundred years.

The architects of St. Peter's deserve a special place as agents for developing the new style. Pope Julius II decided to remove rather than repair the old Constantinian Basilica of St. Peter that had been built on one of the holiest spots in Rome. This gave the first architect, Bramante, an opportunity not usually afforded architects up to that time, for most churches were remodeled rather than built from the ground up. Bramante (1444–1514) began the building in 1506. His plan called for a monumental structure in the form of a Greek cross. After his death his associates continued his plans for a few years, but by 1520 everyone who had had anything to do with the original plan was dead. Between 1520 and 1546, when Michelangelo (1475–1564) took over the direction of the building, there were several modifications of the original plans, but no architect who would push through the construction. Bramante had begun the great pillars that were to carry the dome; Michelangelo returned to the original plan of a Greek cross, and designed the great dome to cover it. When his stone work spanned the great space, the baroque style was born.

Michelangelo's immediate successors continued to follow his plan, but in the opening years of the seventeenth century it was decided that the church was not large enough for the services that were held in it, and Carlo Maderna (1556–1629) added three bays and the vestibule to Michelangelo's church, transforming it from a Greek to a Latin cross. Later in the century, Bernini (1598–1680) designed the vast piazza with the Doric colonnades to give a setting to the building. The result of all their labors was the construction of the most imposing religious structure in the Latin West.

The fact that so many architects contributed to the final result accounts for the inner contradictions in the great cathedral. Neither the dome nor the façade quite succeed in dominating the entire structure. From the west, Michelangelo's dome stands forth clear and frank as the most important feature; from the east, Bernini's piazza and Moderna's façade dwarf or at least cut off the dome and become the center of interest. Bramante's great contribution, the monumental conception of the church, may actually be the most important feature after all, for a visitor only has to stand in the church or walk the length of the piazza to understand how completely this building dwarfs all others. The Corinthian pilasters applied to the nave are eighty-five feet high, the entablature adds another twenty feet, and the barrel vault is one hundred and fifty feet from the floor. To grasp the size, we should realize that the decorative cherubs are actually ten feet high! Yet Bramante's basic plan started with such sound proportions that the heroic size is only comprehended by comparing it with familiar objects.[1]

The Gesù Church is more unified in design. It was planned by da Vignola (1507–1573), and completed by his student, della Porta, between the years 1568 and 1584. The present interior decorations were completed in 1683. Like St. Peter's, this building is an example of space organization on a grand scale: the barrel vault and the soaring dome create the illusion of even greater space than exists. The design dramatically focuses attention on the high altar, and also provides a secondary point of interest in the pulpit. The Jesuits were preachers as well as militant fighters for their faith.

Baroque church architecture continued to develop in those parts of Catholic Europe where the service encouraged the construction of ornate and imposing buildings. The use of twisted pillars, blocks of contrasting colored marble, rich carving on the capitols, and heavy gold ornamentation created

[1] The cathedral at Montreal, Canada, is a scale model of St. Peter's; the fact that it is not as big as the original prevents it from being a monumental expression of power.

The Gesù Church in Rome is one of the most important baroque monuments; it has been copied in nearly every capital of Europe, in Latin America, and even in the Portuguese colonies of Asia. (Foto-Enit-Roma)

striking structures that offended the taste of that part of Europe that had become Calvinist and that demanded simplicity in church architecture. The decoration of these baroque churches was sophisticated, even intellectualized, in its forms; there was none of the naïve representation of saints and sinners found in medieval churches.

Perhaps Jesuit intellectualism rather than Franciscan or Dominican simplicity supplied the inspiration. Today in some places the almost dramatic contrast between the Gothic and baroque styles may be studied easily. The Calvinist iconoclasts in the Lowlands destroyed much of the medieval decoration in the churches there. After the end of the Dutch wars, the Spaniards undertook to redecorate many of those churches. In Ghent the results were striking. The cathedral is a pure Gothic structure; the altar and the decoration inside are pure Spanish baroque in black and white marble. When a visitor gets over the contrast, the dramatic quality of the new construction becomes apparent. Some of the constructions of the latter seventeenth cen-

The interior of the Cathedral of St. Bavon in Ghent tells a dramatic story. The medieval altar and statuary were smashed by the Calvinists in 1566. After the war, the interior was rebuilt in baroque style by the Spanish. The result is a striking contrast between the gothic church and the baroque altar.

tury seem to be in the same spirit that motivated those of the sixteenth, but it is probable that they were actually erected to atone for the sins of princes or to bring honor to the state rather than to God alone.

The same period that saw the building of great baroque cathedrals also witnessed the pacification of the countryside so that country houses could be constructed without high walls. The notion of a château for pleasure rather than for security had to await the centralization of power in the bureaucratic-police state. In the sixteenth and early seventeenth centuries châteaux were still built with ponds and walls that allowed some defense against a popular uprising. Only by the end of the seventeenth century could they be built without serious thought for defense. In Italy the existence of Roman ruins, the writings of Palladio, and the taste of the upper classes led to the construction of châteaux adapted from classical architecture. The château and its gardens came to be regarded as a single project: walks, waterfalls, fountains, arbors, garden houses, and even the patterns made by the trees, were all ordered to conform to the château. It was the château garden that made critics complain that the baroque architect forced all of nature to conform to his will in a man-made order. Most of the early baroque châteaux were built for cardinals, Italian princes, politicians, and wealthy merchants. Since this was the period when the upper classes of all Europe felt that a visit to Italy was necessary for the education of a well-rounded man, these private dwellings gained a European reputation.

The only great palace built in the early years of the baroque was the Escorial in Spain. Philip II was Europe's greatest prince, and Philip's Spain was Europe's first state: the Escorial was his architectural monument proclaiming these facts. It was the "Pentagon" of the sixteenth century. Built of gray granite and placed in a hillside, the palace seems almost to be part of the mountain itself. It was at once a royal residence, an office building, and a monastery. In shape it is a huge quadrangle with towers and courts dominated by a striking chapel. The ground plan recalls the grid upon which St. Lawrence was roasted alive. One of the windows of the king's bedroom opened on a view of the chapel door. (A hundred years later Philip's great-grandson, Louis XIV of France, built Versailles with the king's bedroom as the center of the palace and the chapel off to one side.)

The Escorial was the first building of this size to be constructed in western Europe with a unitary plan. There are eighty-six staircases and 2673 windows in the palace, all of the same style. The spirit of the palace reflects that of the king who built it. It is a powerful but forbidding building; over it all seems to hover the ideals of monastic life and the presuppositions of the Counter-Reformation. It is not a château for worldly pleasure, such as Versailles was to become a hundred years later.

Baroque architecture came to France with Marie de Medici when she became the wife of Henry IV at the opening of the seventeenth century. By that time France had already developed a style of château architecture suitable to the needs of the new society. The Italian style did not completely replace the native one, but it considerably modified it. Marie and Henry IV made an addition to the Louvre, and after the king's death she built the Luxembourg palace (1615–1624). Her son, Louis XIII, was unable or unwill-

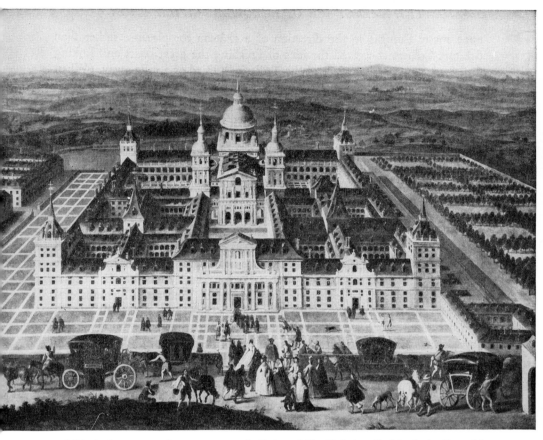

This is the great palace-monastery built by Philip II. It is called both the Escorial and the Monastary of St. Lawrence. It is built on a grid to recall the martyrdom of that saint.

ing to continue to build on such a scale for much of his reign was filled with wars that used up more money than he collected. Richelieu, however, built the Palais Cardinal (the Palais Royal, but considerably less elaborate than it is today). During the regency and the period 1643–1660, when Louis XIV was still a minor, the wars continued to make heavy demands on the treasury. There were a number of private châteaux constructed (the palace of the Duke of Orléans at Blois, for example), and Mazarin built the two wings of the château at Vincennes, but France had to wait for the reign of Louis XIV to become the leader in the development of the new style.

Both Louis XIV and his great minister, Colbert, believed that a king should decorate his capital city to impress both his own subjects and foreigners with his grandeur. Louis' first project, an addition to the Louvre, was just such a building. The Louvre had originally been a fortification on the river dominating both the city and its water approaches; by 1661 it had undergone many changes in the direction of a château for pleasure rather than defense. Colbert conceived the idea of finishing the great court and linking the structure with the palace of the Tuileries a third of a mile away. (When Louis became interested in building at Versailles, this project was dropped and not taken up again until the time of Napoleon III in the mid-nineteenth century.) A number of architects were called in to prepare the plans, including the great Bernini. (He made a famous bust of the king at the same time.) The final construction was under Claude Perrault, who skilfully combined the Italian and French styles. This colonnade wing of the Louvre became the pattern for later construction of that palace, and had tremendous influence on the development of the French baroque style.

Louis XIV, however, was never really at home in Paris. During his adolescence the Fronde had taught him the dangers of the city mobs, and his own love of the country made the city seem closed in to him. Mazarin had indicated the advantage of having a palace near enough to Paris to keep the city under surveillance yet far enough away for security when he had begun to build the château *inside* the great fortification of Vincennes. The medieval walls and towers would guarantee safety, while the beautiful château assured comfort. Between the years of the mid-1650's and the 1670's, however, the development of the police power of the state made a fortification like Vincennes unnecessary; it had become safe to build in the open country without even the protection of a moat or lake. The historian of the city of Paris must wonder what would have happened to the development of that city had Louis followed Mazarin's suggestion. Paris surely would have been different had the royal orientation been toward Vincennes on the eastern edge of the city rather than Versailles to the southwest.

Louis XIII had constructed a hunting lodge at Versailles. This original structure should not be confused with a cabin, yet it was modest when compared with the palaces at Fontainebleau or St. Germain. Louis XIV decided to make his château a residence suitable for the first king of Europe. The original structure was not destroyed; the new palace simply enclosed it. Versailles was a site that would appeal to the architects of the baroque era: it had no natural advantages; all its beauty and charm would depend upon the handiwork of man.

The first remodeling at Versailles was done under Le Vau (1612–1670), but the important construction came under Mansard (1645–1708) and his staff in the bureau of royal buildings. The major work was begun in 1678 and was completed, except for the chapel, by 1687. Like the cathedral of St. Peter in Rome, Versailles has to be seen to be appreciated. It is of little use to give the dimensions of the famous Hall of the Mirrors, or to call attention to the fact that the garden façade is a quarter of a mile long. The public rooms, the royal chambers, and the corridors are all spacious; on the other hand, the multitudinous apartments that were once occupied by courtiers, ministers, and bureaucrats are small and without privacy. The whole building has a unified conception in its design with the exception of the chapel roof which does not conform to the rest of the skyline. In our day this great palace is a dead hive, a sort of museum and public office building that hardly reflects the splendor of its great period. Even so, the imposing yet graceful mass of the château recalls the intention of its builder.

The gardens surrounding the château were designed by Le Notre (1613–1700), probably the most famous gardener in all history. Clipped trees, statues, fountains, alleys, reflecting pools—all were designed in relationship to the château, and the surrounding country fell under the same spell. The great roads leading to the town of Versailles and also the town itself came to be dominated by the building. Versailles dramatically pointed up the work of garden and city planners of the preceding century, and became an object lesson in the organization of space characteristic of the baroque style. This central idea of space planning in part goes back to Michelangelo's laying out the Campidoglio Square on the capitol hill in Rome, to the building of the Piazza di Spagna in the same city, and to the development of the great square in front of St. Peter's. It was to have its influence on city planning all over the western world. Washington, D.C., was laid out by an engineer whose inspiration for a city plan came from Rome *via* Versailles, and when St. Paul, Minnesota, began a project to "lift its face," the conception of space developed at Rome and Versailles was the natural starting point for the city planners.

3. THE BAROQUE PAINTERS AND SCULPTORS

While the architects were learning to organize space to dramatize their monumental conceptions and were creating buildings that glorified either God or the king, the painters and sculptors developed new methods of expression that gave dramatic value to their work. Counter-Reformation artists desired to present the traditional stories of the Bible and the saints so vividly that they would stir the audience. The group around the dead Christ in a Rubens picture are really grief-stricken, and transmit their sorrow to the observer. One of Pilon's statues, a St. Francis, proved to have so powerful a reaction that it had to be removed from the museum of the Louvre, because the votive offerings people left before the statue became a source of considerable inconvenience to the museum. After all, the Louvre is not a church. Thus we see that dramatic force was one of the original characteristics of baroque painting and sculpture. At first the artists painted God and the saints; in the latter seventeenth century they painted "Louis Crossing the Rhine," a landscape of a great harbor, or a portrait of a distinguished servant

These three Davids beautifully illsutrate the difference in the spirit of the sculpture of the fifteenth, sixteenth, and seventeenth centuries. Donatello portrays a stripling youth who has killed his enemy, perhaps during an afternoon stroll. Michaelangelo depicts David as a Greek god, a beautiful, athletic youth carrying a sling. Bernini finds David at his most dramatic moment, preparing to launch his rock at Goliath. Only the baroque artist gives us a dramatic sense of the event.

Donatello, "David" (Florence, The National Museum).

of the king. Both religious and secular paintings tended to have theatrical effects.

In many of them there is also a strong tendency to use motion to accentuate realism. For example, the Renaissance sculptors Michelangelo and Donatello each created a David; Michelangelo's is an Apollo, a beautiful, heroic, calm nude, while Donatello's is a shepherd boy out for a stroll on a summer evening. The great baroque sculptor, Bernini, created David as a youth filled with anger, fear, and hate, his muscles tense from the act of throwing the stone; it is David in action at his most dramatic moment. Several of the painters achieved the same realism by striking use of light and shade; others by the use of color. This was especially true of the Italian and Spanish painters of that period.

Most of the early baroque artists used color to express form and heightened emotion or to accentuate the story. In Italy and in Spain the Venetian Renaissance painters greatly influenced the late sixteenth- and seventeenth-century artists. El Greco (1548?–1614), Velásquez (1599–1660), and Murillo (1618–1682) were the most famous members of the Spanish school; they painted

Michelangelo, "David" (Florence Accademia).

Bernini, "David" (Rome, Borghese Museum).

madonnas and saints, stories from the Bible, and the court of the Spanish Hapsburgs. As colorists they were unexcelled; as dramatic painters they stand at the very top. El Greco used distortion to achieve effect much as a twentieth-century painter might use it. In Italy Carracci (1555–1619), and particularly Caravaggio (1569–1609), used contrasting color, light, and shade, to heighten the dramatic value. Catholic painters emphasized religious subjects and presented them in such a way that the utmost emotional force struck the viewers. In the north, there were two great painters: Rubens (1577–1640), whose color and motion have probably influenced more artists than any other master, and Rembrandt (1606–1669), the most important Protestant painter of this period. Rubens' paintings run the entire course of human interest: religious subjects, classical mythology, historical tableaux, portraits, and allegorical pictures. Much of the work on his canvases was done by his talented assistants, some of whom, like Van Dyck (1599–1641), and Jordaens (1593–1678), earned great reputations in their own right, but all Rubens' work bears the stamp of his own personality. Rembrandt, like Caravaggio, was a great master in the use of light and shade. No painter has ever been able to dramatize the

El Greco, "The Virgin with Saint Ines and Saint Tecla" (Washington, D.C., National Gallery of Art, Widener Collection). El Greco is almost "modern" in his distortions of the human figure made to achieve striking effects. This picture shows his debt to the Venetian school as well as his place among the early baroque artists.

Rembrandt van Ryn, "Portrait of the Artist" (New York, Metropolitan Museum of Art, Bequest of Benjamin Altman, 1913). Rembrandt was the master of light and shade. Baroque artists were often preoccupied with the problem of depicting light from a given source as a dramatic means of presenting their subject.

essential action of his pictures more successfully than he; he focused the light perfectly to explain the story.

After the mid-seventeenth century the schools in Spain, the Lowlands, and Italy declined in vigor, while the French school prepared to take over the leadership in painting. At first, the French school was under the influence of Le Brun (1619–1690), who became first painter to Louis XIV and head of the French Academy. He was a disciple of Raphael, the master of design, and he emphasized the works of the mid-century French painters Poussin (1594–1665) and Lorrain (1600–1682) who had studied at Rome and were greatly influenced by Raphael's works. When the great palace of Versailles was decorated, Le Brun imposed the "Poussinist" tradition upon the painters who worked under him with the result that the great palace was decorated in a uniform style, but one that is somewhat insincere and flat. After Le

Nicholas Poussin, "Death of Germanicus" (Minneapolis Institute of Arts). Poussin was a French artist who spent most of his life in Italy. His subjects included mythology, history, landscapes, and religious topics.

Brun's death, French painting lost its dictator, so that at the opening of the eighteenth century a great battle raged in the French artistic world between the proponents of color (Rubens) and those of design (Poussin). The so-called Rubensists won out over the Poussinists, and France early in the eighteenth century took and held the place in painting that had belonged to Italy and Flanders in the preceding three hundred years. The fruits of this labor are to be found in the rococo painting of the eighteenth century.

It is interesting to note the changes in subject matter considered suitable for the painters. By the end of the seventeenth century landscape, still life, and portrait painting had become the most popular, at least if we consider the canvases that were exhibited in the salons of the period. Even the historic paintings that had been so popular in the mid-century seem to have lost ground. The explanation is not difficult to find. By the end of the seventeenth century painters everywhere were becoming more dependent upon sales of their works in the shops of art dealers rather than upon the command pictures of wealthy patrons. The art dealer was selling pictures to be hung in private homes rather than in royal palaces, and a landscape proved more suitable than an historical tableau. There were, of course, many religious paintings still, but even in those there was a subtle change. The tragic scenes of the crucifixion, the betrayal, and the entombment that had been popular in 1600 gave way to the happier stories about the life of Christ or his saints. And some of the "religious" paintings took on very secular themes; it is surprising how popular were the stories of Lot and his daughters, Suzannah and the elders, Bathsheba, and other such Biblical tales that would permit the painting of a beautiful nude.

4. BAROQUE MUSIC

The development of musical thought followed the same pattern as the other arts. In the latter sixteenth century religious music bulked largest by far; by the opening of the eighteenth century secular music had taken first place, and the religious music that was produced had a strong secular tinge. Like the other arts, music was put to the service of the reformed churches, particularly the Catholic Counter-Reformation movement, as an inspiration to devotion and as a manifestation of faith. With the increased secularization of society in the seventeenth century, the princely courts and, later, all who could pay the price of admission were entertained by operas and concerts, and the musicians responded to those demands.

Italy was the music master of the baroque era. In Naples, Rome, and Venice, as well as in several other lesser centers, there were great schools of music where young men learned to play, write, and sing. Since Italy could not support all its talent, the students had to migrate. From Moscow to Boston, from Stockholm to Constantinople, the Italian music master was a common sight. He taught native children, organized musical entertainment, and took charge of church music. Some became famous and rich, some made only the most precarious livings, but rich or poor they were important representatives of Italian culture during the late sixteenth and seventeenth centuries. By the eighteenth century they had transmitted enough of their learning to Germans, Frenchmen, and others so that non-Italian schools began to appear.

One of the interesting characteristics of music in that period was the introduction of new instruments and their adaptation to musical compositions. Medieval and Renaissance men had known about horns and various kinds of reed and string instruments, but in that period much of the most important music was written for the human voice alone. The development of several kinds of violas and viola-cellos in the latter sixteenth century allowed the introduction of a string section and string accompaniment to the voice. These early string instruments, however, were uniformly soft in tone; only in the mid-seventeenth century was the "fiddle," a strident string and bow instrument of the earlier period, transformed into the violin to give the orchestra a strong first voice. Both reeds and horns were also improved, so that by the end of the seventeenth century they could be successfully added to the orchestra. Curiously enough, it was not until the latter seventeenth century that the director appeared in the role of orchestra leader; he became necessary as the size and complexity of the orchestras increased. The piano family went through a similar evolution in the seventeenth century; multikeyboard harpsichords and other experiments were tried to solve the problem of the scale. Only at the end of the century do we see the "well-tempered" clavichord for which Bach wrote some of his most famous pieces.

Perhaps the most spectacular achievement of the baroque musicians was the evolution of the opera. The seventeenth-century operas cannot be given today because they would appear archaic and absurd, and because they nearly all call for male soprano voices, and the practice of castrating promising boy singers has long been discontinued. These operas were fantastic affairs; their plots were even less carefully worked out than those of contemporary Hollywood, but like modern moviegoers, the audience was willing to accept absurdities and improbabilities as part of the convention. The stage settings were often sumptuous, so much so that it might be said that the settings of the opera were the most completely baroque artistic expression of the baroque era.

5. *MIRRORS OF MEN*

Much has been written to prove the existence of a baroque man. His characteristic pattern, his ambitions, and his fears have been analyzed by historians and moralists in an attempt to establish a norm for his behavior. It seems wise, however, to recall that patterns for men change like other things in the world, and therefore it would be difficult to hold up a mirror and see the image of man for a time as long as the hundred and fifty years of the baroque period.

Bishop Fénelon (1651–1715) made the same discovery at the end of the seventeenth century when he wrote with evident surprise that there had been great changes in manners and customs since the days of Henry IV. The wise bishop learned this fact in an age when most of men's assumptions were grounded in static concepts; it was probably possible for him to discover it because the seventeenth century witnessed a more rapid tempo of change than could have been observed for the preceding centuries. Improvements in transportation, increases in the total volume of trade and wealth, centralization of political power, controversies in religious thought, and that profound social movement, the extension of bourgeois influence and values, contributed to this new tempo.

The moral codes that men have been taught in childhood and in their contacts with other members of the group are the most resistant to change in any society. These notions of good and evil seem to many people to be absolutes, unchanging values with universal application. So deep is men's conviction that their moral ideas are "right" that they have difficulty recognizing change when it does occur. Yet changes come in moral values, in beliefs about good and evil, and such changes can be quite profound in extent.

No one in medieval Europe questioned the right of private warfare. The church tried to limit its effects, but did not question its morality. By the sixteenth century the rise of state power had largely put an end to those private wars between the king's vassals, but the duel was still accepted as the normal method for settling conflicts between gentlemen. Actually, in the utter decay of feudalism itself, that feudal moral value seems to have been heightened. The nobleman found the battlefield unsafe as a place to demonstrate his valor because pikes, arrows, and firearms could so easily strike him down; thus personal combat on a private scale gave outlet to his nostalgia for the days now gone. The amount of blood spilled in those conflicts was incredible. In Paris at the turn of the seventeenth century it was not uncommon for two principals, each seconded by ten to fifteen friends, to stage a general battle in the streets, and as many as a dozen men might be left dead. Some writers have tried to label this decadent feudalism with the word "baroque." It was a pattern shown in the literature of all western Europe, and it did seem to be the emotional exaggeration, the flamboyant defiance that some have called baroque. However, it was, in fact, a mere anachronism. The new political and economic society had no place for private wars, and the leaders of that society were determined to end them.

By the end of the sixteenth century both king (urged by his bourgeois ministers) and church (inspired by bourgeois clergymen) condemned the practice of dueling. The Council of Trent and a papal bull of 1592 placed the Catholic church squarely against dueling. The Scottish parliament, the French kings from Henry III onward, and several other governments published decrees forbidding duels. Richelieu even made it a capital offense and beheaded several great noblemen as examples. Neither the church decrees nor the state laws could stop the bloodshed immediately, but after 1650 it became noticeable that the practice had begun to decline appreciably. By 1780 many gentlemen no longer carried even the ceremonial sword that was popular in 1700. There were still duels to maintain honor, but in a society in which men of the pen were establishing themselves as the rulers both in government and in economic affairs, the sword lost its prestige. Public disapproval of violence did not stop with condemning dueling; by the end of the seventeenth century there were even moralists who taught that war between nations was as immoral as was private war; but it was not until the eighteenth century that this idea gained much currency.

The relationships between men and women have been subject matter for moral teaching ever since men became self-conscious. The Christian tradition had placed women in an invidious position. Medieval man had made a cult of the veneration of Mary, the Virgin, but women in the flesh were regarded as the root of evil by many moralists. Men's souls could best be saved by asceticism; the very existence of women made asceticism difficult. Therefore men gave women many uncomplimentary names, probably for no other reason than the fact that they aroused carnal lust in them. The Reformation in northern Europe abolished celibacy in the priesthood, and in a round-about way exalted marriage. "It is better to marry than to burn," said Luther quoting St. Paul. Nonetheless, sixteenth-century churchmen, both Catholic and Protestant, still had unkind things to say about women: "Fond flibbergibs, evil tongues, and worse minded." In discussing the state of matrimony, the moralist still argued in good medieval fashion that the purpose of marriage was to beget children and not "to satisfy men's carnal lusts and appetites." Like their medieval predecessors, the sixteenth- and seventeenth-century moralists displayed their anger at women for tempting them beyond their strength.

Men had long since revenged themselves upon their women by subjecting them to their rule. The perfect wife in the mirror of a popular poet like Jakob Cats (1577–1660) or of a great one like John Milton (1608–74) submitted meekly to her husband's will. Her life was bound by her home and its demands; she kept herself chaste, sober in dress, and ready to serve her husband and family. If she crossed her husband's will, both law and custom gave him the right to chastise her with physical punishment. This seems to have been the code for most of Europe; there is no doubt that it was broken here and there, and it was probably as true of this period as it is of other ones, that a strong-minded woman knew how to have her way with the man she had married. This code of behavior broke down in some levels of society to prepare the way for a revision of the relationship between the sexes. At the court, women found themselves in the role of queens who actually ruled on their own account or regents who ruled for their sons. Others were mistresses of kings and found themselves able to influence policy. These women were obviously not "flighty minded," nor could they be ignored. At the court and among the upper classes, women came to take part in social affairs on a level of equality. Their presence tended to soften the crudity of masculine behavior even if it introduced other problems. Montaigne (1533–1592) noted that in his day drunkenness was declining, while wantonness increased. Both

tendencies can be explained by the more general presence of women in society. The most striking example is to be found in the court of France. In
Henry IV's court the stable was the center of social life; his grandson Louis
XIV made the salon the important meeting place of society. The change is
also traceable in the rise of salons in Paris, and in the more general acceptance
of women as social equals that came about between 1600 and 1685. We see
the tone of society becoming less rude, manners more courteous, and modes
for men more genteel.

If we believe the preachers and moralists, the seventeenth century was the
most debauched period in all history. The Lutheran theologian, Andras Mus-
culus, fairly shouted that "Sodom and Gomorrah and the Venusburg itself
are child's play compared with the immorality prevailing [in Germany]."
The Restoration playwrights in England seemed to confirm this general impression; practically every woman they presented seemed to deceive her husband. The secular laws that were proclaimed to prevent adultery, sodomy,
rape, and fornication might indicate that mankind had reached a new low
in sexual irregularity. The Roman Catholic church recognized the danger
by ending the practice of having the priest hear confessions with the penitent
kneeling at his knee, and introducing instead the confessional booth with the
small window between the priest and the penitent (obligatory after 1614).
However, other evidence does not seem to indicate that men had changed
for the worse; the moralists had merely become more critical of irregular
behavior.

The literary men of the era give us some clue, probably imperfect, as to
the characteristics of their contemporaries. In the latter sixteenth century the
Italian Tasso (1544-1595) and the Englishman Spenser (1552?-1599) produced the best examples of the popular literature of the day: long-winded
allegorical romances extolling the virtues of feudalism. Like dueling, that
literature represents a decadent feudalism. Tasso's *Jerusalem Delivered* is a
Counter-Reformation allegory; the heroes of the crusades, Moslem villains,
witches, wizards, angels, and demons parade through twenty books of elegant
verse. In the end Tasso claims man should pattern himself after Godfrey
de Bouillon and God will stand on the side of His warriors. Spenser's *Faerie
Queen* is a Protestant counterpart to Tasso's work. It is long (twice as long
as the *Iliad*) and very involved. Its purpose was to instill knightly virtue into
the hearts of its readers and to praise England's Queen Elizabeth (Gloriana,
queen of the fairies). These two pieces were the best of a mass of such literature. Like the "Western" novel of our day, they extolled virtues of the society
(in this case feudalism) that had vanished. Cervantes (1547-1616), whose
own life was more exciting than any romance, well knew that much nonsense passed as truth in such writing. His *Don Quixote,* one of the great
literary achievements of western man, a parody and a satire of the high-

est order, was a complete answer to the whole literature of decadent feudalism.

The great playwrights of the first part of the period, Lope de Vega in Spain, Shakespeare in England, and Corneille in France agreed in portraying men who were seized by a great virtue, a great vice, or a great idea that dominated their lives. Certain writers have insisted that this willingness of a man to follow his star even to his own destruction was the characteristic of the baroque man. In a way the young nobleman who threw away his life in swordplay for honor, the explorer who risked almost certain death for fame, the statesman who, like Richelieu, gave his whole life to the state, the soldiers who, like Wallenstein or Condé, followed their own stars even though they might die, and the king who, like Charles I, went to the block perhaps for his ideas, perhaps for his foolish mistakes, may be classified as baroque men. Still it would not be impossible to find them in another epoch, so we must be cautious in stating that this is a unique characteristic of the men of the baroque era. Nonetheless, the dramatists and the novelists (writers of romances rather than novels as they are understood in the twentieth century) assure us that men with such grand fixations did exist and were admired at the opening of the seventeenth century.

In line with that tendency, one of the widely read moralists of the period advocated that man should pattern himself to develop only his greatest virtue. Heretofore the church had insisted upon the virtues of humility, chastity, self-denial, and so forth, as the ideals of a Christian man: the *honnêt homme* was such a person, a bundle of self-effacing, patient, and mediocre virtues necessary to accept the will of God. The Spanish Jesuit, Father Baltasar Gracián, rejected all this. His hero was something like Nietzsche's superman, an exciting creature who cultivated all his talents and emphasized his greatest one, a man who aspired and worked hard to achieve. Such a flamboyant creature could best be conceived by a Spaniard, a man who understood Philip II, Ignatius de Loyola, and Don Juan. Gracián's hero was also a Christian; he was working, striving, driving, only to lay his conquests at the feet of the Virgin. It is notable that it was a member of the educated, sophisticated Jesuit order who proposed this new man. The barefooted Franciscan saint of the Middle Ages was now obviously outmoded.

Both the dramatists and the moralists may have been simply recording one of the facts that the artists and musicians also understood, namely, that the society of Europe was progressively becoming more and more oriented toward the earth and secular affairs. The baroque man was a creature who "saved his soul" in worldly affairs; he was quite unlike the saintly heroes of the Middle Ages who retired to a cave, a monastery, or a desert. The fact that men were learning to find their lives in worldly affairs may account for the exaggerations, the romantic causes, the flamboyant personalities, that appear on the canvases, the stage, or in the pages of a moralist or a romancer. It is interesting to note that by the end of the seventeenth century there begins to emerge a quieter, less colorful picture of the secular man and a more limited conception of his heroics. We will discuss this development in a later chapter.

Louis XIV Visiting the Observatory, 1662 (Paris, Bibliothèque Nationale).
The observatory was a general scientific laboratory or museum where one
studied everything from the stars to skeletons.

Chapter 17

THE SCIENTIFIC REVOLUTION, 1543-1687

1. THE NEW SCIENCE

The century and a half between 1550 and 1700 witnessed a profound change in man's approach to the world. At first this change took place solely among the intellectual elite, but the new ways which were discovered of solving age-old problems of nature and of man were destined to alter the lives and the attitudes of the whole of western society. For the first time in history, men asked questions about the natural world that could be answered with the observational methods at their disposal. Earlier epochs had asked some of the same questions, but, since they did not have the tools for verification, their answers were merely conjecture. Recognition of the fact that questions had to be tested by observation was at the root of the scientific revolution; men found ways of testing the answers to their questions by direct questioning of nature rather than by appeal to "logical" or "rational" deduction from what was already believed to be truth.

As might be expected, the "new science" ran headlong into conflict with the older philosophical and theological learning. Much Christian doctrine was so deeply rooted in Greek thought that any attack upon Aristotle (the philosopher), Ptolemy (the astronomer), or any other of the important Greek writers was regarded in some quarters as an attack on Christian theology. However, whether it was desired or not, an attack was unavoidable because the "moderns" and the "ancients" approached problems differently. In the first place, the new science that the seventeenth century was developing asked different questions about the ways and meaning of the natural world than had traditionally been asked. If we just read Galileo's *Dialogue on the Two Principal Systems of the Universe* (1632), we see that the new learning asked the question, "how does it happen"; whereas the old learning had asked the question, "why does it happen?" The former obviously is interested in the process and ignores the purpose, while the latter wants to explain the meaning of events in terms of man's ultimate destiny, and presupposes that there is a "motive" or purpose behind events. Galileo once remarked that God could have made the world any way He wanted to make it. Man, he said, probably could not comprehend God's reasons for making this particular world, but he could discover *how* it was made. The theological thinkers, on the other hand, were interested in discovering the purpose of God rather than His mechanics; they assumed first that it would be possible to establish God's motives, and secondly that His purposes were related to man and man's needs and destiny.

On another level, the conflict was even more fundamental. The old learning started with an act of faith in the tradition and writings of the Christian community. As good rationalists, the supporters of Aristotle and St. Thomas rejected as impossible anything that failed to fit into their system. The new science also started with an act of faith, but it was a different one. Galileo and his like believed in the validity of their observations and the inferences that they could make from them. Truth, therefore, was something that could be revealed to anyone any time if he were willing to study nature. In a real sense this belief threatened revealed religion, for it suggested that God could be discovered in His works as well as in the sacred writings.

The basic differences in attitude created an ever-widening chasm between the "Aristotelians" and the "moderns." Greek and medieval science ascribed animate characteristics to inanimate objects. There was a "mineral soul," an "animal soul," as well as a human "soul," and all objects in the world shared these "souls," and in them were the feelings and motives ascribed to men. For example, a rock falls because it "wants" to rejoin the earth; water runs down hill because it "desires" to join the sea; nature "abhors" a vacuum, and so on. While such reasoning ascribed will to inanimate objects, the "modern" scientist of the seventeenth century saw only movement in them. Nor was that all. Greek and medieval science made other types of assumptions about the world. For example, there could be only "perfection" and no "corruption" in the stars. Perfection meant that they moved in "perfect" geometrical form, namely, a circle, and that the surface of the stars was unmarred by irregularities. Thus it was shocking when Kepler proved that the earth moved in an elliptical orbit, and when Galileo's telescope revealed "corruption" (imperfections) on the surface of the moon.

The methods of the "moderns" were based upon observation, and by the mid-seventeenth century their kind of scientific inquiry had become systematized and had invaded many areas of life. That was the era in which an assault was begun upon the secrets of nature by measuring, weighing, and taking the temperature of the world. Men now wanted to know how things happened, and proceeded to invent means of finding data that could be analyzed in mathematical terms rather than in terms of will or supernatural agents. To men accustomed to "common sense" explanations, some of their behavior seemed bizarre. Charles II of England laughed when he heard that his scientists were "weighing air." The German peasant regarded the antics of the scientists with the remark, "je gelehrter, desto verkerter" ("the more learned, the crazier"). But neither the scornful attitude of anti-intellectuals nor the hostility of supporters of the old learning prevented the development of the new approach to the problems of the natural world.

2. THE NEW UNIVERSE

Man has a long history of scanning the heavens. The march of the constellations across the night sky, the "wandering" of the bright stars (planets), and the changing pattern of the sun's rise and descent on the horizon must have attracted the attention of men long before they had verbal tools to explain to themselves the meaning of these phenomena. All ancient people seem to have used the stars to mark out a calendar for their agriculture and their feast days, and most of them believed that somehow their own lives and their history were bound up with movements in the heavens. It is not surprising that the sun, the moon, and the planets were worshiped by some, and held in awe by practically all ancient people.

Medieval men also watched the sky—some who wished to discover how the stars revolved "around" the earth, others who tried to identify these movements with events on the earth. Astronomy and astrology (the pseudo-science that tried to foretell the future of a man's life in terms of the stars) were deeply intertwined. At least some men who sought to "read the stars" did try to fathom them. The best guide to astronomy at the disposal of medieval men was a book written by the Greek astronomer Ptolemy in the second century A.D. Like nearly all the earlier astronomers, he did not even question the idea that the earth was the fixed solid center of the universe: common sense told every man that the sun "moves across" the day-time sky. His basic assumption, however, made the movements of the planets somewhat erratic, even though the instruments of observation were not accurate enough to show *how* erratic these movements would be if the earth were really the center of their movement.

In the period between the thirteenth and sixteenth centuries Christian and Moorish (Spanish) astronomers made a number of "corrections" to the Ptolemaic text, but each correction enormously multiplied the complexity of the whole system without providing a suitable basis for accurate prediction of the celestial movements. In the mid-sixteenth century a Christian astronomer named Copernicus (1473-1543) decided that Ptolemy's astronomy had become impossibly complex and that another approach to the problem was imperative.

His own observations had suggested to Copernicus that the earth might not be the center of the universe, and at about the same time the works of certain ancient Greek astronomers who had also postulated a heliocentric (sun-centered) universe became available to him. In the early sixteenth century methods of observation were woefully inaccurate, and actually Copernicus was unable to amass much systematic data about the stars, but the observations he did make seemed to justify the assumption of a heliocentric universe. His book, *On the Revolution of Heavenly Bodies,* was published in Latin at the time of his death in 1543. It fairly bristles with assumptions that were soon to be proved to be wrong, but it offered a major point of departure by showing that it would be easier to fit observations of the movements of the planets into a heliocentric system than into Ptolemy's geocentric system.

Copernicus did not really "prove" the fact that the sun was the center of the solar system; he argued that this assumption was a more fruitful point of departure than was Ptolemy's. His book did not arouse any great opposition from the conservatives. As we noted, he wrote in Latin, and therefore his ideas had only a limited audience, and, furthermore, even the learned world was not converted by his evidence. It could be pointed out that the heliocentric universe was only a theory—a theory that apparently could not be proved true, while common sense declared it to be false. In 1550 the idea that man could prove Copernicus' theory to be correct was not even considered by the vast majority of men who could read his book. Nonetheless, Copernicus provided the astronomers who followed him with a challenging problem.

The credit for the next great step belongs to the Dane, Tycho Brahe (1546–1601), and his assistant, Johann Kepler (1571–1630), who became the great master. Brahe built an astronomical instrument (a tower with slits through which light could enter) with which he could take reasonably accurate measurements of the angles of planetary movement. He himself was unable to organize his mass of evidence into a meaningful synthesis. However, Kepler took the material, and using long-hand arithmetic (trigonometry had not yet been developed) made the calculations necessary to prove the famous three laws of planetary movement. It has been said that only a sun worshiper like Kepler would have had the courage to tackle so gigantic a task.

Kepler's laws were evidence that mathematics could be used to establish the truth of a scientific proposition. Pythagoras (fourth century B.C.) may have *divined* that the world was number, but it was Kepler who proved that it could be described in terms of number. The *first law* was really revolutionary; he showed that the path of the planet is not a circle but an ellipse, and that the sun is at one focus of the ellipse. This buried the great myth of the "perfect figure," for before Kepler's time everyone had assumed that God would "naturally" adopt the circle when he created the world because it was the only "perfect" geometrical figure. The *second law* stated that the speed of the planet changed in the course of its orbit. It was faster near the sun, slower as it receded from the sun. The area of the triangles made by the sun and the radii to any two points on the planet's path were equal for any two periods of time. Hence, if the time taken to pass from M to M_1 is equal to the time needed to pass from X to X_1, then triangle MM_1S will have the same area as triangle XX_1S. These first two laws were announced in a book, *On the Motions of the Planet Mars*, in 1609. Ten years later came his *third*

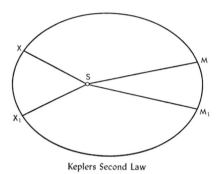

Keplers Second Law

law, a brilliant generalization of his mathematical evidence. In studying the movements of several planets, he noticed that the greater the distance from the sun, the slower the motion of the planet. Kepler then discovered that "the squares of the periodic times are proportional to the cubes of the mean distances of the planets from the sun." Thus, if there were a planet with a mean distance from the sun of nine (3^2) times as great as that of another planet, its year (time taken for the orbit) would be twenty-seven (3^3) times as long. This is approximately the relationship between earth and Saturn.

For anyone with the courage and the mathematical knowledge to read Kepler's books, the heliocentric universe became a fact. But to read Kepler required more knowledge than most men possessed. In 1609 Galileo (1564–1642) constructed a telescope which magnified objects by thirty diameters (nine hundred times), and trained it on the stars. The number of stars increased enormously; the surface of the moon appeared marred by imperfections, and, most important of all, there appeared satellites (moons) moving around Jupiter. Since they and the planets Mercury and Venus showed phases just like the moon, Galileo assumed that they all obtained their light from the central sun and circled around it. Enemies of the heliocentric system could refuse to accept his theory, but for any person willing to trust his eyes, here was proof of the Copernican system. Galileo's first findings were written in Latin in a book called *The Sidereal Messenger* (1610). He was called to Rome, elected to the Academy of the Lynx-eyed, a society of learned men, and given the opportunity to lecture to throngs of laymen and clerics. In the meantime, orders for telescopes poured in from all Europe.

3. ATTACKS ON THE HELIOCENTRIC THESIS

Man will fight for his beliefs, and as often as not he will fight hardest for beliefs that prove to be ill founded. From "the beginning of time" the earth had stood firmly under man's feet; it was a platform, a stage for his life. Its very solidity was proof of man's importance in the universe which had obviously been created expressly for him. All philosophies and theology were deeply rooted in this cosmology (theory of the world); indeed, it seemed to be basic to all speculation about God, man, and the world. As long as Copernicus was simply a theorist writing in Latin for other theorists and arguing simply that reasonableness was on his side, the thesis of the heliocentric universe did not disturb many people. However, Kepler and Galileo produced evidence that proved that the earth *did* revolve around the sun; and their evidence had disturbing effects on the minds of conservative men. As Professor Preserved Smith says: "And now, at one blow from an infatuated stargazer, the world, which had stood so fast . . . for six thousand years, began to twirl giddily on its axis. . . ." Furthermore, it was a fact that had to be contended with, not just a theory that could be considered as an intellectual plaything.

A whole decade before Kepler and Galileo published their findings the conservatives had been alerted to the possibility that the new theory might prove dangerous. Giordano Bruno (1548–1600), a poet-philosopher whose fate enhanced his importance in the eyes of posterity, broke into print with what may well be one of the first "science fiction" books of the modern era. In the manner of that art in our own day, he did not wait for proof of the basic assumptions of the heliocentric universe before announcing the existence of other suns with other earths and other men. Then with poetic insight he discovered "the Deity not as outside of, apart from, and distant from us, but as in ourselves and more within us than we are in ourselves." This new universe and new God were announced in Italian poetry and prose. Bruno's concept shocked many people, including Kepler who remarked that Bruno had "converted God into the universe and reduced Him to circles and points." Bruno was burned at the stake by order of the Inquisition. However, it is questionable whether he should be regarded as a martyr to science, for he died because he openly expressed heretical views about God, not because he accepted the heliocentric idea of the universe. All the same, the conservatives were ready to believe that the whole Christian story rested upon the idea that the earth was the center of all things. If that were not true, what would become of man? What would happen to the proud picture man had painted of himself if he were to become a pitifully small creature inhabiting a little planet revolving around a sun that might also prove to be quite un-important in the universe of stars? This was not a scientific question to be answered in terms of mathematics; the conservatives saw it as a moral ques-tion involving man's measure of himself and his God. If man lost his place in the universe, the conservatives feared that he might also lose his soul and his hope of salvation. It is small wonder that they reacted rather vigorously to counteract the danger.

Thus a counterattack against the new science soon appeared. Among others, a Florentine priest in 1614 chose as his text for a sermon Acts 1:11, "Ye Galileans, why stand ye gazing up into the heavens?" Clearly the writers of the New Testament had foreseen the danger as well as the name of the scientist who heralded it. There was a rash of controversy, with Galileo squarely in the center of the fight: he was a man who loved an argument, especially when he knew that he was in the right. In 1616 the ecclesiastical authorities summoned him before the Inquisition, and warned him to for-sake the false opinion that the earth moved. According to the minutes of the Holy Office, Galileo agreed to do so. There seemed little reason for heroics; he knew that time and evidence were on his side.

For the next decade and a half the controversy simmered. In northern Europe most literate men accepted the heliocentric thesis as proved; in Italy, where the Inquisition was at work, it was treated as an hypothesis rather than a fact, but in the learned world this was recognized as a ruse to avoid argument. In the realm of physics and mechanics, a similar argument de-veloped; the "new" scientists described events in terms of mathematics and process while their opponents insisted upon the system of Aristotle. Galileo entered the lists against the Jesuit scientists, who assumed the role of defend-ers of the old system, with a crushing book on physics, *Il Saggiatore* ("The Scales"), in which he showed how stupid were his opponents' arguments. He waited, however, until his admirer, Cardinal Barberini, became Pope Urban VIII before he again grappled with the problem of the skies; and when he did return to a discussion of the heliocentric system, he explained that it was merely a convention of the time and that, of course, there was "no danger that anyone would ever prove it necessarily true." However, his argument showed that only the obstinate could fail to believe that his thesis was correct.

Galileo's new book was the famous *Dialogue on the Two Principal Sys-tems of the Universe* (1632). He secured the necessary permission from the papal censors to print it on the grounds that it championed neither system: it was supposed to be simply a discussion of both theories. However, no sooner had it been published than all Europe hailed it as a crushing answer to all objections to the heliocentric universe. Galileo did not sum up the con-clusions, but anyone could see that there was no question about them. Campa-nella, congratulating him, wrote, "Even Simplicio, as the buffoon of your philosophic comedy, perfectly revealing the folly of his sect, is skillfully portrayed." The real problem was that the book was written in perfectly lucid Italian, in an era when every educated man would know that language. It was adroit, brilliant, and in its total effect, biting. Even though Galileo was a personal friend of the pope, the Roman church, prodded by the conservatives, could not fail to react against such a book.

Galileo was cited before the Roman Inquisition in the spring of 1633. He argued that he intended only to develop the case for both theories, and finally, under threat of torture, he agreed to recant his whole case for the heliocentric system. Tradition states that he muttered something that sounded like "and even so, it moves," but tradition often includes remarks that should have been made, even if they may not have been. The remaining years of Galileo's life were spent in a not unpleasant semiconfinement. He continued his scientific studies until his eyes gave out, and died in his eightieth year (1642). No one took his recantation seriously, and only the foolhardy could believe that he would have accomplished anything if he had refused to recant and allowed himself to be burned. The blood of martyrs may be useful in propagating the faith, but it would hardly have added any true information regarding the processes of the world.

The trial was a severe shock to many Catholics who had come to recognize the complete victory of the heliocentric theory. Descartes (1596–1650) admitted that his own philosophy must be false if the heliocentric theory were untrue. He finally got around the dictates of the Holy Office by asserting that the earth remained still as a man sleeping on a boat remains still. The boat, of course, moves.

For about fifty years after Galileo's trial his other books advocating the heliocentric theory were on the Index of the Roman Catholic church, but the futility of fighting against the theory became more and more apparent. The stars in their courses, and the telescopes that now watched the skies, belied the old thesis. Some students like Pascal (1623–1662) could not decide which was right, but by the end of the seventeenth century most learned men had accepted the heliocentric world; and the Inquisition sagely allowed them to live in peace.

In 1686 Fontenelle published his brilliant popular book, *Conversations on the Plurality of the Worlds,* in which he taught a beautiful countess the secrets of the universe by means of a series of discussions in a starlit garden. His system was the one proposed by Descartes, in which the worlds become vortices in a "celestial fluid," each planet a subvortex spinning within the larger one. He contrasted this "correct solution" with the various ideas held by other peoples, Europeans as well as non-Europeans, about the universe. The countess charmingly goes through all the emotions from astonishment to fear, adding her sex and her beauty to the interest of the scientific thesis. The book was a huge success as a work of popular science.

The next year the *Principia* of Newton (1642–1727) banished forever

Ptolemy's universe. Kepler's laws had fundamentally shaken the old beliefs; Newton's laws destroyed them. For about a hundred years learned men had accepted Gilbert's (1540–1603) theory that the magnetic needle behaved as it did because the earth was a huge magnet. Galileo's studies of movement and Kepler's laws gave Newton the idea of universal gravitation. He had to wait, however, until Picard accurately measured a degree of longitude (1670) before he could make his calculations. Once those difficult calculations had been made, the evidence for Newton's thesis seemed clear enough to destroy any objections. He showed that the moon was falling toward the earth (that is, away from a straight line) at a constant rate. When he had established the exact distances between the moon and the center of the earth and the surface of the earth and its center, he could also show, by using the law of inverse squares, that the fall of the moon and the fall of an object on the earth's surface were both governed by the same unknown force, gravity. From this Newton argued the case for universal gravitation as the force holding the universe together. The stars and the "apple" were henceforth governed by a single universal law.

Newton's work was in Latin and difficult to read because of the mathematical arguments. Nonetheless, within a generation the rigid space-time machine that he described became an article of faith for educated men, and only a little over a hundred years later the Catholic church accepted the doctrine and allowed its people to read the books that it had formerly banned as erroneous. It should be noted that, while official church action may seem conservatively slow, many of the astronomers of the eighteenth century were good Catholics as well as believers in the heliocentric universe. In the twentieth century apologists for the Roman Catholic church bluntly state that the ecclesiastical commissions that tried and condemned Galileo and the heliocentric theory were in error. Since it was not a question of "faith or morals," the papal position was not involved.

4. PHYSICS AND ANATOMY

The conquests of the new science were not confined to the study of the stars. Indeed it was the discovery of basic laws on the earth that allowed Newton to make his great generalization about the universe. It is not easy to track down the inspiration for much of this study. Obviously the natural curiosity of man has led exceptional individuals to seek answers to problems, but that solution only begs the question, for it does not explain why certain questions are the ones that men ask at a given time. Furthermore, there is obviously a gap between asking and answering questions. The latter act often requires tools and materials that may or may not be available to men at any given time.

In the latter sixteenth century a whole series of questions emerged out of the developing technology of Europe. New mining enterprises required pumps to remove water, but once the pumps were invented it was discovered that their usefulness was limited to lifting water a fixed height (about thirty feet). The development of artillery and the need for discovering the best methods of aiming the new guns opened up a whole series of questions about objects in motion. New metallurgical techniques in the sixteenth century posited questions about metal. The building of canals and locks brought up questions of hydraulics. These and other technological developments posed questions for alert observers.

The sixteenth century also saw the rediscovery and popularization of classical writers on mathematics, mechanics, medicine, and natural science. The humanist scholars turned to these manuscripts as soon as they had about exhausted the literary and philosophical writings of the ancients. Studies on war largely had to wait until the seventeenth century before the printing press made classical writers on that subject easily accessible to all, but by 1600 most of the mathematical and physical knowledge of the ancients was available to anyone who could read. In attempting to understand the intellectual revolution of the seventeenth century the printing presses with their flow of ancient and modern writings must be kept in mind as a central point in the analysis. The so-called "book and reading" culture of modern man finds the printing press at its very core. The readers of books by ancient and modern authors found their curiosity stimulated by problems that demanded attention. When these books dealt with earthly affairs, the questions naturally were about the earth and its processes.

In this history it is obviously impossible either to discuss all the important scientific inquiries or to give credit to the numerous individuals who were responsible for them. Several of their number, however, stand out so significantly that they cannot be ignored. Of these, Galileo is manifestly one of the most important. The fact that he managed to live until he was almost eighty years old may have been responsible for the variety of his achievement; by seventeenth-century standards he had approximately two adult lives. His significant discoveries were in the fields of mechanics, statics, and hydrostatics, as well as astronomy. His were the first discoveries that dramatically introduced the force we call gravity. To come to grips with this uncomprehended force, Galileo had to rid himself of the common sense assumptions about the universe and also of the Aristotelian ideas about physics. He found a force that had nothing to do with the destiny of man and was quite unrelated to human behavior.

One of Galileo's first discoveries was that a body moving freely down an inclined plane accelerates uniformly. He studied the problem by rolling a ball down a plane, and measured the time with a waterclock. He found that the distances traveled were proportional to the square of the time taken. The ball traveled one-fourth of the distance in half the time it took to go the whole course. He concluded rightly that a body falling freely on a perpendicular would behave the same way. The pendulum provided another example of motion. Galileo discovered that neither the weight nor the mass of the object nor the height of the swing determined the time of the oscillation. The duration of each swing depended on the length of the pendulum alone, and was the same for all pendulums of the same length. He also discovered that the duration of oscillation varied as the square root of the length of the pendulum. Thus, if the lengths were 1, 4, and 9, the duration of the oscillation would vary among themselves as 1, 2, and 3. Since the result of this experiment fitted the rule of motion down an inclined plane, Galileo could assume that the same unknown force was operative in each case. His discovery made possible a new kind of clock.

He also discovered that neither the weight nor the mass of a falling body changed the speed of its fall. Thus the cause of the fall was not to be found in matter but rather in the unknown force that attracted all things to the earth. There is a story that in 1592 he dropped objects of vastly different weights from the tower of Pisa to prove this law, but since there is no mention of this fact in Galileo's own writing, it is possible that the story—a good one—is simply a myth.

Galileo further studied the movement of projectiles to determine the laws in question. With all his genius, he never solved the parallelogram of force, but he did discover that a projectile described a parabola; the force of gravitation and the force behind the projectile accounted for the geometric figure. Some years later Torricelli, one of Galileo's most gifted students, showed that a hole pierced in a vessel of water would also create a stream with a trajectory of a parabola. Thus water obeyed the same law when subjected to two forces.

These discoveries allowed Galileo to refute the Aristotelian arguments against Kepler's laws. The principle of the independence and the coexistence of forces acting on a body in motion allowed him to explain the variation discovered by Kepler in the speed of the planet in its orbit. It also explained why an object thrown into the air will drop back to the same place, even though the earth had moved while it was in the air, for the body had, as it left the earth, the speed of the earth as well as the force that projected it skywards.

The new science made considerable discoveries in other areas. Kepler, for example, explained the principle of the eye in terms of the *camera obscura*. He saw that light beams outlined the bright object from which they came. They behaved like strings attached to the corners of an object and passed through the aperture. He guessed that we see the object right side up rather than upside down as it actually enters the eye because we are psychologically conditioned to see it so. He did not solve the problem of color, nor did he understand the "stereoscope" principle resultant from the two eyes seeing the same object from just slightly different positions.

In addition, Galileo wrote about and experimented with sound, optics, and the behavior and pressures of water. In 1638 he brought his own and others' discoveries together in a new dialogue in which he "debated" both sides of the controversy between the old (Aristotelian) and the new science. That was the method that he had used to destroy the old astronomy; it was equally effective in physics. Galileo, however, took the precaution of having this manuscript "stolen" and published in the Netherlands so that, if necessary, he could repudiate it. Like the earlier *Dialogue on the Two Principal Systems of the Universe,* this book was a crushing blow to Aristotelian science. It demonstrated how simple-minded and thoughtless were the doctrines of his opponents.

In exactly the same year (1543) that Copernicus' work on the heliocentric theory appeared, Vesalius (1514-1564) published his study, *On the Structure of the Human Body.* Like Copernicus, Vesalius depended heavily on Greek thought. The complete works of the great Greek anatomist, Galen, had only recently become available—throughout the Middle Ages only summary texts or "digests" had been known. Galen's honesty about his own research led Vesalius to try to probe into the anatomical problems that were obviously unsolved. The new study, based on observation and illustrated by competent artists, gave great impetus to the study of the human body.

The great center of physical as well as of anatomical research was the University of Padua. Supported by Venice, this university was outside the power of Rome and its professors were relatively sure of protection from the Inquisition, no matter what their research might discover. At the end of the sixteenth century Fabrice d'Acquapendento had worked on the veins and blood vessels and discovered the valves in the former. His most gifted student, an Englishman named Harvey (1578-1657), continued the same research, using many different animals in his observations—dogs, pigs, snakes, frogs, mollusks, and even fish—and he realized the relationship between the beat of the heart and the condition of the blood in the veins and arteries. By experiment he proved that shutting off the flow of blood to a limb would result in cutting off the pulse in the area and eventually in gangrene. He also was able to show that the heart was a pump capable of forcing the blood to circulate in the body. His book, *De Motu Cordis,* proclaiming the circulation of the blood, was published in 1628.

In 1648 Jean Pecquet (1622-1694) discovered the circulation of bile in the dog. The Aristotelians objected that a dog was not a man, but a few years later Jargon found the same system in a soldier who had just been killed.

This, then, was another kind of movement that replaced the static system of Aristotle. The blood obviously did not have "spirits" in it; it had a physical function to perform in the body. Just as they had refused to look in Galileo's telescope, so the Aristotelians shrugged their shoulders when Harvey pointed out that he had never seen spirits in the blood. Time, however, was on the side of the men who insisted upon observation as a key to knowledge.

5. *L'ESPRIT GEOMETRIQUE: CARTESIANISM*

As long as the defense of the new science rested in the hands of men like Galileo, it could strike telling blows at Aristotle, but it could not overthrow him. Galileo, Kepler, Harvey, and the others presented facts that made nonsense of much of Aristotelian thought. However, none of them was a philosopher; they neither produced a system to replace Aristotle nor did they elaborate their methodology. For Galileo it was enough to measure and weigh and time the phenomena of the world; he knew that his mathematical descriptions corresponded to reality. For Harvey it was enough to observe exactly, and to check processes; he knew that his observations corresponded to reality. They both assumed a unified universe, but neither bothered to expound it. When Bacon expounded his system, Harvey, his physician, remarked that he (Bacon) philosophized about nature "like a lord chancellor."

Nonetheless, some philosophical explanation based upon the new science had to be made. Sir Francis Bacon (1561–1626), the English statesman (he *was* lord chancellor) and philosopher, proposed a methodology for scientific study. He rejected Aristotle and Plato, but, having little knowledge of mathematics, he was unable to speak intelligently for scientists who were bent upon measurement. Bacon's methodology, however, was almost exactly the same as that to be used by biologists and geologists in the mid-nineteenth century, when the problem was that of collecting and interpreting masses of data and making historical reconstructions: but in his own day his methodology was not particularly fruitful.

René Descartes was the philosopher who provided the new science with a philosophical system. Today we realize Descartes' errors; we see the blind alley that his mechanistic teachings led to, and some historians reject him and praise his contemporary, Pascal, as the man on the "right track." Such an approach, however, neglects the fact that it was Descartes, and not Pascal, who influenced the intellectual life of the next hundred years to the greatest extent. Cartesian philosophy became popular, and, in spite of the objections of the church and universities, Cartesianism became the accepted doctrine of Europe. Thus, whether his influence was good or bad, Descartes was a giant on the stage of his era.

He was first of all a brilliant mathematician. Analytical geometry, which proves that geometry can be reduced to arithmetic, was his great discovery. By analytical geometry movement can be introduced into geometric thought, an idea ignored by Greek thinkers whose systems had been completely static. Descartes' discovery of analytical geometry was necessary for the later discovery of calculus by Newton and Leibniz. The coordinates by which we today show so many movements graphically were his invention. He also experimented with optics and mechanics, but his work in these fields was not particularly significant.

Apparently Descartes' main aim was to bring the new science and Christian thought into harmony. He assumed the unity of truth; therefore this project should be possible. There is a story that Cardinal Bérulle, the venerable leader of the Counter-Reformation forces in France, after hearing Descartes discuss his ambition, insisted that he must complete his work as a matter of conscience. Descartes was profoundly influenced by St. Augustine and St. Thomas, as his writings show: he hoped to do for his age what they had done for their own, namely, as we said, to unify the new trends of thought with Christian tradition. Later Cartesianism became radically anti-Christian, but that in no way justifies a description of Descartes as one who attacked the creed and the church into which he was born. It merely means that he failed to understand the logical consequences of his ideas, and therefore could not achieve the goal that he had set for himself.

Basically the Cartesian system is geometry applied to the world. Descartes realized that geometric truth came from the testing of hypotheses. This, he assumed, was the only method that could yield results. Clearly this notion placed Euclid on Aristotle's throne. But where should he start? Descartes reasoned that man must doubt everything until he finds a proposition that cannot be doubted. This rigorous, philosophical doubt became a basic factor of Cartesianism. What could not be doubted? Montaigne had already suggested it; Descartes put it succinctly into the proposition, *"Cogito, ergo sum"* ("I think, hence I am"). Thus the one thing that must be believed became the *reality* of man. He further assumed that man could feel true experiences from his contact with the world and that he could draw rational conclusions from those contacts. From this basis Descartes proceeded to formulate a philosophy. He proved the existence of God by the fact that man could conceive of God, that is, perfection. This must be an innate idea placed in man's soul by God. When he then approached the world as created by God, we begin to see the seventeenth century's new conception of God. The world that man knew was becoming an orderly machine, made up entirely of motion and extension. The universe, too, appeared to be a vast machine made of subtle celestial fluid and moving in vortices, some of which had subvortices within them (the sun was the center of a vortex; the earth, part of the sun's vortex, was also a vortex itself). It was the handiwork of a master-mechanic-mathematician-God who had created it and given it impulsion. On the earth all was mechanical, all submitted to geometric law. Animals were *automata* (machines) and men's bodies were probably machines. Here Descartes drew back. To preserve man's integrity and immortal soul he proposed the dualism between mind and matter, soul and body, that fitted Christian thought. Thus, only God and the soul of man escaped from Cartesian mechanics; the rest of the world was a machine subject to geometric law.

Once he had arrived at this grand concept of the universe, it was easy to fill in the parts. "Give me motion and extension," Descartes once exclaimed, "and I will create a universe." That is just about what he did. Since his world was so completely integrated by its maker, all that was necessary would be to learn a few true things about it by experience (experiment), and then the whole edifice could be rationally reconstructed. This would save the back-breaking and heart-rending toil necessary for research; it would allow the philosopher to reach the center of things quickly and with great assurance. Descartes did overthrow the Aristotelian hierarchies of value, and substituted for a world of spirit and purpose a world machine of geometric order. However, by creating a world in which man could reason from geometric propositions about reality, he allowed the mathematical symbol to stand for reality, and thereby created another series of beliefs that had to be revalued before scientific progress could escape from his rigid system.

Descartes' most important work was his *Discourse on Method,* published with three essays to illustrate the method (1637). This book had a preface in the form of a confession similar to Augustine's in which he explains, auto-biographically, how he arrived at his methodology. Then he goes on to explain that in science as in geometry man must construct hypotheses about the world, and then, like the geometer, test those hypotheses by experiments or against known truths. The essays showed how that method could be used for actual scientific analyses.

In spite of the fact that Descartes tried at each step along the way to identify the new doctrine with the teachings of the church, his writings were soon condemned to the Index. His philosophical doubt that led to "proof" of the existence of God and that insisted upon "proof" for anything that was to be believed ran contrary to Catholic ideas. He was not the only seventeenth-century philosopher to forget that Christianity is based upon faith, and faith must transcend evidence or the need for evidence. Nevertheless, even though church and university both condemned his teaching, within a generation of his death (1650) Descartes' works were widely read and tremendously in-fluential. Though they may have verbally rejected his doctrine, the bishops, the philosophers, and the learned world almost transformed his name into a verb: "to cartesianate" meant to see the world in terms of a machine, and to assume its logical inner structure. Fontenelle, writing toward the end of the century, insisted that any book, no matter on what subject, would be better written if the author were a geometer. No greater faith could be expressed about the mechanical nature of the world.

In the half century after Descartes' death, Spinoza (1632–1677), a Jewish philosopher living in Holland, wrote one of the world's great moral treatises on ethics, using the geometric method of hypothesis, tests, and proof. Malebranche (1638–1715), a Roman Catholic priest, and the Cambridge Platonists (Anglican theologians) produced books on theology under the influence of Cartesianism, while works on physics, optics, and astronomy teaching the Cartesian system became the common property of everyone. It became so fashionable to read about the new science that it was said that young women hesitated to give their hands to men who had not achieved some scientific status. The lady who carried a cadaver in her carriage, so that she could study anatomy while parading in Paris, was probably extreme, but from the great thinkers to the faddists of the day, Cartesianism set the pattern for thought.

Naturally there were critics. Pascal objected both to Descartes' easy assumption that one could explain the world by "reason" alone and to his lack of deep religious conviction. Pascal was intoxicated by a personal religious experience that was more meaningful to him than were his mathematical studies on the laws of probability. Both Leibniz and Newton criticized Descartes, as did many of the learned men of the era who found him in error in so many of his assumptions and assertions, and yet both Newton and Leibnitz were, basically, themselves Cartesians. They held that the world was a machine subject to the laws of geometry, even though they did not think it so easy to reason about its structure.

6. THE EXTENSION OF THE NEW SCIENTIFIC LEARNING THROUGH COOPERATIVE EFFORTS

As we have seen, Galileo was elected to the Academy of the Lynx-eyed in Rome after he made his telescope. That society represented one of the early attempts to bring learned men together for discussion of mutual problems. In the early seventeenth century such societies existed in several Italian cities to discuss science, literature, or philosophy. One was founded in France, and became the French Academy under Richelieu's patronage. Most of these early societies were organized by private individuals and were governed by their own rules. The secrecy of several of the Italian groups got them into trouble with the police. Learned societies in England and in France, under the patronage of the government, became world-famous institutions.

In 1662 Charles II gave a charter to a group of English gentlemen who had been meeting together for several decades, naming their organization "The

Royal Society for Improving Natural Knowledge." The charter gave the members of the Royal Society the obligation to "examine all systems, theories, principles, hypotheses, elements, histories, and experiments of things natural, mathematical, and mechanical, invented, recorded, or practiced by any considerable author, ancient or modern." It forbade the Society to adopt any official philosophy, imposing upon it the obligation to canvass all opinions. Its objective was to discover useful truth. The Society published its proceedings as well as papers and letters in a journal called *The Philosophical Transactions,* which soon attained international fame as a source for scientific information. It displayed interest in all manner of things from sheep breeding to physics. The accomplishments of its members underlined the practical, useful nature of scientific knowledge as well as the more abstract and theoretical nature of such studies. It was responsible for improving pumps and scales, plows and sheepshears, as well as for encouraging research about weather, the nature of the burning process, the stars, and other such phenomena. It may not be true that the Society was responsible for England's intellectual greatness at the opening of the eighteenth century, yet Huygens was probably right in calling it "an assembly of the choicest wits and finest intellects of Christendom."

The French counterpart was commissioned by Colbert in 1666, and its twenty-one members were each given a pension of 1500 livres per year (perhaps equal to about $6000 in 1960). This society became the *Académie des Sciences;* it had been meeting as a private group with reasonable regularity since the 1630's, when Pascal's father was the leading spirit. Colbert made it separate from the *Académie Française* that Richelieu had supported because he wanted it to specialize narrowly on scientific problems. Its purpose, according to its constitution, was "to work for the perfection of the sciences and arts and to seek generally for all that can be of use or convenience to the human race, and particularly to France." Its publication was called the *Journal des Savants* and immediately it acquired a considerable reputation in Europe. Like its English counterpart, the Society spent much of its time on practical problems. Colbert wanted to be sure that France got her money's worth from the scholars, so he presented them with all manner of questions concerning manufacturing, road and canal construction, navigation, and the like. This does not mean that theoretical science and the problems raised by Cartesian philosophy were ignored. The *Académie* was a hard-working body of men intent upon solving the riddles of the world.

Naturally both groups were the butts of jokes made by men who rejected scientific thought. Butler's poem, "The Elephant in the Moon," tells of a society of scientists which found such a phenomenon, but it turned out to be a mouse in their telescope. Swift ridiculed the Academy of Lagado in *Gulliver's Travels,* and even La Fontaine found time to satirize the *Académie* in his poetry. These were the laughs of men of letters who were often as unsympathetic with the new science as were the theologians, but their sarcasm was no convincing response to the programs of the scientific academies.

In the two generations following the foundation of the English and French academies, similar groups appeared all over the western world. From Connecticut to St. Petersburg, from Berlin to Naples, scientific societies, some of them informal, some subsidized by governments, appeared to popularize the new science. Naturally their quality was uneven, and many times they were victimized by charlatans, but they carried forward as best they could the new Cartesian learning. Even ladies formed learned societies; and some of them were hoaxed by charlatans who announced, prematurely, important discoveries such as the discovery of inhabitants on the moon.

7. SCIENTIFIC PROGRESS

The actual progress of scientific discovery was relatively slow. The world sees few geniuses like Galileo, Kepler, Harvey, and Newton; most men have to be content to work within a more restricted frame of reference. The genius of the era had broken down some of the old assumptions and permitted men to approach some problems with a better chance of obtaining useful results; other assumptions still remained to blind men to whole areas of the natural world.

In physics, Galileo's studies and the work of the instrument makers and the mathematicians who developed logarithms and trigonometry allowed extended research in optics, mechanics, statics, and hydrostatics. The development of good air pumps allowed experiments with vacuum that showed its true relationship to air pressure. (Aristotle's notion about nature abhorrin a vacuum now seemed foolish.) The development of barometers and thermometers allowed studies of weather, while new astronomical insights gave the correct explanation for the changes of the seasons. Studies of rainfall solved the problem of rivers and springs, exploding the older theory of subterranean waters.

In chemistry, Boyle's (1627–1691) studies of the properties of matter gave chemistry independence from alchemy even though his postulates blinded him to the areas where research would be most fruitful. At about the same time, a school of chemists who were also bureaucrat statesmen in Vienna developed the concept of phlogiston, a substance that "facilitates" combustion and calcination. Georg Stahl (1660–1734), who most effectively used this new conception, was able to write equations that would balance; with ø, his symbol for this mystic material, he could explain calcination. The plausible nature of his argument probably was responsible for retarding the development of the more accurate explanation based on oxygen.

The study of the earth sciences was sharply curtailed by the universal belief in the recent creation of the earth. That belief was also to prove a hindrance to Newton's work, but it did not blind men to celestial mechanics the way it shut them off from any study of the processes on the earth's surface. As long as the world had been created about the year 4004 B.C. (the date indicated by biblical studies) the geologist, zoologist, and botanist could only collect and name things; they could not satisfactorily explain them. They were bothered by the discovery of fossils and clam shells on high mountains, and of shark's teeth far from the sea. Some scholars denied the reality of these things, calling them "sports of nature" or the acts of a whimsical creator who made them to amuse man and inspire him to believe in God. Finally, however, the most widely held opinion came to be that the flood of biblical times was the responsible agent. Something had to be discovered to explain the unexplainable mystery, and without a cataclysm there seemed to be no answer. One of the most popular of these theological geology books bore the modest title of *The Sacred History of the Earth, containing an account of the Origin of the Earth and all the General Changes which it hath already undergone or is to undergo till the Consummation of all Things.* This little volume by Dr. Thomas Burnet, a clergyman, was read and praised by the same generation that saw the first publication of Newton's *Principia.* We must remember that although Galileo and a few others began the study of modern physics, most learned men still retained their preconceptions of the world based on earlier postulates. However, this did not mean that students of geology and biology worked to no avail. They collected specimens; they tried to bring order into nature by devising names for plants and animals; they even made discoveries such as the sexual structure of flowers. Only if we remember the chaos that must have existed in regard to ideas about the natural world before it had any orderly nomenclature, can we appreciate the patient labor of naturalists who prepared the way for methodical presentation of the natural world. These men, too, were Cartesians; even though they could not apply geometry to their studies, they could attempt to give them an orderly structure.

8. NEWTONIAN SCIENCE

As we have already noted, in 1687 Newton's *Principia* was published. It made little impression upon the scientific world of the day, for Cartesian science had achieved almost complete acceptance. Newton's world was a vast time machine, operating in an empty universe and held together by mysterious gravity. To the Cartesians this mysterious force seemed to be a superstitious idea; Descartes had lived to banish such notions. For most of the literate population, even those who read Latin fluently, the *Principia* was too difficult to read; a Cartesian scholar might be able to follow Newton's mathematics, but not many other people could. Thus it is not surprising that Herman Moll, the author of the standard English geography of the early eighteenth century (twenty years after the publication of the *Principia*), stated that there was a new theory about the tides (Newton's), but he believed it better to present the older theory.

Nonetheless, Newton's astronomy and his explanations of the universe were destined to become the dogma of the mid-eighteenth century, and to give to scientific research a tone and a method more conducive to useful results than that of Descartes. Newton announced that he would not introduce any propositions in his philosophy that had not been tested by experiment. This banished, although not for all time, the notion that man could grasp a few general truths from experiment and *reason* from them to describe the world. Newton's second general principle argued that of all possible explanations for any phenomena the simplest one must be accepted. This law of parsimony has proved a useful concept for all types of research since that time.

Newtonian science was, in a very real way, the heir to the tradition of Galileo and Kepler. It is Cartesian only in that it assumes that the world can be explained in terms of geometry; its methods and assumptions, like Galileo's, dealt with brute fact rather than theory. And like Galileo and Kepler, Newton had assumptions that he did not take into account. For example, his Cartesian belief that God was a master mathematician-architect who had created the universe blinded him to the fact that the universe had a *long* history and that, in order to understand the universe, its history must be reconstructed.

Newton's discovery of the law of universal gravitation and the very audacity of his great book may have had an unfortunate effect upon the development of science in the early eighteenth century. His prestige as a scientist lent veracity to his book on optics, which proposed a theory of light less susceptible to further research than that proposed by his contemporary, Huygens. The notion that the *Principia* had lighted up the dark corners of the universe seems to have momentarily deterred others from poking around in them. It may be, however, that Newton's theories took men as far as they were ready to go. New postulates about matter and the earth had to be developed before more progress could be made. His book does, however, stand at the end of the seventeenth century as a magnificent milestone marking off the progress that had been made since the days of Copernicus. For the first time in the history of man as an inhabitant of the planet, it was possible to understand much of the mechanics of the universe in which he found himself. In times past, men had *guessed* many things about the world, but seventeenth-century men had devised tools of language (mathematics) and of precision (telescopes, barometers, and so forth) that allowed them to go far beyond mere guesswork. This was the first great harvest of the scientific revolution: by concentrating attention on the *mechanics* of the world, men had developed a new cosmology that was destined to revolutionize many aspects of their lives.

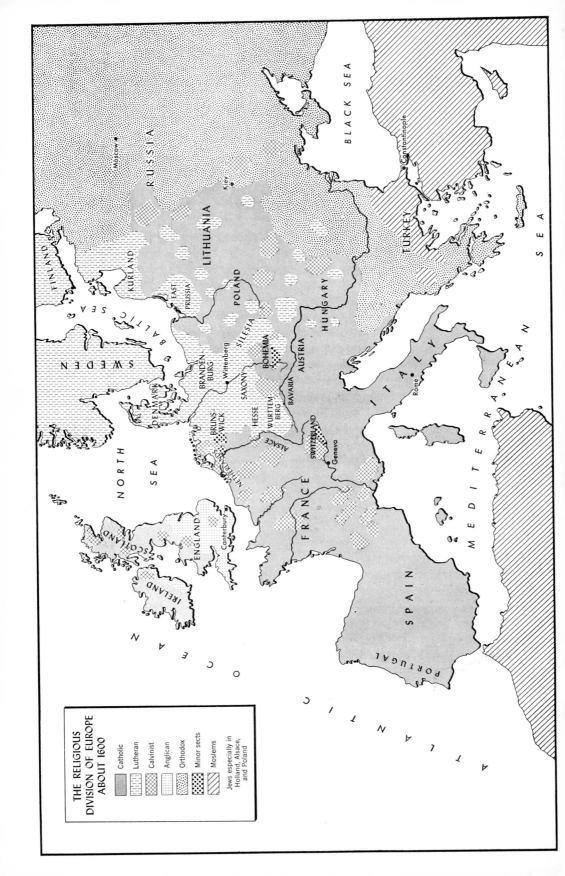

THE RELIGIOUS
DIVISION OF EUROPE
ABOUT 1600

Catholic
Lutheran
Calvinist
Anglican
Orthodox
Minor sects
Moslems

Jews especially in
Holland, Alsace,
and Poland

RUSSIA

Moscow

Kiev

LITHUANIA

FINLAND

KURLAND

BALTIC SEA

EAST
PRUSSIA

POLAND

SILESIA

SWEDEN

BRANDEN-
BURG

Wittenberg

SAXONY

BOHEMIA

DENMARK

HESSE

WURTTEM-
BERG

AUSTRIA

HUNGARY

BAVARIA

BRUNS-
WICK

NETHERLANDS

ALSACE

SWITZERLAND

Geneva

NORTH
SEA

SCOTLAND

ENGLAND

Canterbury

IRELAND

FRANCE

ITALY

Rome

SPAIN

PORTUGAL

MEDITERRANEAN
SEA

ATLANTIC
OCEAN

BLACK SEA

TURKEY

Constantinople

Chapter 18

GOD, MAN, AND THE WORLD

1. CATHOLIC VERSUS CALVINIST

The religious map of Europe at the end of the sixteenth century had already achieved a stability that was to last, with minor alterations, into the twentieth century. Latin Europe, part of the Rhineland, the Spanish Netherlands, southern Germany and Hapsburg central Europe, Ireland, and Poland remained with the old church. Northern Germany and Scandinavia became Lutheran. Calvinism extended from Switzerland down the Rhine to the Netherlands, to England and Scotland, with enclaves in southern France, northern Germany, and Hungary. On the frontiers there were to be minor changes in the two centuries following the reform, and enclaves like those in southern France and Hungary were virtually to disappear. However, the apparent stability of this map masks the fact that the religious ferment did not end with the heroic epoch of the Reformation. Once the unity of the old church was shattered, reformers arose with amazing regularity to demand new reforms in both the old and the new churches.

By the opening of the seventeenth century, Lutheranism had lost most of its revolutionary force. Many of its ministers had become conservative time-servers, interested only in the *status quo*. Since the prince as head both of the church and state had the right to determine the religion of his subjects, there was little need for proselytizing nor much point in working hard to retain church membership. However, while the Lutherans stood still, the Catholics and the Calvinists moved forward. They encroached on Lutheran Europe, and fought each other with all the weapons at hand.

The reforming popes, the decrees of the Council of Trent, the Holy Office of the Inquisition, and the Jesuit, Capuchin, and other reforming orders presented a many-sided Catholic attack upon the reformed churches. The Catholic effort to reconquer Europe embodied a program similar to the ones adopted by earlier reforms in the church; through education of the talented youth and advice and counsel to the governing class, the church hoped to hold and reconvert the elite of society. Through founding orders to perform good works among the poor, the aged, the sick, and the orphaned, it hoped to popularize its program with the people. The Catholic church had always emphasized good works; thus its sixteenth- and seventeenth-century "social security" program merely underlined the church's continued conviction that God's work on earth included caring for the unfortunate. The development of education and advice for the wealthy bourgeoisie, noblemen, and princes, on the other hand, was a new aggressive course of action; the great successes of this labor is often associated with the work of the Jesuit order.

The Jesuits stand out as the most important educational force in the Catholic world. Their schools and colleges were scattered all over Europe, and the quality of their secular education as well as their spiritual teaching attracted the elite among the Catholic population. While they adopted St. Thomas as their theologian, the Jesuits also integrated the new humanist learning in their program of studies. The result was that Jesuit education was "modern" in every way, and rightfully attracted a large student body. The roll call of the Catholic writers, statesmen, and soldiers of the seventeenth century is almost identical with the list of the most prominent of the Jesuits' students. It is astonishing to note how many of the leaders of the period were products of their schools.

On the level of statecraft, too, the Jesuits played an important role. They were the confessors of princes all over Catholic Europe. Their moral teaching may be accused of being lax in political matters, but they kept before their charges the needs of the Catholic church. The Jesuit doctrine of probabilism made permissible any act that *any* moralist had ever condoned, even though all the rest of the moral teachers of the world might condemn it. In a way it became difficult to sin; indeed, a wag spoke of the Jesuits as the men who had taken away the sins of the world. Princes, however, often seemed to need, or at least to appreciate, such spiritual advice. Among the members of the Order were some of the cleverest, best-educated men of the age. Inevitably, they also became the political advisers of princes. The Spanish and Austrian Hapsburgs and the German Catholic princes unhesitatingly employed Jesuits. The French kings relied more upon their rivals, the Capuchins, for diplomatic and political advice and services.

Behind this effort to direct the consciences and policies of princes was the reformed papal curia at Rome. The latter sixteenth- and the seventeenth-century popes were often puritanical men who, for example, ordered fig leaves placed on the pagan statues collected by their more liberal predecessors; they were also vigorous in suppressing abuses and in working for the unity of Catholic Europe. Henry IV found it easy to divorce his first wife when his second was to be Marie de Medici, a granddaughter of a Hapsburg archduke. Marie in turn secured ready support from Rome to help arrange the marriage of her son, Louis XIII, to Anne of Austria, daughter of the king of

Spain. The papacy was anxious to bring together all the forces of Catholic Europe for an assault on the Protestants. However, on many occasions the papal court found itself faced with difficult choices. The policies of Catholic princes were often politically oriented, and the popes therefore had to take care to prevent the papacy from becoming subordinated to Hapsburg or Bourbon interests. Thus, papal policy sometimes appeared contradictory, when in fact it was only trying to retain its independence.

On other levels of Catholic society attempts to reform the church developed political importance. The Council of Trent had given attention to the training of priests. In the early years of the seventeenth century, new seminaries appeared and increased attention was given to strengthening the spiritual mission of the clergy. One of the most important developments was the rise of the Oratory, an organization devoted to the training of clergymen who ministered to the people. Under the vigorous direction of the great French cardinal Bérulle, the Oratory became a spiritual as well as a political force of great importance. On the spiritual side, Bérulle taught an Augustinian doctrine of the necessity to love God with emphasis upon Jesus. His theocentrism was almost violent. On the political side the Oratory became the very center of the so-called "Devout Party" which, as we have noted, advocated a combined Bourbon-Hapsburg assault on the "enemies of God" (the Protestants).

The Calvinists had no centralized direction comparable to that of the Catholics, nor did their beliefs allow them to organize good works to propagandize their cause. Nonetheless, they, too, had fire behind their will to power. The Geneva-trained Calvinist preachers who traveled incessantly from one Reformed community to another displayed a devotion to the "cause" equal to that shown by the Jesuits, and almost seemed to have had as highly centralized a direction from Geneva as the Jesuits had from Rome. Since ability to read was essential for a Christian to have access to the Bible, the Calvinists tried to teach all their people to read. The schools and colleges that then appeared, particularly in the Netherlands but also elsewhere in Calvinist Europe, were excellent for that day. Nor did education end with school. The heart of the Calvinist service was a sermon on theology or doctrine, and thus the church service became a classroom. There were many men in the congregation whose studies would qualify them for a Doctorate in Divinity.

The Calvinists, too, possessed a doctrine with as much appeal in certain classes as the Jesuit doctrines had in others. They taught that all callings were "vocations"; man could serve God as a merchant, a candlestick maker, or a sailor, as well as a preacher or a theologian. All work thus became prayer offered up to God. God for His part blessed the work of His people, and thus worldly success indicated His approval. This was a comfortable doctrine for city people who had heard their profits called sinful usury by Catholic theologians. These people, too, were the ones who possessed the wealth that could be used for God's intentions, even if that included the raising of rebellion.

As statesmen and plotters, the Calvinists were nearly the equals of the Jesuits. As we have already seen, the integration of the Huguenot cause in France under the leadership of the Condé-Bourbon family before Henry IV became king was a masterpiece of political strategy. The diplomacy of the House of Orange-Nassau in the Netherlands that led to independence of those provinces proved the skill of the Calvinists, while the lines of intrigue that surrounded the young Count Frederick of the Palatinate about the time he became king of Bohemia were indicative of their ambitions. Young Frederick's own statements that he wanted the crown for the service of God and "the religion" indicated the considerations that were paramount in his mind.

2. THE UNITY OF CHRISTENDOM AND THE STATE CHURCHES

The idea that the Christian church in Europe could be split into segments was scandalous to many men who considered the unity of Christendom the most important influence for good in the world. This accounts in part for the vigor with which men fought religious wars to force heretics to return to the faith; it also accounts for the enormous intellectual effort made by publicists, theologians, historians, and others to convince their fellow men of the validity of a particular religious belief. Many men, trying to sound the depths of the problem, were astonished that the Christian community had broken apart. Indeed, the religious picture of Europe about 1600 did present a problem. However, the differences between the several competing churches were not really great if either the whole spectrum of man's religious beliefs, or simply the body of Christian teaching were considered. All of the churches accepted the Christian tradition as it was embodied in the Nicene Creed: they believed in a Trinitarian God, the redemption through Christ, the mission of the Christian church. They differed on questions of ritual, salvation (by faith, by good works), predestination or free will, and the real presence of God in the consecrated bread. Many of these differences had also existed within the Christian church throughout the Middle Ages; they were essentially insoluble problems, and in a sense they existed outside the fundamental tenets of Christianity. Charles V and later thinkers like Grotius and Leibniz could not, or at least refused to, understand the divisive factor between the Christian sects. It was the history of the religious rebellion that had created new institutions with divergent notions of church government and organization. It was the history that seared men's souls with religious wars fought with pens as well as with swords. Seventeenth-century men had little knowledge of history and less understanding of the force of historical processes. They could not appreciate the power of the past, and yet it was the past that separated the Christian communities and underlined the current divergences in the attitudes of Christian men.

In the course of the seventeenth century there were several serious proposals for reuniting the Christian community of the West. In 1627 Grotius (1583–1645) published his book *De Veritate Religionis Christianae* in which he argued that it was possible to end the unhappy disorder that had overtaken the Christian church. The book was a success and its author was hailed as a great thinker, but nothing came of it because the book basically failed to take into account the fact that the Christian community had been broken up into a series of rival religious institutions; it was no longer merely a question of differences in ideas. A half century later, after many other similar proposals had been put forward, Leibniz (1646–1716) produced a plan for the unity of the churches of Europe. To his lucid intellect, the problem was simple enough, for he understood that the doctrinal differences were capable of resolution and he had every hope that the influential Bishop Bossuet (1627–1704) would join him in healing the breach. After years of fruitless negotiation, he discovered that time could not be reversed and that Bishop Bossuet was more interested in converting the distinguished German philosopher than in healing the wounds of Christendom. There were to be other plans postulated regarding the unification of Christendom, but all of them were to be shipwrecked upon the same shoals, for by the seventeenth century the work of the Reformation had been incorporated in the political and economic institutions of Europe; great vested interests in the form of state churches had come into being and stood ready to defend their positions and resist any effort to reimpose unity of faith.

In Protestant countries the organization of state churches sometimes presented problems within the church itself, but there was no question about their independence from authorities outside the community (such as the pope). In Lutheran countries the prince assumed control, and appointed bishops or presidents to manage the church in his name. In England Parliament determined church organization and doctrine, but left the management of the church to the episcopal hierarchy. In some Calvinist lands the prince dictated ecclesiastical policy, just as he did in Lutheran states; in others, the church achieved independence of the state as a corporation in the community, and as often as not became the force dictating to the government itself. We should note at this point that wherever the caesaro-papist (king and pope in one person) solution was found (England, Germany, and Scandinavia), church services tended to become formalized and the spiritual interests of the church tended to be subordinated to its administration. The ruling class usually made these state churches into instruments for maintaining its hold on the society. As we shall see, this solution led to secularism and new religious revolts.

In Catholic countries the papal power theoretically remained intact, but actually there also emerged state churches in a very real sense. France is the classic example. The Gallican (French) church has two traditions. The first goes back to the days of the Babylonian Captivity, when the French bishops assumed the right to run the French church. This doctrine had at its heart the right of the cathedral chapter to elect its bishop and the right of the bishops to decide questions of doctrine and government in the church. In its most extreme form in the seventeenth century certain bishops insisted that their position over their diocese was the same as the pope's over his diocese in Rome. Thus, the pope would become first among equals rather than supreme ruler of the church. The second Gallican tradition developed from the early sixteenth-century concordat between Francis I and Rome, by which the king obtained the right to appoint bishops, abbots, and abbesses, while the pope retained the right to install them in office. In effect, the church was made a branch of the king's government. The concordat provided the economic benefits to be shared between pope and king, with the lion's share going to the king.

In the course of the sixteenth and seventeenth centuries royal Gallicanism was expanded and developed to strengthen the authority of the king. At one point, when the Estates-General met in 1614–1615, it almost seemed that, like the Anglican church, the Gallican church might withdraw from the Roman Catholic community. It required all the diplomatic finesse that the friends of the papacy could muster to prevent the Third Estate from demanding a "Gallican oath" that would have, in effect, separated the French church from Rome. The members of the Third Estate blamed the ultramontanes (those men who looked "beyond the mountain" to Rome for guidance) for the murder of Henry IV.

In 1682 under Louis XIV the assembly of the French church tried to define its position toward the papacy by the "Four Articles on the Liberties of the Gallican Church." The first gave to popes spiritual, but not temporal, power; the popes were denied the power to absolve subjects from allegiance to the king. The second, recalling the decrees of the Council of Constance, suggested the supremacy of a General Council of the church over the pope. The third defined papal power in France in terms of custom and treaties; and the fourth granted the pope the right to decide matters of faith pending the convocation of a Council. Although Louis XIV had to back down from his extreme position a decade or so later when his armies were beaten, his finances in disorder, and the need for papal support urgent, yet the "Four Articles" were not out of line with the actual religious policy and program of the Catholic kings of France.

In Catholic countries like Spain or the Hapsburg Danubian states the monarchy tended to maintain control over the church within its boundaries. The kings appointed high churchmen to office, and expected them to act as agents for the extension of the royal power. As a result, from kingdom to kingdom there were numerous differences in the constitution of the Catholic church. Even in matters of doctrine there were problems: for example, the decrees of the Council of Trent were never proclaimed in France; the Spanish and the Roman Inquisitions were different institutions; and the Inquisition was never established in France. Throughout the Catholic community problems of faith were referred to Rome when the local clergy found them too difficult doctrinally or politically to handle, but, nonetheless, the Catholic church, too, had become a state church in most of the kingdoms of Europe where Catholicism was the dominant religion.

3. REFORMERS OF THE REFORMATION SETTLEMENTS

The institution of state churches could not still the cries of men for spiritual reforms, and the great theological debate of the sixteenth century had left unsettled many problems that demanded further exploration. The Reformation era coincided with the development of the printing press, and Europe was flooded with books, pamphlets, histories, and polemics dealing with theology and religion. Most of them did not criticize their own postulates, some of them were violent in their language, but the total effect of this mass of literature was to make religious issues the current merchandise for all who could read. Since Luther and the other reformers had broken with the authority of Rome, it was impossible to impose a dogmatic pattern or interpretation on Europe, and every man, on becoming his own theologian, had a tendency to develop his own heresy.

In general, the continuing Reformation, with variations in Catholic, Calvinist, and Lutheran lands, tended to spiritualize religion and to lay down austere moral codes. The Catholic Jansenist, the Calvinist Puritan, and the Lutheran Pietist, all might well have been surprised to know that an historian would group them together, for they themselves would tend to emphasize their differences rather than their similarities. Nonetheless, they had much in common in their attempts to give greater spiritual content to the state religion, even if that meant opposing the practices of kings. They were also alike in their strict, puritanical code of morals and manners that, to the modern mind, seem narrow-minded but were probably natural reactions to the moral laxity of the seventeenth century.

Jansenism

The Jansenist movement was largely confined to the Walloon Lowlands and France. Cornelius Jansen (1585-1638) was a theologian at the University of Louvain whose studies of Saint Augustine convinced him that the Thomist theology of the Jesuits was erroneous. His own doctrine, though strictly within the framework of Catholic ritual and practice, was theologically closely akin to that of Calvin who was also deeply influenced by St. Augustine. When Jansen's *Augustinus* was published in 1640, it had immediate success among his friends in France. They liked the grandeur of Saint Augustine that shone through the pedantry of the author. In direct contrast to Jesuit philosophy which was trying to open the gates of heaven to all sinners—indeed, trying to explain away sin itself—Jansen's teachings strictly limited the number to whom God would grant grace for salvation. Only the elite could hope to enter the Jansenist heaven.

The church, however, immediately pounced on his doctrine for it made the church unnecessary. In 1642 Pope Urban VIII condemned five propositions of the *Augustinus:* (1) that certain of God's commands are impossible even for a good man to meet, (2) that God's grace is irresistible, (3) that freedom from compulsion, but not freedom from necessity, is requisite for meriting reward or punishment, (4) that man cannot choose either to resist or to accept God's grace, and (5) that Christ died for the elite only and not for all men. There was no doubt that these propositions were within the meaning of Jansen's doctrine, but the French Jansenists did not wish to break either with Rome or with Jansenism. Just as Descartes had to find a "formula" to interpret the church's decree about the heliocentric universe, so the Jansenists looked for a loophole. One of their theological leaders, Arnauld, proved that he was truly the son of a lawyer, for he agreed that the five propositions merited condemnation, but insisted that the pope erred in thinking that they were to be found in the *Augustinus*. What the pope condemned, therefore, was not Jansenism but something else. Not unlike the Puritans in England, the Jansenists in France discovered that their religious beliefs also placed them in opposition to the political aspirations of the king. They disliked Louis XIII and Richelieu as much as the Puritans disliked Charles I and Laud; the development of greater centralized authority and royal power conflicted with their notions of political pluralism. The government responded to their hostility in kind. One of their first leaders, the Abbé de St. Cyran, was imprisoned by Richelieu; the whole movement was involved in the Fronde, and thereby incurred the hostility of both Mazarin and Louis XIV, and Louis continued to persecute them throughout his life.

The movement, as a spiritual and religious force, had as its headquarters the convent of Port Royal which was under the direction of Arnauld's sister. Around Port Royal Jansenist scholars and writers established schools, and the convent was a place of retreat for people anxious to find some peace in the world. When, however, the nuns were dispersed at the order of the government, it was discovered that they were simply pious creatures on whom theological subtleties were really lost. They knew little theology beyond a few catch phrases, but they so ardently desired to be martyrs that they made a nuisance of themselves in the convents to which they were assigned. The teachers and theologians who settled around Port Royal, on the other hand, were serious thinkers, pious men, and sincere Christians deeply influenced by the teachings of their sect. By the mid-seventeenth century their "little schools" were rivals to the Jesuit colleges, and their influence was felt widely in French society. It was in defense of their pious life and to challenge their Jesuit enemies that Pascal wrote his famous *Letters to a Provincial Friend* in which he contrasted the "true Christian virtues" of the Jansenists with the moral laxness of the Jesuits. Pascal's book removed the spotlight of criticism from the Jansenists and placed it upon their detractors.

For the next half century Jansenism hovered between acceptance by the church and summary condemnation as a heresy. Jansenist bishops and theologians, unwilling to break with the church, stood by their formula for evading condemnation by the papacy or the Sorbonne: they admitted freely that the propositions condemned were heretical, but denied that they were Jansenist. Other factors helped them. The Jansenists were sincere men whose Christian virtues could hardly be denied, and when they came before the parlements for trial, both the austerity of the men and the implicit Gallicism of the movement recommended itself to the judges and prevented drastic action. At Rome, too, the Curia was loath to act against men whose lives were so obviously Christian. One pope, Innocent XI, was so friendly to the Jansenists that he was called a Jansenist pope.

Jansenism, however, was incompatible with Catholicism as it was constituted, and eventually it was definitely declared to be heretical. In the early eighteenth century two bulls, *Vinean Domini* (1705) and *Unigenitus* (1713), condemned the doctrine, and Louis XIV ordered the chapel at Port Royal destroyed and the tombs of certain Jansenist saints desecrated. The movement had thus apparently been thrust out of the church, and yet that was not quite so, because many French Catholics, clergy as well as laymen, simply held their peace and waited for an opportunity to obtain a reversal of the decision.

In the early 1730's miracles began to occur at the tomb of a Jansenist deacon in Paris. When the government closed the cemetery, a wit put up the sign:

> De par le roi, défense à Dieu
> De faire miracle en ce lieu.
> ("By order of the King, God is forbidden
> to perform a miracle at this place.")

Professor Preserved Smith remarks: "The Frenchman of the eighteenth century no longer cared who wrote the creeds of his church, if he could write its epigrams." This is not quite true, of course, for Jansenist ideas continued in the French church, and the Jansenists were among those who finally revenged themselves on the Jesuits by helping to secure the dissolution and disbandment of that order. Furthermore, Jansenist tendencies in the French church migrated to Ireland and Bavaria, and from thence to America where they have had great influence.

Puritanism

The seventeenth-century Puritans were much less docile than the Jansenists. Whatever one might think of their tight-laced morals, their meddlesome attitude toward pleasure and art, their narrow-mindedness, and other such "vices," the Puritan doctrine nurtured a race of strong men. Their industry, thrift, and vision carved a commonwealth out of the wilderness in America, overthrew and beheaded a king in England, and provided the backbone for the creation of the state that successfully defied the power first of Spain and then of France. Puritanism as an expression of Calvinist doctrine was found principally in England and the Netherlands. The Puritans developed something of the same theological conflicts that confronted the Jansenists.

After Elizabeth the English church was somewhat Calvinistic in doctrine, but there was also left in England an important doctrinal stream that was closer to Catholicism than to Calvinism. The church in the Low Countries was also divided between the Puritans (high Calvinists) and the *Rekkelyken* or Latitudinarians who owed much of their religious doctrine to Erasmus. This latter group was tolerant and liberal; they, like the "Catholic" Anglicans, took little interest in the theological wrangle between the "supralapsarian" and the "sublapsarian" theories of predestination. The former taught that God had chosen his saints from all time; the latter insisted that Adam had been free, and God only predestined men after Adam's fall.

The man whose name was attached to the liberalization of Calvinism was Jacob Arminius (1560–1609), professor of theology at Leyden. He started out to refute the Erasmian liberals, but developed doubts of his own that led him to propose serious modifications of Calvinist theology. By its insistence upon predestination, Calvin's doctrine seemed to make God the author of sin; Arminius proposed that Christ should be considered the mediator who would save all who reached for salvation. Grace then became something that man could achieve by striving for it. Arminius' doctrine was shocking to the orthodox Calvinists. It implied that infants who died without baptism as well as virtuous heathens could be saved; it also meant that Luther and Calvin were in error, that man was justified by good works as well as by faith.

At the height of the controversy which swept the whole Calvinist community, the Arminians published their "Remonstrance of 1610" in which they pointed out wherein they differed with the conservative Puritans. Eight years later a General Synod of the Calvinist community was held at Dort (Dordrecht) to discuss the question. The majority present was from the Netherlands, even though Scotch, English, Swiss, and German divines were also there, and of the whole group only two or three were Arminians. The result was a foregone conclusion: Arminianism was declared to be heretical, even though the Synod could not agree on the "supralapsarian" or the "sublapsarian" theories.

In England the upper clergy and a considerable number of the theologians were either Arminian or close to the Roman Catholic position. These "High Churchmen" were so out of sympathy with the radicals that the Puritan Calvinists tended to have trouble in the Anglican church, and therefore began to develop sectarian creeds. In the Netherlands, on the other hand, the anti-Arminianists were in the majority and used the religious issue as a political club by which the House of Orange excluded an important segment of the liberal, wealthy bourgeoisie from power. Thus Arminianism tended to smolder in the Netherlands, while in England Puritanism became a revolutionary doctrine directed against the king and the church organization.

The English Puritans, in addition to their strict Calvinist interpretation of predestination, developed very strong opinions about ritual and government in the church. As rigid Calvinists, they wished to banish any formalism that might suggest the Roman church. They became almost fanatical opponents of the bishops and the whole episcopal structure of church government. They proposed three possible (acceptable) solutions for church government. The first was the Puritan church governed by lay commissioners that would exclude all other groups and force all to belong to the Puritan congregation; the second was the Scottish Presbyterian solution of a church controlled by synods and general assemblies; and the third was the congregational organization, allowing each church to determine its own practice. None of these solutions left any place for bishops whose role and office seemed to the Calvinists to be tainted with "Romanism."

The English Puritans were not just debaters. They became the backbone of the opposition to Charles I; they won the civil war; and they beheaded the king. Once in power, their narrow-minded conception of manners and morals, their hostility to pleasure, and their self-righteous assurance that they alone knew God's will made them irksome to the majority of Englishmen; and they were unable to impose their church or their church government on England beyond the limits held by the Puritan army. Thus, when the war and the Commonwealth were finally brought to an end and Charles II had returned to the throne (1660), the English Parliament gladly passed laws excluding the "saints" from toleration.

A twentieth-century critic must be careful in discussing the seventeenth-century Puritans. Like so many of their contemporaries of all religious beliefs, they were firmly convinced that they did God's will on earth. Such knowledge has strength as well as weakness, and its strength gave the Puritans the power to build empires, to write books, and to tear down social structures that they considered an abomination. The execution of Charles I may have made him into an Anglican saint, but it also served notice to future English kings about the temper of England. The fact that the Puritans did not gain control of the Anglican church made them unwilling allies of English Jesuits in fighting for the toleration which was eventually granted to the dissenting sects after 1688. In Milton, the Puritans produced one of the great lofty writers of moral literature; through Bunyan they expressed their naïve world view in the most successful allegory ever written.

Sectarianism

It would not be profitable to examine in detail the varieties of religious doctrine that emerged from the Puritan movement. The Puritan cults that developed in England were the work of men more filled with enthusiasm than learned in the wisdom of the world. The emphasis upon Bible reading and the endless theological discussions led every man to become a theologian, and some showed less stability than others. Literally dozens of sects appeared. The usual pattern included millenary doctrine, emotional congregational participation in oral confessions, and ecstatic exclamations about salvation. These people, "filled with the Lord," made the idea of religious enthusiasm repugnant to their more conservative and perhaps better educated neighbors. Locke, for example, condemned "enthusiasm" (literally, "filled with God") as folly or worse.

One sect that developed in the mid-seventeenth century had the fortune to attract men and women who were better educated than its founder. George Fox (1624-91) was a pure-minded, if somewhat simple man. Like so many others, he felt the call to provide his neighbors with a way to salvation. His meetings were more austere than the usual Puritan service. The congregation sat quietly until a member was "moved" to speak, sometimes in "tongues" that neither he nor the others understood. They called themselves "Friends," but their practice of shaking physically while testifying gave them the name "Quakers." They had many practices that set them aside from the rest of the community: they wore hats on all occasions, they used "thou" instead of "you," they dressed plainly, and they refused to bear arms. Perhaps the most famous single act of the group was the settlement of Pennsylvania, where they found asylum and opportunity to practice their religion without interference. Like most of the sects that developed on the fringe of the Puritan movement, the Quakers actually were as much in the Anabaptist tradition as in the Puritan.

In Germany the spiritual side of Puritanism could not reach the Lutheran community in part because of the conflicts between the two reformed religions. The Calvinists objected to the Lutheran doctrine of the presence of Christ in the bread and wine. They called the Lutheran sacrament *Herrgottsfresserei* ("a gobbling up of the Lord God"). The Lutherans called the Calvinists "Mohammedans." The book and pamphlet war between the two was a disgraceful performance. Yet even though Puritanism did not succeed in Germany, there developed in the Lutheran community a doctrine of practical mysticism, if we may use such a description, called Pietism. In many ways it resembled Puritanism.

The founder of Pietism was Philip Jacob Spener (1635-1705), who wrote books recommending Bible reading, prayer, congregational participation in services, and a strict moral code. As the movement developed, it became the nearest counterpart to the Catholic idea of good works and prayer that could develop in an atmosphere of justification by faith. The Pietists wrote sentimental hymns, urged devout Christian moral conduct, gathered in prayer meetings, and discussed their religious experiences with each other. The movement had difficulty finding popular support in Germany because the state-controlled Lutheran churches were not sympathetic, but its spiritual appeal brought it a wide acceptance among the upper classes of the land. In the eighteenth century the movement flowered in German literature and in the Methodist movement in England.

The most unusual doctrine that tried to remain within the Christian frame of reference grew out of the teachings of Fausto Sozzini (1539-1604), an Italian who denied the trinity and the deity of Christ, but accepted the divine inspiration of the Scriptures. The Unitarian movement was slow to make converts as much because of the novelty of the idea as because of the hostility of both the princes and the established church. Usually wherever toleration was granted to different Christian sects, the Socinian Unitarians were specifically excluded from its benefits. Nonetheless, throughout northern Europe there were independent souls who found Socinian teachings satisfied their needs.

The Jansenists, the Puritans, the Quakers, the Pietists, the Unitarians, and the other sects that sought to reform the State churches of seventeenth-century Europe all played important roles in the society of their day. Their stubborn insistence upon the right of an individual to worship God without the interference of the princes of churches and state was unquestionably one of the important forces in the development of the ideals of individual liberty that have set western civilization apart from all other civilizations of the earth. Their own better educated contemporaries and the more sophisticated generations that followed them have often been unkind in comments and criticism, yet we must not miss the fact that these religious enthusiasts, as much as the great scientists and literary men, were favoring political, social, and religious patterns that became characteristic of western civilization.

4. THE MYSTICS

From its earliest years Christianity has always produced mystics. Some of them, like Thomas à Kempis, have been made saints; others, like the seventeenth-century Molinos, have been declared heretics. In both the Lutheran and in the Catholic community of the seventeenth century, mystics appeared to add variety to the religious picture.

In Germany Jacob Böhme (1575–1624), a cobbler from Görlitz, produced a book called *Aurora* (1612) that became a handbook for German mysticism. It was a curious mixture of Paracelsus, Schwenckfeld, and other mystics who had tried to proclaim the message that God is all and man must bury himself in God. Reason had nothing to do with this doctrine of the *"Urgrund"* which turns out to be both the primordial stuff of the world and an abyss that swallows up everything. Böhme and his followers had had a religious experience by which they identified themselves with the eternal and made the eternal responsible for their will.

In the Catholic community, a Spanish monk called Molinos and a French woman named Madame Guyon initiated a mystic doctrine called Quietism. It developed the curious notion that man's will could be completely absorbed by God, and, therefore, that promptings to action were God's words spoken directly to the human heart. As long as such notions were the property of people whose desires were consonant with Christian ethics, those "promptings" might seem to be the words of God, but when the church discovered that no little amount of moral disorder, particularly sexual behavior, could be excused as God's prompting, the authorities became alarmed. Molinos was tried by the Roman Inquisition and kept in close confinement for life. Madame Guyon's books were condemned. Both of them seem to have been sincere Christians, anxious to do God's will and to humble themselves before the authority of the church. Bishop Fénelon tried to defend Madame Guyon, but when Rome condemned her books, he, too, accepted the church's decision.

Religious mysticism is difficult to understand; it is even more difficult to explain, for explanation involves a rational statement of an emotion, a feeling, a conviction that is itself essentially irrational and unexplainable.

5. LIBERTINES, DOUBTS, AND DOUBTERS

The very violence of the religious debate made other men question the validity of any of the arguments. When Catholic, Calvinist, Lutheran, and Anabaptist all confounded each other and turned their creeds into engines of civil war and bloodshed, a few men stood aside, wondering if *all* the accusations might not be right, all the creeds wrong. Undoubtedly Bishop Bossuet was correct when he pointed out that the differences within the Christian church were at the roots of skepticism about the truths of Christianity, but this intrafaith debate was not the only source for the development of skepticism.

It was natural that the discovery and popularization of the pagan essayists, moralists, and philosophers should convert some men to the pagan conception of life. In the latter sixteenth century Seneca, Epicurus, Zeno, Marcus

Aurelius, Epictetus, and other classical authors were widely read among the upper classes. These authors spoke with a serenity and urbanity unknown to most of the religious writers of the day; they assumed a world with postulates more carefully examined than those developed in the pamphlets of the fanatics who *knew* that God had given them personally the word. Furthermore, the Roman writers spoke about a life and morality more closely related to the comfortable existence of the wealthy than were the stern teachings of the reformers. The word "libertine" that came to be applied to the converts to pagan culture took on a double meaning. It implied both "liberty" from Christian doctrine and looseness of morality.

As the world was organized in the early seventeenth century, it was unwise to be too explicit about unbelief or even doubts. A Montaigne could suggest his questions by subtle essays that never quite joined conflict with the predominant Christian views. Hobbes could write philosophy and political theory based upon assumptions that were surely not Christian, yet he was careful not to disassociate himself from the Christian community. It was asserted that there were fifty thousand atheists (that is, non-Christians) in and around Paris alone, but it would be difficult to identify many of them by any overt words spoken to their contemporaries or left for posterity. Thus, we know about these people who first questioned the dogmatic structure of Christianity from the writings of their Christian enemies more than from their own words. Not until the end of the seventeenth century did the "libertine" tradition become clearly identified and frankly admitted by its followers. These men, many of them men of wealth and education, showed less willingness to be martyrs for their beliefs than the poor, relatively uneducated Puritan fanatics who were filled with religious enthusiasm. It may well be that their skepticism extended to their own beliefs as well as to those of others.

As the seventeenth century progressed, there were other developments that added to the mounting skepticism about western traditions. Of these, none was more important than the gradual realization that there were civilizations other than that of western Christendom and that there were also divergent systems of morality. The sixteenth-century explorers had been soldiers, sailors, merchants, and missionaries; none of these groups had had any special appreciation for the people they encountered. By the seventeenth century, an increasing number of travelers were sensitive men who took the trouble to learn the strange languages and to study the customs of the people they visited. When these men began to write travel books, they raised important questions about morality and religion. Since each quarter of the seventeenth century saw the publication of about twice as many such travel books as had its predecessor, there was by the end of that century a considerable volume of travel literature available in Europe.

After the second half of the seventeenth century, the reading public was also able to obtain "geographies" that were, in effect, summaries of the descriptions found in the travel literature. Thus, the problem of comparative morality and comparative religions became sharply defined as the cultures of the world were placed side by side. Another source of this sharp definition was the inventions of many of the travelers themselves who, disgruntled and dissatisfied with European society, did not hesitate to point up the differences, even to create myths, that could be used to show the superiority of other civilizations over that of Europe or of other religions over Christianity. The ideas of social, ethical, and religious relativism were slow to sink into the consciousness of Europe, but by the end of the seventeenth century they had begun to create a crisis in the thinking of many western men.

This cultural relativism became a public scandal to the Catholic community when certain Jesuit priests proposed to enroll the whole Confucian society of China into the Catholic church. Jesuit missionaries were impressed by the purity of Chinese monotheism and by the lofty nature of Chinese moral teaching. They thought it possible to convert all the Chinese by winning over the emperor, just as the early Christians had won the Roman Empire through Constantine. In Europe, however, far from the influences that were conditioning Jesuit thought in China, such a proposal appeared in a different light. Indeed, it seemed a scandalous proposition. Bishop Bossuet believed that it fundamentally undermined Christianity's claim to moral and religious superiority. Franciscan friars arrived in China attacking the aristocratic Jesuits, and with their aid the opponents of relativism arranged for the condemnation of the Jesuit proposal.

While cultural relativism was beginning to impress itself upon European consciences, the assumptions of the new science made serious inroads upon popular beliefs. People of the seventeenth century were credulous to an extreme. They still believed in all the popular superstitions of their medieval forebears and in a demonology as extensive as that of earlier epochs. There seemed to be nothing too outlandish for some men to believe. In the early part of the century there were outbursts of witch burning all over Europe on a scale unseen in earlier eras. This testimony of belief in the occult extended from his learned majesty, James I of England, down to the meanest peasant filled with fears of the unseen world.

But the occult—demons, witches, and the like—had no place in the world that science was unfolding. The assumption of a world regulated by law, rational as a geometric theorem, simply did not admit witches and wizards who might deal with devils. By the end of the seventeenth century educated men were about ready to give up belief in witches, demons, and other occult forces. A sophisticated English judge dismissed the case of a witch accused of riding a broomstick with the remark that there was no law against riding broomsticks. The great blows to such beliefs were struck by Pierre Bayle and Balthasar Bekker. In the 1680's the comet that Halley described and to which he gave his name created a sensation all over Europe. The ignorant in the streets, the classrooms, and the pulpits assumed that the comet was a sign from God, a prediction of some great event. Bayle used it as the opening gambit for a general attack on superstitions in his book, *Diverse Thoughts on the Comet*. A few years later Bekker's great book, *The Enchanted World* (1691), translated into all the major languages, did much to put an end to the enchantment. He examined and exposed the demonology of his day, so that no intelligent reader could subscribe to it any longer.

Cultural relativism and the postulates of a lawful world order were reinforced by historical studies that also produced questions. For example, Fontenelle's book, *The Oracles* (1686), showed that the oracles of Rome were undoubtedly frauds, and hinted that St. Jerome, St. Augustine, and St. Justin Martyr were either charlatans or dupes when they attempted to bolster Christian doctrine by using the testimony of the oracles to prove Christian truths. Chronologists, too, got into an argument over the date of the creation of the world. Was it 4000 or 4004 B.C., they asked. Historical students turned from Jewish accounts to Egyptian and Chinese to find the answer, only to discover that if Adam had arrived in 4004 B.C., according to these other records, he would, in fact, have been a late comer. This debate was so disturbing that Bishop Bossuet altered his last edition of his *Universal History* to take it into account. He extended time backward to nearly 6000 B.C., but he admitted that he could *not* account for the errors of the calculations.

Even more confusion developed when Father Richard Simon, a priest of the Oratory, published in succession *A Critical History of the Old Testament* (1679), *A Critical History of the Text of the New Testament* (1689), *A Critical History of the Versions of the New Testament* (1690), and *A Critical History of the Commentaries on the New Testament* (1693). It made no difference that his books were placed on the Index and banned from France; the deed had been done. Father Simon had treated the Biblical text just as he would any other, and with a thorough knowledge of Hebrew he showed that errors, additions, omissions, and transpositions had crept into the text. He thought he would bring confusion on the bibliolatrous Protestants and reestablish the true word of God, corrupted by centuries, but what he actually did was to throw doubt on the religious tradition of Christendom. "Nothing," wrote Father Arnauld, "could be more favorable to the Socinians."

Then Bayle added to the confusion by publishing his *Philosophical Dictionary*. This book became one of the most influential works of the whole period because it inspired the writings of most of the co-called *philosophes* of the next century. Bayle was the first to apply internal criticism to the Biblical stories. His entry on David, for example, was an attack on the morality of that Hebrew king as well as an argument against the divine inspiration of the Old Testament. His discussion of heresies of the past as well as of other cults reminds one of Gibbon who taught that all religions were equally true and equally false. These men were firing the opening shots of the eighteenth-century skeptics who were to attack the Christian tradition.

6. CARTESIAN ETHICS AND THEOLOGY

As we have noted, the scientists accepted a world governed by natural laws that could be expressed in terms of mathematics. Descartes assumed a world that was mechanical, that had been created by a master architect-mathematician God; Euclid, the geometer, had taken the place formerly held by Aristotle. Naturally then, both theology and ethics had to consider this new approach to the world. If truth were one, then these new truths could be brought into harmony with the truth of the Christian religion.

Descartes himself was deeply concerned with the theological implications of his work. He set out at once to prove the existence of God and to establish the relationship between the old doctrine and the new learning. His proof for the existence of God rested upon an assumption of innate ideas placed in the minds of men by their creator. His rationalization of the machine world and God involved acceptance of the dualism mind-matter, body-soul that was already familiar to Europeans. His theology, deeply influenced by St. Thomas, was orthodox in its orientation.

While Descartes shrank from the implications of a monist explanation of his machine world, Baruch Spinoza (1632–1677) had no such hesitations. Like Descartes, he was a mathematician. Perhaps his Jewish background allowed him to cast aside theological assumptions and thus to build a new pattern of explanation for the world. Instead of a Creator-God, Spinoza made creation itself God. "It follows solely from the perfection of God," he wrote, "that God never can decree nor ever has decreed anything but what is; that God did not exist before his decrees and the world did not exist without them." Such a doctrine was not for men who wanted a personal God interested in their welfare. Thus, both Christians and eighteenth-century Deists recoiled from Spinoza's strict logical deductions.

The Christians called Spinoza an atheist; the Deists later made fun of his system by schoolboy-type jokes that showed only how much they had missed the meaning of Spinoza's pantheism. The times were unready to listen to a philosopher who said that the soul is mortal, since it is united with the body, but immortal, since it is also united with God. Spinoza wrote a book on ethics which shows him to be one of the great Jewish prophets, an Isaiah or a St. Paul. In line with the mathematical thought of his era, his ethical system is presented in geometric terms with theorems, corollaries, definitions, axioms, and the rest of the apparatus of geometric thought. His language is sometimes difficult, but in its entirety it is a lofty statement of man's duties toward other men in the world. Despite his religious bent, however, Spinoza was expelled from the Jewish community and never accepted by his Christian neighbors. He made his living grinding lenses in Amsterdam. He had a few friends among the educated Dutch bourgeoisie, but for the most part he was ignored or neglected even by those who could understand what he was trying to do. By the nineteenth century, men could see that Spinoza had built a perfect temple on the limited beliefs of his era, a temple that could also be a mausoleum for the idea of a mechanical world.

In England and in France Christian theologians attempted to assimilate Cartesianism and the new science in the Christian tradition. The English Cambridge Platonists and a French priest, Malebranche (1638–1715), were the most conspicuous examples of this attempt. The problem appeared to be simple indeed. The scientists seemed to have "found" a world that had been created with a mathematical pattern of laws regulating its existence. Thus God could be deduced from His work. Difficulties arose, however, when the God who emerged as a master architect had to be identified with Jehovah of the Old Testament or Christ of the New. The impersonal God of the world-machine did not resemble the jealous and at times capricious Jehovah any more than He did the loving, forgiving, gentle Christ. As one of its critics pointed out, the new theology somehow overlooked the fact that it was not Christian.

In an effort to find a formula that would join the new age of science with the old Christian thought, the great chemist Robert Boyle (1627–1691) left a will in which a lecture fund was established to bring Christian truth to the world. One by one the English divines, Anglican and Dissenters, occupied the Boyle Chair for an exposition of their Christian philosophy. The results, however, were not universally satisfactory. As one wag put it: "No one ever doubted the existence of God until the Boyle lecturers tried to prove it." In the eighteenth century much of the intellectual effort that was expended to unify the new learning and Christianity was pounced upon by the Deists to prove their point. All that was needed was to reject revelation, and what was left was the Deist's God of Nature, a God revealed by the scientific discoveries of the era.

The first Deist books appeared at the end of the seventeenth century. John Locke, following his generation's urge to make Christianity agree with the learning of the day, wrote a book called *The Reasonableness of Christianity*. He had just reread the biblical account of the life of Christ and was struck as much by the personality of Jesus as by the fact that there were no creeds, no thirty-nine articles, and no theological discussion in the New Testament. His first convert, however, was the Deist John Toland, who added his contribution with the book, *Christianity Not Mysterious*. If mystery had no part in Christianity, why faith? Toland was of a very small company of men who were harbingers of the religious revolt of the eighteenth century, a rebellion that largely remained in the realm of philosophy but that was, in its way, as fundamental as the one led earlier by Luther and Calvin. The Deists, however, were unable to make an institution out of their beliefs before they were overwhelmed by ideas more radical than their own, and also answered by Christian thinkers who again returned to earlier patterns of religious expression.

BOOK IV

The Eighteenth Century: Threshold of a New World

In many ways the eighteenth century seems to be the opening of the contemporary era of European history; it also appears to be the threshold of the first era of world history. These two statements are but two sides of the same coin: contemporary European history begins at the point in time when European civilization began seriously to challenge the civilizations of men living in other parts of the globe. Non-European peoples were thereby forced to deal with European military and economic power as well as European moral and political values. Unfortunately it is impossible to fix this point in time with any real precision. Some scholars will insist that it cannot be announced until the mid-nineteenth century when steam power and cheap iron gave western men an overwhelming advantage over other peoples of the earth. Yet since the eighteenth century saw the maturing of colonial societies in the Americas, the beginning of the firm establishment of European military and economic hegemony in large parts of Africa and Asia, and the calm assumption by European men that they could explore the world and make themselves masters of whatever lands or peoples they found, it is not improper to assume that world history, whatever the definition of that term, was about to begin. In other words, by the eighteenth century the commencement, if not the more completely realized development, of a world order in which peoples could not ignore each other for long was at hand.

Anyone will readily see that the dynamic force behind the merging of the histories of the several civilizations of the earth into a world history was rooted in European development. It is therefore important to probe into the problems and processes of Europe to understand the thrust that European men were able to exert in the world. Obviously there are several levels of action and influence, and it is not easy to untangle them or to assess the relative value of their importance.

On the political level, the emergence of a secular society with goals and aspirations frankly limited to the earth and more or less completely divorced from theological modes of thought, marked the end of century-old patterns by which men were governed by kings who claimed God's sanction for their rule or, in more ancient times, by emperors who elevated themselves to the status of gods. It was no simple thing to shift from government created by God to government responsible to the world of men, nor could such a step be taken in a single generation; and yet such a step was probably necessary before European men would be prepared to urge their hegemony over the whole of the earth. In 1715 Louis XIV, king by grace of God, died in his bed; in 1793 a descendant of Louis XIV was executed in Paris in the name of popular sovereignty. In less than a century there had been a dramatic shift in men's assumptions about political legitimacy. Not all Europe fully accepted the implications of the beheading of Louis XVI; nonetheless Europe was not to be ruled much longer by kings who justified their government by divine sanctions. Secular society was an imperative necessity for European civilization to become the dynamo for a world history; it was also the source for future ideological conflicts among Europeans as well as non-Europeans, on a national and an international plane, for once society became secular, salvation in society presumably could be reached in this world, and not all men were agreed on the route that should be followed.

While the secular structure of government was becoming characteristic of European society, the tendency toward conflicts between the states of Europe became more and more pronounced. Before about 1500 most of the clashes in Europe had taken the form of civil wars: that is, struggles between a king or the Emperor and his powerful vassals. After 1500 the rise of the bureaucratic-military states and the consequent rivalry between them became more pronounced. The seventeenth century witnessed the development of a balance of power as an instrument for the government of Europe as a whole, but it was so disorderly a method of providing government that a few advanced thinkers began to demand the creation of a superstate for all European society. The diversity of Europe proved to be too great for the emergence of any such institution, and so Europeans continued to try to govern themselves through the agencies of diplomacy, military installations, and relatively frequent wars. In the eighteenth century the recognition of limited objectives for international action prevented these conflicts from becoming fatally destructive, but man's failure to find some means of avoiding them created a legacy dangerous to the onward march of European civilization.

On another level too, undoubtedly interrelated with the political order, a series of developments heralded the emergence of European society as the dynamic force in world history. The eighteenth century saw an enormous expansion in the volume and value of commerce. In the preceding two or more centuries Europeans had sent their ships over the high seas to trade with the world, but those ships were small and relatively few in number. By the eighteenth century ships had reached the maximum size possible for a technology that was dependent upon wood for its principal building material, and the numbers of the ships expanded strikingly. As a result, an increasingly greater percentage of the population of Europe became involved in the commercial structure of the society both as consumers and as purveyors of goods originating beyond the seas. At the same time, European technological skill produced more powerful wind and water mills, and finally a usable steam engine, and European inventive genius extended the use of machinery to both industry and agriculture. It was perhaps only a painful beginning, but by the end of the eighteenth century the technological civilization for which Europeans were to become world famous was already assuming its characteristic forms.

Undoubtedly connected with the rising economic power of Europe was the concomitant rise in European population. It had been static or near static for centuries, but after 1715 the population of Europe again began to grow. This demographic movement is unquestionably an important harbinger of the contemporary world; it marks the beginning of the development of better public health (water supplies, sanitation, and so on), better medical care, and perhaps most important of all, better and more secure supplies of food. The population spiral that began in eighteenth-century Europe has been extended in the twentieth century to the entire world to release a population flood of unprecedented proportions.

Closely related to the secularization of society and the rise of wealth was the development of the intellectual movement that we call "the Enlightenment." It may well be argued that some of the most important roots of the process of secularization were in the scientific and philosophical revolutions of the seventeenth and eighteenth centuries when men focused their attention on the *processes of* the earth rather than on the *reasons for* or *purposes of* things and events on the earth. By asking the question *how* rather than *why* men discovered that they could expand their empire of understanding tremendously. It mattered not that some of their basic assumptions blinded them to many of the processes that they were attempting to understand; their research yielded striking results. In the eighteenth century, the scientific and philosophical revolution was both extended and popularized, and by the end of that century it was becoming clear that European men had developed intellectual patterns that were to give them hegemony over the earth.

Historians always seek to explain their world by studying the origins and development of the historical processes that seem responsible for the characteristic forms that men find in the world. Thus, while the eighteenth century is obviously heir to the history that preceded it (and unquestionably that century's society was itself formed by processes that had their origins in the more remote past), it was also the real threshold of modern world history. It only required the tumultuous political and social revolutions that began in France in 1789 and the equally far-reaching economic dislocations that came with the generalization of cheap iron, steam power, and mechanical technology, to launch European men fully in the roles of teachers and of exploiters of the rest of the peoples of the earth.

BIBLIOGRAPHY FOR BOOK IV

GENERAL HISTORY OF THE EIGHTEENTH CENTURY

The three volumes named below from *The Rise of Modern Europe* (William Langer, ed.) present an excellent picture of the eighteenth century.

Dorn, Walter L., *Competition for Empire, 1740–1763,* New York, Harper, 1940.
Gershoy, L., *From Despotism to Revolution, 1763–1789,* New York, Harper, 1944.
Roberts, Penfield, *The Quest for Security, 1715–1740,* New York, Harper, 1947.

INTERNATIONAL POLITICS AND NATIONAL HISTORY

Buffington, Arthur, *The Second Hundred Years' War, 1689–1815,* New York, Holt, 1929.
Cobban, A., *History of Modern France, 1715–1799,* London, Penguin, 1957.
Ergang, R. R., *The Potsdam Führer,* New York, Columbia University Press, 1941.
Fay, S. B., *The Rise of Brandenburg-Prussia to 1786,* New York, Holt, 1937. A Berkshire Study.
Ford, Franklin, *The Robe and the Sword: The Regrouping of the French Aristocracy,* Cambridge, Harvard University Press, 1953.
Gaxotte, P., *Louis the Fifteenth and His Times,* trans. J. L. May, Philadelphia, Lippincott, 1934.
Gipson, L. H., *The Great War for Empire,* New York, Knopf, 1954.
Gooch, G. P., *Frederick the Great,* New York, Knopf, 1947.
Gooch, G. P., *Maria Theresa and Other Studies,* New York, Longmans, Green, 1954.

Gooch, G. P., *Louis XV*, New York, Longmans, Green, 1956.
Hassall, A., *The Balance of Power, 1715–1789*, New York, Macmillan, 1914.
Mowat, R. B., *Europe, 1715–1815*, New York, Longmans, Green, 1929.
Mowat, R. B., *The Age of Reason*, Boston, Houghton Mifflin, 1934.
Palmer, R. R., *Age of the Democratic Revolution, 1760–1800*, Princeton, Princeton University Press, 1959.
Reddaway, W. F., *Frederick the Great*, New York, Putnam, 1904.
Robertson, C. G., *Chatham and the British Empire*, New York, Macmillan, 1948.
Veale, F. J. P., *Frederick the Great*, London, Hamish Hamilton, 1935.
Williams, B., *The Whig Supremacy, 1714–1760*, Oxford, Clarendon, 1939.
Wright, Gordon, *France in Modern Times*, Chicago, Rand McNally, 1960.

On the War for American Independence, the two new *American Nation Series* volumes are excellent:

Alden, J. R., *The American Revolution, 1775–1783*, New York, Harper, 1954.
Gipson, L. H., *The Coming of the Revolution, 1763–1775*, New York, Harper, 1954.

ECONOMIC AND COLONIAL HISTORY

Burt, A. L., *A Short History of Canada for Americans*, Minneapolis, University of Minnesota Press, 1942.
Dietz, F. C., *The Industrial Revolution*, New York, Holt, 1927.
Dodwell, H., *Duplex and Clive*, London, Methuen, 1920.
Haring, Clarence, *The Spanish Empire in America*, New York, Oxford University Press, 1947.
Kraus, Michael, *The Atlantic Civilization: Eighteenth Century Origins*, Ithaca, Cornell University Press, 1949.
Mantoux, Paul, *The Industrial Revolution in the Eighteenth Century*, rev. ed., trans. M. Vernon, London, Cape, 1928.
Newton, Arthur, *The European Nations in the West Indies, 1493–1688*, New York, Macmillan, 1933.
Packard, L. B., *The Commercial Revolution, 1400–1776*, New York, Holt, 1927.
Savelle, Max, *Foundations of American Civilization: A History of Colonial America*, New York, Holt, 1942.
Wright, Louis B., *The Atlantic Frontier: Colonial American Civilization, 1607–1763*, New York, Knopf, 1947.
Wrong, G. M., *The Rise and Fall of New France*, New York, Macmillan, 1928, 2 vols.

INTELLECTUAL AND CULTURAL HISTORY

Becker, Carl, *The Heavenly City of the Eighteenth Century Philosophers*, New Haven, Yale University Press, 1932.
Brandes, Georg, *Voltaire*, New York, Boni, 1930.
Brinton, Crane, *Of Ideas and Men*, New York, Prentice-Hall, 1950.
Cassirer, Ernst, *The Philosophy of the Enlightenment*, Princeton, Princeton University Press, 1951.

Gay, Peter, *Voltaire's Politics,* Princeton, Princeton University Press, 1959.

Hazard, P., *European Thought in the Eighteenth Century,* London, Hollis & Carter, 1954.

Morley, John, *Diderot and the Encyclopaedists,* London, Macmillan, 1923.

Mornet, D., *French Thought in the Eighteenth Century,* trans. L. M. Levin, New York, Prentice-Hall, 1929.

Palmer, R. R., *Catholics and Unbelievers in Eighteenth Century France,* Princeton, Princeton University Press, 1939.

Randall, J. H., *The Making of the Modern Mind,* Boston, Houghton Mifflin, 1940.

Smith, P., *The History of Modern Culture,* vol. 2, New York, Holt, 1934.

Torrey, N. L., *The Spirit of Voltaire,* New York, Columbia University Press, 1938.

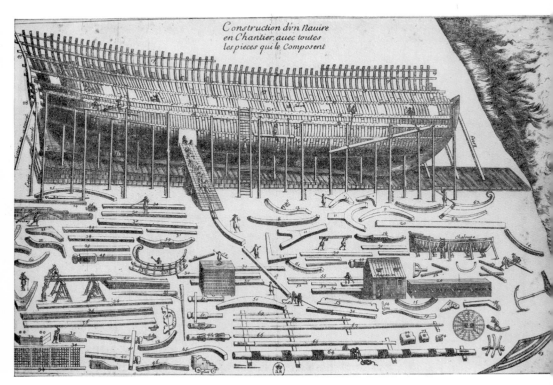

Construction d'vn Navire
en Chantier, avec toutes
les pieces qui le Composent

The building and fitting of a large ship draws upon the full technological powers of any society. That was as true in the eighteenth century as it is today. One may say that the great wooden warships, armored with oak, powered with towering sails, and prepared to fling a broadside of singing metal at an enemy, were as perfect an expression of the civilization of the eighteenth century as were the writings of Voltaire, the pictures of Watteau, or the music of Bach. (University of Minnesota Library)

Chapter 19

THE EIGHTEENTH CENTURY: WESTERN EUROPE

1. THE LEGACY OF THE FIRST WORLD WARS

Between 1713 and 1721 a series of treaties ended the wars that had raged with only a short interruption since 1683. The treaties of Utrecht and Rastadt brought peace to the west; those of Stockholm, Frederiksborg, and Nystadt, to the north; and that of Passarowitz to the Balkans. Taken together, these treaties gave shape to the characteristic form of the political world of the eighteenth century by recognizing the political facts that emerged from the wars. The most important of these were the emergence of England, the Danubian monarchy, and Russia as great military powers with resources and populations that enabled them to challenge successfully the France of Louis XIV and the Sweden of Charles XII. They also marked the end of the Spanish Empire of Philip II. It was partitioned between his heirs, the German Hapsburgs and the French Bourbons. The partition was to have important consequences both to the colonial affairs soon to assume a major role in power politics, and to the Netherlands and Italy, where Philip's territories were thus joined to Hapsburg Austria rather than to Spain. Finally, limits had been placed upon the power of France. In 1680 France could and did terrify all Europe; after 1715 she had an important place in the balance of power, but she no longer could pretend to the hegemony of Europe.

The treaties ending the war in western Europe proclaimed the emergence of England as the most important political power in the West. At the same time, they made English revolutionary theory a postulate for international law. The so-called Glorious Revolution of 1688 established the thesis that a king rules his lands by virtue of a contract with his people rather than as a gift from God. Thus, if a king no longer lived up to that contract or disobeyed the law, he could be dethroned. This fact made royal authority dependent upon the political situation rather than on divine will. By declaring in the treaty settlement that King Philip V of Spain could not inherit the French throne even though the death of Louis XV might make him next in line, the revolutionary principle that a king could be deprived of his throne became part of the law of Europe, for a political agreement, rather than divine right, had been recognized as the determining factor in the succession to the French throne. It is difficult to say what would have happened if Louis XV had actually died without a direct heir; the *Parlement* of Paris might well have insisted that the ancient Salic law and the doctrine of divine right should apply. Since Louis XV did produce an heir, the thesis was not tested. Nonetheless, it is important to note that the revolutionary idea proclaimed by the Whigs and generalized by their great theorist, John Locke, had become an accepted principle. It was a bourgeois principle; it was proclaimed two whole generations before the French Revolution forced a French king to submit to the wishes of the bourgeois class.

The era of warfare left important marks upon the developing political institutions of Europe. Some historians have argued that the changes taking place in the economy and the social structure of Europe would have brought about the same result had there been no wars. This thesis is questionable, but even its proponents will admit that the wars accelerated the process. The rise of bureaucratic institutions and the centralization of power at the expense of the landed nobility were almost universal. In order to fight the war, it had been necessary to encroach upon the power and prerogatives of the old order. The process greatly increased the importance of bourgeois statesmen in the service of the king. For several centuries kings had been employing lawyers and financiers from the bourgeois class, but as late as 1600 the royal councils everywhere in Europe were still predominantly staffed by princes of the blood and great noblemen. By 1715, however, men with bourgeois backgrounds had elbowed the nobles aside. Many of these "new" men called themselves by proud titles, but often enough their grandfathers had sold cloth or grain. Naturally the nobility resented both the royal encroachments on their ancient political position and the rise of a class of bureaucrats who were usurping the traditional role of the nobility. The nobles fought a rearguard action against the trend, but the process was too strong for them. In France they succeeded in pushing their way into the councils of the regent, but the results only emphasized their incapacity to govern. The victory of men of the pen in the seventeenth century could not be reversed.

The most important institutions that emerged from the era of warfare were standing armies and navies. For the first time since the decay of imperial Rome, there were large armies and navies at the disposal of the central authority. These military institutions were henceforth to be characteristic of western European political civilization, and they were to have important implications for the whole of society. Armed and equipped with standardized weapons, clothing, and heavy war material, the armies and the fleets became the businessmen's best customers—customers who encouraged the rise of mass-production methods. To supply barracks and depots with food, ammunition, and weapons became the biggest single business in every important country. The whole establishment placed a heavy financial and administrative load upon the king's government. Large staffs of officials were required to administer the military departments. The very existence of armies and navies required the governments of Europe to adopt economic policies desired by the bourgeois taxpayers, or designed to help those taxpayers to bear their burden without complaint. Political economy was often reduced to the proposition that policies had to be adopted that would make it easier to collect taxes to supply the military.

The bourgeoisie was not the only group affected by the new military institutions. The army and the fleet also provided "honorable" employment for the nobility at a time when the rising bourgeois class was threatening either to destroy them or force them to accept bourgeois values. Throughout the eighteenth century the nobility attempted to make appointments to the officers' corps their exclusive right. The same impulse accounts for the development of the "officer's code" that was actually little more than a refurbishing of the ideals of decadent feudalism. Undoubtedly the fact that kings tended to accept the pretensions of the nobility had significant effects upon the development of military theory. The idea of an officer's "honor" as something that the bourgeoisie could not achieve gave a curious twist to the mythology of the soldier, and tended to make at least part of military thinking quite unrealistic.

While military command tended to become the monopoly of the nobility, the ranks were filled largely with marginal elements of society. Social thinking in this period opposed the recruitment of "economically useful" men in the ranks, hence the recruiting officers concentrated upon vagabonds, beggars, and social misfits (even students sometimes) whose absence from civilian life would not be much regretted. Many of these poor wretches were brought into the army by force (dragooned) or by guile. Those who have read Voltaire's *Candide* will recall that the hero "joined" the army of the king of the Bulgarians by mistakenly drinking the king's health. Once in the army, the recruit became a professional soldier. In times of peace this meant that he was drilled to "spit and polish" perfection, and kept in line by vigorous discipline. In times of war, while desertion was not uncommon, he was kept in line as much by fear of his officers as by any feeling of *ésprit de corps*. In either case, the recruit was expected to regard the army as a long-time career rather than merely as a short-term tour of duty.

The standing army not only affected the economic status of the king's subjects, but also played an important role in both the internal and the international political structure. A hundred years earlier royal governments had not been much stronger than some of the great noblemen who were theoretically subject to them; from England to Russia, from Sweden to France, Italy, and Hungary the century 1550–1650 saw revolts inspired and directed by men who could command military power approximately equal to that of the king. This was no longer possible in the eighteenth century; even in Hungary rebellion was smothered by military power. The French Revolution that came at the end of the century did not start with a military rebellion led by a subject; if it had, Louis XVI would have known how to act.

In international affairs, the standing armies accentuated the fact that the idea of a frontier and the conception of sovereignty were still ill defined in 1715. When it became possible for a prince to send his army, on short notice, into a neighboring state, there were many excuses available for such action. In other words, the problem of international war was aggravated by the existence of ready weapons. The fact that both military and political theory adopted the idea of "limited warfare" (that is, war that affects the civil population as little as possible and is confined to modest aims) did not conceal the dangers inherent in the new military system.

Another very significant legacy of the era of warfare (1683–1715) were the debts that hung over every government of Europe. The wars of 1683–1721 cost much more than those of any previous era. In France the government was bankrupt long before 1713. The United Netherlands was still solvent, but on the verge of bankruptcy. The German princes, with their slender credit resources (their debts were personal, rather than of the state), had exceeded their borrowing power long before the wars ended and had been forced to live on subsidies. Only England carried her war debts relatively easily, largely because her debts were state obligations, passed and guaranteed by Parliament. As we shall see, it was the problem of the royal debts that sparked the Revolution in France in 1789.

2. THE ECONOMIC DEVELOPMENT OF WESTERN EUROPE IN THE EIGHTEENTH CENTURY

The end of the wars released economic energy that had been building up since the explorations of the sixteenth century. In 1550 European commerce with the world had been a mere trickle; by 1650 it had become a small stream, and by 1763 it was a broad river. The difference between the tiny Portuguese vessel that so painfully made its way around Africa and the proud East India merchantmen of the eighteenth century tells only part of the story. The number of ships sailing the seven seas had increased even more spectacularly than their size and their speed. These ships carried the treasures of the New World, Africa, and the Orient in their holds. Manufactured goods of eastern design, drugs, spices, coffee, tea, tin, copper, jewels and objects of art from the Far East; slaves, ivory, gum arabic, and tropical wood from Africa; sugar, hemp, rice, indigo, dye woods, tobacco, fish, furs, and naval supplies from the Americas: these were only a few of the items that poured into European ports from beyond the seas.

Important developments in shipbuilding and navigation had made the expansion possible. During the eighteenth century, men learned to build longer, heavier, and more graceful sailing ships. By copperplating their bottoms, they were made faster and more seaworthy. Men also learned to trim their sails with more canvas than ever before and to steer their ships closer to the wind. The construction of chronometers with real accuracy, better instruments for shooting the sun to establish latitude, and the publication of more usable navigation charts made sailing less hazardous. The sailor of the mid-eighteenth century was much closer to his successor in the mid-nineteenth century than he was to his predecessor in the seventeenth century.

Ater 1715, England seized the paramount place in the commercial world. Like those of the Netherlands in the seventeenth century, England's ports now became the depots for foreign trade. From the Baltic and the White seas, from the Mediterranean and the Levant, from the great river systems of Germany, European goods, foodstuffs, and raw materials came to England to be exchanged for the goods in English warehouses. The Bank of England, private banking houses, English exchanges for stocks and commodities, and companies specializing in insurance developed to assist the extension of English commerce. This flow of goods in and out of her ports became the most important single factor about the British islands, and the very driving wheel of English political and economic life. To a lesser degree France and the United Netherlands played the same economic role, but England outdistanced them as the "shopkeeper of Europe." The Dutch recognized the inevitable, and became, in effect, a junior partner in the English enterprise. Dutch money was invested in English chartered companies and in English state bonds, and Dutch merchants avoided the competition that had made them so famous a century earlier. In return, the British navy protected Dutch ships, and England allowed the Dutch to keep the spice colonies in the East Indies. The French were not so docile. They attempted to cut into English trade in India and in America; as one of the by-products of this rivalry, England and France fought three wars in the middle of the century.

The spectacular rise in the total amount of money and credit available for commercial enterprises was one of the most important factors stimulating this upsurge of commerce. After almost a century of stagnation, the world's production of silver again turned upward in the eighteenth century. Every two decades following 1720 saw an increase of between twenty and thirty percent in the amount of new silver flowing into Europe. In addition to the precious metal, the use of paper money in England and the Netherlands (the practice was tried in France with bad results) added to the stock of money available for business. Finally, a great expansion in the use of letters of credit and bills of exchange, practices which had been begun in the Middle

Ages, further added to the total volume of money and credit. All this currency had a buoyant effect upon prices. Prices had risen in Europe throughout the sixteenth and early seventeenth centuries; from 1640 to about 1740 they had leveled off; after 1740 they again resumed their upward course. Rising prices are not necessary to economic prosperity, but they seem often to accompany it.

To finance the new enterprises more capital than one man or one family could control was required, so partnerships and stock companies were founded to provide the money. In the preceding hundred and fifty years the great chartered companies had been financed by the sale of stock; their monopoly positions and government sponsorship usually meant that their stock was a profitable investment. The many companies founded in the eighteenth century did not always enjoy so sound a position. Some of them failed to pay off because speculators pushed the stock prices to absurd heights; others because the promoters were selling "blue sky" with the intent to swindle the investors. In both England and France the decade following the wars witnessed a stock market boom with the accompanying bust.

The project that set off speculation in France proved to be a successful experiment in the twentieth century, but in the eighteenth men were too inexperienced in finance to make it work. A Scotsman named John Law persuaded the regent in France to let him found a bank that would hold two-thirds of its capital in state obligations. This bank would then issue paper money against its capital to finance a trading company to do business in the New World. In 1718 the bank became a royal enterprise, and the company's activities were enlarged to include all the French colonies. Unwise propaganda about prospects for profit and easy money (the bank's paper money) pushed the value of the company's stock from five hundred to eighteen thousand livres a share. When the company paid what would have been a handsome forty percent on the five hundred livres, the dividend amounted to little more than one percent on the market price. A wave of selling started a full-blown business crisis. There was a run on the bank, and everyone presented paper money for payment in gold. Law, of course, was not prepared to redeem all the paper money since most of the bank's capital was in government bonds that were anything but fluid. The bank had to close its doors; and for almost a century the very word "bank" was suspect in France. The next one that opened discreetly called itself a *Caisse d'Escompte*. Even though the speculators who hoped to make easy profits lost much money, the Law enterprise was hardly the complete failure that many writers have claimed it was. It is all very well to say that Law "sold stock on the profits from beaver skins when they were still on the beaver in the upper Mississippi"; but it is also true that his enterprise had much to do with opening the upper Mississippi to French trade.

The English "bubble" was the result of the *Asiento* clause in the Treaty of

Utrecht (1713) which gave English merchants a foothold in the slave trade with the Spanish colonies as well as the right to send one ship a year to trade. The price of the shares of the South Sea Company, which secured the *Asiento* rights, mushroomed on the market. In the general excitement a "bull" market developed for stocks in other English trading companies, thus pushing their value beyond reasonable expectations of profit. Of course the prospects had been exaggerated; when the South Sea Company's ships appeared in Spanish America, they found the market already glutted with English goods. Smuggling had developed into a major business during the era of warfare. The "bust" followed the boom, and many people sustained severe losses. An old German proverb which says, "If you have a sheep, you must shear it" applies to many of the market operations that became characteristic of the new economy.

However, market fiascos did not stop the spread of stock companies. In the course of the eighteenth century, companies were formed for insurance against losses at sea, through fire, theft, death, marriage, and other hazards that men face. Such companies did not become common in industry, but commerce, finance, and insurance provided outlets for capital and opportunities for investment.

This commercial activity inevitably affected the development of industry. Many of the exports of Europe were in the form of raw materials or agricultural products, but both the colonies and the Orient were markets for finished and semifinished goods as well. Indeed, if Europe had not found things that the orientals would buy, the East-West traffic would have died because Europe could not send precious metals for all the commodities she wanted in the East. Nor was the production of goods for export the only stimulus for the expanding industrial activity. Many of the items that came from the tropics or the forests of America still had to be worked up before they became usable. Molasses had to be made into sugar and rum, hemp into rope, tobacco into snuff, beaver pelts into hats; these and other industries came into existence to care for the goods flowing into Europe.

In the nineteenth century, historians, fascinated by the story of the rise of the English textile industry in the latter eighteenth century, pronounced the period one of "industrial revolution." The principal component of this "revolution" seems to have been that after about 1770 machines came to be used to speed up production. Actually, as a glance at the great Encyclopedia published in France in the mid-eighteenth century will show, the whole period from the sixteenth century onward had been marked by improvements in techniques and machines. The arms industry of the seventeenth century went through a period of mechanical inventions as spectacular as the textile industry of the eighteenth. What seems to have happened is that the historians took seriously the idea proposed by d'Alembert, when he asked how is it that "the names of these benefactors of the human race [the inventors] are almost entirely unknown, while the history of the destroyers, that is to say, the conquerors, are known to everyone." The nineteenth century elevated certain of the inventors of textile machinery (spinning jenny, spinning mule, power loom, and so forth) to the status of heroes and insisted that their work had constituted a "revolution," probably because they were ignorant of the work and progress of other inventors who had gone before them.

There were, however, two achievements in the eighteenth century that were destined to have tremendous impact upon the world's economy: the forging of iron ore with coke, and the building of the steam engine.

By the eighteenth century some parts of Europe were facing a serious crisis as the result of deforestation. Wood was the all-important commodity in this period: with it men made ships, houses, tools, furniture, and machines. In the form of fuel, it was needed to forge or smelt all their metals, so that in a sense all things made of iron, copper, tin, and other metals were actually made of wood (charcoal). With wood, men heated their houses and stoked their fires for industrial production. Ever since the Middle Ages the use of coal had been increasing, but only in cities near good water transportation, and only for uses that the "humors" in the coal would not affect (soap, candles, beer, and the like). Coal and even coke could not be used to forge iron because the "humors" in it made the iron brittle. Men did not know chemistry and so could not identify the processes that were taking place when they tried to forge metal with coal. Thus the pressure on the forests became so great that one "economist" complained that in his part of Ireland hides had to be shipped untanned (tanning was done with oak bark), because the iron forges were eating up the forests.

There were many projects for using coal (coke) in place of (wood) charcoal to produce iron ore. The British Parliament offered rich rewards for a practical process, and it was obvious that wealth awaited the inventor. In the third decade of the eighteenth century an English ironmaster named Darby found a solution by accident. Iron ore blast-fired with coke and limestone produced malleable iron; that was, perhaps, the most important discovery of the century. It freed the forge from the forest. Heretofore men had had to rely upon the annual yield of wood to produce metal; henceforth he could tap the reserves of solar energy accumulated in the remote past and stored in the fossil fuels of the coal fields.

Like all such inventions, it was a long time before this one was generally used. By the last quarter of the eighteenth century most of England's iron was being produced with coke and limestone, but not until the middle of the next century did ironmasters on the continent generally use the process. In England, however, it was responsible for a transformation of the iron industry. Freed from the necessity of following the forest and stream, the iron foundries settled down near the coal fields and began to grow. What had formerly been an enterprise for an ironmaster and a few assistants became a large-scale industry employing many people. A distinguished French visitor to England in the 1780's remarked on the heavy machinery for lifting weights, the huge hammers, the forges with bellows driven by steam engines, and the great amount of iron produced. English iron became cheaper and plentiful. Before the end of the eighteenth century it was used to build items as widely separated as bridges, barges, chairs, coffins, and guns.

The other great invention was the steam engine. Since Roman times men had discovered only one prime mover—the gun, and its usefulness was strictly limited, because the piston (projectile) was thrown away each time it was used. Thus, eighteenth-century men had only the same power for industrial uses that had been available to the Egyptians: wind, water, and the muscles of animals. They had learned to build better windmills and water wheels than their medieval predecessors had known, but these were still weak in power and chained to the vicissitudes of the weather. Latin scholars had turned up accounts of a vapor engine made by Hero, a Greek of the third century A.D.; it had been used to open temple doors, to roll the eyes of an idol, and such relatively uneconomic work. Several people were able to reproduce the Hero engine, but, like the original, these machines were heavy and costly to operate. The problem was simply this: it was possible to force the piston to rise in the cylinder by the introduction of steam, but to make it fall, the steam in the cylinder had to be condensed, and that meant cooling the cylinder. It was extremely inefficient to have to heat and cool the cylinder at each stroke.

At the opening of the eighteenth century an Englishman named Newcomen did build a steam engine that solved the problem by introducing cold water into the cylinder when the piston reached the top of the stroke. It was relatively costly to operate, but miners in England were desperate for some machine to work pumps and so they installed these awkward, clanking monstrosities at the pit heads. In the 1760's James Watt (1736–1819) designed a steam engine that solved the problem of removing the steam by a system of valves. He and his partner, Boulton, succeeded in building the engine after they hired watchmakers to do the machine work; other workers were not accustomed to the necessary precision work. Watt and Boulton installed their engine on a rental contract wherever there was a Newcomen engine. They charged a rental fee of one third of the savings that resulted, and became rich from the proceeds. It was fifteen or twenty years before the Watt engine was used widely for anything but pumping water, but in the 1780's iron forges and textile mills began to install steam engines to take the place of water wheels. It was not until after the Napoleonic wars that the steam engine made any impression on the continent.

These two inventions—the steam engine and the new process for producing iron—prepared the way for the industrial era of the nineteenth century.

The eighteenth century, except for a small part of England, still lived in the era of wood, wind, and water; the new inventions made possible the nineteenth-century era of iron and steam.

The same impulses that led men to seek new sources of power and better ways of making iron also stimulated the development of a more effective organization of production. In the seventeenth century many of the goods that reached the market were produced in the homes of peasant workers using their own tools or in small craft shops operated by guildsmen in the traditional fashion. During the eighteenth century in England, and to a lesser degree in France and the Netherlands, there was a tendency for the businessman to gather the production operation under one roof and thereby turn the workers into an urban proletariat. The process was encouraged by the invention of machines that could be best driven by power (water, wind, or steam). Such machinery had already created similar factories for the production of weapons during the seventeenth century; in the eighteenth, the production of paper, textiles, sugar, snuff, and many other commodities followed this pattern. The other factor that encouraged the process was the more widespread acceptance of the principle of the division of labor.

Adam Smith's description of the manufacture of pins has become a classic statement of the process: by division of labor a crew of workers could produce many more pins than would be possible if each of them made the entire pin. Smith was describing a method of organizing production that did not necessarily depend upon the use of machinery. However, once production was broken down into a series of acts, the idea of substituting a machine for a man was the next obvious step. Toward the end of the century an American, Eli Whitney, conceived the idea of standardized production with replaceable parts. It is not surprising that the item first produced was a musket for the army. It should be noted, however, that the use of interchangeable parts and factory assembly did not become widespread until the twentieth century.

The stimulating effect of commerce upon industry was felt in the port cities all along the Atlantic and North Sea coasts. Sugar refineries, rope factories, coffee roasting mills, distilleries, and many such enterprises using raw materials from beyond the sea were to be found in dozens of cities. In England the rise of a cotton textile industry depending upon imported fiber was one of the sensational developments. The India Company first imported Indian cotton cloth and made calico and gingham the "rage" for ladies of the court. At the request of English textile manufacturers, the importation of those materials was curtailed, but the Company then imported the cotton fiber. After the development of spinning and weaving machinery in England, the Company re-exported the English-made cloth to India and undersold the Indians in their own market. This was a striking example of the saving that could be made by the new manufacturing techniques; the colonel's lady ceased to wear cotton, but Molly O'Grady could afford to buy it.

Agriculture was also affected by the economic stimulus that was turning England into a great workshop. Since the sixteenth century numerous English landlords had secured the right to "enclose" part of the pasture land. Their aim was to convert the land to sheep grazing or more efficient grain production; the effect was to squeeze out the small peasants who could not survive when the common lands were enclosed. Many peasants were thus turned into urban proletariat, into rural poor, or forced to migrate to America. The land of England had become too valuable to leave it under the traditional system of agricultural exploitation. There was another factor that encouraged development of more effective techniques; the squires and small gentry who owned much of the land were often enough first- or second-generation "city men." It had long been customary for wealthy merchants to retire to the land. These people still had bourgeois notions about profit, and many of them directed the exploitation of their own lands with the aim of earning a profit. In this way the English country gentlemen differed from their continental counterparts.

To the modern mind the new agricultural practices do not seem revolutionary, but they were the first important break in the traditional methods of farming. Jethro Tull, Lord (Turnip) Townshend, and other English gentlemen experimented with crop rotation and selective breeding of animals, with important results. Tull was particularly famous for developing new methods of cultivation. After watching French vineyard workers cultivating their crops, he devised machinery pulled by horses or oxen for drilling the seed in rows and for cultivating the crop to keep down the weeds. The results were spectacular. He grew grain on the same plot for over a decade and reaped larger crops and used less seed per acre than his neighbors who broadcast their seed. Tull's book on agriculture (1731) combined sound information on cultivation and machinery with nonsense about the harmfulness of manure. Lord Townshend was also an important innovator; he learned that crop rotation using turnips, clover, barley, and wheat produced larger crops than the time-honored practice of allowing the soil to remain fallow periodically. Furthermore, the turnip and clover crops provided forage for animals, and thereby offered a means of breaking through the "vicious circle" of European agriculture.

Following Tull and Townshend, between 1760 and 1790 Robert Bakewell introduced new selective animal breeding that resulted in developing cattle, hogs, and sheep with more good meat than bone and sinew; his work proved to be the beginning of the revolution in animal husbandry that gave the world the short horn and Hereford cattle, the Berkshire hogs, and Leicester sheep. In the half century 1740–1790 the average weight of English sheep and cattle doubled, and their number, supported by forage crops, greatly increased. The cities with their ever-growing population of well-to-do citizens whose diet included meat were now assured of adequate supplies for their butcher shops.

English methods made little impression upon the continent until after the Napoleonic wars. In many ways the generalization that Europeans lived at different times at the same time is almost correct. If we had moved eastward in Europe in the eighteenth century, we would have seemed to go backward in time. England was the most advanced society; France and the Lowlands came next; the ring around France from Spain to Germany next; and the east and southeast last of all.

3. THE POLITICS OF THE WESTERN STATES

England

The great conservative prime minister of England, Disraeli, once referred to the Whig government of the eighteenth century as a "Venetian oligarchy." Whig historians, who have written much of the history of England, tried to gloss over the corrupt aspect of the regime and to emphasize the fact that England grew rich and powerful and developed her representative institutions in this period. Both explanations are probably true: English society in the eighteenth century was dominated by the rich, and the kingdom became the great economic and military power of Europe. The constitution of the kingdom, as amended by the revolution of 1688, was further developed. By no stretch of the imagination, however, should the England of this period be confused with liberal, democratic, and socialistic England as we know it today.

The revolution of 1688 and the laws enacted to ensure the continuation of the new regime gave a new orientation to the ancient constitution of the kingdom. The great power in the land was Parliament; that is, the king, the House of Lords, and the House of Commons assembled. Parliament made the laws, and Parliament stood as watchdog to see that they were obeyed. The revolution also created an independent judiciary; judges were appointed for life, removable only if due reason for impeachment could be produced. Montesquieu, a French political theorist, visiting England in the eighteenth century, saw the king's government and the two houses, Lords and Commons, as separate powers; thus he concluded that there was a three-way division of power in England between the administration, the legislative houses, and the judiciary. Montesquieu's conception of the British constitution had great influence on the founding fathers of the United States. They consciously tried to create a constitution with division of power, checks and balances, between the three branches of government. In view of the primitive nature of political definition, Montesquieu's mistake was not as silly as it has seemed to nineteenth-century theorists who *knew* how the English constitution actually did develop by *their* time.

The reason for Montesquieu's error lies in the fact that the relations between the king and the two Houses of Parliament were incompletely defined by the revolution of 1688. The ministers were the king's ministers, paid by him out of his civil list, and removable by him at will. The king and his ministers determined policy, prepared laws, and administered the kingdom; the army and the navy were under the king's command. The ministry appointed the officials in the country: the lords lieutenant who commanded the local military forces, the sheriffs who enforced the decisions of the government, and the justices of the peace who had both a judicial and an administrative role to play. To Montesquieu this indeed looked like an independent power. What he failed to appreciate was that the king's government was dependent upon the legislative houses for an annual appropriation and the annual passage of the Mutiny Act. Without these bills, the king could not pay or discipline his military forces and maintain his government. The revolution of 1688 had been primarily concerned with preventing the king from acting contrary to the will of Parliament. Thus the treasury officials had as their most important job the education of the country gentlemen who sat in the House of Commons in the intricacies of finance and royal policy. Their approval was necessary to run the government.

A closer look at the make-up of Parliament reveals that there were considerable differences hiding under a common cloak. The House of Lords was composed of the lords, both temporal and spiritual; the bishops who sat in it were appointed by the king for life, and so tended to belong to the party in power at the time of their appointment. Some of the temporal lords were from old families whose lands and titles dated to the Middle Ages, but the majority were families that had achieved prominence in the Tudor and Stuart eras. Some of the latter reached their positions through military or political service, others because of favors to the ruler, others because of their wealth. The upper house was not homogeneous at all except in its respect for property and the interests of agriculture and industry. In the opening years of the Hanoverian period Parliament passed an Act forbidding the king to appoint a large number of new peers who might support one of his policies. This Act recognized the potential weakness of the upper house; if it opposed the king's government, the creation of new peers, favorable to the king or ministry, could reverse the decision. The Act of 1717, however, proved unnecessary; during the eighteenth century the number of peers actually declined rather than increased.

The House of Commons, too, had considerable diversity under its roof. A mid-eighteenth-century report on the members disclosed that there were thirty-six army and navy officers (probably younger sons of peers or country gentlemen), thirty-six merchants, ten planters, thirty-six practicing lawyers, and three hundred and fourteen country gentlemen. This latter group, however, might mean a member of an old country family, or one of the city folk who recently retired to the country. The former was more usual, but the latter also were elected. An Act of 1711 required every member of the lower house to have an income of at least £600 a year; since many people in England never saw £5 a year, this was a tidy sum. Only "gentlemen" sat in Parliament.

The most important fact about elections to the lower house was the antiquity of the election districts; for centuries there had been no reapportionment, so that the representatives from the boroughs, in particular, were often elected by very few people, and often enough the borough became the property (pocket borough) of this or that family. Election corruption was widespread in those districts where the election was not a foregone conclusion and the local officials were in a position to influence choices. Thus, even though a few thousand people might have the right to vote, the actual decisions were made by a few hundred of them. The mass of the population had no articulate voice. The king's ministers could not always force the election of their candidate, but they often could buy the man who was elected. This fact made corruption a major premise of English political life throughout the eighteenth century.

As a legacy of the Civil War and the Restoration in the mid-seventeenth century, there were two parties competing for power. Looking at them closely it becomes clear that, like the Republican and Democratic parties in the United States, they were internally very diverse. The Tory party tended to represent the descendants of the Cavaliers of the Civil War. Their chief support came from the fox-hunting squires who were ultra-conservative in religion, isolationist in foreign policy, and royalist in internal affairs. The revolution of 1688 had left this party in a difficult position. Many of its most influential leaders believed in the divine right of kings, and therefore supported the deposed Stuarts rather than the new Hanoverian dynasty. These "Jacobites," as they were called, made the first two Georges suspicious of the Tories, and thus assured favor to their political foes. Tory religious ideas also set them sharply apart from the Whigs. The Tories were probably no more religious than their neighbors; they merely wished to force anyone who had anything to do with the nation's affairs to belong to the established church. During the greater part of the eighteenth century, the suspicion of "Jacobite" leanings kept the Tory party in the opposition. George III briefly tried to bring them to power toward the end of the century.

The Whig party tended to recruit the grandchildren of the "roundheads" of the civil war era. In 1688 they successfully insisted upon the right of the nation to impose the law upon the king by dethroning James II for breaking the "law." Their doctrine was that there was a contract between king and people, and this seemed to them to be the important absolute of politics. Their conception of the government of England eventually led to the enthronement of Parliament as the real power in the realm. In Whiggish doctrine the king became a "royal president" of a bourgeois (landlord and capitalist) society, leaving the conduct of affairs in the hands of ministers who could maintain a majority of votes in Parliament to ensure the passing of their measures. The chief support for the Whigs came from the city money men, the squires who recently came from the merchant class, and the great lords with Whig traditions. Curiously enough, the fact that so many bishops refused to recognize William and Mary gave the Whigs a chance to appoint most of the ecclesiastical peers. Since the Tories held power only a very short time in the period between the revolution (1688) and the death of Anne (1714), they were unable to alter this situation. (Most of the parish curates were Tories, but the bishops were Whigs.) The spiritual lords helped to secure a majority in the upper house. In domestic policy, the Whigs were favorable to industry, commerce, and nonconformist religious sects; in foreign affairs they were ready to use England's power to maintain the balance of power on the continent and to encourage English commerce.

George I came to the English throne in 1714 bound by the provisions of the Act of Settlement (1701) that gave the throne to his family. He had already had a reasonably distinguished career as a soldier and statesman, and thus was not without some political skill. He was careful to pay his trusted German advisers out of his German income, but he also listened to their suggestions about English affairs. He picked Whigs for his English ministers, and both he and his successor, George II, continued to rely heavily upon the Whigs as long as there was serious danger of a Jacobite rebellion. It used to be said that George I, unable to speak English, did not take an active interest in English affairs, and that his disinterest led to the development of the cabinet system. This alluringly simple solution is unfortunately untrue. George and his ministers all spoke French, and he did take an interest in English affairs.

The cabinet system of government did, however, begin to emerge during the reigns of the first two Georges. It would be folly to say that any one man was responsible for the cabinet system in England, and yet it is true that Walpole (1676–1745) deserves great credit for his part in establishing this form of government. Before his time, the king had been able to dismiss any of his ministers without affecting the status of the rest of them, and a minister could oppose the policies of his colleagues without being obliged to resign his post. Walpole initiated the tradition that made the cabinet as a whole jointly responsible for policy, and placed it under the direction of a first or prime minister. As long as the prime minster could command a majority in Parliament, his policies were those of the government. This implied cabinet discipline as well as responsibility to Parliament. It matters little that Walpole often maintained his majority by methods that smelled of political corruption, the point is that the principle he established was an important development. It was to be challenged during the reign of George III, but by the nineteenth century it had become a fixture of British government.

In the mid-eighteenth century, when England was at war with France, the elder Pitt came to power. He wished to create a government of all the talents (Whig and Tory) and to dispense with the system of corruption developed by Walpole. His war leadership was brilliant. His political and financial genius, combined with the military genius of Frederick the Great of Prussia, directed the wealth and power of the alliance that won the Seven Years' War, the high point of England's eighteenth-century political, military, and economic power. Pitt, like Walpole, rested his power on the support of Parliament as well as that of the king. His government was evidence of the strength of the English government when king, ministry, and Parliament were in agreement.

In 1760 George III ascended the throne determined to be king in fact as well as in name. Theoretically the royal prerogatives were still largely intact; all that was required was a king who would insist upon them. George III and his advisers, Lord North, Townshend, and others, tried to reverse two trends in English political life: one in the colonies that had progressively given local legislative bodies more and more power, and the other at home which had progressively increased the powers and prestige of Parliament. The king might have won the second of these fights had not the first resulted in great losses for the commercial and financial leaders of England. England was a plutocracy, and the rich and the wealthy would not long put up with a system that damaged their interests. By 1780 George III had lost both battles; the one resulted in the creation of the United States, the other more firmly established Parliament's control over the administration of the country.

France

Louis XIV died in 1715 leaving his great-grandson (Louis XV, 1715–1774), a mere child, to inherit his throne. A magnificent era, filled with grandeur and disaster, had ended, but the problems created in that period were still essential parts of French civilization. The king and his ministers had created a system of government that excluded both the old nobility and the judges of *Parlement*[1] from any voice in political affairs; the former directed all affairs. Louis XIV gave his ministers high-sounding titles, but he recruited them from the bourgeois class to ensure that they would be utterly dependent upon him for their power and prestige. Two families, the Colberts and the Le Telliers, supplied most of the men who directed his government. Such concentration of power had naturally aroused considerable opposition,

---

[1] As we have seen the French *Parlements* were the highest courts of the land, staffed with hereditary officials.

especially when disastrous wars brought the political wisdom of both the king and his ministers into question.

After 1715, the regent, the Duke of Orléans, modified the great king's system as soon as he assumed power. In the first place, to secure registration of changes in the king's will, he granted *Parlement* the right of remonstrance which the late king had denied. He then gave the nobles an opportunity to re-enter the government by adopting the system of *Polysynodie* (many councils) suggested several years before by Bishop Fénelon. There was the Council of the Regency at the top with eleven members, all but three of them princes of the blood or great nobles. Under that council, there were seven subcouncils (covering religious affairs, foreign affairs, war, finance, navy, interior, and commerce). These councils were also staffed by noblemen who proved their incapacity to handle affairs. When this system became bogged down, a wag put his finger on the problem with a bit of verse that assured the French that the regent could avert disaster, since he had seventy ministers to council him. After a few years of such government, the councils were dissolved, and the government reverted more or less to the system developed by Louis XIV.

The fact that there was no opportunity for regular expression of political ideas, no forum for political debate, and no established method for introducing new ideas, made French politics more complex than England's and also much less effective. There were, for example, no regular political parties to act as buffers between the conflicting interests of the country; political figures acted as individuals rather than as representatives of a group, and yet they had to deal with group interests. Political opposition was expressed by individuals, and yet it was often representative of class and economic interests without being able to establish that fact. Had there been no serious problems, the French political structure might not have caused difficulty; but given the economic and political problems of the Bourbon monarchy, some breakdown was probably inevitable. It came at the end of the eighteenth century.

The position of the nobility was ambiguous: on the one side, it had great social prestige as one of the two most privileged orders of society; on the other, the centralization of power under the three Bourbon kings of the seventeenth century had deprived the nobles of much of their social and political usefulness. They were rapidly becoming a parasitic class, enjoying privileges without giving service for them. They did insist upon their paramount right to the officer commissions in the armed services, but that only underlined the observation of the Duke of Antin, "that men of this class [nobility] are not suited to government affairs, that they are only to be killed off in war." They also insisted upon their paramount right to fill the ranks of the upper clergy, but even this claim backfired against them since too few of the nobility were willing to make the moral commitments required of a good bishop. With the nobility as a recruiting ground for the upper clergy, a man like Bossuet or Fénelon was rarer than libertines and wastrels.

The magistrates of the *Parlement* and the officials of the king's government occupied a unique position. Their offices were more or less hereditary; to dismiss one of them, the king had to arrange for repurchase of the position, and as long as the incumbent paid the annual tax (*Paulette*), the office could be sold or willed like any other property. The men of the *Parlements,* particularly, regarded themselves as a special order. They pretended to the right to "judicial review" of the king's decrees by virtue of the ancient practice that allowed them to remonstrate if the king's decrees were, in their opinion, unwise or out of line with the law.

Louis XIII and Louis XIV had effectively kept them from playing any such role, but under weaker governments in the eighteenth century the *Parlement* tried—sometimes successfully—to restore their "rights." While its members were often able to enlist the support of the urban masses as well as the rest of the bourgeoisie, it should be noted that they did not in fact have a record for defending the interests of the people of France; their chief interest was to defend their own "rights" and to shift the burden of taxation from their shoulders to those of others. Voltaire was probably not far afield when he called them rather sharp and unrepeatable names. Both Louis XV and Louis XVI periodically exiled members of *Parlement* who were obstructing their government, but neither ruler was strong enough to act effectively against them.

Alongside the two older privileged orders of nobility, there was emerging another wealthy class that also demanded a voice in government. The bourgeoisie, of course, was not really a new class except in that it had acquired many new members and therefore bulked larger in the society. The enlightened despots of the seventeenth century had developed policies that encouraged commerce and manufacturing; in the eighteenth century the tremendous expansion of trade accelerated the growth of commercial capital and with it the number of businessmen, lawyers, brokers, financiers, and other professional people. As in England, the commercial bourgeoisie were the most vital class in the population, and therefore they soon sought to impose their own values and needs upon the nation.

The bourgeoisie wanted and received consideration from the French government. They secured the gradual suppression of many of the laws that Colbert had imposed to control commerce and industry, so that we might say that the "liberty" demanded by the revolutionaries began to appear long before the Revolution broke out. At their demand, the government also established the *Corps des Ponts et Chaussées* (1738), an agency to construct roads and bridges and give unity to the communication system of the kingdom. This was of great importance to the business community, for commerce depended upon good roads. It might be noted in passing that nowhere in

Europe were there really good roads, but by the end of the eighteenth century France had some of the best roads on the continent. The government also began to take business statistics and furnish consular assistance to French commercial enterprises abroad. The Council of Commerce provided aid and information to French businessmen. Like seventeenth-century governments, those of the eighteenth attempted to interest the nobility in investing money and energy in commerce. The results, however, were mediocre, since many of the nobles still clung to their ancient prejudices against commerce.

The governments of Louis XV and Louis XVI did not satisfy all the demands of the businessmen who wanted the suppression of the privileges of the nobility, but not necessarily of the feudal rights that accompanied ownership of land since many of them had bought estates with seignorial rights. They also wanted suppression of the *corporations de métiers* that Colbert had established to take the place of the old guilds; especially they wished to suppress the special tribunals that regulated the processes of production and thereby prevented the development of new techniques. Turgot yielded to this demand (1776), but the *corporations* were re-established a few years later. Since there was no organ of government that could provide a regular forum for expressing demands and ideas of this kind, the upper bourgeoisie tended to become frustrated. They developed reading and literary societies where books and pamphlets were made available and kindred souls could discuss public affairs. These only helped to reinforce the ambition of the upper bourgeoisie to gain some sort of control over the royal budget and policy.

Recent studies of French society in the eighteenth century point clearly to the fact that the wealthy bourgeoisie were also frustrated because entry into the nobility of the robe and the sword was almost closed to them. The blue-blooded noblemen contracted marriage alliances with wealthy bourgeois women, but only to "manure" their fields with the dowry. The officials of the *Parlements* and the king's bureaucracy who held their positions as hereditary rights tried to exclude the "new" rich from their ranks. Even the financiers (tax farmers) were in the process of making their positions into an hereditary caste that was difficult to penetrate. Since the bourgeoisie uncritically accepted the idea that trade was somehow ignoble and that government, the church, or the army were the only prestige professions, the closed doors were doubly frustrating. Indeed, their uncritical acceptance of the social values prescribed by the nobility made the social barriers more significant than they otherwise would have been. They became walls that could only be scaled or destroyed by violence.

Had France been governed by kings of the mold of a Louis XIII or Louis XIV, it is possible that the "new" men would have received the advantages that they clamored for, even though they probably would have been excluded from direct exercise of power. The bourgeoisie were essentially "statists," that is, they wanted to see the government have real power to forward their interests. That attitude would have appealed to the seventeenth-century kings, but Louis XV was not in the model of either his great- or his great-great-grandfather. He was a handsome, intelligent, and sensitive man without much personal courage; his great-grandfather was his ideal, but he was not of the stuff to realize the regime of Louis XIV. He did not have the courage to stand up to a minister, a courtier, or even his mistresses. He would agree to their proposals, and then intrigue against them behind their backs. The result was that France drifted back and forth, for the constitution of the kingdom depended upon the monarch. Ministers, courtiers, and mistresses vied for control, and the king was caught between them without the courage to act forcefully. Louis XV was not the lusting monster that many French historians have made him out to be; he was a timid man whose good intentions in the early years of his reign earned for him the title of "Louis the Well beloved," and whose incapacities left for posterity the belief that "after me, the deluge" were, or should have been, his last words.

Louis XVI (1774–1792) was an even more unfortunate man. Though reared to be a king, he would have made a better locksmith. He was a good man, a good father, a faithful husband, and had there been no serious problems, he probably would have been a good king, for he wished to rule his people well. But there were problems, and Louis XVI was unable to take decisions easily. He was a poor judge of men and he had a weak will. Such a king was not the man to rule the France that was rapidly becoming a bourgeois society, and in the end the bourgeoisie deprived him of both his throne and his life.

Frederick William's tall soldiers captured the imagination of his contemporaries as well as in later times. One must not fail to see the real reforms of this Prussian king while concentrating on his grotesque guards. (The Bettmann Archive)

Chapter 20

THE EIGHTEENTH CENTURY: CENTRAL AND EASTERN EUROPE

1. BACKWARD AND CONSERVATIVE EASTERN EUROPE

The eighteenth-century traveler who rode eastward from the Rhine made a voyage in time as well as in space, for eastern Europe was from one or two hundred years behind the west of Europe in its political and social structure. The great commercial cities and flourishing towns so characteristic of the countryside in western Europe were farther and farther apart as the traveler journeyed eastward. In England and France the peasants were beginning to secure some control over the land; but in the east the peasants were still serfs. Even before reaching Russia's frontiers, the forms characteristic of eastern Europe were already familiar: great landed estates covering whole counties and under the absolute control of aristocratic families gave form to the social and political society. In Hungary, Poland, Germany beyond the Elbe, in Bohemia-Moravia, and in Russia the pattern was much the same: the land was owned by noblemen and worked by peasants who were virtually slaves.

In eastern Europe there seemed to be a society and an economy with a nearly timeless character. Agriculture was determined by tradition. In the far north, buckwheat rather than wheat or rye provided the bread crop; oats, peas, beans, and barley still formed the base for porridge, soup, and beer. There were differences traceable to climate or soil, but the similarities were great. Just as it had been in the Middle Ages, agriculture was organized in the "field" system that kept the land fertile by leaving part of it fallow each year. In a rich area like the plains of Hungary, great landowners could export their surpluses and could live like princes; in parts of Prussia, where a sandy, glaciated terrain provided poor return from labor, the Junker noblemen had to send their sons into the service of the prince's army or bureaucracy to make ends meet. Forces for change were present, but they worked slowly. Toward the middle of the eighteenth century the grain trade in the Vistula, Danube, Oder, and other river valleys brought more of eastern Europe into economic contact with western Europe, but even at the end of the eighteenth century most people in the east remained largely isolated from the market structure of the Atlantic states.

However, there is almost an inevitability about the impact of economic forces that makes the historian give them great importance in his analyses. In the eighteenth century colonial goods (including coffee, tea, tobacco, cocoa), the traditional wares from the Orient (including spices, drugs, tea, fine cloths), as well as the commodities produced in western Europe (including textiles, hardware, glass, china), did begin to flow into central and eastern Europe in an ever-growing stream. Cities like Frankfurt am Main, Stettin, Danzig, Stockholm, and St. Petersburg, to mention only a few, became the distributing centers for these goods. From the port cities they trickled into the country towns and estates. To pay for these articles, commodities produced in the lands beyond the Rhine had to be sent westward. Wheat, especially after 1763 when England began to import grain on a large scale, became increasingly important as an export from Russia, Poland, Silesia, Bohemia, and Hungary. Cloth came from Germany and the Hapsburg lands; pig and bar iron from Sweden and Russia; furs, skins, tallow, pitch, hemp, wood, and sail cloth from the Baltic lands. Many commodities were the traditional exports of eastern Europe; it was the increase in quantity that marked the expansion of the eighteenth century. Some of the items doubled in volume every decade; all of them showed significant growth.

There were many different forms of organization for the production and export of these products from eastern and central Europe. In Russia, for example, the iron industry developed into a large-scale enterprise. Hundreds of families of serfs were "bound" to the forges that produced the exportable pig and bar iron. In Silesia, linen production was highly organized on a "domestic" system; merchant-manufacturers provided tools and in some cases raw materials for peasant workers who produced the rough cloth. It was bleached, sized, dyed, and pressed in the larger urban centers, sometimes before, sometimes after, being exported to the markets of western Europe. The grain market at Danzig, which dated back to the Middle Ages, became the great cereal mart of the east, for the Vistula river and its tributaries provided transportation from the estates on the Polish plain. The grain merchants and their agents ranged over the whole area collecting cereals for the western market.

While all this gives an alluring picture of an expanding economy, it would be unwise to assume that the economy of eastern Europe was approaching a point where even a sizeable minority of the inhabitants of the area were involved in the market. The manufactured goods, the fine wines and brandies, as well as most of the colonial products that trickled into eastern and central Europe, were consumed by the wealthy elite. Only a small part of such goods ever reached the urban poor or the village peasants. The merchant in his cart was undoubtedly a harbinger of the world to come, but most of eastern Europe still lived under a subsistence economy almost unrelated to the great economic markets beyond the horizon.

2. THE DANUBIAN MONARCHY

The era of warfare that ended with the Treaties of Utrecht and Rastadt (1713–1714) gave considerable impetus to the process that was making a state out of the German, Bohemian, and Hungarian lands in the Danube basin. As we have seen, from the sixteenth century onward the threat of the Turks had kept these peoples in a kind of unity under the House of Hapsburg, but within that loose confederation there were many forces operating to separate them. Provincial loyalties transcended any feeling for the Hapsburg state, and the great families who owned the land jealously guarded their privileges against the authority of a central government.

After his victory over the Bohemian rebels at the White Mountain (1620) and the successes of his armies in the Thirty Years' War, Ferdinand II reduced the Bohemian nobility to submission, and created a government in that kingdom that assured the Hapsburg family a measure of control. Leopold I (1658–1705) did almost the same thing in Hungary when his armies defeated both the Turks and the Hungarian "malcontents" and captured the whole kingdom (1683–1688). Under his rule the Danubian monarchy of the German, Bohemian, and Hungarian lands began to take shape, but it remained a state in which each linguistic group, each traditional kingdom or province, retained special rights and privileges. Even so, Leopold's reign saw the beginnings of a centralized bureaucracy and the idea that the lands of the German Hapsburgs were indissolubly linked together. Leopold's political and economic advisers talked about a *Generallandtag* (a parliament for the whole empire), and managed to introduce many reforms that affected all the empire, but they did not really create a state on the model that was current in western Europe.

The treaties of 1713–1714 complicated the problems of the statesmen in Vienna by giving the Catholic Netherlands and several provinces in Italy to the Hapsburgs. While Leopold had struggled to make a state out of the Danubian lands, his son, Charles VI (1711–1740), now had to govern an empire that was scattered from the English Channel to the Mediterranean. To the traditional problem of bringing Germans, Bohemians, and Hungarians together, was added the difficulty of adjusting to Netherland-Walloon and Italian interests.

In the first decade after the peace of 1713, the cares of the government in Vienna were further complicated by the conquest of Serbia. Prince Eugene, Leopold's greatest general, led a war against the Ottoman Empire, and at Passarowitz forced the Turks to cede Belgrade and most of Serbia, as well as other territory on the southeastern frontier. This introduced a new Slavic-speaking, Greek Orthodox element into the Empire. The Orthodox Serbs were soon dissatisfied with their new Roman Catholic masters; the real emperor, who in their opinion was the heir to the eastern tradition, ruled over the Orthodox Russian community in Moscow and St. Petersburg. The mere fact that he was not yet ready to assume his role as protector of the Slavic Orthodox churches did not deter them from offering him their loyalty. The southern Slav problem was to continue to plague Austrian statesmen as long as the Danubian Empire lasted (1918). Differences in religion, language, and culture were too great to allow their assimilation in a German-Hungarian-Bohemian state. Within a generation, the effort to hold the lands south of the Danube proved to be too much for the government in Vienna. In the last years of Charles VI's reign, the Turks reconquered Serbia with French and Greek aid, and by the treaty of Belgrade in 1739 secured a peace that returned the Serbs to the Ottoman Empire.

Failure to retain the loyalty of the Serbs was only one of the minor problems that plagued Charles VI. Perhaps his greatest personal disappointment was his failure to secure the throne of Spain. He had been driven out of Spain along with the English and imperial armies by Philip of Bourbon, and the treaties of 1713-1714 fully recognized the victory of his rival. Nonetheless, he continued to surround himself with Spanish and Italian advisers, friends of his youth, who had little or no understanding of the problems of his Danubian lands. The old officials who had served both his father, Leopold I, and his brother, Joseph I (1705-1711), still continued to work for the economic and political development of the monarchy, but without enthusiastic or understanding aid and support from the emperor, who remained personally oriented towards Spain until the day of his death.

Charles VI is remembered primarily as the man responsible for the Pragmatic Sanction, the document by which he attempted to guarantee his daughter's right to succeed him on the throne. All Charles' children were girls—a regrettable fact, since several of his lands excluded women, or heirs through women, from the throne. The German Hapsburg inheritance was a complicated assortment of crowns, and even though Leopold I had proclaimed that all those lands and crowns were indissolubly bound together, it was by no means certain that they would remain so. Charles' failure to produce a male heir threatened to result in their separation, and to prevent this he worked from 1713 until his death to secure recognition of his daughter, Maria Theresa, as his sole heir. Thus, Charles had to bribe the various estates and diets of his lands, grant favors to members of his family, and make concessions to the powers of Europe. While the emperor hardly saw more than the dynastic implications of his action, the Pragmatic Sanction was in fact one of the charters that made the Danubian monarchy into a state.

Historians as well as some of his contemporaries have criticized Charles VI for spending time and money to obtain paper guarantees for his daughter's right to follow him on the throne. Had he provided her with an adequate military organization, strong frontier fortifications, and a full treasury, the paper guarantees might not have been necessary. She could have mounted his throne and defied opposition. There is undoubtedly much to be said for this argument, but it overlooks the traditional policy of the Hapsburgs. They ruled a diverse collection of peoples and provinces with different laws, customs, and languages without attempting to impose a single rule upon them; a policy of unity was attempted twice, and each time it proved to be a failure. From the days of Ferdinand I (1556–1564) onward, the Hapsburg policy had been to patch up the central authority by modifying the governmental institutions of the several lands rather than by destroying or completely bypassing the local institutions. Charles may have been in error in his attempt to save his daughter's throne by charters and treaties, but he was acting in accordance with the characteristic pattern of his family. He cannot be blamed for not foreseeing his neighbors' failure to honor their agreements, any more than for not anticipating that the next century would produce the doctrine of nationalism to destroy the state he tried to hold together.

When Charles died in 1740, Maria Theresa (1740–1780) mounted his throne only to be faced with eight years of warfare for the privilege of remaining on it. Her right to rule was challenged from two sources. Frederick II of Prussia (Frederick the Great), who had also just mounted his throne, invaded Silesia to establish the questionable rights of his family over that province. Charles Albert of Bavaria not only invaded Bohemia and the Hapsburg lands in Germany, but also arranged for his election as Holy Roman Emperor. Only in Hungary, where the nobles had traditionally rebelled against the Hapsburg rule, did Maria Theresa find aid and comfort. The Hungarian magnates would not desert the beautiful twenty-three-year-old woman who appealed for their assistance; her beauty proved to be as strong a weapon as her cousin Charles Albert's sword.

As we shall see in a later chapter, the war of the Austrian Succession became involved in the colonial conflict that was developing between the Bourbons of France and Spain on the one side and England on the other. The English were glad to have Austria distract the power of France on the continent; they even acted as intermediary to secure a peace between Prussia and Austria so that the Hapsburg armies could devote their full attention to the Franco-Bavarian forces. By surrendering Silesia to Prussia, the Hapsburg-English forces were able to drive out the other invaders and finally secured a peace (Aix-la-Chapelle, 1748) that recognized Maria Theresa as the ruler of her father's lands. The loss of Silesia, however, was a blow to the young queen's sense of justice, and its recovery was thenceforth her fond ambition. The Seven Years' War (1756-1763) was, as far as Austria was concerned, fought in a vain attempt to recover that province.

Maria Theresa's beauty and motherly character may have attracted loyalty, but neither she nor her ineffectual husband, Francis Stephen, had any real appreciation of the political problems of their age. She had courage and perseverance, and she was a type of universal mother. Her own large family, her husband, her people—she saw them all as objects of motherly love. Anything that she wanted was "justice"; the acts of her enemies were "diabolical violence." Only the fact that she had clever advisers has given her reign a limited fame. Of these, Count Kaunitz was her ablest foreign minister, Count Haugwitz her most effective minister for internal affairs. Count Kaunitz' diplomacy almost encompassed the ruin of her antagonist, Frederick the Great; Count Haugwitz was the architect of the Theresian reforms that continued the labors of her grandfather, Leopold I.

The Prussian victory in Silesia provided the object lesson for Austrian statesmen. With a strong central organization little Prussia had been able to raise and supply armies much larger and better equipped than those which Austria could raise from lands many times as big. Clearly a centralized administration was needed to collect taxes and superintend the army and the police. Neither the Bohemian Diet, which had treasonably sworn allegiance to Charles Albert, nor the German provinces, where Ferdinand II and Leopold I had successfully overruled the *Landtäge* ("estates"), were in any position to resist the movement for reform. The administration of all these lands was combined in a single chancery in Vienna; the elected diets even lost most of their control over the assessment of taxes as well as their right to collect and adminster much of the revenue of the province. This meant that the central bureaucracy could determine the amount and collect the taxes without consulting the elected representatives of the estates. A judicial reform accompanied the administrative and fiscal measures. For the first time in their history the judiciary was separated from the administration in those lands. The most important result was the decline in the importance of the great landed noblemen as governors of the countryside. In place of the feudal relationships that had been common in the past, there emerged a bureaucratic system by which officials of the crown governed both in the provinces and in Vienna, while judges, trained in Roman law, administered justice.

Hungary presented another problem. She had helped to reconquer Bohemia and the German provinces; thus the Hungarians were not rebels who could be forced to accept the queen's pardon in return for the loss of their traditional rights. Leopold's constitution for Hungary (1688-1689) had left the great magnates in control of much of the machinery of royal government and all local administration; it would have been hazardous as well as ungrateful for Maria Theresa to attempt to deprive them of those rights. One historian has called the queen's Hungarian policy "soft violence." Instead of depriving them of control over their lands, she invited the most important of their number to her court, where she showered them with honors, persuaded them to act as her ambassadors abroad, and to lead her armies at home. Her flattery weakened their will to resist her wishes. The Hungarian magnates learned to speak German, married their children to those of German and Czech noblemen, and gradually identified themselves with the fortunes of the Danubian state. Hungary remained feudal in character, for it was not really integrated into the administrative and legal system of the empire, but, for the time at least, the leaders of Hungary were loyal to the Danubian empire.

During the last years of her reign, Maria Theresa associated her son, Joseph II, with her government, and on her death he followed her on the throne. Joseph II (1780–1790) was an admirer of Frederick the Great, and a doctrinaire reformer in the spirit of the "Enlightenment." His sincerity cannot be doubted; his intelligence was unquestionably superior; and his intentions were undoubtedly generous and benign. Nonetheless, his attempt to reform the government and laws of his lands led to rebellion. Many of the measures that Joseph II tried to accomplish were the same that the French Revolution sought to effect a few years after his death. We shall examine some of the problems of his government in a later chapter on the political aspects of the "Enlightenment."

3. BRANDENBURG-PRUSSIA: DUALISM IN GERMANY

If the total picture of European development in the eighteenth and nine-teenth centuries is considered, it is likely that the "land hunger" of Branden-burg-Prussia would be regarded as one of the most revolutionary forces acting upon the society of Europe. In 1700 Brandenburg-Prussia did not ap-pear to have a more promising future than any one of three or four other German states; by 1914 it had become the core of a mighty empire that could challenge all the rest of Europe. It is small wonder that modern historians have paid considerable attention to the story of the Hohenzollern family that governed this state.

Like other German states, the lands and provinces that constituted the in-heritance of the House of Hohenzollern gained quasi-independence from the imperial authority through the Reformation and the religious wars. The Treaties of Westphalia (1648) and Nijmwegen (1678) gave every German princeling the right to behave as an independent sovereign. That "right," however, had meaning only in so far as the prince in question was able to muster the necessary military force to play such a role. No one understood this better than Frederick William, the young prince, who came to the elec-

CENTRAL EUROPE, 1740

Hapsburg Possessions
Hohenzollern Possessions
Venetian Possessions
Holy Roman Empire

toral throne of Brandenburg in 1640. His experience in the Thirty Years'
War taught him clearly that a German prince could either pay a powerful
ally for protection or take the risk of protecting his state by building up his
own military power. There was no third alternative. Frederick William

decided to follow the second path; he earned for himself the surtitle of "The Great Elector," by building up an army and acting as a principal in the politics of Germany and Europe. He was not always able to pay for his military forces out of his own pocket, so he avidly sought allies who would give him a subsidy; and thus the Brandenburg-Prussian army often looked very much like a condottiere force; it also gave that army a meaning that transcended the interests of any single part of the lands under the Hohenzollern princes.

In fact, it might be said that the army made the Hohenzollern lands into a state. When Frederick William ascended the electoral throne, he found himself lord over a string of provinces which spread from the Rhine to the Niemen; they were united only by the fact that all of them had the same prince as ruler. The Hohenzollern family had gained the electoral crown of Brandenburg at the opening of the fifteenth century. When the Reformation secularized many of the ecclesiastical states of Germany, the family had acquired several bishoprics. Even more important, a Hohenzollern prince was Grand Master of the Teutonic Order, and became the first duke of Prussia, which was a fief of the Polish crown. By 1640 the Prussian inheritance had been added to the Brandenburg line. The treaties of Westphalia gave the family its Rhineland provinces and confirmed the acquisition of territory adjoining Brandenburg. Each of these lands, however, had its own traditions, laws, and government; in each the nobility jealously sought to exclude foreigners from any post of confidence, and by foreigners they meant anyone not born in the province itself. Each had a diet or *Landtag* that resisted the use of revenue raised in the province for any purpose outside the boundaries of the province. As long as such provincialisms dominated the scene, there could be no central policy, and no military force to carry out policy for the Hohenzollern lands as a whole.

Frederick William's most important work was his ruthless overriding of the provincial privileges; without that there could have been no Brandenburg-Prussia. He bypassed or ignored the provincial diets, and organized bureaucratic institutions with authority in all of his lands. The first of these was a tax collecting and police agency that managed the farm lands belonging to the prince (the Hohenzollerns were the richest landowners in the provinces), collected the taxes that the prince managed to impose, and organized a primitive police force. The second managed his army: it became a sort of embryonic war ministry that placed the soldiers under the rule of bureaucrats. In developing staffs for the bureaus, Frederick William inaugurated a civil service that was eventually to become the most famous in all Europe. His bureaucrats and the officers of his army were drawn from all his lands; in the service of the prince they lost their identity as Rhinelanders, Prussians, Brandenburgers, or Pomeranians, and became conscious of their loyalty to Brandenburg-Prussia as a state which included all the Hohenzollern lands.

The Great Elector was responsible for the two most important characteristics of the Prussian army. In the first place, from the very beginning he maintained an army much larger than the population of his provinces would seem to justify. When compared to the armies of other states in Europe, the Brandenburg-Prussian army was much larger than the provinces of Brandenburg-Prussia could be expected to support. This in itself was a revolutionary force, for the Hohenzollern princes were always pressed to secure more land and revenue to support their army. The second characteristic was the efficiency of the army. In an effort to play a military role more important than his provinces could support, Frederick William tried to make his army the most efficient in Europe. He recruited the sons of his Junkers (rural noblemen) as officers, and made their promotion dependent upon effective service. He began with the cadet schools and embryo of the Prussian general staff to increase the efficiency of his soldiers.

He did not, however, build up the army without formulating a plan for using it. The army gave him the power to suppress rebellions when local noblemen tried to oppose his unifying policies; it also provided the power that allowed him to act in the wars that raged in the east (Poland versus Sweden) and in the west (the wars of Louis XIV). By judicial use of diplomacy and force, the Great Elector secured recognition of Prussia's freedom from the Polish crown through the Swedish-Polish wars. Thus the Hohenzollerns became independent sovereign dukes of Prussia. His interest in the Dutch War (1672–1678) gave Europe notice of the power of the Brandenburg army through its conquest of Swedish Pomerania, but Louis' victories in the west deprived him of the fruits of his conquest. At the end of his life, Frederick William was again ready to join in a war against Louis XIV, a war that his son fought without the distinction gained by the father.

Frederick (III) I (1688–1713), the son of the Great Elector, had the misfortune to be a man of mediocre talents, although both his father and his son were remarkable individuals. Had it not been for the comparison with them, Frederick (III) I would have enjoyed as much or as little fame as most of the German princes who were his contemporaries. He did succeed in one notable achievement, namely, he secured the recognition of a new title for his house—King in Prussia (Frederick I). This was more than an empty dignity, for it seemed to place the family on a par with the Saxon prince who had become king of Poland and the Hanoverian who was about to become king of England. However, the fact that in the last years of his reign Frederick was unable to maintain the military power of his house meant that the title was a little tarnished by the time of his death. He loved display and pomp more than the work that was necessary to built a state.

When his son, Frederick William I (1713–1740), came to the throne, he gave his father a magnificent funeral and then initiated a regime of severe austerity. The new king understood well that Prussia had lost much since the death of his grandfather, and he was determined to regain the lost ground. As in his grandfather's time, there were three requirements: soldiers, officials to superintend the soldiers, and money to pay both. To get the money required first that his subjects should pay taxes, and second a system for collecting those taxes. The problem was as simple and as difficult as that: Frederick William I spent his whole life solving it.

In his reign the Prussian army and the Prussian state assumed their characteristic forms. His officers and bureaucrats were trained for their tasks and fully indoctrinated with ideals of loyalty and devotion to the state and to their prince. The Prussian officer, unlike his English and French contemporaries, could not buy his commission; he had to win it by service and efficiency. Some historians have ridiculed Frederick William I because he recruited a regiment of giant soldiers, and carefully avoided using either the giants or the rest of his army in a real war. However, the important point was not the use of this army, but its existence. The Prussian army was many times larger in proportion to the number of the king's subjects than any army in Europe, and the discipline and skill of its officers actually made it the equal of armies much larger than itself. It was this army that continued to develop the "land hunger" of Prussia. More land was needed to provide increased tax revenue and recruits, so that the army could grow. At the same time the army was the tool with which the son of Frederick William I acquired more land. Frederick II earned the surtitle "the Great" because his father left him an army and a political machine suitable for conquest.

Furthermore, the political machine that controlled both the army and the state was largely the work of Frederick William I. He ruled his state as an old-fashioned businessman managed his plant; it was a patriarchal establishment, and he poked his nose into every nook and cranny of its management. To do this effectively, Frederick William combined the bureaus that collected taxes, managed farms, ruled the police, and superintended the army into one administrative machine. It was staffed by men who had to pass examinations and depend upon "efficiency" reports for advancement. An eighteenth-century political machine must not be confused with one in the twentieth century; there were no typewriters, railroads, telegraph or wireless transmission, filing cabinets, and the like, to facilitate government. However, Prussia did develop the most efficient government that emerged in the eighteenth century; it had to do so or it could not have supported the Prussian army.

The ever growing military establishment was a heavy burden on the subjects of the Hohenzollern state. Soldiers could be recruited from other parts of Germany, but the money had to come from taxes levied upon his own subjects or from the prince's own agricultural activities. Thus we find the government of Brandenburg-Prussia deeply interested in assisting its people to make more money so that they could pay more taxes. The paternalism that was to be characteristic of the entire history of the Prussian-German state is rooted in this problem. Frederick William I encouraged workers with special skills to migrate to his lands. He passed legislation to aid commerce, industry, and agriculture. His famous son was to be known in history as an "enlightened despot" for carrying on the work begun by Frederick William I. The objective, however, was not to provide greater comfort for the people living under Prussian rule; it was to provide the revenue necessary to maintain the political and military apparatus that made Prussia into a state.

Of all the princes of Prussia, Frederick William I had the poorest "press." He governed without the polite amenities that were becoming characteristic of eighteenth-century society; his so-called "beer and tobacco cabinet" met to discuss affairs of state in a strictly masculine atmosphere. His language was coarse, his manners even coarser, and his proverbial stinginess extended especially to his own needs and those of his family. His treatment of his talented son was nothing less than brutal. His wife and daughter revenged themselves upon him for his boorishness by their letters and memoirs in which they painted the very uncomplimentary picture of this "garrison king" which historians have ever since passed on to their readers. No amount of apology could make Frederick William I into a lovely character; he must be seen as a state builder, a disciplinarian, perhaps even as something of a tyrant. Many of the vices and also of the virtues that we call "Prussian" acquired their characteristic form during his reign.

Frederick II (1740–86) ascended the throne on his father's death. A talented, sensitive, and intelligent young prince whose ambitions prompted him to be a philosopher, a scholar, and a musician, he became the first soldier of his era and the model for all statesmen who aspired to be enlightened despots. In following chapters we shall touch upon his career as a soldier and diplomat and as a philosopher-reformer king. It is enough at this point to explain that his ascent to the Prussian throne seems to mark the end of an old era and the beginning of a new. The Holy Roman Empire was already fully in decay at the beginning of his reign, but it was not until 1740 that the freedom which the German princes had acquired through the treaties of Westphalia and Nijmwegen produced fruit. Frederick II, by seizing Silesia from the Hapsburgs, proclaimed the fact that in addition to Austria, a second great power existed in Germany. The freedom of the princes in central Europe had resulted in the rise of the dualism that was to continue for over a century and a half. Until 1740 the tradition, if not the fact, of a Hapsburg emperor and Hapsburg hegemony had given form to the embers of the Holy Roman Empire. After 1740, Protestant Prussia and Catholic Austria were to be the two points of power in the government and direction of German affairs. The tension that developed between them was at the heart of the so-called "German Question" between 1740 and 1866 when the Austro-Prussian war extruded Austria from Germany.

4. RUSSIA AFTER PETER THE GREAT

As we have seen, Peter I of Russia earned the title "the Great" by turning his kingdom upside down in a mighty effort to defeat the military power of Sweden. Fiscal, military, administrative, religious, and social reforms followed in the wake of his titanic struggle with the Swedish hero-king, Charles XII. Undoubtedly Peter believed that he was Europeanizing his country, but Russia revenged itself by Russianizing Peter's reforms. The European proverb, "Scratch a Russian and you will find a Tartar," like all such easy generalizations, was only half true, but enough of the old Russia survived the Petrine revolution and enough of the western reforms were deformed by Russian ways of life to give it a valid ring. Russia did not lose her traditional character in such a short period as the life of one ruler, no matter how vigorous he may have been.

Nonetheless, Peter did perform political miracles. His wars led to the creation of a modern army and navy, armed and organized in the manner of those of western Europe. His military forces probably were not the equal of those of the west, but the gap between them was closing. His organization of the provincial and central governments of Russia provided the money and the men to maintain this military establishment. It is true that his government was not as efficient as its western models, and it might well be alleged that his fiscal policies were a sort of legal brigandage, but to say that is only to reaffirm the fact that Russia remained Russia, no matter what Peter tried to do. In many areas he only succeeded in creating a burlesqued caricature of the western model, but in at least one aspect of Russian life he succeeded in giving a heavy western veneer to a segment of Russia's population. The nobility, the bureaucracy, and the soldiers learned to dress and behave, outwardly at least, in the western manner, and the nobility gradually learned to talk and to think like their western counterparts. By the end of the eighteenth century they had been transformed into a caste with notions about the world and social customs vastly different from the rest of the Russian people. Along with the bureaucracy, they had become a body of "foreigners" managing the society of Russia. In the long run, this may have been the greatest and the most disastrous of all of Peter's reforms.

Peter would not name his heir as long as he was in good health, and on his deathbed his words became unrecognizable. With the master gone, however, the men around the throne came into their own. Peter had forced his nobles to serve him, and had made nobles out of those who did; individually he often treated them brutally, but at the same time he pampered them as a social class. His crack regiment, the Guards, was composed entirely of the sons of noblemen; upon his death, the Guards were in possession of the military power as well as the will to dictate his successor. They named Peter's second wife, Catherine, a pretty peasant girl with a questionable background, to the throne, but they did not thereby give up the right to dictate policy. For the next century the Guards and the nobility at the court made and unmade the rulers of Russia; the right of palace revolution, and with it the right to murder the czar, almost became an integral part of the Russian constitution. The rulers of eighteenth-century Russia well understood that they had to satisfy the men around the throne or suffer the consequences.

Naturally with the rise in their political prestige, the nobility also strengthened their social and economic position. The idea that the nobility held land in return for service to the ruler was an ancient conception that Peter had reinforced. In the century after his death, however, the nobility largely freed themselves from the contractual relationship that imposed upon them the duty of service to the state. The whole nobility, old and new, emerged as patrimonial landlords, owning their lands by hereditary right. The services that they rendered to the state were paid for from the state's treasury, quite unrelated to the lands that the officeholder might possess. While they succeeded in freeing their economic status from the traditional service contract, they also managed to gain control over the high offices of state, so that the czar's government really became an instrument of their will. The senate, which under Peter had merely been an administrative agency, became a policy-forming institution and was largely staffed by men with great names. The humbler offices in the bureaucracy remained in the hands of little people who became the lackeys of the nobility.

In the country, too, the position of the nobility was strengthened by the hold that they were able to fasten upon the peasants. Peter's need for money and soldiers had led him to give the noblemen an increasing measure of control over the peasants who worked the land. To assure that they could pay their tax obligations, the lands under peasant cultivation for their own use were placed under the direction of the *mir* or village council and redistributed every year. This assured each family enough land to pay taxes, but it also deprived the peasant of any feeling of real ownership in land, since one year he would hold one piece, the next year another. Furthermore, the landlords were invested with additional authority through the process that assured recruits for the czar's army; the nobles and their appointees as headmen of the *mir* had the obligation to name the young men that had to serve in the armed services. This "selective service" made the czar's army "immortal," for he could demand a new recruit to fill any place vacated by death, dismissal, or desertion. It also gave the noblemen a powerful lever over the lives of their peasants. With such controls, the nobility were able to subject the peasants completely. At the opening of the seventeenth century the Russian peasant had gradually been attaining freedom; by the mid-eighteenth century most of them had sunk to the status of serfs who could actually be sold from the land or transferred from one estate to another at the pleasure of the landlords.

In the course of the eighteenth century, the Russian nobility slowly acquired an almost complete veneer of European civilization. Like the nobility of other countries, they accepted the superiority of French culture. They spoke French, read French literature, built their château in the French style, and sent their children to Paris to widen their education. Often enough the culture that they pretended to have was very thin. Their taste for strong liquor and their boorish manners made many of them objects of amusement and possibly scorn in the eyes of their contemporaries in western Europe.

The rest of the nation remained Russian. The peasants entertained all the superstitions that had been accumulated over the centuries; they were a "dark people" in the judgment of Russian intellectuals. The city classes, far from the vital marts of trade in the west, were only slightly stimulated by the forces that were changing the society of western Europe. The result was that the bourgeois class was both weak and ineffectual and remained so even in the nineteenth century. Western notions finally did produce a class of intellectuals, but in the eighteenth century it was of no importance.

The fact that it was perhaps easier to control a woman than a man probably accounts for the fact that eighteenth-century Russia was largely ruled by czarinas (Catherine I, 1725–1727; Anna, 1730–1740; Elizabeth, 1741–1762; and Catherine II, 1762–1796). The male figures that flitted between the reigns of these women were pitiful characters; they neither had, nor would have been allowed to show, the vigor of the great Peter I. Of the czarinas who ruled the land, the last on the list was a remarkable woman. A German princess who became more Russian than any of her court, Catherine II gave Russia as enlightened a rule as the land was ready to accept. She glamorized her court with western intellectuals; she went through the motions of reforms in the western manner; and she extended the frontiers of her kingdom. She has been called the "Great," and listed as one of the enlightened despots of the eighteenth century.

In retrospect, much of the work of Catherine II seems to have been inspired by the traditions of Russia rather than by the *philosophes* of the Enlightenment. From the outset of her reign Catherine depended upon the great landed nobility to command her military forces and manage her government. Several of the nobles were her lovers, but most of them served the throne because the throne served their political and social interests. Catherine did make a much advertised reform in the administrative structure of the kingdom, but the result was not self-government, nor even control over local government by the gentry. The reform left the reality of powers in the hands of the central authority while it made the Russian gentry, like the Prussian Junkers, responsible, as unpaid servants, for local administration. Catherine, who was hailed as a Russian Justinian, succeeded in strengthening her own power by legal and administrative reforms.

The position of the majority of the Russian people, namely the peasants, deteriorated sadly under Catherine. In the first decade of her reign, she was confronted with a peasant revolt led by a Don Cossack, Pugachev, who posed as Peter III. Supplied with cannon from factory workers in the lower Urals and with cavalry from the Bashkir herdsmen, Pugachev won victories that brought his armies almost to St. Petersburg. His slogans, "seize, execute, and hang all landlords," "pay no taxes," "refuse military service," won him wide support wherever his forces could make contact with the peasantry. The rebellion left behind it a trail of flaming châteaux and drove before it the terrified gentry. But Pugachev's forces were no match for the regular army whose rank and file could not "hear" the slogans. He was defeated, captured, drawn and quartered. "This severe penalty," writes Professor Gershoy, ". . . helped to make his erstwhile followers more accommodating."

The Pugachev revolt put an end to any possibility that Catherine might reform the laws regulating the peasantry. The pattern, started by Peter I, that gave the peasants' life and labor over to the landlords was more firmly fixed in Russian law. The landlord, in return, kept the peasants from disturbing the peace, drew on their young men for soldiers to fill the ranks of the army, and took from them the taxes due the government. In other words, Catherine was an enlightened despot in the manner that Peter I had been. Voltaire, writing a history of Peter I, hailed him as a great enlightened prince even though to do so he had to "forget" much of Peter's reign. The *philosophes* who welcomed Catherine into their ranks because she distributed pensions and patronized the arts and sciences seem also to have been blind to the fact that Catherine was a Russian despot rather than an enlightened one. Like many other political reputations, Catherine's fame was fashioned of a little fact and much printer's ink.

5. THREE DECLINING EMPIRES: SWEDEN, POLAND, AND TURKEY

Sweden

Between the frontiers of Russia and those of western Europe there were three states that proved incapable of maintaining their power and influence. The Swedish empire rapidly went into decline after the death of Charles XII (1718); the dual monarchy of Poland-Lithuania suffered a similar fate in the years following the War of the North (1700–1721); and the Ottoman Empire continued to suffer from the forces of decay that had set in during the seventeenth century. The causes for decline were different in each case; the only thing that they had in common was that Russia came forward as the heir

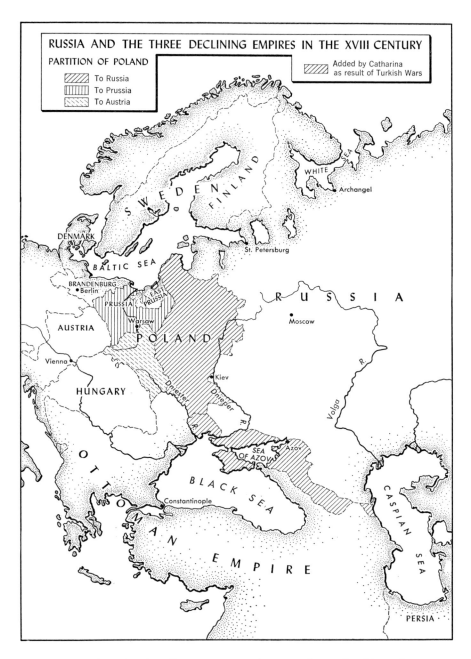

RUSSIA AND THE THREE DECLINING EMPIRES IN THE XVIII CENTURY

PARTITION OF POLAND

To Russia
To Prussia
To Austria

Added by Catharina
as result of Turkish Wars

apparent to their lands. The expansion of Russia from the fifteenth century onward had been at the expense of declining political societies on the Russian frontiers.

As we have seen, the Baltic empire that Gustavus Adolphus and his followers had established for Sweden was the first casualty in the path of the rising

Moscovite state. When Peter had challenged the Swedish power in 1700, his armies had been no match for those of the hero-king, Charles XII. Even with odds of eight to one against them, the Swedes won the early battles. However, Sweden was then at the height of her power; Peter had only started to create a Russian armament. After a little less than a decade of warfare, the size of Russia and the persistence of its czar had turned the tables against the Swedish army.

The troubles of Sweden's Baltic empire arose from the fact that it was not really an integrated state. Both the so-called Baltic provinces and the German lands were ruled as conquered or foreign areas, so that neither their nobility nor their townsmen acquired any real loyalty to Sweden or Sweden's kings. The Swedish provinces had supplied the energy and also the manpower to create the empire, but they proved too narrow a base for a government of the whole territory. In the crisis of the War of the North, they were unable to supply Charles XII with the money and men necessary to defeat his enemies. When we consider the basis for Swedish power at the opening of the eighteenth century, the astonishing thing is not that Charles XII was finally defeated by Russia and Poland-Saxony, but that he was able to fight as long and as well as he did. His father, Charles XI, had been the great reformer in Sweden who had left his son the army and the governmental machine that provided the force to hold out against the Russian forces for almost two decades, but it was not strong enough to match the power that Peter's reforms could squeeze out of Russia, a land mass many times larger and more populous than Sweden.

Swedish historians have differed in their judgment of the hero-king, Charles XII. Those whose attention has been drawn to the financial disorder of the kingdom, to the fact that for a generation the women greatly outnumbered the men, or to the loss of the empire, have condemned Charles as a madman. Those who see Russia as the great menace to the west regard Charles as the hero who tried to stem the Russian tide. Charles XII himself would not have understood either of these judgments. His contempt for Peter's army blinded him to the potential military power of Russia; his unwillingness to consider the welfare of Sweden as the central objective of his government would have made incomprehensible the notions of the men who considered him to be mad. Charles was a ruler with a very limited conception of government; he fought his great war to punish the villains that had tried to rob him of his patrimony. He had no idea of his place in the world historical process.

Historians are agreed upon the change that developed in Sweden after Charles' death. The Caroline era (1660–1718) is known in Swedish history as the "time of strength"; the period that followed it was called "the time of freedom." Charles' death gave the nobility a chance to assert their ancient privileges and powers that had been denied them since about 1680. The crown had spent too lavishly of its wealth and prestige in the wars, and the nobility was able again to bring it under their influence. Thus, Charles' failure to stop Russia also entailed the subordination of the crown and the royal authority to the interests and needs of the landed nobility. This development is obviously in the form characteristic of much of eastern Europe, where the nobility seized control over the government whenever the prestige of the crown could be subordinated to their interests. From Charles' death to the coup d'état engineered by Gustavus III in 1772, the nobility governed Sweden. Their regime threatened to lead to a situation similar to the one that ended in the territorial extinction of Poland. Only the forceful reassertion of the rights of the crown by Gustavus III reconstituted the central authority.

During the era of "liberty," there were two parties in Sweden. The Hats who favored a war of revenge against Russia, and the Caps who wished to remain at peace. The issue, however, was not a real one, for Sweden was so weak that war was next to impossible. In 1741–1743 the Hats tried to recapture some of the lost Baltic provinces, but Russia was too strong, and the effort ended in disaster. The Sweden that had placed so great a role in the seventeenth century had become an unimportant politico-military force in the eighteenth.

Poland

The fate reserved for Poland was even more drastic. The Polish-Lithuanian kingdom was a dual monarchy with an elected king; its constitution prevented any effective action on the part of the central government. Thus, in an age that elsewhere saw the extension of the authority of the centralized power in government, the Polish state was condemned to a pattern of politics that rapidly became anachronistic. The Polish kings were bound by complicated election oaths guaranteeing the traditional laws of the kingdom and by an extensive array of rights and privileges asserted and defended by the landed nobility. Their power to legislate for the kingdom was limited to action through the Diet, and any member of that assembly could veto any action by a single vote. The *Liberum Veto* that placed all policy at the mercy of the most irresponsible member of the Diet was freely used; in at least one case a member of the Diet evoked the veto "just to see what would happen." Nor did the contingent anarchy end with the Diet's inability to act. Each palatine, a great landlord who was governor of a circle or province, had the right of "confederation" which, in effect, meant the right to ally with other great noblemen and make war on the king. Polish noblemen had tender consciences about dethroning a duly elected king, but they thought little of making civil war against him if they felt their interests were endangered.

Such a constitution fairly invited foreign intervention. At each election in the seventeenth century Hapsburg, Bourbon, and Vasa money came from

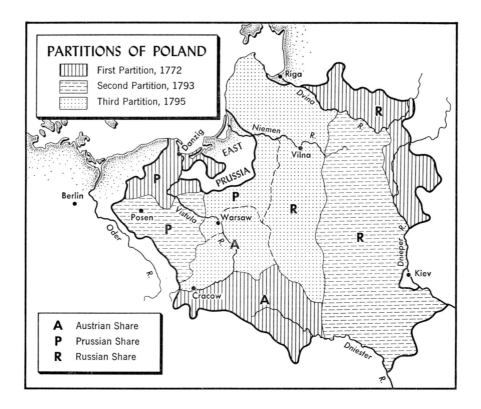

A   Austrian Share
P   Prussian Share
R   Russian Share

Austria, France, and Sweden to influence the choice of the monarch, and once a king was elected, he was confronted by noblemen who took money, arms, and advice from foreigners. Polish politics became a plaything of Poland's neighbors. In the eighteenth century, especially after the victory of Russia over Sweden (1709–1721), Poland fell more and more under the spell of her eastern neighbor. Neither a Saxon nor a native king could maintain himself without foreign aid. Poland developed no army worthy of the name, no war chest, and no effective means of collecting money; thus the kingdom became a politico-military vacuum, waiting for its neighbors to step in and divide the land between them.

The first partition of Poland (1772) was the result of the rising power of Prussia and Russia that came after their victories in Germany (Prussian annexation of Silesia) and in southeast Europe (Catherine's war with the Turks). Her neighbors (Prussia, Austria, and Russia) simply annexed Polish frontier provinces that would round out their own frontiers. The second and third partitions of Poland (1793 and 1795) were as much the result of the weakness of France during the early years of her Revolution as of the weakness of Poland. France's inability to interfere or to demand compensation invited the eastern powers to enlarge their lands at the expense of the impotent kingdom that they surrounded. The partitions have been branded as political brigandage; they might be understood better if the question of morality is dropped, and they are seen as the inevitable result of a politico-military vacuum; a whole kingdom cannot be devoid of political order and military force without inviting intervention from without.

Turkey

The process of disintegration had begun in the Ottoman Empire even before the opening of the seventeenth century, but there were also forces operating to keep the Turkish state from going to pieces completely. The central problem of the empire was that its government was dependent upon the existence of a strong personality at the helm. Created by a line of vigorous sultans, it had no mechanism to operate the government if the sultan happened to be weak and unimaginative. After the death of Suleiman the Magnificent (1566), there were few sultans who could fill the role to which they had been born; as a result, the Janissary corps became an unruly palace guard that made and unmade sultans. Harem intrigue took the place of state deliberation, while the provincial authorities increasingly tended to act without consulting the central government. For a few years in the seventeenth century a series of strong viziers, mostly from the Kupruli family, gave the state the semblance of its old power, but after 1683, when Kara Mustafa's huge army was driven from Vienna, the Ottoman Empire was clearly disintegrating, despite the efforts of reforming viziers.

The day of its destruction, however, was postponed until the nineteenth century, first because in its peril the empire of the Turks found that it could secure aid from at least one of the states of Europe that opposed the expansion of another, and, second, because its Greek subjects decided that submission to the empire was preferable to absorption by the Latin powers of Europe.

France was the first western state to come to the sultan's aid. Louis XIV, fearing the expansion of the German House of Hapsburg, intervened in the Rhineland in 1688 when the Austrian capture of Belgrade had opened the route toward Constantinople. Louis' instructions to his ambassador left no doubt as to his fears or his intentions; he wanted to keep the Ottoman Empire as a counterweight to Austria. After France had been temporarily removed from her dominant position in Europe and weakened by the fact that her king, Louis XV, was a minor, Austria again invaded the Balkans. Prince Eugene recaptured Belgrade, and at Passarovitz (1719) forced the sultan to cede most of Serbia, but in the following decades France reappeared as the patron of the sultan, and in the 1730's the Austrians were forced to give up Serbia (Treaty of Belgrade, 1739). At that time a Franco-Ottoman treaty, the result of Turkish gratitude, gave France rich commercial, cultural, and political advantages in the Levant. Later in the century, when Catherine

II of Russia began to press the Turks hard, the Austrian government was at first a Russian ally against the traditional enemy, but as soon as the Treaty of Kuchuk Kainarji (1774) revealed the extent of Russia's territorial ambitions, the Austrian government decided to reverse its traditional anti-Turkish policy. In the next two centuries Austria, France, England, Germany, and finally the United States, came to the aid of the Turks against the southward pressure of Russian expansion.

In addition to the air that came from without, the Ottoman Empire received important assistance from within its own frontiers. The Greek population of the empire was active in commerce and industry. They owned much of the shipping that flew the Ottoman flag; they had clever legal and commercial manipulators in their community who knew western languages and laws. The Austro-Venetian victories in Hungary, Transylvania, Serbia, and the Morea (1684–1699) showed them that there were worse rulers than the Turks. Italian merchants and Roman Catholic monks followed the Christian armies. The one undercut the Greek commercial position; the other threatened the Greek Orthodox church. One way to avert these evils was to enter the Ottoman service and bolster the tottering empire. The men who joined the sultan's bureaucracy were called Phanariot Greeks from the section of the city where many of them lived. Their intervention provided the sultan with personnel to take the place once occupied by the great servants of the Janissary epoch. In those days the sultan needed soldiers; after the eighteenth century he needed diplomats and administrators, positions that the Greeks were admirably suited to fill. So many Greek civil servants rose to high rank that it almost seemed that the Greeks had taken over the Ottoman Empire for themselves. They and the great powers staved off the day of final reckoning for the Turkish state, even though they were obviously unable to revivify it and give it a real chance to play a great role in the politics of Europe.

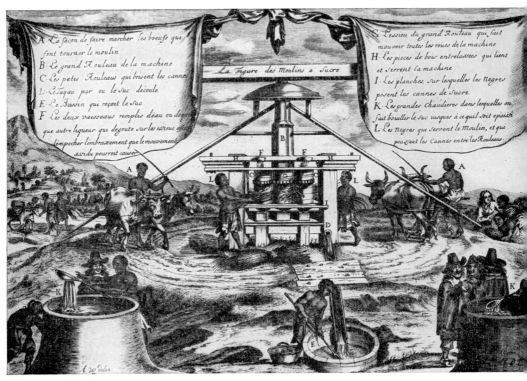

A. La façon de faire marcher les boeufs qui font tourner le moulin

B. Le grand Rouleau de la machine

C. Les petis Rouleaux qui brisent les cannes

D. Le Tuyau par ou le Suc découle

E. Le Bassin qui reçoit le Suc

F. Les deux vaisseaux remplis d'eau ou de que autre liqueur qui degoute sur les essieux pour empecher l'embrazement que le mouvement assidu pourroit causer

La Figure des Moulins a Sucre

S. L'essieu du grand Rouleau qui fait mouvoir toutes les roues de la machine

H. Les pieces de bois entrelassees qui lient et serrent la machine

I. Les planches sur lesquelles les negres posent les cannes de Sucre

K. Les grandes chaudieres dans lesquelles on fait bouillir le suc iusques a ce qu'il soit epaisir

L. Les negres qui servent le Moulin, et qui poussent les Cannes entre les Rouleaux

Sugar Mill in the Antilles. Oxen furnish the power while slaves feed the cane stalks into the rollers that extract the juice. (University of Minnesota Library)

Chapter 21

COLONIAL EMPIRES

1. THE SPANISH EMPIRE IN THE NEW WORLD

In the seventeenth century Protestant enemies of Spain re-edited the works of the historian Las Casas to prove how brutally Spain had treated the Indians. Las Casas' original writings had been intended as an indictment of the Spanish inhabitants of the colonies; edited and enlarged by Protestant propagandists, he was made to say that the whole history of Spanish America was one of bloodshed and massacre. In the nineteenth century certain apologists for Spanish colonial policies reached the opposite conclusion. In their writings no government or colonial administration in the history of the world had ever been as humane and as solicitous for native welfare as the Spaniards. However, both the opponents and the apologists failed to see the mechanics of Spanish policy; they failed to concern themselves with the realities of life that made the Spaniards behave as they did.

Neither the Spaniards nor Columbus had any intention of founding an empire when he sailed under the flag of their king. They thought that the voyage might result in the discovery of a shorter route to the Orient. Columbus even called the miserable half-naked savages he found on the islands by the improbable name, Indians. He assumed that he would soon contact the Chinese mainland and the court of the emperor. It was almost three decades later before the Spaniards finally realized that they had blundered onto another continent, that their calculations about the size of the earth were wrong. The Americas were at first an obstacle; only later were they recognized as valuable in themselves.

The Spanish court, even if it had understood what was before it, was too weak, too poor, and too occupied in Europe to undertake to direct the exploration and conquest of the New World. As we have already seen, the rulers of sixteenth-century Spain were interested in bringing some unity to the Spanish kingdoms. They were involved militarily in Italy and the Lowlands; they had to contend with Moorish and Berber pirates; and they had to face the possibility of a new invasion by Islam. The islands of the Antilles were far away. The mainland of the Americas was even farther. The only possible solution was to allow private individuals to organize and direct the exploration and conquest as private adventures under the general supervision of the crown. The conquistadores who were allowed to consolidate the Spanish empire provide excellent examples of the effectiveness of private initiative dedicated to personal gain.

These conquistadores were usually supported financially by some wealthy patron; their military forces consisted of friends, family, and hangers-on who were willing to risk their lives against possible profit. They performed astonishing feats. Cortés conquered Mexico with four hundred foot soldiers, fifteen cavaliers, and seven cannon. Pizarro conquered Peru with about a hundred men and sixty horses. Naturally both were aided by Indian enemies of the Aztec and Inca empires. The conquistadores received a royal grant that amounted to quasi-sovereignty over immense tracts of land including the right to levy taxes and a *corvée* on the natives, as well as to exploit whatever wealth could be found. The king of Spain reserved his share, usually twenty percent of any treasure discovered. The conquistadores also became laden with honors. Cortés, for example, became captain-general, governor, and Marquis del Valle de Oajaca.

From our point of view the conquest seems to have been remarkably easy. Native military and political power proved unable to match the armor, horses, and firearms of the white men. Superstitious belief that the Spaniards were the "expected white gods" aided Cortés; the inner weakness of the Inca empire aided Pizarro. The Spanish were convinced that God was with them; they were men trained in wars in Europe, hardened by their lives in Spain, and avid for gain. Their successes emboldened them to greater efforts, and once the Incas and Aztecs were defeated they encountered no further serious opposition. The poor Indian who assumed the mounted horseman to be *one* creature could not be expected to put up much resistance to such wonderful animals!

As soon as the first wave of the conquest was past, the government in Spain began to extend its authority over the land. Royal courts, called *audiencias,* were established and endowed with administrative as well as judicial powers: they acted as councils for viceroys. The list of Spanish colonies in America grew rapidly: Hispaniola, 1511; Mexico, 1521; Panama, 1536; Lima, 1544; and so forth. A captain-general in charge of soldiers was placed beside the courts to assure obedience. Gradually, in the emerging towns and cities officials characteristic of Spanish local government appeared. Toward the middle of the sixteenth century the work of the viceroys, the courts, and local officials came to be supervised by the famous Council of the Indies in Madrid. The Spanish crown ruled all its land with royal councils;

the Council of the Indies became the most famous colonial agency the world saw before the rise of the nineteenth-century British Empire.

From the earliest days of the conquest there were differences of opinion as to how the natives should be treated. Those on the islands were for the most part either exterminated or enslaved, and in slavery they died out as a race; but on the mainland the natives were too numerous for the successful application of such a policy. Furthermore, the friars objected to the brutal treatment of the natives; they even rejected the idea that the Indians should be converted by force.

Sixteenth-century European men raised no question about the Spanish king's right to rule the Indians; the pope granted him sovereignty over every land that his subjects discovered. The government in Madrid, particularly after Charles V became king, ruled over many peoples: Italians, French, Netherlanders, Germans, and several Spanish kingdoms. That government was disposed to see the Indians as just another people, equal in status with the rest of its subjects. Convinced as they were of the superiority of Castilian culture, the men in Madrid assumed that the Indian could be taught to speak a little Spanish, worship as a Christian, and conduct his economic life within a Spanish framework, but that in other respects he would remain an Indian. Royal ordinances throughout the sixteenth century were based on these assumptions.

The Spaniards who settled in America took a somewhat different attitude. They regarded the Indians as dangerous, and they wanted to exercise a conqueror's rights. In the colonies a race-conscious, aristocratic society developed in control of the land and the principal sources of wealth in the cities. These people wished to enslave the Indians and keep them in the status of second-class men. They only found slight support in Spain, but even though the government might be largely against them, their positions of power as soldiers, governors, and landowners in America allowed them to implement much of their policy, and at the same time to ignore the more humane attitude of the government in Madrid. Las Casas wrote his memoirs to force the government to act against these people, but no mere book could change the deeply ingrained social and racial prejudices of white men surrounded by a sea of natives.

The natives were widely different in culture and adaptability. From the simple savage cannibal tribes on some of the islands to the complex empires of Mexico and Peru, there was a tremendous gap in civilization. Like the peoples of Europe, the indigenous peoples of the Americas presented a wide diversity of cultural achievements. In the case of the more advanced societies, the Spaniards substituted themselves for the aristocratic upper crust that had previously ruled; in the case of the less organized societies, some were "domesticated," some exterminated, and some driven into the interior, where they made trouble on the frontiers for the Spaniards and their protégés. Throughout the first three centuries following the discoveries, there was a great difference between European understanding and ideas about the Indians and the actual realities in the New World, and that accounts for much of the misunderstanding about America.

The growth of the Spanish colonial empire was largely conditioned by the fact that gold and silver were found in Mexico and Peru. To operate the mines, labor, food, textiles, leather, iron, and many other commodities were required. In the early years, the native process was used to extract the silver, but that was extremely costly in fuel. Later, German technology introduced the process utilizing mercury. It was less costly, but hardly a simple solution. Fortunately the quicksilver that was necessary for the German process was also found in the New World. The economic demands did not stop at the mine and the smelter. The ore was found far from the sea, and to carry it to market and to supply the mines necessitated transportation routes along which towns and cities appeared to provide services and goods. Since the mines produced the metals that could easily pay for such services, by the end of the sixteenth century a vigorous, healthy economy had developed in the Spanish New World.

The amount of treasure exported per year gives some indication of the pressure behind the growth of the colonies. Up to about 1535 it was of minor importance, except as a promise of things to come, but from then until 1600 the amount of treasure taken from the mines increased spectacularly every year. After 1625 it began to taper off, and by 1660 the flow of precious metal was again at the level of 1535. In the years 1521 to 1660 the Spanish colonies produced about eighteen thousand tons of silver and two hundred tons of gold. Compared with modern mining, this is not a large amount, but in the sixteenth and seventeenth centuries it provided a very considerable addition to existing stocks in Europe.

By 1650 there were about eighteen thousand Spaniards in the new world. They organized the mining enterprises, operated the government, provided military protection, built the towns and cities, and supervised the introduction of European animals and plants into the New World. Plantations and ranches sprang up all the way from Cuba to Peru, where Spaniards introduced their agriculture. Pigs, sheep, goats, and particularly cattle were acclimated easily to the new environment. The cattle did so well on the virgin pasture that the cows dropped calves before their second year. Since leather was more important than meat, and would long remain so, large herds alone could be profitable. Before the opening of the seventeenth century we hear of ranches with ten thousand to a hundred thousand head of cattle tended by mounted vaqueros. Because of the obvious military value of the horse, the Spaniards tried to restrict its use to whites alone. This, of course, proved impractical and impossible. By the seventeenth century, horses, both wild and tame, were to be found throughout the Spanish empire, and far up the Mississippi valley, where they produced a revolution in the way of life of the Indians on the plains.

The Spaniards also introduced their bread and porridge crops, of which wheat and beans soon became staples throughout the colonies. They began the cultivation of citrus fruits, the grape, cocoa, coffee, sugar, indigo, rice, and tobacco; all the crops that would flourish in tropical or semitropical climates were planted. Sugar and cocoa immediately became popular, for the habit of drinking chocolate spread rapidly among the upper classes in Spain. The Spanish princesses, Anne and Maria Theresa, introduced the custom to the French courts of Louis XIII and Louis XIV. Negro slaves imported from Africa were used for the tropical and semitropical plantation type agriculture, after it had become clear that the Indians simply died when subjected to such labors. The cereal and vegetable agriculture was more suited to the Indians' way of life and could be adapted to fit their society.

Most of the staple agricultural produce was consumed in the colonies, while "colonial wares," that is, coffee, cocoa, sugar, and the like, were of importance as exports; but it was gold and silver that were the foremost exports from the Spanish colonies. All this traffic was rigidly controlled both in the New World and in Spain. Bullion and goods had to be assembled at specified ports in the Americas, and were carried to specified ports in Spain; the government had to be sure that it got its tax and its share of the treasure. In practice this resulted in the periodic departure of the "treasure fleet." From Spain it carried textiles, hardware, spirits, and luxury items to the New World, where they were sold at exorbitant prices because of the government's deliberate policy of limiting the supply. The fleet then brought back precious metals, leather and colonial goods, that were exchanged for French, Dutch, Italian, English, and German commodities sent to Spain. Thus did the precious metals flow to all Europe.

The scarcity of European goods in the colonies combined with the fact that the military forces in most of the port cities were small and the amount of gold and silver at their disposal large, made the colonies attractive to smugglers. Foreigners were forbidden to trade with the Spanish colonies, but interlopers from England, France, or Holland could sail their ships into a colonial harbor, and, with the connivance of the residents, hold it under their guns and force the colonists to buy their goods. Not all smuggling was that brash, but in the seventeenth century smuggling increasingly became a standard practice. The treasure fleet, the smugglers, and the general lack of naval control infested the waters off the "Spanish Main" with a lawless element. These pirates could set themselves up on one of the uninhabited islands, and from there operate against both the legitimate and illegitimate commerce of the area. Some of the island possessions claimed by the northern powers in the Antilles were first of all nests for "gentlemen" who flew the skull and crossbones.

The vigor of Spanish administration had begun to decay even before the flow of precious metals had dwindled. As we have already seen, neither Philip III nor Philip IV were kings of the mold of the sixteenth-century Charles V and Philip II, and in the latter seventeenth century Charles II was a king who was scarcely a man. The effectiveness of the Council of the Indies began to wane, and worst of all, the mines yielded less wealth. Inevitably, poor government and declining wealth brought in their train changes in the structure of the colonies. By 1715 the forms characteristic of the next century and a half had come into existence.

By the opening of the eighteenth century cities that had once been important centers of trade had become sleepy, poverty-ridden provincial towns. In many places the English and Dutch were surprised to see the Spaniards move away from the coast into the interior, because there was no longer enough trade to keep the ports open. The treasure fleets ceased to make regular voyages; several years passed without a departure. The commerce that there was in many places was simply illegal traffic with smugglers. But the empire did not cease to exist: it merely changed its form. Everywhere one institution arose to give stability to the society. The hacienda, an estate, a plantation, or a ranch of some sort, became the center of life. The haciendado, its owner, took on the characteristics of a great lord or seignior. He administered justice, organized whatever military power there might be, managed political life, and in general controlled the destinies of the people on his hacienda, which had become a self-sufficient political and economic unit. As the amount of money available diminished, the hacienda became increasingly self-sufficient.

Where the Negro slave had not become the source of labor, the villagers fell into a sort of servitude. They owed money to the haciendado beyond anything they or their children could hope to repay. Called peons, their peonage was not dissimilar to the serfdom that had held European peasants in bondage in the Middle Ages. The peons tended the flocks, worked the fields, and supplied the labor to man the haciendado's household and run his enterprise. The clergymen who tended to their spiritual needs were also creatures of the haciendado. Society resembled that of Europe in the seventh and eighth centuries.

Not all the haciendas were owned by laymen. The friars had established missions in the settled country and on the frontiers with the object of converting the Indians. The missions were usually fortifications, even possessing cannon, so that they provided places of security for the more civilized Indians against the inroads of lawless tribes. The friars were quite successful in Christianizing the Indians, even though it was not uncommon for the superstitious natives to pay homage to their old gods as well as to the new one. The superior culture and more effective economy acted as compelling agents in the struggle. Thus, the friars gathered around them Indian villages under their tutelage in a society not dissimilar to the layman's hacienda. They did not encourage the Indians to become priests, so the same white-native gap that was evident elsewhere existed also in the missions.

The Jesuits wished to isolate the natives from evil contacts with both the merchants and the slave raiders. After failing in Portuguese Brazil to save the Indians from contact with bad white men, they persuaded the Spanish king to allow them to control Paraguay. There they set up a theocratic society isolated completely from other Europeans. Much nonsense about the evils of this experiment has been written by people who hated the Jesuits and wished to profit from exploitation of Paraguay. The fact remains that the Jesuits produced an economy that banished fear of hunger and guaranteed, by military force, security from attack. They introduced tea, and forbade alcohol; they made laws that did not include the death penalty at a time when there were hundreds of offenses that merited hanging in Europe. The experiment came to an end when the Jesuit Order was banished and dissolved in Catholic Europe in the mid-eighteenth century. The natives were quite unable to operate this society without Jesuit aid.

The Jesuits as well as the friars created variations on the hacienda system. Perhaps only such a socioeconomic political unit will work when the economy can no longer be "oiled" with money. It resulted in a decentralization of power that made any attack on the empire a vain effort, for there were no vital points that could be used to control the whole. On the other hand, the system did actually allow for a kind of defense because the coastal waters came to be patrolled by "private" Spanish forces (the hacienda system adapted to the coastal waters) that may have appeared to be little more than legalized pirates, but could in any event act against the unwanted inroads of other pirates. It was this informal defense system that led to conflict between Spain and England in the mid-eighteenth century.

In addition to the colonies in the Americas, there was one other relatively important Spanish colony, that of the Philippines. Although the pope gave these islands to Portugal, Spain still held on to them as a window or a door for trade with China. The Manila galleons carrying oriental goods sailed across the Pacific to the Isthmus of Panama, whence their cargoes were transported overland and then shipped to Europe. Just as they did in America, the Spaniards taught some of the inhabitants of the Philippines their language, their religion, and their economy. Up to the twentieth century, Manila was a Spanish city with the institutions and the architecture of the Spanish empire. The hacienda system never became as widespread as it had in the Americas, but in the Philippines, too, it appeared when Spain began to lose her power, her wealth, and her vigor.

SPANISH AND PORTUGESE
AMERICA IN THE
18TH CENTURY

Spanish Possessions

Portugese Possessions

2. THE PORTUGUESE EMPIRE

As we have seen, the Portuguese commercial empire was the result of years
of careful preparation and exploration. Where Spain blundered into an empire, Portugal labored to found one. Her great mariners who pushed down
the African coast and finally reached India were determined to turn the
flank of Islam and to contact the East without Mohammedan interference.
When they reached India, they turned farther east to the spice islands,
China, and even Japan. In the sixteenth century, except for the meager entry
afforded the Spaniards through Manila, the Portuguese had a monopoly of
the European trade with this vast area.

The Portuguese pattern was to secure port rights and a compound or
"factory" area as a base for trade with the country. In India the Mogul power
was uninterested either in sea power and commerce or in the fate of the

Arab merchants, so the Portuguese had no trouble getting the limited concessions they wanted. Farther east, the Portuguese secured similar rights in Macao near Canton and in one or two ports of Japan. They also established themselves on the island of Timor in the East Indies. To reach these commercial centers in the small ships of the sixteenth century, the Portuguese established settlements on both sides of the African coast (Angola and Mozambique), where vegetables and other supplies could be assembled for the ships that made the long voyages eastward.

Although the Portuguese assumed little or no responsibility for the government of the lands with which they traded, their empire was nonetheless held together and extended by military power. In the first quarter of the sixteenth century, their cannon swept the Arabs off the Indian Ocean and the Arabian Sea, and in every port where a Portuguese factory was established the local authorities knew that, when it arrived, the Portuguese fleet would be the preponderant military power in the city. Thus military force secured for the Portuguese merchants a favored position in trade. However, Portugal was a power that did not outlast the sixteenth century. When the Dutch and the English began to sail southward in the closing years of the sixteenth century, Portugal, under Spanish influence, was too weak to prevent the intruders from elbowing their way into the oriental trade. Little Portugal lacked the wealth and the manpower to monopolize the oriental trade after the growing wealth of Europe transformed the trickle of goods that came from the East in the fifteenth century into the broad stream of commerce of the eighteenth. In this changed world situation the Portuguese had to be content with a minor role in eastern commerce.

Portuguese Brazil is another story, but one that was also conditioned by the smallness of Portugal's population. In 1199 Pope Innocent III claimed for the papacy the right to govern the world. On the basis of this claim, in 1493 Pope Alexander VI divided the world beyond the sea between Spain and Portugal at a line one hundred leagues west of the Azores. The next year the Treaty of Tordesillas revised that line to leave most of the territory that was to become modern Brazil in the hands of Portugal.

Early in the sixteenth century this territory became important, because of the demand for Brazil wood from which red and purple dyes could be made. French as well as Portuguese traders landed on the coast, and persuaded the natives that European beads, knives, axes, textiles, and so forth were worth the labor of cutting the wood. The agents put ashore found the native women particularly agreeable, with the result that by the mid-sixteenth century there was a half-breed population that could be used to extend European influence. The Portuguese successfully drove out the French who, curiously enough, had planned in terms of a Calvinist-Huguenot settlement and could, consequently, get no help from Catherine de Medici and her sons. The sons of Frenchmen and native women, however, remained in the province.

Colonial settlement in Brazil is a checkered story. The Jesuit fathers were the first to establish successful plantations, but they were eventually driven out by planters who objected to the fathers' native policy. The slavers drove the Jesuits to Paraguay, where they established their theocratic society. By the seventeenth century there were six or seven well-established centers or captaincies on the Brazilian coast, and a plantation economy flourished there. The fact that the Portuguese and Spanish crowns were united under Philip II made no difference in the relations between Lisbon and Brazil, but it gave the Dutch, particularly after 1624, license to attack and pillage Portuguese colonial installations. Indeed, for over a decade the Dutch West India Company ruled Brazil.

By the end of the seventeenth century the pattern of Brazilian society was well developed. There were relatively few Europeans in the colony, and the few that were there were usually of mixed blood. The plantations were operated by slave labor—Negroes, because the Indians did not make good slaves. In the cities a few merchants and craftsmen supplied goods for rural areas and for workers at the plants that processed the sugar, brazil wood, cocoa, and coffee. The life of the owners on the plantations was easy and luxurious. The Indian and Negro women who were their wives and mistresses taught the planters to eat a diet suitable to the climate, to bathe daily, and in general to live the languid existence of the tropics. The wealth that came from their crops allowed them luxuries that made Brazilian life seem sensuous and fabulous to visitors.

By the eighteenth century a new race and a new civilization was emerging in Brazil. Indian and Negro words as well as the different Negro accents that softened vowels and slurred consonants gave Brazilian Portuguese a distinct character defying the schoolmaster's attempts to keep it pure. At the same time, the eighteenth century saw Brazilian wealth increase and with it the culture of its cities which, in spite of native influences, was Latin in most of its expressions. In the eighteenth century racist doctrines appeared in Brazil, and wealthy Brazilian men sought white mates in Europe, but the amount of Indian and Negro blood in the population made anyone with any European blood a "white" man. Brazilian racism could never be as exclusive as that which developed in the Spanish, French, and English colonies.

3. THE DUTCH COLONIAL EMPIRE

The Dutch colonial adventure began as a by-product of their war for independence. In the first three-quarters of the sixteenth century Dutch seamen were the carriers for Europe. They brought colonial and oriental goods from Spain and Portugal to the north, and northern goods—such as furs, timber, wheat, copper, naval supplies, and amber—to the south, and thus turned their homeland into the market for the goods of the world. The wars for independence in the latter sixteenth and first half of the seventeenth centuries shut off their legitimate entry into Spanish and Portuguese ports. At first, as pirates and privateers, they waylaid the Portuguese Indiamen and the Spanish galleons; when the Spanish and Portuguese developed fleet convoys for protection, the Dutch sailed directly to the East themselves.

Their entry into the western hemisphere was even more conclusively the result of the war with Spain. The West India Company was organized (1621) primarily to carry the war to the Spanish Americas. It established a series of bases from New York to Brazil, but the Netherlands was not populous enough to man this western empire as well as the one in the East, and before the end of the seventeenth century most of the western bases had been lost.

In the East more permanent installations were established by the Dutch East India Company (1602). It was a remarkable institution controlled by the bourgeois elite of the Netherlands. Through interlocking directorates, the same people ruled the Company, the Bank of Amsterdam, and, for the most part, the Estates-General of the United Provinces. They secured for the India Company the right to monopolize the oriental trade, to raise armies, to arm their merchantmen like warships, to annex and govern territory, and to conclude treaties of commerce and alliance with foreign states. In the East the India Company was, in effect, an independent extension of the United Netherlands.

By the middle of the seventeenth century the forms that were to be characteristic of the empire until the nineteenth century had come into being. The first port of call was a Dutch colony at Capetown, where Dutch and Huguenot farmers (Boers) raised food to supply the ships. The next was Mauritius in the Indian Ocean, where a similar way-station was prepared. The empire in the East had two axes: Ceylon and Java. From these two island bases, Dutch influence spread out to the harbors of India, Malaya, Indonesia, China, and Japan, where Dutch agents established factories on the model of the Portuguese. The Company avoided territorial involvement on the mainland, where there was no easy limit to the commitments necessary to hold the installations. On Ceylon and Java, by a combination of diplomacy and war, it came to control both the ports and the hinterlands. Both these islands were fantastically wealthy and, therefore, excellent bases for the Dutch mercantile economy.

Commerce rather than conquest was the reason for the existence of the Dutch East India Company. All year long goods were assembled in the factories to be transported home. About Christmas time the fleet would leave the Indies laden with its cargo. The time of departure was determined by the monsoon winds of the Eastern Ocean. In the holds were to be found Indian cotton, Chinese silks, Persian carpets, and the delicate translucent fabrics made throughout the Orient that were so different from the substantial stuffs made in Europe. There were also teas from India, China, and Ceylon; cloves, nutmegs, cinnamon, and pepper from the islands; coffee from Arabia and Java; saltpeter, copper, and tin from Japan and Malaya; brass boxes from China; pottery and lacquerware from China and Japan; and carved, painted, and glazed objects of art from all over the Orient. After calls at Mauritius and Capetown, the fleet would arrive at Amsterdam early in the summer. The voyage that took almost two years in 1500 could be accomplished in six to eight months in the eighteenth century.

Of all these items, the spice trade virtually became a Dutch monopoly. They were hardheaded about excluding other Europeans and even Chinese from the spice islands; their cruelty, indeed, their barbarous brutality, became almost a watchword. As the sole buyers of spices, they controlled the price. However, when the supplies of spices became too abundant and thereby threatened the price in Europe, the Dutch did not hesitate to destroy plantations. Once or twice they were so systematic in their destruction that the price of pepper remained at scarcity heights for a number of years. Since the plantations were largely in the hands of natives or Chinese, the Dutch themselves suffered no loss.

The Dutch maintained themselves by their own force until the opening of the eighteenth century, but after 1713 they came to rely more and more upon English protection. In the eighteenth century there was a commercial and financial entente between the two countries based on the fact that the Netherlands became a market for English state bonds and that the shares of the Dutch companies, including the India Company, were sold in the London as well as the Amsterdam bourse. The Dutch tended, more or less voluntarily, to withdraw from the India market in favor of the growing English East India Company, and to concentrate their efforts farther east. There was also a substantial decline in profits. Instead of the one hundred to three hundred percent per year often made in the seventeenth century, the Company had to content itself with a modest twenty-five to thirty percent figure. This hardly meant bankruptcy, but it was not as satisfactory to shareholders as the earlier returns had been.

4. THE FRENCH COLONIAL EMPIRE

French seamen and merchants who tried to establish colonial bases in the sixteenth century received painfully little encouragement from the Valois kings. French energy was being absorbed by foreign wars with the Hapsburgs and by rebellions at home, and there was little left to expend upon colonial effort. In the seventeenth century, when the monarchy increased its authority and mercantilist doctrines began to gain currency, Henry IV, Richelieu, and Louis XIV in turn took an interest in colonial adventures.

The French embarked upon three quite different types of colonial ventures. In Asia and Africa they developed a commercial empire modeled upon the Portuguese and the Dutch. In the islands of the Caribbean they founded a plantation society that relied upon Negro slaves for labor. In North America they undertook to assimilate a vast territory with its aboriginal inhabitants into the French kingdom as a new province. The government of France took a keen interest in the organization and government of the colonies, and was able to establish a large measure of control over them from Paris. In the seventeenth century political machinery developed which may or may not have been beneficial to the French colonies—machinery unknown when the Spaniards and Portuguese had founded their empires.

Although French explorers visited Canada before the Antilles, the island colonies came to be regarded as the most important part of France's overseas empire. Between 1630 and 1660 French merchants and colonial agents occupied eight or ten of the Antilles islands: Guadeloupe, Martinique, Dominica, St. Christopher, Grenada, St. Bartholemy, St. Croix, and several others. St. Kitts, where salt was to be had, they shared uneasily with the British; several others they shared with the Spaniards. Spain pretended to sovereignty over all the islands, but the unfriendly cannibalistic habits of the natives plus the vast amount of land at their disposal had prevented the Spaniards from occupying them: by the time the French arrived, they were too weak to prevent the intrusion.

At first there were several different kinds of original charters or grants to the colonizers, but by the latter part of the seventeenth century they had all been brought together under a common pattern. A French governor with military forces at his disposal was assisted (and watched) by an intendant appointed by the crown. At the same time, sovereign courts, with powers roughly coterminous with those of the *parlements* in France, administered justice as well as supervised many of the rights of the crown. The local inhabitants, French, native, or servile, had little or no official voice in their own government, but the wishes of the white population were easily made known to the governor on the island and to the king's government in Paris. The islands were administered with the needs of the wealthy colonists and the merchants in view, but the fact that any man could easily free himself from European controls because of the immensity of the New World made the rulers take note of the wishes of all Europeans in the Americas.

Louis XIV confided the administration of colonial areas to Colbert and his new Ministry of the Marine. This action affected the structure of their government throughout the eighteenth century. As Dorn says, "The French colonies were governed as if they were war vessels permanently at anchor." It is small wonder that bureaucratic controls often crippled the development of new ideas in colonial life, for the French navy was no more progressive than navies elsewhere, and the French Ministry of Marine was almost completely tied up with the regulations modern governments call "red tape."

The West Indian islands' economy was almost entirely of the plantation type. By chance the French had occupied several of the most fertile spots in the whole Caribbean area. Martinique and Guadeloupe, in particular, became veritable gardens. They produced cocoa, tobacco, indigo, rice, brazil wood, and, above all, sugar. In the early eighteenth century the French Antilles were called the sugar bowl of Europe.

To operate the plantations servile labor was essential. Since the Indians made poor slaves, either Negroes or white *"engagés"* (indentured servants) had to be used. The planters preferred to use Negroes, since the indentured servants could become free men at the end of three years and establish themselves as small planters in competition with their erstwhile masters. Thus, as the economy of the islands grew, the proportion of Negroes tended to increase until the blacks were a preponderant part of the population. The famous *code noir* of 1685 defined their status. The black men's souls were to be cared for by the church, their lives were under the protection of the state (the power of life and death did not belong to the planter), but their persons were regarded as chattels that could be sold and forced to labor. The conditions of their life were regulated somewhat to insure reasonable treatment, but their economic value rather than the law probably secured for them as adequate living conditions as were possible.

As in all of the plantation economies of the seventeenth and eighteenth centuries, disease and the hard conditions of labor made sharp inroads into the Negro population so that it was necessary to renew its numbers continually by importation from Africa. French slavers operated out of Senegal and off the Gold Coast to supply the required workers, but the demand often overreached the supply so that smuggling Negroes in Yankee and English slave ships proved to be a profitable business and one that caused considerable difficulty between England and France.

The white population of the islands was nearly all of French origin. The large planters were either noblemen or wealthy bourgeoisie; the small planters were ex-*engagés*. All three groups developed a strong racial attitude against the Negroes; the few whites in a sea of black men had to protect themselves by taboos and laws that kept the latter in an inferior status. Mixed marriages were forbidden, and the few Negroes who were freed, either because of some extraordinary service or because they were children of white men and Negro concubines, had to occupy an inferior status in the society.

The physical installations on the islands betrayed their French origin. The cities reflected those of France; the plantation buildings were markedly French in their architecture. By the eighteenth century a luxurious, wealthy society occupied the top of the social structure. It sent its sons and daughters to Paris to complete their education and to find mates suitable for their wealth and position. On the islands they lived the sensuous, easy life of white men in the island tropics.

The productivity of the sugar islands inevitably gave them international importance. Quantities of cheap fish and corn to feed the slaves as well as a steady flow of human chattel were required to carry on the work. The planters wanted hardware, textiles, drugs, glassware, porcelain, and many other different manufactured items. In return they could trade sugar, molasses, and other colonial goods. The three-cornered trade developed for all the Antilles islands. Molasses was shipped from the islands to be made into rum in New or old England or France; the rum was then traded for slaves on the Gold Coast. The slaves were then traded for more molasses. This trade in spirits and human flesh was a source of great wealth; many of the "first families" of bourgeois France, England, and British North America owed their position in society to the gold made in this three-cornered traffic. Through navigation laws, colonial codes, and such restrictions unsuccessful attempts were made to channel the commerce of the islands so that no foreigner would benefit from it. International conflict developed from the failure of that legislation.

It is interesting to note that several of these islands are still under the French flag. The treaties of 1763 and 1815 awarded most of France's colonies to England, but the planters who managed the economy of the English sugar islands did not want to compete with the French islands in the English market, and therefore English politicians were not anxious to annex them. On the other hand, the French were more willing to give up all of Canada than to part with the Antilles islands. They regarded the islands as more valuable than all French North America. The two attitudes provide insight into the colonial problem of the eighteenth century.

There were two aims behind early French exploration in North America (Canada). The one was the perennial dream of Europe, namely, to find an easy passage to the Orient (a dream which modern man has some difficulty in understanding). The other was to establish fishing grounds off the Newfoundland coast.

The sixteenth- and early seventeenth-century fishermen had taken their catch, salted it wet, and hurried back to France, where the fish easily commanded a premium price on the Rouen and Paris markets. This method, however, was expensive, and so another practice developed—namely, to land the catch on an island, and clean and dry it before bringing it back to France. Since codfish were plentiful, a full shipload could be caught and dried easily. The price was somewhat less than that commanded by the wet cod, but the large cargo brought in considerably more money. This type of fishing enterprise began in the later sixteenth century; by the eighteenth, it had become an important business supplying cheap food for France and her island colonies. It is likely that the fisheries would have prospered even if Friday had not been proclaimed a meatless day by the church, since most of the people who ate dried cod did not eat meat the other six days of the week, for meat was much more expensive than fish.

The early French settlements in Acadia (Nova Scotia) were made to supply the fishing fleet, and therefore they were the first targets of their competitors in the British North American colonies. Even when the English and French kings were allies, the fishermen and colonists of the two countries were at sword's point on the fishing banks. When the first series of modern Anglo-French wars came to an end, Acadia was annexed by England (Peace of Utrecht, 1713). Longfellow's "Evangeline" tells, somewhat romantically, the story of the human tragedy that resulted from the transfer.

The exploration of the St. Lawrence river and the Great Lakes was primarily an attempt to find the northwest passage. As that dream disappeared in the forests of North America, a new idea of empire emerged. Like the Spanish Hapsburgs, the French Bourbons accepted their destiny to rule over many peoples, not necessarily just Frenchmen. Their realm in Europe included men who spoke French, Flemish, German, Italian, Spanish, and Provençal; there was no reason why other subjects might not speak Iroquois or Huron. It was assumed that it would be easy to teach the Indians the Christian religion and European manners, and once that was done, they could be assimilated in the French monarchy. North America thus would be a province like Burgundy or Languedoc. Had they read carefully what Champlain wrote about the Indians, they might have had fewer illusions about that civilization and its adaptability.

To facilitate the attempt to teach the Indians to live like Europeans as well as to get a firmer grip on the land, the royal government gave grants of land in the St. Lawrence valley to patrons or grand seigniors who would agree to bring peasants to work it. Thus the early immigrants were peasants who were "introduced" to the land by a lord, and established on it under a sort of feudal contract. In the areas around Quebec, where these settlements proved most successful, the result was that a part of France with its institutions, customs, and pattern of life was introduced into the New World. Their influence upon the Indians was negligible, but they did establish a French society in America.

The vastness of the land and the opportunities offered on the frontiers resulted in important modifications in the structure of French society as soon as it appeared on the banks of the St. Lawrence river. The *habitan* who in France was a peasant largely controlled by landlord and church almost immediately became a man freed from his obligations to lord and priest. The land was large and the number of *habitans* strictly limited; it was impossible to keep them under control; if they became dissatisfied with conditions of life, they could easily escape to the frontier in the west. Almost from the outset of the settlement, both the church and the seigniors met the terms of the *habitan,* sometimes gracefully, sometimes regretfully, but in any case they had no alternative. Thus, French Canada gained its distinctive character; the frontier modified French feudalism so much that it was emptied of meaning and force; the Canadian *habitan* was as much a free man as were his neighbors in English colonies to the south.

The French empire in North America was a vast extent of land that made the settlement around Quebec seem small indeed. By 1660 French explorers had visited much of the coastline of the Great Lakes system. By the 1670's they were in Illinois and on the upper Ohio river, as well as in the upper waters of the Mississippi. In 1682 La Salle completed his exploration of the Mississippi from St. Louis to its mouth and claimed the river and its tributaries for Louis XIV under the name "Louisiana." Obviously the little settlement around Quebec with its few thousand farmers and craftsmen was not to be reproduced throughout this vast wilderness.

In the seventeenth century the vogue of wearing felt hats as well as the rise of a widespread taste for fur trimming on the clothing of both men and women made the forest empire valuable. The rivers and streams of North America teemed with beaver, and the Indians were adept at capturing them. The Indian hunters willingly traded these furs for "firewater," knives, guns, beads, and other European goods. As the "vision of empire" progressed, the French government came to see Quebec as a capital and depot for a trading empire. French soldiers and merchants could contact the natives, keep the peace, and defend the land from invaders. It could be linked together by water transportation routes and a series of simple fortifications that would act as points of security and also trading posts. French mission priests were expected to teach the natives Christianity and civilization.

In the development of this empire the process of assimilation often worked in reverse. The operation of such an enterprise required bold, footloose men who could handle themselves in the wilderness. From the agricultural settlements and from France itself they came, many of them misfits in the civilization into which they had been born. They fanned out into the Great Lakes region, up the Mississippi and the St. Croix, up the Ohio and the Missouri, in search of furs. They were called *coureurs de bois* (vagabonds of the woods). The very land on which this book is being written (the Wisconsin Indian head country) was crisscrossed by their trails. They put on Indian clothing, used Indian transportation (the canoe), and took on Indian manners, morals, and women. By the mid-eighteenth century the Indian-French half-breed had become common in the forest-lake empire of France. The Jesuit fathers may have Christianized some of the natives, but the natives had also given their way of life to some of the French.

By the eighteenth century another important fact began to develop. As geographical knowledge filled in the gaps on the globe, it became apparent that the French wilderness empire had cut across the hinterland of the British North American colonies. The St. Lawrence and the Great Lakes had been highways into the center of the continent. The Allegheny range had been a barrier. But the French had only a thin settlement of men to hold their great domain, while the English colonies became populous. Inevitably the English began to cross the mountain range, and the result was the commencement of the struggle for North America.

The other areas of French imperial interest were in Africa and Asia, where commerce rather than colonies was the principal aim of French policy. In the sixteenth century, French merchants bought oriental goods from the Arabs in the Levant and from the Portuguese at Lisbon. In the seventeenth century, Amsterdam became a principal source for these goods. When Louis XIV and Colbert began to direct French commercial policy they decided to contact India directly. Somehow they expected the Dutch to help them out of gratitude for past French favors to the United Provinces, but they soon discovered that on the route to Asia Europeans had no friends except their own cannon.

Two companies were chartered to monopolize the traffic. The French African or Senegal Company dealt in slaves, ivory, gum, woods, and other African products. The French East India Company set out to trade with the Orient. These two companies grew less vigorously than their English and Dutch rivals for several reasons. First, they came late into a field where competing companies were already established. Then, too, French merchants were reluctant to invest in so distant a venture, and there was meddlesome governmental interference. Finally, Louis' wars against England and the United Provinces unleashed Dutch and English warships and privateers to attack French commerce. Nonetheless, by the opening of the eighteenth century, the French had established themselves in a half dozen Indian towns and at the mouth of the Senegal river.

After 1713, when there was comparative peace in Europe, the French, like the English, were in a position to profit from the breakdown of the Mogul power in India. The Mogul empire that had looked so brave in the seventeenth century fell prey to the raiding Afghans from the hills. It was the age-old pattern from Mesopotamia to India. The agricultural and commercial society lost its vigor, became effete and inefficient, and the hillsmen came down upon them to loot. The Afghans were unable to create a government to substitute for the Mogul power; they took their booty and retired to the hills whence they had come. India was left as a politico-military vacuum in which petty principalities emerged, each struggling for power. This was the situation that made possible the extension of French territorial interest. With the aid of sepoy troops the French and the English played a political game. They made some of the natives their allies; others they conquered. Eventually they found themselves opposing each other as well as certain Indian princelings. Then India, like America, became an important factor in the politics of Europe.

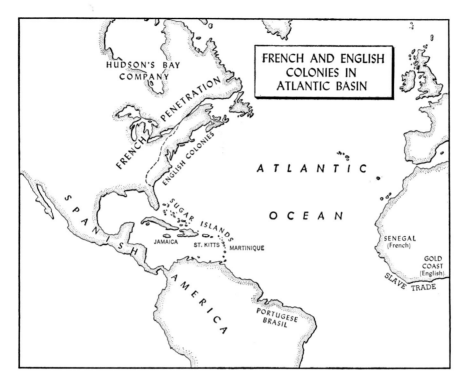

FRENCH AND ENGLISH
COLONIES IN
ATLANTIC BASIN

HUDSON'S BAY
COMPANY

FRENCH PENETRATION

ENGLISH COLONIES

SPANISH

SUGAR ISLANDS

JAMAICA   ST. KITTS   MARTINIQUE

AMERICA

PORTUGESE
BRASIL

ATLANTIC

OCEAN

SENEGAL
(French)

GOLD
COAST
(English)

SLAVE TRADE

5. THE ENGLISH COLONIAL EMPIRE

Like the French, sixteenth-century English explorers went westward in quest of the northwest passage and treasure. They sought gold on the mainland of North America and by waylaying Spanish ships. Soon the fishing banks off North America attracted English fishermen, but neither fish, the northwest passage, nor gold was the foundation on which to build an empire on the coast of America. Not until the seventeenth century do we find the English economy strong enough to support an active policy of colonization; it required both men and money to establish colonies on lands where agriculture was the basis of the economy.

Although the North American colony founded by the Pilgrims (1620) may have been the most publicized English settlement in the New World, the islands that Englishmen occupied in the Antilles were long considered to be the most important. In the eighteenth century the "shugger islands" held an important place in the minds of English merchants and statesmen; they were considered to be much more valuable than the colonies on the North American mainland which competed with English manufacturers and seamen. The establishment of English settlements on Jamaica, Barbados, the Bermudas, the Bahamas, Anguilla, Antigua, and other West Indian islands coincided in time with the French ones in that same area (1630–1690) and, with variations, they reproduced the economy and problems found in the French island colonies. The same crops (sugar, indigo, tobacco, cocoa, and so forth), the same racial and labor problems, and the same luxurious way of life for the planters were characteristic of all American plantation economy from the Carolinas to Brazil.

Again like the French colonies, the planters on the islands tended to come from the well-to-do classes in England. A few ex-indentured servants may have established themselves on plantations, but the type of agriculture there required capital unavailable to poor men. Even more than among the French whom Latin culture made more racially tolerant, the English planters developed strong racial barriers to maintain the gulf between themselves and the sea of black servile humanity that surrounded them. English slaves were as well treated as any chattels, but they and any free Negroes that might appear were held down strictly in a lower social and economic position.

The labor force was the big problem. Six to eight years was the life expectancy of a Negro field worker. The wretched Negroes were usually the victims of slave raids or intertribal wars, so the number of males, for whom there was a premium price, tended to predominate. Thus there were relatively few female slaves in the islands. This meant that the slave supply had to be continuously renewed from Africa. In the seventeenth and eighteenth centuries Africa did little to benefit its own civilization, but it poured forth two streams of human chattels that greatly benefitted the rest of the world. To America went the men who worked the fields and created the wealth of the colonies. To Arabia and Asia went the females and castrated males who did the household work and cared for the harems of Islam. Sombart, the German economic historian, after reviewing what Africa had sent to the Americas, remarked that it was no wonder that Europe had become rich, since whole peoples had died to make it so. While his verdict is too severe, it is true that Europe derived considerable wealth from the exploitation of negro slaves.

The slave trade was not the only traffic that depended upon the use of black men for workers, although that trade was of great importance in the total trade of Europe. The slaves had to be fed and given at least some kind of clothing. The land of the islands was too vital a source of sugar to be put into food crops. This meant that contact with the cod fishermen of New England and the corn-growing farmers of mainland colonies was important to both parties. The manufacturers in Europe who made tools, cloth, leather goods, and a host of other items also had an interest in the black population of the islands. There were few cities in either England, France, or the English mainland colonies that did not benefit from the slavery in the Antilles.

The English colonies that emerged on the mainland of North America depended very little upon Negro servile labor. By the eighteenth century they had a relatively large white population. That transfer of people from England to America was one of the most important and, from the point of view of human behavior, most interesting migrations in history. Historians have asked how it was possible for seventeenth- and eighteenth-century England to export so many of its people. By way of explanation, those interested in religious toleration have pointed to the intolerance of both the Puritan and Anglican churches in England and the willingness of the rulers to allow religious dissenters to go to the colonies. Puritans in New England, Quakers in Pennsylvania, Catholics in Maryland, Baptists in Rhode Island, and so on, by migration retained their religious convictions as well as their role as subjects of England's king. Other writers, impressed with the dislocations of the Civil War that sent Cavaliers to Virginia and Roundheads to New England, stress the political and military disorders of the mid-seventeenth century. Those historians who see economic forces as paramount explain that seventeenth-century warfare in Europe (the Thirty Years' War, the Franco-Spanish War, the wars of Louis XIV) disturbed markets and forced English merchants to look elsewhere. At the same time, the practice of enclosing common lands to raise sheep drove large numbers of workers from the English countryside, making them available for migration. Still other writers point out that the stringent, indeed barbarous, legal code in England imposed imprisonment for minor offenses and filled the jails with men and women who were really excellent human material for transportation. The criminal code hanged real criminals; those who were sent abroad were usually guilty of only minor offenses.

All these factors undoubtedly operated to send the sons of beggars, farmers, artisans, merchants, and squires to the New World. Nor were Englishmen alone in the company that settled North America. Dutchmen in New York and Swedes in New Jersey were evidence of the attempts of other governments to colonize the mainland. Palatine Germans in Pennsylvania and French Huguenots in the Carolinas and elsewhere found refuge from religious intolerance as well as a land of opportunity. The glowing promises and pictures painted by colonial agents of companies and proprietors, the tales of "unlimited opportunity" that originated in the seventeenth century and eventually permeated all Europe, the possibility of freedom from an intolerant state church, these were some of the visions that persuaded men to leave their homelands. Some paid their own passages; some came as indentured servants to men who paid their fares. Some established themselves handsomely; others joined the city poor or were forced to the frontier, where land was plentiful but conditions hard. In the mythology of the people these "hardy pioneers" who fought for their living on the cutting edge of the frontier became the true heroes of the land.

The ever-growing tide of population with its relatively undisciplined tendencies led to difficulty with the natives. It is untrue that the English colonist deliberately developed the notion that a "good Indian was a dead one"; such thinking only came after misunderstandings and perhaps chicaneries on both sides had led to conflict. Neither the Indian nor the white man realized when they made treaties about the land that so many whites were going to move into the area. The Indian thought he was selling the right to coexistence and use of the hunting lands. When the whites became a legion, the Indian had either to migrate westward into the lands of other hostile tribes or fight the whites who were displacing them. It was a tragic choice and one that could only end with the destruction of the Indian. "King" Philip's war of the third quarter of the seventeenth century was characteristic of the pattern. Frustrated by the white invasion, "King" Philip began to massacre frontier communities. The white forces, better armed and disciplined, annihilated the whole of "King" Philip's tribe.

The pattern of conquest of the mainland very early assumed the form that was to be characteristic of much of the westward movement. Frontiersmen with axes and rifles were the explorers, the Indian fighters, and the men who established the first crude settlements. Soon afterward other colonists drifted in and usually bought up the rights of the first comers who with ax and rifle repeated the process. The Indian, whose economy depended upon hunting, was gradually pushed out of the land or annihilated, since there was no place for him in the agricultural economy that the colonists were introducing. On the other hand, the colonists who came to possess and work the land were usually men with some capital; they were not the "pioneers" who had first entered the wilderness.

From about 1688 to 1763 the pattern of English-Indian relations was further complicated by the fact that England and France were at war during much of the period. The French, whose vision of empire made room for the Indians, got on better with them than did the English, so the English colonists tended to suffer more from raids inspired by the high politics of Europe than did the French.

The economy of the English mainland colonies was variegated to a high degree. In the Carolinas and Virginia the colonists raised tobacco, indigo, and other plantation crops; in the middle and northern colonies, where the small farm became standard, the land produced beef, pork, and field crops. The pickled meats (corned beef and salted, smoked, or brined pork) were as exportable as corn and wheat. Near urban areas an even more variegated agriculture appeared early to supply town needs. If we are to judge by the volume of trade, the plantation crops, particularly tobacco in the eighteenth century, provided the most profitable agricultural exports. The planters of the southern colonies enjoyed great prosperity throughout most of the century. In New England the cod fisheries became the great enterprise—the golden cod still hangs above the speaker's chair in the Massachusetts legislative hall. With the fisheries came the development of a shipbuilding industry, the production of naval stores, and eventually a great commercial fleet that hunted whales and carried goods all over the world. In the early eighteenth century New Jersey was for a time one of the important iron producing areas of the western world, but metallurgical industry and mining did not loom large in the colonies. New York and the Hudson valley were long the center of the English fur trade.

As the population grew, the townspeople began to manufacture articles: hardware, whiskey, leather goods, rum, textiles, glass, hats, barrels, wheels, nails, and an ever-expanding list. This type of development was not encouraged by the mother country. The dominant colonial theory conceived of the colonies as raw material producing areas that would buy manufactured goods from Europe. Between 1650 and 1775 a series of acts (on navigation, trade, and manufacturing) attempted to control the production and sale of goods in the colonies. By bounties and rebates certain types of agricultural production were especially encouraged; by tax and prohibition much colonial manufacturing was discouraged. England needed colonial goods, naval supplies, and iron; she wanted to pay for these goods with manufactured merchandise.

Efforts to regulate either trade or manufacturing in the colonies were doomed to frustration, or perhaps we might say, those efforts were not seriously attempted. England did not possess either the bureaucratic or the police power to control the economy. In Europe, smuggling between France and England even in wartime could not be prevented. What chance was there of controlling a sparsely inhabited coastline like that of North America? Smuggled goods leaked everywhere as through a sieve. The eighteenth century was probably the greatest era of smuggling—in Europe as well as in America—in the history of the West. The colonial governors simply did not have the forces necessary to police their frontiers. Perhaps that can never be done anyway if the profits from smuggling are large enough; twentieth-century America will long remember the liquor traffic in the prohibition era.

The governments in all the English colonies, insular and mainland, began as chartered companies or proprietory grants, usually of a large degree of autonomy in local affairs. Between 1660 and 1688 the differences between the governments tended to diminish, as the crown assumed the right of control. The characteristic pattern that developed included a royally appointed governor and council that controlled the military forces of the colony, both militia and regular, and administered the affairs of the colony. In addition to the appointed officials, there was usually an elected assembly with the power to petition, to pass certain legislation, to accept or protest rulings from London, and to vote the colony's budget. These assemblies were elected by a limited suffrage (property qualifications), but they tended to have the support of the whole articulate population of the colony. The control exercised from London was relatively light. The reason was that there was no official specifically charged with the administration of the colonies, and therefore several agencies shared the work. The board of trade, the secretaries for both the north and the south, the treasury officials, and any other member of the king's government corresponded with the royal governors and received letters from other colonial officials. The result was that no one was really responsible, and so the government from London was lax, mild, and inefficient. When men in London tried to assert their right to control the colonies, thirteen of them revolted against English rule; the other seventeen for various reasons accepted the authority of London.

This mildness of the seventeenth and early eighteenth centuries was well taken, for from the very beginning the colonies showed a spirit that would brook little interference with their affairs. This does not mean that colonial assemblies were never browbeaten or bribed by royal governors, but they often showed initiative and independence. Indeed, under James II (1685–1688), when royal governors in New York and Boston, acting on orders from England, tried to suppress colonial "rights," there was a movement that might well have resulted in rebellion had not the revolution in England (1688) forestalled it. In the eighteenth century, as long as French and Indian military power threatened their existence, the colonists were more docile, but once that menace was removed, they again manifested a spirit of independence that developed into revolt. In a later chapter we will discuss the factors responsible for that revolution.

The other part of England's imperial program emerged from the great chartered English East India Company. This Company was similar to the other sixteenth- and seventeenth-century chartered companies: the Levant Company for trade in the Near East, the Muscovy Company for trade with Russia, the Hudson's Bay Company for fur trade in North America, and the like. The East India Company was founded in 1600 and was given a monopoly on English trade with the Orient. Its privileges included, among other things, the rights to make treaties, acquire land, hire armies, and arm merchantmen. In the first three quarters of a century after its initiation, the English East India Company was dwarfed by its Dutch rival. Civil War in England and the weakness of English commercial development did not encourage much development until the end of the seventeenth century. From about 1700 onward, however, the English East India Company made tremendous strides, and by the mid-eighteenth century it was the most important and powerful of all the European firms trading in the East.

As we noted in the case of the French Indian interests, the eighteenth century saw a considerable number of political changes in India. The decay and disintegration of the Mogul empire, the failure of the Afghans to take advantage of their military superiority, and the rise of native princes all over India provided a situation that gave the India companies a real foothold. The conquest did not come until the end of the eighteenth century, but in the first half of that century both the French and the British maneuvered themselves into a position to establish an empire in India. After the French had been eliminated, the British began the conquest, as we shall see later.

European expansion into the Americas and Asia was undoubtedly evidence that European civilization was outstripping the other cultures of the world in economic and military efficiency. On the other hand, the fact that this expansion into the world somehow extended from five or six centers of power (Spain, the Netherlands, Portugal, England, France, and later, Russia) made its total impact on the non-European world somewhat chaotic and irrational. European expansion was obviously undirected; indeed one might almost say that it occurred in spite of the inter-European conflicts that almost checked its development. Nor was the impact that Europeans made upon the outer world more rationalized than were the methods by which they established their hegemony. They had no formula for conquest, nor did they have any single program of action; somehow they carried with them the institutions they had at home and adapted them to non-European conditions in a rough and ready way. In much of South America, the result was the creation of a society not dissimilar to that of Europe in the prefeudal era, when each manor had been an independent social and political unit. In North America, French and English institutions, modified by the liberty assured by the frontier, opened new vistas of political and economic life to European men. In Asia, the great trading companies, as representatives of European civilization and commerce, became the harbingers of political and economic conquests to come. But before Europeans could really impose their will on the non-European world, they fell to fighting among themselves. Perhaps it was only this pattern of inter-European conflict that prevented them from completely dominating all the other peoples of the earth.

Frederick the Great at the Battle of Lowositz, October 1, 1756. According to one legend, during the battle Frederick noticed a soldier with a head wound and gave him a handkerchief with which to bind the wound. The soldier then dashed back into battle. Later, when Frederick came upon the soldier dead, he was greatly moved and said, "There was a whole squad of men!"

Chapter 22

THE MID-EIGHTEENTH-CENTURY WARS: THE BALANCE OF THE CONTINENTS

1. THE STATES SYSTEM

The middle decades of the eighteenth century were filled with wars involving not only Europe but also America and Asia. The astonishing thing about this period is that just when western men seemed locked in a life and death struggle at home, they were also preparing for eventual conquest of much of the rest of the globe. Thus, we must try to keep in focus both Europe and European interests beyond the continent, so that we can understand the historical process that was at work.

In Europe, most enlightened men still regarded themselves as members of a single culture rather than as representatives of a particular national or princely state. General acceptance of French ideas and French manners tended to give reality to this belief. At the same time, there were other forces at work tending to separate the interests of men and to accentuate the differences between the political units of government. In the sixteenth century princes had been concerned with personal dynastic ambitions. The political issue of the seventeenth century had been the creation of bureaucratic-military-police states; each of them had armies and navies, and each was becoming conscious of "state interests." By the eighteenth century, princes, as the "first servants" of their states, were deeply involved in "state interests." Out of their struggles had emerged the government of Europe, the balance of power. Since there was no organization, no law that could impose order on Europe as a whole, war or the threat of war was the sole recourse in the conflict of interests. Therefore, even though enlightened Europeans may have felt a common heritage of western culture, the political liberty of Europe was dependent upon force or the threat of force.

However, current political ideas and the inner structure of the states somewhat ameliorated the threat of that situation. While the rulers and their ministers were deeply conscious of their "state interests," they also tended to regard those interests as the private affairs of the men who actually governed the state. The people were "subjects" rather than "citizens," and as such were often personally uninterested in their princes' wars. For their own part, the rulers also respected this convention. They expected their subjects to pay taxes and keep out of the way; they wanted neither advice nor criticism from the people. In return, soldiers and sailors were never recruited from the "respectable" or "important" segments of the population excepting, of course, that segment which sought to secure employment as officers. Once in the army, the vagabonds and other marginal people who filled the ranks were placed under a strict discipline that separated them from the rest of the population. The disorders of the Thirty Years' War were not to be repeated in the more orderly eighteenth century. Indeed, the extent to which soldiers had to depend upon supply magazines restricted their sphere of operations so that even in war armies lacked mobility.

The dualism between princes and their subjects also importantly affected the military institutions of the eighteenth century. Not only was it difficult to secure large numbers of recruits since the "respectable" and the "productive" classes were largely immune from military service, but it was almost equally difficult to increase the tax revenue paid into the prince's treasury. This was the greatest problem of continental princes; for all their pretentions to "absolutism," they were restrained in their ability to reach into the pockets of their subjects. Lack of money and of recruits meant that the soldiers in the armies of the eighteenth century tended to become highly trained professionals, strictly limited in number and almost too valuable to be risked in battle since it was difficult to replace any casualties. They were risked, of course, but the results were disastrous. Frederick II of Prussia discovered in the course of the Seven Years' War that he could replace neither his aristocratic officers nor his trained troops with men who already knew or could be easily trained in the art of war. Thus, the military institutions of the era joined with the conventions separating state and private interests to turn the conflicts of the eighteenth century into "limited wars" in the classic tradition.

Two quite different problems were responsible for the outbreak of wars in the mid-eighteenth century. On the one side, the expanding economic interests of England and France resulted in competition between the two countries all over the world. The current notions about trade led men to believe that the total amount of commerce that was possible was fixed. This gave point to the belief that war was justified as a method of excluding a rival from a market. On the other hand, the rise of the military power of Prussia-Brandenburg upset the balance of power in middle Europe. Her growing army made Prussia into a "land hungry" state, for she needed more land to support it, and, in turn, the army provided the instrument for acquiring land. This is a simple generalization; at its heart lies one of the most revolutionary movements of eighteenth-century Europe, a movement that eventually was to give new form to Germany.

The men who directed the wars and fought over land and commerce recognized quite cynically the reasons for their conflicts. Since they did not have to justify themselves to their subjects, they did not find it necessary to produce extensive rationalizations for their actions. In a society which was not organized on democratic principles, it was unnecessary to create ministries of propaganda to convince men that they had good reason for making sacrifices. Princes merely prevented the publication of ideas hostile to their policies; no more was necessary.

2. ENGLAND'S TRADE WAR AND THE WAR OF THE AUSTRIAN SUCCESSION, 1739–1748

The conflicts that merged into the first great war of the mid-eighteenth century started over Anglo-Spanish commercial conflicts in the West Indies and the Spanish-American colonies. By the Treaty of Utrecht (1713) the English had been granted the *Asiento* that allowed their slavers and merchants a limited share in the Spanish-American market. This trade had proved disappointing to the English, and the ruses that they developed to enlarge it brought protests from the Spanish. With both sides dissatisfied, it is small wonder that there was considerable friction. Nor was this the only issue. As we have already seen, the Spanish government tried to maintain a virtual monopoly over trade with the New World, so that commerce would yield large tax revenues; Spain fleeced the colonists wherever possible. Thus prices in the colonies were high, and therefore smugglers were in a position to make large profits. While other people also smuggled goods to the Spanish colonies, the English were most active in flooding the colonial market with commodities on which tax had not been paid. There may have been colonial merchants who would have preferred to deal with the Spanish *Flota* (the officially sponsored trading fleet) but to do so might mean being undersold by competitors. Thus, wherever the *Flota* arrived, it found the market already well stocked. This fact may have been responsible for its infrequent sailings; for instance, at one time there was an eight years' interval. It also accounted for the irritation of the government in Madrid.

Spain, however, did not have sufficient naval power to patrol all the coasts of Spanish America. Therefore the Spaniards hit upon a new plan. They commissioned private merchants and ship captains to act as *guarda-costas* ("coast guards"), with the right to capture and sell ships and cargoes of the smugglers. As one might expect the *guarda-costas* looked and behaved like pirates in the eyes of the English merchants whose trade was thus interrupted. The chorus of shrieks of indignation was heard as far away as London.

The Walpole government in England was quite unprepared to fight a major war; the navy was in disrepair, the army even less prepared. However, a war party developed that demanded that the government should do something drastic to save English commerce and English seamen. Walpole was forced to accept their program, and declared war on Spain (1739). Professor Dorn calls this "England's purest trade war."

The English naval campaign in the West Indies fizzled out in ignominious failure and opened the way for French intervention, for the Spanish colonial trade interested France too, since French merchants supplied much of the goods that went into the holds of the Spanish *Flota*. They were also trying to expand their own markets in America by fair, as well as illegal, means. The government of France under the sage direction of Cardinal Fleury had long been preparing for just such a situation as the one that arose. Fleury saw that a showdown with England over colonies and commerce was probably inevitable, so he had negotiated a series of treaties and alliances to prevent the rise of an anti-French coalition similar to the ones that Louis XIV had encountered on the continent. France and Spain together had a very good chance of winning a naval war against England, if their energies could be concentrated on England alone. Thus, to Fleury the English attack on Spain provided a good excuse for a French war on England. This war, too, was to be commercial in origin.

However, before the French could do much more than lay plans to take advantage of England's apparent weakness in the West Indies, another issue appeared which forced a change in French foreign policy. The new problem was that of the succession to the crowns of the Austrian Hapsburgs. As we have seen, the Hapsburg holdings on the Danube basin were slowly emerging as a political unit. Held together by the threat of Turkish invasion and the dynastic interests of the Hapsburgs, by the opening of the eighteenth century the German, Bohemian, and Hungarian peoples had become a federation of states and kingdoms. The Emperor Charles VI, however, failed to produce a male heir, and that fact alone threatened to break up the federation. As we have already seen, Charles VI tried to ward off the disruption of his state by a paper charter, the Pragmatic Sanction, that would allow his daughter Maria Theresa to inherit all his lands. He spent the best part of his life securing the consent of his own people and the states of Europe to this solution, and on his deathbed, in 1740, he assumed that he had assured his daughter's place on his thrones.

Maria Theresa ascended her throne just a few weeks after Frederick II of

Prussia had acquired his ancestral crown, and Frederick was determined to make his reign an eventful one. The House of Hohenzollern had certain claims to territory in Silesia; however, these claims were questionable and had already been surrendered by Frederick's grandfather for Hapsburg support a half century earlier. Such details did not bother Frederick. Thus, on the death of Charles VI, in spite of the counsel of his advisers, he boldly announced that he was annexing all Silesia to satisfy his ancestral rights. His Prussian army immediately invaded the province (1740). Just as his advisers had predicted, this bold act of piracy became the axis of Frederick's policy for the next quarter of a century; Prussia had to fight and endure cruel devastation to establish her ruler's right to Silesia, but its acquisition greatly increased the power of Prussia's kings, and eventually assured that state the status of a great military power.

Unlike England in the West Indies, Prussia was equal to the military task imposed upon her by its warlike ruler. Old Frederick William I had not trained and equipped his army in vain. At Mollwitz (April 1741), the Prussian and Austrian forces met; Frederick himself lost his nerve, and fled the field, but his army under General Schwerin won a complete victory. The political consequences of this battle decided the fate of Europe for the next two and a half decades. Immediately every prince in Europe who had any possible claim to Hapsburg lands began to ransack his archives for plausible evidence. Charles Albert of Bavaria came up with a document, manifestly a forgery, called the "Testament of Emperor Ferdinand I," whereby he proved his right to all the Hapsburg lands save Hungary! He hoped to be elected emperor, but without more territory than just Bavaria he could hardly support the imperial dignity. While he was claiming lands in central Europe, the Spanish government dusted off claims to Hapsburg lands in Italy, and at Nymphenburg (May 1741) the Spaniards and Bavarians signed a treaty of mutual assistance. However, the Spanish and Bavarian projects were mere dreams unless Prussia and France were willing to supply the military power to give them reality, for neither Spain nor Bavaria was any match for the Austrians. It was at this point that Cardinal Fleury and his government had to reconsider French policy; the Austrian problem would change the naval war which he planned against England into a land conflict in Germany and the Netherlands.

Curiously enough, Cardinal Fleury, an old man in his eighties, argued for the "modern" proposition that French interests demanded concentration on the commercial and colonial problem, that is, war with England. A group of young men, led by Belle-Isle, returned to the policies of the Valois and early Bourbon kings and insisted that France must oppose and destroy Austria. This latter policy had become outdated, for Austria was no longer a threat to France. However, tradition proved stronger than Fleury's arguments, and Louis XV agreed to enter the war on the side of Bavaria and Spain to divide the Austrian inheritance. All assumed that Frederick of Prussia would also continue his war with the Hapsburgs, and so the game appeared relatively safe and victory assured.

Indeed, Maria Theresa's plight was a serious one. Before she knew where to turn, she found her resources escaping her as the German and Bohemian lands were occupied by her foes. Only Hungary remained, and the Hapsburg family had had so much trouble with revolts in Hungary for the preceding two centuries that contemporary observers felt that she might as well appeal for help from the devil as from Hungary. Yet there was nothing else to do. As we noted, her youth, her beauty, and her plight brought forth warm response from among the Hungarian magnates. Perhaps they also sensed that this was their opportunity to safeguard themselves against the process of centralization that had threatened them for a century; Hungary's special position in the Hapsburg empire of the nineteenth century dates from this period when the timely aid of the Hungarian magnates saved the Hapsburg throne. In any case, Hungary came to Maria Theresa's aid, and thus she was able to stay in the war until more substantial help could arrive.

The English, frustrated in their war with Spain, saw the continental war as a chance to counteract Franco-Spanish cooperation. But English statesmen did not want to fight against Prussia as well as France; England's king was also prince in Hanover, and as such was influenced by German interests and policies. Since Hanover could not be defended against a determined Prussian attack, the English came to Maria Theresa's aid on condition that she first make peace with Frederick II of Prussia. By this time Charles Albert of Bavaria had succeeded in getting himself elected Holy Roman Emperor, and Bavarian and French troops had occupied Bohemia and much of Austria. The young queen hated Frederick as a robber, a highwayman, and an atheist, but she had no choice but to follow the English proposal. The English bungled her plan for limiting Frederick's conquest by offering him the maximum concessions immediately. Perhaps that was, in fact, the only way to get Frederick out of the war.

The generous offer to Prussia was more than Frederick could resist. Even the remonstrances of the French had no effect upon him; he had no desire to become a puppet of the French king. When he found that the French would neither fight the war as vigorously as he wished nor agree to a negotiated peace that would leave him with the bulk of his gains, he made a separte peace with Austria (the Peace of Breslau, 1742). This earned for him the reputation of being an untrustworthy ally, but it also gave him title to Silesia.

There is no point in following the details of the campaigns. We will just note that after Prussia withdrew, the Austrians were able not only to reconquer Bohemia and Austria, but also to drive the French and Bavarians out of Germany. In Italy, too, the Austrians and their English allies were successful—so much so that Frederick re-entered the war in 1745 because he feared that Austria was becoming powerful enough to reconquer Silesia. The Prussian army again proved its strength, and Frederick once more allowed himself to be assured by treaty that Prussia could keep Silesia (the Treaty of Dresden, 1745).

Elsewhere, the Anglo-French struggle was continuing. In America, where the Anglo-American colonies were fighting "King George's War," the English had captured Louisburg, the principal French base for attacking the English commerce on the North American coast. In India, however, the French under Dupleix captured Madras from the English and held it against the forces of the Nawab of Arcot. Dupleix's little army of some four hundred Europeans and a few sepoy troops showed themselves to be militarily superior to an Indian army of over ten thousand men, and this proved to be of great importance for the future history of India. The French were also victorious in the Netherlands where Marshal Saxe managed to keep a firm grip on the whole province in face of all Anglo-Austrian attacks. In other words, the war had reached a stalemate with both sides holding valuable "real estate," and no apparent possibility of either side's winning a decisive victory.

British statesmen, weary of war and fearful of bankruptcy, deserted their Austrian ally and opened negotiations for peace. The French were equally anxious to come to terms for, despite their victories in the Austrian Netherlands, the English navy was strangling their trade. Thus, peace was concluded at Aix-la-Chapelle in 1748. The only treaty that could be written was one that restored the status quo that had existed before the war. With minor alterations, that is just what the powers agreed upon. The situation created in 1713 at Utrecht was essentially reaffirmed in 1748. The sole striking exception was the European guarantee given to Frederick for Silesia. Prussia was not even a party to the Treaty of Aix-la-Chapelle, but both France and England were anxious to court the favor of Prussia's great king, and so they freely recognized his claim to Maria Theresa's lands. This in effect assured Prussia of the status of a great military power.

The peace, of course, was not really a settlement of the problems that had caused the wars. On the contrary, it reaffirmed all of those problems, even the contest of power between Prussia and Austria. Commercial and colonial rivalries still made relations between England and the Bourbon kingdoms of France and Spain uneasy. In India and in North America, contests for land and markets clearly indicated that the peace was only a truce. In Europe, Austria was not satisfied to forget Silesia, yet Silesia only intensified the land hunger of Prussia. Thus, the years following the treaty of 1748 showed promise of a renewal of war.

3. COLONIAL RIVALRY AFTER 1748

The Treaty of Aix-la-Chapelle seemed to release an enormous increase of commercial energy in both England and France; peace provided a general commercial tonic. While much of the expanded commerce was strictly between the states of Europe, nonetheless overseas trade bulked larger than ever before. European taste for sugar could not be satiated; the fad for oriental goods, particularly decorative objects of art, took root and greatly broadened the traffic of China; the tea and coffee houses, as well as a demand for those exotic beverages for home use, provided markets for ever increasing amounts of tea and coffee. European consumption of tobacco for snuff and smoking, European requirements for furs for hats, for trimmings for clothes, for naval supplies that could no longer be found in sufficient quantities in Europe, all added to the enlarged market.

With this growing commerce the colonies gained a new position of importance in the national economies of England and France. In both countries, the colonies provided employment opportunities for younger sons of important families, either in commerce or in the military and administrative machinery of the colonies. But this was only a part of the importance of the colonial trade. In the port cities of France and England sugar refineries, rum distilleries, cloth works, felt makers and hatters, and many other enterprises relied upon the raw stuffs that came from abroad. In turn, merchants depended upon the shipments from overseas for transshipment to the interior of their own countries and to the rest of Europe. If we add to those who had a considerable immediate interest in the colonial trade all the people who had purchased shares in companies dealing in colonial goods, it becomes obvious that colonialism involved the interest of a large percentage of the important, or at least politically articulate, families in both France and England. Even the great landed families in England that were still interested primarily in the grain trade were marrying their children to men who were involved in colonial interests. In France, the nobles who disdained commerce as ignoble sent their sons abroad as soldiers, sailors, and administrators and invested their money in colonial ventures. One French historian has insisted that the high politics of the mid-eighteenth century were entirely dominated by the rising colonialism that had become important to so many of the influential people of both England and France.

Since men believed that the only way to increase their own trade involved the destruction of that of their competitors, it is not surprising that there was also a willingness to fight over commercial questions. The treaty of peace in 1748 neither solved any old questions nor provided a platform for discussing new ones, so it was probably inevitable that Englishmen and Frenchmen were soon fighting again in North America, India, the West Indies, and Africa.

The situation in the West Indies was tailor-made for conflict. High French tariff policies made the price levels in the French islands somewhat higher than those in the English possessions. At the same time, the French government, in an effort to protect French brandy manufacturers, limited the importation of molasses into France (molasses-rum). Thus, while commodity prices were high in the French islands, molasses was both plentiful and cheap. Here was a perfect invitation to the smugglers and interlopers from New and old England. Sometimes the goods were smuggled in; sometimes the trade was "legitimate" when a ship would put in for "repairs" that could only be paid for by the sale of its cargo. Both the French and British governments regarded this trade unfavorably, for it introduced cheap French molasses into the English markets, and cheap English goods into the French in competition with "legitimate" traders and producers. The part played by the New England ships was particularly provocative to disputes between London and Paris. The Yankee traders had scant respect for the regulations and laws of either England or France.

Even more thorny was the problem arising out of several islands that were, so to speak, unoccupied. French and English planters, smugglers, pirates, and other marginal people had settled on these little points of land, but their status in international law was quite undecided. If either France or England did occupy them, the islands would automatically become a threat to the nonoccupying power as potential bases for privateers in wartime, yet to occupy these islands would be expensive and economically not very useful. The French tried to circumvent the problem by inviting Frederick II of Prussia to claim sovereignty over them, but he refused to commit himself to a defense problem that was beyond his resources. After several years, during which the English and French authorities watched each other suspiciously, the French finally broke the deadlock by occupying St. Lucia (1756). French and English forces were already shooting at each other in the north Atlantic and in the Ohio valley: the conflict had now been extended to the West Indies.

Almost as explosive as this situation was that which developed on the West African coast, where French and English slavers competed in the market for human chattels. By the mid-century the British ships were taking two slaves from Africa to one taken by the French, and by building a string of forts on the Gold Coast they were laying plans to crowd the French out of the trade entirely. Several years before the Seven Years' War broke out in Europe, bloody encounters between slavers on the African littoral had become a common occurrence. The French answered English attempts to crowd them out by arming certain African tribes against other tribes that were working for the English, so that the Anglo-French rivalry led to native wars before the conflict between the principals broke out. It should be noted that, in spite of the competition, both the French and the English enjoyed a volume of trade in Africa and the West Indies greater than they had had before the War of the Austrian Succession.

In India, the situation was less clear. In the first place, the Indian trade was nowhere nearly as important as that with the West Indies. The French had some difficulty justifying their Indian venture at all, and while the English East India Company paid reasonably good dividends, it no longer made the profits characteristic of the preceding century. Europe was importing more oriental goods than ever before, but the trade was less profitable. Secondly, the problem in India was complicated by the fact that the Europeans had to deal with non-European people as well as to compete with each other. India was confronted with a serious crisis in the mid-eighteenth century. The Mogul empire was in the process of disintegration. Its decline was hastened by Afghan invasions on the northern frontier; the Afghans raided the land for loot, disrupted what organization existed, and then retired to the hills. The old Mogul empire had never been a closely knit organization, and it now broke up into a crazy-quilt pattern of independent and semi-independent sovereignties. The European East Indian companies operating from the coast did not realize that they were in a position to inherit the empire of the Moguls, for India had never before been conquered from the sea and the companies were organized for trade rather than conquest. Yet that was indeed the situation: India was ripe for conquest by the first power which had adequate military force to give it some degree of order and government.

The Europeans stumbled into the policies that made this conquest possible. The French and English East India companies had fought each other during the War of the Austrian Succession. In the course of the hostilities, the French governor, Dupleix, had learned an important fact, namely, that Indian military power was no match for European. A few European troops and Indian soldiers, trained and commanded by European officers (they were called sepoy troops), had proved able to defeat Indian armies many times their size. When the war ended in 1748, Dupleix had some fifteen hundred to two thousand French soldiers at his disposal, and the situation in India provided him with a theater for their use. Even though his directors in Paris could not understand that the conquest of territory in India would create a source of profits, Dupleix seems to have partially comprehended that it was the historic destiny of Europeans to establish their rule in India.

However, Dupleix himself probably did not fully understand the precedent that his action was to establish. He had to provide for the troops under his command, and the funds for paying them were hard to find. He even paid them out of his own pocket until he discovered that they could be used to secure control over land that would support them. By allying with one Indian princeling against another and obtaining a share in the spoils of war, the European company could build a firm foundation for its future power. Trade alone will not support soldiers, but the trading company could secure

money from taxation when it had established itself as a sovereign over territory. It could also make alliances with other powers that would pay subsidies
in return for protection. In the six years between 1748 and 1754 Dupleix was
the most important personality in India; he initiated the process that was
eventually to give his English rival control over the entire subcontinent.

Dupleix received little or no support from France. The directors of his
company were interested only in profits; they did not want adventures that
might lead to a war with no foreseeable end. Nor did the government under
Louis XV wish to be pushed into war by the actions of "wild" men thousands
of miles from France. Thus Dupleix had to hide the true proportions of his
policy and develop it without adequate forces to achieve his objectives. Perhaps the government in France was more clear-sighted than he, for France
probably could not have embarked on a successful conquest of India without
naval superiority in both European and Asiatic waters. Since the French
government of the mid-eighteenth century did not try to create a navy powerful enough to dominate both the Indian Ocean and the route to India, it may
well be that its failure to support Dupleix was based on good reasoning, while
the historians who have criticized the decision were unrealistic dreamers.

Thus, the most important result of Dupleix's policy was to arouse the English against it. At first the English were awkward and backhanded in their
attempts to check the brilliant Frenchman, but Saunders, the English governor, soon learned the rules of the new game. In a short time the English
and French were virtually at war with each other because of the conflicts between the Indian states under their "protection." It is unnecessary to follow
the intricacies of Indian politics to see how this curious war became the
center of Indian affairs, nor is it very important to try to decide which side
had the better of the situation by 1753, because the French withdrew their
support from Dupleix in an effort to check the course of the struggle. The
really important fact is that this period set the pattern for the English conquest of India in the next half century. Dupleix was recalled to Europe,
where he wrote a justification for his policy. Clive, the most successful of the
English generals, remained in India, and he and his successors brought the
whole of India under the influence of England.

In North America, too, Anglo-French interests conflicted. France ruled
Canada, the Great Lakes basin, and the vast, sprawling wilderness of the
Mississippi, Ohio, Missouri river systems. To say "ruled" perhaps overstates
the case, for, with the exception of a part of Canada, the lands were held
with little force. The French had an ambivalent attitude toward their possessions. Voltaire's point of view was not uncommon; he wished "Canada at the
bottom of the Arctic Sea together with the reverend Jesuit fathers." Many
Frenchman shared the notion that Canada was a wilderness of ice and snow,
a political, military, and economic liability to the mother country. Louisiana,
on the other hand, was a land not too unlike southern France, and therefore

a valuable possession. Other Frenchmen, however, felt that Canada was valuable for the fur trade and important to retain for the prestige of the kingdom.

The actual situation in French North America seemed to justify the more pessimistic French attitudes toward the colony. The fur trade was the most important inland commercial venture, and fifteen ships could easily handle that traffic in a good year. The fisheries were important, but they depended upon the islands rather than on the mainland colony. The settled area between Quebec and Montreal was lightly ruled by the king's officials, the church, and the great landlords. Since every able-bodied man was required to serve in the militia, the settlement also provided a force for its protection. Beyond Montreal, however, the situation was different. Traders, trappers, outlaws, and others who had deserted civilization to live with the Indians ranged over great spaces. The government at Quebec tried more or less unsuccessfully to provide a rudimentary sort of government by making agreements with Indian tribes and establishing a series of small forts on the Great Lakes and in the Ohio valley. Even though the land did not seem very valuable, the French were in no mood to give it up, and when the English attempted to intrude beyond the Allegheny Mountains, the French stood ready to repulse them.

The English colonies on the North American coast also presented problems for the mother country. They had already manifested a spirit of independence toward her and developed trade rivalry with some English merchants, so that there were men in the mother country who were ready to abandon them to their own fate. The development of commerce and industry in British North America, as well as the general extension of the agricultural interests of the colonies, were evidence that they were approaching an economic maturity matching their spirit of political independence. It is not surprising that there were some men in England who feared their competition and resented their independence. Others regarded them simply as a valuable market for manufactured goods or as an opportunity for political or military employment. Lastly, the general rivalry between France, Spain, and England made these colonies and their preservation matters of prestige for England.

The colonists themselves had divergent notions about their relationship with England. Most of them were of English or Scottish stock, and had a tradition of loyalty to the king and their mother country common to eighteenth-century men, but England was particularly important to them because of the geographical position of the colonies. To the north and the west were the French, who not only posed a military threat but were also a barrier to English expansion into the Ohio and Mississippi river valleys. There were important people in the colonies with money and influence who regarded the western lands as a natural outlet for Anglo-American energies as well as an opportunity for land speculation. It was probably no accident that the first conflicts broke out in that area, where the interests of Virginian land speculators clashed with French military forces. The Spanish settlements in Florida, Mexico, and South America were not dangerous to the colonists, but the Indians on both sides of the frontiers were a continual threat to the tranquility of the settled areas. Thus the colonists needed England to protect them from French, Spanish, and Indian "aggression," as well as to sustain their claims to the fishing banks, the western lands, and the right to trade in the West Indies.

Clashes with the French in the Ohio basin and in upper New York convinced the Anglo-Americans of the necessity for closer organization among themselves. In 1754 a Colonial Congress was held at Albany to create some form of colonial federation. Benjamin Franklin and a few of his friends succeeded in preparing a type of constitution that the Congress adopted. However, when it was returned to the several colonial legislatures local interests proved too strong to secure ratification. Nonetheless, the fact that a Colonial Congress had been convened acted as a precedent for future cooperation among the English colonies. Perhaps even more important was the fact that the struggles on the Ohio frontier also aroused the government in England to decisive action. English troops headed by General Braddock were sent to America with instructions to open the Ohio to English settlement.

When the British soldiers were sent to North America, the French felt that they had to counter the move by a similar expedition. Thus, while the English ministers and the French ambassador in London were assuring each other of the peaceful intentions of their respective governments, preparations were being made for war in America. The French managed to get all but two of their ships up the St. Lawrence river; the British captured the *Alcide* and the *Lys,* the first overt act of war that gave the signal for hostilities to begin from Newfoundland to the West Indies. On land, General Braddock, supported by some colonial militia, invaded the Ohio valley; the French and their Indian allies were waiting for the English column, and successfully destroyed it. Braddock was killed, but George Washington managed to get the remnants of his army back over the mountains. Thus by 1755 the English and French had become involved in an undeclared war in North America and the West Indies.

In Africa, too, Negro tribes supported by the English were fighting other tribes backed by the French; and in India an uneasy peace had been agreed to after four years of wars between English and French Indian allies. War was not declared in Europe until 1756, but the Anglo-French colonial conflicts could not wait for the problem of Silesia and the balance of power in Germany to provide a formal opening of hostilities.

4. THE DIPLOMATIC REVOLUTION

Just when the Anglo-French colonial interests reached an impasse that seemed to demand war, a sudden and dramatic regrouping of the alliance systems on the continent of Europe precipitated a general conflict. Curiously enough, only one of the participants of the war was actively working toward such an outcome; the logic of events and the fears of men rather than their wishes plunged Europe into the Seven Years' War (1755–1763).

It had been traditional since the days of Louis XIV for English statesmen to regard the United Netherlands and the Danubian Hapsburg state as their natural allies. Since the Elector of Hanover was also King of Great Britain, that state, too, was within the English orbit. Hapsburg Austria, in turn, was the patron of the small German states that were fearful of Prussia following the War of the Austrian Succession. Austria also maintained an alliance with Russia against a common enemy, the Ottoman Empire. This Anglo-Austrian system was in general turned against France and her "natural" allies in the borderlands of central Europe, Poland, Sweden, the Ottoman Empire, and Prussia. Bourbon France was also allied with Bourbon Spain as a check to England's overseas power. This system of alliances provided the basis of the balance of power; it rested on traditional roots as well as on recent experience. Any serious change in the system could mean a breakdown in the political structure and might well be a cause for war.

Without meaning to do so, the English foreign minister, the Duke of Newcastle, set in motion a series of events that resulted in a serious reversal of the key alliances in this system. He believed that money could buy anything in high politics, a curious conception held by politicians before and since his time but rarely vindicated by events. When the overseas conflict with France seemed about to flare into a hot war, he recalled that in the last war France's successes in the Netherlands (the Belgium of today) had been enough to reverse English victories in the colonies and at sea. Therefore, the problem of holding the Netherlands and with them Hanover was one of prime importance. To achieve this, Newcastle made a treaty with Russia by which he "bought" the Russian army to hold France's ally, Prussia, out of the war in the west. By this treaty, Russia organized an army in Livonia and agreed not to negotiate with "the common enemy" (September 1755). To the Russians, this meant Prussia and France. It should be noted, however, that England's policy was not necessarily anti-Prussian; it was intended to prevent Prussia from aiding France or attacking Hanover.

The Anglo-Russian treaty is of importance only when considered in connection with the total picture of Europe between September 1755 and the following summer. The most important factor in that picture was the grand design of Count Kaunitz, the Austrian foreign minister. How this free-thinker succeeded in becoming the dominant personality in the government of the pious Maria Theresa is a story that illuminates the contradictions of politics. Count Kaunitz not only convinced the Austrian government that his mechanistic conception of politics was sound, but also persuaded his pious queen that it was necessary to lie a little (*bissel Falschheit*) in conducting politics. To Kaunitz, politics could be reasoned as one reasons mathematics, and as he drew up his system with its pros and cons, his hearers were left without reasonable reply. Had his cold logic been able to account for the vagaries of life that defy logic and perhaps for the vigor of a personality like Frederick the Great, his conclusions might have been correct. Newcastle believed that money could do everything; Kaunitz believed that the world was a machine, and therefore that reason could penetrate its secrets. Both men failed to grasp the fact that their system only built a little world inside a greater one.

Kaunitz was resolved to destroy Prussia, to re-annex Silesia, to re-establish the traditional Hapsburg leadership in Germany. This program exactly suited the ideas of Maria Theresa; she never forgave the theft of her Silesian province, nor did she really mean to allow Prussia to keep that territory. To achieve the Kaunitz project, France and Russia would have to be linked in a grand system that would leave Prussia without allies. To bring France into such a scheme required considerable skill. Louis XV was surrounded by pro-Prussian ministers, and the whole weight of French tradition as well as the logic of France's position in Europe was contrary to any plan to aggrandize Austria. However, Kaunitz knew that Louis XV could be reached through secret channels, and that he actually enjoyed negotiating behind his ministers' backs. Even so, Louis was indecisive. A diplomatic bombshell in the form of the Treaty of Westminster, signed in January 1756, produced results that all of Kaunitz' diplomacy had failed to achieve. Upon hearing that Frederick had agreed to neutralize Germany, Louis was ready to sign a treaty with Austria.

The Treaty of Westminster was an agreement between England and Prussia to neutralize Prussia and Hanover in case of a general war. The background to this treaty is extremely complex and difficult to unravel. When Frederick got wind of the negotiations for Kaunitz' grand coalition against Prussia, he became greatly concerned. Then Newcastle's Anglo-Russian treaty thoroughly frightened him. His first reaction was to invite the French to occupy the Netherlands and Hanover. In the light of the Anglo-French conflicts in America, Africa, and Asia, such a measure did not seem unreasonable, and it would have had the virtue of assuring the Franco-Prussian forces control over northern Europe. Frederick had long regarded a treaty with France as the cornerstone of his policy; both France and Prussia had stolen Hapsburg territory (Alsace and Silesia). If they wished to keep their provinces, it seemed wise to cooperate with one another. The French response to his suggestion to occupy the Netherlands and Hanover appalled

Frederick. Louis XV wanted peace, and, despite all the English provocations in America, he had no intention of occupying Austrian or English territory. The hint that France would not object if Frederick occupied those countries only convinced the Prussian king that France was not serious. At that moment the English offered him a chance to neutralize Germany.

Had the Duke of Newcastle wanted to blackmail Frederick into signing a treaty with England, he could not have hit upon a better method than the Anglo-Russian treaty of 1755. The objective of English policy was relatively simple. With the outbreak of violence in America, George II wanted to keep the war that was looming on the horizon out of his German territory, Hanover, and if possible, to localize it in the colonies. The treaty with Russia would not really guarantee Hanover from Prussian attack; therefore England also offered Prussia a treaty guaranteeing Prussian territorial integrity in return for a Prussian guarantee in regard to Hanover.

If Prussia could be neutralized, a possibly dangerous antagonist to English plans would be removed from the scene. Thus, the English offer to Prussia was not a reversal of English policy. Like the Russian treaty, it was designed to prevent Hanover and the Netherlands from interfering in the war beyond the sea. Frederick also understood that this proposal did not necessarily imply a reversal of his pro-French policy. Since the French had already told him that they had no intention of invading Hanover, he felt that he was in no way deserting his ally when he agreed not to invade that territory in return for an English guarantee to Prussia. Frederick refused to agree to the neutrality of the Austrian Netherlands, for he assumed that the French would surely occupy that province if the war in America continued. One serious mistake that he made was the failure to tell the French that he was going to sign the Treaty of Westminster until after it had been ratified. In Paris, men with and without Austrian money in their pockets cried out that Prussia had betrayed them, and recalled that this was characteristic of Prussia's untrustworthy king.

Maria Theresa was also scandalized by the news. She had counted on England to assist her to recover Silesia, not to neutralize Germany. Only Kaunitz was jubilant; his projected alliance with France and the probability of an Austro-French-Russian coalition could now be realized. To be sure, the alliance that he secured with France (May 1, 1756) was only a defensive agreement, for Louis XV wanted above all to remain at peace if it were possible; nonetheless, Kaunitz well understood that the logic of events would transform it into a more aggressive treaty.

His judgment seemed further vindicated by the reaction of Russia to the Treaty of Westminster. For years the English ambassador at St. Petersburg on orders from his government had urged the destruction of Prussia; now that same English government guaranteed Prussia against the very troops that English money had bought by the Anglo-Russian subsidy treaty. Had

Czarina Elizabeth (1741–1762) had her way, Russia would have at once made a treaty with Austria, but her chief minister had English money in his pocket and knew that the czarina was old, and that her heir, Peter, was an admirer of Frederick II of Prussia. The Austrians finally persuaded Elizabeth to act in spite of the advice of her minister, and in the late summer of 1756 an Austro-Russian treaty agreed upon an invasion of Prussia for the next spring. To be absolutely sure of success, Kaunitz then negotiated a treaty with Sweden, whereby, in return for assistance against Prussia, the Swedish king would be given Prussian Pomerania. A three-pronged attack seemed to assure victory.

When his spies brought him news of the rise of a coalition against Prussia, Frederick II decided to act quickly to frustrate Kaunitz' design. "If Austria is pregnant with war," he remarked, "I shall offer the service of the mid-wife." Before attacking her, however, he asked Maria Theresa to state her intentions, and specifically to assure him that she did not contemplate attacking him in 1757. Several of her councilors urged an honest answer, but Maria Theresa, yielding to Kaunitz' insistence that a few "trifling mendacities" were necessary, put Frederick off with an indirect answer. On August 29, 1756, the Prussian army marched into Saxony whose ruler Frederick had mistakenly taken to be the real center of the coalition against him. The war that thus began was soon linked with the Anglo-French conflicts beyond the seas, for France and Russia came to Austria's aid, and the English government in time supported Frederick. The war lasted seven years, and derived its name from the period of its duration.

5. THE SEVEN YEARS' WAR, 1756–1763

The invasion of Saxony, instead of producing a striking victory, released all the anti-Prussian feeling in Europe. The French joined with Austria, Russia, and Sweden, and the majority of the German states also agreed to send such forces as they possessed with those of the emperor (the husband of Maria Theresa) to punish Prussia for the breach of the peace in Germany. Nor did the English government immediately rush to the defense of Prussia. George II and most of his ministers were anxious to avoid military commitments in Europe; their policy had been to neutralize Germany, not to make it a battlefield. Therefore, the Anglo-Hanoverian general in the Rhineland was instructed to come to an agreement with the French that would neutralize Hanover. It seemed that Frederick and his Prussia must surely be severely punished.

In the early part of 1757 the war went badly for Frederick. He won a minor victory in Bohemia, but was unable to move against Vienna since the Austrians had one army shut up in Prague and another moving toward

Silesia. In the east, the Russians won a victory over one of Frederick's best generals, and moved on Koenigsburg, while in the north the Swedes invaded Pomerania. At this critical moment, Frederick learned that the Anglo-Hanoverians had come to an agreement with the French that allowed a French army to enter central Europe. Prussia seemed about ready to collapse; the Prussian king had either to win striking victories or to surrender.

Frederick, however, was not a man to give up easily, and the Prussian army had yet to show its real capabilities. Resolved to hold on to Saxony, Frederick marched westward to meet a Franco-Austrian army twice as large as his own. At Rossbach, November 5, 1757, he placed his enemies in a position that allowed him to attack their flank. The Prussian army could maneuver more effectively than its foe, and by its freedom of movement it won a complete victory. Without waiting to consolidate his forces, Frederick then turned eastward to seek out the Austrian army that was invading Silesia. On December 5, 1757, he won an even more brilliant victory at Leuthen. In one month the Prussian army had reversed the whole course of the war and earned for its king the surtitle of "the Great." No one could again scoff at the harsh discipline of the Prussian army or question the military genius of Prussia's king.

Throughout Europe, friends and foes alike paid honor to the new military genius. The cosmopolitan eighteenth century recognized merit without nationalistic prejudices. In England, men celebrated the Prussian king's birthday with illuminations; the English Methodists professed to believe that Frederick was a Protestant Gideon! The French *philosophes,* who knew Frederick's religious views rather better, hailed him as one of their company, and ridiculed the generals of their own king. More important, the Prussian victories in Saxony and Silesia gave new direction to the war in England; with them came the rise of Pitt, the man who was to organize the English war effort.

It was obvious to all that the Prussian king was a man of war; it soon became obvious to all that a man of war had come to power in England, too. William Pitt had long been a thorn in the side of the English government. Elected to the House of Commons in 1735 from a "pocket borough," he had been constantly in opposition. Not a revolutionary, Pitt's hostility had been directed against weak policies, corruption, and bad judgment. He had no friends among the Whig chiefs, but he was very popular in the country and among the rank and file in the House of Commons. The Whig politicians unsuccessfully tried to get him to join their government in a subordinate role; only the urgency of the crisis of the summer and fall of 1757 and the victories of the Prussian king finally forced them to admit him to the government on his own terms, namely, that he should have full direction of the war.

The reasons behind the rise of Pitt are not hard to find. In America and in Asia British military policy suffered humiliating reverses, and the neutralization of the Anglo-Hanoverian army in Germany appeared for what it was, a pusillanimous retreat. It took little imagination to see what would happen if the Franco-Austrian-Russian coalition should dominate the continent. England would be without friends, and her position would soon be untenable. Pitt came to power with a policy of action. He poured subsidies into Prussia; he sent ships and soldiers to America and India; he organized and strengthened the British navy to destroy French commerce and frustrate French military projects. Pitt was one of a long line of English statesmen who had proved that the English knew how to maneuver to defend themselves and their interests. France was defeated by English sailors and soldiers like Boscawen and Howe, Clive and Wolfe, but it was the spirit of Pitt that gave them their force.

It is impossible to tell here the complex and sometimes very dreary story of the years of warfare that followed Frederick's invasion of Saxony. The Prussian king lost about as many battles as he won; his style of fighting, imposed upon him by the conditions of his era, would not allow the entire outcome of the war to depend on the results of one afternoon. Europe would have to wait another generation to see Napoleon and the crushing military tactics that became possible when a whole nation could be harnessed to a soldier's chariot. In Frederick's day it was difficult to find new recruits to fill the ranks; it was even more difficult to raise large sums of money. The political philosophy of the era disassociated the people from the acts of their princes, and the soldier had to respect the nonbelligerent. Frederick, therefore, had to fight a war of raids, maneuvers, and inconclusive battles; his greatest achievement was his ability to keep his enemies apart, and to block off their efforts to occupy his little state. The conflict in central Europe was actually two wars: in the west, the Anglo-Hanoverians, often led by a Prussian general, dueled with the French; in the east, Frederick fought the Russians, the Swedes, and the Austrians. The whole German war depended upon Pitt's subsidies; English money just provided the cork needed to keep Prussia afloat until a "miracle" (the death of Czarina Elizabeth in 1762) saved Prussia from defeat.

The war at sea and in the colonies was also largely a story of raids and isolated battles, but in the long run England's superior sea power led to victory. The Anglo-Americans called the conflict "the French and Indian War." It reached a climax in the capture of Quebec (1759) and of Montreal (1760). In the West Indies, one of the French islands after another was occupied with disastrous results to French merchants and sea captains who had depended upon the sugar industry for their livelihood. In India, the conflict seemed to be as much a war between Indian states as between the French and English, but the English had the advantage of sea power and in the end they were almost completely victorious.

The "miracle" mentioned above brought Czar Peter III (1762) to the throne in Russia. He was an ardent admirer of the Prussian king, and his first act was to reverse the role of the Russian army in Germany. His actions changed the Russian forces that had invaded central Europe from enemies of Prussia into allies. The czar's reversal of policy was not quite as capricious as it appeared. In 1759, when the Russians were victorious over the Prussian armies, the Austrians refused to join them in a final push to defeat Frederick. Even though Czarina Elizabeth did not resent this, there were many Russian leaders who thereafter regarded Austria suspiciously. As an ally, the Russians were not of much use to Frederick, but their withdrawal from the war gave him a breathing space and an opportunity to concentrate his full attention on his Austrian neighbor. Soon after mounting the throne, Peter was strangled, allegedly because he was changing Russian military manners to match the Prussian ways. The real reasons were somewhat more complex. In any case, his wife took over the rule of Russia as Catherine II (1762–1796), and her first act was to withdraw from the war entirely. Thus the "miracle" was not undone by the palace revolution in Russia, and Frederick was able to secure a peace that satisfied him.

By 1761 there were political problems in France and England that forced the conclusion of the war. Pitt may have been the personification of the English will to war, but he was never popular with his colleagues in the government. When George II died in 1760, Pitt's position was further compromised by the character of the new king, George III (1760–1820), who was the first in his dynasty to be really an Englishman rather than a transplanted Hanoverian. He was also the first of his line to insist upon the recognition of the rights of the crown and the royal prerogative. Lord Bute, his confidant, was introduced into the ministry, and the king's Tory friends assured him of his right to rule, no matter what "Mr. Pitt" might think. The English constitution was still so unformed on this point that Mr. Pitt could not act against the king's will. As a result Pitt was forced to resign, and Lord Bute, the king's man, came to power.

In France, the war was not popular either with the king or with the people, but French reverses in America and in India made it impossible to withdraw until victories somewhere could right the balance. Unhappily, such victories were hard to secure. The man who finally came to direct French policy, Choiseul, was faced with the problem of organizing a regime that was shot through with disorder and defeatism; he could not hope to save the kingdom from defeat. A grandiose plan to invade England failed utterly because France did not have the naval power necessary to effect it. His alliance with Spain (a Bourbon family compact) came to fruition only when English victories in the West Indies convinced the new Spanish king, Charles III (1759–1788), that further English victories would endanger his American empire. However, when Spain entered the war it became evident that the Spanish alliance had added problems and not power to France's war effort.

As Choiseul exclaimed, "Had I known what I know now, I would have been very careful not to cause to enter the war a power which by its feebleness could only ruin and destroy France." Had not Lord Bute been anxious to make peace in order to carry out his master's plans at home and avoid the return of Pitt to the government, the Spanish alliance might well have resulted in England's acquiring much of the Spanish as well as the French empire.

Thus, by 1762, all parties were anxious to make peace, but instead of one conference and one treaty, there were two. In 1763 England, Spain, and France made peace at Paris, and Prussia and Austria at Hubertusburg. This dramatically reflected the fact that the accession of George III had changed English policy. He and Lord Bute were willing to jettison the German war; with unbelievable arrogance they assumed that England could dictate peace to France and ignore the rest of Europe. The seeds of the disaster that overtook England in North America twenty years later were thus planted at the end of the Seven Years' War. Lord Bute succeeded in antagonizing all Europe, and Europe revenged itself by isolating England. Choiseul's policy was strikingly different. He carefully kept his alliances with Austria and Spain intact without offending Prussia; he was ready to admit defeat, but already he was making plans for the next war that would reverse it.

The Treaty of Paris gave England the lion's share. France was excluded from the North American continent; she gave Canada and the lands east of the Mississippi to England; she ceded Louisiana and her rights west of the Mississippi to Spain; Spain ceded Florida to England in return for Louisiana. As we have already noted, the important French sugar islands were returned as much because the French would have carried on the war rather than surrender them, as because the English sugar plantation interests did not want the competition of the French islands in the empire. The French restored Minorca and ceded Senegal to England in return for Belle Isle and Goree, which were necessary to the French slave trade. They also retained two small islands, Miquelon and St. Pierre, off the fishing banks of North America and with them the right to take fish in those waters. This was all that remained of the great dream of a French North America. In India, Choiseul got everything that he wanted, namely, trading rights in certain Indian towns, but he left the subcontinent open for the British conquest by withdrawing French influence from native politics.

The Treaty of Paris had an impact upon the entire political structure of the European world. With the French out of North America, the English colonists lost their urgent need for protection, and with it, their dependence upon England. When the colonies were ready to assert their independence, the continental states, alienated by Lord Bute's policies in 1763, were prepared to turn the rebellion in North America into a European war.

The Treaty of Hubertusburg was almost equally important for the future of central Europe. It restored the status quo in Germany as it had existed on the eve of the war, thus leaving Prussia in possession of Silesia. In return, Frederick agreed to vote for Archduke Joseph, the heir to the Hapsburg throne, in the coming imperial elections. The simplicity of its terms is in striking contrast to those of the Treaty of Paris. While the Austrians were quite unhappy to admit the loss of Silesia to Prussia, they were henceforth obliged to face the fact that reconquest would be impossible. In the spirit of eighteenth-century politics, the statesmen at Vienna sought compensations for their loss. After 1763 events in central and eastern Europe moved rapidly to provide the opportunity to win compensations. In 1768 the Ottoman Empire declared war on Russia to prevent Catherine II from dominating Poland. As the war developed, it soon became evident that both Poland and the Ottoman Empire were in a position to be partitioned. Since England had little or no interest in central Europe and since France was still recovering from the defeat of 1763, neither of those western powers was in a position to prevent a readjustment of territory, or to put it more bluntly, the plundering of the weaker states. The victorious Russian army operating against the Turks not only placed Russia in a position to annex large segments of the Turkish empire, but also prepared the way for a Russian-Prussian-Austrian partition of Poland. By partitioning Poland, Austria and Prussia could compensate themselves for Russian gains on the north coast of the Black Sea, at the expense of the Ottoman Empire.

The first partition of Poland (1772) simply detached the frontier provinces of that anarchic kingdom and presented them to Poland's three neighbors; with the Turkish army in full retreat and the Polish royal government paralyzed by internal anarchy, there was no force in Europe that could prevent the action. It was a bold-faced "land grab" similar to the one that Peter the Great, August the Strong, and Frederick of Denmark had tried to make in 1700 when they planned the partition of the Swedish empire, as we saw in an earlier chapter. Since the plotters of 1772 did not have to contend with a soldier of the calibre of Charles XII, they could bolster up their action with moral reasons by pointing to the disorders in Poland, and at the same time they could accomplish their piracy undisturbed by anyone.

Two years after the first partition of Poland, the Russians concluded a treaty of peace with the Ottoman Empire at Kuchuk Kainarji (1774). This treaty was perhaps even more important for the future of European politics than the partition of Poland. Peter the Great had almost established Russian power on the Black Sea, but in 1711 he had been forced to give up all his conquests in that region. Catherine the Great's victory in 1774 not only gave Russia most of the north coast of the Black Sea, but also the right to "protect" the Greek Orthodox Christians living in the Ottoman Empire. At a stroke of the pen, Russia became the most important single factor in the Near East. The pressure that she was to exert on the Ottoman Empire and its successors began at Kuchuk Kainarji, and that same treaty might also be used to date the British and Austrian support of Turkey against Russia. England feared Russian control of Constantinople and the Straits; Austria feared Russian encirclement in the Balkans.

Thus, in India, in America, in central and eastern Europe, the treaties that ended the Seven Years' War released political movements of great moment; in many ways the year 1763 might be considered the most important dividing point of the eighteenth century.

Chapter 23

THE CRISIS IN THE BRITISH
EMPIRE, 1763-1786

1. ON THE MORROW OF THE TREATY OF 1763

In 1775 a rebellion broke out in the English colonies on the North American mainland, and quickly developed into a war that spread to Europe, the West Indies, and Asia. In both Europe and America the Treaty of Paris (1763) stands out as a signpost pointing to that war, but only the naïve will assume that it was really the cause of conflict. The English colonies on the North American coast had reached a degree of political and economic maturity by 1763 that made them impatient of controls exerted from beyond the sea, and the treaty that removed the French from Canada and the Ohio basin allowed those colonies to express their feelings of independence. Likewise the Anglo-French rivalry did not stem from the treaty that gave Britain control of America and India: ever since William of Orange mounted the throne in 1688, France and England had been at odds over commerce and colonies, as well as over the hegemony of Europe. The Anglo-Americans understood the situation well: King William's War (1688–1697), Queen Anne's War (1702–1713), King George's War (1740–1748), and the French and Indian War (1755–1763) were the names they had given to the century of Anglo-French conflicts that had involved their own destinies as well as those of Europe. Thus, it was the structure of the Atlantic society of the eighteenth century rather than the treaty of 1763 that we must see as responsible for the outbreak of the conflict and also for the course of the war. From the European point of view, this war was only one phase of the second Hundred Years' War between England and France that was to last until the defeat of Napoleon in 1815.

A Cannon Foundry in 1772. It was in such a workshop that the guns used in the war for American Independence were made. Note the presence of onlookers as well as workers. (University of Minnesota Library)

Both Louis XV and his minister, Choiseul, fully realized that the Treaty of Paris was not the end of Anglo-French rivalry; before the treaty was signed they had begun to prepare France for the next war. Choiseul poured money into the French navy, initiated reforms in the army, and mended the fences of his continental alliances. The incredible arrogance of the English government toward its erstwhile German allies, as well as French propaganda painting England as "perfidious Albion" grown fat with the spoils of war, gave him reason to hope that the next war could be fought as an Anglo-French duel without the diversion of a war on the continent. Thus, when the crisis in the English colonies reached the point of explosion, the French government was prepared. Although the French were to blow hot and cold about participating in the war before they finally did intervene, from 1763 the most important project of French foreign policy had, in fact, been the coming war with England.

Choiseul's efforts had considerable success. In 1763 France had only forty ships of the line and ten frigates; twelve years later the figures had climbed to sixty-four and forty-five respectively. More important, he had injected into the service a new spirit that gave promise of better performance than had been usual in the previous war. The army, especially the artillery, also responded favorably to his reforms, and although the most important results of these did not come until the Revolutionary and Napoleonic wars, the new French army was a better instrument than the old had been. Alliances with Austria, understandings with the other German powers, and the family compact with Spain completed Choiseul's preparations. The Franco-Spanish navies on paper and on the sea were at least a match for the English, and in the war they proved to be the decisive factor in the English defeat at Yorktown (1781).

In 1774, when Louis XVI mounted the throne, Vergennes assumed Choiseul's place as foreign minister. He, too, was an unyielding Anglophobe and in full agreement with Choiseul's policy of preparation for a war of revenge. He may even have been more subtle than Choiseul in his diplomatic preparations for war: by 1777 Vergennes had most of the continent lined up on France's side.

2. BACKGROUND OF THE STRUGGLE IN NORTH AMERICA

While France prepared for another showdown with England, events in the New World also provided opportunities for conflict. By the second half of the eighteenth century men had been living in the English colonies on the North American coast for over a hundred years. The crude settlements characteristic of the earlier days were still to be found on the frontiers, but the seacoast and many miles inland were now dotted with towns and villages, where men's lives were as secure as they were in Europe and where poverty and misery so characteristic of the old world were relatively absent. By 1763 there were almost two million[1] inhabitants in the thirteen colonies; they had built about a dozen towns ranging from ten to twenty-two thousand in population, where public opinion could be formed by newspapers, pamphlets, and public meetings and transmitted to the surrounding smaller communities and countryside.

While there were striking differences in the economy and background of the colonists, the vast majority of them looked to the British Isles as the home of their forefathers, and to the laws, customs, folklore, literature, and general tone of British society as their cultural heritage. Of great importance was the concept that Englishmen were free men possessing rights against tyranny, for the colonists were the descendants of the men who had executed one king and exiled another. Indeed, it may even be true that the social and political ideals developed in England found fuller expression in North America than they did in the British Isles themselves. Moreover, in addition to their common heritage they faced similar problems in dealing with the world that they found in North America. While living conditions in New England were different from those in Georgia, the New World had many things that affected all of the colonists alike, and thereby produced new variations on the traditional English conception of man and his place in society. Even before the Revolution, many people on both sides of the ocean realized that in the New World there was emerging a new man, the American, who was different from his English cousin.

By the mid-eighteenth century the colonies were economically very much alive. From the plantations in the south to the fisheries in the north they exploited the abundant natural resources of the land and the sea. Ironworks in New Jersey, shipyards in New England, and dozens of other shops manufacturing rum, silverware, shoes, furniture, and many other articles of household use testified to the fact that the colonists need not look to Europe for all the things they needed. The ships, shops, and warehouses of the thriving merchants in every city and town bore witness to the essential prosperity of the society. The Americans were obviously becoming economically mature enough to wish to control their own affairs.

On the other hand, the colonies, like any area on an underdeveloped frontier, were faced by many economic needs. They did not have enough capital to develop their resources; they needed credit, more money, and more technical assistance. There were still many articles that they had to buy abroad —capital goods and items of luxury as well as of everyday use. Such commodities were costly, and their own exports sometimes seemed to bring in little by comparison. As they came to realize that their own economy was

---

[1] England's population was only about seven million.

growing in strength, the natural conflicts between the frontier society and the older economy were accentuated. This pattern was destined to repeat itself over and over again as the expanding frontier moved westward across the continent. The underdeveloped community always saw itself as the victim of the merchants and bankers to the east. Thus, the colonists' ideas of their own interests, as opposed to those of England, inevitably produced friction when the government in England asserted its right to control colonial affairs in a way that seemed detrimental to the colonists' interests.

The political development of the colonies had at least kept pace with their economic progress, and the colonists fully understood that their political and economic institutions were interdependent. In each colony there was a popular assembly, elected on a more or less restricted suffrage, but nonetheless the agent of popular power. The popular assemblies closely watched developments in England and regularly claimed for themselves the privileges won by the English Parliament, such as the right to elect their own speaker, freedom of members from arrest, the right to initiate legislation, and the like. They voted taxes, and, among other things, they also tried to print paper money, to pass lax bankruptcy laws, to stay the collection of overdue debts, to attempt to control the sale of public lands, and to assume the right to regulate trade. In other words, they represented the debtor economy of the colonies, and did all that they could to alleviate the problem that faced it. However, the assemblies were not independent. In each colony there was also a royal governor who represented the crown and who had the right of veto; in distant London the Board of Trade and the Privy Council represented the imperial interests of England, and assumed the right to disallow the actions of the legislatures. The British could not allow the colonists to pass laws that violated contracts between their own and colonial merchants or cheapened money to cheat British investors; nor could they tolerate colonial control over trade. It was this very fact that was at the core of the rebellious spirit in the colonies. Traditions and past practices may have been on the side of the Board of Trade, but in every one of the colonies there was growing up a spirit of independence that boded ill for the future of regulation. When colonial legislatures developed the thesis that they were the responsible agents of the crown and that the British Parliament had no right to control their actions, then the conflict over economic interests became inevitable.

Before 1763 most of the conflicts between colonists and the king's government had concerned purely internal policy. Regulations controlling seaborne trade had been accepted or evaded without much discussion. In the name of imperial unity the Board of Trade had made regulations to control and direct trade. The colonists seemed to accept those regulations because they realized that, while the controls were a sort of tax placed upon them by the mercantile interests of the mother country, their own products had a privileged position in the English market and protection from the English navy. Furthermore, since a generally lawless atmosphere prevailed in the waters of the western hemisphere, evasion of unpopular laws was possible, so the regulations of the Board of Trade were ameliorated by smuggling. Any ruling that proved too onerous simply was not obeyed. It ought also to be said that, while smuggling was a large-scale industry in every European country during the eighteenth century, in America it probably was proportionately even larger. For example, even during time of war the colonists supplied the French in Canada with food and other items, and bought sugar and molasses from the French islands in the West Indies. In peacetime illegal traffic probably was greater than legal. Any attempts on the part of the British government to curtail smuggling met with popular resistance. When the courts granted law enforcement officers Writs of Assistance that would allow them to search for illegal goods, a veritable hornets' nest of protest and violence was aroused. The colonists seemed willing to pay lip service to imperial regulation as long as they could evade its consequences when it seemed unjust.

The lax attitude of the English government before 1763 may well have been responsible for the political maturity of the colonies. It has been asserted that no one bothered to read the reports of the governor and so no one in England knew or cared about the course of events in the colonies. This is undoubtedly an exaggeration, but it is nonetheless true that in the first hundred odd years of their existence the colonists largely managed their own internal affairs. Thus, they developed into free societies governed by consent, rather than the bureaucratic and police system that was becoming so common elsewhere in the western world. The fact that they were free societies was only imperfectly understood in England. As the British read history, there was every precedent for legislation in regard to the colonies by the home Parliament. From the time of Cromwell onward the Navigation Acts had regulated commerce, or at least pretended to do so, and this tradition was interpreted to mean that Parliament had the right to impose imperial taxes when they were needed. Although there may have been good legal precedents to justify taxation from London, it turned out to be poor political judgment to insist upon them. The same era that produced the precedents for imperial legislation developed the tradition that the colonists submitted to government only by free consent. As free societies they could not be forced to accept alien rule.

In London after 1763 there were problems that made some kind of colonial taxation appear imperative. Heavy taxes had been imposed as a result of the recent wars, and little chance of early relief seemed in sight. Furthermore, English taxpayers felt that they had taken on these burdens to protect the colonists from the French, and therefore saw no reason why the colonists should not also pay taxes to support the empire. In point of fact, colonial taxes were much lighter than those in England. Thus when the Proclamation of 1763 organized the newly won colonies of Canada, the Ohio basin, and the Floridas, the government in England looked to the colonies for money to help support the cost of police and occupation. The Proclamation closed the trans-Allegheny lands to settlement from the thirteen colonies, and thereby frustrated the ambitions of farmers and land speculators. In London, the government did not realize that it could not keep the Americans out of the Ohio valley by a paper proclamation, nor did it understand that the colonists would resist any efforts to tax them to pay for imperial purposes.

The taxes came in quick succession. In 1764 the Revenue Act, better known as the Sugar Act, placed a tariff on sugar, molasses, and rum. In 1765 the Stamp Act imposed a tax on paper (newspapers as well as legal documents). In 1767 the so-called "Townshend Acts" placed a duty on paint, glass, tea, and several other items of general use. Since these taxes were not heavier than Englishmen were accustomed to, the majority of Englishmen who knew anything about such matters were surprised and irritated by the furor that broke out in the colonies.

In America, however, these taxes looked very different than they did in England. They had not been voted by colonial legislatures, and they fell with particular force upon certain mercantile interests. Merchants, distillers, and others opposed the Sugar Act; the newspapers were outraged at the Stamp Act, and merchants regarded the Townshend Acts as pure tyranny. Arguments did not take long to develop. The colonists had to recognize the right of Parliament to make regulations for imperial trade and to impose tariffs on goods borne at sea; but they claimed a distinction between tariff for regulation and taxes for revenue. They denied absolutely the right of Parliament to impose an "internal" tax; that was the sole prerogative of the colonial legislatures. Thus, for example, they opposed the Sugar Act because it was a low tax, intended for collection, rather than a high tax intended as a barrier to importation of foreign sugar.

There was no lack of eloquent voices to espouse the colonists' case. By the mid-eighteenth century in every city there were lawyers and merchants who knew how to represent colonial interests, and even before the French surrendered Canada the colonists had begun to develop the thesis that their legislatures were on a par with the Parliament of Great Britain. From New England to Virginia a large company of men were searching in English law, in French philosophy, and in the traditions of the English revolutions of the seventeenth century for evidence to prove that acts of Parliament were not effective in the internal affairs of the colonies. The revolutionary slogan, "Taxation without representation is tyranny," did not appear at once; but when Otis denounced a statute of Parliament as unconstitutional because it legalized the Writs of Assistance (1761), and when Patrick Henry protested the king's right to nullify a law passed by a colonial legislature (1763), the colonists were preparing the theory to justify revolt.

As might be expected, men who were accustomed to running their own affairs did not stop with the development of a *theory*. Americans early developed a penchant for action. The Sugar Act virtually became a dead issue at once, because of the extent of smuggling; there simply was not sufficient force to prevent the illegal entry of sugar and molasses, and all attempts to end smuggling led to violence. The Stamp Act resulted in the calling of a "Stamp Act Colonial Congress" (1765) attended by representatives from all but four of the colonies. There was also general movement to boycott all things English and to refuse to pay debts due to English merchants. Even more spectacular was the treatment given to the men who were supposed to collect the stamp tax. Mobs wrecked their homes, applied tar and feathers to their persons, and generally displayed so much temper that the Act was never enforced.

Parliament and the government of England beat a strategical retreat when the Stamp Act aroused so much opposition, and withdrew the tax, but insisted upon the right to impose taxes. The Townshend duties were a vindication of England's right to tax. In America opposition to the duties produced one of the classic pamphlets of the Revolutionary era, John Dickinson's *Letters from a Farmer in Pennsylvania*. Dickinson elaborated the theory that the colonial legislatures bore the same relationship to the crown as the English Parliament. Therefore, acts of Parliament could not apply to the colonies. Among other things, he called for a renewal of the nonimportation agreement between the colonists to boycott English goods.

The reaction to Dickinson's pamphlet and dozens of others like it was immediate. Americans did not need to be urged to resort to violence; it was deeply ingrained in their traditions. All along the coast, but particularly in New England, customs officials were intimidated, ships that had been seized were rescued, and mob action interfered with the application of the law. The governor of Boston, believing that the colony was on the verge of revolt, persuaded the government to send troops to the city; elsewhere tempers were equally shaky, and men who called themselves "sons of liberty" agitated against tyranny and began to drill with muskets.

For a century or more American histories blamed King George and his ministers for the acts that drove the colonists to rebellion. This judgment now needs some revision. The acts that Americans came to regard as tyrannical were passed by overwhelming votes in Parliament, and were sponsored by ministers of varying political faiths. A majority of the people in England who pretended to know about politics saw no reason why the colonists should not pay taxes, nor were they impressed by the arguments about colonial legislatures and their rights. The government backed down when confronted by English merchants who faced ruin because Americans were refusing to

buy goods or to pay bills, but its retreat did not signify that the American arguments were accepted. The English were as irritated over the unreasonable attitude of the colonists as the Americans were over the "tyranny" of the government in London; and the Americans' recourse to violence only stiffened the English decision to insist upon Parliament's rights.

There was little room for compromise. The political activists in America were resolved not to be intimidated, and the English authorities were equally aware of their rights. In 1770 the first blood was shed, when English soldiers, at the end of their patience, fired on a Boston crowd. We need not inquire into the cause of the Boston "massacre" beyond noting the fact that the redcoats were stationed in Boston and were hated by the "sons of liberty." Five people were killed and others injured, and up and down the coast newspapers and pamphleteers had a field day further widening the chasm between England and America. After 1770 the chances for reconciliation declined with each passing year, for both England and the colonies were prepared to settle the problem through force.

3. FROM REBELLION TO WAR

The unwillingness of the colonists to accept Parliament's legislation and the generally lawless attitude of a large segment of the population in colonial America convinced many Englishmen that stronger measures were necessary. Certain English soldiers had the notion that the colonists were cowards who would seek cover before a show of force, forgetting that they themselves had considerable faith in force, and that the colonial militia companies had been drilling and collecting military supplies for just such an occasion. The English government reached the conclusion that the appearance of the redcoats would sustain English authority; rarely have men been more wrong about the probable behavior of others.

By 1773 the colonial theorists had fully evolved a doctrine that was unalterably opposed to the imposition of taxes by the government in London. The "American doctrine" about the British Empire envisaged a confederation of free societies under a common crown, of which the government in London represented only the oldest and most dignified. Each of these free societies, so ran the argument, had the right to control its own affairs, and particularly the right to impose its own taxes. Taxation, except when voted by representatives of the people on whom it was imposed, was alleged to be tyranny. Possibly the British Parliament would have accepted representatives of the American colonies on its benches had that been desired, but that was not the American program. The colonists had already developed the ideas that would eventually create the British Commonwealth of Nations, but in the 1770's no one in power in England had enough vision to see the advantages to be derived from such a confederation. Thus, in America radical opinion became increasingly extreme, and many of the leaders were secretly convinced that only independence could assure liberty.

The particular crisis that led to violence was rooted in the Tea Act of 1773. When it became evident that the Townshend duties could not be collected, they were all repealed except the one on tea. This tax was small, but it represented Parliament's right to tax. The colonists refused to buy legally imported tea, even though the Dutch black tea smuggled in did not suit American taste. At that time the British East India Company was in serious financial straits, because of the military commitments that it had been forced to assume in India. The Tea Act attempted to solve the Company's financial problems by providing a market for its tea in America; but it also imposed more governmental controls upon the Company's activities in India. This confluence of American and Indian history was hardly accidental, for the treaty of 1763 had cleared the way for the conquest of India as well as for the strife between England and her colonies in North America. As far as the "sons of liberty" were concerned, however, the Tea Act appeared to be a monstrous piece of economic imperialism. It gave the East India Company the right to sell tea directly to the Americans, a right that would have ruined, or at least greatly restricted, the profits of merchants in every city of America. Company tea, after the tax had been paid, would have been even cheaper than the smuggled Dutch tea. But was not that the monstrous scheme? The colonists would have to pay the hated tax, and by paying it would recognize the right of the English government to impose a tax.

Long before any tea crossed the ocean, protests in America clearly indicated that trouble was in the air. Indeed, the Company had difficulty in finding ships that would transport the tea to American harbors. When the tea arrived in Boston, the governor found himself isolated; his council, the House of Representatives, and the people of Boston and the neighboring towns arrayed themselves against permission to land the tea. Great public meetings, mob demonstrations, and much oratory convinced the governor that the issue was between legal government and mob rule; the same events convinced the popular leaders that American rights and liberties were at stake. On December 16, 1773, a band of "Indians" boarded the ships, broke open the tea bales, and threw the tea into Boston harbor. The "Boston Tea Party" was the first act of the rebellion. It was both a defiance of English authority and a clarion call for action by Americans. All along the coast of North America ships carrying tea were unable to land their cargoes, or if they were landed, the tea was impounded and not offered for sale.

This refusal to allow the East India Company to sell its tea might be compared to the shelling of Fort Sumter several generations later. Wisely or not, King George III and his minister, Lord North, did not hesitate to reply to the American show of defiance. The port of Boston was closed to commerce until the East India Company had received compensation for its loss, and the customhouse was transferred to the port of Salem (March 30, 1774). A third bill, passed the same month, provided that persons accused of capital offenses in the performance of their official duties might be tried in some other colony or in England at the discretion of the governor. This measure was designed to protect officers who might otherwise be convicted by a colonial court if they attempted to enforce laws that the court refused to recognize. A fourth bill was passed in June allowing the governor to quarter troops in empty buildings, barns, and other places more suitably located than the barracks. There was some opposition to the four so-called "Coercive Acts," but a substantial majority of both Houses in London accepted them.

In addition to those four measures, Parliament passed another act that vitally affected the colonies, but it was purely accidental that it came at the same time. The Quebec Act (June 22, 1774) extended the province of Quebec to include the Ohio and Illinois country which had been left without regular government by the proclamation of 1763. It then proceeded to give the Quebec colony a charter that recognized the predominantly French Roman Catholic character of its inhabitants. The Quebec Act not only offended

Protestant sentiment in the colonies, but also seemed to place definite limits upon the expansion of the seaboard colonies to the west. Furthermore, since the Act did not provide for a popular assembly or trial by jury, Quebec remained essentially a "French" colony within the British Empire, a colony in which Englishmen and Americans would hesitate to settle. Many colonists from Georgia to New England believed that they had fought the late war against France to assure their own rights in the Ohio country; the Act seemed to deny their claims and to exclude them from that land.

The Coercive Acts probably made rebellion inevitable. Colonial newspapers reprinted the speeches of Burke, Fox, Chatham, and others who had opposed the measures in Parliament, and added the opinions of leading colonial lawyers and publicists. The Tea Act had aroused the Anglo-Americans, the Coercive Acts made them into Americans. On September 5, 1774, delegates from all the thirteen colonies except Georgia met in Philadelphia in the First Continental Congress. With the precedents of the Colonial Congress of 1754 and the Stamp Act Congress of 1765, the colonists already had models for some kind of unified action. It is interesting to note that several other British colonies in the New World had also opposed the taxation levied from England, but only those English-speaking colonies with contiguous land frontiers were able to act as a unit. The island colonies were exposed to the coercion of the British fleet, and their organization as plantation economies was in addition a probable check to rebellion. The First Continental Congress served notice upon the English Parliament that Americans did not consider themselves bound by its laws except in the regulation of imperial trade. It warned the king that the exercise of royal prerogatives would be considered inconsistent with American liberties. Men were not quite ready to use the word "independence," but they acted and spoke very independently.

By 1774–1775 in England and in America men were drifting toward war apparently without realizing its possible implications. In Parliament and in the circles of informed opinion, Englishmen re-echoed Dr. Johnson's diatribe against the colonists. They did not regard taxation as tyranny, and like the sage scholar, many Englishmen believed that the colonists were at best rascals; at worst, robbers and pirates. The government was no longer willing to retreat. In America local Committees of Correspondence continued to link the thirteen colonies in an informal sort of unity, and in several of the colonies legislative bodies were elected to meet outside the governor's jurisdiction. Such a meeting in Massachusetts levied taxes, gave commissions, raised militia soldiers, and in general acted like a sovereign power. All up and down the coast of North America men were drilling as well as talking. Possibly less than a majority were willing to rebel, yet the "sons of liberty" were the articulate people, and they did not hesitate to intimidate their less politically minded neighbors.

As everyone knows, the actual spark that ignited the conflict was the shot "heard round the world," fired at Lexington April 19, 1775. The "patriot" version of the "atrocity" at Lexington became the official story of the event in all of the colonies and in most of Europe (even in England) for decades to come. This was one of the great "propaganda victories" of modern times; it branded the British troops as murderers of small children and old men, plunderers, and arsonists who behaved worse than savages. No better rallying cry could have been provided for the "sons of liberty" who were bent upon reaching some conclusions with England; within a few months the articulate sentiment in the colonies had separated the loyalties that had formerly been attached to England from those that held men to their own land; the colonists were fast ceasing to be Englishmen and aggressively becoming Americans.

The breach between the Anglo-Americans and the mother country was not solemnized until the summer of 1776 when the Continental Congress proclaimed the Declaration of Independence (July 4). This document asserted the American case against England, and acted as a catalytic agent to separate the "patriots" and the "loyalists" in the colonies. Probably neither of these groups commanded a majority, yet the Declaration of Independence gave the "patriots" a flag and a slogan that could be used to convince or intimidate their more cautious neighbors, and drive into the open the "loyalists" who were unwilling to support the rebellion. This famous document also became the property of the entire western world; in Europe it was interpreted in a dozen ways that were dangerous to the established order.

It is interesting to note that the leaders who organized the rebellion and directed the war were, by and large, respected, conservative citizens. The Continental Congress that met in Philadelphia was not a gathering of "fire-eaters" who wanted war at any cost; indeed, probably not more than a third of the members could be classified as "radical." The logic of events rather than any preconceived ideas forced them to take the path of organizing an army, granting commissions, raising funds, and finally declaring independence. Perhaps the fact that the Congress was not a radical body prolonged the war. Its members were slow to take the decisive military action that might have cleared North America of British troops before they could be reinforced from Europe.

It was only during the course of the conflict itself that the Continental Congress finally became the legal representative of the Confederation of States that was fighting the war. The "Articles" that bound them together gave very little real power to the Congress; the thirteen colonies were fighting a war to repel a centralized authority; when they became states they had no intention of creating such an authority to rule over them. The Congress conducted most of its business by committees, and, considering its limitations, its conduct of military operations and of foreign and domestic affairs was a credit to the new nation. Finance presented the supreme headache. Before the war was over, the Congress had had to employ Robert Morris as treasurer to bring some kind of order into the chaos. In any war the problem of finance always looms large as an obstacle; in eighteenth-century wars it was the most important single problem, for without money, soldiers could not hope to win victory. The Congress financed its part of the war effort by requisitions, loans, and paper money. Between 1775 and 1779 it issued over $240 million in bills that presumably would be redeemed by the states on a quota basis. The loans were raised in Europe and America, with French money supplying about half of the total amount. In America, requisitions of food and supplies by military officers added a mass of debts that presumably would be paid sometime by the Congress. The total amount of these obligations cannot be estimated, because the issues of continental and state paper money led to inflation which destroyed values. The Congress was never able to supply its armies with money or material on a scale that would allow Washington and his officers great freedom of action, but it did succeed, with the aid of France, Spain, and the Netherlands, in keeping an army in the field. If a force of thirty thousand men seems small for a population of over two million, it should be recalled that there was no machinery by which the Congress could tax the states or draft an army.

As might be expected, the states also participated to a considerable extent in organizing the war. The erstwhile royal officials proved unwilling to fight for their positions once the war had actually broken out, so wherever the British army withdrew, there was no opposition to new constitutions and officials. The states issued paper money, raised militiamen, and assumed the obligations of government. The poor quality of the militia that they raised should not obscure the important work that was done by the new state governments. The fact that many of the constitutions that were adopted at this period lasted far into the next century seems to be evidence of the political maturity and wisdom of the men who seized power.

The course of the war proved to be discouragingly slow. After winning initial victories in upper New York, where they captured some cannon, and then at Boston, where, in spite of the British victory at Bunker Hill, they forced the redcoats to evacuate the city (1776), the Americans ran into a series of reverses. They failed to capture Canada; they were driven out of New York City; and finally even lost Philadelphia. Washington was able to win minor victories by campaigning in the winter, but other than the fact that his army was in being, he and his staff had little room for satisfaction. The real heroism of the men who made up that little army consisted as much in their stubborn persistence in face of terrible odds as in their behavior on any battlefield. It was two years before the stupidities of the British commanders finally gave the Americans their chance to win a victory that justified foreign intervention. The British plan to split the colonial forces in two by an invasion from Canada and an attack from New York was undoubtedly sound, but Howe and Burgoyne (the British commanders) failed to coordinate their efforts. General Gates and his men were thus able to capture the whole British expedition at Saratoga (1777). This was the first real victory of the war.

4. FROM A COLONIAL TO A EUROPEAN WAR

At Versailles men watched the gathering storm in British North America with great interest; it promised an opportunity to settle an old score with the enemy. Yet Louis XVI hesitated to give open assistance to the colonists. His ministers, too, vacillated between reasons to enter the war and objections against taking action. Some feared that the belligerents might make up their family quarrel if France became involved. Others objected that it might be unwise for a king by divine right to assist rebels against another king. Problems in Germany and Poland threatened to erupt into a European war that might possibly produce a world situation similar to that in 1740. The Bavarian succession interested both Prussia and Austria; it resulted in a "cold" war which might well have become serious had Louis XVI wished to intervene. Vergennes and his king, however, were determined to hold their fire for a contest with England; as far as Germany and eastern Europe were concerned, their policy was to maintain peace.

While the French government could not justify active intervention in America until the colonists had proved themselves by winning an important victory, the French court did give considerable covert assistance to the Americans. Louis XVI himself secretly provided money to buy war materials, and encouraged his subjects to volunteer aid either in money or as soldiers. American warships found unofficial asylum in French harbors, and Washington's army in Pennsylvania was armed with guns and powder and clothed with cloth shipped in the holds of French vessels. The men involved in these secret negotiations have already attained immortality in the annals of both France and America. Benjamin Franklin, the unspoiled "natural" man and the darling of the French court and the French people; Beaumarchais, the librettist-courtier and exporter of war supplies; and Lafayette, the hero of two worlds—these were only a few of the many who cemented the forthcoming Franco-American alliance even before Burgoyne's surrender made possible active French intervention.

The secret aid France gave may have helped to keep the American army in the field, but what she gave as a neutral was entirely inadequate for achieving victory. Even though the English government could not raise an army in England large enough to overwhelm the Americans, King George III did rule over a powerful Empire, and the Americans had to face the fact that the English navy could blockade their coasts, while English money could hire soldiers to force them to obedience. The Americans had space on their side, for it was a formidable problem to subdue a thousand miles of coastline and the thinly settled hinterland, but the British could blockade the principal ports and occupy the more important cities and wait until the colonists capitulated—that is, the British could unless European military and naval power were thrown into the balance.

With the news of Burgoyne's surrender at Saratoga, the French government felt justified in recognizing the Americans and making an alliance with them, and in 1778 Louis XVI declared war on England. This act officially opened French ports to the American privateers and naval vessels, the French money market to American securities, and the French military storehouses to the American army. French gifts and assistance no longer needed to be given secretly. Even more important was the fact that the French navy would be able to fight with the British for command of the seas, French privateers would be able to join the Americans in harassing English commerce, and a French army would be able to cross the seas to give direct aid in the New World.

Moreover, when France declared war the whole apparatus of French foreign policy went into operation. At Madrid, Vienna, Berlin, The Hague, and St. Petersburg, French ambassadors closeted themselves with responsible ministers to discuss the war. The most important of these negotiations was with Spain, whose navy could help contain the British fleet. The Spaniards were reluctant to join colonial rebels against their mother country. Spain also possessed colonies that might get ideas. However, the Spanish government was willing, for a price, to come to the aid of France (1779), and this action eventually led to cooperation with the Americans. Spain's role was very important, for with the Spanish navy as an ally the French had, on paper, naval superiority which at critical times could be translated into real control of the seas. The Spanish harbors in the West Indies were also bases for the transshipment of supplies as well as centers for naval operations.

Of somewhat less importance was the role of the Dutch. When France declared war on England, the Netherlands proclaimed her neutrality and immediately embarked upon an extensive triangular commerce with Europe, the Dutch West Indies, and the Anglo-American ports. Under guise of neutrality the Dutch became purveyors of war materials to the American army at a profit to themselves. Unable to stop this traffic, the British government finally decided that it would be easier to control the Dutch activities if they were actual enemies, and so England declared war on the Netherlands (1780). Dutch participation in the war was not at all decisive; England's navy ravaged the Dutch West Indian harbors that had acted as first-stage depots for war supplies, so that loss of a supply route had to be balanced against the work of Dutch privateers and naval vessels.

The experience of every war since the era of Louis XIV and William III had indicated the importance of central and eastern Europe in an Anglo-

French conflict. Through continental allies, England had always forced the French to fight on two fronts: a sea and colonial war with England, a land war with one of the German powers or the Netherlands. This time, however, Louis XVI and his ministers foiled England's attempts to extend the war to the continent. Neither Frederick of Prussia nor Catherine of Russia would have considered the pleas of the American colonists, but they did listen to Vergennes. At the end of the Seven Years' War England had antagonized most of Europe, and the arrogant behavior of the British navy in trying to control the flow of war supplies increased this feeling of hostility. As a result, instead of forming an alliance that would embarrass the French, the eastern states (Russia, Prussia, and Sweden) organized the League of Armed Neutrality (1780) to protect their own commerce. It was largely directed against England, and its principal effect was to give aid to the powers that were assisting the colonists in their war.

Furthermore, French efforts were not confined to the diplomatic isolation of England and the despatch of money and war materials to the Americans. French soldiers landed on American soil, French warships prowled the waters of the western hemisphere, and French raiders harassed British commerce. By 1780 the conflict that English statesmen had entered into with some enthusiam had become a serious problem; the war had spread to the West Indies, the Mediterranean, the African coast, and India, and it was by no means certain that England would win.

In America, the English army seemed to be able to hold the coastal towns, but whenever it attempted to invade the interior, swarms of militia joined the continental soldiers; and even though they might win an occasional victory, the English could not establish effective control over much of the land. With the French soldiers in New England and the continental army under Washington operating in the middle colonies, the British tried to establish their control over the south. This maneuver resulted in an important victory for the Franco-American forces when Rochambeau joined Washington and they besieged the only English field army in America at Yorktown (September–October, 1781). Lord Cornwallis, its commander, depended upon the British navy to get him out of a difficult position, but at the critical moment the French squadron under De Grasse took over control of the mouth of the York river, and sealed Cornwallis' doom. The presence of the French army and navy at Yorktown emphasized the fact that this was an important battle in the third world war since 1740.

After Yorktown, it became obvious that England could not force the colonies to submit. Lord North resigned, and peace negotiations became the order of the day. Once the British recognized that they had lost the war, they were more generous to their erstwhile colonials than to their long-time enemies in Europe. For their part, the American delegates were also willing to listen to suggestions of peace and negotiate behind the backs of their allies.

Such behavior was not as reprehensible as later generations might think; every peace treaty from Westphalia onward had seen similar separate and secret negotiations at the expense of allies.

By the treaty of 1783 the English returned Santa Lucia, Taboga, and Senegal to France; the Floridas went back to Spain. The independence of the thirteen American colonies was recognized, and the entire territory east of the Mississippi river was ceded to the Confederation of American states. The claim to this vast territory had been established during the last years of the war by the expedition of George Rogers Clark into the Ohio and Illinois country. At the time no one could have understood the full importance of the trans-Allegheny territory; the statesmen in Paris knew only that they were negotiating over sparsely inhabited forest lands that might one day have some significance. France's share in the spoils was relatively small, but her king and his ministers took satisfaction in the fact that their rival had been humbled and that at least a part of the Treaty of 1763 had been reversed. Neither Louis XVI nor Vergennes understood the value of India, and so they made no claims there; also, they had agreed not to seek the return of French North America (Canada).

For France the outstanding legacy of the war was not written into the peace. The stirring words of the American Revolutionary documents and the heroic deeds of the leaders in the New World had greatly stimulated the imaginations of Frenchmen, while the tremendous expenses of the war had placed intolerable burdens upon the French treasury. Thus, in a very real way the American Revolution was the first act for revolution in France.

5. THE RISE OF A NEW NATION

The end of the war, unlike the end of a romantic novel, cannot be related in terms of everybody's living happily forever after. The new republic in North America immediately faced enormous problems. Without the protection of the British navy, American commerce ran afoul of port authorities and pirates in many parts of the world, while at home problems of paper money, returned soldiers with claims, unpaid bonds and warrants, and a score of other pressing difficulties threatened the stability of the new states. Since the Confederation that had served to fight the war was little more than a close-knit alliance, it was not strong enough to deal with all the economic and political problems. Talk of tariffs against each other, the problem of the division of the western lands, standards of money, and many other such things threatened to nullify the Confederation. Obviously the Anglo-Americans had won only their independence; they had yet to be formed into a nation.

Historians looking back upon successful political experiments tend to sanctify the origins of those institutions by praising the choice made and condemning all alternatives. Thus the movement that resulted in the writing of the new Constitution of the United States of America has usually been treated as a quasi-sacred affair. Of the wisdom and judgment of the men who persuaded their fellow citizens to adopt the Constitution of 1789, there can be no question, but it may be that the alternatives were not as fraught with danger as they have been painted. The men who settled Anglo-America had already served a long apprenticeship in self-government, and it is inconceivable that they would have succumbed to anarchy had it proved impossible to adopt the Constitution.

The move for revising the Articles of Confederation was in effect a counter-revolutionary movement. Its backers wished to establish a central authority with many of the powers that had been refused to the British crown. The convention that met in Philadelphia was sent there to revise the Articles of Confederation, but once assembled, it became apparent that what was needed was a wholly new constitution. The convention was composed of the most respected leaders of the several states; their decision to write a new constitution was the act of sober statesmen assembled to secure what they considered to be the best interests of their country. In their wisdom, they built upon the existing society and only modified their traditional institutions to secure a stronger federal union. One school of American historians makes much of the fact that the federal Constitution of 1787–1789 was a frank copy of the Americans' idea of the British Empire before 1763. This is somehow conceived to be a conservative political action in spite of the radical means. In any case the result was a Constitution flexible enough to allow for growth and free enough to provide for the rise of unwritten constitutional practices, as well as written legislation that eventually made a nation of the states. In marking out the lines for the continuing development of the United States, the makers of the Constitution of 1789 created a new and potentially very powerful European state in the western hemisphere. It was destined to play an important role in the affairs of the Atlantic and European communities.

The Constitution and the first ten amendments that were adopted as a "bill of rights" outlined a central authority in which the power to govern was roughly divided between the administrative and legislative branches of government. By providing for a supreme court with irremovable judges, the document also became the basis some years later for the doctrine of "judicial review" which added a third agency, the court, to share power. The Constitution wisely remained silent on many points of procedure, thereby leaving to experience and custom the problem of adjusting the organization of power in the federal union. The amendments to the Constitution reflected the spirit of English traditions and the teachings of the eighteenth-century political philosophers by guaranteeing the "rights" of citizens against the inroads of power. All powers not specifically delegated to the federal government were retained by the states with the reservation that the states could not pass legislation that contradicted federal treaties or constitutional rights. The fact that the Constitution could be amended by due process provided for necessary changes in the future.

Perhaps the most striking and revolutionary development that made the thirteen states into one nation was the flood of liberalizing legislation in the decades following independence. The removal of a "ruling class" soon led to the separation of church and state, and this ended the tyranny of "squire and parson" that was associated with remnants of feudalism in Europe. The arrogant contempt for the people that had characterized so much of the ruling gentry's attitude gave way to a more democratic approach to education and social advancement. Furthermore, many of the great families that had owned vast tracts of land or had the right to collect quitrents lost their property. Divided into smaller farms, these lands and those on the frontier became solid economic bases for the new social democracy that was emerging in America (1780–1830). Other inequalities also disappeared as local statutes were revised in the new spirit. Religious liberty ended a host of vindictive legislation, while legal reforms swept some of the more brutal and barbarous aspects of the legal system. These reforms were also finally effected in Europe, but not until almost three-quarters of a century later. In America they were easier to accomplish, perhaps because the frontier society was immeasurably freer than that of the old world. This "new man," the American, was preparing himself for the role that history would demand of him.

6. THE BRITISH IN INDIA

During the years that England and the North American colonies were fighting the war that created the United States of America, English interests in India were preparing themselves for the colossal task of establishing England's Indian empire. The same treaty of Paris (1763) that was so fateful in America had almost equally important effects in India, for the French were reduced to commercial contacts with five Indian coastal cities, leaving the political field free for the British East India Company. The government in Paris gave up intervention in Indian affairs without deep regrets, since it had never been favorable to the politico-military policy that Dupleix had espoused in the mid-century. India had never been conquered from the sea, and, as we noted, probably could not be conquered without more naval power than France could hope to assemble. After 1763 the English, on the other hand, were in a position to exploit their advantages in India, and with the examples that Dupleix and Clive had established, they were aware of a method for conquest.

The situation in India in the middle of the century seems to have invited

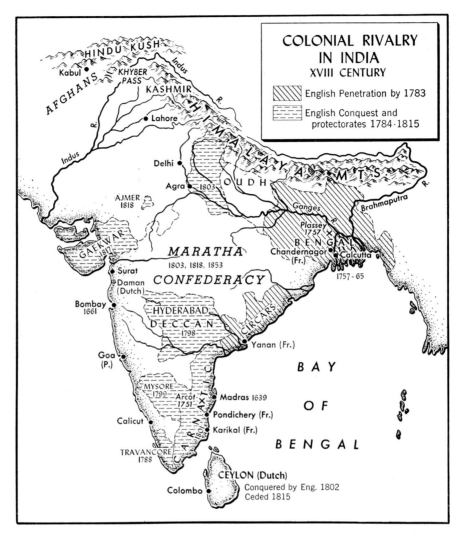

conquest. From the beginning of the eighteenth century the power of the
emperor at Delhi had been declining. In the east, Bengal and Oudh emerged
as independent states; in the middle of the subcontinent the Maratha Confederation practically ended the emperor's authority over most of India, and
in the west the states of the Sikhs were also independent. If military power
were to be the key to the future of India, the Maratha Confederation and
the Sikhs seemed best able to assume the powers that had belonged to the
Mongol emperor. There was, however, one other force involved. On the
northwestern frontier were the Afghan tribes who also took advantage of
the growing weakness of the empire to raid deep into India. In 1761 a swarm
of Afghan cavalry practically annihilated the military power of the Maratha
states at the battle of Panipat. The Afghans could destroy, but they could not

organize; after looting everything that could be carried away, they again retired to the hills with the promise to return.

The aftermath of the Afghan raids was disorder. All India seemed to dissolve into petty warring principalities, none of which was forceful enough to
calm the countryside. Communications broke down, trade declined, and raiding parties reduced whole provinces to starvation. Intervention of some sort
was essential for the recovery of the land.

Intervention came from Europe. In part it took a form characteristic of the
aftermath of each great European war since the War of the Spanish Succession. European soldiers of fortune, unable to adjust to the peace that "broke
out" in Europe, offered their services to princes and potentates in the so-called
backward areas. Every European war since 1713 has sent those soldiers of
fortune to Turkey, Egypt, Persia, China, India, Latin America, or other
lands, where their military talents could find some employment. In the mid-
eighteenth century German, French, Flemish, Italian, and other unemployed
soldiers drifted eastward to find service more congenial that that open to
them in Europe. The other form of European intervention was more regular
and consistent. The British East India Company, drawing on English soldiers
and administrators, became a force in India which brought order into the
anarchy resulting from the collapse of the Mogul empire and the failure of
the Indian princes either to stave off the Afghans or to resolve their own
conflicts.

Some of the European soldiers of fortune were men who had already
fought in India as agents of the French East India Company; others like the
German Richard Sombre, the Savoyard de Boigne, and the Flemish and
Italian soldiers were men dislocated by the wars in Europe. Several of them
were really excellent soldiers. De Boigne, for example, first developed the
"hollow square" as an infantry tactic suitable for checking Afghan cavalry;
and that tactic, taken to Europe by Wellington, was used at Waterloo to
defeat Napoleon. Although the Europeans fought against the Afghans, the
fact that so many of them joined Haidar Ali, Tippoo Sahib, and other bitter
enemies of the English, suggests that many of them were transferring their
personal war with England to India. At least one of them, Michel Raymond,
so captured the imagination of the Indians that young men made pilgrimages to his tomb until the twentieth century.

Unquestionably, these European adventurers slowed up the process of the
English conquest of India by giving native rulers European military techniques, but they were quite unable to defeat the English advance. Indian
princes were not culturally ready to adopt European methods, their subjects
were not committed spiritually to military resistance, and Indian technology
was not far enough advanced to fight successfully against the English. These
were some of the factors that operated to prevent these soldiers of fortune
from buttressing the Indian states against the British conquest.

The English conquest really began during the Seven Years' War, when Clive defeated the French and their Indian allies. The battle of Plassey (1757) gave the English control over Bengal, a magnificent base for continuing the conquest. After the Treaty of Paris had excluded the French as a vital force in India, Clive proceeded to secure from the emperor at Delhi a commission that made the English India Company an imperial officer; in point of fact the Company was fast becoming a sovereign power in India. By 1767 Clive had brought the nabob of Oudh and the rajah of Benares under the "protection" of his government.

At this point the Company ran into difficulties both at home and in India. Most of the Company's wealth had to be used for military purposes since Indian politics were so fluid. Because its stockholders tended to prefer profits that could be made into dividends to military gains that might have future advantages, the East India Company faced a crisis. At the same time, the shameless display of wealth and indifferent morality exhibited by some of the Company "nabobs" who returned home heavy with gold, aroused indignation that was at once moral and jealous. The result was the India Act of 1774 that reorganized British activities in India and sent tea to Boston. The India Act made the crown a partner in the Company's activities. The governor-general was henceforth named by the government, and his power was limited by a council appointed by the Company and by the government. Both the Company and the government were to be kept informed, and a court of justice was established in Calcutta with the power, among others, to veto Company decisions.

The first governor, Warren Hastings (1774–1785), turned out to be an energetic empire builder. While the English were fighting with their backs to the wall in the American war, Haidar Ali allied with the French. For a short time the Franco-Indian forces were successful, or at least they had a slight advantage over Hastings' forces, but by 1784 Haidar Ali's son and successor, Tippoo Sahib, signed a peace which re-established the status quo. Mysore was also a thorn in the English side. Warren Hastings successfully managed the war against that state during the years when England could give no aid because of her commitments in America. When it was over, his enemies were determined to ruin him, and finally succeeded in forcing his recall to stand trial for his actions. Then a new India Act was introduced and passed in 1784 that was destined to be the basic statute for India for the next three quarters of a century. By this act the Company was again permitted to name the governor, subject to revocation by the government in London, and a royal council for India, seated in London, was named as the correspondent to which the Company had to send all its reports. This was a strange political base for what happened in India. The privately owned East India Company was at once a vassal and an agent of the emperor at Delhi, a creature controlled by the India Council in London, sovereign or quasi-sovereign lord over Bengal and several other Indian states, and the commercial agent of its stockholders. It is almost incredible that in the next two decades this political power became the great military force in India, and set for itself the program of conquest that eventually replaced the emperor at Delhi with a British viceroy.

Much ink has been spilled justifying the revolution of the thirteen American colonies; more ink has been and still more will be spilled condemning or justifying the British conquest of India. Somehow neither justification nor condemnation makes much sense. The significant fact seems to be that the crisis that confronted English statesmen after 1763 became the basis for three great political experiments. In the western hemisphere there arose a new nation that was destined to become one of the great politico-military powers of the twentieth century. At the same time, the experience of the American Revolution was destined to become the object lesson that taught English statesmen the way to create the British Commonwealth of Nations. In the East, the British conquest of India made possible the political unification of the territory that has become India and Pakistan, both of which countries were eventually to take their places as important political forces in the twentieth century. From this point of view, the crisis in the British Empire from 1763 to 1784 becomes the source of great political institutions in Europe, America, and Asia.

Eighteenth-Century Holiday Promenade on the Ramparts of Paris (Paris, Bibliothèque Nationale). Note the Chinese Pavillion, the outdoor restaurant, and the varied attire of the men and women.

Chapter 24

THE CIVILIZATION OF THE FRENCH CENTURY

1. PATTERNS OF LIFE

Eighteenth-century civilization will long be known for its frivolous elegance and its underlying brutality. It was the age of powdered wigs, snuff-boxes, the minuet, delicate furniture, and beautiful costumes; it was also an epoch of barbarous legal codes, public executions, and grinding poverty. It probably provides the most striking contrast between the standards of living of the rich and the poor that can be found in the history of the West, not so much because the poor were more miserable, but because the rich had more elegance. The time was still far distant when the culture of an era could be culture for everyone. The civilization of the eighteenth century with its artificiality, its rich ornamentation, and its extreme politeness was solely for the kings, the nobles, the wealthy bourgeoisie, and for the handful of intellectuals who managed to climb the social ladder despite their lack of aristocratic breeding or of money.

The annals of the poor, the ignorant, and the downtrodden are quickly told; they did not make history in the grand sense of the term until the end of the century, when revolution released their political energy and warfare harnessed their military potential. On the other hand, the elite of the eighteenth century have written a broad page in the history of the artistic and intellectual culture of the western world. On the eve of the French Revolution of 1789, the elite of Europe had developed a brilliant civilization. Its principal components were French, but it was in a way the result of the intermixture of all the European societies, making the nearest approximation to a cosmopolitan culture that the western world had seen since the Roman era.

The conditions of eighteenth-century life were particularly favorable for this wealthy highest social class. In the preceding century the rise and development of the bureaucratic state, buttressed by standing military forces, had reduced the incidence of disorder to a minimum. It was no longer necessary for every man to provide for his own military security; the king's officials, his police, and his soldiers forced the lawless elements to recognize the law and to keep the peace. While the political order guaranteed personal security, the economic system poured wealth into the laps of the upper segment of society. Colonial markets, European commerce and manufacturing, and a buoyant economy contributed to the increase in wealth that allowed country gentlemen to rebuild their houses, merchants to erect city homes, and great nobles, soldiers, and politicians to build châteaux. No one considered it necessary to share this wealth with the masses, and since the poor had no organization or articulate spokesmen, no one really demanded that it should be shared.

However, it is difficult to explain the forms of a grand culture without oversimplifying it or giving the idea that it was somehow static. This latter notion is the most common and the most simplified. A grand civilization is never a tableau, picture, or stage setting; like all other worldly affairs, it fluctuates and changes. We have only to compare the little pictures we get of society in the reign of Louis XIII with those of the era of Louis XV to appreciate the tempo of this flux. In the mid-seventeenth century stern men, sure of God's law and deeply convinced of their own mission, seemed to march throughout the world; a hundred years later, witty, perhaps frivolous characters who regarded ability to live and to die graciously as the important mission of man had moved into the spotlight. In 1635 men dressed in exaggeratedly flowing clothes, carried swords, fought duels, and postured bombastically; by 1750 flowing wigs and whiskers had given way to clipped elegance, flowing costume to tailored sophistication, and the dueling sword to a cane. Women's styles changed as radically as men's. The formal elegance of eighteenth-century women makes their grandmothers of the seventeenth century seem crude or prudish.

2. ARCHITECTURE, PAINTING, AND SCULPTURE

These changes and many others reflected the deep currents in western society: the processes of secularization which were turning men's attention to the earth and worldly things; the rise of political stability which deprived men of the right and the need to act as completely free agents; and the development of wealth that allowed many men a larger measure of leisure and greater possibilities for self-expression. These deep currents were readily reflected in architecture, painting, music, and literature. Perhaps the most dramatic physical expression of the new possibilities of that secular society was the great palace at Versailles that Louis XIV built at the end of the seventeenth century. As we noted, instead of a château which depended upon walls and moats for security, the palace was a blatant announcement that it was protected by the authority and power of the bureaucratic-police state. Its elegance, spaciousness, and grandeur proclaimed that secular interests had combined with wealth to produce a new kind of architectural monument.

It was not long before imitators of Louis XIV had sprung up all over Europe. In one way Versailles was as much of a challenge to Europe as Louis' armies had been; in another it was an invitation to European men to readjust their vision of their lives and to re-evaluate their conception of civilized living. Thus, even before the great wars of the Spanish Succession (1702–1713) and of the North (1701–1721) had come to an end, princes, soldiers, statesmen, nobles, and rich bourgeoisie in all parts of Europe began to build châteaux for themselves. The old-style dwelling with its heavy walls and cramped quarters could hardly be remodeled to fit the modern tastes, so a great proportion of the construction—the habitations of the wealthy—was new. Inevitably, the enormous prestige of France and of Louis XIV influenced the patterns of construction and thereby tended to give to all European architecture a unity that it had not had since the Gothic era of the Middle Ages; neither the Renaissance style of the fifteenth and sixteenth centuries nor the baroque of the later sixteenth and seventeenth had so universal an influence as the *rocaille-rococo* style of the eighteenth century.

Like every artistic form, the *rocaille-rococo* has many roots. The palace of Versailles was unquestionably one of the most important models; but Versailles was a colossal building, stately, imposing, formal, and cold in its massive elegance: it was a suitable residence for a great king, but only he could afford such a residence and be willing to live in such formality. Other people had to cut their patterns to fit their pocketbooks, and demanded living quarters that were more informal and more comfortable. In fact, even the royal family at Versailles could not live with such magnificence. After Louis' grandchild, the talented Duke of Burgundy, married a Savoyard princess, the royal architects were commissioned to remodel the family apartments. The result was a new style, more intimate and friendly, more graceful if less impressive. An American art historian insists that this remodeling was the seed for the new mode, the rococo style, of the eighteenth century.

It is difficult to generalize about architecture. No two buildings are exactly alike, nor are they intended for the same purposes. In general one can say that the châteaux and city *hôtels* built in the eighteenth century were lighter in construction than their predecessors had been. They usually had larger windows and doors, more easy access from living quarters to gardens, courtyards, and terraces, and more handsome decoration than the semifortress structures of the preceding centuries. The interiors had lower ceilings, which meant that the rooms were easier to heat; they were ornamented with mir-

An Architect's Drawing for a Rococo Interior. Note the treatment of the fireplace, the bed, and the doors. This style of interior decoration was suitable for a great château or a small city house. (University of Minnesota Library)

rors over the fireplace and on opposing walls, so that the rooms not only could come alive with motion but also seemed much larger than they really were. Elaborate chandeliers with prisms and tinkling glass reflected light and provided pleasant noises with each passing breeze. The decoration was varied, but plaster bas-reliefs of one kind or another filled the corners of the room or encircled the ceilings. This left only small panels for the artists to fill in with pastoral or mythological scenes. The colors used tended toward pastels rather than the bold primary colors of the earlier era; gilding was also much in evidence. Since the furniture and the clothing of the period matched the ornamented walls and the inlaid floors, the whole effect of this rococo was elegance par excellence, if somewhat artificial and fragile.

In France the new *rocaille-rococo* style tended to show restraint, but further east in Europe it became more and more elaborate. The walls of churches and châteaux melt in the motion of the carvings and decorations that cover them: a profusion of flowers, cupids, monkeys, musical instruments, and birds cascade from the ceilings. Some of the buildings were in horrible taste. In Bayreuth the whole exterior of the ducal château is studded with seashells and crystals; the expression "Bavarian rococo" is synonymous with exuberance and movement. It is small wonder that in the latter part of the century there was a reaction against the style.

The new mode of life as well as the new architecture imposed novel patterns on the painters and sculptors of the era. As long as kings and the church were the principal patrons of the arts, heroic subjects, grand portraits, and religious scenes were the style, but such art is quite unsuited to more intimate living. Eighteenth-century men wanted pictures of themselves and their families in familiar poses, pictures of landscapes, festivals, or daily life that would give pleasure and amuse rather than inspire and impress. Furthermore, they wanted smaller pictures that could be fitted into the wall decorations of their new châteaux, not large canvases to cover an entire wall. The sculptors experienced similar new demands. Heroic statues or tableaux were still required to decorate public places or to embellish churches, but portrait sculpture and clever, attractive figures for decorating gardens made up a greater proportion of the orders that came to the sculptors' studios.

Like the architecture, the art of the eighteenth century originated in France. Of course, French art depended in its turn upon earlier forms from Italy and the Lowlands. The squabble that broke out in the French academy when Le Brun (Louis XIV's "czar" of the arts) died gives a clue to the roots of French painting. On one side, were the Rubenists or colorists who drew upon Flemish and Venetian models; on the other, were the Poussinists who drew upon the Florentine and Roman Renaissance models, particularly Raphael, the master of design. The issue of this quarrel was shown in the compromises made by the great eighteenth-century painters whose characteristic style owes much to the great Watteau.

Watteau (1684–1721) combined design and color, but, more than that, he painted in the mood of the new century. Most of his important works were completed between 1711 and 1721. He painted colorful, frivolous *fêtes gallantes*. His pictures of gay companies of young men and women, elegantly costumed in rich fabrics, enjoying the beauty of romanticized rural scenes or forests seem to have set the tone for elegant social life for the next half-century. On other canvases Watteau painted the actors of the Italian opera, soldiers on the march, or gay scenes from classical mythology. He reflected the eighteenth century in that his art insisted upon the stylized exterior of life as true value of life. When later eighteenth-century painters depicted the king (Louis XV) and his mistress (the Marquise de Pompadour) as children playing at love in the garden, or portrayed the romantic bucolic life that Queen Marie Antoinette pretended to live in her make-believe peasant village, they were following the pattern set by Watteau. Fragonard (1732–1806), Le Greuze (1725–1805), and other eighteenth-century French masters vied with each other to paint the fragile beauty of nature, gracefully costumed young men and women, and picturesque, sentimental scenes. In this they set the pattern for European painting, for French art captured the imagination of all Europe.

The portraiture of the French eighteenth-century masters even more completely dominated all European portrait painting to the degree that Englishmen, Netherlanders, and Germans of that period all seem to look like Frenchmen as they peer at us from their canvases. The portrait painter tends to give the style to his subject, and it in turn is conditioned by his training. The grand style of portraiture was fixed at the opening of the century by Rigaud, who painted his subjects surrounded by the symbols of their office or accomplishment, and glorified in their worldly honors. As the century wore on, painters developed more intimate presentations of character, but the handsome men and beautiful, elegant women who grace the canvases of the eighteenth century owe no small part of their glamor, if not their reputations, to the brushes of these painters who glamorized an era with their portraits.

In the mid-eighteenth century one group of French artists introduced a new technique of portraiture in colored chalk (pastels). La Tour was perhaps the greatest of these pastelists. Their pictures were more intimate, and the pastels allowed clearer, more brilliant colors than the oil paints of the eighteenth century could hope to produce. In the second half of the century these pastel portraits were all the "rage"—everyone who was "anyone" had to be drawn. The result was that many fine examples of this art form have come down to our time to suggest that the pastelists of the eighteenth century, like the oil painters, glamorized their subjects, gave them style and, at the same time, produced pictures that will probably never be excelled in the pastel medium.

French sculptors found as great a demand for their products as did the painters. The châteaux always included gardens either of the formal Versailles type or, in the latter eighteenth century, of the romantic English variety. The gardens provided dramatic backdrops for pieces of sculpture in fountains or on pedestals. The rooms of the châteaux, too, were often garnished with a bust of the owner or some pleasing romantic piece. City building also created a market for sculpture. The grand style of the seventeenth-century baroque city planning continued into the eighteenth century. The great Place Louis XV in Paris (Place de la Concorde today) was the most striking example, but open squares created in cities all over Europe fairly cried out for fountains or monumental statues to garnish them. This type of city building, inspired by the great square in front of St. Peter's at Rome and the parks and avenues centering on the palace at Versailles, became standard for the western world.

Watteau, "The Rural Wedding" (The Cleveland Museum of Art, Elisabeth Severance Prentiss Collection). Watteau was the real founder of the rococo school of French painting. The romantic scene, elegance of costume, grace of movement, and lovely color are typical of his many canvasses.

Fragonard, a Detail from "The Lovers" (New York, The Frick Collection). This is one of a series of pictures, romantic in conception, that flattered King Louis XV and his mistress. The artist displays all the frivolity of the rococo civilization of the French court. (University of Minnesota Art Department)

The sculptors who provided pieces for these markets had to produce suitable secular subjects. In place of the saints and biblical characters of earlier artists, they created a galaxy of nymphs, goddesses, animals, and heroes. They learned to express motion in stone and bronze so well that some of the latter eighteenth-century sculpture seems almost violently agitated.

3. FRENCH CULTURAL HEGEMONY

The idea of Europe as a cultural unity has has an interesting history. Medieval Europe, or at least the articulate people of medieval Europe, showed a common culture based upon the Latin Christian Church, the Latin language, Gothic art forms, and the feudal social structure. The period between the fifteenth and eighteenth centuries witnessed a considerable diversification of cultural forms. The vernacular languages, reformed state churches, secularly oriented societies, and regional art forms tended to break down the universalisms of medieval society and created particularism or sectionalism in European civilization. The extension of French civilization in the eighteenth century almost promised to re-establish a sort of universal European culture, at least among the articulate elite of society. It may be either the tragedy or the good fortune of Europe that nationalistic particularism eventually proved to be too strong, and French cultural hegemony too weak to give Europe a common mold.

The eighteenth-century conquests of French culture were accompanied by the rise of the French language to the status formerly enjoyed by Latin, through which all educated Europeans could communicate with one another in the Middle Ages. Latin continued to maintain its important position until the sixteenth century, when Spanish and Italian practically supplanted it as the languages of politics and diplomacy, even though the classical tongue was still widely used for science and philosophy. In the seventeenth century, however, many men began to write important books in their own vernacular, with the result that Italian, English, Spanish, French, Dutch, German, and perhaps other languages were needed to keep abreast of literary, political, and philosophical thought. It was an appalling idea that a man might have to know three or four languages beyond his mother tongue to consider himself educated and to have access to the views of other educated men. In the eighteenth century, the general acceptance of French as the first or second language for all educated men temporarily solved this problem.

The enormous prestige of the court of Louis XIV and the achievements of French soldiers and statesmen undoubtedly contributed greatly to the movement, but the French language did not win its great victory because of the power of French arms. Even when Louis XIV was forced to back down in military defeat, the French language continued to gain acceptance. Although French arms remained formidable, in the eighteenth century, they were clearly in no position to impose the French language upon Europe. Napoleon as a French soldier-statesman was the first to attempt deliberately to force non-Frenchmen to use the French tongue; the result was an intensification of Italian, Spanish, and German nationalistic feeling. The real eighteenth-century victory of the French language was achieved by consent. It is astonishing to see how it leaped over frontiers. In England, for example, the cabinet meetings which George I attended could be conducted only in French or Latin, languages understood by the king, who was a German, as well as by the English statesmen. In Prussia, Frederick II and his whole court used French almost exclusively; the Prussian king's voluminous writings were all in French. The Viennese court of Maria Theresa used French; indeed, the good queen even corresponded with her children in that language. Nor was it surprising that the treaty of peace between Russia and Turkey in 1774 was written in French. Anyone familiar with Tolstoy's *War and Peace* will recall that country gentry east of Moscow used French within the family, just as the salons in St. Petersburg were modeled on those of Paris. In Sweden, Italy, Spain, Hungary, the Lowlands, and Scotland, educated men of the eighteenth century understood and spoke French; it was the language into which any work had to be written or translated to achieve a European audience. The German nobleman who remarked, "I speak French like Diderot and German like my nurse" pointed up the universality of the French language.

The advantages of French over potential rivals were manifold. Richelieu, in establishing the French Academy and endowing it with the power to discipline French vocabulary and grammar, made a language which was already precise even more exact at a time when there was no single German language, only German dialects. Furthermore, seventeenth-century France produced a galaxy of fine writers: dramatists like Corneille, Molière, and Racine; essayists like La Bruyère and La Fontaine; scientists and philosophers who were also fine stylists, such as Fontenelle, Fénelon, and Bâyle; memoirists and letter writers like Saint-Simon and Madame de Sévigné. These people made it worthwhile to learn French in order to have access to their thoughts. They also gave new elegance to the French language, for language is a process purified by significant use. No language is ever the same after it has been used by a great writer. The great German philosopher, Leibniz, was so impressed by its development that he wrote in French rather than in German. The Academy, the men of letters, and the natural structure of the language, all contributed to the purification of the language so that the epigram, "If it is not clear, it is not French," almost became true.

The extension of the French language and culture was facilitated by migrations of Frenchmen to other countries of Europe. In the 1680's thousands upon thousands of Huguenots migrated to England, Holland, Prussia, and elsewhere, taking with them their language, their skills, and their culture. In Berlin, Amsterdam, and a half dozen other cities in 1700, French was almost as common a language of communication as the native tongue. Another way in which Frenchmen and French ideas were sent abroad was through the policy of royal marriages that sent French princesses to Spain, England, Savoy, and Germany, and after Philip V established himself in Spain, the Bourbon family extended French culture to much of Italy as well as Spain.

In the early eighteenth century the financial crisis following the burst of Law's bubble, which we discussed earlier, caused hundreds of French artisans and artists to migrate because there was temporarily no employment for them in France. During the succeeding years, Germany, central Europe, Scandinavia, and Russia drew heavily upon French men and women of various classes to serve as artists, artisans, teachers and scholars, servants and cooks. To a lesser degree, England, Spain, and Italy also attracted teachers of the French language, of dancing and manners, as well as scholars and men of letters. The *émigré* Frenchman was a common sight long before the Revolution of 1789 again forced thousands of Frenchmen to leave their fatherland. When the emigrations of 1789–1815 occurred, the new *émigrés* were astonished to find that men in St. Petersburg, Vienna, Berlin, Rome, Frankfurt, Copenhagen, and Amsterdam spoke their native tongue as well as it was spoken at home.

The fad for things French extended even to cooking, dress, and manners. The French chef and his cuisine were justly famous, but it is surprising to find them so universally accepted. From London to Moscow in 1750, as today, French food was *à la mode*. French manners were never copied as completely; few people were as gentle and polite as the French, and many attempts to follow their manners led to exaggerations. French clothing for men, however, had little competition up to the mid-eighteenth century, and French styles for ladies had none. The natural elegance of the French dressmaker combined with the luxury-oriented French economy to produce the modes of the eighteenth century. Since only the wealthy could dress *à la mode,* there were few limits to the amount or the richness of the fabrics used. The results can best be seen today on the canvases of those eighteenth-century artists who loved to paint female finery.

French furniture, too, acquired European acceptance. In the seventeenth century furniture was still heavy, ornate, and, for the most part, very little adapted for functional purposes. Chairs and tables had to stand stiffly against the walls; they were too awkward to be moved about in the room. These solid, carved pieces were perhaps imposing, but they lacked grace and usefulness. In the eighteenth century, with the coming of the rococo ideal of graceful elegance, furniture became lighter in weight, more easily movable, and differentiated according to use. Even into the twentieth century in both the English and the German languages French words are still used to name several of the pieces that were created for different uses; however, we did not adopt the French term *péché mortal* for the chaise longue. It mattered little where you were in 1750; any house that pretended to modish decor would have been furnished *à la française*.

By the middle of the eighteenth century, French cultural hegemony seemed well on the way to the creation of a common European society. Since the spread of French culture did not depend upon political or military force, its conquests must be recognized as the result of a general acceptance of French artistic, social, and intellectual superiority. The attitude of Frenchmen themselves undoubtedly acted to extend it. Rather than becoming boastful about their own culture, French intellectuals considered themselves cosmopolitan in their outlook. By leaving to others the role of propagandists for their way of life, they exhibited both politeness and sensitivity; perhaps this display of virtue was easy since there were many willing to proclaim the virtues of French civilization. The Italian, Marquis Carraccioli, who wrote the book, *Paris: The Model for Foreign Nations, or French Europe,* not only recognized the excellence of things French, but also the universality of French culture as cosmopolitan. Indeed, the word "cosmopolitanism" came into parlance toward the end of the eighteenth century, and it largely meant the internationalization of French manners, modes, and ideas.

4. NATIONALISTIC RESISTANCE

However, ever since the later Middle Ages Europe had resisted both political and cultural uniformity. It may well be that the German philosopher Herder (1744–1803) was right when he argued that each "folk" had distinctive cultural forms that separated it from every other "folk," and that each strove to work out its own cultural contribution to the civilization of man. The word "folk" naturally presents some problems, but no one who has traveled in Europe will quibble too much about the proposition that there are differences that seem to be related to ethnic, linguistic, historical, and other such forces at work in the population of the continent. Herder further pointed out that those differences are most pronounced among educationally and economically less favored classes; while the upper classes of each "folk" tend to produce some individuals with cosmopolitan attitudes, the lower classes tend to be unaffected by "foreign" ideas. Herder himself was arguing for the unity of the German "folk," so that it might best make its contribution to European culture, but his basic conception can also be used to understand the forces in Europe that resisted the cultural hegemony of any one national group.

From the later Middle Ages onward, the economic forces at work in European society have been progressively elevating individuals from the lower into the upper social classes. The peasant's son who became a master craftsman, the clothmaker's son who became a banker, or a professor, and the banker's son who became a minister of state, each carried with him some of his father's prejudices and ideas. This fluid nature of European society often accounts for the reappearance of social, religious, and political ideas that the sophisticated of earlier periods had long since rejected. It was undoubtedly an important factor in the resistance that European developed to Renaissance Italian culture in the fifteenth and sixteenth centuries, to baroque

Spanish culture in the sixteenth and seventeenth centuries, and to Versailles French culture in the seventeenth and eighteenth centuries. Each of these great movements was persuasive in its time and had large followings among the educated elite, but they were unable to penetrate into the folk-cultural patterns of the mass of the people.

There were, of course, other forces at work to stem the tide of French cultural hegemony. In Italy, Spain, and England, French modes never made the same conquests that they did in central and eastern Europe. The Italians had themselves so long been the schoolmasters of Europe in art, music, and letters that they resented the rise of the French. Spain, after the mid-seventeenth century, had become increasingly remote from the rest of Europe. Spanish society was supported by a decaying economy that even the Bourbon kings of the eighteenth century were unable to revivify. Roads were bad to nonexistent, and accommodations for travel so poor that Boston or Philadelphia was almost closer to Paris than was Madrid. Thus, an economic barrier combined with Spanish pride in the past to resist the inroads of French culture. The English, possibly in part because of their political history as well as because of the sturdy structure of English society, also proved somewhat resistant to the seductiveness of French culture. In the two preceding centuries English men of letters, some of them towering giants like Shakespeare and Milton, had given the English language form and elegance, and in the early eighteenth century the sensational development of English "philosophical thought" led by Newton and Locke temporarily gave England an intellectual hegemony in the western world. These English men of letters, science, and philosophy undoubtedly strengthened England to resist the inroads of French culture.

In central and eastern Europe men possessed no such fortresses against French culture. The popular languages were as yet undeveloped by great literature and neither political nor artistic traditions supplied standards behind which men could rally to support their own culture. In Germany, dozens of dialects competed with each other, with the result that Frederick was probably right in scorning the "peasant's language," for the German spoken in towns and villages had little music and no elegance; even the German used by many university professors was coarse, crude, and guttural. The Polish and Russian languages were in an even worse state than the German; they were literally "peasant tongues," and the educated nobleman or bourgeois was happy to learn French as a vehicle for polite communication. Even into the twentieth century these dialects persist as the language of the poor and the ignorant, and it is easy to see why the educated sought intellectual refuge in another tongue. In France, too, the poor and the illiterate did, of course, speak patois tongues that lacked the elegance of the French of Paris and Tours.

In Germany some of the first opposition to French culture came from men so uncertain of their own traditions that they urged the adoption of English forms rather than French. They had access to English culture, because English books were translated into French. In the second half of the eighteenth century the German language and German forms also began to emerge as competitors to French civilization. The German university and bourgeois figures in science, philosophy, and literature were responsible for refining the German language as a vehicle for serious thought. Once that had been done, the Germans could also begin to resist the French cultural invasion.

It is difficult to describe the eighteenth-century reaction against French culture without overemphazing it. The historian must always be aware of the beginnings of movements and yet resist the temptation to write about them as if they were the characteristic pattern of the period. The really important resistance to French culture and the great surge of nationalistic feelings did not come until the French revolutionary and imperial armies made things French hated from Moscow to Madrid. In the period just before the French Revolution, for every example of a criticism of things French, there were striking examples of free acceptance of French civilization: but the criticisms are significant for they are part of the characteristic pattern of the nationalist movements that were destined to play so important a role in the history of the nineteenth century.

Interestingly enough, the form of the criticism of things French created a fictional picture of France and Frenchmen that has continued with some variations into the twentieth century. The courtesy of the French was assumed to be insincere and the elegance of their speech and dress came to be regarded as "effeminate." French frankness about sex became licentiousness. The gaiety of Paris became wickedness. Thus there emerged a stereotyped and quite unflattering image of the Frenchman; it was purely fictional, but it served as a measure to discredit French culture by comparison with others.

Some of the anti-French criticism was foolish in the extreme. For example, the German who opposed eating salad with a fork rather than in the "good old German way" with fingers cannot be taken more seriously than the Englishman who insisted that roast beef was more honest than *râgout!* Nor can the campaign against French courtesy be accorded much consideration. There may have been some justice in the assertion that French manners were exaggerated beyond sincerity, yet in the crude and often boorish society of the eighteenth century such lessons in good manners were hardly amiss. There was little danger that the country gentry of Europe would become overpolite.

As might be expected, the French language was the most important target of the Francophobes. Cultural conquest has always been fought out on the linguistic frontier. In the eyes of the critics there were two questions involved. On the one hand, they objected to the ever growing use of French as a general means of communication among the upper classes; on the other, they resented the increasing use of French words by all classes when speaking their own language. This "aping" the French by adopting French vocabulary seemed to spell corruption for all other languages. Attacks on the French language as such were sometimes bizarre. Even Goethe contributed his bit by suggesting that the French language was useful for mendacious or perfidious purposes, but not for honest, straightforward German frankness. To clinch his point, he argued that in German the equivalent of the French word *perfide* (perfidious) was *treulos* (lack of truth). Somehow the negative character of the German word gave the language frankness! Another critic argued that French bubbles too easily. "It is the language of men who talk more than they think." Another said that it was insinuating, insincere, frivolous, and not to be employed for serious thought or communication. Much of the criticism was probably the result of envy. French had developed subtleties and elegance beyond the other vernacular languages.

The objection to the use of French words and the insistence upon "purification" of the native language were destined to become characteristic of nationalist movements. For example, Rumanians in the twentieth century "purified" their language of Turkish and Slavic words; the Nazis in Germany tried to exterminate all Greek and Latin roots from German speech. This process began in the eighteenth century when Spanish, Italian, English, and German critics spoke out against the use of French words when a "good native word" would serve the purpose better. As early as 1711 Addison's *Spectator* spoke up for the integrity of the English language and against the invasion of French words. Some of the complaints seem petty in the extreme. The Spaniard Vasquez argued that it was more elegant to use the Spanish *jeje de cocina* instead of the French *bonnet de nuit* (nightcap). The Italian Casari objected to the expression *brava* for *valoroso* or *Armate* for *esercito*. One German insisted that *schön* was better than *élégant*. One does not have to know these languages to understand what the critics were talking about. It was as if a twentieth-century American should object to the use of the word *blitzkrieg* for "lightning war" on the ground that the English equivalent is more honest.

In Germany a widespread movement developed in the universities, the most important seats of German culture, to check the invasion of things French. German scholars supported Shakespeare over the French dramatists, classical antiquity over French taste, and the German language over French. The vogue for Shakespeare still so strong in Germany probably resulted from the excellent German translation of the English's bard's plays. The interest in Graeco-Roman classical style as opposed to the French was directly related to the German scholars who founded the science of archeology. The fact that the latter eighteenth century produced a number of German authors who would have been important figures no matter what language they used, strengthened and purified the German language. The great lights of the late eighteenth-century German *Aufklärung* (Enlightenment)—Herder, Fichte, Schelling, Goethe, Schiller, Lessing, Kant, and others—all wrote in German. This was in sharp contrast to the great Leibniz and Frederick II, both of whom wrote in French.

5. THE ENGLISH INVASION

The Seven Years' War that ended in 1763 gave England undisputed control of a world empire and thereby assured the English language of a broad area for its expansion. It also closed important areas to further expansion of the French language by largely excluding France from North America and the Orient; and it lent prestige to "things English." The culture of the victor always seems more virile, more effective than that of the vanquished, and therefore attractive as a model. As we have already noted, the Germans adopted English cultural forms to defend themselves against the French, but it is even more significant to note that English modes, styles, customs, and words invaded France as well as the rest of Europe. This movement which was only a trickle before 1763 grew apace after that date.

It is quite astonishing to see how popular things English became in France. The post-1920 popularity of American cultural forms in France is the only comparable example. Horse racing, English afternoon tea, the English club from which women were excluded, whist, whisky, and roast beef were only a few of the invasions. Few Europeans went so far as the French restaurant that advertised *rost bif de mouton* ("roast beef of mutton"), and it is unlikely that the French menu actually duplicated English culinary patterns. The French adopted a whole series of English words: redingote (riding coat), jockey, jury, whist, humor, pamphlet, club, and many others, which indicate the invasion from across the Channel. Oddly enough some English words were returned to France after having stayed in England since the Norman conquest. The French word *boeuf* had become *beef,* and returned in the eighteenth century as *bif;* the word jockey came originally from the French diminutive for Jacques ("Jack"), and budget had originally gone to England as *bougette,* a pocket or sack of leather. Not all Frenchmen accepted the English words: De Maistre, for example, sarcastically asked how Sully and Colbert had worked without English words for financial operations.

In the fields of gardening, architecture, and home furnishing, too, English modes entered France as well as the rest of Europe. The popularity of English landscaping is really surprising considering the traditional "classicism" of French taste. The English garden was one with unexpected turns, curved paths (but not geometrically so); walks, trees, and shrubs that were allowed to grow naturally, and romantically placed garden houses, often Chinese in architectural design, were situated at unexpected places. In short, they were almost exactly the opposite of the formal settings of the landscape gardening at Versailles. English gardens appeared not only in Munich and Dresden but also at one corner of Versailles! The garden of the Bagatelle and the Parc Monceau also reflect this Anglomania. Even today a part of the great Luxembourg Garden is carefully cultivated as "the English garden."

In addition English architecture was influential, even though it was obviously "English" only in so far as Wren and other English architects had adapted Palladian, classical, and baroque styles. The Pantheon in Paris, for example, was partly inspired by St. Paul's Church in London. At another level, the furniture style generally called Louis XVI seems to have been influenced by the work of the famous English designer, Robert Adam.

English literature in French and German translations enjoyed a great vogue on the continent too, particularly toward the end of the century. Defoe's *Robinson Crusoe* was not only translated but also imitated many times over; the most famous adaptation, *The Swiss Family Robinson,* is still read. Richardson, Goldsmith, Gray, and many lesser English writers were eagerly studied, in part because of their intrinsic worth, in part as a counterweight to French influence.

The very fact that the French were willing to adopt so many English cultural patterns argues for the flexibility of French culture and seems to justify the idea that French society was the basis for a European cosmopolitan culture. Thus, it has been argued rather effectively that the upsurge of nationalism in the nineteenth century was a violent assault upon the "Europeanism" of the eighteenth century. However, such an interpretation of the development of Europe omits a very important fact, namely, that the French cosmopolitan culture was characteristic of only a small segment of the total population of Europe. The men and women of the princely courts and other men of great wealth with their hangers-on had a share in this culture, but the mass of the population both in France and in Europe was only slightly affected by it.

Just below the French veneer that appeared on the surface of all the societies of Europe, there were other classes that were also making progress in the refinement of manners, speech, and culture, even though they may have lacked the elegance characteristic of French civilization. These emerging national cultures were the fruit of expanding economic horizons, as well as of maturing urban society below the level of "high society." Wealth, leisure, and education were no longer the exclusive rights of noblemen, officials, and great merchants; the bourgeoisie and their allies among the professional people were able to live comfortably, even graciously, within the traditional patterns of society.

It was those people who in France, Germany, the Lowlands, England, and to a degree in Italy and Spain, were unknowingly preparing themselves for their great historical role in the nineteenth century. However, it was not until the French Revolution presented them with slogans and a vision of their destiny that they—men who represented best the several national cultures—were able to act out their parts on the stage of European history.

On the lowest levels of eighteenth-century society there was no indication of the brilliance characteristic of the uppermost. It is not true that the urban or rural masses suffered greater humiliations and deprivations in the eighteenth century than they had in the preceding one. This is the myth of the school of historians that saw the early development of industrial society as a blight upon mankind. However, it is equally untrue to paint the lot of the masses in glowing colors. The vast majority of men in the eighteenth century simply had no place or part in the culture of the elite. They could not ape the manners of their social "betters," nor did they expect to do so. The time was still relatively far away when Europeans would think of creating a civilization in which everyone could participate.

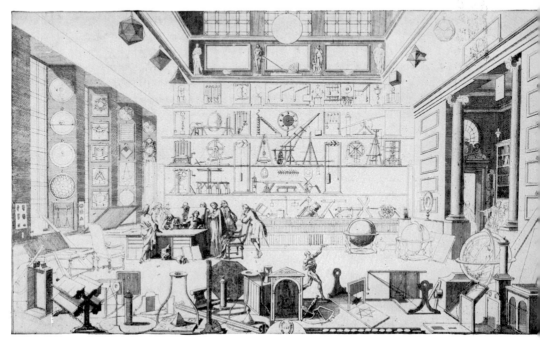

Laboratory of Sebastien Leclerc (Paris, Bibliothèque Nationale).

Chapter 25

THE ENLIGHTENMENT: SCIENCE, PHILOSOPHY, AND LEARNING

1. THE SPIRIT OF THE CENTURY

In England men of the eighteenth century called their era the "Enlightenment;" in France, *"le siècle de lumière"* (century of light"); in Germany, *"der Aufklärung"* ("the clearing of the skies"). Painters and engravers portrayed men hopefully marching forward into the full light of the sun, while the dark clouds of superstition, ignorance, and fear melted away. After centuries of pessimism and doubt about man and his destiny, an era had finally dawned in which men looked optimistically to the future of life on the earth.

There were many streams that fed energy into this new intellectual society. The vigorous expansion of the economic structure of the West provided money and also contact with the larger world beyond Europe. The scientific revolution of the seventeenth century, symbolized by the names of Descartes and Newton, bequeathed to men a whole new set of assumptions about the nature of the world as well as new understanding of its functioning. The emergence of the bureaucratic-police state, endowed with the power to impose order, opened new vistas for the political imagination of men. The awful destruction of the religious wars had finally burned out much of the vitality of the post-Reformation theological debate, so that men could turn their attention to other matters. A century of religious wars had proved the impossibility of imposing religious views upon a people by force. Men were still interested in religious questions, but, like the Methodists and Pietists of the eighteenth century, they were losing faith in the identification of a religious doctrine with the state's power.

This loss of faith in the ability of the state to impose religious truth may even have been the most important single fact about the new era. For the first time since the days of classical Rome, the West was predominantly under secular rather than religious controls. Ever since the high Middle Ages, society had been gradually adopting a more secular outlook, and it is impossible to say at which point in time secular interests became more important than clerical or religious considerations. It is evident, however, that by the eighteenth century theology was no longer the queen of the sciences; painters, sculptors, and musicians no longer chose religious subjects for their most important work; architects no longer received churches for their principal assignments; and the leaders of political society no longer assumed that they were merely carrying out God's will. For good or for evil, the process that had destroyed the religious unity of Europe and created the new state system had also concentrated much of man's attention on the earth and earthly affairs.

With this secularized society there came also a secular viewpoint about the world. The Cartesian and Newtonian sciences saw the world as a mechanical thing, created by God but completely responsible to the natural laws of mechanics. Newton's space-time machine, the universe, was subordinate to the mathematical laws of gravity that ruled its entire behavior. This was the central hypothesis of the new era. Thus, the new language for describing the universe was mathematics, and it is therefore to be expected that men of the period regarded their era as being under the star of geometry. *"L'esprit géometrique* [the geometric spirit]," said Fontenelle, the secretary of the French Academy of Science, "guides the thoughts of men."

An integral part of the idea that geometry was the queen of the sciences was the further assumption that the social, economic, and political world could be explained in terms of physics. This implied a very strict determinism for all aspects of the world. Men's institutions, like the stars, were bound by laws that controlled their destiny. This conception of natural law that came from Newton's discovery of the universal application of the law of gravitation fascinated the men of the eighteenth century.

Together with this mechanistic conception of the universe there was a new set of assumptions about man and his psychology. At the end of the seventeenth century the English philosopher, John Locke, expounded the doctrine that man is born into the world without any innate ideas, that each mind is a clean slate or piece of paper upon which the world writes its lessons in the form of experience. This original doctrine wiped out ideas that had been honored for centuries, and laid the foundation for a new theory of knowledge that was to prove very fruitful for science (this in spite of the error of Locke's assumptions that would be indicated by present-day psychobiological theories). There is a time-honored question: "How do you know?" After Locke many men answered that question by insisting upon experience (experiment) as the basis of knowledge, and rejecting any information not based upon experience as hearsay, useless for understanding of the world.

Just as the artistic culture of this rococo century was limited to the wealthy, so, too, was the Enlightenment limited to a narrow segment of the population. The poor and the ignorant of the eighteenth century were superstitious, often brutal, and despised by their more fortunate neighbors. However, of the men who stood between the poor and the rich, the petty and middle bourgeoisie and the relatively impoverished country nobility, a surprisingly large number were more or less affected by the cross currents of the new learning. Naturally most of them continued to act upon and believe in the traditional assumptions of their society; it is a commonplace that human beings can believe several mutually exclusive ideas at the same time. As the century progressed, however, more and more of the ideas advanced by the scientists and their propagandists, the *philosophes,* trickled down in society to modify the traditional notions about the world. This does not mean that the burgher of Dresden or the merchant in Le Havre would be as well informed as Diderot, the editor of the *Encyclopedia;* but the formation of literary societies, private reading groups, and libraries, accounted for a wide dissemination of Diderot's ideas. The ever growing audience was eloquently shown by the increasing popularity of books and by the rise of a relatively extensive periodical press. When we write about the importance of the printing press in the sixteenth century, we often forget to point out that its influence increased with geometric progression in each succeeding generation. The eighteenth century provides imposing evidence of this fact.

However, the rise of a reading public had not yet solved the financial problems of the creative spirits of the era. The time was still to come when an author could make a secure living from the products of his pen alone; subsidy either by princes or by wealthy bourgeois and noblemen was still frequently necessary to support learning. In the eighteenth century the governments of Europe provided generously for many scientific and literary enterprises. Botanical and zoological gardens, astronomical observatories, money for expeditions for scientific exploration, and pensions for distinguished men were provided by the governments of France, England, Prussia, Russia, and other countries. Scientific societies, some of them royal academies, others less pretentious provincial organizations, gave prizes and grants as well as providing an audience for the learned of the period. Neither were these efforts supported solely by secular organizations; before they were disbanded, the Jesuits published an important journal in which science and the new philosophy had a prominent place, while in Rome the papacy patronized some of the research that men were carrying out to discover the nature of the world.

2. SCIENCE

The era of the Enlightenment has been aptly called the age of mathematics, or, as we have seen above, of *l'esprit géometrique.* Most of the important figures of the era regarded themselves as mathematicians and made significant contributions to that branch of knowledge. Even so, the principal mathematical work of the eighteenth century was confined to elaborating and explaining the possibilities of the important mathematical inventions of the preceding century. Analytical geometry and calculus were the great new discoveries of seventeenth-century mathematicians; the eighteenth century demonstrated the numerous uses for these calculating devices, and explored the frontiers of their possible development.

The strife that raged between the followers of Newton and those of Leibniz somewhat discredits the idea that scientists were seeking knowledge for its own sake. Both men had independently developed the calculus as a means of describing a line with changing direction or an object with changing speed along a given direction. It does Newton little credit that he insisted that Leibniz "stole" the idea from him; and the controversy that raged for over a generation proves that pettiness is not confined to men of little education. Leibniz seems to have understood better than Newton that the notation used to express a mathematical concept is almost as important as the concept itself. In any case, his system of notation was widely adopted on the continent, and became the "language" for most of eighteenth-century mathematics. For a whole generation English scholars deprived themselves of this superior system of notation out of loyalty to their great scientist who had also discovered the calculus.

As we noted earlier, in 1687 Newton's *Principia* was published, but three to four decades had to pass before his ideas found near universal acceptance even among the learned. The idea of a force such as gravitation holding together so complex a machine as the universe was hard to believe; the further notion that this idea dispensed with the need for a "subtle fluid" to float the earth, planets, and suns was even more difficult to accept. Many of the enlightened men of 1700–1720 regarded Newton's hypothesis as pure superstition. Had not Descartes given his life to dispel such ideas? Before 1750, however, Newtonian astronomy had achieved complete recognition, and men all over Europe were busily at work filling in the details of the space-time machine that Newton had "found."

There were several interesting problems in Newton's system. He asserted that the gravitational pull on the earth was not quite centered at the equator, and therefore, that the earth's shape would not be a totally perfect sphere. The top of the earth should be relatively flattened. This was an assertion that could be tested by actual measurement. One French expedition visited the equator at Peru; another went to the Arctic circle. Maupertius and de Clairaut went to Lapland at the end of the Gulf of Bothnia, where they measured the 76th degree of latitude north (1736). It proved to be 378 toises (about 636 meters) greater than Picard had found the 50th degree of latitude north. Thus the earth did tend to flatten toward the pole. Still, 378 toises out of over 57,000 was a small amount; Maupertius could have been in error. A few years later, when La Condamine and Bruguer with an enormous effort of work measured the 3rd degree of latitude north, in Peru, they found that degree to be 663 toises (about 1292.1 meters) less than the 50th degree north. This seemed unquestionable proof that Newton was right, and it gave prestige to his entire thesis.

Another point was solved by the same expeditions. Newton assumed that weight was the *result* of gravitation pull; therefore it was not an attribute of matter. If this were true, then an object would weigh less at the equator, where the centrifugal force created by the earth's turning would be greatest, than it would weigh at the pole, where this centrifugal force would diminish. Again Newton was right. Observations in Peru and Lapland justified his theory.

Furthermore, Newton had noted that the paths of the planets were not always exactly as they "should" be. He assumed that the space-time machine at times got out of order, and assigned to God the task of putting them right. During the course of the eighteenth century increasingly precise observation filled in gaps in men's knowledge, so that by the time that Laplace, the great French astronomer, wrote his treatise (1796), it had been proved that these irregularities were the result of the same gravitation that governed the regular course. The planets effected a slight gravitational pull on each other, which could account for the irregularities and the return to course without calling upon God to repair the damage.

The comets that shot through the skies in 1729, 1742, 1744, 1747, 1748, and particularly Halley's comet which returned in 1758 as predicted, increased men's faith in their astronomical understanding. In 1762 Clairaut received the grand prize from the Imperial Academy of St. Petersburg for his book on comets in which he demonstrated that they, too, were governed by the laws of gravity.

As a result of the development of more accurate telescopes, astronomers also enlarged their knowledge of the nature of light beams and the actual motions of the earth. The sum total of their efforts was synthesized by Laplace at the end of the eighteenth century (*Exposition of the System of the World,* 1796). The observations and the calculations of the hundred years between Newton's *Principia* and his own book gave Laplace great faith in his findings. "Astronomy," he wrote, "has all the certitude that results from the immense number and variety of phenomena rigorously examined and the implicity of the principle that is sufficient by itself to explain them. Far from fearing that a new star might upset this principle, one can assert in advance that its movement will conform to it." Such assurance seemed eminently justified to Laplace's generation. The time was still distant when men would question the basic assumptions behind the "space-time machine" that they believed their universe to be.

In other fields as well progress was made toward understanding the world. During the first half of the eighteenth century the development of accurate thermometers gave physics and medicine novel instruments. There were some eighteen-odd different types of thermometers in use by the middle of the century. The one developed by the Danzig instrument maker, Fahrenheit (1724), was the first really useful one, and it became widely accepted in the English-speaking world. The Frenchman, Réaumur, evolved the thermometer most widely used in Germany; Professor Celsius of Upsala, Sweden, made the first centigrade instrument but scaled it 0° for boiling water and 100° for freezing (1742). Eight years later, his colleague, Strömer, reversed the scale, and launched the thermometer that eventually acquired nearly universal use in Europe. These new heat-measuring instruments failed to open up great vistas for the physicists largely because of their misconceptions as to the nature of heat. It was assumed that heat was a subtle fluid, a very elastic material that somehow distributed itself in proportion to the attraction of objects or the capacity of objects to absorb it. With such assumptions, the laws of thermodynamics were effectively hidden until the next century. Eighteenth-century men scorned their medieval forbears for lack of vision and for their superstitions, without realizing that all men are limited by their assumptions about the world.

In the area of electricity researchers made discoveries during the century that both astounded and amused their contemporaries. They did not advance beyond static electricity in their experiments, but they learned something about its properties. The Leyden jar, by which a big charge of electricity could be built up and then released suddenly, was perfected in 1745. Thereafter experiments were conducted to show that an electric charge could be created that would pass through and shock a large company of men. On one occasion one hundred and eighty French guards and on another three hundred monks held hands and received the shock. Naturally such charges soon assumed "curative" effects for all sorts of illnesses, even though they shed little real light on the nature or use of electricity.

An American experimenter, Benjamin Franklin, made several of the most important electrical "discoveries" of the period. He showed first of all that lightning in the sky was an electrical discharge like the one produced by the Leyden jar, only much larger in extent. During preceding centuries men had thought that God or gods produced lightning to chastise or to warn them, or perhaps just as playful activity. Franklin's discovery that there was a simple, natural explanation for this flaming phenomenon of the sky was almost as much of a shock to the superstitious and the gullible as were the bolts themselves. Franklin also found that the spark from the Leyden jar would jump farther if it were received by a pointed rather than by a blunt object. This led him to speculate about protection against lightning, and finally to the development of the lightning rod.

Several observers independently discovered the positive and negative charges and, by the end of the century, men were on the verge of determining ways to generate an electric current; but the nature of electricity was hidden behind the barrier of the assumptions that these men held about it. To Franklin electricity was a "common element" to be found in all matter; if more than normal, the charge was positive; if less, it was negative. Coulomb and Du Fay explained the phenomenon as two fluids with repulsion and attraction acting at a distance; the fluid unfortunately was without weight. Men had to wait until the nineteenth century for Faraday to break through the walls which concealed the nature of electricity.

The chemists, too, were bound by traditions as well as by the inherent difficulty of finding a solution to the problem of matter. The latter seventeenth- and the eighteenth-century chemists "knew" that the ultimate stuff of the world was made up of hard, impenetrable particles (atoms!), presumably all alike. Some such explanation for the nature of matter had been bruited around ever since the Greeks, but it was not very useful as a basis for experimentation. Several times in the seventeenth century experimenters were on the verge of discoveries that might have shed light on the subject, but each time their preconceived views hindered them. It was perhaps an important advance when a group of German scholars, of whom Dr. Stahl was the most famous, decided that the processes of calcination and oxidization were related, and then proceeded to postulate a subtle substance, phlogiston, which acted in each case. Equations that would balance enabled them to explain the burning of a substance, but these gave them no insight into the atomic table.

It was at the end of the eighteenth century that an Englishman, Priestley, and a Frenchman, Lavoisier, laid the foundation for all later chemistry by discovering that there were a number of "different" elements rather than "hard impenetrable particles of a single kind" at the base of all matter. (Of course we *know* today that the elements, in turn, are made up of other things.) Priestley discovered a way to produce oxygen and carbon gas, and finally showed that oxygen explained respiration, combustion, and calcination, the fundamental chemical actions on the earth. Lavoisier developed a precise balance scale that became the basic instrument for research, and thus founded the science of quantitative chemistry. The balance gave him insight into the nature of matter and allowed him to discard the concept of phlogiston. In a communication to the Academy of Sciences (1772), he wrote, "I have discovered that sulphur in burning gives birth to an acid augmented in weight; it is the same with phosphorus. This augmentation of weight comes from the fixation of a considerable quantity of air. Calcinated metals equally increase their weight; it is because there is a similar fixation of air. . . ."

Lavoisier also urged a changed nomenclature for the new science. At this time chemistry had such words as flowers of zinc, butter of arsenic, oil of tartar, phagedemic water, algorth, and the like. He pointed out that such names were difficult to remember and that "they give birth to false notions." As the result of Lavoisier's proposals, Fourcory, Berthollet, and Lavoisier himself set to work in 1787 to establish simple names for known substances and processes. Thus appeared the words "oxygen" to name the gas and "oxide" to identify metals or other substances that had become calcinated. In acids, the suffixes identified the state of the substance; hence, sulphuric and sulphurous acid. With a new vocabulary as well as a new method, the science of chemistry was to accomplish a fantastic development in the next century.

The earth sciences, too, were severely handicapped by age-old beliefs until near the end of the eighteenth century. The most difficult problem was to understand the enormous age of the earth and the fact that the earth, its fauna and flora, had a history. As long as men believed in a creation of a recent date, they could not penetrate the secrets of the earth's crust. This left naturalists in the role of mere classifiers, and it should be said that the eighteenth century did a magnificent job in that respect. Many men should be mentioned, but Linnaeus, the Swedish naturalist, deserves particularly great credit for evolving the system of nomenclature for plants and animals that has been used ever since. The epigram of the age summed up his work thus: "God created the plants and animals of the world; Linnaeus catalogued them."

As the eighteenth century continued, students of the earth's surfaces came to novel conclusions about it. The development of a volcanic island off the Italian coast provided evidence that important changes in the surface were possible. If an island could rise out of the sea, might not something similar have happened at an earlier time? Could that account for the fossil remains of shark and other fish found at the tops of Italian mountains? Thus was born another school of thought as to the origin of the earth, and with it the realization that it was undoubtedly older than the scriptural text seemed to imply. Some men continued to teach that great floods of water, like Noah's flood, were responsible for the changes in the crust of the earth; others were sure that volcanoes had been the principal architects of change. By the end of the eighteenth century the young Goethe considered these two dominant theories about the earth's surface, the volcanic and the diluvial (flood), and decided in favor of the latter. He had no evidence that seemed incontrovertible for either position, and so he chose the classic doctrine of "flood" rather than "fire," because it was "less violent."

However, neither the volcanic nor the diluvial theorists insisted upon the biblical time period. Instead of the date 4004 B.C. that the seventeenth century had accepted for the creation, men of the latter eighteenth were willing to think in terms of 75,000 to 100,000 years. They had only the slightest notion of the astronomical time upon which the nineteenth century would insist.

As the concept of more and more time became credible, however, students of the zoological and botanical sciences also began to alter their ideas. The great French naturalist, Buffon, was perhaps the first, or at least the foremost, man of his century to go beyond the belief of separate creation for each species of animal and plant. Systematic classifications made by Linnaeus and others had, for example, placed all the cat family together, all the horse family, all the dog family, and so forth. Once there was enough time to account for change, Buffon made the next logical step, namely, that of assuming that dogs, horses, and cats had a common ancestor. He first assumed that a donkey was a degenerated horse, affected by climate; then he decided that it might well be that all the animals had a common ancestor whose descendants, either by perfecting themselves or by degeneration, had produced the great variety found in the world. Buffon did not state the first doctrine of evolution; that was reserved for Lamarck, the tutor of Buffon's son, to announce early in the nineteenth century. Nonetheless, Buffon's book, *Epochs of Nature* (1778), with its optimistic notions of progress, was the immediate forerunner of nineteenth-century biology.

3. THE STUDY OF MAN

This "century of light" developed new conceptions of man as well as of the world around him. Buffon placed man among the animals, related physically perhaps to the great apes, but this provided little information as to the nature of man and his society. The historians, the philosophers, the students who were struggling to develop the study of anthropology, sociology, and political science—these were the men who were to give man and his destiny a meaning in terms of the earth.

There were several streams of information that fed these studies. Travelers whose bizarre observations had at first only amused their readers piled up ever-increasing funds of information about the diversity of the societies of men living on the earth. By the end of the seventeenth century travel literature was the most popular literary form, and its effect was to acquaint educated Europeans with the fact that there were other men, with civilized manners and lofty morality, who lived under conditions vastly different from their own. These strangers lived by religious and ethical teachings quite unconnected with western Christian traditions. At first it was shocking to learn that there were words and meanings for "good" and "evil" other than those honored in Europe, but Europeans gradually realized that morals, manners, and customs were probably relative matters.

In the course of the eighteenth century this notion was stated in several different ways. Voltaire (1694–1778) attempted to give it an objective orientation in his *Essay on Manners* (1756) in which he tried to show how historical, climatic, and other factors, some of them pure chance, were responsible for differences in social organizations. A few years earlier Montesquieu (1689–1755) had demonstrated that political society and social laws were conditioned by climate, soil, religion, and historical traditions (*Spirit of the Laws,* 1748). In their books Voltaire and Montesquieu attempted to remain relatively neutral, but there were other writers who used the differences to criticize European society. By contrasting the "wise Chinese," the "sage Egyptian," the "noble savage" with the decadence of Europe, the idea that morals and manners were relative rather than absolute became a club with which to assault the society of the day. Voltaire himself contributed to this literature in a witty novel about a Huron Indian who, transplanted to France, was absolutely incredulous when confronted with French beliefs and practices.

Of equal importance to the collection of literature about other peoples was the accumulation of documents about former societies. The Jesuit and Benedictine scholars who set out to write the *Lives of the Saints* developed standards of criticism for historical documents that may be considered the very foundation of modern historical thinking. Mabillon's *De Re Diplomatica* (1685) established tests to prove the honesty of most documents as well as the falsity of impostors. Collections of documents on Roman and Greek history, on early Chinese, Persian, and Indian history, and investigations of more recent events in Europe had somewhat the same result as had the publication of travel literature. As Fénelon commented, the changes in manners, even in the short period of the seventeenth century, were astonishing. When men considered changes that took place over centuries, the impression of relativism in customs was strongly reinforced. Even without breaking the secret of Egyptian and Babylonian writing, it was seen that great changes had taken place in the life of European men since the time of Homer's Greeks who had apparently lived in a society with a political and social organization similar to that of the Iroquois Indians in America.

This same idea was imposed upon men from another angle. In the seventeenth century the discovery that Aristotle and the Greek and Roman philosophers and scientists did not know as much about the world as contemporary men knew came as something of a pleasant surprise. It also became apparent that the literary and philosophical thought of the age could be compared favorably with that of the classical era. At the end of the seventeenth century a furious debate broke out between the "ancients" and the "moderns," in which men argued about the relative merits of modern and classical culture. In the eighteenth century this conflict was largely resolved in favor of the moderns. Again it was Voltaire who examined the problem as a scholar-philosopher-historian. His study on the *Age of Louis XIV* (1751) was an entirely new kind of history. Manners, morals, economy, literature, and other human activities came under his scrutiny, and he concluded that the period of Louis XIV was to be compared favorably with other great periods like the Athens of Pericles (440–430 B.C.), the Rome of Augustus (first century A.D.), or the Italy of the Medici (1450–1550).

The question had inevitably to be asked: what caused these many—and sometimes violent—changes in man's history? Such a question probed into the innermost problem of man's life on earth, and even though no satisfactory answer could be evolved, it forced men to consider a whole series of other questions about human destiny.

The massive historical backdrop of the western world provided an object lesson for studying the problem of decadence in society. Had not the brilliant Roman Empire of Augustus given way to the rude society of the "Dark Ages"? Why had such a catastrophe overtaken men? Two men wrote learnedly about the decay of Roman society: Montesquieu (1689–1755) and Gibbon (1737–1794). Montesquieu's *Grandeur and Decadence of the Roman Empire* (1732), however, was only one product of a busy life of study. It bears the stamp of the man who wrote the *Persian Letters* as a thoughtful critique of his own age and *The Spirit of the Laws* (which we shall discuss later) as an analysis of the nature of political and social organization.

Gibbon, on the other hand, devoted a lifetime to his monumental work, and produced one of the really great historical studies written by western scholars. His dignified yet lucid style of writing, his considered judgment on the sources for his history, and his brilliant insights into the problems of the people whom he discussed have combined to make *The Decline and Fall of the Roman Empire* one of the most significant books written in the English language. Gibbon had the vision to paint his picture on a large canvas. His reader is transported from the sandy deserts of Arabia to Spain and England; from central Asia to North Africa; and attention is focused upon all sorts of problems from taxes to religion. As a deist, Gibbon had no love for Christianity, but it is hardly fair to say that he interpreted the decline of Rome solely in terms of the "unfortunate victory" of "Christianity and barbarism." He who rereads Gibbon (a formidable task, by the way, since this book runs into several fat volumes) will soon discover that the author understood the complexity of the problems which confronted Rome between the second and the sixth centuries. The Christian church emerges in these pages as only one of many factors that diverted men from the task of saving the Empire. Such a rereading will also show that Gibbon, perhaps better than many of his nineteenth-century successors, understood the meaning of Byzantine history. It is significant that he concluded his history with the fall of Constantinople in the mid-fifteenth century.

While historians were pondering the fact of change, as demonstrated by the Roman Empire, other philosophers, in whom we see the forerunners of anthropology and sociology, devoted their efforts to a consideration of progress in society. The realization that Homeric Greeks lived in a primitive society not too different from that of the Iroquois inevitably posed the question: how, then, were they able to develop the era of Pericles? While many men wrote about the problem of progress, three—Vico (1668-1744), an Italian; Herder (1744-1803), a German; and Condorcet (1743-1794), a Frenchman—deserve special attention.

Vico's analyses of social change led him to assume some special social force with creative power, the group mind. This group mind was the common understanding of their own development by all the people in a society. Later in the century Rousseau (1712-1778) translated Vico's idea of "group mind" into "general will." It thus became a mystical social force that at the same time contained the social histories and traditions and directed the social development of a society.

Herder "discovered" the root of every society in its primitive culture: that meant to him in its language, its folklore, its gods, and its rural social organization. These forces were at first inarticulate, but as the society developed they acted as guide posts to direct its cultural development. Thus Herder accounted for the achievements of peoples; the Greeks in philosophy, art, and letters; the Romans in law and administration; the English in commerce; the French in war, art, and polite society. His ideas did not achieve wide success in the Europe of his day, because he added a mystical spirit of God as a prime moving force. This did not satisfy the men who saw Newtonian physics as the model for philosophy. Herder's findings, however, were to become very important for German nationalists who saw clearly that German destiny could be achieved only when the cultural roots of the German people were united.

Condorcet's great treatise, *Sketch of an Historical Tableau of the Progress of the Human Spirit* (1794), was the social counterpart of Buffon's work on the *Epochs of Nature*. Condorcet discovered "the ten epochs" or periods through which men progressed from the most primitive society to the highly developed one of his own day. His scientific rigor was so superior to that of his predecessors that we can see in his book the inspiration for much of nineteenth-century sociological thought.

The idea that man's history was the story of man's progress had a strong appeal to educated minds of the eighteenth century. After the discovery of the Newtonian universe, it was not hard for them to believe that the human mind was a perfect instrument for penetrating the truths about the world. It was further easy to believe that if men would discover the true laws of nature and cooperate with them, men could achieve perfection. Therefore, the idea of progress was an integral part of their struggle to find a heaven on earth. Perhaps their growing lack of faith in a heavenly paradise added strength to their belief in one on and of the earth.

While historians and sociologists studied man's past and attempted to probe the dynamics of his history, other students of man worried about his political institutions. Two individuals stand out as very important for their contributions: Montesquieu, the author of *The Spirit of the Laws,* and Rousseau, the author of *The Social Contract*. Both books deserve attention.

The Spirit of the Laws was an attempt to classify the political institutions of all peoples and to draw from these classifications some general principles about the nature of politics. Montesquieu ransacked history and the writings of travelers to non-European lands for his evidence. His basic assumptions led him to regard the political institutions of men as being influenced by, indeed created by geographical, social, and historical forces. While the statement unjustly simplifies his great book, it might be said that Montesquieu was a political physicist. He discovered that each people had to be governed by different political institutions because each people lived under different conditions. While he seemed only to be a scientist searching for understanding of the mechanisms of politics, Montesquieu nonetheless did draw moral judgments from his evidence. He pointed out, as had Aristotle, that there were different forms of government: despotism, monarchy, aristocracy, and democracy. In the real world, however, these rarely appeared in pure form; mixed government was the rule, and it takes little insight to see that Montesquieu thought that the British government was the highest expression of political wisdom reached by man. It is impossible to do justice to *The Spirit of the Laws* in a short statement; it was without doubt one of the most important books produced during the eighteenth century and it became the very bible for politicians and statesmen who ran governments, as well as those who, in the American and French revolutionary eras, attempted to give new form to their states.

In contrast to *The Spirit of the Laws,* Rousseau's *Social Contract* seems to be a mere pamphlet. It displays little of the erudition or the research that characterizes Montesquieu's book, and yet it is in every way as important a contribution, perhaps even a greater one. Rousseau reached his conclusions intuitively, but in a searching way he probed into the central problems of politics. After an introductory bow to a mythological history of man in which he tried to show that men contracted together to make society, Rousseau introduced an idea that became the very core of much of the political and philosophical thought of the next century. His man is a creature born into a society and conditioned by it to accept that society's ideas about good and evil. But these ideas are not static, fixed, or universal; they are the result of history, and history in its onward march can change them. Thus, the law becomes something written not in statute books, but in the hearts of men by their life in society. The core of the *Social Contract* assumes a mystical agent which Rousseau calls the "general will"; volumes have been written to explain it and yet it remains a mystical concept. Roughly, however, the "general will" was the *real,* as contrasted to the selfish, wish of all the people of the society. The notion that all the people in a society were part of its political life and that recalcitrant individuals could, indeed should, be "forced to be free"—that is, to will the "general will"—was destined to have tremendous influence on the political and philosophical ideas of the next generation. The idea that society was an *organic* thing that *grew* rather than a *machine* made by fixed forces was equally important as a new concept for men to apply to the problems of life.

While Montesquieu and Rousseau emerged as great intellectual lights in the field of political theory, there were other men who were working out some of the implications of the social ideals of the era in terms of politics. Perhaps the most significant of these was the realization that the new learning and ideas about man's destiny on the earth could not be universal unless they included all men. Christian doctrine had been willing that all men should be saved if they would only refrain from offending God, but many Christians had not shown themselves to be equally generous in the distribution of earthly goods. It was one thing to share heaven with the poor and quite another to share the world with them. Indeed, the inhumanity of men toward their fellow men can only be explained if we realize that the rich and the powerful really did not consider their less fortunate neighbors to be men like themselves. However, when philosophers began to talk about perfecting society, when they made plans for a heavenly city on this earth, they had to consider means of ameliorating the conditions of life for all people. In this were the roots of a new movement: humanitarianism. Propagandists and publicists began to attack evils on a broad front: some urged the abolition of the slave trade and of slavery; others the reconsideration of the law, especially as it applied to the offenses of the poor; and others attacked the treatment of criminals, of the insane, and of orphaned children. If human beings were to experience their true meaning in the dignity of man, then conditions of life would have to be changed to assure the dignity of man to all men. To conservatives, the reformers seemed to be wild men intent on overthrowing society; to others, they were men of good will anxious to eradicate evils in the world of men. A distinguished American historian has brilliantly described their teachings as "Faith, Hope, and Charity in secular dress."[1]

4. THE PHILOSOPHES AND RELIGIOUS THINKERS

If there was a *Summa* for the eighteenth century corresponding to the theological work of St. Thomas, it was the *Encyclopedia* edited by d'Alembert and Diderot. In many ways this great work was to the eighteenth century what St. Thomas' masterpiece had been for the Middle Ages, and no single book between the two had as important a place in men's minds. Like all such works, the *Encyclopedia* had its predecessors. Bayle's *Philosophical Dictionary*, published in the last decade of the seventeenth century and the in-

[1] Leo Gershoy, *From Despotism to Revolution, 1763–1789*, New York, Harper, 1944.

spiration for so much of the work of the *philosophes,* was its important forerunner, but Bayle had only a limited vision of the area that should be encompassed by an encyclopedia, as well as a limited objective for his own project. Voltaire also produced a *Philosophical Dictionary,* but, like Bayle's work, it had a narrow basis. There were several other similar works in both French and English, but none of them had the universal appeal of the *Encyclopedia.*

The first volume of this great book appeared in 1751. It announced its grandiose plan to provide a compendium for all knowledge. In its final form it had seventeen huge volumes of text and eleven volumes of plates. There were over 130 contributors, including lawyers, professors, doctors, priests, officials, industrialists, manufacturers, and men of commerce; it was the supreme intellectual effort of the French upper bourgeois class which represented the intellectual culture of the period. Voltaire, Montesquieu, and Diderot may have been the most famous collaborators, but the whole list is an impressive array of the names of men who had specialized information of importance for understanding the civilization of eighteenth-century Europe.

The tone of the book is utilitarian and positivist, rational and secular. In the spirit of the century, its editors demanded clarity of presentation as well as careful analyses of causality and procedure. They tried always to relate the subjects under discussion to man and his needs. The result was a monumental compendium of scientific, philosophical, and useful information that played an important role in the education of men for the next century, and became the model for all later encyclopedic collections.

The men who wrote for the *Encyclopedia* have been grouped together under the name *philosophes.* This term was used more or less indiscriminately to include the savants of the era of the Enlightenment: philosophers, historians, literary lights, scientists, all were *philosophes,* and particularly so if they took up their pens to propagandize for the new learning, for the enlightenment of their fellow men. It is not quite correct to equate the *philosophes* with the writers and researchers who were not clerics for there were priests within their ranks, but the term can be equated to the intellectuals whose interests and inspirations were derived from the new learning of the era.

The majority of the *philosophes* were deists. They accepted the Newtonian cosmos and with it the idea that God had created the world and organized its government by eternal laws which He could not alter. In such a case it was useless to pray to God and equally unimportant to follow any religious rites or sacraments. Man's only obligation was to discover the eternal laws and live by them. Thus, a God of Nature who might or might not have any interest in Man, His creature, emerged as the picture of the Godhead.

Some of them optimistically assumed that God was good, and hence had created the world with man in mind. Their reasoning indicated their own

Christian background, for the *philosophes* accepted much of Christian theology, rejecting only the biblical justifications and the rituals of the Christian
sects. They regarded very seriously the critics who were studying the Bible
with the same rigor that earlier generations had examined other texts; on the
basis of those studies, they insisted that the Bible could not possibly be a
divinely inspired book. However, when they developed their own religious
convictions they often included the Christian doctrine that God had created
men in His image and would probably reward or punish him for his behavior in a life after death. Instead of the inspired Bible, these *philosophes*
considered that nature was the witness of the glory and grandeur of the
Creator.

Others, led by Voltaire, were not quite so optimistic. Nature could be as
harmful to men as she could be helpful—as the earthquake in Lisbon (1755)
dramatically demonstrated. It shocked many people to learn that the good
folk who happened to be in churches when the quake came suffered more
severely than their less pious fellows who were in the streets or fields. Voltaire's *Candide* was inspired by this event. Cloaked in an innocently simple
story, his book posed terrible problems for both Deist and Christian, for
Voltaire's story was the story of "evil." As Candide and Cunegunde wander
through the world, it becomes evident that evil is no respecter of place, position, or previous behavior. The evils that march across Voltaire's pages are
sometimes selective, but only insofar as youth seems to be susceptible to certain evils, old age to others. Men with wealth are plagued with evils that do
not bother the poor, but the poor in turn have their own. Neither virtue nor
vice seems to have much to do with the problems that plague men. *Candide*
did not explore all the evils that befall mankind, but it catalogued a goodly
list of them. In the eighteenth century, as in later days, men comforted themselves with Voltaire's parting advice, "cultivate your garden," as a way of
avoiding direct contemplation of the awful problem that the book actually
presents.

There was a small company of thinkers who dispensed with the idea of
God entirely, but these atheists were of no real importance for their doctrine
was out of tune with the universally accepted concepts of the Newtonian
world. The eighteenth-century *philosophes* required belief in God as the
Creator of the world. Their idea that God had given the world a law, ex-
pressible in mathematical terms, which even He had to obey, made their
God into a sort of constitutional monarch who, after granting a charter to
the world, had also to live under its rule. This idea was appealing to men
who admired the English government in which the king was subject to the
law and bound by the constitution of the kingdom.

Taken as a group, the Deists were formidable enemies of the traditional
churches. Their articulate pens branded much of the dogma and practice of
Christianity as superstition or foolishness. Voltaire, for example, spent the last

quarter century of his life striking out viciously at the churches, and while Catholicism was perhaps his main target, some of his most biting sarcasm was leveled at the Calvinists. Under his leadership one of the most vigorous antireligious campaigns the world ever saw was fought in the presses of Europe.

The state churches seemed to give way under this assault. In France and Germany, for example, where all the highest levels of the Catholic clergy were appointed by the king, many of the bishops were men without real religious orientation. To a lesser degree this was also true of the Anglican Church and of the Lutheran state churches. Many of the clergy actually accepted deism themselves; even though they continued in their offices, they were in effect unbelievers. It is said that the archbishop of Paris privately admitted his disbelief in the Christian God. The papacy itself seemed to "go soft" as the assault continued; in the middle of the century it agreed to the disbandment of the Jesuit Order. These "Janissary guards" of Catholicism found haven in the realm of the unbeliever, Frederick of Prussia. Such apparent victories made many of the *philosophes* assert with Voltaire that the next generation would see the end of the Christian church.

However, the *philosophes* proved wrong in their judgment. They failed to see that their doctrines were aimed at the intellectuals rather than at the people; that their rationalism had little or no appeal to the human emotions; and they wholly missed the fact that institutionalized Christianity probably could not be destroyed unless some other institution appeared to take its place in the hearts and minds of the people. The Deists had no such institution. The nearest approach to one was the Masonic Lodge, but it was open only to the upper crust of society, and so could not hope to substitute for institutionalized Christianity. Masonry, starting in the British Isles, offered a sort of deistic substitute for the Christian religion in its mystic symbols, its avowal of the Supreme Being, and its emphasis upon good works, but it was too aristocratic and too intellectualized to take the place of the churches in the hearts of the people of Europe. The *philosophes* also failed to see that a large number of the clergy, both Protestant and Catholic, served their offices for love of God and their fellow men. They clung to the faith of their ancestors, and made life meaningful to themselves and their congregations through devotion and service. The *philosophes'* picture of the lecherous priest, the stupid clergyman, the unbelieving bishop told only part of the story, for Christian churches still had considerable vigor and purity in many parts of Europe. The mere fact that these clergymen were not so articulate as their enemies should not obscure their existence.

As a matter of fact, some of the most vigorous manifestations of the Christian religion were almost as revolutionary as Deism in respect to the established churches. The sixteenth-century revolution in the church had resulted in the creation of state churches which in Protestant and in Catholic countries were largely submissive to the rulers. In the seventeenth century there arose, largely from Calvinistic seeds, sectarian movements that attempted to free the church from state control. This, in effect, was the movement to reform the Reformation. In the eighteenth century the process of sectarian reform continued. In England it produced, in addition to the earlier groups, the Methodist movement. In France and in Germany the reformers strove to work within the traditional church through Pietism and Jansenism.

Methodism was at once a response to the formalism and coldness of the Anglican state church and to the unbelieving Deists. The founder of Methodism, John Wesley (1703–1791), got some of his ideas from the revivalist hymn-singing sectarians who had emerged in mid-seventeenth-century England when the word "enthusiasm" (meaning "filled with God") was coined to explain the ecstatic behavior of the congregation when it was stirred up by a revivalist preacher. Some of his ideas came from German Pietism, a practical sort of Christianity that combined personal meditation, strict morality, and something suspiciously like good works. The "right" people in England regarded the "enthusiastic" Methodists askance, but among the little people of the land—shopkeepers and artisans particularly—the doctrine of the risen Christ and belief in personal salvation were fervently received.

In Germany the Pietist movement that originated late in the seventeenth century made a considerable number of converts among the bourgeoisie and the gentry. Lutheranism had become cold and impersonal as a state-supported church; the Pietist movement emphasized home services, Bible reading, meditation, and good works that made Christianity meaningful in terms of faith. The Pietists, like the Methodists, were essentially anti-intellectual, so that they were untouched by the vicious arguments of the *philosophes;* for them religion was faith and experience, and any attempts to justify or to condemn it on intellectual grounds seemed beside the point. It is probably no accident that most of the German literary men who made the latter eighteenth century a great epoch in German letters were the sons of Pietist clergymen. Their emphasis upon personal experience and purity of manners as well as the refined atmosphere of their lives gave the Pietists a sense of personal worth and mission that was characteristic of German letters.

The survival of Jansenism in France, in spite of the efforts of the papacy and the state to stamp it out, is one of the interesting problems of the eighteenth century. Like their seventeenth-century forebears, the eighteenth-century Jansenists refused to admit that the papal condemnations of their "heresy" applied to their doctrines, and after the death of Louis XIV the government of France took a more lenient position toward them. Eighteenth-century French Jansenism was the counterpart of Pietism in Germany. Jansenist priests taught a strict morality, and emphasized the personal contact between God and man. Their Augustinian theology was a buttress against the unbelieving *philosophes* just as their exemplary lives provided inspiration for their followers. From France, Jansenist teachings of morality spread to Ireland and southern Germany where they were integrated with Catholic doctrine.

Methodism, Pietism, and Jansenism were only the most important of the Christian movements in the eighteenth century; the Quakers and others might also be mentioned. All of them were attempting to personalize Christianity and to break down the formalism of the state churches, and their common aim sheds abundant light on the moral problems of the age. Each insisted upon the importance of the individual soul. In a world that astronomy and science were depersonalizing, these religious movements reaffirmed the traditional Christian faith in a personal God who became man and died to save everyone. In the early nineteenth century they were to be joined by the romantic and idealistic philosophers and men of letters in an assault upon the mechanical rationalism of the eighteenth-century *philosophes*.

BOOK V

The French Revolution and Empire

By common consent western historians have spoken of the period before 1789 as the *ancien régime*[1] with the apparent implication that there had been a clean break with the past, that the Revolution that proclaimed the rights of man and unfurled the slogan "Liberty, Equality, Fraternity" had opened up a new era in human history. In many ways this fiction is not only useful but also well within the realm of credibility. Although we understand that many of the political and social forms that seem to be the direct results of the French revolutionary epoch actually have their roots deep in the eighteenth century, it is still unquestionably true that the Revolution greatly accelerated their growth. The ideas of popular sovereignty, of civil equality, of individual liberty were not unknown before 1789 nor were they completely translated into institutional reality by the Revolution, and yet they are undoubtedly the legacy of that Revolution. The enlightened rulers of the seventeenth and eighteenth centuries possessed the ideal of administrative unity and efficient centralized authority, and yet the administrative reorganization of Europe was the work of the revolutionary era. Finally, although most of the liberal mythology, or *mystique*, of the revolutionary era was borrowed from the eighteenth-century *philosophes*, during the hundred years following 1815 it was to the Revolution rather than to the *philo-*

---

[1] Often translated "old regime," but "former regime" is more accurate.

sophes that men who were anxious to give new form to their political society looked for inspiration and arguments. Clearly, there are emotional and political, as well as social and intellectual reasons, for regarding the French Revolution as a great break with the past.

However, when we see the French Revolution, the era of Louis XIV, or any other epoch as the beginning or the end of a particular movement or even of several movements in history, we do not imply that there was a complete break with the past. For example, the French Revolution had little or no effect upon the movement that many historians regard as the most significant aspect of western civilization, namely, the rise of the new scientific spirit of inquiry into the processes of the world. It also only partially affected the artistic and humanistic thought of western man: the so-called "Empire style" (neoclassicism) had already been born before Louis XVI lost his head, and the movement known as romanticism had been well launched by Rousseau, Herder, Kant, and others before Napoleon entered the king's army as a subaltern officer. The same observation could be made about the emerging industrialism based upon steam power. Indeed, the Revolution actually retarded the new industrialism on the continent by imposing war and embargo between England and the rest of Europe. If we are ever to understand the history of our society, we must see that Clio, the Greek muse of history, has to be joined by Janus, the god with two faces who could look in two directions at the same time. History must always look forward and back, for only in the "Janus pose" can she teach men sophistication about their origins and understanding of the processes that frame their lives.

No matter whether the French Revolution is the beginning or the end of an historical era, it presents one of the most fascinating problems of modern history, and has attracted the labors of some of the most gifted scholars of the modern age. It started with a reform movement in France and ended with a series of international congresses that attempted to restore order and tranquility after twenty-odd years of rapid and violent change in Europe and the world. This simple statement exemplifies the multifold nature of the political problems generated by the Revolution. In its inception it was no more than an attempt to give a more rational order to the constitution of France, but the dynamics of the movement spread its ideas and its influence into the rest of Europe and generated a twenty-odd years' war that involved military action from Madrid to Moscow, from the Nile to the Niemen. It proved that the Europe that emerged into the modern world had become a community, but a community in which centralized direction was as yet impossible. Neither the Revolution nor the Empire could develop political ideas or institutional forms broad enough to bring any large part of Europe under one rule.

For the student of human behavior in the arena of politics, the era of the French Revolution provides a wonderfully rich opportunity for observation. It is always difficult for men to see the political alternatives before them, in part because men are ignorant, in part because they are blinded by passions, prejudices, and presuppositions. Nowhere can better examples of the political problems of choice (both domestic and international) be found than in the great conflict of interests that began as a reform movement in 1789. Nowhere can better examples of the problems of human behavior when great issues throw angry and violent men into positions of power be found. Great interests were at stake, and men tried desperately to give form to their society. At the same time, the dynamics of that society itself imposed form and direction on the movement of politics, vitiating with nice impartiality large parts of the programs of the radicals and also of the conservatives. Such a mine of political experience is worth studying for itself alone, as well as for its place in the emerging story of the wonderful and unique civilization of the West.

BIBLIOGRAPHY FOR BOOK V

THE ERA OF THE FRENCH REVOLUTION AND NAPOLEON

The following two volumes from *The Rise of Modern Europe* are excellent:

Brinton, C., *A Decade of Revolution, 1789–1799*, New York, Harper, 1934.
Bruun, G., *Europe and the French Imperium, 1799–1814*, New York, Harper, 1938.

There are a number of good general accounts of this period. The first three books cited below are textbooks; the others are specialized interpretations of the Revolution.

Aulard, F. V. A., *The French Revolution: A Political History, 1789–1804*, trans. Bernard Miall, New York, Scribner, 1910, 4 vols.
Gershoy, L., *The French Revolution and Napoleon*, New York, Appleton-Century-Crofts, 1933.
Gottschalk, L., *The Era of the French Revolution, 1715–1815*, Boston, Houghton Mifflin, 1929.
Lefèbvre, G., *The Coming of the French Revolution*, trans. R. R. Palmer, Princeton, Princeton University Press, 1947.
Madelin, Louis, *The French Revolution*, New York, Putnam, 1928.
Mathiez, A., *The French Revolution*, trans. Catherine A. Phillips, New York, Knopf, 1929.
Mathiez, A., *After Robespierre: The Thermidorean Reaction*, New York, Knopf, 1931.
Taine, H. A., *The Ancient Regime*, New York, Holt, 1876.
Taine, H. A., *The French Revolution*, New York, Holt, 1878–1887.
Thompson, James, *The French Revolution*, New York, Oxford University Press, 1945.

A large volume of literature has been written concerning the so-called "old regime" as background for the Revolution; the following books are only an introduction.

Bruun, G., *The Enlightened Despots*, New York, Holt, 1929. A Berkshire Study.

Cobban, A., *The Myth of the French Revolution*, London, 1955.

Ducros, L., *French Society in the Eighteenth Century*, trans. W. de Geijer, with foreword by J. A. Higgs-Walker, New York, Putnam, 1927.

Funck-Brentano, F., *The Old Regime in France*, trans. H. Wilson, New York, Longmans, Green, 1929.

Johnson, A. H., *The Age of the Enlightened Despot, 1660–1789*, 15th ed. rev. (revised by his son and C. T. Atkinson), London, Methuen, 1933.

Sorel, A., *Europe under the Old Regime*, Los Angeles, Ritchie, 1947.

Tocqueville, A. de, *The Old Regime and the Revolution*, New York, 1856.

The "heroes" of the era have been the subjects for many studies.

Brinton, C., *The Lives of Talleyrand*, New York, Norton, 1936.

Fisher, H. A. L., *Napoleon*, New York, Holt, 1913.

Geyl, Pieter, *Napoleon: For and Against*, New Haven, Yale University Press, 1949.

Gottschalk, L., *Lafayette between the French and the American Revolutions, 1783–1789*, Chicago, University of Chicago Press, 1950.

Kircheisen, Friederich, *Napoleon*, New York, Harcourt, Brace, 1932.

Madelin, Louis, *Danton*, trans. Lady Mary Loyd, New York, Knopf, 1921.

Marat, Jean Paul, *A Study in Radicalism*, New York, 1927.

Padover, S. K., *The Revolutionary Emperor, Joseph the Second*, New York, Ballou, 1934.

Padover, S. K., *The Life and Death of Louis XVI*, New York, Appleton-Century, 1939.

Palmer, R. R., *Twelve Who Ruled: The Committee of Public Safety during the Terror*, Princeton, Princeton University Press, 1941.

Thompson, James, *Napoleon Bonaparte*, New York, Oxford University Press, 1952.

There are many studies of military history.

Oman, Charles, *Studies in the Napoleonic Wars*, London, Methuen, 1929.

Tarlé, Eugene, *Napoleon's Invasion of Russia, 1812*, New York, Oxford University Press, 1942.

THE CONGRESS OF VIENNA

Cecil, Algernon, *Metternich*, New York, Macmillan, 1935.

Nicolson, Harold, *The Congress of Vienna: A Study in Allied Unity, 1812–1822*, New York, Harcourt, Brace, 1946.

Webster, C. K., *The Congress of Vienna, 1814–1815*, London, Oxford University Press, 1919.

Webster, Charles, *The Foreign Policy of Castlereagh, 1812–1815*, London, Bell, 1931.

An Eighteenth-Century Engraving, "Born for Toil." This illustration depicts the French peasant on the eve of the French Revolution. The tool on his shoulder is a flail with which he threshes the grain. (University of Minnesota Library)

Chapter 26

SOCIAL AND ECONOMIC PATTERNS ON THE EVE OF THE FRENCH REVOLUTION

1. FORCES FOR SOCIAL CHANGE

In the latter eighteenth century three interrelated social and economic forces were at work to induce change in European society. First, after several centuries of near equilibrium, the population of western Europe entered an era of phenomenal growth. Second, commerce that had been expanding gradually for centuries took on a new tempo after the Seven Years' War (1756–1763). With the growth in commerce came also increased demands for manufactured goods. Finally, about the middle of the eighteenth century price levels, which had been relatively stable for about a century, again resumed their upward spiral. Population, commerce, and price inflation—these were dynamic forces that poured energy into European society on the eve of the French Revolution.

It is unlikely that eighteenth-century women bore more children than their predecessors: examinations of earlier parish records reveal floods of births. These, however, were necessary simply to maintain the population level in the eras when death was so determined to reap his early harvest. The secret of the rise in population in the eighteenth century seems to be found in the processes that gently but firmly stayed death's hand while the birth rate continued. The eighteenth century was the first in western Europe's history that was not regularly plagued by famine. Improved methods of agriculture accounted for this in a small part, but primarily this new security against starvation came from the commercial structure and transportation systems that could bring grain from great distances to feed the hungry in times of crop failure. Internal waterways and roads, larger ships on the high seas, and effective market organization: these were the factors that decreased death by starvation and from the diseases that accompany it. Europeans were still far from secure against want, and even farther from a universally adequate diet, but they were at last freeing themselves from the continuous threat of starvation. To this reduction in the incidence of famine should probably be added a slight over-all improvement in the quality of diet of Europe that came with the greater abundance of sugar, rice, and meat as well as wheat. Better diet may have altered the balance slightly, but it would be unwise to emphasize its effect because only a few people enjoyed the improvement in the quality, as well as the quantity, of available food.

Thus, a few more children grew up to become adults and a few more young women lived on as adults to bear children. Very little is required to upset population balances: when the incidence of death is reduced, the population will grow until a new balance has been achieved. It is noteworthy that this law of population growth first became apparent in the latter eighteenth century when the spectacle of a growing population forcibly called Malthus' (1766–1834) attention to the "iron laws" that govern it. Human reproduction, he noticed, tended to outstrip the production of foodstuffs. Therefore, men can increase their numbers only at their own peril, for eventually they must again face starvation as a check on their growth. Few eighteenth-century men worried about that future hazard, for Europeans had long known famine and disease as a fact of their existence; the novelty of a situation that seemed to assure food for all made the majority uninterested in Malthus' pessimistic predictions. It was not until the nineteenth century that his ideas attracted attention.

While the villages apparently shared in the population growth to some extent, its most spectacular effects were to be found in the urban areas where growing population created demands for goods and housing, and opened up wide opportunities for labor. There was hardly a city in western Europe that did not burst out beyond its walls in the second half of the eighteenth century, and since the pattern of warfare had begun to make walled fortifications obsolete, this time-honored check to city growth was removed. The building of the fine homes that the wealthy required in the new urban developments, as well as the provision for some sort of shelter for the rest of ever-growing city populations gave work to an army of construction workers, to manufacturers of building materials, and to the men and horses who hauled wood, stone, sand, and lime into the cities. From the mid-eighteenth century onward these urban areas, no longer constrained by walls, sprawled out wherever there were key commercial and manufacturing centers. The labor required to build the cities gave employment to many of the men recruited from the land to swell their size, while the ever-growing value of urban property made the bourgeoisie who owned the land and the buildings increasingly wealthy.

In turn the new cities were largely responsible for the upsurge of commerce in the latter eighteenth century. Demands for sugar, rice, coffee, tobacco, cocoa, textiles, ironware, and a host of such things followed the upward swing of well-to-do urban dwellers, who had to depend upon commerce for practically all their goods, whether they were items of consumption or raw materials to be made into manufactured goods. This is a familiar pattern. Since the inhabitants of the cities made their livings by manufacturing, commerce, and special services, there had to be an interrelation between the rise of urban population and economic development. Indeed, it may be said that the history of the urbanization movement is in large part the story of rising demands for goods. This movement seemed to spurt ahead more vigorously in the latter eighteenth century than at any previous time.

It might be worthwhile to pause here and note that historians of western Europe have found that the urban dweller was a vital element in developing social change from medieval times onward. However, if we look closely at any era before the eighteenth century, it becomes apparent that, while the urban dweller was undoubtedly important, his power and influence were often dwarfed by the nobility whose wealth came from the land. While we seem unable to discover "laws" in history, there are certain obvious tendencies, and one of these has always been that power and wealth tend to be interrelated. Thus, the rise of the bourgeoisie to power is probably indicative of the fact that urban wealth was becoming as important as rural wealth in the political world. Kings, noblemen, the church, and even at times the peasants had in the past often played roles equal to or more important than those allotted to the bourgeoisie and their more humble allies, the urban workers. In the eighteenth century this situation began spectacularly to reverse itself as the number, wealth, and social influence of the bourgeoisie grew by leaps and bounds. They were obviously ready to occupy the seats of power, and thus on the eve of the French Revolution the actors were in the wings and had rehearsed their curtain calls well.

While the growing cities and expanding trade testified openly to the importance of the city dwellers, the rise in prices that had been interrupted for about a century again spiralled upwards, and brought with it a golden flow of riches to merchants and financiers. Ever since the Middle Ages price trends in Europe had been upward. In the fourteenth century, and again in the seventeenth, the inflationary movement had halted momentarily, but in the sixteenth and eighteenth centuries silver and gold flowed from the New World in quantities that buoyed up prices. Indeed, in the eighteenth century Europe was drenched with as much precious metal as had flowed into European markets during the preceding thousand years.

Just as the growth of cities particularly enriched the bourgeoisie who owned the land and buildings, so the flow of precious metals and the subsequent rise in prices especially enriched the merchants and financiers who had the knowledge and skill to take advantage of it. Country landlords have always had trouble adjusting their income upward to meet rising prices, and since there were no labor unions to urge and to fight for salary adjustments, the day workers of the eighteenth century were almost in the same disadvantageous position as the men whose salaries were paid by the quarter or by the year. None of them was quite able to keep up with the inflationary price rises. The result was that the merchants and financiers were the ones best situated to enjoy the buoyant economy. Rising prices are nearly always coincidental with increased activity in the market, and this was true of the latter eighteenth century. Thus, inflation joined with the population increase to stimulate trade and augment the wealth of the bourgeoisie.

A student needs to be cautious in making an evaluation of the complex problems presented by social and political change. Clearly, there are deep underlying forces which are very difficult to explain. Nonetheless, it is important to understand that the interrelated factors that brought about the rise in population, the extraordinary expansion of commerce, and a price inflation together tended to aggrandize the strength, wealth, and importance of the urban bourgeoisie. Therefore, these forces must be kept in mind in the subsequent discussions of the social structure of western Europe on the eve of the French Revolution.

2. THE BOURGEOISIE

European society in the eighteenth century has usually been described as a social pyramid: at the apex were the nobility and the officials of the princely governments; at the base were the peasants and artisans; in between were the middle classes, the bourgeoisie. This is a loose generalization at best, for, as we shall see, these general terms cover great diversity. Yet no student of the era will deny that a social pyramid did exist in some manner. Perhaps the most important fact about this social structure is that, in general, the bourgeoisie were responsible for change, while the nobility were conservative and resistant to change. The peasantry and artisans showed little or no vision of their role in society, and although their activity was a definite factor in the organization of Europe, it was largely blind and insensitive to any of the larger aspects of the social problem.

The importance of the bourgeoisie can hardly be overestimated if we confine our attention to the western societies of England, France, and the Netherlands. In these states, bourgeois wealth was increasing at an astonishing rate, and bourgeois values, manners, morals, and general view of life were beginning to impose themselves upon the whole society. The distinctions that had separated noblemen from bourgeoisie a century before were breaking down. In England, the men of the "city" (the financial center of London) were every bit as important in setting the social mores as the noblemen who flocked to the court or hunted foxes in the country. In France even Louis XVI lived his personal life *en bonne bourgeoisie* as a family man. The nobility might still scorn the lowly born whose hands were "dirty" from trade, but the vigor of the bourgeoisie, their wealth and their assurance, were making deep inroads on the patterns of society.

Who were the bourgeoisie? The term becomes vague the minute we try to pin it down firmly. Perhaps the best representative statement would be that the bourgeoisie were "non-noblemen" who drew all or part of their income from investments. It might be further stated that, by and large, the original source of their wealth was from trade, manufacturing, or professional services rather than from the land. However, this generalization does not describe the actual diversity of the class. Some of the French bourgeoisie, for example, were practically indistinguishable from the nobility: their forefathers had purchased hereditary offices in the king's service, and they and their children had intermarried with the "noblemen of the sword." The financiers who farmed the taxes on contract, who operated the banks, who facilitated the exchange of money, not only lived on a scale that most noblemen could not emulate, but also found it easy to marry their children to anyone whom they were willing to accept as "family." At the other extreme were the bourgeoisie whose pattern of life and need to work scarcely distinguished them from the artisans: the little shopkeepers, the little entrepreneurs, the impecunious professional people who made up the petty bourgeoisie of all countries, were also part of the bourgeois class. There was a continuum between the little people and the great ones at the top in which we find men at all levels striving to increase their stature and position within the limits of the class. Twentieth-century sociologists, observing a similar situation, have called this a society with a "striving for upward mobility." This terminology may be useful for it calls attention to the fact that these people were socially ambitious. But it should be used cautiously because "mobility" was confined to relatively few individuals. Social change in the eighteenth century was constant but slow; this fact often resulted in envy and hatreds within the bourgeois society itself.

As a class the bourgeoisie were better educated than any other. They sent their sons to schools where they learned languages, some literature, simple mathematics, and came in contact with the stimulating thought of the really learned men of their era. At universities some of them received professional education in law, medicine, theology, or the arts; others were attached to the countinghouses of bankers or merchants, where they learned to manage affairs. Perhaps the most striking evidence of the superior education of the bourgeoisie in the latter eighteenth century was the development of literary and library societies all over western Europe. There was hardly a town of any size that could not boast at least one society where men could read the latest reviews and books and find companions with whom to discuss new ideas. These societies in France were ready-made political cells when the bourgeois revolution took power out of the hands of the king's officials. Thus, while commerce supplied them with wealth, their education gave the bourgeoisie direction and the urge for power.

The bourgeoisie were in far from complete agreement about the courses they wished to follow, yet there was considerable unanimity about the problems that they faced, and, in general, they were ambitious to elbow aside the noblemen who occupied the seats of power. This attitude was particularly true in France, where traditions and royal policy frustrated their ambitions. Both the army and the church were, in effect, closed to the French bourgeoisie because noblemen traditionally had preference in those professions. Most of the important clerical positions were passed on from uncle to nephew. The miserable livings and the country parishes were open to anyone, but only the very pious, the unimaginative, or the unambitious wanted to labor in those vineyards. The bourgeois youth might secure commissions in the artillery or the engineering branches of the army, but higher ranks in the cavalry and infantry were, to all intents and purposes, closed to them, since the mythology of the military service assumed that only a nobleman could understand the code of honor of those services. The bar against bourgeois officers was temporarily suspended in Prussia during the Seven Years' War when so many of the nobles were killed that there was a shortage of officer material. However, the generalization that the armies of Europe were officered exclusively by noblemen is virtually true. In the navies a few bourgeois officers rose to the command of ships, although even in this service the nobles or, as in England, their relatives received preference over the bourgeoisie, because of their allegedly greater patriotic spirit and devotion.

Furthermore, the "blue-blooded" noblemen were not the only frustrating barrier to bourgeois ambitions. Both the government bureaucracy and the judiciary were staffed by "noblemen of the robe" who held their offices as an hereditary right as long as they paid an annual tax known as the *Paulette*. Most of these families went back to the time of the great king, Louis XIV— some of them even to Henry IV; and they showed no disposition either to step aside or to admit newcomers to their ranks. These "venal" offices were thus, in effect, hereditary property. It is small wonder that talk of the equality of man, of the right to equality of opportunity, found in the writings of the more radical *philosophes,* appealed to the ambitious bourgeois youth who saw glamorous and lucrative careers closed to him by hereditary claims of others no more able than himself.

In addition, the bourgeoisie were confronted with another source of frustration resulting from class privilege. The best and safest investment of the eighteenth century, indeed of all centuries preceding the nineteenth, was land. Land provided a security not to be found elsewhere. Therefore, the well-to-do bourgeoisie eagerly sought to buy land, only to be confronted time and again with the distinction between the land of noblemen and that of commoners. In Prussia, commoners could not buy "noble land" at any price, and everywhere they found that the "fiefs" were owned either by great noblemen or by the king. Then too, as in France, for example, once the commoner owned land, he found himself taxed differently from his noble neighbor, who evaded certain taxes on the fictitious ground that he paid a "blood tax" as a soldier in the army.

In still another way the political order of the eighteenth century outraged the desire of the bourgeoisie for equality. The bureaucratic-police states that seventeenth- and eighteenth-century statesmen were trying to mold into political units were the result of nearly a thousand years of political evolution. They were made up of provinces and towns that had come under the hand of the ruler at different times and under varying conditions. Each had its own character, its collection of royal grants, its complex of privileges; the enlightened French rulers in the seventeenth century may have forced their provinces and towns to recognize the royal authority, but neither Louis XIV nor either of his successors was able to deprive them of their distinctive privileges or to force them to accept a common charter of rights. Like so many of the earlier meetings of the French Estates-General (parliament), that in 1614 had floundered on this very point: none of the privileged areas was willing to give up its peculiar prerogatives in return for general guarantee of right. These special territorial privileges were a constant source of irritation to the bourgeoisie and the peasants. They implied unequal assessment of taxes, unequal access to justice, and unequal personal status—all simply because of the accidents of historical geography.

No less urgent was the bourgeoisie's desire to free their commercial and industrial enterprises from the controls of the state. In the seventeenth century the royal authority had in part achieved its mission by usurping the traditional role of the towns, as well as of the guilds, as the regulators of commerce and industry. It had seemed wise in Colbert's time to substitute royal order for the patchwork of traditional controls that were confusing the economic life of the nation. These royal ordinances undoubtedly had a beneficial effect on the economy; they "cured" specific evils, solved specific problems, and achieved specific results. Studying this so-called "mercantilist" legislation, the impression grows that the ordinances were a series of "new deal" reforms designed to carry the seventeenth-century economy over a series of crises. But the regulations of economic life that had been reform measures in 1670 became strait jackets by 1740 and intolerable tyranny after

1763. As the conditions of economic life changed, the rules and regulations that had previously worked reasonably well no longer suited existing conditions, and therefore needed reorganization.

The rising chorus of demands for relaxation of the "mercantilist" regulations began almost immediately after the deaths of Louis XIV in France and of Anne in England, and, as a matter of fact, much of the politico-economic legislation of the eighteenth century might be discussed in terms of a liberalization of policy toward economic laissez faire. As the century progressed, the notion that the state should withdraw from the field of economic regulation and allow businessmen to conduct their affairs as they wished was widely expressed in both England and France. The "physiocrats" were the first and most eloquent exponents of a laissez faire doctrine which they cleverly combined with the advocacy of a single tax on land. Thus they desired not only to free the bourgeoisie from regulation, but also to force the landlords to pay all taxes, since the latter's wealth came not from their own labor but from the beneficence of God or nature. In the last quarter of the century Adam Smith's *Wealth of Nations* (1776) became a bible for the bourgeoisie in England, since Adam Smith, too, insisted that the economy was a machine governed by economic laws that could function properly only if the state ceased to interfere with the business community. Thus laissez faire became a sort of flag for the bourgeoisie, a catchword that urged liberty as a class aspiration.

The bourgeois intellectuals found it easy to ally themselves with their brothers in the market place, and in fact they provided them with arguments to buttress the middle-class demands. The lawyers and others who read Montesquieu's *Spirit of the Laws* and pondered the problem of "creating" a constitution for society came to believe that somehow it might be possible to legislate a good society. Others who read Rousseau's *Social Contract* or Locke's *Reflections on Government* gradually realized that power and authority were separate entities; the people granted power to their magistrates, but authority (that is, the *right* to govern) they retained themselves. Indeed, Rousseau conclusively "proved" that the people could not possibly surrender this authority, for the government must carry out the "general will" or be turned out by a government that would do so.

Reform was in the air of the eighteenth century, and bourgeois demands for equality of opportunity, equality before the law and the tax collector, equality in society, and liberty in economic and social affairs loomed large in the reform program. The winged words of the American Revolutionary proclamations asserting the right to "life, liberty, and happiness," as well as the right of a people to control their own destiny, were echoed in the confident pages of the *philosophes* who assured western men, and particularly the bourgeoisie, that change was the order of the day, and that change and progress were synonymous.

3. THE NOBILITY AND THEIR ALLIES

If the bourgeoisie might be called the eighteenth century's "party of movement," the nobility was its "party of resistance." The revolutionary developments of the seventeenth century had dealt the nobility almost lethal blows. Throughout Europe the rise of royal authority had been at the expense of the traditional authority of the noblemen. The great feudal overlords with fiefs scattered all over the kingdom, as well as the petty country gentlemen, had been deprived of the social and political functions that had traditionally justified their existence. Royal officials appeared in the provinces armed with the right and power to dispense justice, collect taxes, and foster public works and public education. The noblemen saw the king interpose himself between the lord and the peasant in such a way as to deprive the former of his traditional role in society. It was this change that had been one of the important roots of the rebellions that took place from Spain to Petrine Russia in the seventeenth century. Richelieu and Louis XIII and Mazarin and Louis XIV won the victory in France; elsewhere from Savoy and Hungary to Sweden and Prussia similar victories were chalked up for royal power at the expense of the nobility. The rise of standing royal armies blasted the nobleman's chances of successful rebellion, just as the rise of the bureaucracy placed him in the toils of the royal administration.

In the eighteenth century the nobility attempted to regain its former position by "capturing" the machinery of government. After the deaths of Louis XIV in France, Charles XII in Sweden, Peter I in Russia, to mention a few examples, the nobility in those countries staged a sort of counter-revolution by seizing the governmental machinery that the great kings had developed. However, the political trend was against them. If there was a characteristic political form for all European society, it may be stated in terms of an ever-increasing concentration of power in the hands of the central authority directed by officials of humble origin. In Poland, where the great nobles successfully resisted this pressure, the result was the partition of the kingdom by its powerful neighbors, which we have already discussed.

Thus, the nobility of Europe developed a pattern of resistance to further encroachments upon its traditional rights. In a way they were fighting a battle on two fronts: on the one, they had to stave off the encroachments of the king's officials; on the other, they found themselves challenged by the bourgeoisie whose wealth allowed them to live as well as any nobleman. Individually impoverished noblemen might marry their children to members of the bourgeoisie to secure a fortune, but as a class the nobles resented and affected to despise them. They tried to insist that blood and breeding rather than money and ability should be the criteria for social as well as political preference. Unfortunately for the nobles, they had few articulate spokesmen to champion their cause. As a class they failed to acquire a liberating education, and, in addition, the intellectual climate of the eighteenth century did not encourage conservatives to state their case. We have to wait until the Revolution of 1789 shocked the English philosopher-statesman, Edmund Burke, to hear a lucid conservative argument.

Perhaps the inner disunity of the nobility was responsible for its failure to regroup in face of threats from both king and people. Not all noblemen probably were as rank conscious as the Duke of Saint Simon who worried unconscionably when another duke with a title less ancient than his own pushed ahead of him at a court function. Even so, there was little feeling of unity between the great court noblemen and the poor country gentlemen whose coats-of-arms and pedigrees were their most important asset. These poorer noblemen sent their sons to military schools on scholarships; themselves went to court almost as a "vulture class" to repair their fortunes; or squatted miserably in their country places watching their world collapse around them. They furnished the soldiers and also the politicians for the French Revolution. The great noblemen despised them as much as they despised the upstarts who bought titles or received titles for services they had performed for the king. The nobles who thought well of themselves had to inquire about the wealth and the ancestry of their fellows before accepting them as equals.

As a class the nobility was relatively less educated than the bourgeoisie. Goethe's biting remark, "learned as a German squire," was meant to cover the whole tribe of country gentlemen whose lives revolved around horses, dogs, food, and drink. Hunting and rustic entertainment were the principal occupations of the countryside; the nobleman who could and actually did read much seems to have been the exception. The great noblemen who lived at court were equally indisposed to serious study. Manners were more important than philosophy, and although many noblemen toyed with the intellectual movement we call the Enlightenment, they did not turn it to the advantage of their class. Ability to turn a phrase or repeat a witty epigram was more important than the heartbreaking labor of analyzing a political or social position.

However, even though they may not have been articulate enough to produce effective political spokesmen, most of the noblemen were conscious of their economic problems in a changing world. In France, for example, where most of the great nobles still held feudal fiefs, price inflation cut heavily into that portion of their incomes that was fixed by a money payment. Some of the peasants still paid their *cens* in kind or in labor; others paid in coin. The latter, of course, benefited greatly from inflation, since their obligations were fixed to a definite sum of money. Conversely, the noblemen in such cases found their real income decline sharply. It is not, therefore, surprising to see that the landlords tried to extend their "take" from the villages when inflation began to pinch. Old rights were resurrected and pushed for their fullest yield, so that at the end of the eighteenth century French peasants had good cause to resent the feudal *corvées* ("forced labor"), *banalités* ("public utilities": wine press, bake oven, and the like), and other impositions.

Nevertheless, some of the nobles in France, the Netherlands, and the Rhineland were in a relatively strong position to meet the economic problems of the eighteenth century, since they or their forebears had already altered the legal arrangement regulating their land holdings by suppressing feudal contracts entirely and consolidating their own holdings into land that could be rented annually either for money or on shares. The former (tenant money-rent contracts) were relatively common in the grain areas, while the *métayage* (sharecropper) contracts were used mostly in the vine and olive lands of the south. The landowners who had thus consolidated their situation were in a reasonably good position to ride the inflation of rising prices; at the same time, their legal control over the land was "modern" rather than "feudal," and therefore remained intact throughout the revolutionary epoch that followed.

The French nobility escaped the *taille* which had originally been imposed as a war tax centuries earlier, but which had become a source of general revenue by 1750. They were excused from this tax on the grounds that they, theoretically at least, paid a blood tax in its place. Actually, anyone reading the letters of French ladies at court or of noblewomen in the country during a period of warfare will see that the blood tax was a very grim reality to many families, even if some did succeed in escaping it altogether. In addition to it, they paid heavy "fines" upon inheriting their titles, for each new heir had to have his title registered in *parlement* to make it legal. The nobles were also subject to excise taxes on luxury and other goods as well as the several special taxes that the French kings found it necessary to impose. Thus, though they did not pay the *taille,* they certainly did contribute to the king's treasury. The point that must be made is that they did not contribute in proportion to their wealth, and in this they were in good company with the clergy and the upper bourgeoisie.

Two other socially favored groups in France and, indeed, in many other parts of Europe, were closely allied to the nobility: the upper clergy, composed largely of the children of noblemen, and the magistrates, whose daughters, at least, were often enough the wives and mothers of noblemen.

The Concordat Francis I had made with the pope in the early sixteenth century had, in effect, turned the church benefices into political plums at the disposal of the king. To get some idea of their numbers, it may be sufficient to point out that in the kingdom of France there were about 130,-000 secular and regular clergymen. Of these, under ten thousand were upper clergy (bishops, abbots, abbesses, vicar generals, and so forth), sixty thousand were lower secular clergy (parish priests), and sixty thousand were regular clergy (monks and nuns). The total was somewhat under one percent of the population of the kingdom. Appointments to the offices of bishop and archbishop, of abbot and abbess, and of the *abbés* of the more profitable parish churches, were made by the king—not necessarily on religious grounds. By tradition some of these higher clerical offices were inheritable from uncle to nephew; others were given as favors or rewards for political or military service. We have seen that throughout the eighteenth century it had become increasingly difficult for a man who was not a nobleman to obtain one of these offices, no matter how well qualified he might be.

As a result, the personnel of the upper clergy tended to identify with the interests, as well as the way of life, of the nobility. Bishops who were more interested in horses, dogs, and women than in their ecclesiastical offices did not help the church: indeed, they softened its armor in face of the assaults of the deistic *philosophes*. At the same time, the education of the lower clergy was inevitably neglected, so that from top to bottom the church suffered from a malady that was political and social, rather than religious.

The church in France drew its income chiefly from two sources. First, as a landlord it collected between eighty and a hundred and twenty million livres annually from its properties; but most of that income went to a favored few among the upper clergy who had the right to administer and collect it. The second main source of wealth was the tithe which was theoretically imposed on all, but which actually weighed most heavily on the peasantry. The tithe was no longer ten percent; in some districts it amounted to not more than one-sixteenth; in others it was about one-eighth. Tithes brought in about a hundred and twenty-five million livres a year and this money also went largely to the upper clergy. The parish churches and the lower clergy received little consideration from their ecclesiastical superiors. Some of the bishops, like the one in Strasbourg, had enormous incomes (four hundred thousand livres); the majority, however, had to get along with thirty thousand to forty thousand livres, while a parish priest was lucky to get a few hundred.

Clerical income was largely free from direct royal taxation, for the clergy customarily presented the king with a "free gift" in lieu of a direct tax. The remainder was not entirely used to gratify the worldly tastes of worldly men, for the church did support education and charity; it cared for orphans, the insane, the sick, and the aged. Unquestionably, too much of the church's income was used for nonreligious or even irreligious purposes, but critics should also realize that the church as a whole served a number of important roles in society that were only indirectly connected with the sacerdotal office.

The other group closely associated with the nobility was the magistracy. In France judges and civil officials purchased their offices and held them as property that could be sold or willed to an heir as long as the incumbent paid an annual tax (the *Paulette*). Since state offices were not only a secure form of investment but also an assurance of social prestige, such positions were eagerly sought after and properly cherished by the upper crust of the bourgeoisie. They came to be regarded as the "nobility of the robe," and although the "nobility of the sword" tended to look down upon them, their wealth made their children desirable marriage partners; so much so, in fact, that whenever a great nobleman died, there were probably as many of the magistrates in "mourning" as authentic noblemen.

Inevitably the "nobility of the robe" also acquired vested interests and prerogatives. In the era of Louis XIV their number had increased greatly as the wars required more and more money. The wit who assured Louis that God would create a fool to buy any office the king might create reflected the expansion of this class. In the eighteenth century, without a strong king like Louis XIV to curb their pretensions, the descendants of the seventeenth-century magistracy became a social phalanx guarding its own rights, but not necessarily dispensing either justice or administration effectively. By the middle of the century men like Voltaire despised the magistrates as contemptuously as they did the other parasitical class in society. Their critics, however, should not overlook the fact that this hereditary magistracy had certain advantages. Many of these families provided a considerable number of upright and honest royal servants whose traditions and honor acted as an inspiration to service. It was of some value to the office for a boy to grow up knowing that he some day must fill the position that his father and grandfather had honorably occupied before him.

4. THE PEASANTRY AND CITY WORKERS

It used to be customary for historians to introduce any discussion of the causes of the French Revolution with a distressing tableau depicting the miseries of the peasants. La Bruyère's famous description of the "wild animals" living in the fields gave excellent "color" to such accounts, even though he wrote almost a century before the Revolution actually broke out. However, there is little evidence to show that the peasants had much to do either with the origin of the Revolution or with its course after 1789. The additional assumption, too, that the French peasants were particularly disposed toward revolution because of their miserable condition will probably not stand up under careful examination. Very likely they were no worse off in the eighteenth century than they had been in the preceding centuries. They had always lived a precarious economic existence; at least one-half of the kingdom rarely produced more food than was absolutely essential to support the life of the men who raised it. The mid-twentieth-century tourist driving through the mountainous areas of France can still see the abandoned farms, terraced on the hillsides, where peasants formerly tried vainly to make a living. In fact, it would be difficult to prove that they were appreciably worse off in 1789 than they had been in 1600.

At the end of the eighteenth century rural France was strongly reminiscent of the past, even though here and there harbingers of the future might be perceived. For the most part, the culture of the peasants had changed little in three hundred years. To be sure, newer methods of plowing, planting, and harvesting were to be seen occasionally, but the time-honored patterns were largely predominant. The historian is always at a loss to explain that, although a system of agriculture seems to remain unchanged, there is nevertheless some progress; if he emphasizes either the static or the dynamic, the other is virtually overshadowed. In eighteenth-century rural France there were few horse-drawn implements for planting or cultivating the fields, and yet some did exist. For the most part, the fields were ordered as they had been traditionally, and yet there were places where the new "English" system of crop rotation was beginning to replace the traditional three-field order.

The peasants in France were nearly all free men. Only a handful of serfs, bound to the soil, remained as a reminder of earlier periods. Many of the peasants considered themselves to be free proprietors. In point of fact, however, most of these were not real proprietors but owners of hereditary leaseholds of land belonging to great noblemen. For the lands they had to pay a *cens* either in coin, in kind, or in labor to the overlord. In turn, they could sell or will their rights in the land as real property. The plots, however, were small and their owners had to rent more land for money or on shares (*métayage*), work for a noble neighbor, or depend upon cottage labor such as spinning, weaving, dyeing, and the like, in order to support their families. Thus, the process that created the small peasant plots in France had begun long before the Revolution of 1789, and even that Revolution did not increase the size and number of the plots enough to enable a large percentage of the peasantry to live off of their own land.

By the eighteenth century many of the ancient feudal rights had ceased to be important in the villages. In most parts of France the manorial courts, in which a nobleman's bailiff dispensed justice for a price, and the *corvée* had all but disappeared. However, the nobles still retained the right to impose a tax for transfer of title when a peasant died or sold his right in the land, and, an even greater cause of annoyance to the peasantry, he also retained the monopoly on the public utilities of the village (the *banalités*). The peasant had to use these "public services" and to pay relatively high fees for the privilege. Almost as vexatious were the many tolls and market dues which the feudal nobles retained from ancient times and which raised prices artificially in rural areas. Lastly, the peasants were still bound by the ancient hunting rights of the nobility which forbade them to kill or molest game that damaged their fields, but allowed the nobles to ride through the fields in pursuit of their quarry, damaging crops wherever they went.

Such a brief account of rural France does only slight justice to the problem. Frequently more than a thousand years of historic background of many of the villages had endowed them with characteristics different from their neighbors, while the diversity of crops, culture, soil, and rainfall that marked the ancient kingdom had given each district its own problems and its own interests. The peasantry of France, like that of all Europe, was beset with one overwhelming ambition that could not be fulfilled, namely, to secure more land—i.e., enough—and to own it completely. In the latter eighteenth century this ambition became further frustrated as the population rose sharply while the amount of land remained constant. Rural France swarmed with landless men, as did the rest of rural Europe: beggars and day workers who could not hope to realize the peasants' dream. In 1789 about one-fourth of all the inhabitants of rural France neither owned nor could rent land to cultivate on their own, and another half had to supplement income from their own property by labor on the land of others. They were too poor, too ignorant, and too inarticulate to count much in eighteenth-century society, but their very existence presented problems of moment for those who tried to rule the country.

The other underprivileged group in eighteenth-century Europe was the urban worker class. Communist historians and others who follow the Marxist ideology like to refer to these city workers as the urban masses, but such terminology is too loaded with twentieth-century overtones to be useful for describing the social conditions of the eighteenth century. In the first place, eighteenth-century workers were largely artisans who plied a trade that had taken years of apprenticeship to learn, and they worked for patrons who, often enough, were themselves artisans and worked at the next bench. For the most part they were employed in establishments with not more than a dozen workers, some of whom would be mere boys learning the trade. The "factory" worker employed as only semiskilled labor at huge plants was almost unknown except in England's textile industry and here and there in the metal working trades. Thus the eighteenth-century worker, even when he was a hewer of wood, a drawer of water, or a puller of a cart may hardly be described in terms of twentieth-century proletarian ideology.

Furthermore, these artisans were largely unorganized and nearly completely inarticulate in terms of their own interests. The building trades and a few of the others had loosely connected mutual benefit societies called *compagnonnages*. Of ancient origin, these societies had social and some professional goals: a worker far from home could find companionship; the sick could be cared for; the dead buried; and occasionally a strike would be undertaken to secure advantages. But they were a far cry from a labor union. The general ignorance of the workers was a barrier to any union or united action. Unable to read or write, they could not hear spokesmen who might urge their interests or leaders who might bring them together for united action.

The artisans suffered severely from the inflation, for their wages tended to lag behind the rising prices. At the same time, the growth of urban population tended to crowd them more tightly in their already overcrowded quarters. Since there was no one to explain these economic phenomena to them in either bourgeois or proletarian terms, they simply became blindly bitter against their fate. This bitterness made them dangerous, for the general brutality of an age of public executions, barbarous legal codes, crude manners and morals, furnished little to ameliorate the behavior of the poor. We hear that they were polite, perhaps servile, but also capable of shocking acts of individual and mass violence. The traditions of the Parisian mob from the fourteenth century onward retold stories of barricades in the streets and savage outbursts of violence. The urban poor of the eighteenth century had no experiences to soften these traditions.

In general, the urban workers identified their interests with those of their patrons, the bourgeoisie, and saw themselves opposed to the nobility as natural enemies. Thus, when the bourgeoisie wanted to threaten violence, they had men at their disposal who could be depended on to make a demonstration in the streets. It is not so much that the "masses intervened" on the side of the bourgeoisie, but rather that the bourgeoisie were able to stir up the "masses" as allies, even perhaps as stooges to carry out their wishes. This was to be the pattern at least until the middle of the nineteenth century when the workers began to develop a sort of political maturity.

5. EUROPEAN PATTERNS

Most of this discussion of the class structure at the end of the eighteenth century has been centered on France, because it was France that made the bourgeois revolution of 1789. Elsewhere in Europe, as has been occasionally noted, bourgeois patterns bore a resemblance to those of France. In the Low Countries and the Rhineland the situation was almost exactly the same. Beyond the Rhine the bourgeoisie became less and less "mature" as a class; that is to say, they were fewer in number, not so well educated, and much less conscious of themselves as a social group. Beyond the Elbe the bourgeoisie were practically of no political importance. In Italy and Spain there were towns where for hundreds of years a mature bourgeois society had existed on a town level, but the political institutions of both countries were such that this group had achieved little political importance on the higher levels of politics. In England during the seventeenth century the bourgeoisie had won considerable power as well as recognition of their interests, so that they were, by and large, reasonably satisfied with their position in society.

The relations between the peasants and the land were also somewhat different from one section of Europe to another. Again on the continent France was most advanced in the direction of the new emerging society. Beyond the Elbe the peasants tended to be serfs, too much under the control of their lords to conceive of a more equitable situation. In the Lowlands, the Rhineland, and central Germany, the patterns of France were reproduced in varying degrees, while in Italy and Spain the landlord's control was almost as complete as it was in the East. England again was a special case. Throughout the eighteenth century the English landlords were in the process of buying out or squeezing out the yeomanly class of peasant landowners, and as a result England had a large landless group of rural poor. This landless group migrated to North America as indentured servants, filled poorhouses, and provided a labor supply for the industrialists who were experimenting with mass production methods in textiles and metallurgy, but they were in no position to start a revolution without bourgeois assistance, and that was simply not available.

The lot of the urban artisan class of the rest of Europe also somewhat resembled the situation in France. Like the French workers, they were organized in guilds or corporations that were no longer the semidemocratic institutions developed by medieval Europe. However, even though these artisans and the beggar-laborer class of the cities might be available for a popular uprising, without leadership from the bourgeoisie they were incapable of developing a revolution on their own or even of urging reform.

Thus, throughout Europe there were sociopolitical problems inherent in the fact that European society had already been in existence for over a thousand years, and that many social patterns had become almost fossilized. The tensions that give dynamic force to European history seem to result from the struggle between the tendency of society to form stationary, almost immovable social classes and the inevitable forces of change at work in a society with a growing population and an expanding economy. At the end of the eighteenth century the princes of Europe were trying to come to grips with this problem, but before they had done much toward solving it a revolution broke out in France. This revolution not only readjusted the socioeconomic patterns of Europe, but also opened up a whole series of new political problems with which men had to grapple.

Jacques Louis David, "The Tennis Court Oath" (Paris, The Louvre).

Chapter 27

REFORM AND REVOLUTION

1. ENLIGHTENED DESPOTISM: A REFORM MOVEMENT

The student's first introduction to the study of European history is often a frustrating experience because the same problems seem to reappear unsolved at each stage of the story. The whole history of the rise of modern Europe could be told in terms of the gradual breakdown or, perhaps, evolution from feudal institutions. Yet were it so told, the story would seem endlessly repetitious, for when did the forms characteristic of the Middle Ages actually disappear? The answer is, of course, that some of them still exist. Likewise the story could be explained in terms of the unfolding of the modern state, and yet at each period of the state's history the student will discover that what seems to be a mature development is only the beginning of the next phase of an ongoing process. Thus, an historian of medieval Europe finds in the early fourteenth century a mature society, and often speaks of it as the period of decline of the Middle Ages, while the historian of the seventeenth century sees the same fourteenth century as a seed bed for the development of the period of his interest.

In this history the reader has been introduced to successive phases of the process that was forming the modern world. Medieval kings joined hands with city dwellers to fight feudal anarchy. Renaissance princes consolidated their power by using condottieri troops, Roman law, dynastic politics, and other such "tools" for the integration of their realms. Seventeenth-century rulers subdued the great lords and the estates, created military and civil bureaucracies, police power, and courts, and set the pattern for the reforms of the eighteenth-century enlightened despots. Nevertheless, despite this imposing progress, at the end of the eighteenth century the ancient patterns of life still continued in large segments of society. Land ownership, traditional systems of cultivation, labor and rent contracts, time-honored and often fossilized tolls, tariffs, and taxes, and old laws and customs: these were the very fabric of life for the majority of the people, and they were tenacious, conservative forces in society. Thus, in spite of the new patterns of commerce, industry, and finance, new systems of government, diplomacy, and war, and even new classes in society, much of eighteenth-century Europe had resisted the processes of change.

However, in that century men did become more conscious of the problems that confronted them. The *philosophes* "understood" that change meant progress; the commercial, industrial, and financial bourgeoisie recognized change as essential to their prosperity; and the advisers of kings, digesting the experience of enlightened rulers like Louis XIV, came to see change as essential to political development. Of these three groups, the *philosophes* had the clearest voice, but the bourgeoisie and the rulers were still in possession of the realities of power. It was this self-consciousness about the process of change that produced the movement known as enlightened despotism. The intellectual usually likes to credit the *philosophes* with being the driving force behind this movement, and if their propaganda is taken at face value, it is easy enough to assign this important role to them. The great political theorists of the eighteenth century—Locke, Montesquieu, and Rousseau—tried to examine political life without having recourse to any supernatural force. Thus, the justification for any government had to rest upon purely human and earthly grounds.

Monarchs continued to call themselves kings by the grace of God, and to be anointed and consecrated with religious rites, but it was becoming increasingly clear that enlightened men regarded such ceremonies as mere pomp. The real justification for a government had to be established in terms of its service to the community. John Locke had separated power (the ability to govern) from authority (the right to govern), and endowed the ruler with the one and his people with the other. As his doctrine gained converts, enlightened men increasingly expected their rulers to govern in the general interest, for if they did not, the people retained the right to remove their governors (i.e., revolution).

The *philosophes* did not stop by pointing out that princes must recognize their duty to society. Once men understood that change was a process of development, their economic and political interests as well as their ethical values became guideposts for that change. Thus the so-called "Enlighten-ment" came to bear upon the process of politics. The majority of the *philosophes* were rationalists who believed that it might be possible to discover the laws governing political life just as Newton had established laws governing the stars. While none of them was anxious to overthrow the existing order, they were nonetheless critical of the many abuses and irregularities that plagued eighteenth-century society. As we have seen, they were critical of the cumbersome and unfair tax structure, the brutal legal and penal system, the existence of serfdom and slavery, and the care given to the insane and the sick. This first stirring of humanitarianism was fundamentally based on the "liberal" assumption that all men had a certain basic dignity and rights as a part of their membership in the human race. However, such an idea did not imply any democratic presuppositions that all men also have a right to a voice in public affairs.

In politics, the majority of the *philosophes* were firm believers in despotism. Like the princes, they looked back to the first twenty-five years of Louis XIV's regime to see how royal power could be used to eradicate certain evils, and even though many of them wished to replace Colbert's program of regulations with a program of freedom, they nonetheless approved the idea that government should extirpate evils. Somehow they assumed that an absolute despot, if he were properly instructed, might rationalize society and give man a government that would end abuses. This belief that the political world was a "machine" that would work well if the laws were discovered and rigorously applied later gave men faith in the idea that they could write a constitution for a society and expect it to function. The words of a Rousseau speaking about law as something engraved in the human heart were not able to penetrate such a mechanistic notion that even Rousseau seemed at times to share.

There was a company of princes in the latter eighteenth century that professed to believe in and to act upon the teachings of the Enlightenment. Of these so-called "enlightened despots" Frederick II of Prussia was unquestionably the most famous, both in his day and later, but Catherine II of Russia, Joseph II of Austria, and a coterie of lesser lights in Spain, Portugal, Tuscany, and Scandinavia also posed as disciples of the Enlightenment, and several of them actually tried to govern their lands in the spirit of the age.

There were numerous "stock" reform programs that seemed to provide important work for kings. Legal and court reforms, administrative reorganization, the reduction or abolition of unreasonable tolls, tariffs, and other regulations of commerce and industry, and land reforms that would relieve the peasantry and provide incentives—these were projects that could be profitably followed. Draining marshes, clearing forests, building roads and harbor facilities, and other public works, the creation of banking and credit facilities, and the patronage of schools were further opportunities for royal activity.

However, on looking closely at the actual accomplishment of the enlightened despots, it becomes apparent that their programs were largely determined by the traditions and past history of their states, rather than by the teachings of the *philosophes* or even the example of the Sun King. Frederick the Great (1740–1786), for example, was most successful when he followed in the footsteps of his father (Frederick William I, 1713–1740) and great-grandfather (the Great Elector, 1640–1688). Frederick II well deserved the title of enlightened despot for his insistence upon efficient and honest government, for his preoccupation with the prosperity of his kingdom (so that it could produce more tax revenue), and for his wise and tolerant administration of justice. Even more than Louis XIV, he deserved the title of which he was most proud—first servant of the state. Like his illustrious forebears, he actually administered his kingdom himself as if it were a business or a farm controlled by a patriarch.

All the same, Frederick was guided by no abstract notions about brotherhood or equality of man or of liberty. His forefathers had developed a state out of the unpromising array of provinces they had inherited, and the needs of that state were enough to satisfy Frederick as the taproot of policy. Thus, he engaged in wars for the conquest of Silesia that bled his people almost white; he joined his neighbors in the first partition of Poland (1772) to extend his holdings and assure land contact between Prussia and his provinces inside the Holy Roman Empire; and he maintained an army far out of proportion to the number of subjects who were expected to support it. No one can claim that his measures were ineffective or futile, but they were motivated by reasons that were completely divorced from the reforming ideals that were supposed to direct the work of the enlightened despot.

Catherine II of Russia (1762–1796) was even more cynically in line with the traditions of Russia rather than with the preachments of the *philosophes.* Her "enlightened despotism" completed the process that reduced the Russian peasantry to complete serfdom and gave power without responsibility to the landowning nobility. Her foreign policy followed the expansionist program marked out by Peter I, while her administrative and fiscal reforms were more in the spirit of Ivan IV and Peter I (the Great) than in that of Louis XIV. Yet Catherine patronized the *philosophes,* and like Peter the Great before her, encouraged Russian propaganda in Europe to conceal the true situation in her kingdom. It would be quite unjust to label all of Catherine's "westernizing" reforms mere "dust in the eye" to hide the essential Russian society from the foreigner; they were more of the same kind and in the same spirit as the reforms that Russian rulers from Ivan II to Stalin have tried to impose upon the burgeoning society of Russia. The central problem in Russia was deeply rooted in geography and history. There were no natural frontiers, and yet expansion only aggravated the problem of organizing government for so large an area. Catherine, like her predecessors and successors, sought to expand to defensible frontiers and to strengthen the power of the central authority of the state.

The royal reformer who most clearly tried to put into effect the notions of the *philosophes* was Joseph II of Austria (1765–1790). He had been his mother's (Maria Theresa) associate some years before he became ruler in his own right, but she had restrained his urge to reorganize their ramshackle assortment of kingdoms and provinces. After her death (1780) Joseph embarked upon a program of land and legal reform. Almost overnight the serfs were freed, land laws liberalized, administrative organization rationalized, court systems overhauled, and the church severely restricted in its sphere of activity. "Liberty and equality" seems to have been as much the slogan of Joseph II as of the French revolutionaries, but Joseph applied his "rational" program without reference to reality. The Hapsburg inheritance was not a state in the modern sense of the word, but rather a confederation of states (the Danubian monarchy, the Netherlands, and north Italy) and even though a rationalist might believe they could be treated alike, they simply could not be so treated. Hungary, Italy, the Netherlands, Bohemia, and German Austria represented at least five different traditions, and Joseph's reforms brought all of them either to rebellion or the point of rebellion against the prince whose principal aim was to give them good government. Reforms inevitably hurt the interests of many people who had benefited from the inequalities and injustices. Joseph tried to make reforms without eradicating the social groups (nobles and clergymen) who benefited from the status quo. On his death he left his brother a host of problems and the best military organization that the Danubian monarchy had ever had. Leopold II (1790–1792) liquidated most of Joseph's reforms; his son, Francis II (1792–1806) found use for the army in the wars against the French Revolution.

In Spain, Portugal, and elsewhere in Europe rulers tried more or less successfully to imitate the examples of enlightened despotism set by Louis XIV a century earlier and by Frederick II in their own time. In general it should be noted that the real problems involving social organization could not be solved because the princes were in no position to abolish the privileges and inequalities that made the creation of a rational state difficult. Even Joseph was unwilling to use force against the landlords; he soon discovered, moreover, that they did not hesitate to fight when he tried to cut down their privileges. Likewise, a thoroughgoing legal reform was next to impossible anywhere in Europe because traditional forms and rights had too many defenders to be easily swept aside. Thus, enlightened despotism was successful only when it introduced reforms that patched up the machinery of government to make it more efficient, and removed merely the most crying abuses in society.

However, contemporaries did not draw the same conclusions that we do in the twentieth century. To them it seemed that an enlightened prince like Frederick was actually framing the constitution of his realm in accordance with the natural law, or, if not that, discovering the law and applying it. It is small wonder that such men were able to place great faith in the idea that men could frame a constitution for society. The experience of the thirteen colonies in North America seemed to give added credence to this notion. In France after 1789 men tried to draw up a constitution that would put an end to the problems of the kingdom; that story is one of the most dramatic and instructive in the history of western Europe.

2. ENLIGHTENED DESPOTISM IN FRANCE: LOUIS XVI

When his grandfather died in 1774, Louis XVI (1774–1792) mounted the throne of France. Although not yet twenty years old, this young prince seemed to many Frenchmen to be the hope of the kingdom. His predecessor, Louis XV, had also started his rule in an aura of hope and optimism, but his indecisiveness, his inability either to attract or to retain strong men in his service, his general unwillingness to accept the responsibilities of his office, and the fact that his reign saw two disastrous wars, had all combined to make men forget that Louis XV had once been called "the well beloved." Therefore, Louis XVI could look for inspiration to the reign of Louis XIV, "the Great," or Louis XIII, "the Just," rather than to that of his own grandfather. Those two monarchs had been enlightened kings served by strong men; their reigns had given meaning to the idea of monarchy, as well as a constitution for France.

The young king, however, possessed little of the stern tenacity of Louis XIII or of the grand vision of the "Sun King"; he was a genial man who loved his wife and family and enjoyed working with his hands. He had a sturdy religious conscience that told him the difference between right and wrong, but he was not strong enough to carry out a real reform program based on such moral considerations. Nor was his wife, Marie Antoinette, the right woman to make him into a grand monarch. She was a frivolous lady given to romantic notions suitable to the rococo civilization in which she lived, but utterly unprepared to act as a queen or to help her husband govern the kingdom in time of crisis. Both of them played the royal role best when they were executed as traitors rather than when they sat upon their thrones; like many of their generation, even though they did not know how to govern, they knew how to die "nobly."

When Louis XVI came to the throne he wanted desperately to succeed in the high office to which he had been called. He, too, wished to be an enlightened despot. His first ministry, headed by an old man who had been disgraced by Madame de Pompadour, was supposed to be a reform government, and the presence of Turgot as controller of the treasury seemed to promise success. Turgot had already made a great reputation both as an administrator (he had been an extremely successful intendant at Limoges) and as a writer (he was one of the physiocrat economists). Like Sully and Colbert before him, Turgot gave most of his attention to the problems of efficiency and honesty in the treasury. He liberalized some of the regulations governing commerce and manufacturing, but he could hardly be accused of developing a revolutionary program. However, no French finance minister could long govern the treasury without discovering that the privileged nobles and clergy did not contribute their share to the support of the government. Once Turgot made that discovery, he soon accumulated a sackful of enemies.

His substitution of a money tax payable by all landowners instead of the traditional *corvée* evoked a tempest of protests. Did Turgot think that he could, by implication, impose "road work" on noblemen and clergymen? He was dismissed on May 12, 1776. The queen wanted to send him to the Bastille. His parting words to Louis XVI are said to have been: "Never forget, Sire, that it was weakness that brought the head of Charles I to the block."

Necker, a Swiss banker who had achieved a great reputation as a philosopher and financier, followed Turgot. Since he was a foreigner, he did not became a full-fledged minister. His policy was a return to the regulations of Colbert, but he never had a real chance to demonstrate how his program might work for France drifted into the War of American Independence and soon became the principal financial supporter of the entire coalition. Necker's enemies point out that by 1781 he had increased the national debt by six hundred million livres; they somehow failed to add that the war had something to do with the debt. Necker left power with even more enemies than Turgot had acquired because of the publication of the *compte rendu,* the first frank analysis of the French budget. This book became a best seller, and soon everyone knew of the pensions, gifts, and extravagances of the great nobles at court. It was easy for men who had little real conception of the total mechanics of government to see the scandalous financial situation of Versailles as the real root of all the trouble in the kingdom. Naturally those who had been exposed resented the man who had disclosed their greedy assaults on the king's treasury. From Necker's dismissal onward, the government of Louis XVI lived on borrowed time.

There was one other finance minister who had the ability necessary to see the problem clearly, but he did not dare attack it because of the fate of his predecessors. Calonne, called in 1783 from the office of intendant at Lille, made a desperate effort to increase the revenue of the treasury by stimulating business in the kingdom. He came to power just at the time when the economic crisis that was soon to overwhelm the kingdom was beginning to strangle commerce and manufacturing. From the 1780's onward these periodic "depressions" became characteristic features of European economic life. Calonne, like a number of statesmen after him, tried to solve the crisis by borrowing money and "priming the pump" of the economy. For a program of deficit finance to function there must be substantial confidence in the fiscal stability of the regime; and such confidence could be acquired only if the government is able to tax all the potential sources of revenue. Calonne recognized these facts, but any measures that he proposed inevitably encountered the opposition of the privileged. Both the *parlement* and the court were opposed to reforms that might invade their traditional privileges.

In 1786 Calonne proposed a general land tax on all property, without any exceptions. He linked this proposal with a program according freedom of commerce in grain, the suppression of interior tariffs, and the establishment of provincial assemblies elected by all taxpayers without distinction of class. This was a revolutionary program achieving at one blow liberty of commerce, equality of men before the tax collector, and, by implication, the equality of all landowners no matter who their fathers might have been. Had he been able to count on the support of the king, Calonne might have achieved his program, but Louis XVI was not the man for that particular job. Instead of imposing Calonne's program on the kingdom as an act of royal will, Louis presented his proposals to an "assembly of notables." Since they were chosen and appointed by the king, it might have been expected that they would have been as subservient as the "assemblies of notables" that Richelieu and Louis XIII had used as sounding boards for their policies. However Louis XVI did not let Calonne tell his assembly what was wanted; he asked their advice. Since the men of the Assembly were all *privilégiés*— noblemen, clergy, parlementarians, and officials—they could hardly be expected to be enthusiastic over a program that would annihilate many privileges and reduce all the well-to-do to the bourgeois class. The "assembly of notables" side-stepped the king's requests by demanding that he call an Estates-General to consider the condition of the kingdom, and was dissolved (May 1787).

The *Parlement* of Paris was scarcely more helpful. It allowed the king to free the grain trade of regulations, but declared the land tax unconstitutional. Then, when the king exiled two of its members, the *Parlement* also condemned the king's *lettres de cachet*[1] in the name of individual liberty. The *Parlement* took up the refrain that the king should call an Estates-General. When Louis suppressed the *Parlement* of Paris, the provincial *Parlements* became centers of similar agitation that occasionally flared up into violence, such as the "day of the tiles" when the citizens of Grenoble attacked the royal troops with their roof tiles.

Thus the privileged classes, acting through an "assembly of notables" and the *Parlements,* refused to accept any alteration in their privileges. Somehow they conceived the idea that they could use the political crisis to recapture the authority and influence that their ancestors had enjoyed before the rise of the Bourbon bureaucratic-police state. They believed that they could return to the situation as it was before 1615, when the last Estates-General had been dissolved. At that time the clergy, the nobles, and the third estate had almost been in a position to control the kingdom, with the first two orders holding the balance of power. Neither the parliamentarians nor the nobles and great clergymen seemed to realize the changes that had taken place in French society since 1615.

---

[1] The *lettres de cachet* allowed the king arbitrarily to arrest or exile any person without giving cause. This instrument of absolutism was mostly used at the request of fathers who could not control their sons and appealed to the king to help them enforce discipline by putting the young men in jail for a while, but it was also used to impose the royal will on other occasions.

Thus by 1788 Louis XVI, as an "enlightened despot," had reached a point of crisis. Turgot, Necker, and finally Calonne had been repudiated by the privileged classes as soon as they had attempted to invade their privileges, and Louis XVI had been incapable of supporting any of his financiers. Joseph II of Austria had encountered revolts because he had attempted reforms without first pulling the teeth of potential opposition; Louis XVI was never able to introduce real reforms because he could not face up to the power of the privileged classes who would suffer from them.

On their side, the privileged nobility, clergy, and magistrates who used the power of the court, the "assembly of notables," and the *Parlement* against reforming ministers, little understood that their demand for the convocation of an Estates-General would accomplish what they most feared, namely, the destruction of their privileges along with the destruction of the ancient forms of the monarchy. The next "enlightened despot" to sit on the throne of France was destined to be a soldier, the Emperor Napoleon, who was placed there by the forces which were released when Louis XVI called the Estates-General of 1789.

3. THE RELEASE OF REVOLUTIONARY FORCES IN FRANCE

The year 1788 was an unfortunate one for the privileged classes to pick as the year of their revolt. In the 170-odd years since the last Estates-General had been called, the bourgeois class had grown greatly in numbers, wealth, maturity, ambitions, and hostility toward their "social betters." They could no longer be depended upon to send magistrates and city officials to represent them in an Estates-General. Furthermore, they could count upon the support of the peasantry and artisans in any contest of power with the privileged classes. This was especially true in 1788-1789, when an economic crisis seriously threatened the livelihood of the artisans, peasants, and petty bourgeoisie and tended to concentrate the wrath of the poor and the oppressed against the privileged ones.

The problem of the economic crisis of 1788-1789 was complicated. Calonne's policy of freeing the grain trade had envisaged a rise in the price of bread as a sure way to encourage the introduction of better agricultural methods. Economists had long recognized that controls on the price of grain had had a stagnating effect on agriculture. This policy of "expensive bread" might have had the desired results if the harvest had been normal, but in 1788 hail, high winds, and drought combined to produce a poor crop. The result was that the price of wheat went up fifty percent between 1787 and 1789; the price of rye, the mainstay of the people, mounted one hundred percent in the same period. The price of vegetables and wine, which also were in short supply, followed that of bread.

It might be thought that farmers would benefit from such a rise in prices, but the contrary was true for a majority of the French peasants. An ordinary crop yield rarely left them much grain to sell after they had paid the church, the lord, and the state. When the crops failed, these dues still had to be paid, and paid out of grain that was needed for keeping the peasants' own families alive. The peasantry had long harbored grievances against the nobles and the clergy, but when hunger stalked the villages those grievances were fanned into hatred.

The rise in the price of bread also had disastrous effects on urban economy. Bread had normally accounted for about half a worker's salary, and when it mounted skyward, the workers were soon in distress. Nor did their problems end with the rising bread prices. Agriculture was the principal industry of France, and so when it got into trouble, other industries soon felt the effects; these were aggravated by the fact that in 1786 the government had signed a treaty with England reducing tariffs on textiles and hardware in an effort to sell more French wines, brandies, and grain in England. Thus, just when the French market was restricted by agricultural distress, French producers of textiles and hardware had to meet competition with England. Widespread unemployment among the workers arose in 1789, and continued for the next three years.

The other group to be hit hard by the economic depression was the petty bourgeoisie—the host of little shopkeepers who eked out a living in normal times, but whose financial resources were too slim to carry them over any severe economic strain. There were hundreds of such people in every small town, in every quarter of the larger cities, and they were literally being forced into bankruptcy by the depression.

Both in the country and in the towns men had only the vaguest notions about the economic order that was in derangement. Like many human beings in distress, they struck about for someone or something to blame. Freedom of the grain traffic, the trade treaty, the disorder in the royal finances, the insistence upon collection of taxes and talk of new ones, even a scandal involving the queen, a high prelate, and a necklace—such occurrences made it evident that the government was to blame, while the exactions of the nobility and the church made it equally clear that the privileged classes were to blame. This economic crisis and the feelings that went with it were exactly contemporary with the politico-financial crisis facing the government of Louis XVI.

Louis XVI could not evade the convocation of an Estates-General, but what was that institution? Everyone knew that it was representative of the orders in the kingdom: the clergy, the nobility, and the third estate, but men were uncertain about what it would do or how it would function. The last meeting, held in 1614–1615, had ended in frustration. The three orders had been at loggerheads with one another, and all of them had appealed to the royal authority to save the kingdom. During the "War of the Three Henrys" in the sixteenth century, an Estates-General, dominated by the Catholic League, had threatened to depose the last Valois king and settle the succession on the House of Guise. Obviously Louis XVI and his ministers wanted no such revolutionary body. There were further questions. How many deputies should be elected? How should they be elected? How should they be seated? What provisions should be made to insure some sort of action? That is, should decisions be unanimously voted by all three houses, by a simple majority of the houses, or should all three orders sit together and vote as individuals rather than as orders? By pamphlet and by oral discussion, France, as well as the king's government, discussed these problems, and in the process began to organize the machinery that was to give rise to the Revolution of 1789.

The privileged classes, the nobility, and upper ranks of the clergy had one answer that tied all of the questions into a neat little knot. They insisted that the three orders must sit in three "houses" and deliberate separately; any action must be approved by all three before it could become law. If this proposition were granted, the other questions were meaningless. It would not matter how deputies were elected or how many there were—the privileged classes would have a veto on any action that might threaten their interests. Taken all together, the *privilégiés* were but a small percentage of the population (about two percent), but their pretensions were great and their demands highly vocal. It was not long before they were known as the "aristocrats," and another party, the "patriots," quickly appeared to oppose their program.

The patriot party arose almost by magic. In the flood of pamphlets, many loud voices echoed the ideas presented by Abbé Siéyès in his *What is the Third Estate?* It is everything, or should be everything, was his conclusion, and a strong body of opinion was prepared to insist that this conclusion be respected. By recognizing the "patriot" demand that the third estate should have as many members as the other two estates combined, the government seemed momentarily to agree with the patriot party. The king ordered the election of three hundred clergymen, three hundred nobles, and six hundred deputies to the third estate.

The most important result of all this discussion was the rise of "clubs" in every town of France. These "clubs" were often former reading or literary societies; some of them were new creations, but all acted as molders of public opinion, and in due time they became virtual rulers of their communities. Here the enlightened bourgeoisie studied their interests, and by exchanging journals, pamphlets, and letters, as well as speakers, they became a network of "cells" of the patriot party covering the whole kingdom. They dominated the elections to the Estates-General, and they avidly followed the political problems that developed at Versailles when that body met. It was the clubs, with the printers who published their pronouncements and their pamphlets, which were the very backbone of the Revolution.

The other important group affected by the movement of ideas were the French troops of the royal army. Naturally the foreign soldiers, mostly Swiss, were unaffected, but the French troops, quartered with the general urban population, could not be quarantined against the bourgeois propaganda, and they soon learned that their interests and those of the patriot party were similar. Their own aristocratic officers were in no position to convince them otherwise. Mutinies in the army occurred before the assault on the Bastille, as evidence that the soldiers were preparing themselves for their role. A picture of the storming of the Bastille made at the time shows clearly what everyone knew, namely, that without the military muscle of the soldiers, the bourgeoisie would have had some trouble imposing their will upon the king's government.

However, the elections for and the discussions of the coming meeting of the Estates-General gave no clue to the stormy events that were to come after 1789. France still believed itself to be profoundly loyal to its king. If the *cahiers*[2] are to be trusted, the deputies went to Versailles to secure the redress of specific grievances, not to initiate a revolution. Yet the first act of those deputies was not to adjust grievances, but to start a revolution.

The Estates-General first met on May 4, 1789, but the question of seating prevented all action. The nobles insisted upon seating separately by orders; the third estate refused to consider anything but seating in a single body and voting as individuals. From May 4 to June 27 this argument went back and forth, and in the course of the discussions the patriots' position hardened to the belief that the only possible solution was to unite the three houses in one. With the king and the aristocratic party against them, a large segment of the third estate, supported by some of the minor clergy and a few liberal nobles, on June 17 declared themselves to constitute a National Assembly and took an oath on June 20 not to disband until they had written a constitution for the kingdom. This "tennis court oath," so called because of the building in which the deputies were assembled, may be said to be the formal beginning of the Revolution. Seven days later Louis XVI reluctantly ordered the Estates-General to meet as a single body—thereby admitting that it had in effect become the National Assembly.

In the next two months the patriot party indelibly imposed its will upon the kingdom. Whether Louis XVI and the aristocrats actually planned to use force to dissolve the Assembly is at best an academic question, since the people of Paris were in any event convinced that they intended to do so. In the "official" French republican historical tradition, there is no doubt about

---

[2] The *cahiers* were the instructions drawn up at the time of the elections to guide the deputies when they reached Versailles.

the evil intention of the king, but this "official" story may well contain an element of myth. There are good reasons for believing that Louis XVI had no intention of molesting the deputies, and that the whole story of the "royal plot" for July 1789 was the fabrication of political activists in Paris. It was not difficult to stir up the population of Paris; like the rest of France, they followed the debates in Versailles, and if pamphlets, posters, and street orators are any indication, the city was completely in favor of the patriots. As early as June there were mutterings about a massacre of the nobles; by July, feeling against the aristocrats was running high, and it was a simple matter for political activists to convince the mob that the third estate was in danger from the king's troops.

The first two weeks of July 1789 were decisive in Paris. News from Versailles reached the city a few hours after events, and was quickly "interpreted" by soapbox orators and pamphleteers. The Duke of Orléans, in the traditional pattern of the king's relatives who were so often the leaders of rebellions, opened the gardens of his palace in Paris to the crowds, and supplied the orators with inside information direct from the court. He was a slippery, ambitious character; in the course of the next few years he took the name *Philippe Égalité,* to attract favor with the revolutionaries, but was unable to keep his head in the later stages of the Terror. It may have been at his suggestion that the people were told that the king planned to use troops against the Assembly. However, it was not simply political events that ruffled tempers in the city. Economic need sorely afflicted the poorer people, so much so that every outbreak, upon close examination, seems to have started over bread rather than politics. The politically minded agitators had, therefore, an excellent seed bed for their propaganda. From the first of July to the middle of the month the city erupted almost daily. The French guards mutinied, the crowd battled with cavalry, the bread shops were pilfered, the Convent of Saint Lazare was pillaged for grain, the Invalides and the gun shops were forced to provide weapons, and finally, on July 14, the great royal fortress, the Bastille, was stormed and forced to surrender. In popular mythology these events have been covered by a sort of heroic mist that any careful examination quickly dispels. Nonetheless, these two weeks of violence in Paris forced the king to recognize the National Assembly, acted as a tocsin for similar violence all over the kingdom of France, and started the Revolution on its way.

Provincial France may not have needed the example of Paris to start revolt. All through June there were stories of riots in provincial cities over bread, at the toll and tariff stations over taxes or movement of grain, and at city gates over food. In rural areas, many of the peasants believed that the grievances they had put into the *cahiers* must surely be adjusted, and so even before July 1 there were stories of peasants refusing to pay feudal dues, killing partridge, and ignoring the commands of the noble's bailiff. When the

Bastille fell these events multiplied many times over. Who knows how they were directed? They seem to have emanated from several "centers" in the countryside, but the total action was quite uneven, for some districts remained at peace while others were shaken by violence. Historical research, however, has not been able to discover the authors of the peasant revolt.

It is hard to sum up the hundreds of events, even though as a whole they form a pretty solid picture. In the cities and towns the old governmental officials were simply chased out of office, and in their places "elected" officers took over the government. Behind these acts there was usually a bourgeois club or council that acted as a general staff, as well as directing agent for the rebellion. In the country the peasants were seized with a "great fear of brigands and evil men," but the object of their attack was usually the château where the records of their taxes and debts were kept. All over France the partisans of violence had a field day, and the government and police were paralyzed.

The first acts of the Revolution in Paris were the creation of a new government, the Commune, and a new military force, the National Guard. The new mayor of Paris, Bailly, was an important member of the patriot party; the commander of the new citizen army was Lafayette, the friend of Washington, soon to be called, ironically, the "hero of two worlds." The National Guard in Paris and the provinces swelled to a million strong, and was the bourgeois "janissary" corps; its rank and file were petty merchants and professional people who elected their own officers and stood ready to defend the interests of liberty and property against all comers. Lafayette had a romantic vision of himself as the power behind the throne, and hoped to use these citizen soldiers to establish himself as the indispensable man.

As the Revolution extended to the provinces, the Guard and the Commune tended to repeat themselves from town to town, so that there arose in the French kingdom hundreds of little "republics," each with its own government, its own soldiers, and its own directing "club of the Revolution." The old officials gave up their places usually without a struggle; the new officials took over the *Hôtel de Ville* ("the town hall"), and cleared the way for a government in the interest of the bourgeoisie. It was not long before the town and city communes, feeling isolated as units, began to federate with other communes in their neighborhood. By 1790 this movement of federation had become nationwide. The Revolution was in the process of making the kingdom of France into the French nation; these federations and the fêtes held to celebrate their progress were considered to be an indication of the brotherhood and the fraternity of Frenchmen.

It did not take long for the news of provincial violence to filter to Versailles: every courtier brought fresh stories of flaming châteaux, of urban rebellion. The National Assembly could not afford to ignore the movement of the people if it wished to continue to be their leader. The result was the great renunciation of August 4, 1789, when representatives of the nobility, the privileged towns, corporations, and provinces gave up the privileges that they had heretofore so tenaciously defended. While this drama seemed to be a spontaneous movement, it had actually been carefully planned in advance by a group of the deputies at the Breton Club that had decided that something had to be done. The peasants were in revolt against the feudal order; therefore, the Assembly had to abolish it. But, as good bourgeoisie, they also wanted to ensure the rights of property. Many of the nobles, thoroughly frightened by the events of the month, were willing to go along with them to cut their losses. They willingly surrendered some of their feudal rights to secure their other property rights. Thus, though the "night of renunciation" seemed to abolish all the rural grievances, when the peasants actually examined the decrees they discovered that they were expected to "buy" the nobles' property rights after all. In the emotional upsurge that ran through the Assembly as the privileged classes dramatically renounced their special rights, the fact that they did not intend to give up their property rights as well had somehow been overlooked.

Nonetheless, no matter what had been the intention of the actors, the "night of renunciation" ended the feudal regime. The hunting and fishing rights of the nobility disappeared. Serfdom was abolished without indemnity. The tithe was suppressed. All positions in the church, army, and administration were thrown open to every citizen, and the sale of offices was prohibited. Justice was henceforth to be free, and a new system of courts was promised. These were the more important of a whole series of social, economic, and political reforms outlined by the decrees that followed August 4. In theory they ended the regime of privilege, and instituted one of civic and social equality. It was now up to the National Assembly to prepare a constitution and other basic laws that would implement the spirit of the movement that had led to the outbursts of violence.

There was one further upsurge of violence in October 1789, when a crowd of women seeking bread turned into a mob of men, women, and children that marched in the rain to Versailles. Lafayette and the Parisian National Guard arrived on the heels of the mob and restored order. However, the next day violence broke out that almost involved the queen, and the final result of the whole disturbance was that the king, his family, and the National Assembly returned to Paris with the crowds. The Parisians sang that they had brought "the baker, the baker's wife, and the baker's child" home with them. They had done much more than that; they had brought both the king and the Assembly under the menace of the Parisian crowds.

4. A CONSTITUTION FOR FRANCE

Between the late summer of 1789 and the fall of 1791, the National Assembly was the spirit as well as the directing force of the French government. For the most part, particularly after the mob forced them to come to Paris in October, 1789, Louis XVI and his ministers had little or no voice in the direction of affairs, and actually did not try to assume any power. There was no more violence after the October march on Versailles. The harvests of 1789 were reasonably good, tax collections virtually came to an end, and grievances against the feudal system were satisfied. Thus, the causes of mob action were temporarily removed. This did not mean, however, that either problems or friction were ended, or that party strife was much abated.

In those two years the Assembly wrote a constitution for France, six important points of which are worth considering: (1) the bill of rights, (2) the royal veto, (3) the suffrage, (4) the system of local government, (5) the financial rehabilitation of the kingdom, and (6) the civil constitution for the clergy. All six of these problems still remained in one form or another as big questions for the government that came to power in 1791. They were not easy to solve.

The "Declaration of the Rights of Man and the Citizen" (August 22, 1789) was hardly more than a promise of what men might hope to achieve, but at least it was a declaration of the aspirations of the bourgeois society of the eighteenth century. English and American precedents helped to guide its framers in announcing that "all men are born and remain free and equal in rights." Fears of the consequences of so radical a statement made the remainder of the document into an abridgement or perhaps a definition of this equality of rights. The final document was a considerably more radical statement than the draft reported by the committee, for the house as a whole, still under the influence of the dramatic and violent events of July, was willing to believe that human rights and property rights need not be in conflict with each other. Thus, while the "Declaration of the Rights of Man" may have appeared revolutionary to a society based on special privileges, it was not a document which was intended to endanger the economic fabric of social life.

The next great problem was to discover a suitable balance between legislative and executive power. The Assembly early rejected the idea of creating an upper chamber as a balance wheel in government, for such a chamber might easily become the refuge of the aristocrats and the tool of royal authority. But what were to be the relations between the king and the unicameral legislature? If the king had no veto, then the legislature could do whatever it wanted without any check or balance. On the other hand, if the king were given absolute veto power, the acts of the legislature would become little more than petitions. The Assembly solved this dilemma by endowing the king with a suspensive veto. His will could force a delay of any measure for four years (two legislative sessions), but could not prevent it entirely. Inevitably a man like Louis XVI would use this veto in a matter of conscience, and equally as inevitably the use of that veto would enrage the radicals who would see him as a reactionary blocking their path.

The problem of the suffrage made the Assembly pause. Few in the latter eighteenth century could conceive of universal manhood suffrage; the ignorant, illiterate masses were simply not to be trusted. Yet how could men speak of equality of rights, and then restrict the right to vote? This Assembly was more liberal in its interpretation of the right to vote than later post-revolutionary constitutions of France which provided for limited monarchy (1815 and 1830), but it fell considerably short of granting universal suffrage. The adult males were divided into "active" and "passive" citizens on the basis of their places on the tax rolls. Some four million Frenchmen were given the right to vote; some two million "passive" citizens were left without a vote. Women, of course, were not eligible to vote. The electoral laws provided further restrictions on eligibility for candidacy. A person could vote if he paid a tax equal to three days' wages, but to be a candidate for the legislature, a man must pay a tax equal to fifty days' wages (the "silver mark"), and possess landed property. These suffrage regulations, less liberal than the ones that had governed the elections to the Estates-General, assured bourgeois control over future governments, and it was this that was the principal concern of the framers.

The system of local government under the former regime had been centered on an intendant, appointed by the king. The revolutionary upsurge of July-August 1789 had eradicated this centralized control and created elected communal governments. The Assembly sought to extend this system by a complete reorganization of the country. In place of the old provinces they divided France into eighty-odd departments of about equal size. These were vaguely reminiscent of the *géneralité* of the former regime, but by giving them names connected with rivers, mountains, and so forth, the departments appeared as new creations. These new departments were supposed to have no connection with the old provinces. Frenchmen were to be Frenchmen—not Provençals, Lorrainers, and so on. The departments were divided into districts and communes. At each level the new government provided for an elective council and elected local officials; this was a complete reversal of the old centralized government. It failed utterly, because there was no way to make contact between the petty republics at the bottom of the scale and the central government in Paris, especially in an era when many of those elected could not even sign their own names. Later regimes established officials who were responsible to the central government in positions of power at the department level.

The problems of financial disorder were most pressing, and became increasingly difficult each month. Old taxes were abrogated, and new ones simply not paid because there was no machinery to enforce collection. The king and his ministers did nothing to help; the Assembly seemed unable to grapple with the problem. What was needed was some source for large amounts of money that could be collected without endangering the rights of property. The lands of the church provided just such a source. The church as a corporation did not have the same property rights possessed by an individual. In a sense, the church's property was a sort of social property, held in trust by the clergy rather than belonging to them. It was not hard to persuade the Assembly that this property should be confiscated. The monastic houses were dissolved after "appropriate" provision had been made for their inmates, and the rest of the church property confiscated after assuring the clergy that the state would assume responsibility for their salaries.

Land and buildings, however, are not media of exchange. The confiscation may have given the Assembly about twenty percent of the land of France, but it did not provide ready money. After several essays at a solution, the Assembly printed paper money, the *assignats,* which were declared legal tender. Since they could be used to purchase church lands, they had real and immediate value. According to the law, the *assignats* were to be burned after being exchanged for land. Several years later the *assignats,* enormously multiplied in number, had become worthless paper; nineteenth-century historians assumed, therefore, that the whole experiment had been a fiasco. Such an assumption is hardly warranted in light of the fact that the *assignats* provided the financial muscle to fight a great war. Twentieth-century men, with broader experience than their forefathers, recognize paper money as a military-economic weapon.

The confiscation of the church property made it necessary to provide for the clergy under state control. The general spirit of the eighteenth century favored such a program even if it had not been financially necessary. The enlightened despot, Joseph II of Austria, tried reforms of the church organization; and it is not surprising to see the National Assembly also attempted to give more rational form to church government. The Civil Constitution of the Clergy was the result. As it was finally passed, it became the source of the most important conflict between Louis XVI and the Assembly; it was also the legislation that divided France into two camps. The "enlightened bourgeoisie" may have been convinced that religion was superstition. Nonetheless, there were millions of Frenchmen who did not agree with them. If anyone wants to understand how shallow an impression the deists and anticlericals had made by 1789, he only needs to study the problem of religious loyalty as it developed in the decade following 1791; most Frenchmen proved unwilling to give up the consolations of the traditional church.

On the surface the civil constitution of the clergy did not interfere with questions of dogma or ritual. It was an attempt to provide a new government and new financial support for the church. Bishops and priests were to be paid by the state. The former suffered severe cuts in income, while stipends for priests were substantially raised. Both bishops and priests were, henceforth, to be elected rather than appointed, and they were forbidden to seek papal authorization for their offices. This was more independence from Rome than any program heretofore proposed, yet it was not the Gallicanism desired by the upper levels of the French clergy who wanted to retain control over the church in clerical hands. When the Assembly decided that the clergy, like all other officers of the state, must take an oath of fidelity to the Constitution, clerical opposition to the Civil Constitution of the Clergy became apparent. Only a few bishops, including Talleyrand, Bishop of Autun, and rather less than half the parish priests were willing to take the oath. Talleyrand may have consecrated new bishops, and new priests may have been ordained, but good Catholics had a strong suspicion that all was not well, a suspicion fully confirmed when Pope Pius VI finally condemned the whole arrangement.

In addition to political measures, the National Assembly also grappled with reforms of the economic order. In general, the deputies were well grounded in the economic teachings of the physiocrats and Adam Smith that could be summed up in the expression, *"laissez faire, laissez passer."*[3] However, in the enormously complex pattern of French society in 1789 it proved impossible to remove all restrictions, even if the Assembly had wished to do so. In general, however, the measures were in the direction of liberty. The corporations (guilds) lost their privileges, the great trading companies lost their monopolies, and the interior tolls and tariffs were abolished. The Assembly piously affirmed that there were no interests except the general good and the rights of individuals, and therefore forbade "combinations" of either workers or employers. The major problem of translating this system of economic freedom into law was left to the jurists who compiled the commercial code.

By the time the National Assembly had completed the basic laws for a constitutional monarchy, many of the problems inherent in such a fabrication had come to the surface for all to see. Perhaps the most important of these was the conflict between Louis XVI and the Revolution that sought to make him into a constitutional monarch. When the Bastille fell in July 1789 Louis donned the tricolor hat of the Revolution, but a number of his friends, including his brothers, quietly left France. As we have seen, Louis with his queen and the dauphin moved from Versailles to Paris on the demand of the crowd, but more of the high-ranking nobility left the country to agitate against the Revolution in Germany, Italy, and Spain. Louis watched the Asssembly remake the status of the crown without enthusiasm for the results, but when the Civil Constitution of the Clergy brought his conscience and his religious faith into the issue, he decided to follow the other *émigrés*

---

[3] No interference with commerce or trade; literally, "allow to make; allow to pass" (on the road).

across the frontier where it might be possible to enlist military support to destroy the work of the Revolution.

Louis' flight was almost successful. He was recognized and detained at Varennes (June 1791) within sight of a frontier that promised him freedom. The king's flight clarified the political confusion that had been building up for two years. The partisans of constitutional monarchy suddenly found themselves without a king they could depend on; no one who knew what had happened placed any faith in the story that the king had been "kidnapped." The radicals who directed the most important political club in Paris, the Jacobins, saw their vision of a "royal Jacobin" on the throne vanish, and overnight they became republicans. The conservatives who had pinned their faith on the monarchy were equally in a quandary; they must soon decide whether the king or the Revolution was more important to them. However, the obvious fact was that the Constitution of 1791, which had taken three years of labor, was a dead letter almost from the hour that it went into effect. A legislative body, provided for by the Constitution, was elected and met on October 1, 1791. Its term lasted less than a year. When it became clear that Louis XVI was not to be an "enlightened constitutional despot" directed by the "enlightened bourgeoisie," some other solution for the political crisis had to be found.

Jacques Louis David, "Death of Marat." David's drawing was a Pietà for the Revolutionary propaganda. (French Cultural Services)

Chapter 28

THE DEVELOPMENT OF
THE REVOLUTION

1. EUROPE AND THE REVOLUTION

Goethe may have sung about the throb of his pulse when he heard about the Revolution in Paris and the "Rights of Man," but the mass of Europeans —the princes and the people—knew little and understood less of events in Paris in the summer of 1789. Here and there isolated groups met and lauded the work of the National Assembly. A Doctor Price in England made a speech that was to become famous only because Burke used it as a whipping boy in his famous attack on the Revolution. In Brussels and several other cities in the Lowlands and the Rhineland, "clubs" on the French model came into existence; and out in Königsberg, the philosopher Kant hailed the new regime as a sign of the future; but none of these people was able and few of them were willing to try to initiate a similar revolution in their own land. The "United States of the Netherlands" formed in Belgium was a rebellion against the reforms of Joseph II rather than an imitation of the American Republic or the French Revolution, and it collapsed completely within a year of its origin.

Public opinion in the latter eighteenth century could not easily be mobilized. The press was only for a select few who could afford such expensive reading material, and it was not always very informative about political affairs; since most of the people who read the papers had little to do with the course of politics, the press had no obligation to keep its readers abreast of the times. Therefore it is not surprising to find that the significance of the Revolution in France was not immediately apparent to the majority of the reasonably enlightened people of Europe, to say nothing of the ignorant masses. Before the decade was over, however, a great number of Europeans were to be affected by the Revolution, and were to be forced willy-nilly to reach some conclusions about it.

The princes were blinded to the situation in France by the eighteenth-century system of international organization. By 1789 Europe was governed by a "balance of power," but not by a "concert," of Europe. Princes tended to see the affairs of neighboring states in terms of the possibilities thereby offered for their own interests. Thus, in 1790 Leopold II of Austria, who was at war with the Ottoman Empire, did not seriously contemplate giving aid to his sister, Marie Antoinette, when she and her husband got into difficulties with their "loyal" subjects. He was persuaded to make a declaration against the revolutionaries (at Pillnitz, 1791), but his threat of intervention was qualified by a huge "if" (*alors, et, dans ce cas*), so that it meant nothing at all. In fact, even though all the eastern monarchs (Prussia, Austria, and Russia) cordially disliked the "hydra with one thousand, two hundred heads," as Catherine II of Russia called the Assembly, they were more interested in their own affairs than in the problems of Louis XVI. Who in 1790 or 1791 could have understood that the Revolution in France was so different from earlier uprisings? Revolts in the past had resulted in weakening the affected state, not in the development of aggressive imperialism that threatened neighboring powers.

The Revolution had obviously weakened France, and the German powers regarded this as a signal for their own expansion. Both Poland and France could now be partitioned. Here was an opportunity to recapture Alsace-Lorraine which the French had "stolen" earlier from the Houses of Hapsburg and Lorraine, now happily united in the person of Leopold II. Here also was an opportunity to make another partition of Poland. In 1772 Russia, Austria, and Prussia had detached parts of the anarchic, disorganized Polish kingdom; between 1792 and 1795 they divided up the rest between themselves. This bold-faced robbery of territory could be accomplished only when Poland's natural ally, France, was momentarily incapacitated. Thus, instead of seeing the Revolution in Paris-Versailles as a movement that would eventually topple thrones, the eastern princes regarded it as a boon.

The Revolution, however, did not permit Europe to remain totally unaware of its dynamics. After July 1789 the *émigrés* from France, headed by the king's own brothers, were everywhere preaching the danger of the French revolutionary "infection." They were probably not given more attention than the world usually gives to *émigrés*, but at least they were an articulate group trying to explain the dangerous movement that had driven them from their homelands. Soon their voices were seconded by those of another group of men with a legal complaint against the Revolution. Alsace was a province of the French king, but the great treaties of the seventeenth century had not completely separated it from the Holy Roman Empire. Hence its bishops and many of its noblemen regarded the emperor as the final legal authority. When the Revolution deprived the clergy of all their property and the noblemen of their feudal rights, they appealed to Leopold

II as Holy Roman Emperor to secure redress. The position of the papal state of Avignon was a further source of complaint. Since 1417 the popes had lived at Rome and governed Avignon as a distant province. Papal government was mild, and the province was reasonably prosperous; as long as France lived under a similar political and social order no problem arose between France and this papal enclave. However, the Revolution could not be stopped at the Avignon "frontier," and soon a revolutionary group in Avignon was clamoring for revolutionary reforms and annexation to France. Whether or not papal "rights" would thus be violated did not bother the revolutionaries. The fact that His Holiness refused to accept either the Civil Constitution of the Clergy or the fundamental liberal philosophy of the Revolution made it easier for them to annex Avignon, but in the eyes of Europe the annexation branded the Revolution as an expansionist, aggressive movement.

Thus by 1791 there had arisen a number of problems, although none of them necessarily implied military action. In fact, when Louis XVI went to the Assembly and formally accepted the Constitution of 1791, Leopold II seemed to sigh with relief; there no longer appeared to be any reason for intervention if Louis and the Assembly had made peace. Edmund Burke[1] in England may have understood that the Parisians were on the verge of upsetting Europe, but no one else seemed to perceive that fact.

2. THE REVOLUTIONARY MACHINE AND THE WAR PARTY

Even if Europe was largely blind to what was happening in France, the revolutionary machinery that was destined to upset the apparent tranquillity of the western world had begun to assume firm outlines. At the very heart of that machinery were the two thousand-odd political clubs scattered throughout the French kingdom. Most of them had become federated under the leadership of the Jacobin Club[2] of Paris. There were many other clubs, but the Jacobins early outdistanced and in some cases absorbed their rivals. At one time or another nearly all the important figures of the Revolution, from Lafayette to Robespierre, belonged to the Jacobins. However, after the patriots had won their initial victory over the aristocrats, the club became increasingly radical, and groups broke off from it to form new clubs—the

[1] Edmund Burke wrote his *Reflections on the French Revolution* (1790) as an attack on the "rationalistic" conception of politics demonstrated by the Revolution. This occasionally long-winded but brilliant analysis has become a classic both because of the grandeur of Burke's style and the vigor of his political thought. It is almost unbelievable that it could have been written as early as 1790.

[2] Its real name was the Society of Friends of the Constitution; it was called Jacobin because the Paris Club met in the library of the Parisian Jacobin monastery.

Feuillants, for example—so that by 1792 the clubs bore some resemblance to political parties.

The revolutionary clubs came to be run by a relatively small group of politicians who possessed oratorical skill to sway the members, and political patience equal to the task of organization. That is to say that the clubs soon fell into the hands of professional politicians, often enough lawyers without many clients. As a group, these men were mostly petty bourgeoisie and therefore easily became "radicals" in a monarchical society. They saw no difficulty in dispensing with the king, even though most of France was monarchist; they knew "their Rousseau, their Montesquieu, their Locke"; they "understood" the American Revolution and the English revolutions of the preceding century. They were rationalists who never questioned the possibility that it might not be wise to try to overthrow the history and tradition of the nation and to start relatively afresh. Like revolutionaries at all times, they grew to "know what ought to be done," and ruthlessly proceeded to do it regardless of the consequences. Unfortunately for France and for Europe, the reactionaries who opposed them were equally doctrinaire in their belief that they, too, knew the will of God, and curiously His will very often coincided with their own property interests.

Revolutionary propaganda was also spread by dozens of ephemeral newspapers. Marat's *Friend of the People* may now be the most famous, but *La Bouche de Fer* ("Iron Mouth"), the *Journal de la Société de 1789* (by Condorcet), the *Courier de Versailles,* the reactionaries' *Actes des Apôtres* ("Acts of the Apostles"), and dozens of others carried the word from many tongues to the people. To these more or less established newspapers must be added hundreds of pamphlets that poured off the presses, in which men with or without ideas unburdened themselves for the benefit of their fellow citizens. As the Revolution moved forward, and especially after war broke out between France and Europe, only the radical Jacobin voices continued to be heard. This, too, seems to be characteristic of revolution; the minority of activists that gain control over the political machinery cannot tolerate dissenting opinion. They may have posed as liberals at the beginning, but their "liberalism" did not include "liberty" for their opponents.

Another important method of advertising the ideals of the Revolution was the public festival. Every possible occasion provided a stage for oratory and pageantry. The great anniversaries of the Revolution gave Paris a chance for parades, fireworks, speeches, and elaborate tableaux, but these were only the most important of many such public displays. The pageantry of these public festivals recalled the great displays of the days of Louis XIV. The church (as long as it supported the Revolution), the National Guard, the army, the organized clubs—all were represented in the tableaux of fireworks and papier-mâché. These "festivals of the nation" may well be evidence of the "religious" character of the nationalistic sentiment that was developing. How

effective these patriotic displays were in stimulating patriotism and enthusiasm among the people cannot be measured, but their repetition shows that
the leaders at least thought that they were useful.

Thus by 1791 the movement that had started with the "revolt of the privileged classes" had created a political machine to control the nation. Like any
such movement in any land, there were many politicians standing by ex-
pectantly in the hope of imposing their own views on the nation and gaining
riches and fame as political leaders. These politicians ranged from the Marquis de Lafayette, who envisioned himself as mayor of the Palace, through
such moderate revolutionaries of noble extraction as Barnave and Dupont, to
men like the Girondins, who were really radical republicans, and finally to
the groups that were to control the Jacobin Club after 1793 and were to make
the word "Jacobin" mean radical democratic republicanism. This latter
group, the Robespierres, the St. Justs, and their colleagues were the men who
developed the Terror as an instrument of republican policy. In 1791, however,
there still remained a whole year of fumbling by the Legislative Assembly
before the radical parties emerged from the wings to take over the leading
roles in the drama.

The Legislative Assembly elected in 1791 was composed entirely of new
faces, since one of the last acts of the National Assembly had been to rule
that none of its members could be elected to the first legislature assembled
under the Constitution of 1791. Naturally the new men arrived anxious to
make good, but the fact that the king was no longer to be trusted, that friction existed between France and the rest of Europe, and that the institutions
provided for by the Constitution obviously needed revision boded ill for the
life of this Assembly. Furthermore, in the preceding two years literate France
had been discussing constitutions. The members of the Legislative Assembly
would hardly have been "normal" if they had not developed some ideas about
the framing of a constitution that they would like to write into law.

The Legislative Assembly very soon came into conflict with the king over
problems that arose out of the Civil Constitution of the Clergy. The church
could hardly be expected to approve a law that deprived the clergy of their
property, abolished monastic foundations, and upset traditional lines of authority. Yet Pope Pius VI held back a condemnation until it became clear
that the revolutionaries had no intention of meeting his objections even half
way. In the meantime, the National Assembly had commenced action against
priests who refused to take the oath to support the Constitution. Thus in the
spring of 1791, when Pope Pius VI condemned the measure, there were already two kinds of clergymen in France: those who would support the Civil
Constitution (juring) and those who would not (nonjuring). The pope
excommunicated the one group; the state outlawed the other. Louis XVI
had a strong conscience that would not allow him to support clergymen
whose ministrations might send men to hell. He vetoed a bill of the Legisla-

tive Assembly compelling nonjuring priests either to take the oath or face expulsion. The juring clergymen, by their oath, sacrificed their right to act in the name of the church of Rome.

The religious question was soon overshadowed by foreign affairs. When an internal crisis becomes acute, many people see a possible solution in a war that will allow a readjustment of power. Louis and his queen came to believe that the only solution to the Revolution was a war in which France would be defeated and the revolutionary politicians discredited. To this end they conspired with the queen's relatives in Vienna. There were others in France who also thought that a war might serve their interests. They fell into two approximate groups. The first was the radical party called the Brissotins, after one of their leaders, or the Girondins, because so many of them came from the Gironde (one of the departments). The leaders (Brissot, Vergniaud, Guadet, Ducas, and others) were really republicans; they had no confidence in Louis XVI, and they firmly believed that France, perhaps assisted by Prussia, could easily defeat Austria. Such a war would make the king declare himself either for or against the Revolution. The other war party was that of the *Feuillants* led by Lafayette, Barnave, Lameth, and Dupont. These men were conservative nobles, constitutional royalists, many of whom had had experience in America. They believed that a war would give them control over the army and, if necessary, they could then force a coup d'état to establish a regime satisfactory to their own interests and ideals. The queen, who also wanted war, was sure that her brother's army would march on Paris and re-establish the monarchy. Only a small group of Jacobin deputies led by Robespierre, who was not a deputy himself, opposed the idea of war. Robespierre was certain that a war would result in catastrophe for the Revolution.

The pretext for war was the presence of the *émigrés* in the Rhineland. They not only propagandized against the Revolution, but were also building up a small army to start a civil war. The war party in the Assembly practically forced Louis to send the electoral bishop of Trier an ultimatum giving him a month's grace to expel and disperse the *émigrés*. Leopold II of Austria persuaded the elector to yield, and then notified France that he considered the incident closed, but added that if France should attack Trier, he would defend the province. Leopold clearly wanted peace; he also wanted security, for he made a defensive treaty with Prussia which abandoned Poland to Russo-Prussian partition in return for possible help against France. He might have staved off the war, but he died on March 1, 1792, and his more aggressive and adventurous son, Francis II, became emperor.

The revolutionary government in Paris was determined not to be reasonable. Narbonne, the foreign minister, and Dumouriez, the war minister, threw their weight behind the Girondist war party in the Assembly. Provocative notes were addressed to Francis II; then an ultimatum; and, finally, on April 20 Louis XVI proposed and the Assembly declared war on "the king of Hungary and Bohemia."

3. THE WAR EXTENDS THE REVOLUTION

Somehow everyone in the Legislative Assembly except a few of the radical Jacobins believed that winning the war would be easy. They had assumed that Prussia, as her traditional ally, would join France, and that the Austrian army would not present serious opposition. However, the Prussians joined Austria, and the Austrian army actually proved to be as good or better than the Prussian. Francis II and his advisers had equally unrealistic assumptions. The *émigrés* and secret letters from the court in Paris had convinced them that the war would be a military parade, that France and the French army waited only for a chance to surrender to the "defenders of monarchy." Both suppositions were false, and in exposing the errors of those judgments, the course of events worked havoc on the men who so optimistically and light-heartedly went to war.

The Revolution had taken its toll of the French army; by 1792 more than half its high-ranking officers had migrated, and Jacobin propaganda in the ranks had caused serious breaches of discipline. Yet the army was potentially a formidable instrument. The military reforms of the preceding two decades had given France the best artillery in Europe and had reformed the basic drill with emphasis upon speed rather than spit-and-polish precision; a Prussian army might be able to march over a plowed field without disturbing the line, but a French regiment could move from column to line and back again more quickly than the ponderous Prussians. In fact, the loss of over half of its officers did not prove particularly harmful to the French army. Of Napoleon's twenty-five marshals, nineteen had belonged to the pre-Revolutionary army, nine as officers, ten as non-commissioned officers or privates, and only six had been civilians in 1789. In other words, the human material to command the army was also available and already in the ranks, even though the emigration seemed to have wrecked the organization of command. Lastly, the Revolution introduced a new spirit in the army. Henceforth French soldiers were fighting for their fatherland and for the ideology of their revolution. When the volunteers and later the conscripts learned the art of war from the regulars, they gave to the whole army a tone and a morale unknown to the German regiments that opposed them.

However, in 1792 the faults rather than the virtues of the French military machine were apparent, partly because of the inexperienced command and partly because of the disorderly political structure in Paris. The king did not want to win; many of the highest officers lost the conviction that they could win; the soldiers in the ranks had no confidence in their commanders, and many of them deserted in the face of the enemy. Furthermore, the Girondist war party was deprived of office when the first campaign failed. The result was frustration that convinced the radical party that the king and his government were all traitors. Robespierre, who had opposed the war, called for the summary punishment of the defeated commanders. The commanders blamed the troops. The king and his queen were in actual contact with the enemy, and had undoubtedly committed treason. When the Assembly declared the fatherland in danger on July 11, 1792, it was indeed in peril.

Out of this confusion emerged a plot to overthrow the constitutional monarchy and to create a republic. Economic conditions in the form of a hungry Parisian mob placed a dynamic force into the hands of the plotters. There were several reasons for the scarcity of bread in Paris during August and September 1792. The harvest had been scanty, and had not at that time been turned into flour. The war had dislocated the economy both by funneling supplies toward the frontier and by forcing the government to print more *assignats* to finance the struggle. As a result, the *assignats* rapidly lost value, and France experienced an inflationary spiral that further dislocated the economy. Taken together these factors resulted in the renewal of bread riots similar to those of 1789. It would be folly to describe the French Revolution as a movement caused by economic distress, but it would be even greater folly to tell the story without mentioning the fact that people were moved to violence by hunger as well as by politics.

The plotters who took advantage of these conditions were a group of Parisian politicians in the poorer sections[3] of the city. While they used the machinery of Parisian city government to achieve their objectives, they were also closely linked with the radical party in the Jacobin Club. Thus Danton, Robespierre, Marat, and others may not have been directly responsible for the Parisian uprising of August 10, 1792, yet they were surely not without some part in it.

If a spur were needed to speed up their movement, it was provided by the July 25 manifesto of the Duke of Brunswick, the commander of the Prussian army. Neither the Duke who signed the manifesto, nor Louis XVI who had requested some sort of a statement from the invaders, had anything to do with its actual text, nor did either of them approve of it. A simple-minded *émigré* nobleman had drafted it and no one had had enough political sense to recognize the stupidity of publishing it. The manifesto proclaimed the allies' intention to re-establish Louis XVI with full powers, and threatened the military destruction of Paris if any harm came to the royal family. It was useless for Louis to disavow the document; no one believed him, and bad news from the front convinced the French that Brunswick would make

---

[3] Paris was divided into forty-eight sections or wards, each with a popularly elected "assembly." These assemblies became political clubs, and, in federating, became instruments of power.

good his threat if they did not act quickly. Thus the war begun by revolution became a powerful impetus for expanding the revolutionary action.

Late in June 1792 a crowd had broken into the Tuileries palace, perhaps to "warm up" for the grand "day." On August 10 the people stormed into the palace again, and this time they were acting in accordance with a well coordinated plan. The Parisian radicals were reinforced by a large number of provincials, national guardsmen, and *fédérés* who had come to Paris for the festival of July 14 and who had remained there for just such an emergency. The Jacobins were thus armed and supported by several groups with political convictions as well as by the hungry Parisian mob as they stormed the palace. At the last moment, the commander of the Paris National Guard, loyal to the king, was removed and murdered so that one of the plotters could take his place. Thus the king was without adequate military protection when the crowds attacked. His Swiss guards fought valiantly; the king and his family sought refuge in the Assembly. The crowd massacred everyone caught defending the king, as well as some Parisian porters who had the misfortune to be called "Swiss." By a simple act of mob violence the monarchy and with it the Constitution of 1791 had been overthrown. The Legislative Assembly suspended Louis XVI, and ordered the election of a National Convention to formulate a new constitution and to defend France against her enemies.

Between August 10 and the convocation of the National Convention on September 22, 1792, the provisional government was practically impotent. Early in September there occurred a series of lynchings and jail deliveries known as the September massacres, which were too well organized to be spontaneous uprisings. The National Guard was about to depart for the front to try to stem the Prussian advance. Longwy had fallen, then Verdun; the road to Paris was open. Could the patriots go out to defend the fatherland, leaving traitors, mostly priests who would not take the oath, behind to undo their heroic work? The radicals gave their answer in the week following September 2 by murdering, with only the semblance of a trial, priests and noblemen in the prisons and, if they caught them, on the streets. In their enthusiasm the butchers also murdered petty thieves and prostitutes who happened to be in prison. A similar outbreak of mob savagery swept through the provincial towns, giving France and the world a foretaste of the Terror. Much has been written in the past to excuse these gory massacres, but it is no longer fashionable to defend the actions of the "cannibals."

On September 20, 1792, a cannonade at Valmy dramatically reversed the fortunes of the war. Like the battle of the Marne in 1914, the Battle of Valmy was not really a battle. The French artillerymen convinced the Duke of Brunswick that they had the superior power, and so in good eighteenth-century tradition, the Duke ordered retreat rather than fight. There were several reasons for the failure of the invading army: military inefficiency and torrential rains that separated the flour, the bake ovens, and the Prussian troops; dysentery caused by ripe grapes (Goethe tells the story amusingly); and, finally, the enterprise and skill of their French antagonists. Although French historians rarely mention it, there was one other element of chance in the picture. At the very moment that Brunswick was retreating, another splendid Prussian army was occupying a large section of Poland. These Polish provinces had been the price of the Austro-Prussian alliance. The troops that occupied them, if they had been used in the west, might well have occupied Paris. However, no matter what were the reasons, the cannonade at Valmy ended the danger to the fatherland, and the National Convention that met for the first time the next day could now decide what face the French Revolution should assume.

4. THE CONVENTION AND THE REPUBLIC OF VIRTUE

When the Convention which had been elected in 1792 met, it was obvious that only revolutionary France was represented there. Electors with other ideas stayed away from the polls under threats from the patriots. However, although all the members were revolutionaries, they were not all in full agreement about policy. Political parties, as we know them, did not exist, but there were three reasonably well defined groups in the Convention.

The first was the Girondin deputies who now emerged as moderate republicans, representative of the interests of the wealthy, provincial bourgeoisie, and suspicious of the influence of the city of Paris, as well as of the radical leveling tendencies that were developing in the Jacobin clubs. The Girondists had urged the prosecution of the war and were anxious to carry it forward; they were shocked at the excesses of the September massacres and hopeful that they could check the democratic tendencies that were developing among the extremists. The second group was the Jacobins or the Mountain (so called because they sat on the high benches on the left). Although many of these men were almost identical in social origins with the Girondins, following Robespierre they had opposed the war, but once engaged, they, too, avidly supported it. Their political program might be called radical republicanism, but as the economic crisis deepened, they also became willing to support the radical economic measures of the Parisian artisans and workers. They accepted the September massacres and the Terror as a legitimate means of destroying their enemies of the Revolution. Each of these extremist groups had less than two hundred members; the bulk of the deputies to the convention, called the Plain or the "Marsh," sat between them, and joined first the Girondins, then the Jacobins, and, finally, after the vigorous and sometimes violent leaders had died, took over the government machine and made it their own. Most of the members of the "Plain" had been elected earlier either to the Estates-General of 1789 or to the Legislative Assembly of 1791; they were bourgeois revolutionaries, many of them anxious to feather their own nests, as well as to make France safe for the middle class. They were the men who directed or at least supported the main development of the Revolution from 1790 to 1814.

Outside the Convention were other important political groups. The Parisian politicians and journalists who had engineered both the attack on the Tuileries and the September massacres belonged to and controlled the Cordelier Club, the radical section assemblies, and the Commune of Paris. As their followers found it increasingly difficult to get bread, one group came to be called "The Enraged Ones," because of their social radicalism. Marxist historians have pondered many documents about those Parisian *sans-culottes* (the long trousers worn by the honest working class revolutionaries gave them their name—under their covering, all legs became equal!) in an effort to make them their own—to portray them as early communists. Their success has been at best mediocre.

In the provinces the political situation was most confusing. There were the *fédérés,* who had been responsible for the first revolution in local government and now wished that France would become a simple federation of independent communes. Such an idea would have been fatal to the war effort and was completely unacceptable to the Jacobins who knew their Rousseau. The Jacobins were also of importance in the provinces; every town had its club dominated by the republican activists, and when the Jacobins finally got control over the Convention, these clubs virtually became organs of government. In the provinces, too, there was all manner of opinion, ranging from conservative monarchist to the most radical revolutionary activist, with the result that the problems that developed in Paris were often re-echoed there with amplification.

The first months of the Convention were simplified by the victories of the republican armies. Although the overthrow of the monarchy and the September massacres had resulted in new desertions among officers with blue blood in their veins, the French army took the initiative after Valmy and cleared the Austro-Prussians out of the Netherlands, Rhineland, and Savoy. In these conquered provinces revolutionary clubs promptly appeared, demanding that the provinces be annexed to France.

The Convention took up this gambit quickly, voting the "propaganda decrees" which turned the French armies into "liberators," agents of a peoples' "crusade against aristocrats and kings." This move was soon followed by outright annexations that attempted to impose the revolutionary laws as well as the depreciated *assignats* on the peoples beyond the French frontier. Unfortunately for the men in Paris, the facts could not exactly mirror their beautiful propaganda blasts. To wage war costs money, no matter whether it is for "liberation" or "aggression" or both, and practical men were soon trying to make the "liberated" people pay for their share. Besides, "liberation" in the Rhineland was not just what it seemed to be in

Paris; not everyone there welcomed the foreign soldiers, and even fewer people welcomed the inflated French currency. The result was that before they had occupied their neighbors' territory for long, the French Jacobins were in conflict with the people as well as with the latter's erstwhile masters.

Europe became acutely aware of the threat to monarchical institutions when the revolutionaries cut off the head of the French king; the "crusade against aristocrats and kings" thus became a grim reality. There was little chance that the king could have been saved, even if his accusers had not found papers in a secret safe that proved he had been in contact with France's enemy. The basic assumption behind the attack on the palace on August 10 was that the king was a traitor; his suspension from office had come before his enemies had real proof of his guilt. However, the Gironde party in the Convention attempted to save Louis' life by postponing the trial, by suggesting that the nation be consulted, and by other maneuvers. They believed that only by saving the king could the Revolution make peace with Europe. The Jacobin-Mountainards were not to be balked; they insisted upon a trial and pushed through a verdict of guilty by 387 to 334 votes, a motion to postpone the execution was defeated by 380 to 310. The next day, January 21, 1793, Louis XVI was guillotined. In the Terror that followed the queen and many of the important, as well as the insignificant, noblemen and clergymen were beheaded; the guillotine was overworked in an effort to eradicate treason. When noblemen were no longer available, the guillotine consumed the men who had instituted the Revolution.

Revolutionary "imperialism" and the execution of Louis XVI brought most of Europe to the support of Austria and Prussia. Had this first coalition been directed so that the entire military force of its members could have been applied against France, it might well have resulted in the overthrow of the Revolution; but Prussia, Russia, and Austria were also engaged in partitioning Poland, a problem that occupied most of their best troops. The eastern powers were every bit as interested in aggrandizing themselves as they were in checking the spread of revolution. England was ruled by men who were still convinced that money rather than blood could win wars, and who were actually using some of her best officers in India, where the East India Company in cooperation with the English government was conquering an empire. Neither Spain nor the Italian states could bring great pressure to bear on France. Even so, in spite of disorganization within the coalition, the tide of battle again turned against France in the first months of 1793.

When the armies of the coalition regained the offensive, the situation in Paris became critical. General Dumouriez's[4] treasonous actions made each

---

[4] Dumouriez went over to the enemy when he decided that the Jacobin politicians in the Netherlands were undoing the Revolution by their excesses. First he tried to get the army to follow him back to Paris to restore order; when that failed, he deserted.

man fearful of his neighbor. Dumouriez's friends, the Girondins, became particularly open to suspicion, and with them any officer or politician who had any connection with the nobility. When the Convention called for a levy of soldiers, trouble broke out in the provinces where peasants and provincials inspired by religious, political, and economic motives refused to support the Convention, and in several places even raised the flag of revolt. Added to the threats from without and civil rebellion at home was a mounting economic crisis that created shortages of bread in Paris. Invasion, treason, civil rebellion, and economic distress: these were the problems facing the Convention in 1793.

From the very beginning of the Convention the Girondin and Jacobin parties had been rivals for power, and at first the majority of the center or Plain tended to support the Girondins who were less radical and violent than their opponents. However, as the crisis deepened, and the treason committed by trusted officers seemed to question all men's integrity, the Girondins began to slip from favor. It was, though, the radical politicians of the city of Paris, rather than any deliberations by the Convention, who finally determined their fall. The same people who had engineered the attack on the royal palace that dethroned the king and the September massacres that so shocked the world, turned the Paris masses against the Girondins. The Convention, threatened by the crowds that invaded the hall and blocked all the exits, voted to purge the Girondins and to place the Jacobin leaders in power. This was not to be the last time that Paris imposed its will upon "representatives of the people" without consulting the wishes of the rest of France.

It was manifestly impossible for the Convention to present France with a new constitution while the country was in mortal danger, so it assumed the responsibility for governing the nation, suppressing rebellions, and conducting the war. In the summer of 1793 the revolutionary political machine of the Convention came into being; it took the form of two committees: those of Public Safety and General Security.

The Committee of Public Safety was the real driving force. Established in March 1793, by the late summer of the same year it had developed into an effective war agency or cabinet, and as long as its twelve members worked together in relative harmony, it was able to govern France. The Committee of Public Safety drafted decrees, recruited and supplied soldiers, and sent "Deputies on Mission" to watch generals, govern provincial France, and carry out the dozens of tasks which had formerly been performed by Louis XVI's intendants. The Committee of General Security was a police and justice agency to ferret out treason and to try people suspected of treason. It was one of the principal agencies of the Terror. The Convention passed a "law of suspects" that gave wide powers to the revolutionary tribunal to act against traitors and prospective traitors.

Of the men who manned these committees during the critical years of 1793–1794, Robespierre is the most famous—perhaps because he was an articulate preacher of the Jacobin "religious cult;" or because, having less work to do than most of his colleagues, he could talk more; or because his enemies tried to make him the sole author of all the wickedness of the Terror after they had accomplished his downfall. The other eleven men, however, were important; several of them much more significant in regard to the conduct of the war than Robespierre. The distinguished American scholar Leo Gershoy has written of them: "All were well educated, all were experienced and capable. Their sincerity and devotion to their cause were uncontested. All were scrupulously honest and, with unlimited opportunities for corrupt practices, remained poor and above considerations of personal profit." The war, treason, and economic distress had brought these men to power; their own backgrounds, their ideas about politics, their skill as leaders of men and organizers of affairs, and their conceptions of their role as saviors of society both introduced the Terror with its Jacobin-Rousseau-istic religious implications, and defeated or contained the internal enemies of the regime and also the foreign armies of the First Coalition.

The Terror in its first instance was merely the natural continuation of the September massacres. The decree that the fatherland was "in danger" led to the execution of those traitors and other enemies who might strike from behind. "The Law of Suspects," however, was so loosely drawn up and later instructions to the Committee on Public Security so vague that it was easy to make almost anyone into a suspect, and from that point on it was hard for the victim to avoid the verdict of "guilty." Guilt by association tarred many; anyone born a noble or ever consecrated a priest was in danger of being a "suspect." Men who talked loosely or complained openly, men who critized the conduct of affairs, friends of soldiers like Lafayette or, later, Dumouriez, were under suspicion. Many innocent people were guillotined on the slightest pretext as the Revolution protected itself from potential internal enemies.

Then the Terror became a political weapon as well. Party opposition was silenced by the guillotine. First, the leaders of the constitutional monarchists were either driven into exile or executed; then the Girondins, as moderate republicans, were persecuted; finally, the Jacobins themselves furnished victims for the Terror. By 1794 any opposition to the policy of the ruling clique had come to be regarded as treason. Thus Danton and his friends, moderate Jacobins who wanted to check the Terror, as well as Hébert, Desmoulins, several members of the Cordelier Club, and radicals from the Paris sections were condemned to death; in all cases the charges assumed that these opponents of the regime were inspired and paid by foreigners. Only after having seen Stalin's Terror in the 1930's and the pathologically suspicious fears that haunted post-1945 Russia does the French Terror become credible. The fanatics were convinced that any opposition was inspired by their monarchist enemies.

The Terror went even further. The men whom history had thrown to the pinnacle of power were simon-pure Jacobins. As Professor Brinton has so brilliantly and convincingly argued,[5] their thoughts were grounded as much in theological assumptions as in political ones. The whole revolutionary movement had been building up toward the substitution of some kind of deism for Catholicism. Under the Terror this "Cult of Pure Reason" with its God of Nature, its public festivals (as obligatory as attendance at mass had been), and its conceptions of required virtue, blossomed into full bloom. It was an arid business to anyone but a true believer. Robespierre's "sermons" at the Jacobin Club and at public festivals must have been as good as any of that type of literature, yet to anyone not completely immersed in a theological mysticism they sound hollow and uninspired. His articles of faith, the existence of a supreme being and the immortality of the human soul somehow lacked the color that had surrounded Catholic worship, and yet sounded like superstition to more confirmed skeptics. When to the religious cult was also added the Jacobin conception of Rousseauist political theory, the use of Terror to achieve the Republic of Virtue becomes understandable. They somehow failed to grasp what Rousseau had to say about law, custom, and historical process, but they did seize upon his notion that men should be forced "to be free," that is, be forced to will the General Will. Since these fanatics, like "true believers" of twentieth-century political cults, were convinced that they knew the General Will, they had no scruples in using the guillotine as a broom with which to clean up society. It was this phase of the Terror that turned the guillotine against harlots, profiteers, grafters, and other malefactors. The Parisian crowds cried out for victims who could be blamed for the economic distress; the guillotine claimed them. It was apparently to be the symbol of virtue and civic righteousness.

Were the Terror the sole outcome of the rule of the Committees of Public Safety and General Security in 1793–1794, the Jacobin movement would stand utterly condemned by French and European historians. The government, however, did more than behead its internal enemies; it also defeated the enemies of France in the field. In 1793 with rebellion flaring up in many parts of France, with a royalist army waging a full-fledged civil war in the Vendée (Western France), and with Austrian, Prussian, English, and Spanish armies pressing on French frontiers, it seemed as though the revolutionary experiment would receive short shrift. The defeat of these dreaded enemies was the work of the government of the Terror. Carnot, who earned the title "organizer of victory," stands out as one of the most important

[5] Crane Brinton, *A Decade of Revolution, 1789–1799*, New York, Harper, 1934.

members of the Committee of Public Safety, but he was only one of the twelve who worked to supply arms, train men, and direct the over-all strategy of the war, as well as to handle foreign affairs, administer the country, and see that Paris was fed. To the twelve must also be added the dozens of deputies on mission, some of whom carried the Terror to the provinces, some of whom were venal, some efficient, some of whom were stern believers who drove France and her military power to victories that saved the republic.

Several Marxist historians have attempted to make Robespierre and the Committee of Public Safety into socialist politicians, because they were willing to interfere with free trade in grain and the so-called "laws of supply and demand" for the necessities of life. Their efforts were doomed to fail, for the revolutionaries were all bourgeois at heart, most of them petty bourgeoisie in spirit and action. It was the necessities of the hour—the threats of the hungry Parisian mob and the insistence of the radical Parisian politicians who had helped to overthrow the Girondins—that practically forced the closing of the Bourse, the passage of the law of the maximum (a price setting device), and a number of similar measures of governmental control over the economy. These were war measures, not laws inspired by socialistic theories; Colbert could have promulgated such rules as easily as Robespierre.

In the process of fighting the war a new army came into being. The crisis of 1793 led to a *levée en masse,* a general conscription of all able-bodied males aged eighteen to twenty-five years. Thus, the ranks were swelled, and men from the "better" segments of society, who had theretofore escaped service in the armies of Europe, were brought into the army. Such men, loyal to the regime, raised the morale of the army, and once they had learned the art of war, made better soldiers than the impressed vagabonds and homeless conscripts of the earlier period. Furthermore, since conscription could fill the ranks and replace losses, their officers could use the new troops more daringly and aggressively. Long before Bonaparte showed how good a weapon the new French army could be, republican generals had used it to defeat the armies of the First Coalition.

However, before Robespierre, St. Just, and their friends could harvest the fruits of these victories, the Terror that they had seemed to personify overtook and destroyed them. As long as the members of the Committee of Public Safety worked together, they acted like a well-functioning machine, but early in the summer of 1794 disagreements appeared within the Committee; Robespierre actually ceased attending its meetings. He apparently believed that his control over the Convention was strong enough to allow him to reorganize the Committee more to his liking. In the meantime, Fouché, a deputy on mission and a man with a shady background, became convinced that he was "on Robespierre's list," and began to organize a plot among members of the Convention—ex-deputies on mission and several members of the Committee of Public Safety. Many of these men had reason to fear Robespierre, the "incorruptible one." On 8 Thermidor[6] (July 26) Robespierre convinced them of their danger by making vague, unspecified accusations in a speech before the Convention. His speech frightened a lot more people. The next day Robespierre was denied the floor, while his enemies testified against him, and finally accomplished his downfall. Arrested and placed in prison, the Robespierrists became a rallying point for the Parisian radicals, and Robespierre allowed himself the position of fomenting a rebellion against the Convention. The uprising failed. Robespierre and his immediate friends were guillotined on 10 Thermidor II. In the twentieth century, too, we have had examples of important revolutionary leaders who have fallen from power and ended up with a bullet in their skulls. Revolutions have a way of murdering their enemies and then devouring their own sons.

5. THE THERMIDOREAN REACTION AND THE END OF THE FIRST COALITION

The men who displaced Robespierre had no intention of stopping the forward process of the Revolution. Equally with Robespierre, they too were revolutionaries with great personal interests involved in the success of the movement. They had voted for the death of the king, most of them had acquired either church or *émigré* land, their whole training and background made them distrust the Roman Catholic church, the nobility, and the king; and yet these men were responsible for the reaction that practically ended the forward movement of the Revolution.

By the time they had seized power from Robespierre, the armies of the republic had rolled back the enemy in the Rhineland and the Netherlands, and soon both Prussia and Spain would seek peace. The internal situation, too, had cleared up; except in the Vendée, the rebellions had all been quelled, and the apparatus of the Republic had things well in hand. Under such conditions it was safe to start dismantling the machine that had made the Terror, and to initiate a policy of amnesty toward suspects and "deviationists." Moreover, public opinion in France accelerated the process. Hardly was Robespierre's head in the basket when opposition sprang up on all sides, and the program of vilification that equated the Jacobins with monsters and Robespierre with the devil was begun. The politicians of the Plain as well as some terrorists from the Jacobin "Mountain" hastened to whitewash themselves of any association with Robespierre. The very men who had voted his measures pliantly for over a year, now washed themselves of their former contact, and thereby accelerated the reaction. They even closed the Paris Jacobin Club, and forced the dissolution of the Jacobin federation.

[6] The Convention created a new calendar, starting with 1792 as the year 1 and giving the months new names. Thermidor was the month of heat (July).

A "white terror" broke out in the winter of 1794-1795. Scenes resembling those of the September massacres occurred in a dozen provincial cities. Only this time royalists murdered Jacobins. In Paris wealthy young men, sons of profiteers in many cases, armed with clubs, terrorized the Jacobin sections of the city, smashed busts of Marat, and generally behaved like bullies. The re-opened salons praised this "gilded youth," and encouraged their excesses.

The amnesty policy seems, in a way, to have reversed and unwound the engine of the Terror. Each in turn—the Dantonists, the Girondists, the con-stitutionals—were allowed to come back. The Girondin deputies, some of them actually guilty of armed rebellion against the Republic, were allowed to resume their seats in the Convention. Their subsequent behavior would indicate that while expulsion had taught them very little wisdom, it had in-spired deep hatreds and desires for revenge.

The winter of 1794-1795 was a hard one. The Dutch fleet became frozen into the ice and captured by the advancing French armies—which gives some indication of the weather. In France the Thermidoreans repealed the law of the maximum controls over grain trading, and other "socialistic" wartime measures of the Terror. The result was disaster for the poor. Prices mounted beyond all past experience; bread, even when rationed, was in such short supply that death by starvation was not uncommon in Paris. The wealthy merchants approved of the free trade measures, but the poor spoke of the good old days under Robespierre. However, without leaders their uprisings proved fruitless. Several attempted riots were broken up by military force (the National Guard from quieter sections of the city) with the sole result that more of the ex-Mountainards were guillotined for stirring up the crowd. Of the twelve members of the Committee of Public Safety of 1793-1794, only three were still alive in Paris by March 1795.

In 1795 both Prussia and Spain made peace with the French Republic (Treaty of Basel). Prussia, after absorbing the best part of Poland, embarked on a ten-year period of isolation and neutralism. Spain was persuaded to be-come an ally of the French Republic in the war against England, only to lose most of her overseas empire. The Dutch, too, after being overrun by the armies of the Republic and seeing part of their territory annexed to France, became "allies" of the Republic, and promptly lost Ceylon and Capetown to the British. With Savoy, the Austrian Netherlands, and the left bank of the Rhineland annexed to France and integrated into the French defensive sys-tem, and both England and Austria negotiating for peace, the Thermidoreans and the Convention as a whole could consider drafting a new constitution for France. This was the purpose for which the Convention had been elected in 1792. Obviously the draft constitution it had written that first year, the Constitution of the Year I, was now obsolete, so a second one was hastily drawn up.

When the new constitutional laws of the year III were drafted, one fact

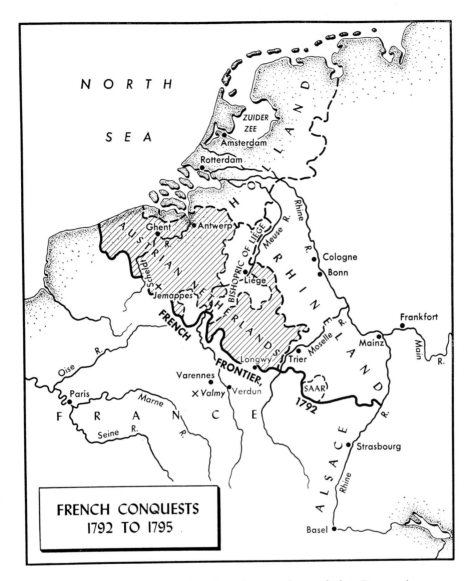

**FRENCH CONQUESTS
1792 TO 1795**

became quite evident, namely, that the members of the Convention were
unwilling to give up public office. The Constitution provided for a two-
chamber legislature, the Council of Elders (250 members) and the Council
of Five Hundred (500). But an additional law made it obligatory that 500
of the total of 750 should be selected by the voters from the ranks of the Convention that had drafted the Constitution. The rest of the Constitution of the
year III (1795) provided for a Directory of five members (vaguely similar
to the Committee of Public Safety) nominated by one of the legislative houses
and selected by the other. The separation of the legislative and executive
functions was so complete that unless extralegal institutions should arise to

bridge the gap, conflict was probably inevitable. Suffrage for voting in an indirect system of elections was restricted to taxpayers; further qualifications for office were high enough to assure the upper bourgeoisie control over the whole government. Even more obvious to everyone was the fact that the "conventionals" were themselves assured of the control of the new government.

By insisting that its members should have a majority in the new legislative chambers, the conventionals roused considerable ire. The nation immediately labeled them "the perpetuals," many of whom were corrupt speculators with a record of cruelty during the Terror and of corruption during the Thermidorean reaction. Their districts were literally crowded with men who wanted to vote against them. A plot was prepared for a coup d'état to overthrow the Convention. This time the plot was initiated in the wealthier sections of Paris, and a good part of the Parisian National Guard was on the side of the insurrection. When the day came, 13 Vendémiaire III (October 5, 1795) the crowds that stormed the Convention numbered at least twenty-five thousand reasonably well-armed men. Barras was in charge of the Convention's defenses; he had about four thousand troops and some hastily armed "Jacobins" from the poorer sections, but he also had among his forces a young artillery officer who knew how to use guns.

Napoleon Bonaparte had first called attention to himself through his brilliant artillery work at Toulon against the English several years earlier. On 13 Vendémiaire his guns blasted the insurrection completely. This famous "whiff of grapeshot" made it clear that future coups d'état would have to be planned by the army rather than by a Parisian mob. Napoleon was the first to show that a few well-trained troops armed with artillery could easily defeat a city crowd many times their number.

It would be unfair to leave the Convention (1793–1795) without pointing out that, in addition to victory over foreign enemies and civil rebellion, it was responsible for much of the important work of the Revolution. Its legal reforms were the basis for the codification of the laws that came later under Napoleon. Its educational reforms laid the groundwork for a new system of schools, as well as creating numerous educational and scientific institutions that are still the glory of France: the Museum of the Louvre, the School of Public Works (polytechnic school), the Museum of Natural History, the National Conservatory of Arts and Industries, the National Institute, and the National Library, to mention the more important. The Convention introduced the metric system and attempted to make the French language of the Isle de France standard for all lands under the tricolor flag. Its attempt to substitute a "rational" religion for Christianity failed; even before the Convention gave way to the Directory government, Catholic services were again being held in many parts of France.

Many nineteenth-century historians who tried to divide the past into neat little packages asserted that the French Revolution ended with the Convention. It is perhaps true that this was the government that inscribed the words "Liberty, Equality, Fraternity," on public buildings, institutions, and even in the hearts of many men, but it is a static, mechanistic conception of the historical process that would argue for "periods" so clean-cut or so brief.

Jean August Ingres, "Bonaparte, First Consul." This was the period in which Napoleon made himself the darling of France by ending the war, conciliating the church, and bringing peace to the countryside. (The Bettmann Archive)

Chapter 29

FROM REPUBLIC TO EMPIRE

1. THE DIRECTORY, 1795–1799

While the course of development of the French Revolution cannot be assumed to embody any universal "law" for understanding revolution in general, it is nonetheless instructive, because it did follow patterns that give insight into the problem of revolution. Twentieth-century men are, therefore, well advised to know something of the forces and the direction of the process that gave rise to both great disorder and important new institutions in France and in Europe at the opening of the nineteenth century.

The Thermidorean reaction (1794) that overtook and destroyed Robespierre and ended the Terror led directly to the Constitution of the Year III, a political system resembling somewhat the Convention, but presumably guaranteeing the two legislative houses more power vis-à-vis the five Directors than the Convention had had vis-à-vis the twelve members of the Committee of Public Safety. The new government that assumed power was largely composed of old faces. The two-thirds rule had forced the electors to return majorities from the ranks of the Convention to both legislative houses, thus assuring a continuity that had been lacking when the National Assembly of 1789–1791 had denied its members the right even to run for the Legislative Assembly (1791–1792). Indeed, the Directory that emerged in 1796 was so completely a continuation of the Thermidorean system that real differences did not appear for almost a year.

The Convention left its successor a host of problems. The war against the First Coalition appeared about to end. Prussia, Spain, the Netherlands, and all the petty states of Germany and Italy had made peace, while both England and Austria were negotiating for treaties. The French armies were firmly posted in the Rhineland and the Netherlands, and no foreign troops were on French soil, while Spain and the Netherlands (now the Batavian Republic) were allies of France. It was not clear, however, that either England or Austria would make peace on terms suitable to France, or that, if such a peace were made, it would be more than a truce. One fundamental fact seemed to argue for a speedy peace that would leave France in possession of her conquests. Austria, Russia, and Prussia had greatly enlarged their territories by the partitions of Poland (1792–1795), and it might be reasoned that France had a right to compensations in the Lowlands. Since the Thermidorean politicians no longer talked so blatantly about "liberation" and "the war of peoples against kings and tyrants," these propaganda measures might be forgotten in a general peace. Such at least were the hopes of the optimistic; they did not know that a young general would soon give another face to the problem of war and peace.

If the foreign situation looked promising, the domestic one still presented problems. Rebellions against the Republic had been suppressed, except for the royalist forces in the Vendée where a full-fledged military campaign was still necessary to destroy the rebel army. However, the mere fact that there were no other rebel armies in the field was cold comfort: France swarmed with bands of desperate men whose lawless ways made travel on the highway hazardous to life as well as to property. The police system of the former regime had broken down, and the system of provincial administration was in near chaos. To restore order would be a herculean task for any government, and one which war and political intrigue prevented the Directory from ever solving satisfactorily.

Perhaps even more difficult was the religious question. The vast majority of those elected to the legislative houses of the Directory were not Christians. They ranged from Deists believing in the Robespierrian supreme being to skeptics who did not know what they believed, beyond the fact that they had a strong prejudice against the church. The large majority of Frenchmen, on the other hand, were undoubtedly Christian and devoted to the ritual and teachings of the Roman Catholic church. In the excitement of the early stages of the Revolution, and especially during the period of the Terror, the anti-Catholic Jacobins had had a field day smashing churches and church decorations, and driving priests underground or to the guillotine. The results of this anti-Catholic movement are still to be seen all over France. Except for a few churches like the magnificent cathedral of Albi, the artistic efforts of generations were destroyed by these men whose hatred of the church blinded them to the artistic merits of church buildings. In some cases, explosions of powder inside medieval churches wrecked priceless glass windows, while clubs and axes destroyed statues and paintings. The masses, inarticulate and fearful, allowed their churches to be desecrated, their priests to be persecuted, and their ecclesiastical organization to be wrecked, but they did not transfer their loyalty to the new cult of the Supreme Being and Pure Reason. Even the Jacobin bourgeoisie found it difficult to sustain great enthusiasm for such a cult. With the death of Robespierre, the Roman Catholics began to come out of hiding, and nothing that the Thermidoreans or the Directory could do seemed able to stop France from returning to the church. The Directory tried to hold on to the cult of the Supreme Being, but the people were returning to their ancient beliefs. Between the church and the state there was a barrier: the confiscated lands of the church and the Civil Constitution of the Clergy which the pope would not accept. Thus the Directory had no solution for the religious question. It apparently did not occur to anyone in France at that period that church and state could be separate entities, each free from the authority of the other. There was too long a tradition of a united church and state for any idea of separation to appear satisfactory to either party.

There were also internal problems; the 1790's were beset with economic crises. Like the depressions of the twentieth century, these eighteenth-century crises bore most heavily upon the poor, whose margin of economic safety was narrow. Since the economic crisis was accompanied by war and the inflation of *assignats* to pay for the war, it also provided unusual opportunities for stockbrokers, speculators, and profiteers. The problems that accompanied this inevitable social dislocation were not easy to solve. Men of the eighteenth century had a more primitive notion of the economic structure than we have today. Also, the fiscal and taxation policies of the government were controlled by the very men who most profited from the economic chaos and who therefore were unwilling to take measures to correct it. Tax collection, for example, was in complete disorder; there was apparently no way to force payment of the arrears.

At another level the problem of bread for the poor was as serious after 1795 as it had been before. The laissez faire economic theory of the Thermidoreans ended Robespierre's laws governing prices and markets of grain with excellent results for speculators and merchants, but disastrous ones for the poor. The Directory had to face at least one threat of rebellion from the poor of the city of Paris that had at its root the food problem. It finally proved impossible to maintain a policy of laissez faire; modified controls over the grain trade were developed to assure Paris its bread at reasonable prices.

The constitution of the Directory was not the least of its problems. It was rigid in its conceptions of the state as a mechanism. Its authors apparently assumed that they had "solved" the problem of government forever. Their constitution did not provide for easy amendment, nor did it take into account the political passions of the era in which it was launched. On the other hand, once in control, the authors did not hesitate to change it without any pretense of legality. The "perpetuals" who had forced France to elect them to the legislative assemblies of the new regime would not scruple to use ruse or force to keep themselves in office. This was especially true since the alternatives seemed grim in regard to their own personal fortunes. Most of them had voted for the death of Louis XVI, and so had every reason to fear a return of the Bourbon monarchy. All of them were well-to-do bourgeoisie who had nothing but mistrust for the democratic teachings that were arising among the masses. They regarded their regime as the "happy mean," and were willing to do anything to maintain themselves in office.

In any conflict between their own political interests and the letter of the constitution, men trained in a revolutionary era inevitably acted to preserve the former. The result was that the Directory was troubled by periodic coups d'état. Both the radicals and the royalists provided excuses for political "arrangements" not provided for by the constitution. Nineteenth-century historians, with a deep respect for constitutional provisions, regarded these illegal actions as ample reason for condemning the Directory "lock, stock, and barrel." Curiously enough, many of those same historians found it easy to praise Napoleon, who founded his regime on the last coup d'état against the Constitution of the Year III, and governed France more arbitrarily than any Directory government. The coups d'état can safely be regarded as evidence that the Constitution of the year III was an artificial creation quite unsuited for the violent political forces that were at work in France. They were the work of men who were trying to control those forces in their own interests rather than allow them to run their course.

2. THE RISE OF NAPOLEON BONAPARTE

The problems of the republic's foreign policy after 1795 were complicated by the meteoric career of Napoleon Bonaparte. Before he appeared on the scene, the Directory had planned its policy to consolidate France's position in the north and east by annexing the Belgian lowlands and the left bank of the Rhine. The general doctrine of "compensation" accepted by most eighteenth-century statesmen would have recognized such annexations as justified in the light of the partitions of Poland by the eastern powers. At the same time, such a program of expansion in the Low Countries (present-day Belgium) had very deep roots in French history. Francis I and Louis XIV would both have approved. However, Napoleon suddenly interjected new issues into the problem by reorganizing Italy, creating a series of satellite republics, and then invading the Levant (Egypt and Syria) as a means of breaking England's hold on India. Far from being able to make a peace that might have compensated France for the gains of Austria, Prussia, and Russia in Poland, Bonaparte's new revolutionary imperialism aroused a second coalition against France and carried with itself the germs of a French Empire under Napoleon.

Napoleon Bonaparte was in his mid-twenties when a combination of factors thrust him into command of the army in Italy (1796). A Corsican by birth, his first political activity had been in support of Corsican nationalism.

Napoleon was one of the bright young men who had been given a military education under the Bourbons and used that education to give strength to the armies of the republic. As we noted, he first called attention to himself at Toulon in 1793, when his brilliant artillery work made the harbor untenable for the British fleet. It was Robespierre, though, who had befriended him and given him his first command as a general officer; when Robespierre fell, Bonaparte only barely escaped the guillotine. Again he got his chance when Barras needed a soldier to defend the Convention in 1795; at the time of the 13 Vendémiaire uprising, Napoleon Bonaparte was the artilleryman whose grapeshot showed that street warfare against cannons is folly. Within a year he had married Barras' ex-mistress, Josephine; malicious gossip had it that he had been given command of the army in Italy for taking her off Barras' hands.

Not yet twenty-seven years old, this short, emaciated, Italian-looking "General Vendémiaire" appeared at the camp of the French army near Genoa as its commander in chief. The Directory expected little from this army; the "big push" on Vienna was to be made by another army on the Rhine. It was not long, however, before both France and the army of Italy discovered that a new personality with new policies had appeared on the horizon. Veteran commanders like Generals Augereau and Masséna, as well as the men in the ranks, accepted without question his right to command, once Napoleon had demonstrated his uncanny skill as a soldier.

His first proclamation indicates the incentives that inspired his troops: "Soldiers," he wrote, "you are naked and hungry. The government owes you much, but can give you nothing. Your patience and your courage are admirable, but they can win you neither glory nor prestige. I will lead you to the most fertile plains in the world. Rich provinces and great cities will be in your power; there you will find honor, glory, and riches. Soldiers of Italy! Will you lack courage or constancy?"

In less than three weeks Napoleon's army had overrun Savoy, Piedmont, and Lombardy, and had driven the Austrians to Mantua, where they hoped to block French passage to the Tyrol and Vienna. Those three weeks sealed the fate of Italy, and filled the treasury of the army as well as the pockets of its officers and men. Sixty million francs in currency, the English goods found in Milan, Leghorn, and Tuscany, enormous loot in the form of pictures, statues, and libraries—these were the "official" payments Italy made for its "liberation." Unofficially, the extortions and plunderings of the army matched the promises Napoleon had given at the beginning of the campaign. Soldiers have traditionally "liberated" whatever they found on their campaigns, especially if they were victorious.

The second phase of the campaign involved the fate of the fortress of Mantua and with it the Venetian republic and the Austrian empire. Mantua was doomed by the battle of Rivoli on January 14, 1797, when Napoleon and

Masséna defeated the German troops who were supposed to relieve the siege. Bonaparte was then able to push on toward Vienna, and on April 18, 1797, before the French army on the Rhine had been able to achieve anything to help him, Napoleon signed the preliminaries of peace at Leoben. Austria was now also out of the war, but the French, much against the wishes of the Directory in Paris, were committed to an "Italian system." At the same time, Bonaparte repudiated the Directory's project for the annexation of the whole left bank of the Rhine. The Directory had made peace with Prussia, and had agreed to help Prussia against Austria; Napoleon now made peace with Austria and agreed to help Austria against Prussia. The victorious general saw no reason for accepting or respecting the political program of his government in Paris. His brusque action introduced new problems into the European political system that were not to be solved for over a decade. The Directors, however, ratified Napoleon's plans for a treaty; they needed his support against the conservative, royalist reaction that had become apparent in the elections of 1797.

The definitive peace signed with Austria at Campo Formio (October 1797) was Napoleon's full responsibility. Austria received the republic of Venice and the bishopric of Salzburg as compensation for her losses in the Netherlands, the Rhineland, and northern Italy. The student of history might pause for a moment to note that thus fell the proud Venetian republic that for over a thousand years had played so significant a part in Europe's history. As a result of the treaty of Campo Formio, the French republic acquired "natural frontiers" on the Rhine and the Alps, and created friendly "republics" that were mere satellites in Italy and the Netherlands.

The implications of Napoleon's "Italian system" began to unfold almost immediately after the treaty had been signed. Within a year the French armies had "reorganized" Switzerland to create another "satellite republic" that would give France easy access to Alpine passes. Continuing expansion of the Cisalpine republic indicated clearly the imperialist tendencies of the new French system. The "satellite" republics were unstable political units; their very existence invited the extension of the system to the neighboring territories. Within a year and a half after the treaty of Campo Formio, France was again at war on the continent. Austria, Russia, and Turkey, along with several minor states, joined England in the Second Coalition. Napoleon's peace was only a truce.

When he returned to Paris after making the peace of Campo Formio, Napoleon was greeted as a hero by the government and by the people. Heroes, however, must be kept busy or they have a tendency to get into trouble, so the government assigned to him the task of invading England. One look at the situation in the English Channel convinced Napoleon that there must be a better way to fight England than by invasion. At this moment the idea for a campaign into Egypt was born. Talleyrand may deserve

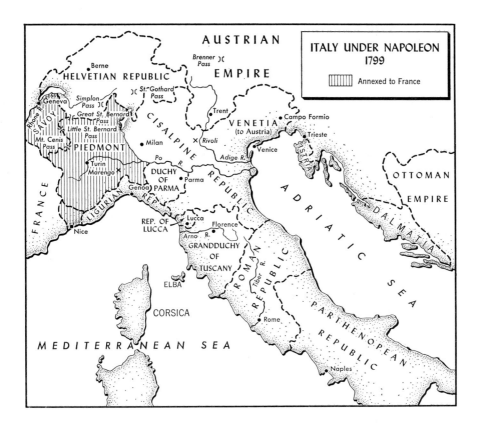

ITALY UNDER NAPOLEON
1799

Annexed to France

the credit for first conceiving it, but the idea well suited Napoleon, too. The project was simple. An army of French veterans would conquer Egypt, and then transfer operations to India, where a fabulous character named Tippo Sahib, the sultan of Mysore, whom we mentioned previously, was waiting to join forces with the French army. England's commercial empire would be ruined. The scheme was not as farfetched as it seems at first sight, nor did the English, who were fighting Tippoo Sahib as well as the French, consider it a harebrained idea when they saw Napoleon's army land in Egypt.

For Napoleon the Egyptian campaign was an opportunity. First of all, he was out of France and hence in no way responsible for the Directory's troubles at home. Secondly, he was far enough away that his campaign's success or failure could not easily be judged by the people at home. Furthermore, like an enlightened despot, he took along a group of intellectuals (linguists, archeologists, historians, and artists) who could advertise his actions in the best light. Among other discoveries, these men found the Rosetta Stone which provided the first key to the writing of Egypt, and thereby established Egyptology as one of the decorative sciences of our civilization.

However, the real political results were not impressive. After taking Malta, the French army landed in Egypt and easily defeated the Mameluke armies, but Lord Nelson's English squadron finally caught up with Napoleon and destroyed the French fleet. Without a navy Napoleon could neither supply his army in an invasion of Syria nor even consider leaving the Levant for India. Thus, though in France it seemed that Napoleon had won great victories, the lack of sea power forced him to retreat from Acre, and bottled up his army in the Nile basin. In the meantime, the situation in France had become such that it seemed to Napoleon that it might be advantageous to return. His "escape" from Egypt in the face of the British fleet was daring; foes regard it, however, as desertion of his army.

The reason for his return was intimately tied up with the course of the war. The English did not make peace in 1797, nor did they cease to negotiate for a reorganization of the coalition against France. French meddling in Switzerland and Italy, Napoleon's invasion of Egypt, and the general fears that inevitably resulted from French annexations and satellite states assisted English diplomats in their negotiations. By 1798 England, Austria, Russia, Turkey, and several of the smaller states had joined in the Second Coalition against the French Republic.

The first campaigns went badly for France. The English invaded the Lowlands; the Austrians and Russians cleared Italy of French troops, and pressed into Switzerland and the Rhineland. The government in Paris became panic stricken; some demanded the re-establishment of the Committee of Public Safety. Laws were passed requiring *émigrés* and others to give up their children as hostages for good behavior. The republic conscripted all able-bodied men into the army; some talked wildly about the possible return of the Terror. Fortunately for many innocent people, the tide of battle turned in the Low Countries, and saner councils prevailed in Paris. Yet enough had been done to drive the Vendée back into rebellion and further to undermine faith in the government of the Directory.

There had been a minor coup d'état in 1796 when the Parisian radicals seemed to threaten society, or rather perhaps, when the existence of a handful of radicals was used to "convince" France of that danger. There was another in 1797, when the elections seemed to indicate that the royalists might capture the machinery of government. There was a third in 1798, when a series of elections was annulled to check the Jacobin extremists. In other words, the Constitution of the year III (1795) had become a thing of rags and tatters before Napoleon returned from Egypt, and at the very time he did return a little group of politicians was preparing a fourth coup d'état.

The central fact of all of these events rested upon the existence of the group of men who had made a career of the Revolution. A majority of them were lawyers of one kind or another, a fact that often brought on them the scorn of the soldiers who had won their wars. As we have already noted, many of them had been deputies to the Estates-General (1789–1791), members of the Legislative Assembly (1791–1792), in the Convention (1792–1795), or served the government of the Committee of Public Safety as deputies on mission or in other functions. They were the "perpetuals" who had assured their election to the councils of the Directory by a constitutional law. Whenever elections threatened to turn them out of office, they sought to protect themselves. Regicides, ex-terrorists, administrators, speculators, politicians, and occasionally a statesman—these were the men who wanted to guarantee for themselves a secure future out of the Revolution they had made. Behind them were the people who had purchased the lands of the church and of the *émigrés,* the peasants who had finally freed themselves of all their feudal obligations without compensating their late lords, and the soldiers who had made a career in the republican army. Like the politicians, these groups were fearful of the return of the monarchy, and the people and policies that would inevitably surround a Bourbon king.

One of the cleverest of the politicians was Siéyès, the same man who, as Abbé Siéyès, had written so eloquently about the Third Estate in 1788–1789. When asked years later what he did during the Convention, he replied, "I lived." Such a response was characteristic of the man. Siéyès was a skillful politician and a compromiser, but not the man to risk his neck for an ideal. An ex-priest, he was too skeptical of all truth to espouse any too firmly. In 1799 Siéyès, himself a Director, was convinced that the Constitution of the year III required revision. Since no extensive coup was possible without military force, his first thought was to find a soldier to help him make the necessary revision. Napoleon was not his first choice, but Talleyrand, who was also promised rewards, assured Siéyès that Napoleon would serve the purpose satisfactorily.

The coup d'état of 18 Brumaire (November 9, 1799) was carefully organized. The legislative councils were moved from Paris to Saint Cloud, presumably for their own safety, and Napoleon was given command of the troops around Paris. Republican generals not in the plot (Augereau, Jourdan, and Bernadotte) were carefully watched while the plotters sprang their coup. Soldiers under Napoleon's command occupied the building housing the councils, and the plotters announced their intention to alter the Constitution. The Council of the Elders had already been won over to accept the coup d'état but in the Council of the Five Hundred Napoleon was greeted by cries of "Down with the dictator!" and "Outlaw him," and some of the deputies tried to reach him with daggers. Only the skillful intervention of his brother Lucien, who was president of the body, saved him from bodily harm. Then the troops entered and cleared the chamber; this show of force ended the Directory.

The men who had seized power as a provisional government immediately promised the French people the right to vote on a new constitution within three months. Their announced policies were to end the civil war in the Vendée, to bring order into the national finances, to codify the revolutionary legislation, and to arrange an honorable peace to Europe. This was a tall order indeed, but it was exactly what the people wanted the most. Indeed, by fulfilling this program, Napoleon endeared himself to the nation and assured his elevation to the imperial throne. Siéyès had not planned to give Napoleon a position that would allow him to take the center of the stage, but Siéyès was not a man to fight a determined thrust for power. The politician who believed in compromise could not control the violent forces released by the Revolution.

3. THE CONSULATE: PRELUDE TO EMPIRE

Most of the European history written in the half century following 1870 was predicated on the general proposition that the western world, if not the whole world, was inevitably moving in the direction of liberal democracy. This optimistic assumption gave historians the right to praise all movements that seemed to be leading toward their goal; to damn or ignore all actions that diverted men from it. The French Revolution and the *philosophes* who preceded it were thus classified as the roots for the eventual triumph of democracy; some writers were troubled when it became difficult to fit all the evidence into this simple frame of reference, but not so troubled that they were unable to do it. Thus, standard textbooks in European history written for American students before 1929 usually placed the English revolutions of the seventeenth century and the French Revolution of the eighteenth century in a common frame of reference. They easily could be interpreted as movements of the people against royal authority; and liberal historians relished telling the story of the people against the king. In doing so, they often overlooked the fact that the "people" were also a minority, and one not always inspired by the lofty idealism of the historians. Furthermore, by combining the English and French revolutions in a common pattern, they neglected the great differences between them and further beclouded their meaning by the assumption that somehow both were democratic movements with aims and ambitions similar to those of the historians who wrote the books.

The facile conclusion that the rise of liberal democratic governments in most of western Europe in the latter nineteenth century was evidence that this was the goal of the whole history of Europe was a fallacy similar to the one made by the distinguished early nineteenth-century French historian Guizot, who believed that all occidental history had been a preparation for the final triumph of the upper bourgeoisie. M. Guizot's equally distinguished contemporary, Karl Marx, went even further by proving that all history was directed toward the eventual triumph of the proletariat. Mid-twentieth-century historians have come to see that it is perhaps wisest to try to discover the characteristic form of the process of the history of Europe, and not to assume that we know the goals toward which that process is, or seems to be, working. It may even be that such "goals" do not exist at all except in the minds of men who want them to come into being. In other words, liberal democracy may be a laudable goal for men to set for themselves, but it would be folly to assume that its desirability would make it the inevitable outcome of the historical process.

The very fact that the revolutionary decade, 1789–1799, ended with the Consulate (1799–1804), a government largely under the control of a soldier-statesman, should give us insight into the historical processes at work. Just as France a century and a half earlier had willingly accepted the authoritarian government of Mazarin and Louis XIV in return for order and a more efficient administrative organization, so she again hailed a new authoritarian government that assured a return of order and personal security. It would be a serious mistake to underestimate the disorder and insecurity that have been the common lot of Europeans or to discount their desires to escape from these evils. The individualist may urge freedom and opportunity, but many men are simply interested in security. Napoleon was probably right when he assumed that liberty did not mean much to many people; the vast majority of his fellow citizens wanted equal justice, personal security, and relief from the disorders of both the revolutionary epoch and the preceding monarchical regime.

At the beginning of the consular regime it was not so evident that power was concentrated in the hands of Napoleon, yet before two years had passed it became apparent that the Constitution of the year VIII (1799) had placed power in the hands of Napoleon, while Siéyès and his friends kept the strings of patronage.[1] The new Constitution created a three-chamber legislature. The Conservative Senate that passed on the constitutionality of measures and proposed new changes in the Constitution, the Tribunate which discussed measures but did not vote, the Legislative Chamber which voted but could neither discuss nor amend measures before it were all well paid, and the members were elected by a complicated system that assured the voters no real voice at all. The executive was entrusted to three consuls, of which the First Consul was the important one; the Second and Third were merely his agents. Siéyès had not planned so strong an executive, but Napoleon, who insisted that he should be First Consul, could not imagine himself consenting "to settle down like a pig fattening on so many millions." The heart of the executive power was the Council of State, an administrative court that drew up legislation, passed on administrative law and procedure, and provided the First Consul with a training ground for his executive officers.

[1] Professor Bruun estimates that Siéyès controlled the appointment of 460 functionaries with the combined salary of 6,000,000 francs annually as his share. The "perpetuals" obviously had reached a safe haven.

France freely accepted this new Constitution as a relief from the old. Whatever may have been the people's attitude toward the "lawyers" who hung onto the coat tails of the coup d'état, the popularity of Napoleon served to secure the necessary vote of confidence. This was a fact that Napoleon made sure his associates understood, and one that assured little opposition to the programs he chose to adopt. This was indeed not to be the last time that a popular soldier guaranteed a measure of stability for a political system.

The first task of the new regime was the pacification of the west. The Vendéean revolt had been quelled in 1795–1796, but the *chouans*[2] kept their arms, and in 1799, with the proclamation of the laws of hostages and universal conscription, the whole of western France from Poitou to Normandy flared up in revolt. The five or six bands did not actually unite in a single rebel force, but their activity effectively tied down the so-called "army of England" and posed a serious threat to the government. Napoleon repealed the law of hostages, and granted religious toleration in the belief that the rebels were more interested in their church than in their king. He then announced to the leaders that since France now had a government that everyone could trust, there was no further need for opposition. With one hand he offered the rebels amnesty; with the other he strengthened the army against them, and promised to hunt down and execute anyone who remained under arms. Such energetic measures produced results; in seven weeks Napoleon solved a problem that the preceding regimes had failed to solve in seven years.

The financial difficulties were less easily removed, but in that area Napoleon had the advantage of the rigorous, if unpopular, work of the Directory without having to accept the odium of these measures. He also had the services of the Third Consul, Lebrun, a constitutional royalist with a fine understanding of fiscal problems. However, the most important tasks had already been fulfilled. In May 1797 the Directory had given up all paper money and reverted to metallic currency. This ended the *assignat* inflation and stabilized values. It was an unpopular measure, but absolutely essential for public credit. In September 1797 the Directory had given the owners of government bonds drafts payable to the bearer for two-thirds of their holding; the other "consolidated third" was turned into bonds bearing five percent interest. Since the paper drafts immediately depreciated to near zero, this measure amounted to a two-thirds' repudiation of the national debt; it was undoubtedly one of the factors responsible for the discontent with the Directorate. Lest it may be thought that Napoleon's prestige immediately buoyed up the consolidated bonds, it should be noted that in 1802,

---

[2] Insurgent rebels, mostly peasants with a few noblemen as their leaders. The word in French almost equates to "guerrillas," originally a Spanish word.

the period of his greatest popularity, they were quoted at from forty-eight to fifty-three; par was one hundred. Obviously the bondholders were skeptics in finance, even though they were probably Bonapartist in politics.

However, the Consulate did improve the financial situation of the government. For the first time in its history, France achieved reasonably effective machinery for the collection of taxes as well as a more equitable assessment than had ever been known. The revolutionary idea that every man should be "equal" before the tax collector has never been really effective in France, but the new government came nearer to it than any before. In the year X (1801–1802) the Consulate even "balanced his budget," or seemed to do so, if too close inquiry was not made into various items on the list.

Perhaps one of the most important, and surely the most lasting, of Napoleon's financial reforms was the creation of the Bank of France. Though technically a private institution, its interrelations with the government as well as its privileges almost made the Bank an organ of government. It carried government accounts, cashed coupons on government bonds, discounted bills, and in 1803 acquired the right of the exclusive issue of bank notes. The French, however, were cautious about paper money; Law's paper money a century earlier and the *assignats* of the Revolution had taught them to trust only gold and silver. In 1803 the government standardized the coinage with a decimal system and established the ratio of silver to gold at 15.5 to 1. Commerce may have been injured by tight credit and scarcity of money, but Napoleon was not the man to cure the French of their fear of paper money.

Along with the reform in the system of tax collection came a similar reform in the whole structure of administration. The administrative offices in the provinces became appointments made by the First Consul. The prefects who were the image of the Consul in the departments more than vaguely resembled the intendants of the former regime. However, they were unencumbered by the political and social debris of former epochs, since the revolutionary broom had swept aside those relics of the feudal and the decentralized monarchy. Thus, Napoleon's administrative reforms, unlike those of Joseph II ten years earlier, could be applied without interference from the old order. It has often been observed that Napoleon's reorganization of France was obviously more akin to the work of the great enlightened despots than to that of the liberal democrats who were to follow him in the nineteenth century.

Closely related to the administrative reform, and also in the spirit of the enlightened despots, was the codification of the laws. The Roman law of the south, the customary law of the north, and the legislation of the revolutionary assemblies had to be brought into some sort of harmony. This work had been started by the Convention, but under the Directory little progress had been made. Napoleon pushed it through to completion. The great difficulty was that the preconceptions of the era stood squarely in the way of understanding the nature of law. The *philosophes,* impressed by the fact that God had given a law to the stars (Newton's), could not believe that He would fail to provide one for men. St. Just in 1793 clearly expressed the credo of the era: "Every political edict which is not based upon nature is wrong." Then again: "If man be given laws which harmonize with the dictates of nature and of his heart, he will cease to be unhappy and corrupt." Such an idea of law made codification difficult. What was needed was a code of laws for France and the French, not a law of nature.

Napoleon saw the importance of finishing the codification of the laws of France, and appointed a committee to achieve this project. Their compromises were somewhat less liberal than the early legislation of the Revolution, somewhat less conservative than the chaos of the former regime. When they are taken together, it is apparent that the needs of the bourgeoisie rather than any idea about universal laws for all men had been foremost in the minds of the codifiers. Protection of property was the core of the law; the family, and with it the role and power of the father, was strengthened as against the individualism of the revolutionary legislation. Employers' rights were guaranteed; artisans and day laborers were brought under surveillance by the introduction of the *livret* (a book indicating his employment record which was to be carried by every employee) and by the outlawing of collective action. It would be impossible to review adequately anything as complex as these law codes; perhaps it is enough to say that the *Code Napoléon* provided a firm legal basis for the emerging civilization of France. The civil code was issued in 1804; the procedural code in 1806; the commercial code in 1807; and the criminal code in 1810. Even though this work was not completed until after Napoleon had become Emperor, his prestige and authority as First Consul grew with the work on the law codes. France, like Europe, believed that there was no conflict between authoritarian, despotic government and the liberty of subjects. The student of French history might pause here for a moment to reflect that in the codification of the laws, as in the creation of the administrative system, Napoleon was completing work which had been begun by Louis XIV. The "Sun King," curiously enough, occupied the thoughts of Napoleon just as he had those of Frederick the Great of Prussia. Louis XIV was the first "enlightened" despot, Frederick and Napoleon were the last.

The most important achievements of the Consulate were in the field of foreign affairs. Confronted with the Second Coalition, Napoleon helped to enlarge the growing gap between Austria and Russia with honeyed words directed at the czar, and succeeded in detaching Russia from the coalition. Czar Paul was murdered shortly afterward, but the alliance between Russia and Austria had been broken. The Austrians were then induced to make peace with France by a two-pronged attack on Vienna: Napoleon through Italy and Moreau through Bavaria. Under close scrutiny, Napoleon's victory at Marengo (June 14, 1800) does not sustain the myth of his military genius, but the Austrians, beaten in Italy and in Germany (Moreau defeated the Austrians at Hohenlinden, December 3, 1800) were ready by the end of 1800 to make peace. On February 9, 1801, at Lunéville, they signed a treaty with France more limiting to Austrian power than the Treaty of Campo Formio had been four years before.

England, again the sole survivor of the Coalition, could not be defeated by a campaign, for her naval superiority had mounted tremendously in the decade of war. But England wanted peace, and the government, directed by men who apparently understood very little of the counters of high politics, entrusted negotiations to Lord Cornwallis, a general and war hero renowned for the wars he had fought in North America and India. Probably it would have been hard to find a less qualified negotiator. The result was the Treaty of Amiens (1801) which turned out to be just a truce, since it could satisfy neither France nor England. The treaty tacitly recognized all of France's gains in Europe, including the annexation of the Lowlands and the creation of satellite republics on her eastern frontiers. England, on the other hand, returned all her naval conquests except Trinidad and Ceylon, which had belonged to Spain and Holland. This meant that England compensated herself at the expense of France's allies. "The French," writes Professor Bruun, "endured the losses suffered by their allies with commendable fortitude."

The English government was disappointed with the treaty, but ratified it rather than repudiate their distinguished negotiator. The reasoning seems to have been that actually nothing had been changed by the treaty so long as England's sea power remained strong. It was, therefore, only a truce, easily broken if conditions should warrant a renewal of the war. Napoleon eagerly ratified the Treaty of Amiens as evidence that his government could bring peace to France.

The other great achievement of the first years of the Consulate was the Concordat with Rome (1801), which regularized the relationship between the Roman Catholic church and the French republic. When Austria had to sign the Treaty of Lunéville, the papacy decided that it was time to salvage what it could from the French Revolution. The resultant agreement was rather less than Rome had hoped to achieve. The French government assumed responsibility for maintaining churches and paying the clergy; in return it had the right to nominate the bishops, leaving to the pope the right to install them. Napoleon thus defended all the rights of the Gallican church and at the same time provided for the return of regular church services. The Deists and skeptics in his government and in the three chambers were less happy to see this treaty with Rome than were the faithful. To satisfy the former, all religions, including the Jewish, were recognized. The Roman Catholics were assured only of first place among the others. The Concordat of 1801 remained a basic law in France for just over a century.

Studying the achievements of the Consulate, it is not hard to understand why the Senate proposed and the people accepted, first, the election of Napoleon as Consul for life (1802), and, second, his installation as hereditary emperor of the French republic (1804). The prestige of the First Consul as soldier, statesman, and administrator had risen with each successive triumph, until nothing less than the imperial purple seemed adequate to express France's appreciation.

However, everyone was not as happy to see the rise of a new despotism as it might appear from the plebiscites. After the treaties of Lunéville and Amiens, the war had ended, and the army had returned home. The officers of the army had been picked and indoctrinated by the Jacobin Carnot, and many of them were more staunchly, if naïvely, republican than the lawyers and career politicians. It was not surprising that all of them did not welcome the upstart general as statesman and potential despot, or that some of them wondered what turn of fortune had placed Napoleon on the way to a throne and them on the half pay of retirement. There were also among the lawyer-politicians some who were yet unconvinced, or perhaps only inadequately bribed, while others of them, regicides, were worried that General Bonaparte might turn out to be a General Monk.[3] Before the Empire could come into being, the soldiers and politicians would have to be satisfied.

4. NAPOLEON, EMPEROR OF THE FRENCH, BY THE GRACE OF GOD AND THE CONSTITUTION OF THE REPUBLIC

The constitutional and social forms of the Consulate changed slowly in the direction of the Empire, even before it was actually proclaimed. Napoleon's personal prestige was so great that he had only to say that he disapproved of the extreme décolletage fashion for the feminine style designers in Paris to insist immediately that a new mode was at hand. On another level, the members of the Tribune quickly learned that men who indulged too freely in criticism were soon replaced by others more friendly to the First Consul, and the press that had blossomed so freely in 1799 was under control by 1802. In other words, by suggestion or, if necessary, by force, France was being prepared for the despotic exercise of power; again it became treason to criticize.

[3] The English soldier who restored Charles II to the throne of his father in 1660.

The creation of the Legion of Honor (1802) to reward both soldiers and functionaries for service to the state was the first step in establishing a new nobility and buying off the dissident grumblers. At first there was some tendency to criticize, but since each rank in the Legion carried an appropriate pension for its owner, and since the upper ranks were freely bestowed upon the soldiers, the Order had a tendency to quiet some of the republican consciences of the generals. Furthermore, since the money for the pensions came out of the lands confiscated from the *émigré* nobles, the beneficiaries had good reason to prevent a Bourbon restoration. The senators, whose voices were needed to change the constitution, were also rewarded.

A royalist plot to murder Napoleon and restore the Bourbons was the final act in the drama creating the Empire (1804). Napoleon found out about the plot very early, but waited to spring a trap in the hope of capturing some member of the Bourbon family on French soil. This proved impossible, but he did kidnap the young Duke of Enghien in Baden; the Duke was an authentic Bourbon, but his mission in Baden had been amorous rather than political. Nonetheless, he was tried and summarily shot. A handful of the real conspirators (among them several important generals) were taken. Six or eight were guillotined, the rest banished or imprisoned. Cadoudal, one of the ringleaders, realized that this exposé only heightened Napoleon's position: "We came to give France a king," he exclaimed, "and we have given her an emperor."

There was much truth in Cadoudal's statement. With the execution of the Duke of Enghien, Napoleon, too, had Bourbon blood on his hands, and the regicides in the three houses could regard him as one of their own. As soon as the politicians were ready to act, France was willing to vote. The Conservative Senate proposed a constitutional law confiding the executive power of the French republic to an hereditary emperor, Napoleon Bonaparte. The plebiscite of 1804 confirmed the establishment of an hereditary Empire by 5,572,399 to 2,569 votes. For the next few years the coins of France carried the devices: "French Republic, Emperor Napoleon Bonaparte." Eventually the word "Republic" was dropped.

Immediately the rewards again went to all those who had helped or who had yet to be bribed. The first crosses of the Legion of Honor were bestowed, and all public officials above a given rank were assured of their titles for life together with pensions. The next step was to create an imperial nobility, and within ten years France could count four princes, thirty dukes, four hundred counts, and over a thousand barons in addition to titles that were given to the imperial family. This was a new nobility staffed with men who had deserved well of Napoleon or men who caused him to fear them.

In a way the Constitution of the Empire was a logical development in the process by which the revolutionary regime governed France. During the

Convention (1792–1795) the twelve-member Committee of Public Safety had ruled with a single-chamber legislature which the Committee dominated (or killed). The Directory (1796–1799) reduced the executive to a five-member board, and increased the legislative chambers to two. The Consulate had decreased the executive to three with the First Consul occupying the principal role, and increased the legislative houses to three, none of which enjoyed much prestige. Under the Consulate the central agency of government had soon become the Council of State, the executive court that drafted legislation and ruled on administrative law and procedure; the three houses (Senate, Legislative Chamber, and Tribunate) went into virtual eclipse after 1802. During the Empire the executive, reduced to one, swallowed up the functions of the Tribunate and Legislative Chamber. The former ceased to exist after 1808, while the latter, like the Senate, became subservient to the emperor. The real heart of government became the Council of State, an institution which Louis XIV would have been pleased to have had if his France had been as easy to organize as that of Bonaparte's day.

By the time Napoleon was crowned emperor, the immediate results of the revolutionary epoch were fast becoming manifest. The Revolution had accomplished the legal and administrative reforms that the enlightened despots had unsuccessfully striven to effect, and had inspired in the imagination of the French people an image of themselves as French citizens, as French nationals, and as bearers of a great tradition. The combination of legal and administrative reforms had created equality before the judge, the administrator, and the tax collector, as well as a rough approximation of equality of opportunity to serve the state. The moral content of the Revolution made each Frenchman conscious of his fraternity with all Frenchmen—a harbinger of the political world to come.

Thus two of the Jacobin watchwords—Equality and Fraternity—found a kind of reality under the Empire, a reality that they were to retain throughout the nineteenth century, for they were written into the laws, the institutions, and the minds and feelings of the Frenchmen. The third Jacobin slogan—Liberty—found a less secure haven. Even the Jacobin Robespierre, who has since been made a symbol of democracy by some historians, saw "liberty" as the right to will the "general will," and did not hesitate to use prison and guillotine to "force men to be free," that is, to force them to obey his conception of virtue. Nor did the other revolutionary governments welcome liberty to discuss, criticize, or vote freely unless the people behaved "right," and it was not to be left freely to the individual to decide what really was "right." Napoleon did not hesitate to impose his own image of freedom on the nation. In Europe as a whole, "liberty" was to remain merely a word for the privilege to say and do what was "right" for a long time after Napoleon had gone from the scene.

In 1804 Napoleon's defeat was a decade away. Pope Pius VII journeyed across the Alps to join the company of priests, politicians, and soldiers who gathered together in the cathedral of Notre Dame in Paris to consecrate the new "Charlemagne." Napoleon put the crown on his own head, and stood out before Europe as emperor of the French by the grace of God and the Constitution of the republic. David commemorated the scene with one of the great historical pictures of all times.

Jacques Louis David, "Coronation of Josephine by Napoleon I in Notre Dame" (Paris, The Louvre).

Chapter 30

EUROPE AND THE FRENCH IMPERIUM

1. THE BACKGROUND FOR THE NAPOLEONIC WARS

As we have seen, in the seventeenth century a series of enlightened kings and ministers had reformed the French state. One of the important results of their work was that France had then become immeasurably stronger than her neighbors. In the great wars at the end of the seventeenth century the other states of Europe had either had to adapt the French system of the bureaucratic-police state to their own traditions, or, like Poland where this was not done, face extinction. The reforms of the French Revolution, 1789–1804, again reorganized France, and thereby gave her new military and political power that dwarfed that of her neighbors. Napoleon's contemporaries, like those of Louis XIV, had either to reform in the spirit of the French Revolution or face the possibility of absorption into a French Empire. This political dynamic is obviously at the root of much of the movement in European history. There seems to have been sufficient difference within the political units of European society to make it impossible for any one state to absorb the others, and yet at the same time there was enough homogeneity to make possible liberal borrowing and adaptation of measures and ideas developed in any of them. Thus European society was able to retain its basic diversity as well as its unity.

By 1804 France was easily the largest power in Europe. With the Lowlands (Belgium), the Rhineland, and Savoy as actual departments of the republic, the population of France equalled that of Russia, and her productive capacity excelled that of England. Furthermore, a new bureaucracy governed the territory, and thus made its potential power available to the central authority in Paris. No other state in Europe had such a machine for administration and control. Nor indeed, was that the whole story. To the east there was a tier of satellite republics: the Batavian (Netherlands), the Helvetian (Swiss), and the Cisalpine (north Italian). These states were almost as much a part of the government in Paris as were the French departments. They were not allowed to have ideas or policies that did not fit the program of the First Consul who soon became Emperor.

Perhaps even as important as the actual display of power in the form of provinces and soldiers was the moral force generated by the Revolution. After much talk about the "rights of man" and the unfurling of slogans about "liberty, equality, and fraternity," a hard core of revolutionary ideology that was applicable to laws and institutions emerged as a reality. This can best be summed up under the words *civic equality,* and it easily became the "exportable" ideal of the Revolution. It was simple to understand, and formidable to a Europe organized on the semifeudal monarchical pattern of the pre-Revolutionary epoch. *Civic equality* simply meant that every individual should enjoy the right of equal treatment at law, in the tax collector's office, and in opportunities to serve the state. Napoleon summed it up by saying that "every soldier carried a marshal's baton in his knapsack"; that is, if his talents warranted it.

This notion of *civic equality* as an exportable commodity of the French Revolution was regarded with horror by the aristocrats and rulers who benefited from the inequalities of class-conscious societies. At the same time, it made questionable—even doubtful—the loyalties of the bourgeoisie and peasantry whose governments did not grant this equality. No one in 1804 had ever heard the expression "fifth column." If they had, the term might well have gained currency, for the French could depend upon the support of many people in central and western Europe. Napoleon and his advisers well understood the importance of the idea of *civic equality,* and would not allow any deviation from it in the lands under French control. Of the three great words inscribed on revolutionary documents, "equality" was the most important. Napoleon cynically noted that most men do not wish for liberty, that nearly all men will trade "liberty" for "equality." "Fraternity," the third word, was nearly pure political mysticism, and so could not easily be written into laws or institutions.

In the new Europe reorganized by France, the government in Paris kept a strict watch upon the internal affairs of its satellite republics. When a majority of those voting rejected a French-made constitution in the Batavian Republic (the Netherlands), Napoleon simply forced them to accept it anyway. The French argument was ingenious to the extreme: a majority of all possible voters did not vote; hence they tacitly approved the constitution that the voters had rejected.

The English ambassador at Paris protested Napoleon's highhanded behavior in the Netherlands. He was blandly assured that no country, including England, had any right to interfere with the internal affairs of another.

The Swiss and Italian republics were also "reorganized" from Paris. French intervention in Switzerland had lasting results, for the constitution that Napoleon helped to give the Swiss is still today the basic law of that republic. In Italy, after so many changes that even the Italians must have had trouble following them, Napoleon himself emerged as President of the Cisalpine Republic.

In Germany the rapid march of events between the Franco-Prussian Treaty of Basel (1795) and the Franco-Austrian Treaties of Campo Formio (1797) and Lunéville (1801) led to great territorial changes. When the French swept their opponents out of the left bank of the Rhine, they agreed to the right of Austria and Prussia to compensation in Germany. After the Treaty of Lunéville an imperial court was established to effect a redivision of Germany. This so-called *Reichsdeputationshauptschluss* meant for all intents and purposes the end of the Holy Roman Empire. By rapid blows the ecclesiastical princes were deprived of their territory. Free knights were swallowed up by their neighbors, and about half the petty princes ceased to rule. With the French ambassador behind the scenes as stage director, the readjustments were made in terms of Napoleon's idea of foreign policy. At that moment he reached the decision to make Prussia his ally and to break up Austria. (The shades of Louis XIII, Louis XIV, and Louis XV must have blessed his wisdom.)

Thus by 1804 a new French-organized Germany was about to appear. The minor princes who were willing to be lackeys of Napoleon emerged with new territory; Prussia grew considerably; Austria received very little. When the Austrian ambassador protested in Paris that his ruler had not received a just share, Napoleon suggested that he might win compensations in the Balkans—at the cost of an expensive war, of course. The Austrian emperor could not hope to dominate the new German situation as long as French military and political power was so overwhelming.

In 1804 the Emperor Francis II received another blow when Napoleon also assumed the title of emperor. Obviously the French imperial dignity was supported by real power, whereas the crown of the Holy Roman Empire had become corroded by time and weakened by history. Was there room in Europe for two emperors? Francis II was yet unwilling to give up the crown of the Holy Roman Empire, but he buttressed his right to be called emperor by adding to his honors the new high-sounding title, "Emperor of Austria and Apostolic King of Hungary." Even such titles, however, could not overshadow the crown that Napoleon had assumed in the cathedral of Notre Dame in Paris.

The Spanish government had little alternative to accepting Napoleon's blandishments. Spain had allied herself with the Directory after being defeated by the French armies, and easily fell back into the dependence on Paris that had been her characteristic pattern for a century. Napoleon even flattered the Bourbon Spanish kings by giving them an Italian duchy for a younger son in return for the vast territory of Louisiana. The Spaniards, already burdened with American colonies that paid slight dividends, thought they had made a good bargain, while Napoleon, with dreams of a French overseas empire, was sure that he had made a fortunate deal. He knew that he could "reorganize" Italy any time he wished, and thereby regain the real estate that he had traded for Louisiana. Thus Spain also became a satellite of France; she still retained more independence or at least the *appearance* of independence than the new republics were able to show, but in reality Spanish policy also was decided in Paris.

The other two powers of Europe—Russia and England—regarded the continuous expansion of French power uneasily. Czar Alexander I, who came to the throne when a nobles' plot deposed and strangled his father (1801), decided that Europe could defend itself against the slogan "equality" only by one of equal force. His idea was "justice"; and as early as 1803 he began to talk to the English about an alliance that would guarantee "justice" to all. It was not for nothing that Alexander had been educated by a Swiss Jacobin and a Greek Orthodox monk. His grandmother, Catherine the Great, had ensured that his education would fit him for the world; she would have been not a little surprised to see her grandson's idea of "justice" develop a decade later into the Holy Alliance. When Napoleon executed the Duke of Enghien, Alexander and his Russian nobles recognized in the French emperor all the evil that had characterized the worst phases of the Revolution.

Just a few months after the Treaty of Amiens the English were becoming increasingly conscious that the peace had been a mistake. Indeed, Napoleon did not make it easy for them to see it otherwise. French interference in the internal affairs of neighboring states led to English protests that Napoleon simply ignored. The terms of the Treaty of Amiens were not lived up to by either side, a situation that resulted in further protest and recrimination. Both states began to retaliate by arresting each other's nationals and by impounding merchant ships. Such actions naturally caused a deterioration in Anglo-French relations: there could be no outcome other than war. England knew that both Austria and Russia were willing to join against Napoleon, and their support made her quite willing to risk a war. The sensational growth of French power had completely destroyed the traditional balance of power in Europe: England, Russia, and Austria had to either accept this new Europe in which they would play a lesser role or make war on France to re-establish a European balance more agreeable to their own interests.

Napoleon believed (or at least asserted that he believed) to the end of his days that it was not the political issue that brought on the war, but rather the economic. The new French Empire was attempting to supplant England as the merchant and the manufacturer for Europe. Napoleon insisted that it was his unwillingness to make a trade treaty with England comparable to the one made by Louis XVI and his efforts to extend French economic power that led to the war with England. The economic problems in 1802–1804 were undoubtedly important factors leading to war. In the preceding two or three decades English textile, china, and metallurgical manufacturers had made great strides in the development of new machines and new processes, while the introduction of steam engines to supplement water power had greatly added to the power-potentials available for manufacturing in general. At the same time, road and canal construction in England had opened up much of the back country to commerce, so that English goods of all kinds could easily flow to market. During the decade 1791–1801 this commerce had been handicapped by the war, and, even though new markets in the Americas had been opened up, English exporters and manufacturers eagerly awaited the end of hostilities in the expectation that France would again sign a treaty of commerce like that of 1786 which had reduced duties to let English manufactured goods be exported to France in return for French wines and brandies.

However, the Treaty of Amiens (1802) had not been accompanied by a commercial treaty, nor was Napoleon in any hurry to make one. The reason was not hard to find. In the first place, French manufacturers had bitterly opposed the commercial treaty of 1786 that, in their words, had "flooded" France with cheap English goods. Indeed, they had welcomed the war in 1793 that had again returned the French market to them. Furthermore, the war had resulted in two important developments: it had greatly extended the frontiers of France to include the industrial area of the Netherlands and the Rhineland; it had also encouraged the growth of French industry to supply both the army and the enlarged French market. The satellite republics, too, were economically involved with France, and it required only a little imagination to see the French political system translated into an economic union. In other words, the germ of the famous Napoleonic continental system was already in existence at the time of the Treaty of Amiens.

Napoleon was a soldier, not a liberal economist. The ideas of the protectionists appealed to him, for they seemed to assure self-sufficiency in case of war, while the laissez faire doctrine promised advantages that might well be better for Englishmen than for Frenchmen. Thus Napoleon evaded making a trade treaty, and slowly but surely began to build up a French economic system. He built roads, encouraged industry, aided commerce in the spirit of enlightened despotism, while England and English economic interests were frustrated in their effort to trade in French territories. Undoubtedly these economic problems were important factors in the decision that was responsible for England's renewal of war with France. In any case, it is hard to separate them from the political problems that English politicians of that day alleged to be the cause.

Napoleon apparently regarded the return to hostilities with reasonable equanimity. He greatly strengthened the French navy which had suffered severely from the Revolution, but he soon understood that he could not hope to match England ship for ship. As a political realist, Napoleon realized that he could not hope to hold colonies scattered all over the globe without naval superiority. Furthermore, his hopes for a French American empire were blighted by revolts in Haiti and threatened by the overflow of emigrants from the United States into the Louisiana territory. In an effort to cut his losses in America before war should break out between England and France, he sold Louisiana to the republic of the United States. The money France received was not much, but the sale prevented her enemies from profiting from French naval weakness. His real answer to England's preparations for war was to concentrate the finest army France ever possessed on the Boulogne coast in preparation for a direct attack on England. Both sides were willing to risk armed conflict, and even before Napoleon was crowned emperor (December 2, 1804), France and England had drifted into war; each was watching for a chance to strike down the other.

The war with England lasted as long as the French Empire did; it became a great European war with several phases or interludes. At one point it looked as though Napoleon's ideal of a Europe in which "anyone could travel anywhere and still find himself in his fatherland" might be realized, but the final achievement of the war was not to be universalism for Europe, but rather intensified national particularisms.

2. WAR AND THE REORGANIZATION OF EUROPE

The army concentrated on the Boulogne coast in 1804–1805 was not just a bluff; Napoleon had a grand plan for the invasion of England. He well knew that English money and diplomacy were at work in Russia, Austria, and Prussia in an effort to build a new coalition against him. He also knew that if an army of French veterans could land on England's shore, nothing would come of those negotiations, for with a French army in London he could "wring England's neck," and with it the threat of future coalitions.

Napoleon's plan was grandiose. The French Toulon fleet, evading the English Mediterranean fleet, was to sail to the Caribbean with the allied Spanish fleet. There it would pick up several more French and Spanish vessels, and set sail for Europe, where it would join with two other French fleets. The English Mediterranean fleet, he believed, would have to follow the Franco-Spanish ships across the Atlantic, but it would not arrive in

European waters in time to join the English Channel fleet. Thus the French would momentarily have superior forces, and would be able to seize control of the Channel long enough to transport an army to England. His plan, however, left too much to chance. At first Napoleon had trouble with his admirals, two of whom died unexpectedly, delaying the plan. Then when Admiral Villeneuve finally did get under way, a combination of circumstances forced him to abandon the last phase of the project. Instead of sailing to the Channel, he had to stop at Spanish ports, and finally concentrated his fleet near Trafalgar. Nelson, after following him across the Atlantic and back, also eventually reached Trafalgar, where the Franco-Spanish fleet was practically destroyed in one of the great naval battles of all times (October 21, 1805).

Perhaps Napoleon should have known that his inferior fleet probably could not accomplish such a mission; perhaps he was not really surprised when it failed. In any case, as soon as it had become evident that there would be no invasion of England, the magnificent army on the Boulogne coast undertook other work. Austria and Russia were concentrating their forces, and by August 1805 the Third Coalition challenging Napoleon's right to govern Europe had become a fact.

In *War and Peace* Tolstoy has given a classic description of the Russian army that invaded Europe in 1805. Several of the most brilliant passages of that famous book are concerned with the Austerlitz campaign. The other side of this picture, the story of the French army at Austerlitz, still awaits a novelist of Tolstoy's genius. The French army was probably the best Napoleon ever commanded. In three years of relative peace the veterans of the late wars had taught the new recruits how to be soldiers, and the year of training on the Boulogne coast had hammered out a magnificent fighting machine. As Tolstoy so ably tells us, the Austro-Russian armies were also good according to eighteenth-century standards, but little deficiencies like shortages of shoes, and important complications such as divided command, allied distrust, and uneasy morale in the ranks made those armies no real match for the French in spite of their superiority in numbers.

The campaign was a rapid one. When Austria and Russia appeared as allies of England (August 1805), the army of Boulogne turned eastward. By October it was on the upper Danube, where it captured General Mack's Austrian army at Ulm. In November it occupied Vienna, the capital that had successfully resisted Turks, Swedes, French, and Prussians in the preceding three centuries. The two opposing armies came face to face near Austerlitz in Bohemia on December 1, 1805, the eve of the first anniversary of Napoleon's coronation. At the outset the Austro-Russians had great numerical superiority and occupied the high ground on the battlefield, but they somehow overlooked the marching speed of the French and also the

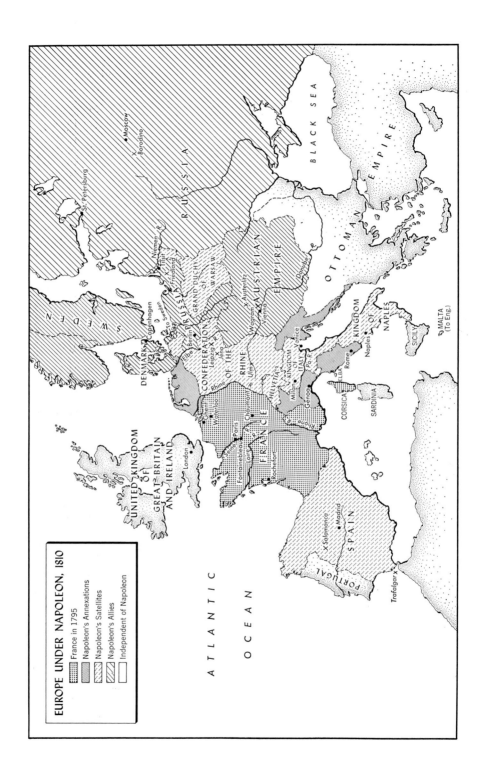

EUROPE UNDER NAPOLEON, 1810

France in 1795
Napoleon's Annexations
Napoleon's Satellites
Napoleon's Allies
Independent of Napoleon

ATLANTIC

OCEAN

UNITED KINGDOM OF GREAT BRITAIN AND IRELAND
London

FRANCE
Paris

SPAIN
Madrid
× Salamanca

PORTUGAL

Trafalgar ×

SWEDEN

DENMARK
Copenhagen

RUSSIA
Moscow
× Borodino
St. Petersburg

PRUSSIA
Berlin

GRAND DUCHY OF WARSAW

CONFEDERATION OF THE RHINE

AUSTRIAN EMPIRE
Vienna
× Austerlitz
× Wagram

KINGDOM OF ITALY
Milan
Venice
Genoa
Rome

KINGDOM OF NAPLES
Naples

HELVETIA

CORSICA

SARDINIA

SICILY

ELBA

MALTA (To Eng.)

OTTOMAN EMPIRE

BLACK SEA

Niemen R.
Friedland
Jena
Leipzig ×
Ulm
Po R.
Danube

Waterloo

Rhine R.

Rhone R.

× Eylau

Genoa

audacity of Napoleon. He brought up sufficient forces to reduce his enemies' numerical superiority in the line to eight to seven, and on December 2 gave battle.

More than any of the other battles that Napoleon fought, Austerlitz was the one that best demonstrated both the flexibility of the French army and the genius of its commander. Tolstoy notwithstanding,[4] the battle did not fight itself. Napoleon's tactics induced his opponents to weaken their center on the high ground, and then he broke through this weak point with a desperate attack that threw his enemies into confusion. The Russian army withdrew from central Europe to recover from its wounds, and the Emperor Francis of Austria sued for peace.

With the Franco-Austrian peace (Treaty of Pressburg, December 1805) and a Franco-Prussian treaty of alliance, the Napoleonic order in Europe took a new turn. Most of the states of central Europe became satellites of imperial France. The Holy Roman Empire and with it the Emperor Francis' shadowy title as emperor disappeared (1806). Very few people shed any tears over either. Prussia, on the other hand, received Hanover from Napoleon, and presumably became the ally of France, but the Prussian king could take little comfort in his new position for the rest of Germany was organized in the Confederation of the Rhine under French auspices. Several German princes emerged as kings in this new organization, but they were, in fact, mere satellites of the French imperium, since both Prussia and Austria were rigorously excluded. In the upsurge of new institutions, Napoleon assumed the title of king of Italy, his brother Louis became king of the Netherlands (Batavian Republic), and his brother Jerome became king of Naples.

Prussia was now in the uncertain position of being an ally or becoming a mere satellite, but when Frederick William III of Prussia heard that Napoleon had offered to return Hanover to England as a pledge of peace, Prussia's true situation became apparent; like Spain, Prussia was fast becoming a dependency of France. The Russian and English ambassadors in Berlin urged the Prussian king to reconsider his political alignments to save himself from destruction. The breach between Prussia and Napoleon came about quickly. French troops were quartered on Prussian territory, and none of Prussia's protests had brought relief. Such treatment was quite unsuitable for the kingdom that had had Frederick II for its ruler. To Napoleon's surprise, Frederick William III chose to fight rather than to sink into the role of a mere satellite. The folly of Prussian pride became apparent in September 1806 when two battles were fought simultaneously at Jena and

---

[4] Tolstoy insisted that it was the chance combination of thousands of petty factors that decided every battle in the war. These factors themselves were determined, not by any grand historical process, but by the thousands of individuals who were brought together in the armies. Thus, accidents of morale rather than the designs of commanders or even the overriding historical forces of an era became the central causative factor in Tolstoy's history.

Auerstädt: in both the Prussian armies suffered defeat. The French victory at Auerstädt, where Marshal Davout commanded the imperial forces, was, in fact, more impressive and decisive than the one at Jena, where the emperor was in command, but in popular tradition only Jena remains as the victory that proved that the new French army was decisively superior to the military machine left by the great Frederick.

The Prussian king retreated to east Prussia, while Napoleon occupied the capital at Berlin; but the war was not over, for a Russian army was moving in, too late to save Prussia, yet willing to give battle. Napoleon almost over-reached himself in this phase of the campaign. The Russians retreated into Poland, and winter closed in on both armies. At Eylau in February 1807 the two armies came to grips with each other. The result was a French victory since the Russians continued to retreat, but French losses were so great that Napoleon could not afford many like it. Fortunately for him, Russian re-serves and reinforcements were mired down in the roadless wastes of Polish mud, and the Austrian army was still recovering from the effects of Auster-litz. By June 1807 Napoleon had brought up fresh troops and supplies, so that he could again assume the offensive. At Friedland on June 14 another battle was fought. This time the Russians were badly beaten owing to the mistakes of their own commander, and Czar Alexander was willing to dis-cuss peace.

The Treaty of Tilsit, June 1807, is usually regarded as the high point of the French Empire. Alexander I of Russia was ready to come to terms both be-cause his armies had been beaten in the field and because a pro-French party was predominant in his government. Napoleon readily accepted a peace be-cause he needed freedom of action to reorganize Europe so that it could be used effectively to combat England.

There were three issues to settle: the problems of Prussia, England, and Turkey. Napoleon wanted to annihilate Prussia because of its treacherous behavior the year before, but Alexander—perhaps from feelings of guilt since he had urged Prussia to fight, perhaps from feelings of gallantry toward the beautiful Prussian queen, or perhaps from the realization that Tilsit might not be the last treaty to be signed—urged moderation. Napoleon therefore agreed to restore Prussia, less various provinces, to the Hohenzollern dynasty; he stripped off Prussia's Polish provinces to make the new Grand Duchy of Warsaw (Poland), and the Rhineland provinces together with Hanover to make the kingdom of Westphalia for his brother. The remaining territories were left to Frederick William III; but the Prussian kingdom was limited in the size of the army that it could raise and was compelled to become a French ally, occupied by French troops.

England and Turkey presented somewhat different problems. Neither of them had been defeated, nor was there an immediate prospect of their oc-cupation. In 1806 Napoleon had urged Turkey to make war on Russia, but at Tilsit he deserted the Turks and assured Alexander of his willingness to let Russia seize both Wallachia and Moldavia while France reoccupied the Ionian Islands. If Turkey should resist, Napoleon and Alexander were prepared to divide the whole empire between them.

The English problem was more difficult. Napoleon merely wanted England to recognize his conquests, and the only way that he knew to accomplish that was to exclude English goods from the continent. Such a blockade, he believed, would force England to come to terms. Alexander agreed to help to close the Baltic and to join the grand project of closing all European ports to English goods. Napoleon persuaded the czar that the Franco-Russian alliance was thenceforth to be the cornerstone of French policy. Russia had taken the place that, in 1804, Napoleon had reserved for Prussia as the protector of the eastern marches of his Empire.

Tilsit gave Napoleon the chance to try out his program of economic warfare to bring England to her knees. The continental blockade, embodied in the so-called Milan and Berlin decrees of 1807, barred all English goods from the continent and forbade all neutrals to trade with England on pain of the confiscation of any ship that stopped at a British port. The theory behind the project was simple enough. Napoleon regarded England as a "nation of shopkeepers" whose existence depended upon their ability to export the goods made in English shops and those that English ships transported from the world beyond the seas. If European markets were closed to English commodities, Napoleon believed that the merchants would force the government to make peace on his terms. With Alexander's Russia as part of a great blockade system, he thought that it would be possible to seal off the whole of Europe from commercial contact with England. The great difficulty was that Napoleon had no navy with which to blockade England, and so he could not actually control the trade of neutrals except by confiscating any ships that engaged in trade with England. This was, however, no substitute for a naval blockade.

Not to be outdone by Napoleon, the English issued Orders in Council requiring all neutral traders to stop at British ports before proceeding to the continent, and at the same time establishing a naval blockade of all the French-occupied harbors of Europe. Since England had a navy with which to enforce these Orders, they proved more onerous to neutrals than did the French "paper" blockade. The English also acted quickly after Tilsit to protect their naval position. When the Danish government refused to sell its fleet to England, a British squadron descended on Copenhagen, and, without warning or declaration of war, destroyed the entire Danish fleet, an act vaguely reminiscent of Pearl Harbor on December 7, 1941. As Professor Brunn remarks, "Napoleon's adversaries were learning to match his methods in speed and exceed them in ruthlessness."

The neutral nation most affected by the conflicting naval blockade was the young republic of the United States. Mr. Jefferson's administration tried to force the belligerents to respect the rights of neutral shipping by refusing to allow American ships to trade with either. He failed to see that international law in times of war is regulated by naval guns. In Madison's administration, English interference with American shipping was one of the factors that led the United States to declare war in 1812. There were, however, other issues more pressing than the commercial one, or Mr. Madison would or should have declared war on France as well as England.

Napoleon's efforts to make the continent refrain from trade with England actually had two purposes. First was his desire to ruin the "nation of shop-keepers" and thereby impose peace, but second was his ambition to supplant English with French goods in the continental markets. His economic warfare thus supplemented his economic imperialism. On the other hand, he did not hesitate to buy for his army such English goods as could not be obtained in France. Nor, curiously enough, did English merchants hesitate to sell their goods to "the enemy of the human race," their distinguished opponent, even though their own government forbade such sales. It was difficult, apparently, for English merchants to distinguish between their "patriotic duty" to smuggle goods into Europe to break the continental blockade, and the treasonable act of trading with the enemy in wartime.

Smuggling became big business after 1807. From Heligoland, from the Ionian islands, Malta, Portugal, and elsewhere, English manufactured goods and colonial products literally poured into Europe. Price differences of one to nine on sugar, coffee, tobacoo, and the like made such commerce extremely profitable. To check it, Napoleon was forced to embark on a new round of aggression.

His brother Louis winked at Dutch smuggling in his kingdom, so Louis was deposed and the kingdom of Holland was annexed to France. The British Heligoland smugglers had such a field day in northern Germany that Napoleon finally annexed the whole southern coast of the North Sea. A Franco-Spanish army marched into Portugal to divide that kingdom. It proved impossible to take Lisbon, defended as it was by Anglo-Portuguese forces and supplied by sea, but the adventure led to the deposition of the Spanish king and the installation of Napoleon's brother, Joseph, as king of Spain. The flow of smuggled goods from the Ionian islands and Malta led to the annexation of the Illyrian coast on the Adriatic, and was one of the factors involved in the annexation of Rome and the papal states. Napoleon might annex all of Europe, but he did not have the personnel necessary to supervise it and stop the smuggling of English goods.

It is undoubtedly true that Napoleon's ambitions and projects wandered far beyond the continental system. We know, for example, that he entertained ideas about an overseas empire that included Egypt and Syria as well as India and the New World, but all such projects were conditional on the defeat of England, and there was no other way to accomplish this than through the route of economic warfare. By 1808 he had subdued the great land powers of Europe, but so long as England controlled the seas he could not obtain peace except on enemy terms. He could not build or buy a navy, and he could not invade England without one. The continental system whereby he tried to shut out England from the markets of Europe was his one trump card.

However, Napoleon did not understand that sea power not only protected England but also opened up new markets for English goods. It would be folly to assume that the continental system did not hurt English commerce, but it is also evident that it did not seriously check the development of the English economy. The loss of continental markets was in part compensated for by the development of new markets in the world beyond Europe. Revolutions in the Spanish colonies in South America rendered accessible to English merchantmen harbors that had never before been available, and the revolutionary armies there needed a variety of goods that could be produced in England. Bolívar and San Martín, the "liberators" of South America, thereby made good some of the economic losses resulting from Napoleon's continental system. In India and the Orient, too, English conquests made at the end of the eighteenth century now paid dividends in the form of new markets, after Napoleon had closed the ports of Europe.

Thus the smugglers from Heligoland, Malta, the Ionian islands, and elsewhere, the markets in South America and the Orient, the colonies, and the United States, as well as the requirements of war in England itself, prevented the English economy from being ruined by Napoleon's blockade. On the contrary, English credit remained strong, and the country's ability to produce the sinews of war for her armies and navy and any others that would help to defeat the "enemy of the human race" actually grew during the conflict. Parliament never had trouble selling the bonds that provided men, allies, and the materials of war, even though Napoleon annexed or controlled almost all the courts of Europe.

3. EUROPE IN REVOLT

"It was a fine Empire." That was Napoleon's considered judgment many years later at St. Helena where, as a prisoner, he created the myth of the "liberal empire" and the belief that the implacable hostility of England alone prevented the unification of Europe. The former aided his nephew to gain the French throne in 1851; the latter provided an alibi for his failures. Actually, of course, Napoleon's empire was jerry-built at every joint, a thing of paper laws and decrees, of paper treaties and agreements, rather than an organic structure for European society. After 1813 no one in Europe, not even the French, wanted to keep it alive. The French were too numbed by despotism and war to be willing to fight when the Russian soldiers arrived; and the non-French parts of the Empire fell apart with the first defeat of the emperor's battalions. By 1814 it had become perfectly clear that Napoleon's power extended to the points of his bayonets, and not much further.

It was too much to ask that the doctrine of *civic equality*, unequally applied, should satisfy all Europe so completely that a universal imperium could be created. Even if the French had been generous, they probably would have failed; but they were not generous, and the idea of equality became a travesty. Men in Italy, Germany, Spain, and Holland did not regard the extortions of the Empire as equality. French agents and the French army looted their libraries, art treasures, and imposed crushing taxes upon them; the *Code Napoléon* seemed little enough in return. Nor did the non-French inhabitants of Europe like the imposition of the French language and customs. As long as "aping French ways" was optional, French culture had made great strides among the upper crust of European society, but when the French language became compulsory, the result was increased hostility to all things French. It is an interesting and instructive fact that the anti-French sentiment in Europe that had been but a murmur before 1789 had become a roar by 1810. In the interval, both the revolutionary and imperial soldiers and functionaries had attempted to impose French culture by force.

As we look back on it now, this Empire ran counter to the strongest political forces that were shaping the destinies of the western world: nationalism and popular sovereignty. Beside these currents, the hostility of England to Napoleon's projects is dwarfed in importance. From Spain to Moscow Napoleon's Empire not only failed to build organic political institutions respected by men, but also, and more important, it aroused an intense feeling of hostility towards France and a new loyalty to the homeland. By 1813 there were German soldier songs with emotional force equal to that of the "Marseillaise" in 1793. The blind anti-French hatred among Spanish and Russian people drove the invaders from both of those countries. In other words, Napoleon's Empire may have forced the body of Europe into a kind of obedience, but it failed to capture the spirit and the loyalties of Europe's people. Therefore, all the arrangements made to build an Empire were and remained mere scraps of paper. The *Code Napoléon* may have tried to give the people of Europe *civic equality*, but his rule raised among the people of Europe the cry for liberty. German historians call this revolt the *"Befreiungskrieg"*—War of Liberation—and tell the story as a people's war for the right to be governed by their own institutions, their own nationals, and in their own interests. Napoleon found that Frenchmen were willing to trade liberty for equality; Europe obviously was not.

Let us look at the story. The first fissures in the Napoleonic system developed in Spain. The Spaniards had never liked foreigners; their leaders were clergymen and noblemen who stood to lose by the application of

French revolutionary measures; and since the Spanish bourgeoisie was weak, in fact, practically nonexistent, there was literally almost no social support for either the Revolution or Napoleonic institutions. Thus, while the Spaniards may have had few real reasons for loyalty to the Bourbon family that ruled them, when Napoleon enticed Spain's king to Bayonne (1808) and forced him to abdicate in favor of Joseph Bonaparte, he conjured up a hornet's nest about his ears. The revolt started with isolated acts of violence, was broadened by guerrilla bands operating from mountain valleys, and finally developed into a full-fledged war with Anglo-Portuguese forces joining the Spaniards.

Spain was a poor field for Napoleonic military strategy. Its mountains favored the "hit and run" tactics of the guerrillas. To hold Spain against even the inferior forces of poorly armed men tied down tens of thousands of Napoleon's veterans who were desperately needed elsewhere. The Spanish war also made excessive demands on the French treasury—demands that Napoleon could ill afford to meet. Historians have called Spain the "running sore" of the Empire. It was more than that; it came close to being the meat chopper for the imperial army.

Even though Napoleon clapped a censorship around the Spanish rebellion, the news soon leaked out to the rest of Europe. His difficulties in Spain made Napoleon more willing to make concessions when he met Alexander at Erfurt in 1808; since his army was unencumbered, Alexander had become the stronger force. Napoleon had to concede the czar's right to take Finland from Sweden and to extend his territory to the southwest at the expense of Turkey, but he found the czar strangely unwilling to make important counterconcessions to him. Alexander realized that the balance of power was tilting in his favor; he had firsthand information about Napoleon's difficulties. Talleyrand, Napoleon's own foreign minister, was advising Alexander to resist him.

In 1808 Napoleon's need for aid from this reluctant ally was real for the Spanish uprisings had also emboldened the Austrians. The Emperor Francis had never really accepted Austerlitz as the final word between France and Austria; even less had his chief military and civil advisers. The defeat had taught the Viennese court that reforms were necessary in both the legal and military institutions of the Empire. When a civic militia, vaguely reminiscent of the French National Guard, appeared in the German parts of the Hapsburg state, men knew that Austria was on the march. The legal and military reforms were accompanied by a propaganda campaign vilifying everything French and glorifying the war heroes of Hapsburg tradition. A war fever ran through the German population. The French ambassador uneasily noted that for the first time the government, the army, and the populace seemed agreed in their enthusiasm for war. The Emperor Francis was reluctant to give the word, but finally, early in 1809, after receiving secret assurances of neutrality from both Russia and Prussia, Austria declared war on France.

This time Napoleon had trouble finding troops to fight the Spanish insurgents, to occupy Europe against possible English invasion or the rebellion of subject peoples, and to fight a major war with Austria. He scraped together an army, but it was not like the one that had fought at Austerlitz. The Austrians, still not masters of the new strategy, obliged him by invading Bavaria and then failing to move their forces rapidly. Even with relatively green troops, Napoleon could concentrate his forces at a point with great speed, a trick that often gave him numerical superiority on a given battlefield even though his enemy might outnumber him in the province. The campaign went badly for the Austrians; they were driven out of Bavaria, and Napoleon again occupied Vienna. However, the Austrian army was still in being, and very anxious to fight. Finally a great battle was fought at Wagram (1809). The carnage on both sides was terrible, and at last the Austrians withdrew. But the situation was not the same as at the battles of Austerlitz, Jena, or Friedland; the Austrians were not disorganized in their retreat, nor were the French in any position to follow them with an annihilating attack. By 1809 Napoleon's army was not as good as it had been in 1805, nor was the Austrian army as poor as the one that had fought at Austerlitz. The disparity between the two was disappearing.

The Emperor Francis, however, made peace after Wagram. Austria could not challenge France alone, the amount of English aid had been negligible, and Russia and Prussia had remained neutral. The Treaty of Schönbrunn stripped more territory from Austria, and, significantly, after this peace an Austrian princess went to France as the bride of Napoleon. Marie Louise, daughter of the Hapsburgs, became the wife of the new Caesar, because Josephine had been unable to produce an heir. That made the emperor of France a son-in-law of the emperor of Austria, but the marriage did not dampen the hatred that the Austrians felt for Napoleon, nor did it make the French emperor more considerate of his father-in-law's subjects. As an example of Napoleon's brutality, the Tyrolese rebel, Andreas Hofer, was executed for supporting the Emperor Francis almost the same day that Marie Louise became empress of France. Napoleon needed to establish a stable, legitimate throne by having descendants; he was not interested in the feelings of his new relatives. His chief regret was that he was not his own great-grandson, a role that would have made legitimate all his pretensions.

After Austria had been beaten down, Russia and Prussia became the hope of Napoleon's enemies. Prussia, particularly, developed into the rising star of German nationalism. After his defeat Frederick William III took as his ministers a group of men who believed that Prussia must experience a revolution similar to the one that had occurred in France, but one more controlled. It is possibly within the German tradition to desire a revolution "with order." Stein and Hardenburg were the civil reformers. They abolished the differences in land and occupation that had separated nobles from commoners, and began the reforms that ended serfdom. *Civic equality,* the key word of the French Revolution, became a fundamental expression of the Prussian reforms. With legal reforms that opened the doors of occupation and state service to everyone, no matter what his birth, came also an educational reform that was to give Prussia the finest educational institutions of any of the great powers. The universities of Halle, Berlin, and Breslau became powerhouses for disseminating the doctrine of German nationalism.

Along with the civic reforms came a reform in the Prussian army. At Jena and Auerstädt an army of serfs and vagabonds, commanded by noblemen whom they feared more than the enemy, had been defeated by the French. Scharnhorst and Gneisenau, who undertook to reorganize the Prussian army, understood that the brutal discipline of the Frederickan army could not be retained in a citizen army. The bourgeoisie would never trust their sons to the sergeant's whip: and yet without the bourgeoisie to raise the *élan* of the ranks, no modern army could be created. Thus, the first reform was in the spirit and practice of discipline. The second measure of reform was imposed upon it by Napoleon. He had limited the Prussian army by treaty to 42,000 men; therefore Prussia devised a program of training recruits quickly and then dismissing them into the reserves. By 1813 this so-called *Krümpersystem* had not been in existence long enough to assure Prussia of a large trained army, but old soldiers, students, and the youth of Germany rallied to Prussia and thereby provided an army capable of fighting the French.

The legal and military reforms accompanied one of the most stirring popular movements that has ever swept a nation. In the latter eighteenth century men like Herder had begun to teach the importance of national cultural development. As German university professors, they opposed the invasion of French culture on the grounds that it crippled the growth of German culture. Until the advent of French troops and commissars in Germany, their teaching had been largely academic, but after 1795 and particularly after 1806 the professors were joined by poets and publicists who began a great propaganda battle for the minds and emotions of German youth. Professor Fichte's *Address to the German Nation* was a triumphant call to action. Arndt, Schlegel, Humboldt, Jahn, and others—poets, philosophers, scientists, and gymnasium teachers—joined the chorus. When the opportunity to fight for Germany finally came, the universities, technical schools, and gymnasia (secondary schools including approximately the age levels from twelve to twenty) were emptied as the elite of the German youth joined the colors. After Austria's defeat in 1809, Prussia became the hope of these ardent nationalists; they, with Prussia's civil and military reformers, envisaged the birth of a new Germany.

The French did not understand the German movement, and fortunately, too, for surely they would have shot Fichte had they known what might be the result of the good professor's teachings. Like so many men who rely on stark force or on money, the French gave little heed to an intellectual movement, even though it soon had developed emotional outpourings similar to those that filled the republic's armies in 1793–1795.

Since Napoleon was quartering about one hundred thousand men on Prussian soil, he did not even consider it possible that Prussia might threaten him. Russia, however, was quite another story. After 1809 Alexander became less and less willing to play the role of ally to Napoleon. There were many reasons. The Russian Baltic nobles were being hurt economically by the blockade. The French were not living up to their promises to support Alexander against Turkey. There was anti-French feeling rampant in Russia, and Alexander understood that to oppose it was to court assassination. For almost a century regicide had been a regular procedure in Russia. The czar opened his ports to English goods; he surrounded himself with anti-French advisers from all over Europe as well as from Russia; and he protested vigorously the growth of the Grand Duchy of Warsaw. Furthermore, French agents discovered that Alexander was negotiating an alliance with Bernadotte[5] and peace with the sultan of Turkey. Such news could mean only that Alexander was freeing his flanks for action against Napoleon.

By 1812 the breach was complete, and in spite of the fact that an English army was fighting alongside the Spanish insurgents in Spain, Napoleon decided to punish Russia and end all threats from the east. Among his papers there have also been discovered grandiose plans for contact with India that have made historians wonder if "Caesar" desired also to be "Alexander." Such plans can probably be dismissed as the stuff that an ambitious man might play with; they never became near to achieving reality.

However, Napoleon did assemble an army of half a million men from all over western Europe and led them against Russia. The French were in a minority; it was an imperial army of Italians, Flemish, Dutch, Spaniards, Poles, Germans, and Frenchmen, bound together only by a promise of

---

[5] In 1810 Charles XIII of Sweden made Marshal Bernadotte heir to his throne on the mistaken notion that Bonaparte would approve. Actually Bernadotte and Napoleon were never friendly, although Napoleon had made the former prince of Ponte Corvo. When Bernadotte became king of Sweden, he reversed the anti-Russian policy of Charles XIII to be on the side of Napoleon's enemies. He commanded one of the armies that finally defeated Napoleon in 1813. At his death men discovered tattooed on the chest of the Swedish king the motto, "Death to all kings." He had started his career as one of Carnot's republican generals.

cities to loot and the will of a great soldier. Most of its regiments had no great desire to fight; this was not the army of 1795 that had defended *La Patrie,* nor that of 1805 that had carried the banners of imperial France through Germany; the soldiers were mostly conscripts recruited into the imperial army against their will and kept in line as much by fear of discipline as by fear of the enemy.

The story of the invasion of Russia in 1812 has been told many times. Tolstoy's account is still the most brilliant, but in *War and Peace* hard fact suffered whenever met by a good story. Nonetheless, no other writer has ever caught the emotional force behind the defeat of Napoleon in 1812. Like Charles XII a hundred years before him, and Hindenburg and Hitler in the century after, Napoleon learned that whoever fights Russia fights against time and space enlarged by poor roads, and a blind hatred in the hearts of the peasants and townspeople along the line of march. Russians have not always made good soldiers, but in modern times when they have defended their own lands they have been as tenacious and brave as the best.

As Napoleon advanced, the Russian army fumbled backward, at first because its leaders could not agree; later, after Kutusov assumed command, the retreat was by design. Thus Napoleon's lines of communication were dangerously extended through hostile territory, while the Russians were falling back to their own sources of horses, food, munitions, and guns. Nor was that all. As they retreated, the Russians of 1812, like those who fought the Swedish Charles or the German Hitler, burned towns, villages, and supplies, so that little of use fell to the advantage of the invader. Napoleon, perplexed and frustrated, pressed on even after he knew that the campaign should be over. Finally, at Borodino the Russians gave battle rather than let the French take Moscow without a fight. Borodino (September 1812) was the battle of Wagram over again, only bloodier; corpses were piled up like cut grain in the fields. Yet neither army broke. Kutusov hoped to renew the conflict the next day, but could not. He withdrew through Moscow, then swung around to the south, where from Tula he could get recruits, cannon, horses, food, and clothing.

This was the first time that the civilian inhabitants of a captured capital fled before the invaders. Napoleon entered Moscow, but it was a deserted city. The wooden houses soon caught fire, and no one seemed able or willing to extinguish them. By October, unable to negotiate with the Czar or to stay in Moscow, Napoleon ordered a retreat. The only road open to him was back over the blackened path that he had already used. The weather of November and December, Russian guerrilla troops, and infuriated peasants made terrible inroads upon his forces. The army left Moscow laden with loot, but both the loot and the bones of the looters were later generously strewn across Russia. A twentieth-century Russian historian, Professor Tarlé, has shown that Russian losses were about equal to those of the French, a fact that explains Kutusov's unwillingness to fight another battle. If this report of losses is true, almost a million men, soldiers and civilians, perished between the day Napoleon entered Russia and the day the remnants of his army straggled back across the frontier. Of a little more than half a million imperial soldiers, about ten percent returned.

The magnitude of the defeat was immediately apparent. General Yorck, commanding a Prussian army, joined the Russians, and announced that his army would force the king of Prussia to help liberate Europe. In the next months the last coalition was formed—Russia, England, Prussia, and finally, after some hesitation, Austria joined together to liberate Europe. To read the proclamations of this last coalition, one would almost think that the Committee of Public Safety had been reconstituted. Liberty, equality, and the rights of nationality, those were words which had once been the undisputed possession of France. Now they were turned against the French emperor, as the armies of Russia, Prussia, Austria, and England became the "armies of liberation."

In 1813 Napoleon raised a new army, but it was impossible to get adequate supplies with which to arm his troops. The cannon, wagons, and muskets scattered over Russia were now desperately needed in Germany. The question was not whether Napoleon could hold Germany, but whether he could reconquer it. He was outnumbered now, overwhelmingly so. At least two men who had won great honor as generals in the French revolutionary armies commanded troops opposing him, while the Prussian, Russian, and Austrian soldiers were led by men who had learned the art of war from Napoleon himself—the bitter way. The campaign of the summer of 1813 was exciting and full of suspense; it inevitably ended with a crushing defeat of the French army at Leipzig, the Battle of the Nations. Napoleon retreated into France, followed by the allies. At the same time, the Anglo-Spanish forces in the peninsula succeeded in clearing Spain of French troops and also began to invade France. The people of Paris did not move when foreign soldiers returned the visits the French had made to Vienna, Berlin, Madrid, Rome, Venice, and Moscow; and Napoleon's own marshals finally forced his abdication at Fontainebleau.

The military story had not been completely told when Napoleon, deprived of the French throne, was given the government of the island of Elba. Louis XVIII and the *émigré* noblemen returned to France. Louis was welcomed by the Napoleonic Senate, by a street crowd bought with Bourbon money through Talleyrand's intervention, and by the allies. However, no one, unless it were Louis XVIII and his family, really welcomed back the *émigrés* who proceeded to demand rank in the French army and offices in the French government on the basis of seniority gained in service in Russia, Austria, or elsewhere. The *émigrés* also immediately commenced a campaign to have their lands restored to them, along with their ancient privileges. Compared with such men, Napoleon looked like a great liberal. The officeholders, soldiers, and purchasers of the confiscated lands began to look to Elba for some sign of relief.

Whether it was deserved or not, discontent with the restored regime did lead to Napoleon's return—for a hundred days in 1815. He landed on French soil, captured the French armies sent against him without firing a shot, and re-established himself in Paris. Then he announced his intention of creating a liberal regime for France, and warned the allies not to interfere.

The allies, engaged in Vienna in making a peace for Europe, could not allow this turn of events to go unchecked, and prepared again for war. It has been said that Napoleon lacked everything but men, and even men were in short supply. Apologists have said that it was the accident of the sunken road at Waterloo that caused the French defeat. Such statements overlook the fact that the English and Prussian armies under Wellington and Blücher outnumbered the French and were much better equipped. Furthermore, behind them, ready to finish off any French forces that might succeed in escaping, were the armies of Austria and Russia. The outcome of the campaign of June, 1815, was even more surely predetermined than the one that produced the battle at Leipzig. Napoleon was defeated at Waterloo (June 18, 1815) by a Europe that his Empire had aroused against him. After Waterloo he was sent to St. Helena in the south Atlantic, where he ended his life as an exile and as an apologist for his career and his Empire.

The Congress of Vienna. Princes and statesmen of Europe, including representatives of the king of France, gathered at Vienna to give Europe a new international law. (Culver Service)

Chapter 31

THE PACIFICATION OF
EUROPE, 1814-1825

1. THE CONDITIONS OF PEACE

Like most peace treaties, those made in 1814–1815 were conditioned by the agreements that had united the victorious powers. In 1812–1813 a grand alliance had come into being to fight Napoleon, and each member of that coalition had exacted terms in return for assistance. The great powers—England, Russia, Prussia, and Austria—had negotiated a whole sheaf of treaties with one another and with the petty kings and princes of Europe. As long as Napoleon was "on the loose," the great powers were in no position to dictate arbitrarily to their smaller neighbors. As a result, the petty princes of Germany and Italy, as well as the kings in Spain, Portugal, and Scandinavia, came to the peace conference more or less assured that their "interests" would be adequately protected. These treaties were, therefore, a primary conditioning factor in the construction of the new Europe. General policies that emerge as great decisions are very often the result of many petty decisions rather than of a rational plan.

Furthermore, the promises did not end with the treaty commitments. The War of the Liberation was a people's war, fought by volunteers as well as by mercenary and conscripted soldiers, and with nationalist ideals. This was the legacy of the French Revolution. To induce the people of Europe to join willingly in this great effort against "the enemy of the human race," the princes of the coalition made many stirring promises for the future. By speech and proclamation the people of Europe were assured of the liberty, equality, and fraternity that the French had failed to give. It was "wonderful" to see Czar Alexander, autocrat of Russia, blow the trumpet of liberty, to hear Frederick William, despot of Prussia, promise a constitution, to see the Emperor Francis, absolute ruler on the Danube, in the role of champion of the rights of man. It was somewhat more difficult to see how they were

711

to accomplish these miracles, especially since by training and temperament they were wedded to the authoritarian tradition. Once the war was won, however, the proclamations and promises came home to haunt the men who had made them. Frederick William, for example, was troubled for the rest of his life because of his failure to develop the constitution that he had promised his people.

Even the French had been given a share of the promises. The allies adopted the fiction that they were fighting Napoleon, not France; and indeed both Alexander and Metternich had good reasons for wishing to see France decide her own destiny without too much foreign interference. Without France as a stable member of the European family, Prussia would become too powerful. Therefore, they assured the French that France alone would decide the question of her own government, and that she would be treated justly in the territorial settlement, provided Napoleon was excluded from the throne. This was, of course, wise; a whole generation possessing political, property, and legal rights had grown up in France, and understandably they should have some voice in their future.

Quite obviously too, the personalities and political ideals of the men who were in command of the armies and the policies of the coalition were conditioning factors in the formation of the peace. Three of them were particularly important: Czar Alexander of Russia, Lord Castlereagh of England, and Prince Metternich of Austria. They played the leading roles in the drama, but there were a dozen or so more or less important persons who had supporting roles. Among these were King Frederick William of Prussia, Talleyrand, that amazing political changeling who came to the surface as the foreign minister of the new Bourbon king of France, and the revolutionary soldier, General Bernadotte, who was now king of Sweden.

Of them all Czar Alexander was perhaps the most colorful. Like Wilson at Paris a century later, he took the part of the visionary who soared toward a world where strife would be banished. Unlike Wilson, he never really lost sight of his own ambitions and interests. As we noted, Alexander had been educated by a Swiss Jacobin tutor, by Greek Orthodox monks, and in the hard school of the Russian court, where assassination was a not unusual way of ending the career of a monarch. He had thus been given access to the idealistic words current in his era, but had not been deprived of a sense of rude political realities. He came to the conference talking about popular sovereignty, about Christian unity, about the brotherhood of monarchs, and about his intention to give Poland a model government. This nice mixture of religious and political mysticism interlarded with a hardheaded understanding of his own interests makes Alexander an interesting case study for historians. In an argument for Russian control of Poland, he first used his idealism to justify his position, but when pushed hard he brutally retorted, "I have two hundred thousand men in Poland. Put me out who can!" Needless to say, Alexander could speak for Russia; he was absolute monarch in a land where assassination was the only redress against tyranny.

Lord Castlereagh, the foreign minister of England, was also able to speak for his government. He had the complete confidence of the Cabinet in London, and was able to make decisions without continually referring to his colleagues for support. He was a shrewd man, utterly devoid of political or religious mysticism. More than most English statesmen, he understood the political problems of Europe and appreciated England's relationship to them. He was fully convinced that the security and prosperity of England depended upon a solid agreement of the great powers to cooperate militarily to prevent a resurgence of French revolutionary or imperial power. He believed that Europe could act together only if the peace settlement created a balance of power that was recognized as reasonable and just by victors and vanquished alike. Thus, Castlereagh strove for a territorial settlement that would satisfy all the parties concerned, the vanquished as well as the victors, and a strong alliance to guarantee the settlement after it had been reached.

The third member of the "big three" was Prince Metternich. His name has ever since been associated with the era 1814–1848, and for almost a century it meant "reactionary politics" to all liberal statesmen and historians. Since 1919, however, Metternich's reputation has undergone considerable reevaluation. After witnessing the failure of the first peace conference of the twentieth century, the architect of the treaties of Paris and Vienna has appeared to historians in a new light.

Metternich was obsessed by the fact that the ideals of nationalism and popular sovereignty were potentially disastrous to the Danubian monarchy that he governed. That state was made up of four major racial and linguistic groups—German, Slavic, Romance (Italian and Rumanian), and Magyar—with at least a dozen distinct languages or dialects. The provinces and kingdoms of the monarchy were "federated" into a kind of unity under the Hapsburg "Emperor and King" at Vienna, but each had its own local rights, customs, and institutions. Such a state could not be held together (and was not) if the nationalists' doctrine that each national group should govern itself were ever to be honored universally. It had, nevertheless, been a useful political unit. It had defended Europe against the Turks; it had been a check on the overwhelming power of Louis XIV and Napoleon; it had acted as a brake on the rise of Prussia-Germany. In the World War (1914–1918) it was to be destroyed in its attempt to exclude Russia from Europe. The destruction of this Danubian monarchy in 1918–1921 left central Europe open to Hitler, to Stalin, and to any power that could produce a military force. However, as Metternich understood the world of 1815, this conglomerate of Germanic, Slavic, Romance, and Magyar people could be held together only by emphasizing the federal rather than the national principle for Europe. He could not know that before another century had passed nationalism was to become a flaming beacon for political and military action.

The Danubian monarchy was in fact a federation of people. Metternich wished to extend that principle by creating a German federation, an Italian federation, and a European federation, each of which would include part or all of the provinces and kingdoms of the Danubian monarchy. Thus the German-Bohemian states of the Danubian monarchy would share in the German confederation, the Italian provinces in the *Lex Italica,* and the whole monarchy in the federal alliance of the great powers. He envisaged other federations (Scandinavian and Iberian, for instance) that might grow up to create a completely overlapping political order for all Europe. The main difficulty with his federal Europe was that it was based upon rational principles, and had neither emotional nor historical appeal for the people of Europe.

Metternich's second guiding principle was a belief in the balance of power. The idea of a European balance of power had emerged out of the two great wars at the turn of the eighteenth century (1683–1714); the Napoleonic era seemed to teach that this power balance was the only alternative to the tyranny of one power. Therefore Metternich wanted to establish a territorial and political order that would prevent any one power from acting to the detriment of its neighbors. This meant in effect that the Danubian monarchy, as well as France, would be constrained by the general power structure of Europe. It also implied that France must be reintegrated into Europe as an integral part of the total government of Europe. In the twentieth century statesmen had to learn the hard way the conclusion that Metternich reached —namely, that the land of the vanquished can not be made into a political and military vacuum without seriously damaging the balance of power.

Other men who were consulted about the settlement of 1814–1815, for example, Frederick William of Prussia and several Prussian statesmen, guarded the interests of their country. Talleyrand skillfully maneuvered himself and France into the roles of protector and sponsor of the rights of small states. He was too experienced a diplomat to be sidetracked into inaction, even though his government had no military force to back up its program. There was also a host of lesser men representing princes and princelings who stood guard on special interests. There was not the melee of tongues that was to haunt twentieth-century peace conferences, but there was a babble that only the skillful could untangle.

2. PROBLEMS OF THE PEACE TREATIES

As we have seen, when the allied armies pressed into France after the battle of Leipzig (1813), the leaders of the Coalition did not have a fixed solution for the French problem. They were resolved that Napoleon and his dynasty must be deposed, but, as we have said, they were not ready to tell the French what sort of regime should replace the Empire. Alexander had assured the French that they would have a voice in their destiny, and both Castlereagh and Metternich were agreed that no government could be imposed upon France.

As is usual in such cases, those with a plan had a distinct advantage. There were several tentative suggestions: a monarchy with a new and untried dynasty; one headed by the Duke of Orléans, a cousin of the Bourbon family; a Bourbon restoration; even a republic was suggested. Talleyrand came up with the winning proposal. With a pocketful of money from the Bourbon interests, he organized a popular demonstration in favor of Louis XVIII (1814–1824), the Bourbon pretender to the throne. At the same time he bribed or persuaded enough politically important Frenchmen in the imperial Senate to accept this solution. For the world and the allies he produced an argument: the restoration of the Bourbons, he pointed out, would be in accord with a principle, the principle of legitimacy. The Bourbons were kings of France by the grace of God and tradition. Any other solution would be mere expediency and inevitably short lived; the Bourbon restoration would be the triumph of principle. Like many intellectuals, Talleyrand could build a sound argument to support the program that he found useful, reasonable, and profitable. Since he also gave assurance that the legitimate Bourbon king would grant France a constitutional charter, both the allies and the French were apparently satisfied to accept the return of the Bourbon dynasty to France.

For over a century many historians read Talleyrand's eloquent defense of the principle of legitimacy, and concluded that the treaties of 1814–1815 were also based on that principle. A comparison of the treaty map of Europe of 1814–1815 with that of 1789 will illustrate how unrealistic is such an assumption. The allies accepted the principle of legitimacy for France because it seemed to assure a stability that would allow that kingdom to play its part in the European balance of power. Elsewhere the principle of legitimacy was used or ignored, depending upon its ability to produce a stable relationship within the European community. It is unjust to accuse the men of 1814–1815 of narrowly following a limited doctrine like legitimacy in their organization of Europe.

Once the Bourbons had been restored, the allies made peace with the new French government. The first Treaty of Paris (May 1814) is an indication of the statesmanlike vision of the victors. They wanted France to return to the family of states as a peaceful member; therefore, they wrote a treaty that would allow Frenchmen to accept the political structure of Europe. They set French frontiers at the point they had reached in 1792, when the Bourbon king, Louis XVI, had been deposed, thus leaving to France some of the territory in the Rhineland that the revolutionary armies had conquered. They imposed no indemnity and no army of occupation on the kingdom. Napoleon was provided for by giving him the government of the island of Elba as a sort of consolation prize. After all, he was the son-in-law of the Emperor Francis of Austria.

After making peace with France, the statesmen of Europe went to Vienna to write a peace for the rest of Europe (September 1814 to June 1815). It was easy enough to restore Spain and Portugal to their pre-Napoleonic governments and to assure the Scandinavian states of their sovereignty, but central Europe presented thorny problems. Germany, Poland, and Italy had been so radically reorganized several times during the preceding twenty-five years that it was impossible to return to the old order, even if men wished to do so. Obviously there was no simple principle such as legitimacy to give form to central Europe.

As we have seen, most of the petty German princes came to Vienna with assurances that they should retain all the lands they had acquired in the reshuffle that had taken place on the destruction of the Holy Roman Empire. At the same time, the powers had also promised some kind of German unity to the intellectuals and others who had played an important role in the War of the Liberation. German unity, of course, could not be established without agreement between Austria and Prussia, the two great powers in Germany, and neither of them would consent to a solution that left the other in control. The peacemakers had considerable land to allocate, for Napoleon had annexed a large segment of western Germany to France, and several of the German princes had endangered their territorial holdings by remaining too long in Napoleon's camp, but these lands had long since been the subject of diplomatic conversations and treaties, so that, in most cases, their "ultimate" destiny was, in a sense, decided before the congress met at Vienna.

Fortunately for the peacemakers, the years 1802–1814 had reduced the number of principalities in Germany from about three hundred to less than forty. It was obviously impossible to reduce the forty to one, as some exponents of German unity wished, but it would be possible to create a federation of the forty states that might satisfy the promises made to the German nationalists. This, of course, was exactly what Metternich wished, since his Austria would necessarily play a large role in such a federation and thereby integrate the states of Germany with the kingdoms and provinces of the Danubian monarchy. Thus the Germanic Confederation (*Deutsche Bund*) was created at Vienna as the only solution that would guarantee the right of the German princes and also provide some sort of unity for Germany. Such a compromise was all that could be had in 1815, and the fact that it did not satisfy the nationalists only emphasizes its character as a compromise.

The constitution of the German Confederation provided for a diet, representing the states of the Confederation meeting at Frankfurt under the presidency of Austria. The most important single article required all the German states to come to the defense of Germany if any one of them were attacked. This, in effect, amounted to an Austro-Prussian alliance to guarantee central Europe from attacks by either France or Russia. The Confederation has often been looked upon as a sorry institution, because it did not provide a permanent solution for the German question. Somehow there have been very few permanent solutions to European problems. It might be better to realize that it guaranteed the frontiers of Germany from attack for over fifty years and, while it may not have satisfied everyone in Germany, it did provide a central political authority that gave the country as a whole some form of order for that period. Unlike the Constitution of the United States of America, it was unable to survive a German civil war in 1866, but it had never had the federal character of the United States Constitution. It was, in effect, a confederation of states bound together for mutual defense rather than a federation of states united in a common political enterprise.

While the Congress of Vienna had achieved a temporary solution for the German question, it proved impossible to work out a similar one for Italy. By an exchange of territories that gave the Austrian Netherlands (Belgium) to the king of Holland and Lombardy-Venetia to the Hapsburgs, the Danubian monarchy extended its political and military authority deep into northern Italy. Since several of the smaller Italian states were also governed by relatives of the Hapsburgs, the government in Vienna was assured of a large share of control over Italian affairs. Indeed, so much power went to Austria that neither the pope nor the king of Sardinia-Piedmont was willing to join a confederation of Italian states (*Lex Italica*) for fear of complete Austrian domination. Thus, the treaty makers at Vienna had to content themselves with a redefinition of Italy's frontiers that strengthened Piedmont-Sardinia as the buffer state between France and Austria, but left Austria as the most important force in Italy.

The Polish-Saxony question almost led to a rupture of the alliance, and possible conflict between Prussia and Russia on the one side, with England, Austria, and France on the other. By a secret treaty Alexander and Frederick William agreed on a transfer of territories that would give most of Poland to Russia and all Saxony to Prussia. There was nothing that could be done about Alexander's Polish demands since he was in occupation of the territory he wished to take over, but neither Austria nor England (whose king was also ruler of Hanover) was willing to see Saxony go to Prussia. As the crisis deepened, Talleyrand cleverly committed France to support England and Austria in case of a war, thereby insinuating himself into the councils of the victors. Fortunately for the allies, the crisis passed when Napoleon suddenly returned to France. It became more important to deal with him than to fight over the spoils. After his defeat, it was evident to all that Prussia should be strengthened by the addition of Rhineland territory from which she could watch France, rather than by Saxon territory in east central Germany.

The return of Napoleon was a dramatic reminder that politics and war are variable problems. In 1814 the situation in France was far from stable, no matter what Talleyrand might say about his "principle of legitimacy." As we have seen, there was a crowd of French *émigrés* who had returned home in the "baggage trains" of the allied armies. They had been exiles for a quarter of a century, and had lost much wealth and position as a result of the Revolution. On their return, they wanted to recoup their losses by re-acquiring their lands and by replacing the civil and military officials who were in control of France. Thus, they threatened everyone who had title to confiscated lands or who held a civil or military position; and all in all, a large crowd of people who also had wealth and talent were affected by the *émigrés*. It is not surprising to learn that plots against the Bourbons began to spring up, or that Napoleon at Elba learned that his services might again be needed.

Napoleon was bored governing Elba; the island was no substitute for governing Europe. When he learned of the discontent in France, he decided to intervene. With a few followers and loud proclamations, he landed in southern France and marched on Paris, winning over every army that was sent against him. After all, no French soldier in 1815 would shoot Napoleon. The Bourbons hastily left France, along with the *émigrés*, and Napoleon proclaimed his intention to establish a peaceful, liberal regime in Paris. As we have seen, such a challenge could not be ignored by the statesmen in Vienna. Now Napoleon really was "the enemy of the human race," and there was no alternative to the remobilization of the armies of Europe against him. The decision came at Waterloo (1815), one hundred days after Napoleon had landed in France.

When the allies arrived in Paris a second time, they were less disposed to be generous to France. The second Treaty of Paris (November 1815) reduced France's frontiers to those of 1789, imposed an indemnity on France to make her foot the bill for the whole Waterloo campaign, and placed an army of occupation in the kingdom to guarantee against any further such development. This treaty was stiffer than its predecessor, but it can hardly be called vindictive.

After the second Treaty of Paris, the allies quickly composed their differences and completed the treaties of Vienna. The final territorial settlement (1815) introduced several new features to the map of Europe. In the east, Alexander emerged as "king" of "Congress Poland." It is hard to say what was the "number" of this partition of Poland; if the first partition was in 1772, this must have been the fifth or sixth, and there were to be more to come. Both Prussia and Austria also received Polish provinces (Prussia was given Posen and west Prussia; Austria, Galicia), but most of Poland went to the Russian czar with the understanding that he would give it a "model constitution."

As we have already seen, the Germanic Confederation gave new form to Germany. The interesting territorial development in Germany, however, was the fact that Prussia lost most of her Polish subjects and acquired a large block of territory in the Rhineland largely inhabited by Roman Catholics. Thus Prussia not only emerged as "defender of the Rhine," but also as a predominantly "German" state with both Protestant and Catholic subjects. This was to become an important factor in the future evolution of a Germany that was to be organized as a national state.

The other interesting feature of the settlement was the emergence of the kingdoms of the Netherlands and of Piedmont-Sardinia as "buffer states." For the first time since the sixteenth century, the Catholic and Protestant Netherlands states were united, this time under the king of Holland. The idea behind this change of territory was that the new kingdom would be able to hold up an attack from France until the Prussian army could come to its assistance. The same theory accounted for the enlarged kingdom of Piedmont-Sardinia; it would hold off the French army until the Austrians, who acquired Lombardy-Venetia, could arrive to support it. The Netherlands "experiment" failed to develop into a state. The traditions of the "Burgundian crown" had not been considered in the reconstruction of the Netherlands; by ignoring the interests and aspirations of the Catholic south, the treaty only succeeded in creating a temporary situation. On the other hand, the buffer state of Piedmont-Sardinia was destined to annex all of Italy within half a century.

The Congress of Vienna was the first European peace congress at which the participants were more or less aware of their position as legislators of international law. Metternich liked to refer to the meetings of the powers as the *areopagus* ("high court" or "supreme tribunal"—he knew both the Greek language and Athenian history) of Europe. After the territorial adjustments had been made, it seemed proper to pass some general legislation to demonstrate both the powers and the temper of the Congress. At the urging of English humanitarians, the Congress decided to abolish the trade in slaves on the high seas. Such an act would at once affirm the power of Europe and the humanitarian impulses of the men who had overthrown the Napoleonic political system.

The slave trade had been a scandalous traffic in human flesh that had outraged humanitarian thinkers everywhere. The Vienna declaration did not, of course, actually end it, but it did give international sanction to English naval action on the African coast against it. Since English ships were thenceforth forbidden to engage in this lucrative trade, English warships undertook to prevent the ships of other nations from enjoying it. There were to be many serious arguments about the right of "visit and search."

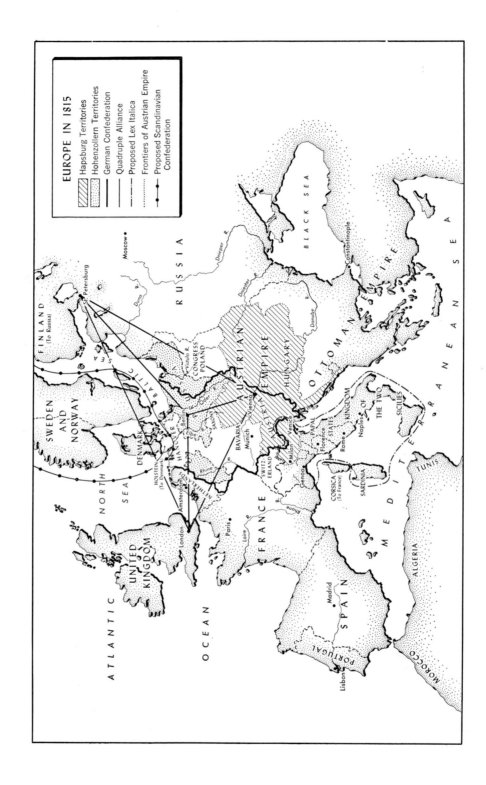

EUROPE IN 1815

Hapsburg Territories
Hohenzollern Territories
German Confederation
Quadruple Alliance
Proposed Lex Italica
Frontiers of Austrian Empire
Proposed Scandinavian
    Confederation

RUSSIA

BLACK SEA

Moscow

St. Petersburg

Dnieper R.

Dniester R.

Constantinople

OTTOMAN EMPIRE

Danube R.

FINLAND
(To Russia)

Dvina R.

Vistula R.

CONGRESS
POLAND

AUSTRIAN EMPIRE

HUNGARY

MEDITERRANEAN SEA

SWEDEN
AND
NORWAY

BALTIC SEA

DENMARK

Berlin

Oder R.

Elbe R.

Vienna

KINGDOM
OF
THE TWO
SICILIES

TUNIS

NORTH
SEA

HANOVER

HOLSTEIN
(To Denmark)

Amsterdam

SAXONY

BAVARIA
Munich

SWITZ-
ERLAND

PAPAL
STATES
Florence
Rome

Naples

SARDINIA

ATLANTIC

London

Paris

Rhine R.

Rhône R.

Loire R.

Milan

Genoa

CORSICA
(To France)

ALGERIA

UNITED
KINGDOM

FRANCE

Madrid

SPAIN

MOROCCO

OCEAN

PORTUGAL

Lisbon

3. INTERNATIONAL ORGANIZATION

In the years following the Treaty of Utrecht (1713), the Abbé de St. Pierre had spent much of his time writing and agitating for the creation of a society of nations to guarantee the peace of Europe. Cardinal Fleury had advised him to send forth a "band of missionaries to convert the hearts of princes"; nothing had come of that plan. Almost a century before St. Pierre's time, Sully, the trusted servant of Henry IV, had also proposed some such society of nations. In addition to those two men, there were a dozen or so others who had in one way or another suggested or urged the European states to form some kind of a league to bring peace to Europe.

Both Metternich and Alexander had ideas about an international organization to guarantee the peace. Metternich thought in terms of a confederation of the victor powers; Alexander wanted a broad alliance of all Christian princes. He had fallen under the spell of a religious mystic who convinced him that he had a "mission." His colleagues, more hardheaded than the czar, were embarrassed by the nebulous proposals that he insisted on making. Nonetheless, they were not able to avoid his plans, for Alexander was the ruler of the greatest land power in the world; in 1815 his armies were without doubt the strongest in Europe. Therefore, when the czar proposed the Holy Alliance (1815), there was little the other statesmen could do but sign. The Emperor Francis said that he hoped his subjects would not believe that he had suddenly become addlepated when they read the treaty. The Holy Alliance was, in effect, a hazy, inexact, and extremely pious-sounding expression of aspirations for international peace and brotherhood. Clothed in words used in Christian religious services, it seemed to be a Christian assertion of truth. After studying it in detail, however, it became evident that it was simply the statement of Alexander's mystic imagination.

Within less than a decade, every ruler in Europe had signed this treaty except the sultan of Turkey, the pope, and the king of England. The sultan as a non-Christian was not invited, perhaps because Alexander had other plans for Turkey. The pope refused to sign so nebulous a document sponsored by a heretic (Frederick William of Prussia) and a schismatic (Alexander I of Russia). The English prime minister could not sign the treaty since he was not "a ruling sovereign," and the English king was temporarily incapacitated so he could not sign. The regent expressed sympathy with the "aspirations" of the alliance, and assured the czar that England would join when her king had recovered from his illness.

While the Holy Alliance spoke of the brotherhood of rulers, the fatherhood of God, and the paternalistic relationship between rulers and subjects, the other treaty of 1815, the Quadruple Alliance, spoke of the exact commitments of soldiers and policy. This latter treaty sponsored by Metternich and Castlereagh was, in effect, a continuation of the Grand Alliance of the four great powers that had defeated Napoleon, and it undertook to insure the fruits of that victory. It guaranteed the status quo created at Vienna and Paris, and *forever* excluded the Napoleonic family from the French throne. It also provided for the mobilization of the allied military power in case France again undertook to disturb the peace. The treaty carefully defined in precise terms the military and political obligations of its signatories, but, recognizing that many conditions cannot be foreseen, the treaty also arranged for future consultation by the heads of the allied governments. In case the peace of Europe appeared to be threatened in any way, any one of the rulers or their first ministers could summon the four powers to a conference to meet the threat. This was the basis upon which the post-Vienna congresses were called to govern Europe.

The treaties of Paris and Vienna provided the territorial settlement of 1815; the Holy Alliance and the Quadruple Alliance established a sort of international structure to govern the Europe that emerged from the defeat of Napoleon. In spite of the objections raised by a few determined revolutionaries and nationalists, the treaties were popular with the vast majority of Europeans at the time, for they provided peace and a measure of stability that had been unknown for twenty-five years. It was as simple as that: in 1815 the people of Europe would probably have applauded any settlement that seemed to insure a degree of tranquillity. As we view these treaties today, they were clearly inadequate to meet the strains imposed upon Europe in the hundred years following 1815. Nonetheless, the main lines of the territorial map of Europe in 1815 are almost the same as those of 1914, and this fact speaks volumes for the wisdom of the mapmakers. Europe actually had a breathing space of a whole century before another war of world-wide scope engulfed its civilization.

4. UNFINISHED BUSINESS: REVOLUTION UNSATISFIED

It was not easy for Europe to become tranquil again. The passions, hatreds, ambitions, and fears of hard-bitten men on the right and left of the political stage could not be assuaged by a document or two signed by kings and prime ministers. In Italy, Germany, France, and Spain small groups of earnest men met secretly to discuss the possibility of another revolution. Some were nationalists, some were liberals, others were Jacobins, and all believed that it would be possible to "save" mankind by some political panacea or another. On the other hand, in the drawing rooms, the countinghouses, the cafés, and even the chancelleries, there were other equally earnest men who discussed ways and means of eradicating the traces of the Revolution from the legal and political institutions of their countries. The latter assumed that the clock could be set back twenty-five years, and then all would be as it had been before the spring of 1789. Revolutionaries and reactionaries, both were equally unrealistic, yet neither was ready to give up hope.

The first meeting of the great powers as a congress of Europe following the peace of 1815 did not officially take notice of the undercurrent of revolution and counterrevolution that threatened the peace. When the powers met in 1818 at Aix-la-Chapelle, they acted as if they believed that the peace was assured. The French government had paid its indemnity, and the powers by formal action withdrew their armies of occupation from France. This act seemed to prove that the Bourbons were not supported in France by foreign bayonets. After withdrawing their armies, the powers signed a new treaty—the Quintuple Alliance (1818)—in which France was included as one of the great powers of the "high court of Europe." They secretly re-signed the Quadruple Alliance—just in case. There was talk of revolutionary threats to Europe's peace, but since no revolution was in evidence, no action could be taken about such fears.

Within one year of this peaceful meeting, the forces of revolution and reaction had begun to produce problems all over Latin and Germanic Europe. In Naples a revolution forced the king to grant a constitution which he had no intention of observing if he could avoid it. In Germany, student groups (*Burschenschaften*) held demonstrations protesting the status quo. When a neurotic youth (Karl Sand) murdered the publicist-playwright, Kotzebue, because he was in the pay of Russia, the "student pranks" assumed a threatening appearance. Obviously, action of some sort was in order.

Since the first two overt revolutionary acts were in Italy and Germany, Metternich was the statesman most concerned. The question of the German students and their nationalist society, the Burschenschaften, seemed to Metternich to be a problem for the Germanic Confederation rather than for Europe as a whole. Thus the Carlsbad Decrees (1819) treated the student agitation as a German question: the student league was driven underground, the universities were muzzled on political questions, and press censorship was tightened. These repressive measures did not prevent the universities from teaching their students ideas that were fundamentally nationalistic and revolutionary, but they did, for the time being at least, place a lid on overt political agitation.

The revolution in Naples was a problem of a different order. The proposed Italian Confederation never came into existence, and so there was no Italian diet to deal with the Italian question. For different reasons Metternich and Alexander resolved to handle the problem as one requiring formal European action. Thus, a congress was called at Troppau (1820) to discuss the problem of revolution in general and the rights of Europe in particular.

The English government, for reasons that we shall develop later, urged

Metternich to act quickly in Naples, but not to generalize the action by a formal principle. Metternich and Alexander, however, went ahead with the proclamation of the Troppau Protocol, a document that established the right of the great powers to intervene in the affairs of any state if conditions in that state threatened the peace of Europe. This was the first statement of the right of intervention ever made. It was supported wholeheartedly by Russia, Austria, and Prussia, halfheartedly by France, and not at all by England.

From Troppau the representatives of the powers traveled to Laibach (January 1821), where they listened to the king of Naples explain the disgraceful way the revolutionaries had treated him and the danger they represented to Europe. The powers mandated Austria to restore the king to his "rights." In the summer of 1821 an Austrian army invaded Naples, and restored "order." In addition to re-establishing the king of Naples, the advent of the army gave Italians a reason for hating Austria.

While the powers were deliberating on Italy, a revolution had broken out in Spain. There were many reasons for this flare-up, most of them unquestionably Spanish or Spanish-American in origin. Nonetheless, with the precedents of the Troppau and Laibach solutions of the Italian revolution, the Spanish revolt, too, assumed a European character. This was especially true since events in France had brought an ultraroyalist government to power whose chiefs argued that France would not forget Napoleon until the Bourbons brought "glory" to French arms. Intervention in Spain seemed to those men to offer a possible avenue to such glory. Since Alexander of Russia also wanted the Spanish revolution suppressed, it was easy enough to call a congress on the Spanish question. Thus, the Congress of Verona (1822) ordered a French army to invade Spain and suppress the revolution. The military adventure, however, produced somewhat less "glory" than the ultraroyalists had expected.

The suppression of the *Burschenschaften* in Germany (Carlsbad Decrees, 1819) and the Neapolitan and Spanish revolutions (Troppau, 1820; Laibach, 1821; Verona, 1822) momentarily blanketed the revolutionary movements in those countries. The assassination of the Duke of Berry by a French revolutionary (1819) had provided the excuse to change electoral and press laws in France, and the revolutionaries there were also driven underground. However, the fires of revolution had not really been extinguished, and the repressive measures only succeeded in making men of moderate opinion increasingly suspicious of the reactionaries. The suppression of a student league, the arrest of a revolutionary leader, even the repression of a revolutionary government drove underground but did not eradicate revolutionary propaganda and organization. The revolutionaries had only to wait until their reactionary opponents had alienated men of moderate opinion.

5. *UNFINISHED BUSINESS: LATIN AMERICA*

When the smoke had cleared in Europe after 1815, it became evident that the epoch of the war had introduced changes into the European world beyond Europe. The young republic of the United States, after fighting a frustrating war with England (that of 1812) was spilling its population into the great midwestern river basins at a tremendous rate, and obviously preparing itself to rule the North American continent. In South America a series of revolutions had shaken most of Spain's colonies loose from their allegiance to the mother country, and were in the process of forming new states, independent of Spain. Within a decade of the treaties of Paris-Vienna, all the Spanish American mainland had thrown off the Spanish government, leaving only Cuba and a few other islands as reminders of Spain's once extensive colonial empire.

However, there was considerable difference between the government of the United States of America and those governments of the Spanish American states to the south. The former was obviously stable, and had been recognized as a member of the family of nations. The latter were often enough politically formless, with indistinct boundaries, undeveloped constitutions, and only a vague promise of stability. Indeed, the government in Spain had not even recognized the *fait accompli* of their independence, and was making plans for their reconquest. The political situation south of the Rio Grande to the Straits of Magellan had yet to be given form. The "liberators" like Bolívar, San Martín, and other lesser lights were soldiers and politicians, but they did not have enough politically educated fellow citizens to assure that their victories would create stable political institutions. After all, Spain's government of her colonies had not been calculated to educate the colonists to handle their own affairs.

England gained the most from this new order in Spanish America. As we noted, when Napoleon closed the harbors of Europe to legitimate trade, English merchants were fortunate to have the harbors of revolutionary Spanish America opened to them. By 1815 the English had become the principal suppliers of the revolutionary armies and the civilian population there. Naturally the English were anxious to see the revolutionary regimes succeed, for were the Spanish colonial regime to be re-established, much of the commercial traffic would come to an end. The revolutionary governments, however, were hardly stable enough to be given *de jure* recognition without running the risk of conflict with Spain. Still the British could aid the revolutionaries, a suitable revenge for Franco-Spanish aid to the thirteen colonies a generation earlier. They assumed that the complete independence of the Spanish American republics was simply a matter of time. However, when Mexico joined the ranks of the rebellious colonies in the early 1820's, other powers began to take an interest in them. Both Russia and France, for different reasons, were willing to consider intervention.

Russian interests were tied up with the needs of the Russian colony in Alaska. That fur and mining colony could not raise the meat, grain, and fruit needed by its inhabitants, and therefore the Russian government was anxious to extend its sovereignty down the Pacific coast of North America to secure a territory that would complement Alaska. Russian explorers and their claims began edging southward into relatively unpromising territory, but if California could be acquired from Spain, Russia reasoned that their problem would be solved. The Russians thought it possible that Spain might be willing to cede California in exchange for military aid against the rebel colonists.

French interests were less exactly defined. The ultraroyalist party believed that the French people would forget Napoleon if the Bourbons could win glory. As we have seen, this notion was behind the French intervention in Spain (1822). If the French army were to go on and suppress the Spanish revolutionary forces in South America, their action would bring glory and probably a colony or so to Bourbon France.

Such reasoning in France and Russia led to diplomatic discussions of the possibility of calling a congress in Paris to order intervention in Spanish America like that which had taken place in Naples and Spain. The project never got beyond the discussion stage, for both the American and British governments opposed the project, and England had the naval power necessary to control the sea lanes to South America. Russian interest in the Pacific coast had come to the attention of the government in Washington some time before the scheme for military intervention in Spanish America had been bruited. John Quincy Adams, secretary of state in President Monroe's cabinet, protested in St. Petersburg that the Pacific coast could no longer be claimed by exploration, since the Spanish, American, British, and Russian claims already blanketed the coast line. He added gratuitously that the United States considered the era of colonial expansion in the western hemisphere at an end. The British secretary of state, George Canning, was also keeping the Russian and French projects under surveillance. As soon as he understood that there was serious talk of a European military expedition to South America, he decided on action. His first move was to propose a joint Anglo-American proclamation indicating the unwillingness of the two governments to allow any such action. Jefferson, Madison, and Monroe at first favored accepting the English proposal, but Adams persuaded them to reject it, and instead issued a statement of United States policy. Adams' reasoning was that England's commercial interests would never allow France or Russia to suppress the rebellions in Spanish America; hence there was no danger that such intervention would occur. If the United States joined England in a manifesto, it would constitute merely a seconding and of no great significance, but if the United States issued its own declaration, it would not risk much and would, indeed, gain greatly in prestige. This was the origin of Monroe's famous Doctrine which closed the western hemisphere to colonization. All of the ideas and most of the words in Monroe's message to Congress in December 1823 came from the letters that Adams had written about the activities of Russia in the Pacific northwest. Bismarck later called the Doctrine a piece of "international effrontery," but none could deny that Adams' reasoning was sound. It worked out just as he had predicted it would.

When the American republic refused to join him, George Canning informed the French ambassador in London that the government of Great Britain would resist with force any attempt on the part of the European powers to send a military expedition to Spanish America. This action not only ended the project, for the British navy barred the way, but also marked the first big breach in the alliance system of Europe. Canning was pleased that his action ended the system of congresses that had marked the years after the treaties of 1815. Henceforth national interest was again to be the sole guiding line for foreign policy.

6. UNFINISHED BUSINESS: THE NEAR EAST

The other area of the European world not discussed at the Congress of Vienna was the Near East. It was not purely accidental that the sultan of Turkey was ignored by the Congress; Russian statesmen had come to regard the problems of the Ottoman Empire as peculiarly in their zone of interest. Most of Russia's rivers flowed into the Black Sea, and Constantinople controlled the outlet of that sea. This situation was pregnant with important strategic and commercial consequences for Russia. Furthermore, the religious question involved Russia. Those Greek Orthodox Christians in the Ottoman Empire who had any political ideas at all regarded Russia as their natural protector, and by the peace treaty of 1774 the sultan had been forced to recognize Russia's legal and moral right to protect them. Finally, the rising tide of nationalism was producing another bond. Russia was the "big brother" to the Slavic people of the Balkans. Many Russians regarded it simply as a matter of time until the Russian flag would float over the Bosphorus, the Dardanelles, and the great city of Constantinople.

However, neither Austrian nor English statesmen were pleased to contemplate this latter eventuality. To the Austrians it would mean that Russia, outflanking the Danubian monarchy in the south as well as in the north (Poland), would represent a threatening political pincer movement against them. Austria also ruled Slavic people. In the last decades of the eighteenth century Austrian statesmen had reached the conclusion that the period of Austro-Russian alliances against the Ottoman Empire was over; henceforth Austrian policy demanded the buttressing of the decadent Turkish state. The English with large commercial interests in the Near East also did not relish the idea of Russian conquest in that area. Like the Austrians, the English were reaching the conclusion that policy demanded that they support the Ottoman Empire as a political necessity. It was not easy, though, to support that state. Its administration, its armies, and its navy were in sorry disrepair, and the subject people were restless. Greeks remembered their classical past; Serbs and Bulgars their medieval past; and the Rumanians, their Roman heritage. Ideas of nationalism and national independence had penetrated the elite of these subject peoples to prepare them for rebellion against the Turks. Greek and Serbian agitators had found welcome and sympathy in Russia, and both assumed that Russia would aid them to secure freedom from the Turks. The Russians were not the only people who were sympathetic. All educated Europeans knew and could read some Greek, and somehow many of them confused the Greece of Pericles with that of their own day. An articulate public opinion arose urging the governments of England, France, and the Germanies to support Greek independence.

The Greeks were the first of the Balkan peoples to stage a successful revolt. Greek merchants were wealthy; they controlled most of the shipping flying the Turkish flag, and thus could supply the Greek rebel armies with weapons and supplies. The rebellion started in 1821, and very soon the Greeks seemed victorious everywhere. Although neither the English nor the Austrian government was too pleased to see Russian protégés establishing a new state, they could not interfere on behalf of the sultan. European public opinion was too deeply committed to the idea that this was a conflict between culture and barbarism, Christianity and Mohammedanism. In their enthusiasm for Hellas, educated Europeans often ignored all the arguments that the Turks had to offer as mere Moslem prejudice.

The sultan, however, had one resource. In Egypt his vassal, Mehemet Ali, had a modernized, French-trained army and navy which he willingly placed at the sultan's service in return for the government of the Morea (southern Greece). The Egyptians turned the tide against the Greeks (1825–1826) and soon Europe was filled with cries for help. Mehemet Ali's armies behaved very badly; they apparently intended to put an end to the Greek problem by killing all the Greeks. Once the tide had turned against the Greeks, Austria and England found it hard to keep Russia from entering the war. To prevent singlehanded Russian action, the British Mediterranean fleet was instructed, with the French, to bring pressure on Mehemet Ali's military forces. The instructions to the English commander were vague, but the situation in the eastern Mediterranean left him little alternative. His orders were to check the progress of the Egyptian army; he could do this only by blockading the harbor from which that army was supplied. In effect, then, he had to blockade the Egyptian navy. Before the statesmen in Paris and London could take stock, a naval battle had been fought at Navarino Bay (1827) and most of Mehemet Ali's navy had been despatched to the bottom of the sea. Following this hasty action, a Russian army marched into Turkey,

French marines occupied the Morea, and the allied navy established a close blockade of Turkey's coasts. The sultan was forced to submit.

When the treaty of peace was made, it became clear that the western powers had no intention of despoiling the Ottoman Empire or of creating a Greek state that might become a powerful factor in the politics of the Near East. Turkey had to recognize Greek independence, but the new Greek state was a tiny fragment of the territory claimed by Greek nationalists. The English, French, and Austrians were quite content to see a "token" Greek state, but not a powerful Greece that could become a Russian satellite. Furthermore, this Greece was loaded with debts incurred in the war, and those debts were guaranteed by the great powers in that they undertook to force Greece to pay them. One disillusioned Greek patriot remarked: "Greece may sometime be independent of Turkey, but she will never be free of the great powers."

Unlike the solution of the South American problems, the action taken in Greece did not end European intervention. The partial success of the Greek revolt was a sort of beacon light for other nationalist groups in the Balkans, and in the next three-quarters of the century Serbians, Rumanians, Bulgarians, Armenians, and even Moslem Arabs were to plot rebellion and call upon the great powers to give them assistance. Thus, the Near East, unlike Latin America, remained a source of friction throughout the nineteenth century. The men who pacified Europe after 1815, either blind to the explosive force of nationalism or unable to recognize its validity, were quite unwilling to compromise their own political and economic interests to control or direct the nationalistic movement in the Near East or elsewhere. Thus, they left the problem to their successors.

In a sense the settlement of the Greek revolt symbolized the end of the post-1815 pacification of Europe and the beginning of the political problems that were to take the center of the stage in the nineteenth century. The statesmen of 1815 hoped to find peace in the classic formula of the balance of power; their faith in political physics was grounded in their understanding of eighteenth-century political processes and their aristocratic assumptions about the world. They did not seem to understand that ideas of nationalism, liberalism, democracy, and other secular ideologies had been released by dynamic forces largely unknown in the eighteenth century, and that those ideas themselves were, in turn, becoming new justifications for political rights, new patterns for political authority, and new springs for political action. The conservativism of the statesmen of 1815–1825 was no answer to these forces; they might momentarily impose peace, but the dynamic movement of European history could not be checked in its course.

INDEX